# DARI

## AN ELEMENTARY TEXTBOOK

کتاب ابتدایی دری

**Rahman Arman**

This textbook, as well as other language materials for Central Asian Languages produced by CeLCAR, is supported by a Title-VI grant from the Department of Education.

Library of Congress Cataloging-in-Publication Data

Arman, Rahman, author.
Dari : an elementary textbook / Rahman Arman
    pages cm -- (Central Asian language series; 5) Includes index.

Summary: This textbook offers a thematically-organized approach to the Dari language for beginning students. The book emphasizes task-oriented, communicative activities that develop the four language skills (speaking, listening, reading, and writing). It introduces learners to both colloquial and standard forms. The topics discussed are of importance to language learners as well as to business people and government officials. The textbook prepares learners to perform at level 1+ or 2 on the ILR scale and at the novice high/intermediate low level on the ACTFL scale. Dari belongs to the Iranian group of Indo-European languages. Along with Farsi and Tajiki, it is one of the three main Persian dialects. Dari is the most-used language in Afghanistan; all official documents are written in the language. It is, with Pashto, one of the two official languages of the country. Dari has more than 40 million speakers worldwide. Large communities of native speakers reside in Iran and Tajikistan and throughout Central and South Asia.

Includes bibliographical references and index.
    ISBN 978-1-62616-109-2 (alk. paper)

    1. Persian language--Dialects--Afghanistan--Grammar.
    2. Dari language--Textbooks for foreign speakers--English.  I. Title.
PK6393.A35.A76 2014
491'.5682421--dc23

2014029454

19 18 17    9 8 7 6 5 4 3 2

Printed in the United States of America
Cover designed by Pamela Pease
Cover image by Abdul Bari Nawzadee

# CONTENTS

# SCOPE AND SEQUENCE

| Chapter | functions | language Structure | Culture Notes |
|---|---|---|---|
| 1. معرفی زبان دری<br>An Introduction to Dari | - Greeting people<br>- Introducing yourself<br>- Learning the alphabet & writing practice<br>- Reading letters | - Forming letters in various positions<br>- Ligatures | - Formally addressing people |
| 2. شمارۀ تلیفون تان چند است؟<br>What Is Your Phone Number? | - Learning numbers 0 to 10<br>- Giving & asking for phone numbers<br>- Reading signs and business cards<br>- Writing a brief description of yourself<br>- Asking about others | - Vowel sounds<br>- Diphthongs<br>- Consonants<br>- Letters used in loanwords<br>- Demonstrative pronouns<br>- Sentence structure in Dari<br>- Pluralization of inanimate objects<br>- Interrogative sentences | - Afghan phone numbers<br>- Afghan business cards<br>- Afghan work week<br>- Afghan days & nights |
| 3. سلام علیکی و معرفی<br>Greetings and Introductions | - Greeting others and asking about how they're doing<br>- Introducing yourself and others<br>- Using "jan" & other personal titles<br>- Talking about place of origin<br>- Asking others about where they live | - Personal pronouns<br>- The defective verb هست/است 'to be'<br>- Negation<br>- Interrogative sentences with the verb "to be"<br>- Possessive pronouns<br>- The addition or ēzāfate '-e'<br>Question words:<br>'Who' کی; 'What' چی; 'How' چطور; 'Where' کجا; 'Which' کدام<br>- The compound verb: زنده گی کردن 'to live'<br>- The preposition 'in' در | - The title: jan<br>- Learning cultural rules of greetings and partings.<br>- Addressing people in formal/ polite form |
| 4. در صنف درسی<br>In the Classroom | - Naming objects in the classroom<br>- Asking for location of objects<br>- Giving a command<br>- Being polite | - Pluralizing inanimate objects<br>- Adverbs of place<br>- Classifiers<br>- Verb داشتن 'to have'<br>- Prepositions<br>- Ezāfate (-e) in writing<br>- Negation<br>- Yes/no questions<br>- Compound verbs using definitive object marker | - Learning about the Afghan classroom<br>- Following Afghan rules of being polite |

| Chapter | Functions | Language Structure | Culture Notes |
|---|---|---|---|
| شما هر روز چی میکنید؟ .5<br>What Do You Do Every Day? | - Telling time & date<br>- Talking about your daily routines<br>- Talking about weekends | - The compound verb with simple verb شدن 'to become, to be'<br>- Cardinal numbers<br>- Question word<br>- Time adverbs<br>- Negative adverbs with the word هیچ<br>- The verbs خوش داشتن 'to like'<br>- Conjunction اما 'but'<br>- More verbs to express likes and dislike | - Time<br>- Calendar<br>- The game of buzkashi |
| خانواده ام .6<br>My Family | - Talking about family using kinship terms<br>- Addressing others using family titles<br>- Using religious titles<br>- Talking about weddings | - The verb بودن 'to be'<br>- Adjectives<br>- Plural suffix ان<br>- The functions of verb شدن<br>- Relative pronouns<br>- Forming simple past tense | - Prayers against the "evil eye"<br>- Religious titles<br>- Afghan women at work<br>- Afghan wedding traditions |
| جای زندگی ام .7<br>My Residence | - Describing your residence<br>- Moving to a new place<br>- Asking/giving directions<br>- Talking about home/campus<br>- Talking about daily routines/ activities | - The suffix خانه<br>- The verb نشستن 'to sit/ live', کوچ کردن 'to move'<br>- Expressing wishes, wants, & abilities<br>- The conjunction بخاطریکه/ چونکه 'because'<br>- Adjectives describing places<br>- Other prepositions & verbs | - Afghan houses<br>- Giving directions in Afghanistan<br>- Traffic and traffic signs<br>- Significance of directions in Afghan society |
| در بازار .8<br>At the Bazaar | - Buying groceries<br>- Learning names of various foods<br>- Expressing likes/ dislikes<br>- Talking about daily meals<br>- Learning how to use Afghan currency<br>- Learning the names of clothing<br>- Shopping/ bargaining | - The auxiliary verbs شاید ، باید 'might, most'<br>- The verb خوش آمدن 'to like'<br>- The suffix فروشی<br>- Defining relative clause که<br>- Use of the present perfect of پوشیدن 'to wear'<br>- Order of adjectives | - Tips for the bazaar<br>- Afghan currency<br>- Weight units<br>- Afghan dishes<br>- Afghan men's clothing<br>- Afghan women's clothing<br>- Clothing sizes |

| Chapter | Functions | Language Structure | Culture Notes |
|---|---|---|---|
| 9. رخصتی‌های تابستانی<br>Summer Vacations | - Talking about the weather<br>- Booking tickets and traveling<br>- Going through the airport & customs<br>- Reserving a hotel room<br>- Renting a taxi | - The verb باریدن 'to rain, to pour down'<br>- Nominal adjectives with suffix ی 'i'<br>- Conditional sentences<br>- Past progressive/ imperfect tense of verbs باریدن 'to rain, to pour down' & وزیدن 'to blow'<br>- Expressing future tense with verb خواستن 'to want'<br>- The generic possessive خود<br>- The past perfect form | - Weather in Afghanistan<br>- Hotels in Afghanistan |
| 10. در جریان رخصتی هایم<br>During My Break | - Checking into a hotel, reading travel brochures/ country guidelines<br>- Visiting a doctor, pharmacy, or traditional doctor about an illness<br>- Calling travel agencies for tickets, information, delays, flight cancellations, lost luggage, etc.<br>- Writing about your travel problems to others, e.g. managers, colleagues<br>- Writing about your travel experiences | - Gerunds<br>- Expressing opinions and decisions<br>- The verb درد کردن 'to hurt'<br>- Deriving place names using the suffix خانه<br>- Wishes and exclamations | - Modern vs. traditional doctors<br>- Modern vs. traditional medicine<br>- Traditional healthcare facilities |

# FOREWORD

The Center for Languages of the Central Asian Region (CeLCAR) is preparing the first set of Central Asian language textbooks published in the United States based on the Communicative Approach to language teaching. *Dari: An Elementary Textbook*, authored by Dr. Rahman Arman, is the fifth such book.

The textbook provides learners with activities that are aimed at helping them perform tasks and functions that native speakers of Dari perform in their appropriate cultural context. The grammar and the vocabulary covered in the textbook are also chosen carefully to help learners perform these tasks and functions at the elementary level and beyond.

The textbook aims to provide students with a foundation of listening, speaking, reading, and writing skills, all four basic skills of language, while, at the same time, offering them various authentic and culturally relevant materials, including videos taped in various regions of Afghanistan, where the Dari language is predominantly spoken. In addition to demonstrating different aspects of the culture of Dari speakers, the book provides contemporary topics of universal interest and does so in meaningful and communicative ways.

*Dari: An Elementary Textbook* incorporates the latest innovations in foreign language teaching and has been prepared with the input of various second language acquisition and language pedagogy experts, as well as linguists. The way new information is presented and the tasks and activities used in the textbook to consolidate this information are all in line with the findings of the latest research in second language acquisition, linguistics, and language pedagogy.

A textbook such as this is possible with the vision and labor of many. We are, first of all, grateful for support from the Department of Education through Title VI funds that helped establish and continue to sustain our Language Resource Center. We are also grateful to Indiana University's College of Arts and Sciences and the new School of Global and International Studies (SGIS) for providing us with logistical support as well as significant internal funds. We would also like to thank the Department of Central Eurasian Studies (CEUS) for providing us with the linguistic and cultural expertise needed for the study of Central Asia as well as for sharing many resources.

Dr. Öner Özçelik
Director, CeLCAR
Assistant Professor, CEUS
Indiana University, Bloomington

# ACKNOWLEDGMENTS

I would like to express my sincere gratitude to Indiana University and to the team at IU's Center for Languages of the Central Asian Region (CeLCAR). I am especially grateful to CeLCAR's directors past and present, expressly the current director Dr. Öner Özçelik, for the opportunity to work on this project and for their careful oversight of my work on the textbook.

I owe a special debt of gratitude to Beatrix Burghardt for providing insightful counsel throughout the project regarding pedagogy and methodology for our materials. I also want to thank Dr. Michael Thompson for his help with English and Dari language grammars, Dr. Rakhmon Inomkhojayev for his assistance with proofreading and advising me on the Dari text, and Zalmay Yawar for participating in audio recordings and proofreading the Dari text. I would like to recognize Dave Baer and Katie Williamson for their contributions proofreading the English texts and Amber Kennedy Kent for helping with layout and design, as well as editing and proofreading the English texts. Special thanks go to Sukhrob Karimov for his help with layout and design and Marzia Zamani for participating in the audio recordings. I owe special gratitude to my wife, Behnaz Zamani, who provided constructive feedback as a course instructor for many years, participated in the audio recordings, and helped with the editing and proofreading both of the Dari and of the English texts. I am in debt to her for the ongoing support throughout this project. Finally, I am grateful to all the students and the reviewers for their feedback on draft versions of this textbook.

I also wish to express my appreciation to CeLCAR in general for providing photos and video materials from Afghanistan and for their technical support that made possible the publishing of this book.

All remaining mistakes are mine.

# PREFACE

This textbook is developed specifically for classroom use. Its purpose is to provide learners and instructors with a wide selection of materials and task-oriented, communicative activities that facilitate in a balanced way the development of the four language skills (speaking, listening, reading, writing). The course introduces learners to colloquial Dari via the audio recordings and to standard Dari via the text (formal Dari as it is spoken in Afghanistan and written in Afghanistan and Iran).

The course is designed for beginners, and thus it does not presume any previous knowledge of written or spoken Dari. The focus is on enabling learners to participate successfully in simple, everyday situations that require both spoken and written skills. The topics discussed in the book are of importance to language learners as well as to business people and government officials. Learners with previous knowledge of spoken Dari might find the book beneficial to improve their writing skills. Special notes are included for people with experience in Persian to help them learn Dari more efficiently.

By the end of the course, successful learners will be able to:
- engage in simple conversations on a number of everyday topics using colloquial Dari,
- read simple texts and understand the main ideas of texts written in standard Dari,
- write short texts using standard Dari,
- answer in writing simple questions on familiar topics using standard Dari,
- participate in simple interactions following social conventions of Afghan culture.

The materials presented in this textbook require a minimum of 160 hours of intensive language instruction. In terms of proficiency, this textbook prepares learners to perform at Level 1+ or 2 on the ILR scale (Interagency Language Roundtable), or on the ACTFL scale (American Council on the Teaching of Foreign Languages) at the levels of Novice High/Intermediate Low.

The textbook is divided into ten thematic chapters. Learning outcomes are summarized at the beginning of each chapter. Chapter-specific goals are described in terms of function, writing, grammar, and culture. Each chapter is divided into three lessons with individually specified learning outcomes, which may also serve as a study guide. Each chapter concludes with a chapter review. This section provides additional activities that aim to recycle previously presented materials in an integrated way.

In addition to presenting language, each chapter includes rich cultural notes on Afghan society, customs, and relevant nonverbal aspects of communication, such as body language and gestures.

Unique features of *Dari: An Elementary Textbook* include the following:
- Topics are selected with care so that they are of immediate use to the learner. These include a wide variety of themes; for example, introducing oneself, shopping, and making travel arrangements.
- Activities are personalized to help students express their personal needs. The primary focus is on language use, and the grammar provides a supporting structure to achieve this focus.
- Passages of text presented here are easy for adult learners to read and understand. In this way, the focus is on language acquisition. The selected texts include both simple authentic texts and short, modified readings.
- Audio recordings and transcripts are included for all listening activities in order to allow for further individual practice and/or checking responses to listening activities.
- Grammar is presented in context and selected with care so that it naturally relates to the topic. Grammar points are presented in both written and spoken contexts so that learners have multiple opportunities to practice them in both modalities.
- All thirty-two letters of the Dari alphabet, including vowels and consonants, are introduced in the book. Letters are presented first as basic character strokes, and then they are combined into words. Vowels and consonants are presented separately. Vowels are presented in their short form first, then in long form, and finally diphthongs are introduced. Consonants are presented in three steps. First, consonants that are most similar to those of English are presented. These are followed by consonants that are represented in English by two letters but by a single letter in the Dari alphabet. Finally, consonants that have no English counterpart are presented. To aid in recognition and acquisition of these sounds, they are transcribed using romanized letters in the first few chapters.

# REFERENCES

Khodjaerov, N. (2009). *Tajiki: An Elementary Textbook* (Vols. 1 and 2). Washington, DC: Georgetown University Press.

Lambton, A. K. S. (1953). *Persian Grammar.* Cambridge, UK: Press Syndicate of the University of Cambridge.

Mace, J. (2003). *Persian Grammar: For Reference and Revision.* London, UK: Routledge Curzon Publisher.

Nek-hat Saidi, N. M. (1969). *The Modern Dari Language Grammar Book.* Kabul, Afghanistan: College of Literature Press.

Thackston, W. M. (1993). *An Introduction to Persian.* Bethesda, MD: IBEX Publishers/ Iranbooks.

# A BRIEF INTRODUCTION TO DARI

Dari belongs to the Iranian group of Indo-European languages. This language is one of three main Persian dialects: Farsi, Dari, and Tajiki.

Dari is one of two official national languages of Afghanistan and is the most commonly used language. All official documents are written in Dari.

Other languages spoken in Afghanistan include:

- Pashto: Also one of the two official languages, it is spoken and written mostly by Pashtuns and used in schools.
- Turkic languages (e.g. Uzbek, Turkmen): Spoken only by Turkic people.
- Other minor languages (Pasha-yi, Balochi, Brahwi, and Pamiri): Spoken only by their ethnic groups.

Dari has more than 40 million speakers worldwide. It and languages like it are used by large communities of native speakers who reside in Iran and Tajikistan. A small community of these language speakers can be found in Uzbekistan, Pakistan, and India, as well. In addition, immigrant Dari-speaking communities live in Saudi Arabia, United Arab Emirates, the United Kingdom, Germany, Sweden, Canada, the United States, and other countries.

Dari has several main dialects in Afghanistan: Kabuli, Hazaragi, Herati, and Shamali. The Kabuli dialect of Dari is the main dialect. Therefore, in this book, Kabuli dialect is used.

# فـصـل اول

## CHAPTER ONE

1

## معرفـی زبـان دری

### AN INTRODUCTION TO DARI

# IN THIS CHAPTER

# Chapter Introduction معرفی فصل

In this chapter, you will learn how to greet others, introduce yourself, say farewells, and state and ask others' places of origin. On completion of the chapter, you will be able to write letters of the Dari alphabet in various positions and connect them, as well as write your name and names of people and places. You will also be able to read simple public signs and titles.

شما از کجا هستید؟

Where are you from?

نام تان چیست؟

What is your name?

او کیست؟

Who is he/she?

**Note:**

The introduction of a new alphabet system can lead to additional confusion during language learning, so to alleviate this confusion, the first few chapters of the textbook will use a modified phonetic transcription based on the English alphabet (to clearly demonstrate the correct pronunciation of Dari words) in addition to the Dari script.

# درس اول: نام تان چیست؟

## Lesson One: What is your name?

In this section, you will learn how to greet people in Dari, how to introduce yourself and say your name, and how to say good-bye.

**Exercise 1:** 🎧 ۱ :تمرین

You will hear two people greeting each other. Number the order of the pictures as they are presented:

**Exercise 2:** 🎧 ۲ :تمرین

A. Listen to the audio of men and women greeting one another.

السلام علیکم!
[salām alaykom!]
Hello!
(Peace be with you)

وعلیکم السلام!
[walaykom salām!]
Hello!
(Peace be with you)

B. 🎧 Now you will hear the people in the picture greet each other in different ways. What differences can you hear between these phrases and the phrases in part A?

> Hello! (Peace be with you) [salām] ‫سلام!‬
>
> Hello! (Peace be with you) [walaykom] ‫وعلیکم!‬

1. Is that phrase shorter? _____

2. Is that phrase formal? _____

3. Is that phrase informal? _____

## Cultural Note    تبصرهٔ فرهنگی

### Formally Addressing People

**Formal Address**

Because respect is such a major component of Afghan culture, you must greet people with the appropriate level of formality. In fact, many learners choose to greet everyone with the formal form, just to avoid inadvertently disrespecting someone. But know that the following situations will always call for the formal form:

- When meeting someone for first time.
- When meeting someone who is older than you or has a higher status.
- When in a formal meeting.
- When talking with high government officials.

**Informal Address**

When in doubt, it is always safe to use the formal form of address; therefore, many people avoid using the informal form. However, instances where the informal form may be used are when talking to a close friend, a younger relative, or one's spouse.

Exercise 3:  تمرین ۳:

A. Formal and Informal Greetings. For each of the following scenarios, mark whether you would use a formal or informal greeting. Check your answers with a partner.

|  | | Formal | Informal |
|---|---|---|---|
| 1. | You meet a young man for the first time. | | |
| 2. | You meet a young girl for the first time. | | |
| 3. | You meet your best friend. | | |
| 4. | You meet a village elder. | | |
| 5. | You negotiate with a government official. | | |
| 6. | You are greeting a coworker. | | |

B. Look at the pictures below. Write down whether you will hear a formal or informal greeting. Then listen and see whether your predictions are correct.

1. _____    2. _____    3. _____    4. _____

C.  Practice greeting your classmates and your instructor using both forms of greeting.

Exercise 4: تمرین ۴:

A. Introductions. First, listen to the following dialogue between **Sādiq** and **Zalmay**.

| Hello! (Peace be with you) | [salām alaykom!] | السلام علیکم! |
|---|---|---|
| Hello! (Peace be with you) | [walaykom salām!] | وعلیکم السلام! |
| What is your name? | [nām-e tān čist?] | نام تان چیست؟ |
| My name is Sadiq. | [nām-e man sāděq ast]. | نام من صادق است. |
| What is your name? | [nām-e šomā čist?] | نام شما چیست؟ |
| My name is Zalmay. | [nām-e man zalmay ast.] | نام من زلمی است. |

B. Working in pairs, use the example in the previous dialogue to introduce yourself to a classmate.

Exercise 5: تمرین ۵:

A. Now you will hear an audio recording of people saying goodbye to one another. Number the order of the pictures in the order you hear them.

_____    _____    _____

B. You will hear how people say goodbye to each other. Listen and repeat.

خدا حافظ!
[xodā hāfĕz!]
Goodbye!

خدا حافظ!
[xodā hāfĕz!]
Goodbye!

Exercise 6:  تمرین ۶:

A. Listen to the exchange between **Zalmay** and **Laylā**. Then, number the order of sentences as you hear them. The first one has been done for you.

| 1 | [salām!] | | سلام! |
|---|---|---|---|
| ___ | [xodā hāfěz!] | | خدا حافظ! |
| ___ | [nām-e man zalmay ast.] |  | نام من زلمی است. |
| ___ | [nām-e man laylā ast.] | | نام من لیلا است. |
| ___ | [nām-e šomā čist?] | | نام شما چیست؟ |
| ___ | [walaykom!] | | وعلیکم! |
| ___ | [nām-e tān čist?] | | نام تان چیست؟ |
| ___ | [xodā hāfěz!] | | خدا حافظ! |

B. Working with a partner, write a short dialogue which includes greeting, introduction, and farewell phrases. Practice your dialogue and then present it to the class.

## 1.1 Dari Alphabet: Introduction

The Dari alphabet is based on the Arabic alphabet; however, the Dari alphabet includes four additional letters (پ، چ، گ، ژ) adding up to 32 letters total. Also, the letter ( ), which only appears at the beginning of words, is sometimes considered a separate, additional letter.

Dari script is written and read from right to left and there are no distinct capital letters.

Like English, Dari writing is not phonetic, meaning that some words do not have a one-to-one correspondence between symbol and sound. For example, sometimes vowel sounds in the medial position (middle) of the word are not written by a distinct letter from the alphabet. Also, some sounds may be written by a different letter or a combination of letters.

Exercise 7: 🎧 تمرین ۷:

A. You will hear an audio recording of the Dari alphabet chart below. Repeat each letter as you listen. Pay attention to the name of each letter as well as to the pronunciation of sounds represented by each letter.

| Transcription used in this textbook | Letter name | | Isolated |
|---|---|---|---|
| [ā] as *aw* in *law* | [alĕf mad] | الف مد | آ |
| [ā] as *aw* in *law*; [a] as *o* in *hot* | [alĕf] | الف | ا |
| [b] as *b* in *boy* | [be] | بی | ب |
| [p] as *p* in *pen* | [pe] | پی | پ |
| [t] as *t* in *teach* | [te] | تی | ت |
| [s] as *s* in *son* | [se] | ثی | ث |
| [j] as *j* in *John* | [jim] | جیم | ج |
| [č] as *ch* in *chain* | [če] | چی | چ |
| [h] as *h* in *human* | [he] | حی | ح |
| [x] as *ch* in German *Bach* | [xe] | خی | خ |
| [d] as *d* in *dig* but softer | [dāl] | دال | د |
| [z] as *z* in *zoo* | [zāl] | ذال | ذ |
| [r] as *rr* in Spanish *perro* but softer | [re] | ری | ر |
| [z] as *z* in *zoo* | [ze] | زی | ز |
| [ž] as *s* in *measure* | [že] | ژی | ژ |
| [s] as *s* in *son* | [sin] | سین | س |
| [š] as *sh* in *shame* | [šin] | شین | ش |
| [s] as *s* in *son* | [sād] | صاد | ص |
| [z] as *z* in *zoo* | [zād] | ضاد | ض |
| [t] as *t* in *teach* | [tā]/[toy] | ظا/طوی | ط |
| [z] as *z* in *zoo* | [zā]/[zoy] | ظا/ظوی | ظ |
| [ ' ] as ʿ in Arabic *Qurʾan* | [ayn] | عین | ع |
| [ğ] as *r* in French *Paris* | [ğayn] | غین | غ |
| [f] as *f* in *fish* | [fe] | فی | ف |
| [q] as *q* in Arabic *Qibla* | [qāf] | قاف | ق |
| [k] as *k* in *king* | [kāf] | کاف | ک/ك |
| [g] as *g* in *gift* | [gāf] | گاف | گ |

| | | | |
|---|---|---|---|
| [l] as *l* in *land* | [lām] | لام | ل |
| [m] as *m* in *myth* | [mim] | میم | م |
| [n] as *n* in *new* | [nun] | نون | ن |
| [w] as *w* in *wet*; [ū] as *oo* in *pool*; [o] and [ō] as *oa* in *coat* | [wāw] | واو | و |
| [h] as *h* in *human*, [a] as *a* in *hat* | [he] | هی | ه |
| [y] as *y* in *yes*; [ay] as *y* in *sky*, [i] as *ea* in *seat*; [ĕ] as in *pen*; [e] as in *may* | [yā] | یا | ی |

B. Look over the above letters and answer the following questions.

1. How many of the letters have similar shapes to another letter (not including their dots and lines)?
   a) 15    b) 16    c) 17    d) 18

2. How many letters have three dots above them?
   a) 2    b) 13    c) 3    d) 5

3. How many of the letters have three dots below them?
   a) 2    b) 13    c) 4    d) 5

4. What is the difference between the letters [ayn] and [ğayn]?
   _____

5. What is the difference between the letters [alĕf mad] and [alĕf]?
   _____

6. What is the difference between the letters [qāf] and [fe]?
   _____

7. What is the difference between the letters [kāf] and [gāf]?
   _____

C. 🎧 Listen to the audio and circle all of the letters that you hear.

| | | | |
|---|---|---|---|
| **1** | آ | ا | ب |
| **2** | پ | ت | ث |
| **3** | ج | چ | ح |
| **4** | خ | د | ذ |
| **5** | ر | ز | ژ |

| | | | |
|---|---|---|---|
| **6** | ص | ش | س |
| **7** | ظ | ط | ض |
| **8** | ف | غ | ع |
| **9** | گ | ك | ق |
| **10** | ی | ن | م |

D. Put the dots and lines on the appropriate positions of each shape. Then, match your work with the table on exercise 7A. Pay attention to whether the dots go above or below the letter, or if they should be this way (⁑), e.g. [پ], or this way (⁂), e.g. [ث].

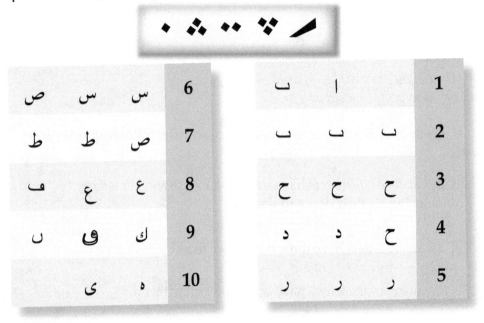

| | | | | 6 | | | | | 1 |
|---|---|---|---|---|---|---|---|---|---|
| ص | س | س | | 6 | ﺐ | | | ا | 1 |
| ط | ط | ص | | 7 | ﺐ | ﺐ | ﺐ | | 2 |
| ﻒ | ع | ع | | 8 | ح | ح | ح | | 3 |
| ﺑ | ﻕ | ك | | 9 | د | د | ح | | 4 |
| | ى | ﻩ | | 10 | ر | ر | ر | | 5 |

Exercise 8: تمرین ۸:

A. Match the following American names written in English with their Dari equivalent.

| a. | | | ا | ل | ر | ک |
|---|---|---|---|---|---|---|
| b. | | | ن | ا | ج |
| c. | | ک | ى | ا | م |
| d. | | ى | ل | ى | ل |
| e. | ا | ک | ى | س | ج |

| Lily |
|---|
| Jessica |
| John |
| Carla |
| Mike |

B. Now match the following Afghan names written in English with their Dari equivalent.

| a. | ز | ى | و | ر | پ |
|---|---|---|---|---|---|
| b. | | ش | ر | آ |
| c. | د | ى | ر | ف |
| d. | ب | ى | ج | ن |
| e. | ت | ر | ص | ن |

| Farid |
|---|
| Najib |
| Nasrat |
| Arash |
| Parwez |

C. Write your own name in Dari.  Be sure to focus on the actual sounds in your name, not the spelling. Remember: Dari is written from right to left.

**Example:** "George" really sounds like "jorj".

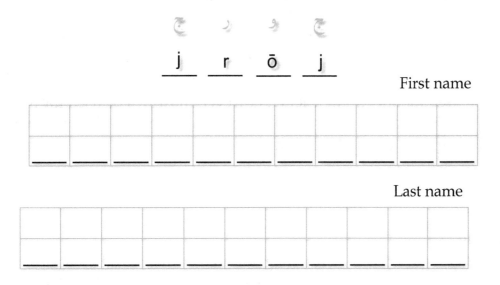

ج    و    ر    ج

_j_    _r_    _ō_    _j_

First name

Last name

Exercise 9: ٩ تمرین:

Sound out the following words in Dari.  Then match them to the corresponding picture.

ر ت و ی پ م ك

ن و ف ی ل ت

ل س ن پ

ی ف ا ك

س ا ل ی گ

## 1.2 Dari Alphabet: Written, Part One

As previously mentioned, the Dari alphabet has 32 letters. If you look closely, you will notice that many of these letters actually look very similar to another letter. In fact, there only 18 basic letter shapes, but some of these are modified using diacritics (such as dots and lines) to differentiate between them. Some shapes will be used for only a single letter, however, most will be used for two or more different letters. To learn how to write in Dari, you will begin by learning the basic shapes.

Exercise 10:   تمرین ۱۰:

Watch the video demonstrating how to write the basic 18 shapes of Dari letters. For each shape, pay attention to the movement of the pen and then practice writing it on the dotted lines provided.

| | | | | | |
|---|---|---|---|---|---|
| ............ | ﻪ | Shape No.10 | ............ | ا | Shape No.1 |
| ............ | ﻑ | Shape No.11 | ............ | ﺐ | Shape No.2 |
| ............ | ﻚ | Shape No.12 | ............ | ﺡ | Shape No.3 |
| ............ | ﻝ | Shape No.13 | ............ | ﺩ | Shape No.4 |
| ............ | ﻡ | Shape No.14 | ............ | ﺭ | Shape No.5 |
| ............ | ﻦ | Shape No.15 | ............ | ﺱ | Shape No.6 |
| ............ | ﻭ | Shape No.16 | ............ | ﺹ | Shape No.7 |
| ............ | ﻩ | Shape No.17 | ............ | ﻁ | Shape No.8 |
| ............ | ﻯ | Shape No.18 | ............ | ﻉ | Shape No.9 |

Exercise 11: 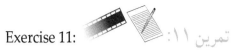 تمرین ۱۱:

The Dari Letters. Now, learn to convert the 18 basic shapes into actual letters. Watch the video demonstrating how to write each letter. Pay close attention to the orientation of the marks relative to the basic letter shape, the placement of each letter between the lines, and the direction and order of the strokes.

| | | | |
|---|---|---|---|
| | ص | | ا |
| | ض | | ب |
| | ط | | پ |
| | ظ | | ت |
| | ع | | ث |
| | غ | | ج |
| | ف | | چ |
| | ق | | ح |
| | ک | | خ |
| | گ | | د |
| | ل | | ذ |
| | م | | ر |
| | ن | | ز |
| | و | | ژ |
| | ه | | س |
| | ی | | ش |

Exercise 12: تمرین ۱۲:

A. Write the correct form of each letter next to the transcription.

| | | | | | |
|---|---|---|---|---|---|
| _____ | [fe] | _____ | [re] | _____ | [alĕf] |
| _____ | [qāf] | _____ | [ze] | _____ | [be] |
| _____ | [kāf] | _____ | [že] | _____ | [pe] |
| _____ | [gāf] | _____ | [sin] | _____ | [te] |
| _____ | [lām] | _____ | [šin] | _____ | [se] |
| _____ | [mim] | _____ | [sād] | _____ | [jim] |
| _____ | [nun] | _____ | [zād] | _____ | [če] |
| _____ | [wāw] | _____ | [tā] [toy] | _____ | [he] |
| _____ | [he] | _____ | [zā] [zoy] | _____ | [xe] |
| _____ | [yā] | _____ | [ayn] | _____ | [dāl] |
| | | _____ | [ğayn] | _____ | [zāl] |

B. Listen to the audio recording and write down the letters you hear. Compare your answers with a classmate.

Exercise 13:  تمرین ۱۳:

A. Provided below are some common words as they're written in Dari. Can you figure out what they are? The first example has been done for you.

| Word: internet | ت | ن | ر | ت | ن | ا | **1** |
|---|---|---|---|---|---|---|---|
| | t | n | r | t | n | i | |
| | | | س | ن | ر | ن | **2** |
| | | ل | ی | م | ی | ا | **3** |
| | ل | ک | س | ی | ا | ب | **4** |
| ر | ت | و | ی | پ | م | ک | **5** |

B. You have been given the transcriptions of some common Dari words along with their scrambled spellings. For each word, rearrange the Dari letters to correctly spell out the given word.

| | | | |
|---|---|---|---|
| ———— | س ه د ی ت | [hasted] | answer |
| ———— | ت ه س م | [hastam] | volleyball |
| ———— | ل ا م س | [salām] | name |
| ———— | ط ر چ و | [čĕtor] | friend |
| ———— | ا م ن | [name] | young man |
| ———— | س ی ت چ | [čist] | picture |
| ———— | ص ل ت خ | [taxalos] | Pashto |
| ———— | ش ا م | [šomā] | apartment |

C.  Spell out your whole name in the boxes below.  First, write the transcription of the sounds in your name. Then, write the corresponding Dari letters in the boxes below. For example: 'Richard' becomes:

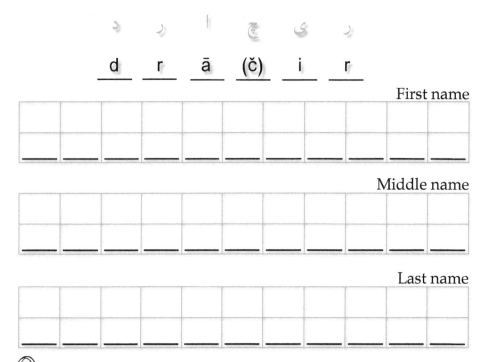

$$\underline{\text{د}} \quad \underline{\text{ر}} \quad \underline{\text{ا}} \quad \underline{\text{چ}} \quad \underline{\text{ی}} \quad \underline{\text{ر}}$$

$$\underline{\quad d \quad} \quad \underline{\quad r \quad} \quad \underline{\quad \bar{a} \quad} \quad \underline{\quad (\check{c}) \quad} \quad \underline{\quad i \quad} \quad \underline{\quad r \quad}$$

First name

Middle name

Last name

D. Listen to the audio recording and spell out the words you hear. Compare your answers with a classmate.

# درس دوم: شما از کجا هستید؟

# Lesson Two: Where are you from?

In this section, you will learn how to say where you are from and ask others where they come from. Additionally, you will learn how to connect letters.

Exercise 1:  تمرین ۱:

A. You will hear people talking about their places of origin on the audio recording. Listen and practice the phrases you hear.

شما از کجا هستید؟
[šomā az kojā hasted?]
Where are you from?

از افغانستان.
[az afğānĕstān]
From Afghanistan

B. Practice discussing various countries of origin, such as the ones below, and ask your classmates where they are from using the question above as a model.

## 1.3 Dari Alphabet: Written, Part Two

In Dari, most letters are connected to each other on both the right and the left by a short horizontal line and have four forms (isolated, initial, medial, and final). These are called four-form letters.

Some letters connect only from the previous letter (on the right), also with a short horizontal line, and have only two forms (isolated and final). These are called two-form letters. Two-form letters won't join with the following letter (to the left), even when they occur in the initial or medial position within a word.

*Note: In summary, 25 letters of the Dari alphabet have isolated, initial, medial, and final forms, whereas 7 letters have only isolated and final forms.*

Connecting or not connecting letters within words is not optional in Dari, like it is in cursive English. It is a requirement for writing the words properly. However, each word is written separately; the last letter of the preceding word cannot be written while connected to the first letter of the next word. The few exceptions are compound words and prepositions, which will be discussed later in the textbook.

Exercise 2: ‏تمرین ۲:‏

Look at the following chart and answer the questions that follow.

| Final آخر | Medial وسط | Initial شروع | Isolated مفرد | Letter Name نام حرف | | Number شماره |
|---|---|---|---|---|---|---|
| ‏ا‏ | – | – | ‏ا‏ | alĕf | ‏الف‏ | 1 |
| ‏ب‏ | ‏ب‏ | ‏ب‏ | ‏ب‏ | be | ‏بی‏ | 2 |
| ‏پ‏ | ‏پ‏ | ‏پ‏ | ‏پ‏ | pe | ‏پی‏ | 3 |
| ‏ت‏ | ‏ت‏ | ‏ت‏ | ‏ت‏ | te | ‏تی‏ | 4 |

| Final آخر | Medial وسط | Initial شروع | Isolated مفرد | Letter Name نام حرف | | Number شماره |
|---|---|---|---|---|---|---|
| ث | ﺸ | ﺛ | ث | se | ثى | 5 |
| ﺞ | ﺠ | ﺟ | ج | jim | جيم | 6 |
| ﭻ | ﭽ | ﭼ | چ | če | چى | 7 |
| ﺢ | ﺤ | ﺣ | ح | he | حى | 8 |
| ﺦ | ﺨ | ﺧ | خ | xe | خى | 9 |
| ﺪ | – | – | د | dāl | دال | 10 |
| ﺬ | – | – | ذ | zāl | ذال | 11 |
| ﺮ | – | – | ر | re | رى | 12 |
| ﺰ | – | – | ز | ze | زى | 13 |
| ﮋ | – | – | ژ | že | ژى | 14 |
| ﺲ | ﺴ | ﺳ | س | sin | سين | 15 |
| ﺶ | ﺸ | ﺷ | ش | šin | شين | 16 |
| ﺺ | ﺼ | ﺻ | ص | sād | صاد | 17 |
| ﺾ | ﺿ | ﺿ | ض | zād | ضاد | 18 |
| ﻂ | ﻄ | ﻃ | ط | toy, tā | طوى، طا | 19 |
| ﻆ | ﻈ | ﻇ | ظ | zoy, zā | ظوى، ظا | 20 |
| ﻊ | ﻌ | ﻋ | ع | ayn | عين | 21 |
| ﻎ | ﻐ | ﻏ | غ | ğayn | غين | 22 |
| ﻒ | ﻔ | ﻓ | ف | fe | فى | 23 |
| ﻖ | ﻘ | ﻗ | ق | qāf | قاف | 24 |
| ﻚ | ﻜ | ﻛ | ک | kāf | کاف | 25 |
| ﮓ | ﮕ | ﮔ | گ | gāf | گاف | 26 |
| ﻞ | ﻠ | ﻟ | ل | lām | لام | 27 |
| ﻢ | ﻤ | ﻣ | م | mim | ميم | 28 |
| ﻦ | ﻨ | ﻧ | ن | nun | نون | 29 |
| ﻮ | ﻮ | ﻭ | و | wāw | واو | 30 |
| ﻪ | ﻬ | ﻫ | ه | he | هى | 31 |
| ﻰ | ﻴ | ﻳ | ى | yā | يا | 32 |

1. How many two-form letters and four-form letters are there in the Dari alphabet?

2. The two-form letters come in which positions?
    a) isolated and medial    b) isolated and initial    c) isolated and final

## 1.4 Dari Alphabet: Two-form letters

The letters alĕf, dāl, zāl, re, and ze in the chart above are two-form letters and connect only to the letter before them (that is, to the letter to their right). Therefore, when a two-form letter occurs in the initial position, it takes the isolated form (not connecting right or left) and when it occurs in the medial position, it takes the final form (only connecting on the right).

Exercise 3:   تمرین ۳:

Watch the following video recording demonstrating writing in the isolated and final forms of two-form letters.

1. Mark arrows on the shapes given to show the movement of the pen.
2. Practice writing each form on the dotted lines.

| Final<br>آخر | Isolated<br>مفرد | Letter<br>حرف |
|---|---|---|
| | | ا↓ |
| | | د |
| | | ذ |
| | | ر |
| | | ز |
| | | ژ |
| | | و |

## 1.5 Dari Alphabet: Four-form letters

Four-form letters can connect to other letters on both the left and the right. There are 25 four-form letters in the Dari alphabet.

Exercise 4:  تمرین ۴:

You will see a video recording demonstrating the writing of various forms of four-form letters.

1. Mark arrows on the shapes given to show the movement of the pen.
2. Practice writing each form on the dotted lines.

| Final<br>آخر | Medial<br>وسط | Initial<br>شروع | Isolated<br>مفرد | Letter<br>حرف |
|---|---|---|---|---|
| | | | | ب |
| | | | | پ |
| | | | | ت |
| | | | | ث |
| | | | | ج |
| | | | | چ |
| | | | | ح |
| | | | | خ |
| | | | | س |

| | | | | |
|---|---|---|---|---|
| | | | | ش |
| | | | | ص |
| | | | | ض |
| | | | | ط |
| | | | | ظ |
| | | | | ع |
| | | | | غ |
| | | | | ف |
| | | | | ق |
| | | | | ک |
| | | | | گ |
| | | | | ل |
| | | | | م |
| | | | | ن |
| | | | | ه |
| | | | | ی |

Exercise 5:  تمرین ۵:

The following words are the names of some countries that you will see and hear in everyday life. For each word, first circle the letters you recognize, then write them in the correct columns below. (Hint: There can be more than one letter in each column.) The first one is done for you.

| Final<br>آخر | Medial<br>وسط | Initial<br>شروع | Isolated<br>مفرد | |
|---|---|---|---|---|
| ا | کـ | مـ - یـ | ا - ر | امریکا |
| | | | | افغانستان |
| | | | | کانادا |
| | | | | مکسیکو |

Exercise 6:  تمرین ۶:

First, identify the names of the following countries by sounding them out using the transcriptions provided. Then, try writing the countries' names in Dari script by using the proper form of each letter. The first example is done for you.

| | Spelling | Pronunciation |
|---|---|---|
| 1. | مـ کـ سـ یـ کـ و | [maksikō] |
| 2. | | [barāzil] |
| 3. | | [rusi-ya] |
| 4. | | [torki-ya] |
| 5. | | [poland] |
| 6. | | [kānādā] |
| 7. | | [farānsa] |
| 8. | | [andoniziyā] |
| 9. | | [pākĕstān] |

Exercise 7:  تمرین ۷:

Ask your classmate the following question: شما از کجا هستید؟

šomā az kojā hasted? Your classmate will choose a country name among the
above names and would say, ... از az ...

Exercise 8:  تمرین ۸:

Watch the videos and practice writing the following words, which consist of
two-form letters in which none of the letters are connected to another.

| | | | |
|---|---|---|---|
| | ا + ز = از | [az] | from |
| | د + و = دو | [dō] | two |
| | د + ر + ا + ز = دراز | [darāz] | tall |
| | د + ر = در | [dar] | in |
| | ر + و + ز = روز | [rōz] | day |

Exercise 9:  تمرین ۹:

You will now watch a video recording on how the two-form and four-form
letters connect. As you watch the video, practice writing the words below.

| | | | |
|---|---|---|---|
| | سلام | [salām] | Hi |
| | نام | [nām] | name |
| | شما | [šomā] | you |
| | چیست | [čist] | what is |
| | من | [man] | I |

| | است [ast] | is |
|---|---|---|
| | از [az] | from |
| | کجا [kojā] | where |
| | هستید [hasted] | are |
| | واشنگتن [wāšengtan] | Washington |
| | کانادا [kānādā] | Canada |
| | مکسیکو [maksikō] | Mexico |
| | فرانسه [faransa] | France |
| | امریکا [amrikā] | America |
| | نیویورک [neyō-yōrk] | New York |
| | چین [čin] | China |
| | کابل [kābol] | Kabul |
| | روسیه [rōsi-ya] | Russia |

Exercise 10:  تمرین ۱۰:

> For each of the following words, you have been given the isolated forms of each letter. Rewrite them in the correct form, connecting the letters as appropriate. The first one has been done for you.

| Answer | | | | | | Letters | | | # |
|---|---|---|---|---|---|---|---|---|---|
| سلام | | | | م | ا | ل | س | | 1 |
| | | | م | ك | ی | ل | ع | و | 2 |
| | | ظ | ف | ا | ح | د | خ | | 3 |
| | | | | | م | ا | ن | | 4 |
| | | | | | ا | م | ش | | 5 |
| | | | | ت | س | ی | چ | | 6 |
| | | | | ت | س | ا | | | 7 |
| | | | | ن | ا | ت | | | 8 |

# درس سوم: او کیست؟

## Lesson Three: Who is he/she?

In this section, you will learn how to introduce a third person and how to write ligatures.

Exercise 1:  تمرین ۱:

You will hear two short conversations on the audio recording: the first is of two men and the second is of a man and a woman. In both, you will hear someone introducing a third person.

Who is she?
[ō kist?] او کیست؟

She is Layla.
[ō laylā ast] او لیلا است.

Where is she from?
[ō az kojā ast?] او از کجاست؟

From Kabul.
[az kabol.] از کابل.

Who is he?
[ō kist?] او کیست؟

He is Farid.
[ō farid ast] او فرید است.

Where is he from?
[ō az kojā ast?] او از کجاست؟

From Kabul.
[az kabol.] از کابل.

Exercise 2:  تمرین ۲:

Turn to your classmate sitting next to you; introduce yourself, ask for his/her name and where they are from. Then point to a person in the classroom and ask his/her name, also.

## 1.6 Dari Alphabet: Ligatures (Connections)

In Dari handwriting and typing there are a few letters that take a special form when connected to each other. These combinations of letters are called ligatures. For example:

1. The combination of letters ك [kāf] and گ [gāf] with letters ا [alĕf] or ل [lām] are joined at a point to make a circle instead of using a horizontal connecting line.

| Handwritten | Printed |
|---|---|
| کل = ل + ك | كل = ل + ك |
| گل = ل + گ | گل = ل + ك |
| کا = ا + ك | کا = ا + ك |
| گا = ا + گ | گا = ا + گ |

2. The combination of letter ل [lām] with ا [alĕf] also takes a different shape.

| Handwritten | Printed |
|---|---|
| لا = ا + ل | كل = ل + ك |
| لا = ا + ل | لا = ا + ل |

3. In some words, the combination of لا may follow کل، بل، سل and گل. In this case, the connection between them that appears as:

| Handwritten | Printed |
|---|---|
| گلا = ا + ل + گ | گلا = ا + ل + گ |
| کلا = ا + ل + ك | کلا = ا + ل + ك |

Exercise 3:  تمرین ۳:

Now, watch the video recording and practice writing some Afghan names that use the ligatures ك [kāf], گ [gāf], ل [lām], and ا [aléf].

| | |
|---|---|
| س + ل + ا + م = سلام | [salām] |
| ك + ا + ظ + م = کاظم | [kāzem] |
| ل + ی + ل + ا = لیلا | [laylā] |
| ك + ا + ب + ل = کابل | [kābol] |
| گ + ل + ا + ل + ی = گلالی | [golālay] |
| ك + ا + م + ل = کامل | [kāmel] |
| م + ل + ا + ل + ی = ملالی | [malālay] |
| گ + ل + ا + ب = گلاب | [gulāb] |
| غ + ل + ا + م = غلام | [ğolām] |
| ج + ل + ا + ل = جلال | [jalāl] |
| ن + ن + گ + ی + ا + ل + ی = ننگیالی | [nangyālay] |
| ل + ط + ی + ف = لطیف | [latif] |
| ع + ب + د + ا + ل + ل + ه = عبد الله | [abdulāh] |

## 1.7 Dari Alphabet: Writing Rule

When letters with the ‌‌ shape ( ‍ [jim], ‍ [če], ‍ [he], ‍ [xe]) occur in medial or final position in handwriting, the preceding letter is written a little above the medial line, even though in the printed form the connection occurs on the medial line. Compare the ligatures in print (A) and handwriting (B) in the following chart:

| B | A | Letters connecting |
|---|---|---|
| سخت | سخت | س+خ+ت |
| تخت | تخت | ت+خ+ت |
| نجيب | نجيب | ن+ج+ى+ب |
| نجار | نجار | ن+ج+ا+ر |
| تجارت | تجارت | ت+ج+ا+ر+ت |
| محمد | محمد | م+ح+م+د |

Exercise 4:    تمرین ۴:

Watch the video recording and write the Afghan names that have the shape ح- in various positions.

| | |
|---|---|
|  | ح + ب + ى + ب = حبيب  [habib] |
|  | ن + ج + ى + ب = نجيب  [najib] |
|  | م + ح + ب = محب  [moheb] |
|  | ح + س + ى + ب = حسيب  [hasib] |

| | [xaybar] خ + ی + ب + ر = خیبر |
|---|---|
| | [sakhi] س + خ + ی = سخی |
| | [ajmal] ا + ج + م + ل = اجمل |
| | [mohammad] م + ح + م + د = محمد |
| | [fatāh] ف + ت + ا + ح = فتاح |
| | [rahim] ر + ح + ی + م = رحیم |

Exercise 5:  تمرین ۵:

The following letters in each column spell a country name. Connect them to each other to make words. The first example is done for you.

| Answer | C1 | C2 | C3 | C4 | C5 | C6 | C7 | C8 | C9 | Ex. |
|---|---|---|---|---|---|---|---|---|---|---|
| امریکا | | | | ا | ک | ی | ر | م | ا | Ex. |
| | | | | | ا | پ | و | ر | ا | 1 |
| | | | | ا | د | ا | ن | ا | ک | 2 |
| | | | | | ن | ا | ر | ی | ا | 3 |
| | ن | ا | ت | س | ن | ا | غ | ف | ا | 4 |
| | | | ن | ا | ت | س | ب | ر | ع | 5 |
| | | | ن | ا | ت | س | ک | ا | پ | 6 |
| | | ن | ا | ت | س | ل | گ | ن | ا | 7 |
| | | | | ه | س | ن | ا | ر | ف | 8 |
| | | ا | ی | ل | ا | ر | ت | س | ا | 9 |
| | | | | | | | ر | ص | م | 10 |
| | | | | | ن | ا | پ | ا | ج | 11 |
| | | | | | ه | ی | س | و | ر | 12 |
| | | ن | ا | ت | س | ک | ب | ز | ا | 13 |

Exercise 6: تمرین ۶:

Ask your classmates their names and where they are from. Then fill in the chart in Dari. For example:

What is your name? [nām-e tān čist?] نام تان چیست؟
My name is Sadiq. [nām-e man sādĕq ast.] نام من صادق است.
Where are you from? [šomā az kojā hasted?] شما از کجا هستید؟
From Afghanistan. [az afğānĕstān] از افغانستان.

| Place [jāy] جای | Name [nām] نام | Place [jāy] جای | Name [nām] نام |
|---|---|---|---|
|  |  |  |  |
|  |  |  |  |
|  |  |  |  |
|  |  |  |  |

# مرور فصل اول

# Chapter One Review

In this section you will review the vocabulary, phrases, grammar, and cultural elements that you learned throughout the chapter.

Exercise 1: تمرین ۱:

A. Listen carefully to the two short conversations and mark if they are formal or informal. Then explain your answer.

| | | | Formal | Informal |
|---|---|---|---|---|
| 1 | Farid فرید | Laylā لیلا | ☐ | ☐ |
| 2 | Jāwed جاوید | Parwez پرویز | ☐ | ☐ |

B. Listen carefully to a conversation between a man and a woman and, in the table below, write down their first names, last names, place of origin, and any other information given.

| Place of Residency [jāy-e bud o bāš] جای بود و باش | Last Name [taxalos] تخلص | First Name [nām] نام | |
|---|---|---|---|
| | | | 1 |
| | | | 2 |

Exercise 2:  تمرین ۲ :

You are traveling in Afghanistan and see the following signs. In each sign you will find alphabet letters you've written in the previous activities. Using what you've learned, figure out what each sign says.

Exercise 3:

Choose the most appropriate answer for each of the following questions.

| | | |
|---|---|---|
| 1. | Which country in Europe uses English as its official language? | ___ برلین |
| 2. | What is the capital city of Germany? | ___ انگلستان |
| 3. | What is the capital of the USA? | ___ نیویورک |
| 4. | Where is the Statue of Liberty located? | ___ واشنگتن دی سی |
| 5. | Which country shares a southern border with the USA? | ___ کانادا |
| 6. | Which country shares a northern border with the USA? | ___ تگزاس |
| 7. | Mexico shares a border with what state? | ___ کابل |
| 8. | What is the capital city of Afghanistan? | ___ مکسیکو |

Exercise 4:

Listen to the audio recording and match the sayings in Column A with their responses in Column B.

| B | | A | |
|---|---|---|---|
| ___ | نام من صادق است. | سلام علیکم | 1 |
| ___ | وعلیکم سلام | سلام | 2 |
| ___ | وعلیکم | نام تان چیست؟ | 3 |
| ___ | نام من زلمی است. | نام شما چیست؟ | 4 |
| ___ | خدا حافظ | خدا حافظ! | 5 |

Exercise 5: 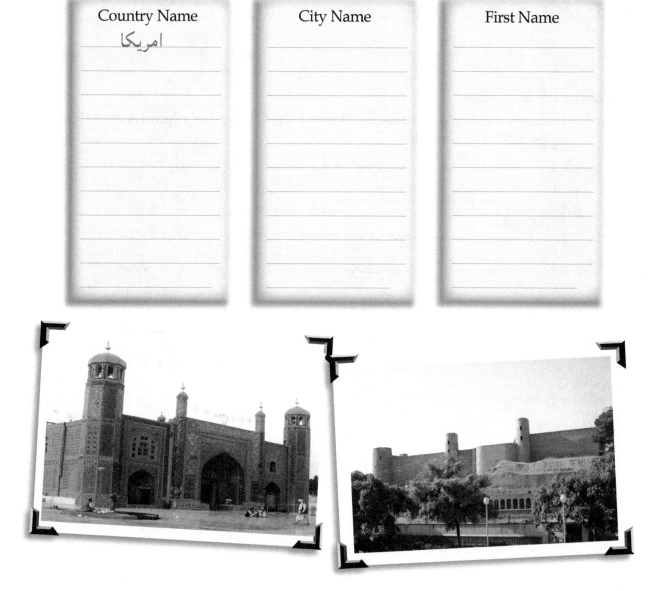 ۵ :تمرین

Look at the word list below and put each word under the right heading. For example: "America" would go under the "Country name" tab.

| | | | | |
|---|---|---|---|---|
| لیلی | کارلا | جان | کابل | امریکا |
| نیویورک | اندونیزیا | مایک | کانادا | پرویز |
| پاکستان | برازیل | روسیه | ترکیه | آرش |
| واشنگتن | جسیکا | برلین | فرید | چین |
| پولند | نجیب | کندهار | نصرت | فرانسه |

| Country Name | City Name | First Name |
|---|---|---|
| امریکا | | |

# لغات فصل اول
# Chapter One Vocabulary

In this part of the lesson, you will review, listen to, and practice pronunciation of the phrases and vocabulary used in the chapter.

## Phrases عبارات

| Hello! (Peace be with you.) | asalām ō alaykom! | السلام وعلیکم! |
|---|---|---|
| Hello! (Peace be with you.) | walaykom salām! | وعلیکم السلام! |
| Hello! (Peace be with you.) | salām | سلام! |
| Hello! (Peace be with you.) | walaykom | وعلیکم! |
| Where are you from? | šomā az kojā hasted? | شما از کجا هستید؟ |
| From Afghanistan. | az afğānĕstān | از افغانستان |
| Nice meeting you. | az didan-e tān xōšāl šodom. | از دیدن تان خوشحال شدم. |
| Me too. | man hamčenān. | من همچنان . |
| Goodbye. | xodā hāfĕz! | خدا حافظ! |

## Vocabulary Words لغات

| America | mrikā | امریکا |
|---|---|---|
| Indonesia | andoniziyā | اندونیزیا |
| Brazil | barāzíl | برازیل |
| Pakistan | pākĕstān | پاکستان |
| Poland | poland | پولند |
| your | tān | تان |
| Turkey | torki-ya | ترکیه |
| China | čin | چین |
| God | xodā | خدا |
| to be happy | xōšāl šodan | خوشحال شدن |

| | | |
|---|---|---|
| meeting, seeing (to see) | didan | ديدن |
| Russia | rōsiya | روسیه |
| you (your) | šomā | شما |
| France | faransa | فرانسه |
| Kabul | kābol | کابل |
| Canada | kānādā | کانادا |
| where | kojā | کجا |
| Mexico | maksikō | مکسیکو |
| I, my | man | من |
| name | nām | نام |
| New York | neyō-yōrk | نیویورک |
| Washington | wāšĕngtan | واشنگتن |
| also | hamčenān | همچنان |

## Dari Vocabulary Different from Iranian Persian

| English Translation | Iranian Persian | | Farsi-e Dari | |
|---|---|---|---|---|
| Washington | vāšĕngtōn | واشنگتون | wāšĕngtan | واشنگتن |
| Mexico | mak-zik | مکزیک | maksikō | مکسیکو |
| Indonesia | andonizi | اندونیزی | andoniziyā | اندونیزیا |

# فصل دوم
## CHAPTER TWO

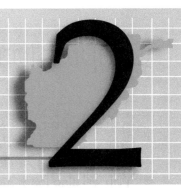

# شمارهٔ تلیفون تان چند است؟
## WHAT IS YOUR TELEPHONE NUMBER?

# IN THIS CHAPTER

- **وظایف** Functions

*Learning numbers 0–20; Asking and giving phone numbers; Reading business cards and signs; Writing brief descriptions about yourself; Talking about classroom objects; Asking "Who is that?" and "How many people are there?"*

- **تبصرهٔ فرهنگی** Cultural Notes

*Afghan phone numbers; Afghan business cards; Afghan work week; Periods of time of day: Afghan days & nights*

- **دستور زبان** Language Structure

*Vowel sounds; Diphthongs; Consonants; Letters used in loanwords; Demonstrative pronouns; Sentence structure in Dari; Pluralization of inanimate objects; Interrogative sentences*

- **مرور فصل** Chapter Review

*Writing short informational notes about people; Reading people's business cards in Dari; Making your own business cards in Dari; Pointing out objects around you*

- **لغات** Vocabulary

*Review phrases and words used in this chapter*

# Chapter Introduction    معرفی فصل

In this chapter, you will learn more about Dari vowels and consonants, numbers from 0-20, and the days of the week. You will be introduced to the letters used in Pashto and Dari loanwords and recognize some common English loanwords. You will also learn how to ask for someone's phone number and ask who that person is and how many people there are.

شمارهٔ تلیفون تان چند است؟
What is your phone number?

بیایید ، به دری حساب کنیم.
Let's count in Dari.

این چیست؟
What is this?

## Note:

On the completion of the chapter, you will be able to ask simple questions in Dari, tell someone your phone number, and read for basic information.

درس اول: بیایید، به دری حساب کنیم.

# Lesson One: Let's count in Dari.

In this section, you will learn Dari numbers 0–20 and more about Dari vowel and consonant sounds.

Exercise 1: تمرین ۱ :

Look at the following picture of a standard cell phone. Find the Dari numbers and draw them next to their English equivalents in the chart below. For example:

| | | 5 |
|---|---|---|
| | | 6 |
| | | 7 |
| | | 8 |
| | | 9 |

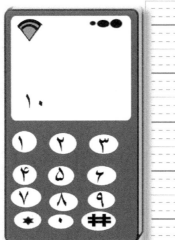

| | | 0 |
|---|---|---|
| | | 1 |
| | | 2 |
| | | 3 |
| | | 4 |

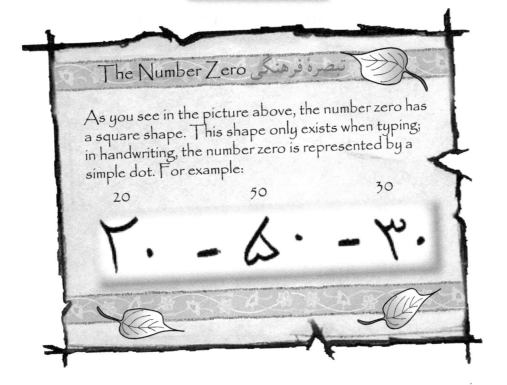

### The Number Zero — تبصرۀ فرهنگی

As you see in the picture above, the number zero has a square shape. This shape only exists when typing; in handwriting, the number zero is represented by a simple dot. For example:

20        50        30

۲۰ - ۵۰ - ۳۰

Exercise 2: تمرین ۲ :

Watch the video recording about writing numbers. Then, for each of the following numbers below:

1. Trace the arrows showing how the numbers are formed.
2. Practice writing the numbers on the provided lines.

| | ٥/۵ | 5 |
|---|---|---|
| | ۶ | 6 |
| | ۷ | 7 |
| | ۸ | 8 |
| | ۹ | 9 |

| | ۰ | 0 |
|---|---|---|
| | ۱ | 1 |
| | ۲ | 2 |
| | ۳ | 3 |
| | ۴ | 4 |

| | ۱۰ | 10 |
|---|---|---|

Exercise 3: تمرین ۳ :

Listen to the audio recording and practice pronouncing each number as it is read. Then for each, write the proper digit under the "numbers" column. Each number will be read twice.

| Pronunciation | Spelling | Numbers | |
|---|---|---|---|
| [sěfěr] | صفر | —— | 0 |
| [yak] | یك | —— | 1 |
| [dō] | دو | —— | 2 |
| [sě] | سه | —— | 3 |
| [čār] | چار | —— | 4 |
| [panj] | پنج | —— | 5 |
| [šaš] | شش | —— | 6 |
| [haft] | هفت | —— | 7 |
| [hašt] | هشت | —— | 8 |
| [noh] | نه | —— | 9 |
| [dah] | ده | —— | 10 |

## 2.1 Dari Numbers

Unlike Dari letters, numbers in Dari are written from left to right, just as they are in English. For example:

**120    390    500    192    201**

۱۲۰    ۳۹۰    ۵۰۰    ۱۹۲    ۲۰۱

Exercise 4:    تمرین ۴ :

Listen to the audio recording and write down the numbers you hear. Then, write the name of the digit in the space beside it.

| | | 6 |
|---|---|---|
| | | 7 |
| | | 8 |
| | | 9 |
| | | 10 |
| | | 11 |

| | | 1 |
|---|---|---|
| sĕ | ۳ | |
| | | 2 |
| | | 3 |
| | | 4 |
| | | 5 |

### 2.2 Dari Vowel Sounds

You may have already realized that in some Dari words, the vowels are not written or that certain letters are pronounced differently when in different positions within a word. For example, the number شش [šaš] 'six' is pronounced with a vowel sound in the middle, but is written using only two consonant sounds( s [š]). This is because Dari has eight vowel sounds of various lengths (e.g. short or long), and the short vowel sounds do not appear in writing:

1. [a] as a in 'cash'.
2. [ā] as a in 'father'.
3. [ĕ] as e in 'let'.
4. [e] as a in 'late'.

5. [i] as ee in 'heed'.
6. [o] as o in 'note'.
7. [ō] as o in 'hole'.
8. [u] as oo in 'pool'.

Exercise 5: تمرین ۵ :

The following chart gives the most common pronunciations of the eight vowels used in Dari. Listen to the words representing each vowel sound, and note that some of the vowels are pronounced a little differently depending on the sounds around them.

| English Meaning | Examples in Dari | | English Words with Similar Sounds | Dari Vowels |
|---|---|---|---|---|
| one<br>seven<br>eight | [yak]<br>[haft]<br>[hašt] | يك<br>هفت<br>هشت | cash | [a] |
| water<br>doctor<br>four | [āb]<br>[dāktar]<br>[čār] | آب<br>داكتر<br>چار | father | [ā] |
| three<br>pencil<br>bicycle | [sĕ]<br>[pĕnsĕl]<br>[bāys-kĕl] | سه<br>پنسل<br>بایسکِل | let (short) | [ĕ] |

| | | | | |
|---|---|---|---|---|
| full<br>table<br>cheese | [ser]<br>[mez]<br>[paner] | سیر<br>میز<br>پنیر | **late (long)** | [e] |
| key<br>milk<br>old | [kĕli]<br>[šir]<br>[pir] | کلی<br>شیر<br>پیر | **heed** | [i] |
| hungry<br>thirsty<br>nine | [gošna]<br>[tošna]<br>[noh] | گشنه<br>تشنه<br>نه | **note (short)** | [o] |
| two<br>football<br>ball | [dō]<br>[fōtbāl]<br>[tōp] | دو<br>فوتبال<br>توپ | **hole (long)** | [ō] |
| sugar<br>south<br>boot | [bura]<br>[jonub]<br>[but] | بوره<br>جنوب<br>بوت | **pool** | [u] |

Exercise 6:

Listen to the audio recording and mark the vowels that you hear in each of the numbers given.

| ĕ | e | i | u | ō | o | ā | a | | |
|---|---|---|---|---|---|---|---|---|---|
| | | | | | | | | صفر | ٠ |
| | | | | | | | | یك | ١ |
| | | | | | | | | دو | ٢ |
| | | | | | | | | سه | ٣ |
| | | | | | | | | چار | ۴ |
| | | | | | | | | پنج | ۵ |
| | | | | | | | | شش | ۶ |
| | | | | | | | | هفت | ٧ |
| | | | | | | | | هشت | ٨ |
| | | | | | | | | نه | ٩ |
| | | | | | | | | ده | ١٠ |

Exercise 7: تمرین ۷ :

You will hear pairs of words with similar vowel sounds on the audio recording; put a check (√) next to the word you hear in each pair.

| ☐ | xār | ۴ | ☐ | tar | ۳ | ☐ | kār | ۲ | ☐ | bām | ۱ |
|---|-----|---|---|-----|---|---|-----|---|---|-----|---|
| ☐ | xar |   | ☐ | tār |   | ☐ | kar |   | ☐ | bam |   |

| ☐ | jāl | ۸ | ☐ | zēr | ۷ | ☐ | muš | ۶ | ☐ | nār | ۵ |
|---|-----|---|---|-----|---|---|-----|---|---|-----|---|
| ☐ | jal |   | ☐ | zar |   | ☐ | māš |   | ☐ | nar |   |

| ☐ | par | ۱۲ | ☐ | dur | ۱۱ | ☐ | tir | ۱۰ | ☐ | pās | ۹ |
|---|-----|----|---|-----|----|---|-----|----|---|-----|---|
| ☐ | pār |    | ☐ | dor |    | ☐ | tēr |    | ☐ | pas |   |

| ☐ | šer | ۱۵ | ☐ | pur | ۱۴ | ☐ | sir | ۱۳ |
|---|-----|----|---|-----|----|---|-----|----|
| ☐ | šir |    | ☐ | por |    | ☐ | sēr |    |

## 2.3 Dari Diphthongs or Semivowels

Dipthongs are formed by two adjacent vowel sounds working together to make one unique vowel sound. Examples in English include sounds such as *coat* (/ou/), *raise* (/ei/), *aisle* (/ai/), and *foil* (/oi/).

The Dari language has two types of diphthongs: a vowel followed by *y* and a vowel followed by *w*. Listen to the following examples of Dari diphthongs.

aw    [naw] نو    [jaw] جو    [šaw] شو    (similar to the sound in "now")
ay    [nay] نی    [sayl] سیل    [mayl] میل    (similar to the sound in "say")

Exercise 8:  تمرین ۸ :

Listen to the audio recording and fill in the blanks with the diphthongs you hear.

| | | | | | |
|---|---|---|---|---|---|
| [ āb___ ] | آبرو | ۴ | [ s___r] | سیر | ۱ |
| [ aft___ ] | افتو | ۵ | [ x___ ] | خو | ۲ |
| [ m___ ] | نی | ۶ | [ k___ ] | کی | ۳ |

## 2.4 Dari Consonants

There are twenty-five consonants in Dari. Eighteen of these should be easy for native English speakers to learn because they are pronounced similarly to some English sounds.

A. Dari consonants that sound similar to English consonants:

| English Example | Dari Example | Dari Consonants | |
|---|---|---|---|
| as *b* in *boy* | brother [barādar] برادر | ب | [b] |
| as *p* in *pen* | five [panj] پنج | پ | [p] |
| as *t* in *train* | phone [tĕlefun] تلیفون | ت، ط | [t] |
| as *s* in *son* | three [sĕ] سه | س، ث، ص | [s] |
| as *d* in *donate* | two [dō] دو | د | [d] |
| as *ch* in *chain* | four [čār] چار | چ | [č] |
| as *j* in *John* | Japan [jāpān] جاپان | ج | [j] |
| as *sh* in *she* | six [šaš] شش | ش | [š] |
| as *z* in *zebra* | woman [zan] زن | ز، ظ، ض | [z] |
| as *su* in *pleasure* or *ge* in *garage* | journalist [žornālest] ژورنالیست | ژ | [ž] |
| as *f* in *family* | family [fāmil] فامیل | ف | [f] |
| as *k* in *king* | book [kĕtāb] کتاب | ك | [k] |
| as *g* gold | warm [garm] گرم | گ | [g] |

## 2.4 Dari Consonants (cont'd.)

| | | | |
|---|---|---|---|
| as *l* in *lots* | lip [lab] لب | ل | [l] |
| as *m* in *myth* | table [mez] میز | م | [m] |
| as *n* in *Nancy* | nine [noh] نه | ن | [n] |
| as *w* in *wet* | time [waqt] وقت | و | [w] |
| as *y* in *yes* | one [yak] یك | ى | [y] |

As you can see in the table, some of the consonant sounds are represented by more than one letter. That is because some of those letters are only used in Arabic loanwords. For more information about Arabic loanwords, see 2.6.

B. Dari consonant sounds with no English consonant sound equivalent: ([q], [x], [ğ], [ž], [r], and ['], [h].)

1. [q] ق This sound is pronounced somewhat like the *k* sound in "kook" except even further back in the mouth, so that *q* has a very low or deep sound compared to *k*. Example: pen [qalam] قلم

2. [x] خ This sound is pronounced by putting the tongue in position for *k* but allowing air to flow between the tongue and the roof of the mouth. Example: home [xāna] خانه

3. [ğ] غ This sound is pronounced by putting the tongue in position for *g* but allowing air to flow between the tongue and the roof of the mouth. Example: Afghanistan [afğānĕstān] افغانستان

4. ['] ع This is the sound of the catch in the throat when you say "uh-oh." In Dari, this occurs in many places, e.g. immediately before or after another consonant. Example: Arab ['arab] عرب

5. [h] ه / ح This sound is pronounced the same in Dari and in English. However, in Dari, unlike in English, it can occur at the end of a syllable. Example: eight [hašt] هشت

6. [r] ر In Dari, r is pronounced with the tip of the tongue and trilled. Example: four [čār] چار

Exercise 9: تمرین ۹ :
Listen closely to the audio recording and put a check (√) next to the word(s) you hear.

| | | ۴ | | | ۳ | | | ۲ | | | ۱ |
|---|---|---|---|---|---|---|---|---|---|---|---|
| ☐ | ğam | | ☐ | ğayr | | ☐ | ğĕlāf | | ☐ | ğolām | |
| ☐ | xam | | ☐ | xayr | | ☐ | xĕlāf | | ☐ | qorān | |

| | | ۸ | | | ۷ | | | ۶ | | | ۵ |
|---|---|---|---|---|---|---|---|---|---|---|---|
| ☐ | kamar | | ☐ | kand | | ☐ | khāri | | ☐ | ğār | |
| ☐ | qamar | | ☐ | qand | | ☐ | qāri | | ☐ | xār | |

| | | ۱۰ | | | ۹ |
|---|---|---|---|---|---|
| ☐ | khār | | ☐ | karam | |
| ☐ | qār | | ☐ | qalam | |

Exercise 10: تمرین ۱۰ :
A. You will hear numbers 11–20 on the audio recording. Listen to it and write the Dari transliteration of each number in the appropriate blank.

| 11 | _____ |
|---|---|
| 12 | _____ |
| 13 | _____ |
| 14 | _____ |
| 15 | _____ |

| 16 | _____ |
|---|---|
| 17 | _____ |
| 18 | _____ |
| 19 | _____ |
| 20 | _____ |

B. Write the written numbers from the box below next to the digits they represent.

شانزده، پانزده، دوازده، سیزده، یازده، چارده، بیست،
نوزده، هفده، هژده

| _____ | ۱۶ |
|---|---|
| _____ | ۱۷ |
| _____ | ۱۸ |
| _____ | ۱۹ |
| _____ | ۲۰ |

| _____ | ۱۱ |
|---|---|
| _____ | ۱۲ |
| _____ | ۱۳ |
| _____ | ۱۴ |
| _____ | ۱۵ |

# درس دوم: شمارهٔ تلیفون تان چند است؟

## Lesson Two: What's your telephone number?

In this section, you will learn how to ask for and give a telephone number and how to get information from a business card or ID.

Exercise 1:  تمرین ۱ :

Listen to the following conversation on the audio recording. For each of the speakers shown below, write the phone numbers in the blanks provided.

Farid

Laylā

## Cultural Note     تبصرهٔ فرهنگی

### Giving your phone number in Afghanistan

Cell phones are very popular in Afghanistan, and like in the US, people use cell phones more than landlines. In fact, typically landlines are not even available in the rural areas and smaller cities, but are available only in a few big cities, so those who don't live in big cities have to use cell phones.

The country code for Afghanistan is (93) and there is no specific code for local areas. So unlike the US, which uses area codes, you can't tell from looking at a number which area it belongs to. However, all cell phone numbers begin with the number zero, and all cell phone numbers are ten digits long.

When you ask someone for their phone number in Afghanistan, they will usually give it in single, double, or triple digits. For example: the number 0119856253 could be given as

0-1-1-9-8-5-6-2-5-3 or

01-19-85-62-53 or

011-985-625-3

Exercise 2:  تمرین ۲ :

Listen to the audio recording and repeat the following phrases.

شمارهٔ تلیفون‌تان چند است؟

[šomāra-e tĕlefun-e tān čand ast?]

What is your phone number?

۰۷۰۲۰۱۲۱۴۵

[0702012145]

0702012145

Exercise 3: تمرین ۳ :

Go around the classroom and ask each person's first and last name and phone number. Then, fill in the table in Dari.

| شمارهٔتلیفون | تخلص | نام |
|---|---|---|
| | | |

Exercise 4:  تمرین ۴ :
  Listen to the audio recording and match each person to his/her phone number.

| | | | |
|---|---|---|---|
| 1. | | ماری | ۰۷۰۰۲۳۱۴۸۹ |
| 2. | | کریم | ۰۷۸۶۷۸۹۹۰۳ |
| 3. | | لیلا | ۰۷۹۹۱۱۲۲۰۰ |
| 4. | | رحیم | ۰۷۹۹۷۷۱۲۰۳ |
| 5. | | فرید | ۰۷۷۷۹۱۰۲۴۸ |
| 6. | | میوند | ۰۷۰۰۲۱۳۹۹۰ |

Exercise 5: تمرین ۵ :
  Read the following business cards carefully and answer the following questions.

۱

دوکان بـــــــــرگـــــر و آیـــسکریـــــم
فـــــــرید
شـــــمارهٔ تلیـــــفون ۷۹۹۰۱۲۳۸۲
آدرس ایمـــــیل: faridburger@yahoo.com

1. What is their phone number? _____
2. Whose business card is this?
   a) Farid      b) Fahim      c) Farshid
3. Looking at the business card, can you guess what types of things this person sells?

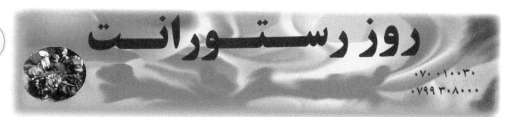

روز رستـــورانـت

۰۷۰۰۱۰۰۳۰
۰۷۹۹۳۰۸۰۰۰

1. What kind of business is this?

_____

2. What is the business's name?

_____

3. What are the phone numbers?

_____

---

داکتر زلمی عزیز
متخصص امراض قلبی

شماره تلیفون: ۰۷۹۹۱۱۲۳۴۵-۰۷۰۰۳۴۵۶۷۱-۰۷۰۰

آدرس: افغانستان ـ کابل-شهر نو سرک گلفروشي

1. What is this person's name (first and last)?

_____

2. What is his profession? _____

3. What are his phone numbers? _____

4. Which country is he from? _____

5. Which city? _____

---

جمهوری اسلامی افغانستان

شــاروالــی کــابل

۰۷۹۹۲۳۱۵۴۴

1. Underline Afghanistan in the title above.

2. What city is mentioned? _____

3. What is the phone number listed? _____

## 2.5 Pashto Letters in Dari

There are several letters that occasionally occur in words borrowed from Pashto. Most Dari speakers pronounce them as the closest Dari sounds. For example, the word 'municipality' [šārwāli] شاروالی used in the business card before is pronounced as as:

| Dari | | | Pashto | | |
|---|---|---|---|---|---|
| municipality شاروالی | ش | šen | municipality ښاروالی | ښ | xen/šen |

Some other examples include the following:

| Dari | | | Pashto | | |
|---|---|---|---|---|---|
| road وات | ت | te | road وات | ټ | te |
| general attorney سارنوالی | س | sin | general attorney څارنوالی | څ | ce |
| a male name زلمی | ز | ze | a male name ځلمی | ځ | dze |

تبصرهٔ فرهنگی Cultural Note
English Loanwords in Dari

Most of the names of new technological devices used in Dari are the same as in English, i.e. blackberry, tablet, etc.

Language scholars tried to replace those words with some Dari/Persian equivalent. However, the result was unsuccessful, because people use the English terms often, and so when someone says the new Dari/Persian terms, it sounds strange to people.

Here are some examples of other common English loanwords in Dari:

| | | |
|---|---|---|
| restaurant | rastōrānt | ریستورانت |
| ice cream | āys-kerim | آیسکریم |
| burger | bargar | برگر |

Exercise 6:  تمرین ۶ :

A. Each picture below represents an English loanword in Dari. First, listen to the pronunciations on the audio recording, numbering each picture in the order you hear it. Then, write the name in Dari below its picture. Check your work with a partner.

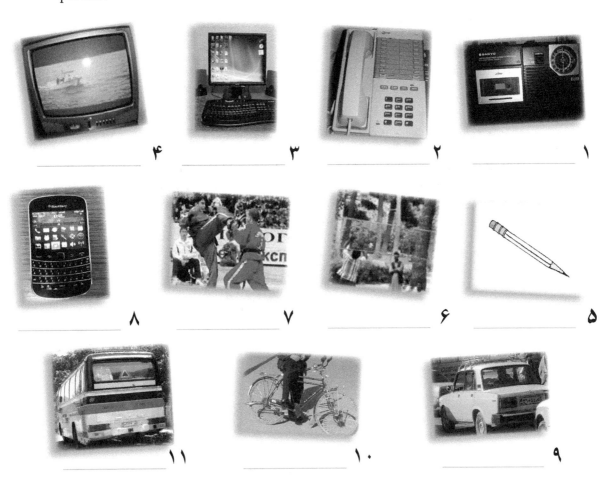

۴ _____ ۳ _____ ۲ _____ ۱ _____

۸ _____ ۷ _____ ۶ _____ ۵ _____

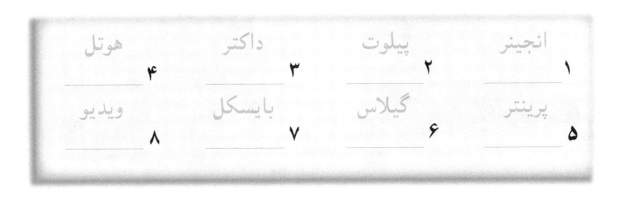

۱۱ _____ ۱۰ _____ ۹ _____

B. Read the following English loanwords in Dari. Can you figure out what each one is? Write its English equivalent in the space below.

| هوتل | داکتر | پیلوت | انجینر |
|---|---|---|---|
| ۴ _____ | ۳ _____ | ۲ _____ | ۱ _____ |
| ویدیو | بایسکل | گیلاس | پرینتر |
| ۸ _____ | ۷ _____ | ۶ _____ | ۵ _____ |

Exercise 7: تمرین ۷ :

> You will hear a conversation between a man and woman on the audio recording. Listen and then answer the following questions in Dari script.

| | |
|---|---|
| 1. What is the woman's name? | |
| 2. What is the man's name? | |
| 3. What is the man's phone number? | |
| 4. What is Karim's phone number? | |

Exercise 8: تمرین ۸ :

> Working with a partner, write a short dialogue in Dari script that includes the following: greeting each other, introducing yourselves, asking where the other is from, asking one another's phone number, and saying goodbye. Practice your dialogue, and then act it out in front of the class.

Exercise 9: ٩ تمرین :

Working with a partner, read the ID card below and answer the following questions.

کارت هویت

| نام | عبدالمتین |
| نام پدر | عبدالسلام |
| تخلص | فیضی |
| کار | انجینر |
| آدرس | کابل |

| شمارهٔ تلیفون خانه | ۲۰۲۲۳۴۶۲۸۱ |
| شمارهٔ تلیفون کار | ۲۰۶۷۳۲۹۱۳۷ |
| شمارهٔ مبایل | ۰۷۹۹۳۰۳۷۲۹ |

| | |
|---|---|
| 1. What is the name of the person on the ID card? (first and last name) | |
| 2. What is his father's name? | |
| 3. What is his cell phone number? | |
| 4. What is his home phone number? | |
| 5. In which city does he live? | |
| 6. What does he do for a living? | |

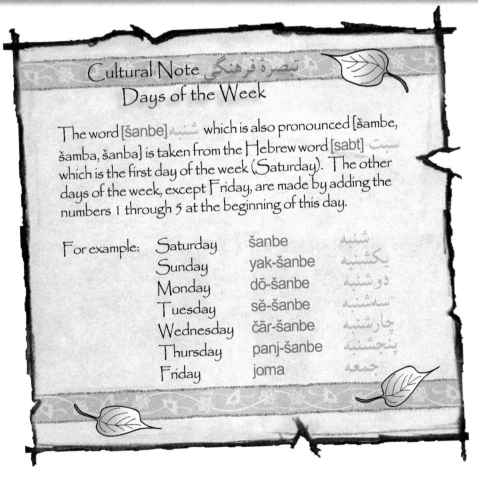

Cultural Note   تبصرهٔ فرهنگی
Days of the Week

The word [šanbe] شنبه which is also pronounced [šambe, šamba, šanba] is taken from the Hebrew word [sabt] سبت which is the first day of the week (Saturday). The other days of the week, except Friday, are made by adding the numbers 1 through 5 at the beginning of this day.

For example:

| Saturday | šanbe | شنبه |
| Sunday | yak-šanbe | یکشنبه |
| Monday | dō-šanbe | دوشنبه |
| Tuesday | sĕ-šanbe | سهشنبه |
| Wednesday | čār-šanbe | چارشنبه |
| Thursday | panj-šanbe | پنجشنبه |
| Friday | joma | جمعه |

Exercise 10: تمرین ١٠ :

You will hear on the audio recording the names of the days of the week in Dari, starting with Saturday and ending with Friday (the traditional order in Afghanistan). Repeat the name of each day and number each in the order that you hear it.

| | | |
|---|---|---|
| _____ | [šanbe] | شنبه |
| _____ | [sě-šanbe] | سه شنبه |
| _____ | [dō-šanbe] | دوشنبه |
| _____ | [joma] | جمعه |
| _____ | [čā-ršanbe] | چارشنبه |
| _____ | [yakšanbe] | یکشنبه |
| _____ | [panj-šanbe] | پنجشنبه |

Cultural Note    تبصرهٔ فرهنگی
## Afghan Work Week

In Afghanistan, people work six days a week and the work week starts on Saturday. A typical work week in Afghanistan runs Saturday through Thursday at noon, with the weekend beginning Thursday afternoon. Most offices are open on Thursdays, but on Friday all offices, stores, and shops are closed. So, if you would like to schedule a meeting with one of the government offices on Thursday afternoon, make sure that they are aware ahead of time so that they can make arrangements to stay open.

Additionally, NGOs (non govermental organizations) are off Fridays and Saturdays as well.

Exercise 11:  تمرین ۱۱:

You will hear a conversation between a man a woman on the audio recording. Write only the days of the week you hear on each line below.

### Cultural Note تبصرهٔ فرهنگی
### Afghan Days & Nights

In Afghanistan, some people will calculate day and night in the way it is done in many other cultures, i.e. a day is from 12:00 am through 11:59 pm. However, this method is not common among Afghan people. Most Afghans calculate that the day starts at the beginning of dusk and ends at dusk on the following day.

For example: If today is Monday, then last night was Monday night. And when the sun sets today, it becomes Tuesday night. And as the sun is rising, it now becomes Tuesday day.

Sunset to Sunrise (approx 6pm – 6am) – Monday night
Sunrise to Sunset (approx 6am – 6pm) – Monday day
Sunset to Sunrise (approx 6pm – 6am) – Tuesday night
Sunrise to Sunset (approx 6am – 6pm) – Tuesday day

Exercise 12:  تمرین ۱۲ :

A. Listen to a short dialogue on the audio recording demonstrating how someone would ask the day of the week in Dari.

What day is today? ĕmroz, čand šanbe ast? امروز، چند شنبه است؟
Monday. dō- šanbe. دوشنبه.

B. Below you see a Dari calendar. Using what you have learned in Exercise 10 and the Cutlural Note on page 58, fill in the days of the week. The first one has been done for you.

| | | | | | | شنبه |
|---|---|---|---|---|---|---|
| ۱ | | | | | | |
| ۸ | ۷ | ۶ | ۵ | ۴ | ۳ | ۲ |
| ۱۵ | ۱۴ | ۱۳ | ۱۲ | ۱۱ | ۱۰ | ۹ |
| ۲۲ | ۲۱ | ۲۰ | ۱۹ | ۱۸ | ۱۷ | ۱۶ |
| ۲۹ | ۲۸ | ۲۷ | ۲۶ | ۲۵ | ۲۴ | ۲۳ |
| | | | | | ۳۱ | ۳۰ |

### 2.6 Letters That Are Only Used in Arabic Loanwords

In the Dari alphabet, there are a number of letters that are only used as Arabic loanwords for sounds that do not exist in Dari. Religiously educated people imitate the Arabic pronunciation of these letters; however, ordinary Dari speakers substitute similar Dari sounds for the Arabic, but keep the original spelling when writing. For example, the word 'Friday' [jom'a ] جمعه is an Arabic loanword which is taken from the Dari word 'collectivity, plural, together' [jam'] جمع . In Dari, the letter [ayn] ع , which sounds like ['], is not pronounced as it is in Arabic. Thus, the word [jom'a] is pronounced as [joma].

## 2.6 Letters That Are Only Used in Arabic Loanwords (cont'd.)

These letters are written and pronounced as follows:

| Letters used only in Arabic loanwords | Letters used both in loanwords and native words | Sound |
|---|---|---|
| ط [tā] | ت [te] | [t] |
| ص [sād] , ث [se] | س [sin] | [s] |
| ح [he] | ه [he] | [h] |
| ظ [zā] , ض [zād] , ذ [zāl] | ز [ze] | [z] |
| ع [ayn] | - | ['], [a], [i], [u], [o] or silent |

The letters (ح ، ظ ، ط ، ض ، ص ، ذ ، ث ) are used in loanwords that come from Arabic. These letters are not used in loanwords from any other language.

Exception: The letter [zāl] ذ is mostly used in Arabic words, but it is also used in a very limited number of Dari words, for example 'parade' [rasmegozášt] رسم گذشت .

Exercise 13:  تمرین ۱۳ :

> Look at the following text carefully. Based on all you have learned about loanwords so far, underline all of the loanwords you see. Then, write each word below and indicate whether it is an English, Pashto, or Arabic loanword.

افغانستان یك كشور محاط به خشكه است كه در اطراف آن كشور های ایران، پاكستان، چین، تاجكستان، ازبكستان و تركمنستان واقع میباشد . افغانستان یك كشور زراعتی است و دارای باغ های مثمر میباشد .
مردم این كشور پركار و زحمتكش اند ، آنها از نظر اقتصادی بسیار غریب و ضعیف میباشند . كشور مذكور سرشار از منابع طبیعی میباشد . سیستم تحصیلی این كشور، سیستم دولتی و خصوصی است. مشهورترین پوهنتون های آن پوهنتون كابل، هرات، مزار، جلال آباد و قندهار است كه هر یك شامل چندین پوهنحئی میباشد .

# درس سوم : این زن کیست؟

## Lesson Three: Who is this woman?

In this section, you will learn how to point out someone, how to make nouns plural, and how to ask questions in Dari. You will also learn about Dari sentence structure.

Exercise 1:    تمرین ۱:

A. Listen to the audio recording and pay attention to the pronunciation of the following terms.

زن
[zan]
woman

مرد
[mard]
man

دختر
[doxtar]
girl

بچه/پسر
[bača/pasar]
boy

همصنفی
[ham-sěnfi]
classmate

استاد
[ostād]
instructor
(college level)

معلم
[moʼalem]
school teacher
(male)

محصل
[mohasel]
college student

شاگرد
[šāgěrd]
student (primary and secondary levels)

B. 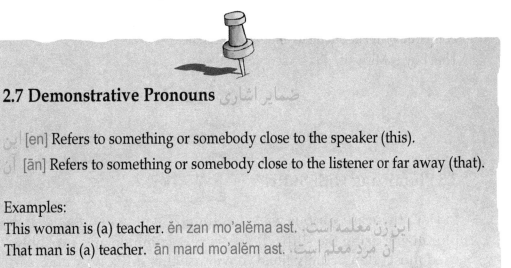 Pictionary.  Make two groups. Each group member writes one of the new words learned above for someone from the other group to act out. Group members should take turns picking cards from the other group and acting out the word they've picked for their team to guess. Each group will have 30 seconds to guess the word.

### 2.7 Demonstrative Pronouns  ضمایر اشاری

این [en] Refers to something or somebody close to the speaker (this).

آن [ān] Refers to something or somebody close to the listener or far away (that).

Examples:

This woman is (a) teacher. ĕn zan mo'alĕma ast.  این زن معلمه است.

That man is (a) teacher.  ān mard mo'alĕm ast.  آن مرد معلم است.

Exercise 2:  تمرین ۲:

Make a sentence for each of the following pictures.  For example:

This girl is (a) student. ĕn doxtar šāgĕrd ast.  این دختر شاگرد است.

 **college student** _____

_____ **student**

 **school teacher** _____

_____ **instructor**

Exercise 3:  ۳ تمرین :

Group work. Going around the room, take turns introducing or pointing out your classmates to each other. For example:

Introduce your classmate to another classmate:
This girl is Layla. ĕn doxtar laylā ast.  این دختر لیلا است.

Point out your classmate to another classmate
That boy is Mirwais. ān bača mirwais ast.  آن بچه میرویس است.

## 2.8 Pluralizing with Suffix ها

In Dari, there are various ways to pluralize a noun, and among these pluralizing using the suffix [hā] ها is very common and probably used most often in daily life. We will use this suffix now and learn the others later.

The suffix [hā] ها comes right after the noun it modifies.
For example:

| Plural | Singular |
|---|---|
| men [mardhā] مردها | man [mard] مرد |
| women [zanhā] زنها | woman [zan] زن |
| boys [bačahā] بچه ها | boy [bača] بچه |
| girls [doxtarhā] دخترها | girl [doxtar] دختر |
| these [ĕnhā] اینها | this [ĕn] این |
| those [ānhā] آنها | that [ān] آن |

Unlike in English, when pluralizing using numbers in Dari, you leave the nouns singular (they do not take the suffix ها). For example:

| Plural | Singular |
|---|---|
| ten woman (women) [dah zan] ده زن | one woman [yak zan] یك زن |
| ten man (man) [dah mard] ده مرد | one man [yak mard] یك مرد |

Exercise 4: تمرین ۴:

First, find the best translation for the following words from the given set of words. Then, change the singular noun to plural.

> *boy, school student, college student,*
> *woman, girl, classmate, teacher*

| English Translation | Plural | Singular | |
|---|---|---|---|
| _____ | _____ | معلم | ۱ |
| _____ | _____ | همصنفی | ۲ |
| _____ | _____ | شاگرد | ۳ |
| _____ | _____ | بچه | ۴ |
| _____ | _____ | زن | ۵ |
| _____ | _____ | محصل | ۶ |
| _____ | _____ | دختر | ۷ |

Exercise 5: تمرین ۵:

Write the Dari equivalent of the following words.

| | | |
|---|---|---|
| five students | _____ | ۱ |
| four teachers | _____ | ۲ |
| eight women | _____ | ۳ |
| nine boys | _____ | ۴ |
| eleven girls | _____ | ۵ |
| eighteen classmates | _____ | ۶ |

## 2.9 Sentence Structure in Dari ساختار جمله

You may already know that English sentences use a subject, verb &
object (SVO) word order. For example:

<table>
<tr><td align="center">This</td><td align="center">is</td><td align="center">a computer.</td></tr>
<tr><td align="center">( SUBJECT )</td><td align="center">( VERB )</td><td align="center">( OBJECT )</td></tr>
<tr><td align="center">1</td><td align="center">2</td><td align="center">3</td></tr>
</table>

In Dari, however, the sentence structure is: subject, object & verb
(SOV). For example:

<table>
<tr><td align="center">( VERB )</td><td align="center">( OBJECT )</td><td align="center">( SUBJECT )</td></tr>
<tr><td align="center">is</td><td align="center">a computer</td><td align="center">This</td></tr>
<tr><td align="center">3</td><td align="center">2</td><td align="center">1</td></tr>
</table>

This sentence structure is the same in all sentences, regardless of the
tense, aspect, or mood. Some examples include:

| | | |
|---|---|---|
| This is (a) woman. | ĕn zan ast. | این زن است. |
| That is (a) man. | ān mard ast. | آن مرد است. |
| This girl is (a) student. | ĕn doxtar šāgĕrd ast. | این دختر شاگرد است. |
| That boy is (a) student. | ān bača šāgĕrd ast. | آن بچه شاگرد است. |

Exercise 6: تمرین ۶:

    A. Let's make sentences. The following sentences are in the wrong order. Unscramble them and rewrite them in the correct format.

| | |
|---|---|
| ۱ | زن این است. |
| ۲ | مرد است این. |
| ۳ | این دختر است معلم. |
| ۴ | است آن بچه محصل. |
| ۵ | این زن است استاد . |

    B.    Write the following sentences in Dari.  Then check your work with a classmate.

| 1 | That man is John. | |
|---|---|---|
| 2 | This girl is Martha. | |
| 3 | That woman is Layla. | |
| 4 | This boy is Karim. | |
| 5 | That man is Maywand. | |

Exercise 7: تمرین ۷:

    A. You will hear a short conversation on the audio recording. Listen and repeat after it.

Who is this woman? [ĕn zan kist?] این زن کیست؟
This woman is Layla. [ĕn zan laylā ast.] این زن لیلا است.

Who is that man? [ān mard kist?] آن مرد کیست؟
That man is Maywand. [ān mard maywand ast.] آن مرد میوند است.

    B.  Now, by using the questions above as a guide, ask a classmate about the other people in the room.

## 2.10 Plural Sentences

As was mentioned before, a noun is pluralized by adding the suffix [hā] ها to it.

In order to make a sentence which has a plural animate object (e.g. men, women) in Dari, you must use the subject, object, and verb in the plural forms.  For example:

| Plural | Singular |
|--------|----------|
| اینها زنها هستند.<br>[ĕn-hā zan-hā hastand.] | این زن است.<br>[ĕn zan ast.] |
| آنها مردها هستند.<br>[ān-hā mard-hā hastand.] | آن مرد است.<br>[ān mard ast.] |
| این دخترها شاگردها هستند.<br>[ĕn doxtar-hā šāgĕrd-hā hastand.] | این دختر شاگرد است.<br>[ĕn doxtar šāgĕrd ast.] |
| آن بچه ها شاگردها هستند.<br>[ān bača-hā  šāgĕrd-hā hastand.] | آن بچه شاگرد است.<br>[ān bača  šāgĕrd ast.] |

Exercise 8: تمرین ۸:

A. You will hear a short conversation on the audio recording. Listen and number each phrase in the order you hear it, and then translate it properly.

___ آن دخترها کیستند؟
[ān doxtar-hā  kistand?]

___ اینها کیستند؟
[ĕn-hā  kistand?]

___ آن دخترها لیلا و نسرین هستند.
[ān doxtar-hā laylā wa nasrin hastand.]

___ اینها اجمل و پروین هستند.
[ĕn-hā ajmal wa parwin hastand.]

New Vocabulary:

| and | wa | و |
|-----|----|----|

B. 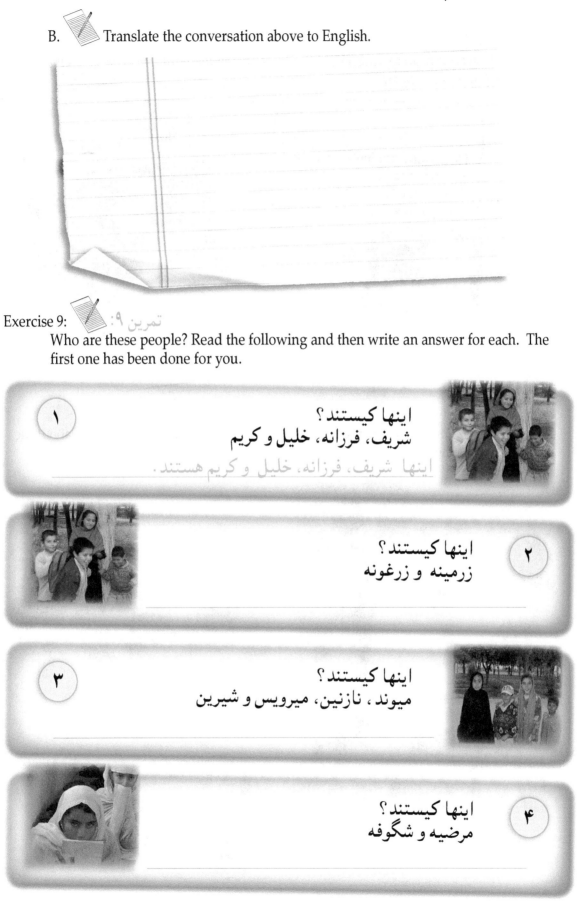 Translate the conversation above to English.

Exercise 9: تمرین ۹:

Who are these people? Read the following and then write an answer for each. The first one has been done for you.

| ۱ | اینها کیستند؟<br>شریف، فرزانه، خلیل و کریم |

اینها شریف، فرزانه، خلیل و کریم هستند.

| اینها کیستند؟<br>زرمینه و زرغونه | ۲ |

| ۳ | اینها کیستند؟<br>میوند، نازنین، میرویس و شیرین |

| اینها کیستند؟<br>مرضیه و شگوفه | ۴ |

Exercise 10: 🎧 تمرین ۱۰:

A. Listen to the following short conversations on the audio recording. Then practice the phrases you hear.

آنها چند شاگرد هستند؟
[ān-hā čand šāgĕrd hastand?]
How many students are there?

ششِ شاگرد.
[šaš šāgĕrd]
Six students.

اینها چند شاگرد هستند؟
[ĕn-hā čand šāgĕrd hastand?]
How many students are there?

سهِ شاگرد.
[se šāgĕrd]
Three students.

B. 🤝 Now, with a partner, point to one of the pictures below and ask about the people in them.

## 2.11 Interrogative Sentences

In English, questions are often formed by changing the word order of the sentence.

**Interrogative sentence**
Is this boy Maywand?

**Affirmative sentence**
This boy is Maywand.

However, in Dari, questions are shown only by changing the intonation of the sentence. The word order does not change. For example:

**Interrogative sentence**
این بچه میوند است؟
[ĕn bača maywand ast?]

**Affirmative sentence**
این بچه میوند است .
[ĕn bača maywand ast.]

Short answers to such questions are expressed with the words نی / نه   "yes" and   بلی / ها   "no." Look at these examples:

| نه / نی | بلی / ها | این بچه میوند است؟ |
|---|---|---|
| [ne] | [balĕ/hā] | [ĕn bača maywand ast?] |
| no | yes | Is this boy Maywand? |

Exercise 11: ✎ تمرین ۱۱ :

A. Using what you have learned, write the following questions in Dari. Then check your work with the instructor. The first one has been done for you.

| انگلیسی | دری | چك | |
|---|---|---|---|
| Is he Ahmad? | او احمد است؟ | √ | ۱ |
| Is your name Mirwais? | | — | ۲ |
| Are you from Kabul? | | — | ۳ |
| Is today Monday? | | — | ۴ |
| Is your phone number 0777205458? | | — | ۵ |
| Is your last name Karimi? | | — | ۶ |

B. By using the interrogative sentences, ask your classmate's first name, last name, phone number, and additionally ask him/her "what day is today?"

# مرور فصل دوم
# Chapter Two Review

In this section you will review the vocabulary, phrases, grammar, and cultural elements that you learned throughout the chapter.

Exercise 1: تمرین ۱:

The following is a portion of an Afghan ID card. Read it carefully and provide the required information in the table below.

دولت اسلامی
افغانستان
وزارت داخله
مدیریت ثبت احوال
نفوس

ولایت : کابل
ولسوالی : پغمان
شمارۀ خانه: ۲۳۴

شمارۀ ثبت: ۱۲۶۳۵۴۱
قیمت: ۱۰ افغانی

| | |
|---|---|
| نام | پروین |
| نام پدر | محمد کریم |
| نام پدر کلان | محمد رحیم |
| تخلص | رحیمی |

New Vocabulary:

| | | | | | |
|---|---|---|---|---|---|
| price | qimat | قیمت | big | kalān | کلان |
| home/house | xāna | خانه | father | padar | پدر |
| register | sabt | ثبت | district | waloswāli | ولسوالی |
| number | šomāra | شماره | province | walāyat | ولایت |

| 1 | Name (first and last) | |
|---|---|---|
| 2 | Father's and grandfather's names | |
| 3 | Country name | |

| 4 | Province name | _____ |
|---|---|---|
| 5 | District name | _____ |
| 6 | Price of the form | _____ |
| 7 | House number | _____ |
| 8 | Registration number | _____ |

Exercise 2: تمرین ۲ :

Read the following business card and then answer the questions that follow.

ورکشاپ رادیو و تلویزیون میوند

ورکشاپ میوند در روز های شنبه، یکشنبه، دوشنبه، سه شنبه ، چار شبنه و پنجشنبه در خدمت هموطنان عزیز میباشد .

آدرس: افغانستان، ولایت غزنی ، شهر نو ، دوکان شماره ۱۲۳
شمارهٔ تلیفون: ۲۲۰۷۵۷۶۲۳۵
شمارهٔ مبایل: ۰۷۰۰۴۰۳۲۶۷

| 1 | What kind of business is the card for? | _____ |
|---|---|---|
| 2 | On which days of the week is this business open? | _____ |
| 3 | What is the name of the business? | _____ |
| 4 | What is the telephone number for this business? | _____ |
| 5 | What is the shop number? | _____ |
| 6 | What is the cell phone number for this business? | _____ |
| 7 | In which province is this business located? | _____ |

Exercise 3: تمرین ۳ :

With a partner, create your own business cards. The business cards should include your name (first and last), address, phone number, and mobile number.

Exercise 4:  تمرین ۴:

Read the information provided with the pictures below. Then, for each one, write a question about the person shown.

۱    نام: جان محمد    از: پروان
تخلص: برمک    تلیفون: ۰۷۰۰۸۹۲۷۸۷

۲    نام: زرغونه    از: کندهار
تخلص: پوپل    مبایل: ۰۷۹۹۷۲۸۳۲۶

۳    نام: گل احمد    از: هرات
تخلص: زرین    تلیفون: ۴۴۱۹۲۳

۴    نام: پرستو    از: کندوز
تخلص: کریمی    مبایل: ۰۷۸۷۹۸۷۲۳۶

Exercise 5: تمرین ۵:

You will hear an audio recording with some missing parts. Listen carefully and fill in the missing parts with the appropriate responses.

| | | |
|---|---|---|
| ۱ | السلام و علیکم ! | |
| ۲ | نام تان چیست؟ | |
| ۳ | تخلص تان چیست؟ | |
| ۴ | شما از کجا هستید؟ | |
| ۵ | شمارهٔ تلیفون تان چند است؟ | |

| | |
|---|---|
| ۶ | امروز چند شنبه است؟ |
| ۷ | تشکر |
| ۸ | خدا حافظ |

# لغات فصل دوم
## Chapter Two Vocabulary

In this part of the lesson, you will review, listen to, and practice pronunciation of the phrases and vocabulary used in the chapter.

### Phrases عبارات

| How many phones do you have? | šomā čand dāna tĕlefun dāred? | شما چند دانه تلیفون دارید؟ |
|---|---|---|
| I have one phone. | man yak dāna tĕlefun dārom. | من یک دانه تلیفون دارم. |
| What is your phone number? | nambar-e telefun-e tān čand ast? | نمبر تلیفون تان چند است؟ |
| What day is today? | ĕmroz čand šanbe ast? | امروز، چند شنبه است؟ |
| Today is Monday. | ĕmroz do šanbe ast. | امروز دوشنبه است. |

### Vocabulary Words لغات

| college instructor | ostād | استاد |
|---|---|---|
| today | ĕmroz | امروز |
| boy | bača | بچه |
| twenty | bist | بیست |
| fifteen | pānz-dah | پانزده |
| boy | pasar | پسر |
| five | panj | پنج |
| Thursday | panj-šanbe | پنجشنبه |
| register | sabt | ثبت |
| Friday | joma | جمعه |

| four | čār | چار |
| Wednesday | čār- šanbe | چار شنبه |
| fourteen | čār-dah | چارده |
| two | do | دو |
| twelve | dōwāz-dah | دوازده |
| Monday | do-šanbe | دو شنبه |
| ten | dah | ده |
| woman | zan | زن |
| three | se | سه |
| Tuesday | se- šanbe | سه شنبه |
| thirteen | sĕz-dah | سیزده |
| student | šāgerd | شاگرد |
| sixteen | šānz-dah | شانزده |
| six | šaš | شش |
| Saturday | šanbe | شنبه |
| zero | sefer | صفر |
| watch | sĕnf | صنف |
| big | kalān | کلان |
| cell phone | mobā-yel | مبایل |
| university student | mohasel | محصل |
| man | mard | مرد |
| school teacher | mo'lem | معلم |
| nineteen | nōz-dah | نوزده |
| nine | noh | نه |
| province | walāyat | ولایت |
| district | waloswāli | ولسوالی |
| eighteen | haž-dah | هژده |
| eight | hašt | هشت |
| seven | haft | هفت |

| | | |
|---|---|---|
| seventeen | haf-dah | هفده |
| classmate | ham-senfi | همصنفی |
| eleven | yāz-dah | یازده |
| one | yak | یك |
| Sunday | yak-šanbe | یك شنبه |

## Dari Vocabulary Different from Iranian Persian

| English Translation | Iranian Persian | | Farsi-e Dari | |
|---|---|---|---|---|
| district | farmāndāri | فرمانداری | waloswāli | ولسوالی |
| province | ostān | استان | walāyat | ولایت |
| eighteen | haj-dah | هجده | haž-dah | هژده |
| four | čahār | چهار | čār | چار |
| Saturday | šanba | شنبه | šanbe | شنبه |
| Wednesday | čahār-šanba | چهارشنبه | čār- šanbe | چار شنبه |
| fourteen | čahār-dah | چهار ده | čār-dah | چارده |
| classmate | ham-kelāsi | همکلاسی | ham-senfi | همصنفی |

# فصل سوم
## CHAPTER THREE

# سلام علیکی و معرفی!
## GREETINGS AND INTRODUCTIONS

## IN THIS CHAPTER

- وظایف Functions

*Greeting others and asking how they are doing; Introducing yourself and others; Using personal titles in appropriate situations; Talking about your place of origin; Asking others where they live and their place of origin; Talking about nationalities*

- تبصرهٔ فرهنگی Cultural Notes

*The title: jān; Learning cultural rules of greetings and partings; Addressing people in formal/polite form*

- دستور زبان Language Structure

*Personal pronouns* ضمایر شخصی; *The defective verb "to be"* هست/است; *Negation; Interrogative sentences with the verb "to be"; Possessive pronouns* ضمایر ملکی; *The addition of ēzāfate '-e'; Question words [ki]* کی, *[či]* چی *and [čětōr]* چطور; *Contractions; Particle* کجا *[kojā]; Conjunction "and"* و; *The preposition [az]* از; *Question words [kojā]* کجا *[kojā]; Conjunction "and"* و; *The preposition [az]* از; *Question words* همچنان، هم ، نیز *and [kodām]* کدام; *The preposition 'in'* د; *The compound verb (to live)* زنده گی کردن; *The preposition 'in'* د; *and [kodām]* کدام

- مرور فصل Chapter Review

*Greeting both genders and various age groups appropriately; Addressing people politely using proper titles; Introducing yourself and others; Place of origin and nationalities*

- لغات Vocabulary

*Review phrases and words used in this chapter*

# Chapter Introduction    معرفی فصل

In this chapter you will learn additional ways to greet in Dari and also to tell someone goodbye. You will also learn how to introduce yourself, including your name, where you live, and place of origin, as well as be able to introduce another person. And you will learn how to ask others their names, where they live, and their place of origin.

معرفی خود و دیگران
Introducing yourself and others

احوال پرسی
Greetings

شما در اکجا زندگی میکنید؟
Where do you live?

## Note:

Throughout the chapter, you will also learn more about the Dari language, including the differences between colloquial and standard Dari; when to use polite (formal) language; and titles you must use when speaking to Afghans. You will also learn more about the structure of the Afghan government.

# درس اول: سلام علیکی.

# Lesson One: Greetings.

> In this section, you will learn how to greet people in Dari, how to ask how they are doing, and how to say goodbye.

Exercise 1: 🎧   تمرین ۱ :

You will hear three short conversations on the audio recording.  The first is between two men (میرویس، فرید), the second is between a woman (لیلا) and a man (فرید), and the third is between two women (لیلا ، پروین).  For each conversation, listen carefully and number the turns of the conversation in the order you hear them.  The first one has been done for you.

| | | |
|---|:---:|---|
| [asalām ō alaykom, mirwais jān!] | ۱ | ۱ السلام و علیکم، میرویس جان. |
| [šomā čětōr hasted?] | | ___ شما چطور هستید؟ |
| [man ham xub hastam, tašakor.] | | ___ من هم خوب هستم. تشکر. |
| [man xub hastam, tašakor.] | | ___ من خوب هستم، تشکر. |
| [walaykom asalām, farid jān!] | | ___ وعلیکم السلام، فرید جان. |
| [šomā čětōr hasted?] | | ___ شما چطور هستید؟ |

| | | |
|---|:---:|---|
| [man ham xub hastam, tašakor.] | ۲ | ___ من هم خوب هستم. تشکر. |
| [šomā čětōr hasted?] | | ___ شما چطور هستید؟ |
| [asalām ō alaykom, laylā jān!] | | ___ السلام و علیکم، لیلا جان. |
| [šomā čětōr hasted?] | | ___ شما چطور هستید؟ |
| [man xub hastam, tašakor.] | | ___ من خوب هستم، تشکر. |
| [walaykom asalām, farid jān!] | | ___ وعلیکم السلام، فرید جان. |

| | | |
|---|:---:|---|
| [man ham xub hastam.] | ۳ | ___ شما چطور هستید؟ |
| [šomā čětōr hasted?] | | ___ من هم خوب هستم. |
| [asalām ō alaykom, laylā jān!] | | ___ وعلیکم السلام، پروین جان. |
| [šomā čětōr hasted?] | | ___ شما چطور هستید؟ |
| [man xub hastam, tašakor.] | | ___ من خوب هستم، تشکر. |
| [walaykom asalām, farid jān!] | | ___ السلام و علیکم، لیلا جان. |

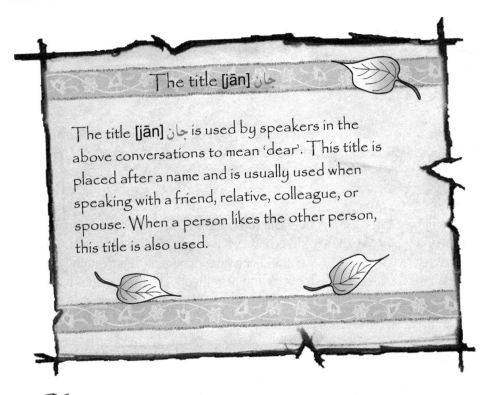

The title [jān] جان

The title [jān] جان is used by speakers in the above conversations to mean 'dear'. This title is placed after a name and is usually used when speaking with a friend, relative, colleague, or spouse. When a person likes the other person, this title is also used.

Exercise 2: تمرین ۲:

Go around the classroom and greet your classmates and instructor incorporating the new greeting phrases you've learned. Remember to use their names and titles جان as seen in exercise 1.

| Hello, Dear Ahmad. | [asalām ō alaykom] | السلام و علیکم احمد جان. |
| Hello. | [walaykom asalām] | وعلیکم السلام. |
| How are you? | [šomā čětōr hasted?] [(šomā čětōr hasten?)*] | شما چطور هستید؟ |
| I am fine, thanks. | [man xub hastam, tašakor.] [(ma xub hastom).] | من خوب هستم، تشکر. |
| How are you? | [šomā čětōr hasted?] [(šomā čětōr hasten?)] | شما چطور هستید؟ |
| I am fine too (me too), thanks. | [man ham xub hastam, tašakor.] [(ma ham xub hastom, tašakor).] | من هم خوب هستم. تشکر |

*Note: The phrases in the parentheses are the colloquial form. For more information see Grammar Note 3.8.

# Note: Rules of greeting

Greeting properly is incredibly important in the Afghan culture. This is because a proper greeting demonstrates one's level of respect toward the other person. As a result, if a greeting is not properly performed, it can result in misunderstandings and might even be taken as a sign of disrespect. There are several rules of greeting that are very important for a visitor to know prior to visiting Afghanistan.

**Greetings between men:**

1. The younger man always greets (and approaches) the elder first, saying السلام وعليكم while shaking with the right hand. (Sometimes both men will clasp their embraced hands with their left lands as well.) Then both men will bring their right hand over their own heart. (Usually, the younger man will give a slight bow when putting his hand over his heart.)

2. Men passing by should greet those sitting or not moving.
   - If you happen to be the man sitting, and the man standing is older than you, you should always stand up as a sign of respect and respond to the greeting.
   - If the man standing is younger than you, you don't have to stand. Simply respond to the greeting (still properly) while remaining seated.

3. When men who don't know each other meet on the street, they put their right hands on their chests and say السلام و عليكم or سلام . (Also, sometimes men raise their right hands and put their left hands on their chest and say سلام or السلام و عليكم ).

4. When men who do know one another (especially if they are close friends or relatives) meet after awhile, they will give each other big hugs to express friendly emotions/feelings.

5. When one man knows the other, they shake with both hands (shaking with the right, with the left hands clasping over the embraced hands) as a sign of respect.

6. Hugging is also common among Afghan men who know one another. When men hug, they make the shoulders slightly touch the other person's shoulders and this is repeated a standard of three times (some people just do it once or twice). After hugging and shaking hands, the men put their hand on the chest to complete the greeting.

## Note: Rules of greeting (cont'd.)

7. When a man meets an elder male relative after a long time, the younger one kisses the back of the elder's right hand to show respect. The elder will then kiss the younger man's cheeks, head, or forehead, and then they will hug and/or shake hands. (During Eid, the younger man always kisses the elder's hand.)

8. NEVER raise your left hand when greeting because this is considered disrespectful.

**Greetings between men and women:**

1. Although shaking hands with a member of the opposite sex is acceptable in Afghanistan, women never hug or kiss when meeting a strange man.

2. Shaking hands between men and women occurs very seldom and most commonly takes place among officials and immediate relatives.

3. If you are a man and want to be sure when to shake a woman's hand, simply wait and if the woman wants to shake hands, she will bring her hand forward. Otherwise, put your right hand on your chest and greet.

**Greetings between women:**

1. When women greet each other, they usually kiss cheek-to-cheek three times and put their right hands on their chest right after kissing.

Exercise 3: تمرین ۳ :

A. How would you greet someone in the following situations? Do you hug, kiss, put your right hand on your chest, shake hands, or do you do all three? Write in the column exactly what you would do to greet the person in the situation described.

| 1. When a man meets a male friend after a long time? |
| --- |
| |
| 2. When a man meets a woman for the first time? |
| |
| 3. When a grandson meets his grandfather after a long time? |
| |
| 4. When a man meets another man for the second time? |
| |

5. When two women meet for first time?

6. When a male pedestrian passes a group of men who are sitting on the sidewalk?

7. When a woman a man doesn't know raises her right hand for a greeting?

B. Working in pairs, check your answers. Then, examine your answers and compare Afghan rules of greeting with those from your own culture. What is similar? What is different? Fill in the chart below.

| Similar | Different |
| --- | --- |
| | |

C. Now, choose one of the greeting forms you have learned and practice this greeting with your partner. Then, act out the greeting for the class.

## 3.1 Personal Pronouns

As you can see in Exercise 1, in the phrase شما چطور هستید؟, the word شما is the personal pronoun for the second–person plural and formal singular form. Here you will learn the rest of the personal pronouns in Dari.

| 1st person singular | I | من (man) |
| 1st person plural | We | ما (mā) |
| 2nd person singular | You | تو (tu) |
| 2nd person plural (singular formal) | You | شما (šomā) |
| 3rd person singular | S/he | او (ō) |
| 3rd person plural | They | آنها (ān-hā) |

Note: The personal pronoun for the third–person plural آنها 'they' has another synonym, which is ایشان and is very formal and rarely used.

Exercise 4:  تمرین ۴:

   A. Match the pronouns to the most appropriate picture.

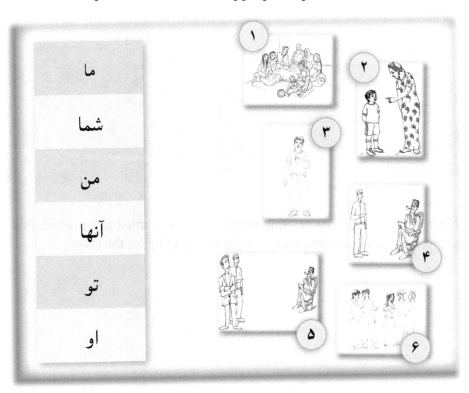

B. Match the singular form of each pronoun to its plural equivalent.

| Plural form | | Singular form | |
|---|---|---|---|
| شما | | من | ١ |
| آنها | | تو | ٢ |
| ما | | او | ٣ |

## تبصرهٔ فرهنگی Cultural Note
## Colloquial Language

In Dari, some words have different colloquial (or spoken) pronounciations not commonly used by the media, in books, or in newspapers.

This colloquial language is used daily and in unofficial situations. For example, one will use colloquial language when buying groceries, but when meeting with a government official, one will use the language that will be more formal and similar to that of the written langauge.

Note: If you learn the written language, you can use it both in informal and formal settings.

## 3.2 Personal Pronouns in Colloquial Dari

In colloquial Dari, the first-person singular personal pronoun من and the third-person plural pronoun آنها are pronounced differently. But the rest are pronounced as written.  For example:

| Colloquial Form | Written Form |
|---|---|
| I (ma) مه | I (man) من |
| They (ō-hā/ō-nā) اوها/اونا | They (ān-hā) آنها |

Exercise 5: تمرین ۵:

You will hear two conversations on the audio recording. One will be in colloquial Dari and the other will be in standard Dari. Listen carefully and then mark each one appropriately.

| Second Person | First Person | |
|---|---|---|
| وعليكم السلام، فريد جان. | السلام و عليكم، ليلا جان. | A. Standard _____ Colloquial _____ |
| من خوب هستم، تشکر. | شما چطور هستید؟ | |
| شما چطور هستید؟ | من هم خوب هستم. تشکر | |

| | Second Person | First Person |
|---|---|---|
| B. Standard _____ Colloquial _____ | واليكم سلام، فريد جان. | سلام ماليكم، ليلا جان. |
| | مه خوب هستم، تشکر. | شما چطور هستین؟ |
| | شما چطور هستین؟ | مه هم خوب هستم. تشکر |

## 3.3 The Defective Verb "To Be" هست/است

You will see in the conversations above the words هستید and هستم, which are the first person singular and second–person formal forms of the verb ("to be") هست/است.

I am fine, thanks. [man xub hastam.] من خوب هستم
How are you? [šomā čĕtōr hasted?] شما چطور هستید؟

As with English verb "to be," the Dari defective verb هست/است has distinctive forms for each subject pronoun. For example:

| I am... | man ... hastam. | من ___ هستم. |
|---|---|---|
| We are... | mā ... hastem. | ما ___ هستم. |
| You are... | tu ... hasti. | تو ___ هستی. |
| You are... | šomā ... hasted. | شما ___ هستید. |
| S/he is... | ō ... ast. | او ___ است. |
| They are... | ān-hā ... hastand. | آنها ___ هستند. |

## 3.4 Personal Endings پسوند های شخصی

As seen in Grammar Note 3.3, the endings of verbs change for each person. These endings are called personal endings.

Most verbs will use the same personal endings as used above with the verb هست/است, except for the third-person singular (which doesn't have an ending and uses the infinitive form for هست/است). Other verbs will use the third-person singular ending shown below.

Personal endings for each person are as follows:

man ___ am. مَ ___ من      mā ___ em. یم ___ ما
tu ___ i. ی ___ تو      šomā ___ ed. ید ___ شما
ō ___ ast. است ___ او      ān-hā ___ and. ند ___ آنها

Personal endings also play the role of the personal pronoun, meaning you can omit the personal pronoun and the meaning of the phrase doesn't change. For example:

**Without personal pronouns**      **With personal pronouns**

[čětōr hasted?] چطور هستید؟      [šomā čětōr hasted?] شما چطور هستید؟

[xub hastam.] خوب هستم.      [man xub hastam.] من خوب هستم.

Exercise 6: تمرین ۶:

     A. Look at the following table and circle the most appropriate personal ending for each person given. Then, write its English equivalent in the blank spaces provided below.

| | | | | | | | | |
|---|---|---|---|---|---|---|---|---|
| _____ | — | ید | ی | مَ | یم | ند | من هست ... | ۱ |
| _____ | — | مَ | یم | ید | ند | ی | ما هست ... | ۲ |
| _____ | — | ید | ند | یم | ی | مَ | تو هست ... | ۳ |
| _____ | — | ید | ی | مَ | یم | ند | شما هست ... | ۴ |
| _____ | — | مَ | یم | است | ند | ی | او ... | ۵ |
| _____ | — | ید | ند | یم | ی | مَ | آنها هست ... | ۶ |

B. Circle the most appropriate verb for each pronoun below.

| | | | | | | | |
|---|---|---|---|---|---|---|---|
| ١ | من | است | هستی | هستیم | هستید | هستند | هستم |
| ٢ | ما | هستید | هستم | است | هستی | هستیم | هستند |
| ٣ | تو | هستیم | هستید | هستی | هستم | است | هستند |
| ٤ | شما | است | هستی | هستیم | هستید | هستند | هستم |
| ٥ | او | هستید | هستم | است | هستی | هستیم | هستند |
| ٦ | آنها | هستیم | هستید | هستی | هستم | است | هستند |

Exercise 7:    تمرین ٧:

A. Using what you have learned so far in this chapter, write the following sentences in Dari.

1. How is she? She is fine.

        ١

2. How is he? He is fine.

        ٢

3. How are you (singular)? I am fine.

        ٣

4. How are they? They are fine.

        ٤

B. Now check your work with a partner. Then take turns practicing the phrases you've written.

## 3.5 The Defective Verb "To Be" هست/است in Colloquial Dari

The personal endings in colloquial Dari are pronounced differently.
For example:

| Colloquial | | Standard | |
|---|---|---|---|
| man ... om. | مه ـــــــ مُ. | man ... am. | من ـــــــ مَ. |
| mā ... em. | ما ـــــــ یم. | mā ... em. | ما ـــــــ یم. |
| tu ... i. | تو ـــــــ ی. | tu ... i. | تو ـــــــ ی. |
| šomā ... en. | شما ـــــــ ین. | šomā ... ed. | شما ـــــــ ید. |
| ō ... as. | او ـــــــ اس. | ō ... ast. | او ـــــــ است. |
| ān-hā ... an. | اوها ـــــــ ن. | ān-hā ... and. | آنها ـــــــ ند. |

For example, for the verb "to be" هست/است, the colloquial personal
endings are as follows:

| | |
|---|---|
| man ... hastom. | مه ـــــــ هستمُ. |
| mā ... hastem. | ما ـــــــ هستیم. |
| tu ... hasti. | تو ـــــــ هستی. |
| šomā ... hasten. | شما ـــــــ هستین. |
| ō ... as. | او ـــــــ اس. |
| ān-hā ... hastan. | اوها ـــــــ هستن. |

Exercise 8: 🎧 تمرین ۸:
   You will hear a conversation between لیلا and فرید on the audio recording. Listen
carefully and decide whether the conversation is in colloquial or in standard Dari.
Place a checkmark next to your choice. Then discuss your choice with a classmate.

| ☐ | Colloquial | ۱ |   | ☐ | Standard | ۱ |

Exercise 9:  تمرین ۹ :

You will hear three short conversations on the audio recording. Listen carefully as you are introduced to some new phrases commonly used among Afghans. After listening, practice the new phrases you've used with a classmate.

١

مانده نباشید ، میرویس جان.
[mānda nabāšed, Mirwais jān.] (mānda nabāšen, Mirwais jān.) *
جور باشید ، فرید جان.
[jōr bāšed, farid jān.] (jōr bāšen, farid jān.)

٢

مانده نباشید ، لیلا جان.
[mānda nabāšed, laylā jān.] (mānda nabāšen, laylā jān.)
جور باشید ، فرید جان.
[jōr bāšed, farid jān.] (jōr bāšen, farid jān.)

٣

مانده نباشید ، لیلا جان.
[mānda nabāšed, laylā jān.] (mānda nabāšen, laylā jān.)
جور باشید ، پروین جان.
[jōr bāšed, Parwin jān.] (jōr bāšen, Parwin jān.)

* [Standard pronunciation] (Colloquial pronunciation)

Exercise 10:  تمرین ۱۰ :

You will hear a conversation between فرید and لیلا on the audio recording. Listen to the conversation and fill in the blanks with the missing words.

| | |
|---|---|
| لیلا | سلام و علیکم، فرید جان. |
| فرید | _____ ، لیلا جان. |
| لیلا | چطور _____ ؟ |
| فرید | خوب هستم. تشکر، _____ چطور هستید؟ |
| لیلا | من هم خوب _____ ، تشکر. |
| لیلا | مانده نباشید . |
| فرید | _____ . |
| لیلا | خدا حافظ . |
| فرید | خدا حافظ . |

# Cultural Note تبصرهٔ فرهنگی
## Other Useful Greeting Phrases

Dari greetings, as well as their responses, are basically used to wish people well. This notion also applies to some phrases borrowed from other languages. For example, the greeting [asalām o alaykom] السلام علیکم و is borrowed from Arabic and means "peace be upon you," and [walaykom asalām] وعلیکم السلام means "peace be upon you, too!"

The following chart presents popular greetings and parting phrases as well as their responses, along with the meaning of each phrase.

Hello (Peace be upon you.) [asalām ō alaykom] السلام و علیکم
Hello (Peace be upon you, too.) [walaykom asalām] وعلیکم السلام

Hello (Peace be upon you.) [salām ō alaykom] سلام و علیکم
Hello (Peace be upon you, too.) [walaykom salām] وعلیکم سلام

Hi (Peace.) [salām] سلام
Hi (Peace.) [walaykom] وعلیکم

How are you? [čĕtōr hasted?] چطور هستید؟
How are you? [či hāl dāred?] چی حال دارید؟
I am fine. [xub hastam.] خوب هستم.
Thanks, it's God's will. [shokor fazle xodāst.] شُکُر فضل خداست.
Thanks to God, I am fine. [al-hamdolelā, xub hastam.] الحمدالله، خوب هستم.

Don't be tired. [mānda nabāšed.] مانده نباشید.
Be well. Live healthy! [jōr bāšed.] جور باشید.
Be alive. [zĕnda bāšed.] زنده باشید.
Live healthy. [salāmat bāšed] سلامت باشید.

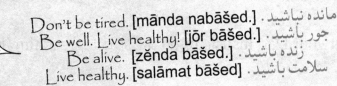

Exercise 11: 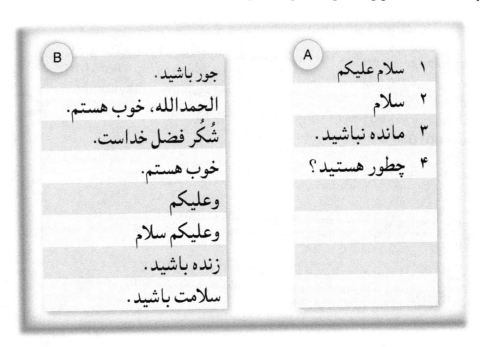 تمرین ۱۱:

A. Match the following greeting and parting phrases in column A to the appropriate responses provided in column B. Then, practice each pair with a classmate.
Remember that the responses to some greetings and parting phrases can vary.

| B | | A | |
|---|---|---|---|
| جور باشید. | | سلام علیکم | ۱ |
| الحمدالله، خوب هستم. | | سلام | ۲ |
| شُکر فضل خداست. | | مانده نباشید. | ۳ |
| خوب هستم. | | چطور هستید؟ | ۴ |
| وعلیکم | | | |
| وعلیکم سلام | | | |
| زنده باشید. | | | |
| سلامت باشید. | | | |

Exercise 12: تمرین ۱۲:

Write a greeting phrase for the following situations.

1. You meet your friend's father at the bus stop; greet him.

_____ ۱

2. You meet your Dari instructor on the street; greet him/her.

_____ ۲

3. You see an older relative after one year; greet him/her.

_____ ۳

4. In class, you see your classmate Tom; greet him.

_____ ۴

Exercise 13: تمرین ۱۳:

You will hear some useful phrases on the audio recording which are used at different situations and times of the day. Listen carefully.

## Initial

| | | | |
|---|---|---|---|
| Thanks. | [tašakor.] | تشکر | ۱ |
| Welcome! | [xoš āmaded!] | خوش آمدید! | ۲ |
| Hope to see you soon. | [ba omede dídār.] | به امید دیدار. | ۳ |
| Goodnight! | [šab baxayr!] | شب بخیر! | ۴ |
| Goodday. | [rōz baxayr.] | روز بخیر! | ۵ |

## Response

| | | | |
|---|---|---|---|
| My pleasure. | [xāheš mekonam.] | خواهش میکنم . | ۱ |
| Thanks. | [tašakor.] | تشکر | ۲ |
| Hope to see you soon. | [ba omede dídār.] | به امید دیدار. | ۳ |
| Goodnight. | [šab baxayr.] | شب بخیر. | ۴ |
| Goodday. | [rōz baxayr.] | روز بخیر. | ۵ |

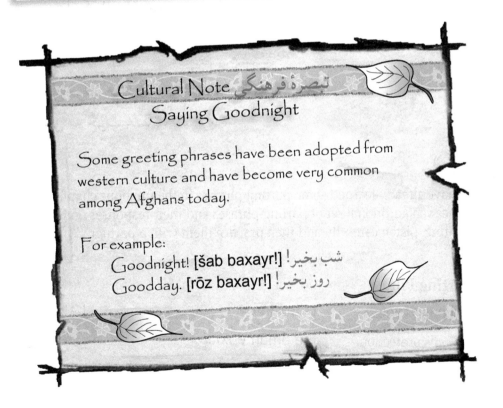

Cultural Note   تبصرهٔ فرهنگی
Saying Goodnight

Some greeting phrases have been adopted from western culture and have become very common among Afghans today.

For example:
Goodnight! [šab baxayr!] شب بخیر!
Goodday. [rōz baxayr!] روز بخیر!

Exercise 14: 🎧 تمرین ۱۴:

A. You will hear a few greeting phrases on the audio recording. Listen and then provide an appropriate response for each.

| | |
|---|---|
| ۱  روز بخیر! | _____ |
| ۲  به امید دیدار. | _____ |
| ۳  شب بخیر! | _____ |
| ۴  تشکر | _____ |
| ۵  خوش آمدید! | _____ |

B. Now go around the classroom and practice saying welcome, good day, goodnight, and thanks to each of your classmates.

Exercise 15: 🎧 تمرین ۱۵:

You will hear a conversation between لیلا and میرویس on the audio recording. Listen and fill in the blanks with the proper missing words. Then practice them with a partner.

| میرویس | السلام و علیکم، لیلا جان. روز بخیر. |
|---|---|
| لیلا | و علیکم السلام میرویس جان، _____ ، _____ . |
| میرویس | _____ ، چطور هستید؟ |
| لیلا | من خوب هستم، تشکر شما چطور هستید. |
| میرویس | من هم خوب هستم. تشکر. |

Exercise 16: 🎧 تمرین ۱۶:

You have already learned some parting phrases in the previous chapter. Now you will hear an additional set of parting phrases and their responses on the audio recording. Listen carefully and then practice them with a partner.

**Parting Phrase**

| God protect you. | [xodā hāfĕz.] | ۱  خدا حافظ |
|---|---|---|
| In God's protection. | [ba amān-e xodā.] | ۲  به امان خدا |

**Response**

| | | |
|---|---|---|
| God protect you. | [xodā hāfĕz.] | خدا حافظ ۱ |
| Be in protection of God. | [ba amān-e xodā.] | به امان خدا ۲ |
| I entrust you to God! | [ba xodā sapordĕm-e tān!] | به خدا سپردم تان. ۳ |
| May God be your protector. | [xodā pošt ō panāh-e tān.] | خدا پشت و پناه تان. ۴ |

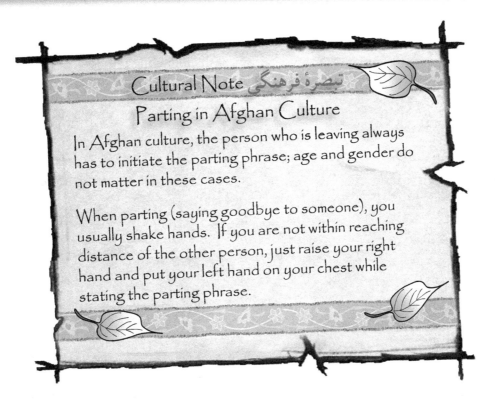

تبصرهٔ فرهنگی Cultural Note

Parting in Afghan Culture

In Afghan culture, the person who is leaving always has to initiate the parting phrase; age and gender do not matter in these cases.

When parting (saying goodbye to someone), you usually shake hands. If you are not within reaching distance of the other person, just raise your right hand and put your left hand on your chest while stating the parting phrase.

Exercise 17:   تمرین ۱۷:
Write a parting phrase for the following situations.

1. You're leaving for school; say goodbye to your roommate.

   _____ ۱

2. Your Dari class has ended; say goodbye to your classmates.

   _____ ۲

3. Your Dari class has ended; say goodbye to your instructor.

   _____ ۳

# درس دوم: معرفی خود و دیگران

## Lesson Two: Introducing Yourself and Others.

In this section, you will learn how to introduce yourself and to introduce other people to one another. You will also learn more about addressing others using polite (formal) forms and culturally appropriate titles.

Exercise 1: ۱ تمرین

A. Listen to the audio recording and repeat the following phrases.

| | ۱ | |
|---|---|---|
| نامم فرید است. <br> [nām-am farid ast.] | | نام تان چیست؟ <br> [nām-e tān čist?]* |
| تخلصم مومند است. <br> [taxalos-am momand ast.] | | تخلص تان چیست؟ <br> [taxalos-e tān čist?] |
| من همچنان. <br> [man hamčanān.] | | از دیدن تان خوشحال شدم. <br> [az didan-e tān xōšhāl šodam.] |

| | ۲ | |
|---|---|---|
| نامم لیلا است. <br> [nām-am laylā ast.] | | نام تان چیست؟ <br> [nām-e tān čist?] |
| تخلصم پوپل است. <br> [taxalos-am popal ast.] | | تخلص تان چیست؟ <br> [taxalos-e tān číst?] |
| من همچنان. <br> [man hamčanān.] | | از دیدن تان خوشحال شدم. <br> [az didan-e tān xōšhāl šodam.] |

B. Now go around the classroom and greet your classmates, asking for their first names and last names. Then say you are pleased to have met him/her.

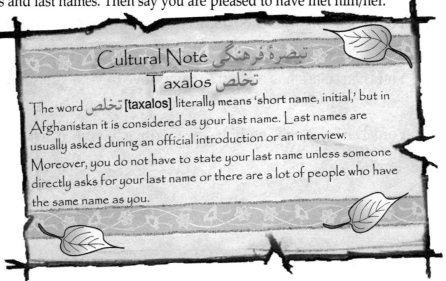

Cultural Note تبصرهٔ فرهنگی

Taxalos تخلص

The word تخلص [taxalos] literally means 'short name, initial,' but in Afghanistan it is considered as your last name. Last names are usually asked during an official introduction or an interview. Moreover, you do not have to state your last name unless someone directly asks for your last name or there are a lot of people who have the same name as you.

## 3.6 Possessive Pronouns ضمایر ملکی

In the conversation above, you see [tān] تان and [am] ام, which are the possessive pronouns for the second–person singular/formal and first–person singular.  Here are the rest of the possessive pronouns in Dari.

| Plural | | Singular | | |
|---|---|---|---|---|
| [mā], [mān] | ما / مان | [am] | اَم / مَ | 1st |
| [tān] | تان | [at] | تَ / اَت | 2nd |
| [šān] | شان | [aš] | شَ / اَش | 3rd |

Also, in Dari, personal pronouns work as possessives by adding the **ezāfate [-e]** to the words that come before personal pronouns. For example:

| my name | [nām-e man] نامِ من | [-e man] من |
|---|---|---|
| our name | [nām-e mā] نامِ ما | [-e mā] ما |
| your name (singular) | [nām-e tu] نامِ تو | [-e tu] تو |
| your name (plural) | [nām-e šomā] نامِ شما | [-e šomā] شما |
| her/his name | [nām-e ō] نامِ او | [-e ō] او |
| their name | [nām-e ān-hā] نامِ آنها | [-e ān-hā] آنها |

Both forms of possessives in written Dari are used and are correct.

**Note:** In colloquial Dari, singular possessives are pronounced differently. For example:

1. am اَم is pronounced as em اِم
2. at اَت - et یت
3. aš اَش - eš یش

### 3.7 The Addition of ēzāfate '-e'

The **ēzāfat-e** [e] which is used in phrases such a [nām-e tān] 'your name' means 'addition.' This element shows the relation between two words and always is attached as a suffix to the first word.

For example:

your name [nām-e šomā] نامِ شما
you [šomā]  شما    name [nām] نام
your book [ketāb-e šomā] کتابِ شما
you [šomā]  شما    book [ketāb] کتابْ

Exercise 2: تمرین ۲ :

A. You've already learned two ways to indicate possession. Column A contains one form and column B contains the second. Write the number from the forms in column A next to their equivalents in column B. The first one has been done for you.

| B | | A | |
|---|---|---|---|
| ____ نام تو | نامم | ۱ |
| ____ نام آنها | نام ما | ۲ |
| ____ نام شما | نامت | ۳ |
| ۱ نام من | نام تان | ۴ |
| ____ نام ما | نامش | ۵ |
| ____ نام او | نام شان | ۶ |

B. Read the following Dari sentences and match them to their meaning.

| B | | A | |
|---|---|---|---|
| ____ Your name is Layla. (f) | نامش لیلا است. | ۱ |
| ____ My name is Layla. | نامت لیلا است. | ۲ |
| ____ Your name is Layla. (inf) | نامم لیلا است. | ۳ |
| ____ Her name is Layla. | نام تان لیلا است. | ۴ |

C. Read the following text and circle the possessive pronouns. Then underline the personal pronouns.

سلام، نامم کریم است، من شاگرد هستم. او مادرم است، نامش رابعه است. او داکتر است. ما افغان هستیم. من جور هستم. مادرم ناجور است.

### 3.8 The Contraction چیست [čist]

The word [čist] چیست, as seen in the conversation above, is formed from two different words 'what' [čí] چی and 'is'[ast] است. The two combined create the contraction چیست meaning 'what is.' In Dari, the 'to be' verb for the third person always contracts with the question words [čí] چی. For example:

what is [čí + ast = číst] چیست = است + چی

Exercise 3:   تمرین ۳:

Read the following questions and write an appropriate answer for each. Then use the proper possessive pronouns for each.

For example:   نامم شریف است.   نامتان چیست؟

| | | |
|---|---|---|
| ۱ | نامم چیست؟ | اجمل |
| ۲ | نامش چیست ؟ | سیمین |
| ۳ | نامت چیست؟ | فرهاد |
| ۴ | نام ما چیست؟ | کریم، نجیب و میرویس |
| ۵ | نام شان چیست؟ | پروین، سیمین و نسرین |
| ۶ | نام تان چیست؟ | عبدالرحیم |

### 3.9 Conjunction 'and' [wa] و

In a series of objects or persons, 'and' [wa] و is only used before the last noun. For example:

نام ما فرید و لیلا است

[nām-e mā farid wa laylā ast.]

The conjunction 'and' [wa] و is borrowed from Arabic and is rarely used in spoken Dari. Its colloquial Dari pronunciation is [ō] and it is not stressed. For example:

نام ما فرید و لیلا است.

[nām-e mā farid ō laylā ast.]

Exercise 4: تمرین ۴ :

A. Listen to the following short dialogue on the audio recording in which [farid] فرید is introducing his friend [sharif] شریف to [laylā] لیلا. Then translate the conversation into English.

| | |
|---|---|
| ۱ | السلام وعلیکم لیلا جان، چطور هستید؟ <br>[asalām ō alaykom, laylā jān, čĕtōr hasted?] |
| ۲ | وعلیکم السلام فرید جان، من خوب هستم تشکر. ایشان کی هستند؟ <br>[walaykom asalām, farid jān. man xub hastam, tašakor. ešān ki hastand?] |
| ۳ | ایشان آقای شریف، دوستم هستند. <br>[ešān āqā-ye šarif, dōst-am hastand.] |
| ۴ | سلام شریف جان، از دیدن تان خوشحال شدم. <br>[salām šarif jān, az didan-e tān xuš-hāl šodam.] |
| ۵ | تشکر، من همچنان. <br>[tašakor, man ham-čanān.] |

B. کار مشترک Working in pairs, use what you have learned to make a similar conversation. Be sure to come up with a scenario where you introduce each other to some of your friends or classmates. Then act it out in front of the class.

### 3.10 Particles   همچنان، هم، نیز

There are three common particles in Dari:

also, too, and as well
همچنان [hamčanān]
نیز [nez]
هم [ham]

Among these, [ham] هم is the most commonly used in colloquial and standard language.

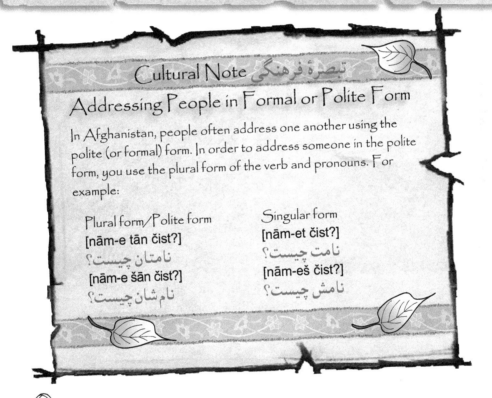

Cultural Note   تبصرهٔ فرهنگی

## Addressing People in Formal or Polite Form

In Afghanistan, people often address one another using the polite (or formal) form. In order to address someone in the polite form, you use the plural form of the verb and pronouns. For example:

Plural form/Polite form
[nām-e tān čist?]
نامتان چیست؟
[nām-e šān čist?]
نام‌شان چیست؟

Singular form
[nām-et čist?]
نامت چیست؟
[nām-eš čist?]
نامش چیست؟

Exercise 5:   تمرین ۵:
Listen to the following short conversations on the audio recording. Then put a check mark next to formal or informal form based on what you hear. There will be a pause between each conversation.

| | Informal | | Formal | ۱ |
|---|---|---|---|---|
| ☐ | Informal | ☐ | Formal | ۱ |
| ☐ | Informal | ☐ | Formal | ۲ |

Cultural Note تبصرهٔ فرهنگی

## Titles

In official meetings and when talking to elders and children in Afghanistan, you should use the correct titles when addressing people. Below is a list of some common titles used in various situations.

People in an official situation
Mrs./Lady [xānom] خانم      Mr./Gentleman [āqā] آقا

People in an official situation
Ms./Mrs.[moh-tarama] محترمه    Mr.[moh-taram] محترم

People in an official situation (after last name and official titles).
Madam [sā-heb, sā-heba] صاحب/صاحبه    Sir[sā-heb] صاحب

A professor
Professor [ostād] استاد    Professor [ostād] استاد

For elder people (respectful)
Dear mother[ mādar jān] مادر جان    Dear father [padar jān] پدرجان

For elder people (respectful)
Dear aunt [xāla jān] خاله جان    Dear uncle[kākā jān] کاکا جان

For younger people (respectful)
Dear daughter [doxtar jān] دختر جان    Dear son[baČa jān] بچه جان

For younger people (respectful)
My daughter[doxtarĕm] دخترم    My son[bačĕm] بچیم (بچه ام)

For people who are same age as you (respectful)
Sister[xā-har] خواهر    Brother[brādar] برادر

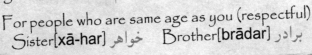

Exercise 6:  تمرین ۶:

For each of the scenarios described below, choose the most appropriate title to use.

1. John works at the university. He goes to talk with a department director. Which one of the following options would be appropriate to use for Mr. Karim, the director?

آقای کریم          برادر کریم          کریم جان

2. Mirwais wants to introduce one of his colleagues, Layla, to John for the first time. What would be the most appropriate title and phrase to use in this situation?

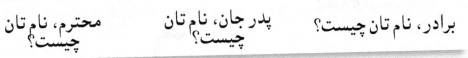

آقای جان!
او خواهر لیلا است.     ایشان خانم لیلا هستند.     آقای جان! او لیلا است.

3. Farid is working in an office and wants to register an older gentleman. The man is sitting on a chair next to Farid. Farid wants to get his attention in order to ask for his name. What would be the best title to use in this case?

محترم، نام تان
چیست؟          پدر جان، نام تان
چیست؟          برادر، نام تان چیست؟

Exercise 7:  تمرین ۷:

Role-play: You want to introduce your father/mother and brother/sister to your teacher and, in return, your teacher to your family. Working in groups of three, draft the introductions. Then, go to the front of the classroom and act out the scenario as a group. Remember to do a formal introduction. For example: He is my father. His name is John. His last name is Williams, etc.

Exercise 8: ۸ :تمرین

Read the following text and then answer the questions.

نامم لیلا است، تخلصم پوپل است، من داکتر هستم. او پروین است، او <u>دوستم</u> است. او هم داکتر است.

نامم رحیم است، تخلصم کابلی است، من خوب هستم،  . نام او فواد است، تخلصش افغان است، او انجینر است، او هم خوب است.

1. Whose last name is Popal? _____

2. Who is Layla's friend? _____

3. What is Mr. Kabuli's first name? _____

4. Based on the context of the text, what do you think the underlined word دوست means? _____

# درس سوم: شما درکجا زندگی میکنید؟
## Lesson Three: Where do you live?

In this section, you will learn to tell people where you are from and ask others where they are from.

Exercise 1:  تمرین ۱ :

Listen to the audio recording and number the words in the order you hear. Each will be read twice.

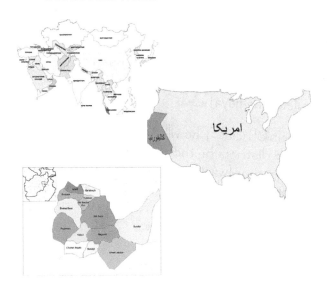

| | |
|---|---|
| State [ayālat] ایالت | _____ |
| Province [walāyat] ولایت | _____ |
| City [šahr] شهر | _____ |
| Continent [qārra] قاره | _____ |
| Island [jazira] جزیره | _____ |
| Country [kěšwar] کشور | _____ |
| District [wolaswāli] ولسوالی | _____ |
| Village [qari-ya] قریه | _____ |

Exercise 2: تمرین ۲ :

A. You will hear a short conversation on the audio recording between two people who are asking each other about their places of origin. Listen and then practice with a partner.

| [asalām o alaykom] | السلام و علیکم | الف |
|---|---|---|
| [walaykom asalām] | وعلیکم السلام | ب |
| [šomā az kojā hasted?] | شما از کجا هستید؟ | الف |
| [man az amrikā hastam.] | من از امریکا هستم. | ب |
| [az kodām šahr hasted?] | از کدام شهر هستید؟ | الف |
| [man az šahr-e šikāgo hastam.] | من از شهر شیکاگو هستم. | ب |

B. Using the previous conversation as a model, ask a classmate where s/he is from (the name of the village, district, city, province, state, and/or country).

## Cultural Note تبصرۀ فرهنگی

## Government Structure of Afghanistan

In order to better understand the government structure of Afghanistan, you must first learn the geographical division of the country.

Afghanistan is divided into 34 provinces [walaayat] ولایت , including the capital, Kabul. Each province has a capital city [šahar/šār, markaz] شهر / مرکز and is divided into several districts [wəloswaali] ولسوالی . Finally, each district is divided into several villages [qariya/deh] قریه، ده .

For example: Kabul province's capital city is 'Kabul City' and it has 14 districts. Each district has several different villages. Similarly, each capital city is divided into several sections called [naa-heya] ناحیه .

Each of these divisions is governed by an official: The villages are run by village elders, [malek/khaan] ملك / خان , the districts by the district in charge [wəloswaal] ولسوال , the provinces by a governor [waali] والی , and the capital city of each province has a mayor [šārwāl/šahar-dār] شاروال / شهردار . The mayor is only in charge of city management; some examples include taking care of construction, canalization, urbanization, and the environment.

The village elders, districts in charge, and governors are the representatives of the central government in local areas. Village elders are responsible for reporting village issues to the district in charge. The district in charge gives district reports to the governor. And governors are responsible for reporting the province issues to the central government.

Selections for these positions are made as follow:
- Governors are appointed by the president.
- The district in charge (district governer) is appointed by a governor and must be a resident of that district.
- Village elders are chosen by the people of the village, who take into account the experience, cultural and social knowledge of the person, age, and sometimes the wealth of the candidate; e.g., mayors are elected through public election.

Exercise 3: 📖 ۳ :تمرین

The following is a list of some countries, major cities, states, provinces, and continents. Read them carefully and put them in the correct place on the chart below.

| امریکا | اروپا | نیویورک | تهران |
|---|---|---|---|
| پاریس | عراق | منهتن | کندهار |
| فلوریدا | مکسیکو | هندوستان | پاکستان |
| لندن | کانادا | اسلام آباد | افغانستان |
| آسیا | فرانسه | ایران | رم |

| ۳ شهر | ۲ ولایت | ۱ ایالت |
|---|---|---|
| | | |

| ۵ قاره | ۴ کشور |
|---|---|
| | |

Exercise 4:  تمرین ۴:

> You will hear a conversation on the audio recording in which people ask the location of cities and countries. Listen first and then, working with a partner, practice asking the location of cities, states, and countries from the chart in Exercise 3. For example:

شهر شیکاگو در کجا است؟ [šahr-e šikāgo dar kojā ast?]

شهر شیکاگو در آیلینوی است. [šahr-e šikāgo dar ĕlinōy ast.]

### 3.11 The Prepositions [az] از and [dar] در

1. The preposition [az] از generally means 'from'. For example:

از افغانستان [az afğānestān]        از کجا [az kojā]

2. The preposition در [dar] means 'in, at'

در افغانستان [dar afğānestān]        در کجا [dar kojā]

### 3.12 Question Words [kojā] کجا and [kodām] کدام

The question word [kojā] کجا means 'where' and [kodām] کدام means 'which.' These functions are the same as in English. For example:

from where [az kojā] از کجا
from which city [az kodā šahr] از کدام شهر
in where [dar kojā] در کجا

Exercise 5:  ۵ تمرین:

Look at the pictures and read the descriptions. Then answer the questions that follow.

| | | |
|---|---|---|
| کریم، شهر مزار | رانی، کشور هندوستان | پروین، ولایت کابل |
| او از کدام شهر است؟ | او از کجا است؟ | او از کدام ولایت است؟ |

| | | |
|---|---|---|
| شریف، ولسوالی پغمان | فرزانه، کشور تاجکستان | مارته، ایالت کینتاکی |
| او از کدام ولسوالی است؟ | او از کجا است؟ | او از کدام ایالت است؟ |

Exercise 6: ۶ تمرین:

Go around the classroom and fill in the chart below by asking your classmates their first name, last name, and where they are from, including the country, state, district, city, and/or village name seen in Exercise 1. Then choose two classmates and introduce them to the rest of the class.

| شماره | نام | تخلص | کشور | ایالت | ولایت | شهر | ولسوالی | قریه |
|---|---|---|---|---|---|---|---|---|
| ۱ | | | | | | | | |
| ۲ | | | | | | | | |
| ۳ | | | | | | | | |
| ۴ | | | | | | | | |
| ۵ | | | | | | | | |

Exercise 7: ٧ :تمرین

A. You will hear a conversation between two students on the audio recording. Listen and then answer the following questions.

| | |
|---|---|
| ١ | تخلص نازنین چیست؟ |
| ٢ | تخلص امید چیست؟ |
| ٣ | امید از کدام ولایت است؟ |
| ۴ | نازنین از کدام ولایت است؟ |
| ۵ | امید از کدام ولسوالی است؟ |
| ۶ | نام قریهٔ امید چیست؟ |

B. Now create a dialogue similar to the one you just heard, using your own name and place of origin. Then act out your dialogue for the class.

Exercise 8: ٨ :تمرین

Fill out the following foreign registration form for yourself.

جمهوری اسلامی افغانستان
وزارت خارجه
فورم ثبت نام
برای اتباع خارجی

نام هوتل _____

نام _____ تخلص _____

نام پدر _____ نام پدر کلان ____

نام شهر _____ نام ولسوالی _____ نام قریه ____

امضا _____ .

تشکر

Exercise 9:  ‏تمرین ۹:‏

A. You will hear a few people introduce themselves on the audio recording, giving their names, places of origin, and nationalities.

نامم میرویس است، من از افغانستان هستم و من افغان هستم.
[nām-am mirwias ast, man az afğānestān hastam wa

man afğān hastam.]

نامم مارته است، من از امریکا هستم و من امریکایی هستم.
[nām-am mārta ast, man az amrikā hastam wa

man amrikāye hastam.]

نامم ایرج است، من از ایران هستم و من ایرانی هستم.
[nām-am eraj ast, man az erān hastam wa  man erāni hastam.]

B. Now go around the room and practice introducing yourself to your classmates. Use the examples above as a guide.

## 3.13 Nationality

The terms for nationality have two different forms in Dari.

1. Nationalities take the suffix [i] ی at the end of the country name. This form divides into three different categories.

A. The first category is country names that end with consonants. These take the suffix [i] ی . For example:

| | |
|---|---|
| Indian [hindi] هندی | India [hind] هند |
| Iranian [erāni] ایرانی | Iran [erān] ایران |
| Pakistani [pākestāni] پاکستانی | Pakistan [pākestān] پاکستان |
| Brazilian [barāzili] برازیلی | Brazil [barāzil] برازیل |

B. The second is country names that end with a vowel [ā, ō & u]. These take the suffixes [y] and [i]. For example::

| | |
|---|---|
| American [amrikā-yi] امریکایی | America [amrikā] امریکا |
| Australian [āstarāliyā-yi] استرلیایی | Australia [āstarāliyā] استرلیا |
| Canadian [kānādā-yi] کانادایی | Canada [kānādā] کانادا |
| Mexican [maksikō-yi] مکسیکویی | Mexico [maksikō] مکسیکو |

C. The third is country names that end with a vowel sound [a]. These take the suffixes [w] and [i]. For example:

| | |
|---|---|
| French [farānsa-wi] فرانسوی | France [farānsa] فرانسه |

2. The second form has spellings that change and don't follow a regular rule, therefore they must be memorized. For example:

| | |
|---|---|
| Afghan [afğān] افغان | Afghanistan [afğānestān] افغانستان |
| Tajik [tājek] تاجک | Tajikistan [tājekestān] تاجکستان |

Exercise 10 تمرین ۱۰:

Listen carefully to the introductions of the following people on the audio recording. Underneath each picture, write the person's place of origin and nationality.

| | | | |
|---|---|---|---|
| کریم ۴ | حلیموف ۳ | صادق خان ۲ | مارته ۱ |
| ثریا ۸ | ژاک ۷ | دیوید ۶ | عالیه ۵ |

Exercise 11: تمرین ۱۱:

Read the following short texts with a partner. Then answer the following questions.

نامم دیوید است، تخلصم ویلیام است، کشورم کانادا است، من از شهر وانکوور هستم و من کانادایی هستم.

نام او پال است، تخلصش فاستر است، او از کشور امریکا است، او از ایالت اندیانا است، او از شهر بلومینگتون است و او امریکایی است.

---

نام من فرید و نام او کریم است، ما از افغانستان هستیم، ما از ولایت کابل هستیم، ما از ولسوالی پغمان هستیم و ما افغان هستیم.

نام آنها سهراب و رستم است، تخلص شان کریموف است، آنها از تاجکستان هستند، آنها از شهر دوشنبه هستند و آنها تاجک هستند.

| 1 | Which district is Karim from? | |
|---|---|---|
| 2 | Who is from Dushanbe City? | |
| 3 | What is Farid's nationality? | |
| 4 | Where is David from? | |
| 5 | Which state is Paul from? | |
| 6 | Who is from Vancouver, Canada? | |
| 7 | What is Sohrab's nationality? | |
| 8 | What is David's nationality? | |

Exercise 12    تمرین ۱۲:

You will hear a conversation between two classmates on the audio recording. Listen to their conversation and then check 'true' or 'false' for each statement in the table below.

| | Sentences | True | False |
|---|---|---|---|
| 1 | Ahmad is from Uzbekistan. | ☐ | ☐ |
| 2 | Ahmad is living in Badakhshan City. | ☐ | ☐ |
| 3 | Maywand is from Kandahar City. | ☐ | ☐ |
| 4 | Maywand is originally from Afghanistan. | ☐ | ☐ |

# 3.14 The Compound Verb 'To Live' زندگی کردن

Compound verbs are sets of verbs that consist of simple verbs, nouns, adverbs, adjectives and other verbs. The compound verb 'to live' [zindagi-kardan] زندگی کردن consists of a simple verb 'to do' [kardan] کردن and a noun 'life' [zindagi] زندگی. The simple verb 'to do' [kardan] کردن is a main verb in formation of the compound verbs. You will learn more compound verbs in the next chapters. For now, let's see how the verb 'to live' [zindagi-kardan] زندگی کردن is conjugated for all persons.

Tips: You've already learned about the defective verb 'to be' هست/است and how it is conjugated in the present tense. The defective verb 'to be' هست/است is simply conjugated for the personal pronouns, and there is no change to the present stem of the verb. But the rest of the Dari verbs have different present stems and a prefix, which is called the present prefix [me] می, is added.

Present Stem: All Dari verbs have different forms from their infinitive that students must memorize. For example: the present stem of 'to do' [kardan] کردن is [kon] کن.

The present prefix [me] می typically comes at the beginning of verbs when in the present tense (there are a few exceptions). For example: the present stem of [kardan] کردن is [kon] کن, and it will change to [me-kon] میکن in the present tense.

Note: The present prefix [me] می can be attached or detached to the present stem. For example:

> Attached to the present stem - [me-kon] میکن
> Detached from the present stem - [me kon] می کن

The verb 'to live' [zindagi-kardan] زنده گی کردن in standard Dari is:

| I live in ... . | man dar ... zendagi me-konam. | من در ... زندگی میکنم. |
| We live in ... . | mā dar ... zendagi me-konem. | ما در ... زندگی میکنیم. |
| You live in ... . | tu dar ... zendagi me-koni. | تو در ... زندگی میکنی. |
| You live in ... . | šomā dar ... zendagi me-koned. | شما در ... زندگی میکنید. |
| S/he lives in ... . | o dar ... zendagi me-konad. | او در ... زندگی میکند. |
| They live in ... . | ān-hā dar ... zendagi me-konand. | آنها در ... زندگی میکنند. |

### 3.14 The Compound Verb 'To Live' زندگی کردن (cont'd.)

The verb [zindagi-kardan] زندگی کردن (to live) in colloquial Dari is:

#### Colloquial

| | |
|---|---|
| man dar ... zendagi me-konom. | من در ... زندگی میکنُم. |
| mā dar ... zendagi me-konem. | ما در ... زندگی میکنیم. |
| tu dar ... zendagi me-koni. | تو در ... زندگی میکنی. |
| šomā dar ... zendagi me-konen. | شما در ... زندگی میکنین. |
| o dar ... zendagi me-kona. | او در ... زندگی میکنه. |
| ān-hā dar ... zendagi me-konan. | آنها در ... زندگی میکنن. |

#### Standard

| | |
|---|---|
| man dar ... zendagi me-konam. | من در ... زندگی میکنم. |
| mā dar ... zendagi me-konem. | ما در ... زندگی میکنیم. |
| tu dar ... zendagi me-koni. | تو در ... زندگی میکنی. |
| šomā dar ... zendagi me-koned. | شما در ... زندگی میکنید. |
| o dar ... zendagi me-konad. | او در ... زندگی میکند. |
| ān-hā dar ... zendagi me-konand. | آنها در ... زندگی میکنند. |

تمرین ۱۳:    Exercise 13:

A. Look at the following table and circle the appropriate personal ending for each person. Then write the English equivalent in the column on the far left.

| | | | | | | | | |
|---|---|---|---|---|---|---|---|---|
| ۱ | شما در امریکا زنده گی میکن... | یم | ند | مَ | د | ی | ید | |
| ۲ | ما در کابل زنده گی میکن... | مَ | ی | یم | ید | ند | د | |
| ۳ | آنها در فرانسه زنده گی میکن... | ید | یم | ی | ند | مَ | د | |
| ۴ | من در کانادا زنده گی میکن... | یم | ند | مَ | د | ی | ید | |
| ۵ | او در ازبکستان زنده گی میکن... | مَ | ی | یم | ید | ند | د | |
| ۶ | تو در ایتالیا زنده گی میکن... | ید | یم | ی | ند | مَ | د | |

B. Write the Dari equivalent of the following sentences in the spaces provided.

| 1 | Ajmal lives in Indiana. | |
| 2 | Layli lives in the District of Columbia. | |
| 3 | You live in Chicago. | |
| 4 | They live in Germany. | |
| 5 | We live in Kabul. | |
| 6 | You live in the Bamiyan Province. | |
| 7 | She lives in America. | |
| 8 | He lives in Africa. | |

Exercise 14: تمرین ۱۴:

Go around the classroom and ask each of your classmates where they live. Then ask them where they are originally from. For example:

Which state do you live in?
[šomā dar kodām ayālat zendagi me-koned?]

شما در کدام ایالت زنده گی میکنید؟

Where are you originally from?
[šomā as-lan an az kojā hasted?]

شما اصلاً از کجا هستید؟

Exercise 15: تمرین ۱۵:

Match the following pictures and their summaries in the left column to their description on the right column.

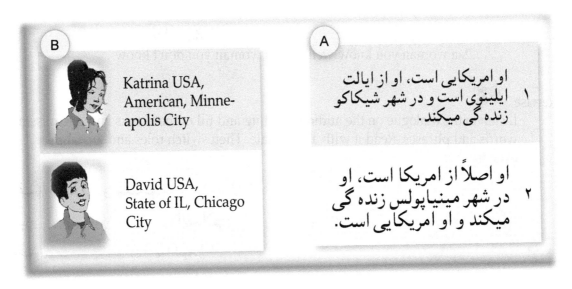

| B | | A |
|---|---|---|
| Katrina USA, American, Minne-apolis City | | ۱ او امریکایی است، او از ایالت ایلینوی است و در شهر شیکاکو زنده گی میکند. |
| David USA, State of IL, Chicago City | | ۲ او اصلاً از امریکا است، او در شهر مینیاپولس زنده گی میکند و او امریکایی است. |

# مرور فصل سوم
## Review of Chapter Three

In this section you will review the vocabulary, phrases, grammar, and cultural elements that you learned throughout the chapter.

Exercise 1    تمرین ۱:

Listen to the following dialogue on the audio recording and number the sentences in the order you hear them. The first one has been done for you.

| | | | |
|---|---|---|---|
| ــــ | تخلص تان چیست؟ | ــــ | ببخشین، نام تان چیست؟ |
| ــــ | تخلصم بارکزی است. | ــــ | نام من میوند است. نام شما چیست؟ |
| ــــ | نامم زبیر است. | ۱ | السلام و علیکم، |
| ــــ | تشکر | ــــ | وعلیکم السلام، |
| ــــ | خواهش میکنم. | ــــ | مانده نباشید. |
| ــــ | به امان خدا | ــــ | جور باشید. شما چطور هستید؟ |
| ــــ | خدا حافظ | ــــ | من خوب هستم، تشکر. |

Exercise 2:    تمرین ۲:

With a partner, greet each other using one of the following scenarios. Then act out your part in front of the class. Imagine that you're in Afghanistan and you have a meeting with:

1. a man you know
2. a woman you know well
3. a man you don't know
4. a woman you don't know

Exercise 3    تمرین ۳:

Listen to the dialogue on the audio recording and fill in the blanks with the missing words and phrases. Read it with a classmate. Then switch roles and repeat the exercise.

| | | |
|---|---|---|
| الف | السلام و علیکم | |
| ب | السلام _____ | |
| الف | _____ نباشید! | |
| ب | _____ باشید! | |
| الف | شما _____ هستید؟ | |

| | | |
|---|---|---|
| ب | من خوب هستم . شما چطور _____ ؟ | |
| الف | تشکر، من _____ خوب هستم. | |
| ب | احمد چطور _____ ؟ | |
| الف | احمد هم _____ است. | |
| ب | لیلا چطور _____ ؟ | |
| الف | او هم خوب _____ . تشکر. | |
| ب | _____ ، خدا حافظ! | |
| الف | به امان خدا! | |
| ب | به _____ دیدار. | |

Exercise 4:  تمرین ۴:

With a partner, greet each other using one of the following scenarios. Then act out your part in front of the class.

    1. Greet your classroom buddy.
    2. Ask your classroom buddy's name.
    3. Ask where s/he lives.

Exercise 5: تمرین ۵:

Match the following questions in column A with their appropriate answers in column B.

| B | A |
|---|---|
| من خوب هستم، تشکر. | ۱   نام تان چیست؟ |
| او فرید است. | ۲   تخلص تان چیست؟ |
| نامم اجمل است. | ۳   او کیست؟ |
| تخلصم وطنوال است. | ۴   چطور هستید؟ |
| من در واشنگتن زندگی میکنم. | ۵   شما از کجا هستید؟ |
| من از شهر شیکاگو هستم. | ۶   شما از کدام ایالت هستید؟ |
| من از امریکا هستم. | ۷   شما از کدام شهر هستید؟ |
| من از ایالت اوآیو هستم. | ۸   شما در کجا زندگی میکنید؟ |

Exercise 6: تمرین ۶:

Read the following text. Then write three questions about it. Working in pairs, practice answering each other's questions.

۱   نام او اجمل اسِت، تخلصش بارکزی است، او از کشور افغانستان است ، او اصلاً از شهر کندهار، از ولسوالی ارغنداب است. او افغان است، او در ولایت کابل زندگی میکند .

۲   نام او کریستوفر است، او کانادایی است، او اصلاً از لندن است، او در کشور کانادا، در شهر وانکوور زندگی میکند. او انجینر است.

**٣** نامم احمد شعیب است، من امریکایی هستم، من اصلاً از امریکا نیستم، من اصلاً از عربستان هستم،  من در امریکا، در ایالت کالیفرنیا، درشهر لوانجلس زندگی میکنم.

_____

_____

Exercise 7: تمرین ۷:

A. Using the following words, write a question for each. Then write an answer for each one. Then take turns and practice reading with a classmate.

| ملالی خوب است. | ملالی چطور است؟ | چطور/ ملالی |
|---|---|---|
| | | ١ کی/او |
| | | ٢ چیست/ تان |
| | | ٣ اجمل و ایمل/ افغان |
| | | ٤ نام شان/ چی |
| | | ٥ او/نام |
| | | ٦ تخلص/شان |
| | | ٧ شما/ کی |

Exercise 8: تمرین ۸:

A. Practice the following conversation with a partner.

| | |
|---|---|
| میوند | سلام احمد جان مانده نباشید ، چطور هستید؟ |
| احمد | وعلیکم میوند جان زنده باشید ، من خوب هستم، شما چطور هستید؟ |
| میوند | من هم خوب هستم، احمد جان شما از کجا هستید؟ |
| احمد | من از تاجکستان هستم. |
| میوند | شما در کجا زندگی میکنید؟ |
| احمد | من در شهر بدخشان زندگی میکنم. شما اصلاً از کجا هستید؟ |
| میوند | من اصلاً از افغانستان هستم. |
| احمد | شما از ولایت کابل هستید؟ |
| میوند | نه، من از ولایت کابل نیستم، من از ولایت کندهار هستم. |

B. Now, using the conversation as a model, write a similar conversation based on your own place of origin.  Then present it to the class.

Exercise 9: تمرین ۹:

A. Write a complete introduction of yourself and a friend. Then read your composition to the class. Make sure to mention your first name, last name, place of origin (country, state, and city), and nationality.

B. Complete the following sentences with an appropriate personal ending. Then write the English equivalent.

| | | | | | | | | | |
|---|---|---|---|---|---|---|---|---|---|
| ــد | ــی | ــید | ــند | ــیم | ــمَ | شما از فرانسه هست... | ۱ |
| ــد | ــی | ــید | ــند | ــیم | ــمَ | ما از شهر نیویورک هست... | ۲ |
| ــد | ــی | ــید | ــند | ــیم | ــمَ | آنها در پاریس زندگی میکن... | ۳ |
| ــد | ــی | ــید | ــند | ــیم | ــمَ | من از کاناداهست... | ۴ |
| ــد | ــی | ــید | ــند | ــیم | ــمَ | او درکشور ایتالیا زندگی میکن... | ۵ |
| ــد | ــی | ــید | ــند | ــیم | ــمَ | تو برازیلی هست... | ۶ |

Exercise 10: تمرین ۱۰:

A. First watch video clips A & B with the sound off and note the various physical ways in which Afghans greet each other. Note age and social status. Then discuss the gestures and cultural norms reflected in the clips with your classmates and instructor.

B. Now watch video clips A & B a second time with the sound on, checking the following greetings, questions, and responses based on what you hear.

| | | | | | |
|---|---|---|---|---|---|
| ☐ | تشکر | ☐ | مانده نباشید. | ☐ | السلام علیکم. |
| ☐ | وعلیکم السلام. | ☐ | زنده باشید. | ☐ | چطور هستید؟ |
| ☐ | من جور نیستم. | ☐ | جور باشید. | ☐ | خوب هستید؟ |
| ☐ | شما چطور هستید؟ | ☐ | خوش آمدید. | ☐ | من، خوب هستم، تشکر |

C. Finally, watch video clips A & B one more time with the sound on and check the new phrases used first by guessing what these phrases mean. Then look up the new words in the vocabulary list at the end of this chapter. Check your work with the instructor.

| | |
|---|---|
| ☐ | به خیر آمدید؟ |
| ☐ | چی حال دارید. |
| ☐ | صحت تان خوب است. |
| ☐ | خیر و خیریت است. |

| | |
|---|---|
| ☐ | سلامت باشید. |
| ☐ | خانه آباد. |
| ☐ | فامیل همه خوب هستند؟ |
| ☐ | شکر، الحمدالله همه خوب هستند. |

| | |
|---|---|
| ☐ | اولاد ها چطور هستند؟ |
| ☐ | قرار قراریست، تشکر. |
| ☐ | خانه خیریت است؟ |
| ☐ | دیگر چطور هستید؟ |

Exercise 11: 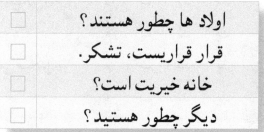 تمرین ۱۱:

A. First, watch video clips A & B with the sound off and note the various physical ways in which Afghans say goodbye to each other. Note age and social status. Then discuss the gestures and cultural norms reflected in the clips with your classmates and instructors.

B.　　　 Now watch video clips A & B a second time with the sound on and check the following parting phrases and new phrases that you hear.

| | |
|---|---|
| ☐ | بخیر بروی. |
| ☐ | خدا یار و مددگارت. |

| | |
|---|---|
| ☐ | به خدا سپردم تان سلامت باشید. |
| ☐ | خدا پشت و پناه تان. |

| | |
|---|---|
| ☐ | خدا حافظ. |
| ☐ | به امان خدا. |

# لغات فصل سوم
# Chapter Three Vocabulary

In this part of the lesson, you will review, listen to, and practice pronunciation of the phrases and vocabulary used in the chapter.

## Phrases عبارات

| Don't be tired. | mānda nabāšed? (mānda nabāšen?) | ماندهنباشید . |
| Be well. Live healthy! | jōr bāšed. | جور باشید . |
| Be alive. | zěnda bāšed. | زنده باشید . |
| Live healthy. | salāmat bāšed. | سلامت باشید . |
| How are you? | četor hasted? | چطور هستید؟ |
| I am fine. | xub hastam. | خوب هستم . |
| Thanks, it's God's will. | shokor fazle xodāst. | شُکر فضل خداست . |
| Thanks to God, I am fine. | al-hamdolelā, xub hastam. | الحمدالله، خوب هستم . |
| What is your name? | nām-e tān čist? | نام تان چیست؟ |
| My name is Farid. | nām-am farid ast. | نامم فرید است . |
| What is the name of your city? | nām-e šahr tān čist? | نام شهرتان چیست؟ |
| The name of my city is Kabul. | nām-e šahr-am kābol ast. | نام شهرم کابل است . |
| Which city are you from? | šomā az kodām šahr hasted? | شما از کدام شهرهستید؟ |
| I am from Kabul City. | man az šahr kabol hastam. | من ازشهر کابل هستم . |
| Which state do you live in? | šomā dar kodām ayālat zendagi me-koned? | شما در کدام ایالت زنده گی میکنید؟ |
| Where are you originally from? | šomā as-lan an az kojā hasted? | شما اصلاً از کجا هستید؟ |
| Thanks. | tašakor. | تشکر . |
| My pleasure! | xāheš mekonam! | خواهش میکنم . |
| Welcome! | xoš āmaded! | خوش آمدید! |
| Hope to see you soon. | ba omeede dídār! | به امید دیدار . |
| Goodnight! | šab baxayr! | شب بخیر! |
| Good day. | roz baxayr. | روز بخیر . |

## Vocabulary Words لغات

| Mr./Gentleman, Sir | āqā | آقا |
| they are ... | ān-hā ... hastand. | آنها ... هستند. |
| they | ān-hā | آنها |
| your (singular) | at | ات |
| her/his | aš | اش |
| my | am | اَم / اَم |
| s/he is... | o ... ast. | او ... است. |
| s/he, it | o | او |
| state | ayālat | ایالت |
| they | ěšān | ایشان |
| unemployed | bi-kār | بیکار |
| capital | pāye-taxt | پایتخت |
| your (plural) | tān | تان |
| last name | taxalos | تخلص |
| you | tu | تو |
| you are... | tu ... hasti. | تو ... هستی. |
| island | jazira | جزیره |
| healthy | jōr | جور |
| how | četór | چطور |
| what | či | چی |
| Mrs./Lady | xānom | خانم |
| well/fine | xub | خوب |
| to live | zendagi kardan | زندگی کردن |
| their | šān | شان |
| you are... | šomā ... hasted. | شما ـــــ هستید. |
| you | šomā | شما |
| city | šahr, šār | شهر |
| madam | sā-heb, sā-heba | صاحب / صاحبه |

| | | |
|---|---|---|
| sir | sā-heb | صاحب |
| continent | qārra | قاره |
| village | qari-ya | قریه |
| country | kešwar | کشور |
| who | ki | کی |
| when | kay | کی |
| we are... | mā ... hastem. | ما ... هستیم. |
| we | mā | ما |
| our | mā, mān | ما/ مان |
| Mr. | moh-taram | محترم |
| Ms./Mrs. | moh-tarama | محترمه |
| I | man | من |
| I am... | man ... hastam. | من ... هستم. |
| and | wa | و |
| province | walāyat | ولایت |
| district | wolaswāli | ولسوالی |
| also, too | hamčanān | همچنان |

## Dari Vocabulary Different from Iranian Persian

| English Translation | Iranian Persian | | Farsi-e Dari | |
|---|---|---|---|---|
| last name | esme fāmili | اسم فامیلی | taxalos | تخلص |
| village | šahrestān | شهرستان | qari-ya | قریه |

# فصل چارم
## CHAPTER FOUR

# در صنف درسی
## IN THE CLASSROOM

## IN THIS CHAPTER

- وظایف Functions

  *Naming objects in the classroom; Asking where an object is; Describing an object's location; Answering in the negative; Giving a command; Responding to a command; Being polite*

- تبصرهٔ فرهنگی Cultural Notes

  *Learning about the Afghan classroom; Following Afghans' rules of politeness*

- دستور زبان Language Structure

  *Pluralizing inanimate objects; Adverbs of place; Classifiers; Verb "to have" داشتن; Prepositions; ezafate (-e) in writing; Negation; Yes/No Questions; Compound Verbs; Definitive Object Marker*

- مرور فصل Chapter Review

  *Describing pictures; Describing activities; Writing verbs in formal and command forms; Conjugating the present stem of verbs*

- لغات Vocabulary

  *Review phrases and words used in this chapter*

# Chapter Introduction                   معرفی فصل

In this chapter you will learn how to talk about objects in your classroom and office, to describe where something is located, to say you have something, to tell someone to do something, and to respond to a command. Throughout the chapter, you will also learn more about the polite (formal) forms of the Dari language and about the rules of politeness in Afghan society.

| کتابم در کجا است؟ | در صنف ما چیست؟ |
|---|---|
| Where is my book? | What is in our classroom? |

در صنف ما چی میکنیم؟

What do we do in class?

## Note:

Remember, starting from this chapter, the Dari transliteration will be omitted.

# درس اول: در صنف ما چیست؟

## Lesson One: What is in our classroom?

In this section, you will learn how to talk about objects in your classroom, say someone has something, and ask what objects someone has.

**Exercise 1:** تمرین ۱:

Listen to the audio recording and pay attention to the pronunciation of each new phrase. Then translate each phrase into English.

این کتاب است.

آن کتابچه است.

این قلم است.

آن پنسل است.

این بکس است.

آن پنسل پاک است.

این خطکش است.

آن کاغذ است.

این میز است.

آن چوکی است.

این الماری است.

آن گوشکی است.

این تخته است.

آن تخته پاک است.

این تباشیر است.

آن صنف است.

این چراغ است.

آن کلکین است.

این دروازه است.

آن کمپیوتر است.

Exercise 2: تمرین ۲:

With a partner, look at the following pictures of some Afghan classrooms. Practice asking one another about the people and objects in the classroom. Then write their correct names in the spaces provided. For example:

Exercise 3: تمرین ۳:

Let's play charades. Form two groups. Each person should write down a
classroom item (in Dari) on a slip of paper. Then someone from the opposite
group should randomly draw one piece of paper from the other group's pile. That
person acts out the word for his/her group. Each group will have 30 seconds to
guess the correct word.

## 4.1 Pluralization of Inanimate Objects

To pluralize inanimate objects in Dari, add the suffix [hā] ها to the objects. For example:

| Plural | Singular |
|--------|----------|
| کتاب ها | کتاب |
| قلم ها | قلم |
| پنسل ها | پنسل |

Unlike in English, you pluralize an inanimate object in a sentence in Dari using only the demonstrative pronoun. The object and verb stay in singular form. For example:

| Plural | Singular |
|--------|----------|
| اینها میز است. | این میز است. |
| آنها چوکی است. | آن چوکی است. |

In colloquial Dari, all three elements (subject, object, and verb) come in plural form.

| Colloquial Plural Form | Standard Plural Form |
|------------------------|----------------------|
| ایها میزها هستند. | اینها میز است. |
| آوها چوکیها هستند. | آنها چوکی است. |

 Exercise 4: تمرین ۴:

Look at the following pictures. Make a sentence for each using demonstrative pronouns. Remember to follow the singular and plural form rules.

Exercise 5:  تمرین ۵:

Match the following terms with objects in the picture. Remember that in Dari, most technology tools have the same name as in English.

| | |
|---|---|
| لودسپیکر | میز |
| مانیتور | کمپیوتر |
| موس | گوشکی |
| تلیفون | چوکی |
| ستپلر | کیبورد |
| سی دی | پرینتر |
| ماشین کاپی | سکینر |

Exercise 6: تمرین ۶:

A. You will hear زلمی describing the things in his office on the audio recording. Listen carefully to his statements and then write the name and number of each of the objects you hear. Finally, ask your partner three questions about Zalmay's belongings.

B. Write about Zalmay's belongings. Then ask a partner three questions about those items.

### 4.2 Adverbs of Place اینجا / آنجا

In exercise 6, you heard the word اینجا. The words 'here' اینجا and 'there' آنجا are place adverbs, and are actually a combination of two words.

آن + جا = آنجا

that + place = there (that place)
refers to an object far from us

این + جا = اینجا

this + place = here (this place)
refers to an object near to us

These two adverbs are used in two different situations:

1. When you want to introduce a place to someone in general, like a country, city, class, office, university, etc., you put the adverb at the beginning of the sentence. For example:

اینجا صنفم است. Here is my class.
اینجا صنف است. Here is a class.
آنجا دفترم است. There is my office.
آنجا دفتر است. There is an office.

2. When you want to introduce the specific location of something, someone, or someplace, you put the adverb right after the object. For example:

کتاب آنجا است. There is the book.
میز اینجا است. Here is the table.
صنفم اینجا است. My class is here.

Exercise 7: تمرین ۷:
Match the following sentences with their meaning.

| B | A |
|---|---|
| Here is the notebook. | ۱  اینجا صنف است. |
| There are the head-phones. | ۲  آنجا دفتر است. |
| Here is a class. | ۳  قلمم آنجا است. |
| There is an office. | ۴  کمپیوتر اینجا است. |
| My pen is there. | ۵  گوشکی آنجا است. |
| There is the computer. | ۶  کتابچه اینجا است. |

Exercise 8:  تمرین ۸:

A. Listen to the following short conversations and practice with a partner.

میرویس جان، اینجا چند دانه میز است؟
Mirwais jan, how many (pieces of) tables are here?
اینجا سه دانه میز است.
Here are three tables.

لیلا جان، آنجا چند دانه کتاب است؟
Layla jan, how many (pieces of) books are there?
آنجا شش دانه کتاب است.
There are six books.

B.  Now, with a partner, point to the objects in the following pictures and ask how many are here or there. Your partner should answer in a complete sentence. For example:

اینجا چند دانه چوکی است؟    اینجا پنج دانه چوکی است.
آنجا چند تا بچه است؟    آنجا دو تا بچه است.

Note: The words [dāna] دانه and [tā] تا are used as classifiers (counting words) like in the English 'two bunches of flowers' (see the language point in Grammar Note 4.3 for more info).

## 4.3 Classifiers

General Classifiers: There are two common classifiers used in Dari: [dāna] دانه and [tā] تا . These are interchangeable with most of the specific classifiers listed below. In fact, it is very common to use these classifiers [dāna] دانه or [tā] تا in place of the more specific ones. The general classifier [dāna] دانه is commonly used with inanimate nouns and the classifier [tā] تا is used for both animate and inanimate nouns interchangeably. For example:

Both [dāna] دانه and [tā] تا can be used

three notebooks سه تا کتابچه /سه دانه کتابچه

three pens سه دانه قلم/سه تا قلم

Only [tā] تا can be used

three teachers سه تا معلم

In written Dari, you usually count objects by giving a numeral followed by a classifier, such as دسته "bunch" in "ten bunches of flowers." This classifier is added to the stem of the numeral and precedes the noun. The following classifiers are the ones you really need to learn:

| | | | |
|---|---|---|---|
| سه نفر شاگرد | for people | [nafar, tan] نفر ، تن |
| سه جلد کتاب | for books and notebooks | [jeld] جلد |
| سه پایه میز | for things that stand | [pā-ya] پایه |
| یك قطعه عكس | for pictures and charts | [qet'a] قطعه |
| یك درجن تخم | for dozens | [darjan] درجن |
| یك بسته سگرت | for a package | [basta] بسته |
| چار دسته گل | for bunches | [desta] دسته |
| سه راس گاو | for cattle | [ra's] راس |
| دو عراده بایسکل | for vehicles | [arāda'] عراده |

Exercise 9: تمرین ۹:

A. The following is a list of some items. Read them carefully and put each under the correct classifier below.

| | | | |
|---|---|---|---|
| خطکش | استاد | کتابچه | چوکی |
| گوشکی | زن | قلم | میز |
| پرینتر | مرد | پنسل | کمپیوتر |
| | دروازه | شاگرد | سکینر |
| | کلکین | معلم | کتاب |

| پایه | تا | دانه |
|---|---|---|
| | | |

| نفر | درجن | جلد |
|---|---|---|
| | | |

B. Now, working with a partner, ask about the objects and people in the classroom. Use the general classifiers دانه and تا. For example:

How many tables are in the classroom? در صنف چند دانه میز است؟
Two tables are in the classroom. در صنف دو دانه میز است.

How many girls are here? اینجا چند تا دختر است؟
There are three girls. اینجا سه تا دختر است.

## Cultural Note    تبصرۀ فرهنگي

### Classrooms in the Afghanistan

A typical classroom in Afghanistan is furnished with tables and chairs and a blackboard with chalk and erasers. However, there are some schools that, because of lack of space and a large number of students, cannot provide even these basic classroom objects. In fact, some of these schools cannot even provide classrooms. Students end up sitting outside in the yards or underneath a tent.

In grade levels where students are taught different subjects by different teachers, it is the teachers, not the students, who change classrooms.

Exercise 10:    تمرين ١٠:

Working in pairs, discuss the similarities and differences between typical classrooms in your home country and typical classrooms in Afghanistan. Then compare your list with that of another pair.

| Afghan Classroom | Home Country Classroom |
|---|---|
|  |  |

### 4.4 The Verb داشتن 'To Have'

The present stem of the verb داشتن 'to have' is دار 'dār' and is conjugated similarly to other regular verbs in Dari. However, unlike regular verbs, this particular verb does not take the prefix می in contemporary usage. However, it does if you are using it in literature.

The present stem دار is conjugated as follows.

| | |
|---|---|
| I have a pen. | من یک قلم دارم. |
| We have a classroom. | ما یک صنف داریم. |
| You have two books. | تو دو کتاب داری. |
| You have four chairs. | شما چار چوکی دارید. |
| S/he has a notebook. | او یک کتابچه دارد. |
| They have three tables. | آنها سه میز دارند. |

Exercise 11:     تمرین ۱۱:

Mark the appropriate pronoun for each verb. Then translate the sentence into English.

| | | | | | |
|---|---|---|---|---|---|
| ۱ | شما | ما | ایشان | سه چوکی داریم. | |
| ۲ | او | تو | من | دو گوشکی دارد. | |
| ۳ | شما | ما | ایشان | چار کمپیوتر دارند. | |
| ۴ | او | تو | من | یک لپتاپ داری. | |
| ۵ | او | تو | من | یک کتاب دارم. | |
| ۶ | شما | ما | ایشان | پنج دانه کتاب دارید. | |

Exercise 12:    تمرین ۱۲:
Write the following sentences in Dari.

| | | |
|---|---|---|
| I have a desk. | | ۱ |
| You have a book. | | ۲ |
| He has two bags. | | ۳ |
| You all have an office. | | ۴ |
| We have two phones. | | ۵ |
| They have three teachers. | | ۶ |
| She has a notebook. | | ۷ |

Exercise 13:    تمرین ۱۳:
You will hear a conversation between لیلا and میرویس as they discuss their belongings. Listen carefully and then answer the questions.

1. How many classmates does Layla have?
   a) 6   b) 16

2. How many of her classmates are boys?
   a) 3   b) 4   c) 8

3. Mark the correct numbers and names of objects in Layla's classroom.

دو دانه کمپیوتر
سه دانه کمپیوتر
یك دانه کمپیوتر

هشت دانه چوکی
هفت دانه چوکی
شش دانه چوکی

دو دانه تباشیر
تباشیر
چار دانه تباشیر

دو دانه تخته
پنج دانه تخته
نه دانه تخته

دو دانه تخته پاك
شش دانه تخته پاك
چار دانه تخته پاك

سه دانه پروجکتور
دو دانه پروجکتور
یك دانه پروجکتور

Exercise 14:  تمرین ۱۴:

Open your backpack or purse. Make a list of the objects you have inside.

Exercise 15: تمرین ۱۵:

A. First, find and write down these words in Dari.

| | |
|---|---|
| | pen |
| | classroom |
| | student |
| | teacher |
| | bag |
| | notebook |
| | chair |
| | phone |
| | computer |

B. Now practice asking your classmates what objects they have in their bags. For example:

Student 1: شما چند دانه کتاب دارید؟      Student 1: شما کتابچه دارید؟
Student 2: من یک کتاب دارم.      Student 2: بلی دارم.

# درس دوم: کتابم در کجا است؟

## Lesson Two: Where is my book?

In this section, you will learn how to ask where an object is and describe an object's location.

Exercise 1: تمرین ۱:
Listen to the audio recording. Then practice repeating the phrases.

**در**

شاگرد ها در صنف هستند.

**در روی**

کتاب در روی میز است.

**در زیر**

کتابچه در زیر میز است.

**در پهلوی**

چوکی در پهلوی میز است.

**در پیشروی**

چوکی در پیشروی میز است.

**در رو بروی**

لپتاپ در روبروی کمپیوتر است.

**در پشت**

چوکی در پشت میز است .

**در بین**

کتاب در بین میز است.

**در بیرون**

شاگرد در بیرون صنف است.

**در اطراف**

چوکی ها در اطراف میز است.

**در طرف چپ**

کتاب در طرف چپ لپتاپ است.

**در طرف راست**

ستپلر در طرف راست لپتاپ است.

## 4.5 Prepositions

The basic preposition [dar] در means 'in/at'; this preposition is used to indicate the location of an object. For example:

The students are in the class. .شاگردها در صنف هستند

In order to indicate the location of an object, the preposition [dar] در is combined with a noun or an adverb. For example:

| on the / on the top of | در روی | in + the top | در + روی |
|---|---|---|---|
| under the | در زیر | in + under | در + زیر |
| next to the | در پهلوی | in+ the next | در + پهلوی |
| in front of the | در پیشروی | in + the front | در + پیشروی |
| across the | در روبروی | in+ face to face | در + روبروی |
| behind the | در پشت | in+ behind the | در + پشت |
| inside the | در بین | in+ between | در + بین |
| outside the | در بیرون | in+ outside | در + بیرون |
| around the | در اطراف | in+ around | در + اطراف |
| on the left side of the | در طرف چپ | in+ left side | در + طرف چپ |
| on the right side of the | در طرف راست | in+ right side | در + طرف راست |

In colloquial Dari, the preposition در is often pronounced as [da] د. Moreover, in spoken Dari you will sometimes see the place prepositions without در or د.

Exercise 2:  تمرین ۲:

A. Nāzanin is searching for her school supplies around the house. Where are they? Look at the picture below and match each item to its location.

| دستکش | | در روی کتاب است. | الف | ۱ |
|---|---|---|---|---|
| کتاب | | در روی چوکی است. | ب | ۲ |
| چراغ | | در زیر چوکی است. | ج | ۳ |
| ساعت | | در پیشروی چوکی است. | د | ۴ |
| بکس | | در بین بکس است. | هـ | ۵ |

B. Split the class into two groups. The first group should wait in the hallway while the second group places some objects around the classroom. When the first group comes back in the room, they should ask someone from the second group to tell them where an object is located, and should then retrieve the object. Then the groups should switch and repeat. For example:

Excuse me, where is my book? الف ـ ببخشین! کتاب ام در کجاست؟
Your book is on the table. ب ـ کتاب تان در روی میز است.

## 4.6 More Prepositions

The prepositions mentioned in Grammar Note 4.5 have a few Dari and Arabic loanword synonyms. These are:

| Translation | Arabic loanwords | Dari synonym | Common preposition |
|---|---|---|---|
| on the / on the top of | – | در سر، در بالای | در روی |
| under the | – | – | در زیر |
| next to the | – | در بغل | در پهلوی |
| in front of the | – | – | در پیشروی |
| across the | در مقابل | – | در روبروی |
| behind the | در عقب | در پشت سر | در پشت |
| inside the | در داخل | در مابین | در بین |
| outside the | در خارج | | در بیرون |
| around the | در چار طرف | در گرد، در دور | در اطراف |
| on the left side of the | در سمت چپ | – | در طرف چپ |
| on the right side of the | در سمت راست | – | در طرف راست |

Exercise 3: 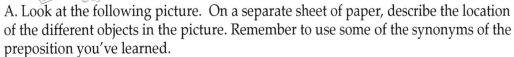 تمرین ۳:

A. Look at the following picture. On a separate sheet of paper, describe the location of the different objects in the picture. Remember to use some of the synonyms of the preposition you've learned.

B.  Look at the picture below and then complete the sentences. You may use a phrase more than once. Try to use the synonyms of the prepositions.

| | | |
|---|---|---|
| ۱ | کمپیوتر _____ است. | |
| ۲ | تخته _____ است. | |
| ۳ | کتاب ها _____ است. | |
| ۴ | یخچال _____ است. | |
| ۵ | تلیفون _____ است. | |
| ۶ | چوکی _____ است. | |
| ۷ | چراغ _____ است. | |
| ۸ | لودسپیکر _____ است. | |
| ۹ | گیلاس _____ است. | |
| ۱۰ | الماری کتاب _____ است. | |

در بالای میز

در سمت راست میز

در داخل الماری کتاب

در پیشروی میز

در بالای یخچال

در سمت چپ کیبورد

در طرف راست تخته

در سر یخچال

در پیشروی کمپیوتر

در بالای کمپیوتر

## 4.7 The Existence of ezāfat [-e] in Writing

As you learned in the previous chapter, the ezāfat [-e] shows the relation between two words. For example:

Dari class  senf-e Dari  صنف دری
My name  nām-e man  نام من

Now you will learn how this element looks in writing:

1. All words that end with consonants take the ezāfat [-e]; however, it isn't written. For example:

dar zĕr  در زیر                    dar pošt  در پشت
dar zĕr-e mĕz  در زیر میز         dar pošt-e mĕz  در پشت میز

2. If a word ends with the vowel sound [a] (most likely appearing as [he] ه), the ezāfat will be represented by the diacritic [hamza] همزه ء at the top of a letter or following the letters [alef] الف and [yā] ی and is pronounced [-ye]. For example, the following forms are both acceptable:

kĕtāb-ča  کتابچه                  taxta  تخته
kĕtāb-ča-ye man  کتابچۀ من       taxta -ye senf-e maa  تختۀ صنف ده
kĕtāb-ča-ye man  کتابچه ای من    taxta -ye senf-e maa  تخته ای صنف دهم

3. If a noun ends with the vowel sound [ā], [o], [ō], or [u] it will take the ending [ye] ی instead of ezāfat [-e]. Usually those words are represented by الف [alĕf] or و [wāw].  For example:

dar ro-ye  در روی                 dar rō  در رو
dar pahlu-ye  در پهلوی            dar pahlu  در پهلو
dar bālā-ye  در بالای             dar bālā  در بالا

4. If a word ends with the vowel sound [i], the ezāfat [-e] is not written (as after the consonant). For example:

čawki  چوکی                       gošaki  گوشکی
čawki-ye man  چوکی من           gošaki-ye man  گوشکی من

Exercise 4:    تمرین ۴:

Using what you have just learned, combine the words given in the right column.
Then, working with a partner, translate each phrase into English.

| English | Combined | |
|---------|----------|---|
| _____ | _____ | [mo'alem/englisi] ١ معلم/انگلیسی |
| _____ | _____ | [senf/dari] ٢ صنف/دری |
| _____ | _____ | [hamsĕnfi/tān] ٣ همصنفی/تان |
| _____ | _____ | [qalam-hā/tān] ۴ قلم ها/تان |
| _____ | _____ | [pahlu/mez] ۵ پهلو/میز |

Exercise 5:    تمرین ۵:

Read the following text and underline the pairs of words that take ezāfat [-e].
Double underline the words that take them in spoken Dari but are not written.

این صنف دری است، در اینجا سه محصل مرد و دو محصل دختر هستند.
در پیشروی صنف، یك تخته، یك میز و یك کمپیوتر است. در بالای میز یك کتاب
دری و یك کتاب انگلیسی است. صنف دری ده دانه میز و ده دانه چوکی دارد.

Exercise 6:    تمرین ۶:

You will hear a conversation between نازنین and شریف on the audio recording.
Listen and answer the following questions.

1. Which book did Nazanin ask about?
   a) Dari book    b) English book    c) Pashto book

2. Where did Sharif first say the book was?
   a) inside of the bookshelf
   b) on the left side of the bookshelf
   c) behind the bookshelf

3. Where was the book?
   a) under the table    b) behind the table    c) on the top of the table

### 4.8 Negation in Dari

To make a negative statement in Dari, the short form of 'no' نه/نی is added to the beginning of the verb. An exception is the verb 'to be,' in which the نی actually replaces the first letter of that verb. The short form of نه/نی is [ـن].

The book is here. کتاب اینجا است.
The book isn't here. کتاب اینجا نیست.

I am a student. من شاگرد هستم.
I am not a student. من شاگرد نیستم.

He is living in Kabul. او در کابل زنده گی میکند.
He is not living in Kabul. او در کابل زنده گی نمیکند.

We have a classroom. ما یک صنف داریم.
We don't have a classroom. اما یک صنف نداریم.

Exercise 7: تمرین ۷:

Change the following sentences from affirmative to negative. Then translate them into English.

| | | |
|---|---|---|
| | | ۱ شاگرد ها در صنف هستند. |
| | | ۲ کتاب و قلم در روی میز است. |
| | | ۳ او اینجا است. |
| | | ۴ اجمل سه دانه کتابچه دارد. |
| | | ۵ کریم در امریکا زنده گی میکند. |

Exercise 8:    تمرین ۸:

Read the following statements describing the locations of the following objects. Decide if the descriptions are right or not.  If they are incorrect, write a negative statement saying that it is not here and a positive statement about its correct location. When finished, compare your answers with a classmate. The first one is done for you.

| | | | |
|---|---|---|---|
| کتاب در پهلوی میز نیست، کتاب در زیر میز است. | 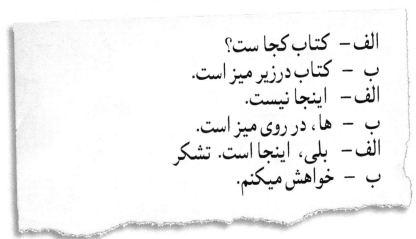 | ۱ کتاب در پهلوی میز است. | |
| | | ۲ آن بچه در پیشروی کلکین است. | |
| | | ۳ ساعت در بالای کلکین است. | |
| | | ۴ میز در پهلوی کلکین است. | |
| | | ۵ چوکی در پشت میز است. | |
| | | ۶ ساعت در زیر میز است. | |

Exercise 9:    تمرین ۹:

Working with a classmate, write a dialogue where you ask about one of the objects that belong to your classmate.  S/he should mistakenly give you the wrong direction. You will go look for it and say that the object is not there.  Then s/he should give you the correct location.  Finally, you should thank him/her. For example:

الف – کتاب کجا ست؟
ب – کتاب در زیر میز است.
الف – اینجا نیست.
ب – ها، در روی میز است.
الف – بلی، اینجا است. تشکر
ب – خواهش میکنم.

Exercise 10: تمرین ۱۰:

A. You will hear a conversation on the audio recording between two classmates meeting one another on the first day of the class. Listen and then choose the best answer for each.

1. Where are Jawed and Sharif's classmates?
   a) in the classroom     b) outside of the classroom

2. Where are the 13 chairs?
   a) inside of the classroom
   b) behind the classroom
   c) in front of the classroom

3. Does Sharif have a book?
   a) yes     b) no

4. Where is Jaweed's book?
   a) in his bag  b) under his bag  c) next to the Jawed's bag

5. Where is Jawed from?
   a) Kandahar  b) Nangarhar   c) Mazar

B. Working with a partner, create a similar conversation. Then act it out in the front of the class.

### 4.9 Yes/No Questions with آیا

The word [āyā] آیا is a common question marker in Dari that always comes at the beginning of the sentence. When you use the question marker آیا, you don't need the intonation, because the word آیا by itself clarifies the question.

Remember that the question marker آیا is not used at the same time as other question words like why, who, when, etc.

Exercise 11: تمرین ۱۱:

Read the following sentences and then make a question for each using the question marker آیا.

| | |
|---|---|
| ۱ | معلم در صنف است. |
| ۲ | قلم در بالای میز است. |
| ۳ | کتاب در پشت کمپیوتر است. |
| ۴ | صنف ما در روبروی دفتر است. |
| ۵ | پنسل در بین کتابچه است. |
| ۶ | چوکی در پشت میز است. |

Exercise 12: تمرین ۱۲:

A. The following texts describe the locations of the objects and the people in the pictures. Read the texts and then look at the pictures. Under each picture, write the number of the text that best describes it.

۳ در صنف پنج مرد، دو زن، سه میز، یک چوکی و یک تخته است. مرد ها در مقابل زنها هستند.

۲ در صنف پنج دختر، ده بچه، هفت میز، سه چوکی و یک تخته است. تخته در پشت دختر ها است.

۱ آنجا دو دختر است، یک دختر در بین دروازه است و یک دختر در پیشروی دروازه است.

۶ در صنف یک استاد زن، دو محصل دختر است. استاد در روبروی محصل ها است.

۵ در صنف یک استاد، دو محصل و سه میز است. استاد در پهلوی محصل دختر است.

۴ در آنجا یک میز، دو تلیفون، یک قلم و یک کتابچه است. تلیفون ها بالای میز است.

B. Working with a partner, point to a picture and ask the location of some of the objects and people in it.

C. Now write the location of at least one object or a person in each of the pictures shown below.

| | |
|---|---|
| | ١ |
| | ٢ |
| | ٣ |
| | ۴ |
| | ۵ |
| | ۶ |
| | ٧ |

# درس سوم: در صنف ما چی میکنیم؟

## Lesson Three: What do we do in the classroom?

In this section, you will talk about classroom activities and learn how to give commands and make requests in Dari.

Exercise 1:  تمرین ۱:

A. Listen to the audio recording in which امید is explaining his daily classroom activities. Match each Dari phrase to its possible English equivalent provided below.

من در صنف کتاب میخوانم.    من محصل زبان دری هستم.    نامم امید است.

ویدیو سیل میکنم.    نوشته میکنم.    گفتگو میکنم.

و نوت میگیرم.    گپ میزنم.    به گفتگوها گوش میکنم.

| | | |
|---|---|---|
| My name is Omeed. | I write. | In Dari class, I read a book. |
| I watch a video. | I converse. | I am a Dari language student. |
| I speak. | I take notes. | I listen to conversations. |

B. What do you do in your classroom every day? Turn to the person next to you and tell them about your daily classroom activities.

## 4.10 The Present Stem of the Verbs ریشهٔ زمان حال افعال

All Dari verbs have different stems in the present tense. The present stems of verbs don't have a standard rule and sometimes don't even match the infinitive form of the verbs. Also, most Dari verbs take the prefix می, which represents duration and continuity of an action.

For example, you heard the following verbs in Exercise 1A.

| Meaning | [PS Prefix]me + | Present stem | Infinitive |
|---|---|---|---|
| to read | کتاب می + خوان.... | کتاب خوان | کتاب خواندن |
| to speak/ talk | گپ می + زن.... | گپ زن | گپ زدن |
| to take | نوت می + گیر.... | نوت گیر | نوت گرفتن |
| to do | گفتگو می + کن .... | گفتگو کن | گفتگو کردن |

After learning the present stem, you can conjugate each verb for each person by adding the proper personal ending.

Exercise 2: تمرین ۲ :

You have already learned how to conjugate the present stem of verbs for each person. For each of the phrases below, circle the best personal ending for each occurrence of the verb خواندن [xāndan].

| | | | | | | | |
|---|---|---|---|---|---|---|---|
| د | ی | ید | ند | یم | مَ | ۱ من کتاب میخوان.... |
| د | ی | ید | ند | یم | مَ | ۲ ما نوت میگیر.... |
| د | ی | ید | ند | یم | مَ | ۳ تو مینویس.... |
| د | ی | ید | ند | یم | مَ | ۴ شما گپ میزن... |
| د | ی | ید | ند | یم | مَ | ۵ او نوت میگیر... |
| د | ی | ید | ند | یم | مَ | ۶ آنها کتاب میخوان.... |

## 4.11 Compound Verbs Using the Simple Verb کردن

The simple verb کردن used with the present stem (کن) can combine with a noun, adverb, preposition, other verbs, or adjectives to make a new compound verb.

For example, in Exercise 1A, you heard the following verbs:

| | |
|---|---|
| to converse گفتگو + کردن | conversation + to do گفتگو + کردن |
| to write نوشته کردن | write (past participle form) + to do نوشته + کردن |
| to watch سیل کردن | watching + to do سیل + کردن |
| to listen گوش کردن | ear + to do گوش + کردن |

The present stems of these verbs are as follows:

| The present stems | | The infinitive of the verbs | |
|---|---|---|---|
| گفتگو میکن | گفتگو + می+کن | to converse | گفتگو کردن |
| نوشته میکن | نوشته+می+کن | to write | نوشته کردن |
| سیل میکن | سیل + می+کن | to watch | سیل کردن |
| گوش میکن | گوش+ می+کن | to listen | گوش کردن |

By adding the personal ending to each verb, you can conjugate them for each person.

Exercise 3: تمرین ۳:

Complete the following sentences with the appropriate verbs and the correct personal endings.

|  |  |  |  |
|---|---|---|---|
| to converse | _____ | ۱ | شما در صنف |
| to write | _____ | ۲ | او در کتابچه |
| to watch | _____ | ۳ | ما در صنف تلویزیون |
| to listen | _____ | ۴ | آنها در صنف رادیو |
| to write | _____ | ۵ | تو ایمیل |
| to talk | _____ | ۶ | من و اجمل |

Exercise 4: تمرین ۴:

Ahmad is a Dari language student. Every day in class he reads books, writes in his notebook, and speaks with his classmates. Write a few sentences about him in Dari.

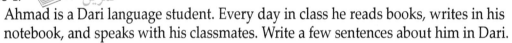

Exercise 5: تمرین ۵:

A. You will hear a conversation on the audio recording between لیلا and فرید in which they are talking about their classroom activities. Listen and write a correct answer to each question.

| ۱ | لیلا هر روز در صنف چی میکند؟ |
|---|---|
| | ............................................. |
| | ............................................. |
| ۲ | فرید هر روز در صنف چی میکند؟ |
| | ............................................. |
| | ............................................. |

B. Divide into two groups and ask each other about the classroom activities that you do. As you ask one another about activities, fill in the following table according to the statements of your group.

| نام همصنفی | کتاب خواندن | نوشته کردن | گفتگو کردن | گپ زدن | ویدیو سیل کردن | گوش کردن | نوت گرفتن |
|---|---|---|---|---|---|---|---|
| | | | | | | | |
| | | | | | | | |
| | | | | | | | |
| | | | | | | | |
| | | | | | | | |
| | | | | | | | |

C. Now, pair up with someone in the other group and take turns reporting your group members' activities.

## 4.12 Definite Object Marker را

The definite object marker is equal to the English word 'the' and its function is to specify the object.

For example:

|  |  |
|---|---|
| I read a book. | من کتاب میخوانم. |
| I read the book. | من کتاب را میخوانم. |
| I watch a movie. | من فلم سیل میکنم. |
| I watch the movie. | من فلم را سیل میکنم. |
| I listen to the conversation. | من گفتگو را گوش میکنم. |
| I listen to a conversation. | من به گفتگو گوش میکنم. |

In colloquial Dari, if the definite object marker comes after a word ending with a vowel sound, the را is changed to [a] ه, and if the word ends with a consonant, it will be pronounced [ra] ره. For example:

| Ends with a vowel | | Ends with a consonant | |
|---|---|---|---|
| Colloquial | Standard | Colloquial | Standard |
| کتابچه ره | کتابچه را | کتابه | کتاب را |
| تخته ره | تخته را | قلمه | قلم را |
| گفتگو ره | گفتگو را | میزه | میز را |

Exercise 6:    تمرین ۶:

For each of the following objects and words listed below, write an original sentence using the definite object marker را in an appropriate way.

| | |
|---|---|
| ۱ | ما/ کتاب/ نوشته کردن |
| ۲ | تو/ کتاب/ خواندن |
| ۳ | شما/ کتاب دری/ خواندن |
| ۴ | آنها/ فلم ستارترك/ سیل کردن |
| ۵ | من/ رادیو/ گوش کردن |

Exercise 7:    تمرین ۷:

Read the following text and answer the questions about it.

آن مرد زلمی است، او از ایالت کالیفرنیا است، اصلاً او امریکایی است، او حالا در پوهنتون اندیانا محصل است، او محصل صنف دری است. زلمی در صنف دری، قصه ها را میخواند، به زبان دری گفتگو میکند و بالای تخته نوشته میکند.

| | |
|---|---|
| university | پوهنتون |
| reading a story | قصه خواندن |
| now | حالا |

1   Where is Zalmay from?

2   Which university is Zalmay in?

3   What does Zalmay do in Dari class?

4   What does Zalmay do with the board?

Exercise 8: ۸ :تمرین

A. Listen to the audio recording depicting some common classroom phrases, commands, and requests. Then, working with a partner, practice these phrases.

اجازه است...؟

May I...?

پرسان دارم.

I have a question.

بفرمایید!

Please (when you offer).

اجازه است، داخل شوم؟

May I come in?

ببخشید.

Excuse me. / Sorry.

لطفآ.

Please.

این واضح است.

This is clear.

فهمیدم.

I understood.

نفهمیدم.

I didn't understand.

B. For each of the following situations, write what you would say.

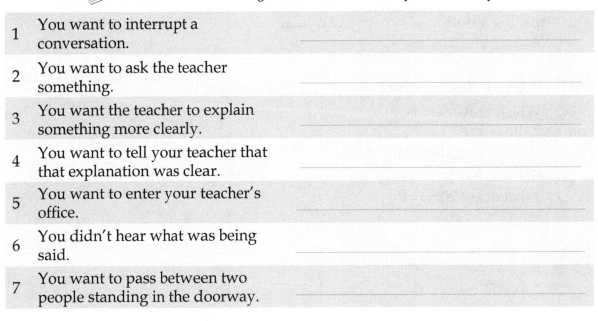

| 1 | You want to interrupt a conversation. | |
| 2 | You want to ask the teacher something. | |
| 3 | You want the teacher to explain something more clearly. | |
| 4 | You want to tell your teacher that that explanation was clear. | |
| 5 | You want to enter your teacher's office. | |
| 6 | You didn't hear what was being said. | |
| 7 | You want to pass between two people standing in the doorway. | |

Exercise 9: تمرین ۹:

A. Listen to the audio recording depicting some common responses to the phrases, commands, and requests given in Exercise 8. Then, working with a partner, practice these phrases.

بیا. / بیایید.

Come. / Come (formal).

برو. / بروید.

Go. / Go (formal).

بخوان. / بخوانید.

Read. / Read (formal).

بشین./ بشینید.

Sit down. / Sit down (formal).

بخیز. / بخیزید.

Stand up. / Stand up. (formal)

گوش کن. / گوش کنید.

Listen. / Listen (formal).

آرام باش./ آرام باشید.

Silence. / Silence (formal).

بگیر./ بگیرید.

Take it. / Take it (formal).

بده./ بدهید.

Give it. / Give it (formal).

دروازه را بسته کنید.

Please close the door.

دروازه را باز کنید.

Please open the door.

تکرار کن./ تکرار کنید.

Repeat it / Repeat it (formal)

نوشته کن./ نوشته کنید.

Write down ./ Please write down.

ببین./ ببینید.

Look. / Please look.

بگو./ بگوید.

Tell. / Tell (formal).

B. Working with a partner, practice giving one another commands, e.g. sit down, stand up, etc. Your partner should act out the commands as they are given. Then switch roles and repeat the exercise.

## 4.13 Commands and Requests امریه ها و درخواست ها

Among the phrases you've just learned are some commands and requests, or imperatives. These are formed by adding the letter [ba] بـ at the beginning of the present stem of the verb excluding the prefix [me] می . For example:

| Commands | Present Stem | Meaning | Infinitive |
|---|---|---|---|
| بـ + خوان | خوان | to read | خواندن |
| بـ + بین | بین | to see | دیدن |
| بـ + شنو | شنو | to listen | شنیدن |

However, as you saw earlier, some of the commands will not take the prefix بـ [ba]. For example:

| Commands | Present Stem | Meaning | Infinitive |
|---|---|---|---|
| نوشته کن | نوشته کن | to write | نوشته کردن |
| آرام باش | آرام باش | to be silent | آرام بودن |
| تکرار کن | تکرار کن | to repeat | تکرار کردن |

To make these imperative phrases negative, the prefix بـ [ba] is replaced with نـ [na] or نـ [na] is added to the verbs that do not take the prefix بـ [ba]. For example:

نخوان    بخوان
نبین    ببین
آرام نباش    آرام باش
تکرار نکن    تکرار کنی

All the commands above are in the singular informal form.

## 4.13 Commands and Requests (cont'd.)

However, in Dari there is another form of commands that takes the personal ending یـد [ed], and this form of command is used for:

- Formal Singular
- Formal Plural
- Informal Plural

| Negative form | | Positive form | |
|---|---|---|---|
| Please don't read. | نخوانید. | Please read. | بخوانید. |
| Please don't look/see. | نبینید. | Please look/see. | ببینید. |
| Please don't sit. | نشینید. | Please sit. | بشینید. |
| Please don't repeat. | تکرار نکنید. | Please repeat. | تکرار کنید. |

For example:

As you see, the only difference between the above forms is the personal ending [ed].

Exercise 10:  تمرین ۱۰:

Read the following commands carefully and change the informal forms to formal. Then write each in their negative form. Finally, match them to their proper meanings.

| Meaning | | Negative | Formal | Informal | |
|---|---|---|---|---|---|
| Write. | | | | بشین. | ۱ |
| Close the door. | | | | بخیز. | ۲ |
| Open the door. | | | | بخوان. | ۳ |
| Repeat. | | | | بگو. | ۴ |
| Give it. | | | | بیا. | ۵ |
| Read. | | | | برو. | ۶ |
| Get up. | | | | گوش کن. | ۷ |
| Sit down. | | | | بگیر. | ۸ |
| Tell. | | | | بده. | ۹ |
| Take it. | | | | تکرار کن. | ۱۰ |
| Listen. | | | | دروازه را باز کن. | ۱۱ |
| Go. | | | | دروازه را بسته کن. | ۱۲ |
| Come. | | | | نوشته کن. | ۱۳ |

Exercise 11:  تمرین ۱۱:

A. Using the rules you have learned, convert the present stem of the following verbs to the imperative (command) form.

| Commands | Present Stem | Meaning | Infinitive | |
|---|---|---|---|---|
| _____ | مان | to put | ماندن | ۱ |
| _____ | بردار | to pick up | برداشتن | ۲ |
| _____ | روشن کن | to turn on | روشن کردن | ۳ |
| _____ | خاموش کن | to turn off | خاموش کردن | ۴ |

B.   Write the following sentences in Dari.

1. Open the book.

_____   ۱

2. Close the door.

_____   ۲

3. Put down the pen.

_____   ۳

4. Pick up the phone.

_____   ۴

5. Give the pencil.

_____   ۵

Exercise 12:   تمرین ۱۲:

A. You will hear a conversation between two classmates on the audio recording. Listen and mark the phrases, commands, and requests that you hear from the list below.

| | | | |
|---|---|---|---|
| بازکن. ☐ | بدهید. ☐ | بفرمایید. ☐ | بردارید. ☐ |
| بازکنید. ☐ | بده. ☐ | ببخشید. ☐ | بردار. ☐ |
| پرسان دارم. ☐ | بگیرید. ☐ | بشینید. ☐ | بمانید. ☐ |
| بروید. ☐ | بگیر. ☐ | بشین. ☐ | بمانید. ☐ |
| برو. ☐ | بسته کنید. ☐ | بخیزید. ☐ | بردارید. ☐ |
| اجازه است، داخل شوم؟ ☐ | بسته کن. ☐ | بخیز. ☐ | بردار. ☐ |

B.   Role-play. Working with a partner, make a conversation similar to the one you've just heard, using the phrases, commands, and requests you learned in this lesson.

## Cultural Note  تبصرهٔ فرهنگی

### Being Polite

In Afghan culture, it is very important to be polite and use the correct form when speaking. By using proper manners, people can earn trust and respect in Afghan society. There are several rules when trying to be polite. Some of the most important ones are listed below.

1. Say hello & greet everybody, especially elders.
   Note: Unknown females are an exception to this rule, unless they are government officials or they approach you first.

2. Always speak formally. Using the plural form of verbs and pronouns in the second person is very important.

3. When an elder enters a room, stand up and greet him or her.

4. Don't remain seated when an elder person is standing and speaking with you.

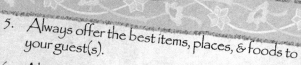

5. Always offer the best items, places, & foods to your guest(s).

6. Always help people in need; i.e., those injured, old people, and small children.

7. Listen to the advice of an elder and talk to him or her in a very soft voice, even if you don't agree with what they have to say.

8. Visit sick people, especially your family, friends, and neighbors.

9. During meals, wait to eat until the elders start to eat first.

10. If you are thirsty and want to drink water, first offer the drink to a younger person. If they don't want water, then you may drink.

There is a proverb, "water is necessary for the young, and food is necessary for the elders."
آب از خوردها، نان از کلان‌ها

Exercise 13: تمرین ۱۳:

A. What would do you do in the following situations if you were in Afghanistan?

1. You are in the office and a village elder enters your office.

2. You are traveling with a group of people and all of you stop to drink water.

3. You are passing by some people.

4. You are speaking to a group of village elders.

5. A person from your office is very sick.

6. You are at a meeting and the governor wants to leave. Right before he leaves, he remembers one important thing to discuss with you, so he turns to talk to you while you are sitting in your chair.

B. Working in small groups, discuss the differences between how you would react to the situations above in your culture and in Afghan culture. Are there any similarities?

# مرور فصل چارم
# Review of Chapter Four

In this section you will review the vocabulary, phrases, grammar, and cultural elements that you learned throughout the chapter.

Exercise 1: تمرین ۱:

A. Look at the following pictures. Then list the objects or people you see in each picture. For example: این صنف یک دروازه دارد.

B. Now, write down the objects and people in your own classroom.

Exercise 2: تمرین ۲:

Look at the following pictures. Then list the objects you see in each picture. For
example: این صنف یک تخته دارد.

Exercise 3: تمرین ۳:

A. You will hear a conversation on the audio recording between لیلا and فرید.
Listen carefully and then answer the following questions.

۱   لپتاپ در کجا است؟

۲   کتاب انگلیسی در کجا است؟

۳   تلیفون مبایل در کجا است؟

B. 🎧 Now listen again to the conversation. This time mark the commands, requests, and phrases you hear.

| | | | | | |
|---|---|---|---|---|---|
| ☐ | بدهید. | ☐ | بفرمایید. | ☐ | ببین. |
| ☐ | بده. | ☐ | ببخشید. | ☐ | ببینید. |
| ☐ | بگیرید. | ☐ | لطفاً. | ☐ | بمانید. |
| ☐ | بگیر. | ☐ | بیاور. | ☐ | بمانید. |
| ☐ | بسته کنید. | ☐ | بیاورید. | ☐ | بردارید. |
| ☐ | بسته کن. | ☐ | بخیز. | ☐ | بردار. |

Exercise 4: تمرین ۴:

A. Read the following verbs and their present stems. Then write each in their formal and informal command forms.

| | | | | | |
|---|---|---|---|---|---|
| ___ | ___ | to open | باز کن | باز کردن | ۱ |
| ___ | ___ | to close | بسته کن | بسته کردن | ۲ |
| ___ | ___ | to see | بین | دیدن | ۳ |
| ___ | ___ | to listen | شنو | شنیدن | ۴ |
| ___ | ___ | to listen | گوش کن | گوش کردن | ۵ |
| ___ | ___ | to tell | گوی | گفتن | ۶ |
| ___ | ___ | to write | نوشته کن | نوشته کردن | ۷ |
| ___ | ___ | to read | خوان | خواندن | ۸ |
| ___ | ___ | to sit down | شین | نشستن | ۹ |
| ___ | ___ | to stand up | خیز | خیستن | ۱۰ |
| ___ | ___ | to go | رو | رفتن | ۱۱ |
| ___ | ___ | to come | آی | آمدن | ۱۲ |
| ___ | ___ | to carry | بر | بردن | ۱۳ |
| ___ | ___ | to bring | آور | آوردن | ۱۴ |
| ___ | ___ | to give | ده | دادن | ۱۵ |

| | | English | Present stem | Infinitive | № |
|---|---|---|---|---|---|
| _____ _____ | | to take | گیر | گرفتن | ۱۶ |
| _____ _____ | | to put down | مان | ماندن | ۱۷ |
| _____ _____ | | to pick up | بردار | برداشتن | ۱۸ |
| _____ _____ | | to eat | خور | خوردن | ۱۹ |
| _____ _____ | | to drink | نوش | نوشیدن | ۲۰ |
| _____ _____ | | to be calm / to be silent | آرام باش | آرام بودن | ۲۱ |

B. Now conjugate the present stem of each verb. The first one is done for you.

| من | ما | تو | شما | او | آنها | Present stem | |
|---|---|---|---|---|---|---|---|
| بسته میکنم | بسته میکنیم | بسته میکنی | بسته میکنید | بسته میکند | بسته میکنند | بسته کن | ۱ |
| | | | | | | بین | ۲ |
| | | | | | | شنو | ۳ |
| | | | | | | گوش کن | ۴ |
| | | | | | | گو/گوی | ۵ |
| | | | | | | نوشته کن | ۶ |
| | | | | | | خوان | ۷ |
| | | | | | | شین | ۸ |
| | | | | | | خیز | ۹ |
| | | | | | | رو | ۱۰ |
| | | | | | | آ/ آی | ۱۱ |
| | | | | | | بر | ۱۲ |
| | | | | | | آور | ۱۳ |
| | | | | | | ده | ۱۴ |
| | | | | | | گیر | ۱۵ |
| | | | | | | مان | ۱۶ |
| | | | | | | بردار | ۱۷ |
| | | | | | | خور | ۱۸ |
| | | | | | | نوش | ۱۹ |

Exercise 5:  تمرین ۵:

Watch the video recording.  What is this person doing?

Exercise 6: تمرین ۶:

Read the following text and write an appropriate answer for each of the following questions.

نامم فریدون است، من از شهر کابل هستم، اصلاً من از شهر مزار هستم، من شاگرد هستم و این صنفم است.

در صنفم هشت دانه میز، هشت دانه چوکی ، یک دانه تخته، یک دانه ساعت،  پنج دانه کتاب و دو دانه کتابچه است.

آن صنف احمد و کریم است،  در صنف آنها دوازده دانه چوکی ، شش دانه میز، یک تخته، یک کمپیوتر، بیست دانه تباشیر ، دو دانه تخته پاک و دو دانه پروجکتور است.

۱    در صنف فریدون چند دانه میز است؟

_____

۲    در صنف فریدون چند دانه کتاب و کتابچه است؟

_____

۳    در صنف فریدون چند دانه ساعت  است؟

_____

۴    آیا در صنف فریدون پروجکتور است؟

_____

۵    آیا فریدون از کندهار است؟

_____

۶    آیا فریدون شاگرد است؟

۷    در صنف احمد و کریم چند دانه میز و چند
دانه چوکی است؟

۸    در صنف احمد و کریم چند دانه تخته و چند
دانه تخته پاک است؟

۹    آیا در صنف احمد و کریم کمپیوتر است؟

۱۰    آیا در صنف احمد و کریم کتابچه است؟

# Vocabulary لغات

In this part of the lesson, you will review, listen to, and practice pronunciation of the phrases and vocabulary used in the chapter.

## Phrases اصطلاحات

| Please (when offering something). | bafarmāyed! | بفرمایید! |
|---|---|---|
| Excuse me! (Forgive me.) | babaxšed! | ببخشید! |
| May I come in? | ĕjāza ast dāxĕl šawam? | اجازه است داخل شوم. |
| May I? | ĕjāza ast? | اجازه است؟ |
| This is clear. | ĕn wāzĕh ast. | این واضح است. |
| I understood. | fahmidan. | فهمیدم. |
| Please. | lotfan. | لطفاً. |
| I didn't understand. | nafamidam. | نفهمیدم. |
| I have a question. | porsān dāram. | پرسان دارم. |

## Vocabulary Words لغات

| to calm/silent | ārām bōdan (ārām bāš/ ārām hast) | آرام بودن (آرام باش/هست) |
|---|---|---|
| to come | āmadan (āy) | آمدن (آی) |
| there | ānjā | آنجا |
| to bring | āwordan (āwar) | آوردن (آور) |
| bookshelf | almāri kĕtāb | الماری کتاب |
| here | ĕnjā | اینجا |
| to open | bāz kardan (bāz kon) | باز کردن (باز کن) |
| to pick up/to leave | bardāštan (bardār) | برداشتن (بردار) |
| to carry | bordan (bar) | بردن (بر) |
| to close | basta kardan (basta kon) | بسته کردن (بسته کن) |
| package | basta | بسته |

| | | |
|---|---|---|
| book bag/backpack/case | baks | بکس |
| classifier for objects that 'stand' (e.g. table, chair, bed) | pā-ya | پایه |
| printer | parentar | پرینتر |
| pencil | pĕnsĕl | پنسل |
| eraser (pencil) | pĕnsĕl-pāk | پنسل پاک |
| chalk | tabāšir | تباشیر |
| board | taxta | تخته |
| eraser (board) | taxta-pāk | تخته پاک |
| book cover | jeld | جلد |
| chair | čawki | چوکی |
| ruler | xatkaš | خطکش |
| to read | xāndan(xān) | خواندن (خوان) |
| to eat | xordan (xor) | خوردن (خور) |
| to stand up | xestan (xez) | خیستن (خیز) |
| to give | dādan (dĕh) | دادن (ده) |
| in, in the, at | dar | در |
| around the | dar atrāf-e | در اطراف |
| next to the | dar baḡal-e | در بغل |
| on the, at the top of the | dar bālāy-e | در بالای |
| between the | dar bayn-e | در بین |
| outside of the | dar birōn-e | در بیرون |
| next to the | dar pahlōy-e | در پهلوی |
| in front of the | dar pĕšrōy-e | در پیشروی |
| behind the | dar pĕšt-e | در پشت |
| behind the | dar pōšt-e sar-e | در پشت سر |
| dozen | darjan | درجن |
| around the | dar čār taraf-e | در چار طرف |
| outside of the | dar xārĕj-e | در خارج |

| | | |
|---|---|---|
| inside the | dar dāxĕle | در داخل |
| across the | dar rōbarōy-e | در روبروی |
| on top of the/on the | dar rōy-e | در رویی |
| under the | dar zĕr-e | در زیر |
| on the left side of the | dar samt-e čap-e | در سمت چپ |
| on the right side of the | dar samt-e rāst-e | در سمت راست |
| on the, on top of the | dar sar-e | در سر |
| on the left side of the | dar taraf-e čap-e | در طرف چپ |
| on the right side of the | dar taraf-e rāst-e | در طرف راست |
| behind the | dar aqĕb-e | در عقب |
| around the | dar gerd-e, dar dawr-e | در گرد، در دور |
| inside of the | dar mābayn-e | در مابین |
| in front of the | dar moqābĕl-e | در مقابل |
| door | darwāza | دروازه |
| bunch | desta | دسته |
| to see | didan (bin) | دیدن (بین) |
| classifier for cattle (head) | ra's | راس |
| to go | raftan (raw) | رفتن (رو) |
| language, tongue | zabān | زبان |
| staple | ĕstĕblar | ستپلر |
| scanner | ĕskenar | سکینر |
| CD | si di | سی دی |
| to watch | sayl kardan (sayl kon) | سیل کردن ( سیل کن) |
| to listen | šanidan (šanaw) | شنیدن (شنو) |
| classroom/ class | sĕnf | صنف |
| classifier for vehicles (vehicle) | 'arāda | عراده |
| classifier for picture  (piece of ) | qet'a | قطعه |
| pen | qalam | قلم |
| paper | kāǧaz | کاغذ |

| book | kĕtāb | کتاب |
| notebook | kĕtāb-ča | کتابچه |
| window | kalkin | کلکین |
| computer | kampi-yutar | کمپیوتر |
| keyboard | kibōrd | کیبورد |
| to speak | gap zadan (gap zan) | گپ زدن (گپ زن) |
| to take | gĕrĕftan (gir) | گرفتن (گیر) |
| to converse | goftago kardan (goftago kon) | گفتگو کردن (گفتگو کن) |
| to tell | goftan (goy) | گفتن (گوی) |
| to listen | goš kardan (goš kon) | گوش کردن (گوش کن) |
| headphone | gošaki | گوشکی |
| loudspeaker | lōd-espikar | لودسپیکر |
| copy machine | māšin ĕsāb | ماشین کاپی |
| to put down | māndan (mān) | ماندن (مان) |
| monitor (computer screen) | mānitor (safha-e kampi-yutar) | مانیتور (صفحهٔ کمپیوتر) |
| (computer) mouse | maws | موس |
| table/desk | mez | میز |
| to sit down | nešastan (šin) | نشستن (شین) |
| to drink | nošidan (noš) | نوشیدن (نوش) |
| people classifier (individual, person) | nafar, tan | نفر، تن |
| to take note | nōt gĕrĕftan (nōt gir) | نوت گرفتن (نوت گیر) |
| to write | nawĕšta kardan (nawĕšta kon) | نوشته کردن (نوشته کن) |
| to write | naweštan (dĕh) | نوشتن (نویس ) |

## Dari Vocabulary Different from Iranian Persian

| English Translation | Iranian Persian | | Farsi-e Dari | |
| --- | --- | --- | --- | --- |
| notebook | daftar | دفتر | kĕtāb-ča | کتابچه |
| pen | xudkār | خودکار | qalam | قلم |
| pencil | medād | مداد | pĕnsĕl | پنسل |
| eraser | medādpāk-kon | مداد پاک کن | pĕnsĕl-pāk | پنسل پاك |
| pencil sharpener | medād-tarāš | مداد تراش | qlam-tarāš | قلمتراش |
| chair | sandali | صندلی | čawki | چوکی |
| window | panjarah | پنجره | kĕlkin | کلکین |
| door | dar | در | darwāza | دروازه |
| class | kalās | کلاس | sĕnf | صنف |

# فصل پنجم
## CHAPTER FIVE

شما هر روز چی میکنید؟

WHAT DO YOU DO EVERY DAY?

# IN THIS CHAPTER

• وظایف Functions

*Telling time and date; Talking about your daily routine; Asking about other people's daily routine; Expressing likes and dislikes; Talking about your weekends*

• تبصرهٔ فرهنگی Cultural Notes

*Telling time; Reading the Afghan calendar; Playing Buzkashi*

• دستور زبان Language Structure

*The compound verb with simple verb* شدن; *Cardinal numbers; Question word* چند; *Using ordinal numbers; Time adverbs; The prepositions 'from'* از, *'until'* تا; *Negative adverbs with the word* هیچ; *The verbs 'to like'* داشتن خوش; *The conjunction 'but'* خوش آمدن; *More verbs to express likes and dislikes* اما;

• مرور فصل Chapter Review

*Narrating your daily routine; Expressing your likes and dislikes; Describing your regular weekend routines*

• لغات Vocabulary

*Review phrases and words used in this chapter*

## Chapter Introduction                    معرفی فصل

In this chapter you will learn how to talk about your daily activities and your work. You will also learn to talk about your hobbies, likes, and dislikes, as well as learn to ask for and give the date and time.

شما چند بجه بیدار میشوید؟
What time do you wake up?

ساعت چند بجه است؟
What time is it?

در روز های رخصتی چی میکنید؟
What do you do on weekends?

# درس اول: چند بجه است؟
## Lesson One: What time is it?

> In this section, you will learn how to ask for and tell the time and date, talk about tomorrow, learn the cardinal numbers 20-1000, and learn Dari ordinal numbers.

Exercise 1: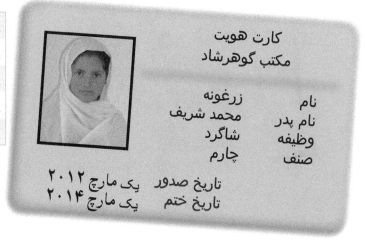

Look at the following picture. For each of the Dari words given, write its meaning on the line beside it.

دقیقه

ثانیه

بجه

ساعت

Exercise 2:

A. Can you find the following words on the ID card shown?

| | |
|---|---|
| date | |
| date of issue | |
| expiration date | |
| fourth | |
| school | |

کارت هویت
مکتب گوهرشاد

نام        زرغونه
نام پدر      محمد شریف
وظیفه       شاگرد
صنف        چارم

تاریخ صدور    یک مارچ ۲۰۱۲
تاریخ ختم     یک مارچ ۲۰۱۴

B.    Now answer the following questions using information from the ID card in Exercise 2A.

| 1. What is the girl's name? | |
| 2. What is her father's name? | |
| 3. What school does she attend? | |
| 4. What grade is she in? | |
| 5. What are the issued and expiration dates on the ID card? | |

C.    Working in pairs, discuss the differences between the way dates are written in Afghanistan and the United States.

Exercise 3:    تمرین ۳:
Match the words shown in the column A to the terms in B.

| B | A |
|---|---|
| year of 2012 | ۱   یك هفته |
| two days | ۲   ماه جنوری |
| five nights | ۳   سال ۲۰۱۲ |
| one week | ۴   دو روز |
| month of January | ۵   پنج شب |

## 5.1 Cardinal Numbers

In order to tell the time and date in Dari, you will need to learn the numbers over 20.

Just like when you learned the numerals 0-20 in chapter 2, you will see that learning the numbers over 20 in Dari is very easy, because you just have to learn a few new terms (سی, چهل, etc.) and then follow a pattern.

| | | | |
|---|---|---|---|
| هفتاد | 70 | بیست | 20 |
| هشتاد | 80 | سی | 30 |
| نود | 90 | چهل | 40 |
| صد | 100 | پنجاه | 50 |
| هزار | 1000 | شصت | 60 |

To form all other numbers up to one million, you combine the numbers as follows:

| | | | | | | |
|---|---|---|---|---|---|---|
| ۲۱ | بیست و یك | 21 | ۲۰ | بیست | 20 |
| ۳۱ | سی و یك | 31 | ۳۰ | سی | 30 |
| ۴۱ | چهل و یك | 41 | ۴۰ | چهل | 40 |
| ۵۱ | پنجاه و یك | 51 | ۵۰ | پنجاه | 50 |
| ۶۱ | شصت و یك | 61 | ۶۰ | شصت | 60 |
| ۷۱ | هفتاد و یك | 71 | ۷۰ | هفتاد | 70 |
| ۸۱ | هشتاد و یك | 81 | ۸۰ | هشتاد | 80 |
| ۹۱ | نود و یك | 91 | ۹۰ | نود | 90 |

Similarly, the following examples show how numbers greater than 100 are formed with صد sad "100". For example:

| | | |
|---|---|---|
| صد | ۱۰۰ | 100 |
| صد و یك | ۱۰۱ | 101 |
| هزار | ۱۰۰۰ | 1000 |
| یك هزار و دو صد و بیست | ۱۲۲۰ | 1220 |

As you can see, the conjunction "and" [wa] و comes between double and multiple-digit numbers and is pronounced as 'o'.

Exercise 4: ۴ تمرین :

A. Write the numbers you hear.

| | ۵ | | ۴ | | ۳ | | ۲ | | ۱ |
|---|---|---|---|---|---|---|---|---|---|
| | ۱۰ | | ۹ | | ۸ | | ۷ | | ۶ |

B. Working in pairs, write 10 random numbers between 20 and 1000. Tell your numbers to your partner while s/he writes what was heard. Then check the answers to see if the numbers match yours.

| | ۵ | | ۴ | | ۳ | | ۲ | | ۱ |
|---|---|---|---|---|---|---|---|---|---|
| | ۱۰ | | ۹ | | ۸ | | ۷ | | ۶ |

Exercise 5: ۵ تمرین :

A. Read the times given, and then draw the hands on the clock to show the correct time.

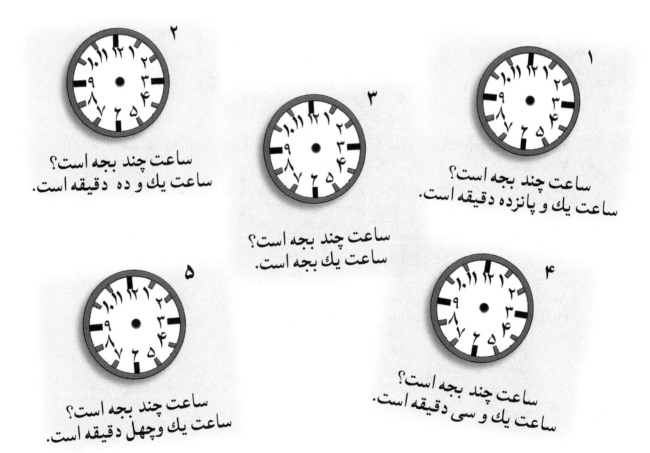

۲

ساعت چند بجه است؟
ساعت یک و ده دقیقه است.

۳

ساعت چند بجه است؟
ساعت یک بجه است.

۱

ساعت چند بجه است؟
ساعت یک و پانزده دقیقه است.

۵

ساعت چند بجه است؟
ساعت یک وچهل دقیقه است.

۴

ساعت چند بجه است؟
ساعت یک و سی دقیقه است.

B.  Listen carefully to the times that are given on the audio recording. For each time you hear, draw the hands on the clock to show the correct time.

C. 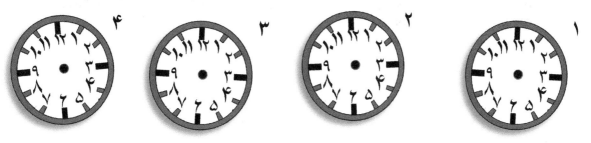 Listen to the conversations on the audio recording and draw the time for the times of each conversation.

## 5.2 Question Word چند

When asking about time, always use the question word [čand] چند
"how many." For example: ساعت چند بجه است؟

Also, in standard and colloquial Dari, you will hear and see
ساعت چند بجه است؟ instead of: چند بجه است؟

It would be incorrect, in Dari, to ask "what" چی as we do in English
(What time is it?).

Exercise 6: تمرین ۶:
A. Ask your classmates "what time is it?" by pointing to one of the following times.

| 9:25 | 7:50 | 8:00 | 1:15 | 1:20 | 4:40 | 3:30 | 2:02 |

| 11:40 | 12:56 | 3:05 | 9:36 | 10:10 | 6:00 | 5:45 | 4:55 |

B. The following clocks represent various countries. Take turns pointing to a clock and asking your partner what time it is that country. When your partner responds with a (made-up) time, draw the given time on the clock. Then have them check your answer. For example:

الف: در افغانستان ساعت چند بجه است؟
ب: در افغانستان چار و پنجاه و پنج دقیقه است.

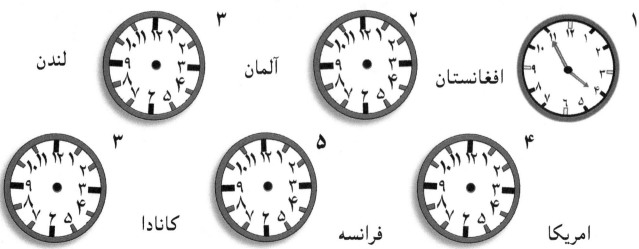

## 5.3 Telling Time in Afghanistan گفتن وقت در افغانستان

The following are very important facts about telling time in Afghanistan:

1. The 12-hour clock is standard in Afghanistan and the 24-hour (military clock) is NOT used at all.

2. In standard Dari, the day is divided into five parts: "morning" قبل، صبح "night" شب and "noon" ظهر، چاشت, "afternoon" بعد از ظهر, "midnight" نیمه شب.

3. "midnight" نیمه شب, "morning" صبح, and "noon" ظهر، چاشت are used for A.M. and بعد از ظهر "afternoon" and شب "night" for P.M.

For example:

| | |
|---|---|
| ۵ بجه صبح | means 5 a.m. |
| ۱۲ بجه ظهر | means 12 p.m. |
| ۴ بجه بعد از ظهر | means 4 p.m. |
| ۱۰ بجه شب | means 10 p.m. |
| ۳ بجه نیمه شب | means 3 a.m. |

4. In spoken Dari, a.m. and p.m. are indicated with "day" روز and "night" شب، شو. These do not correspond exactly to a.m. and p.m., but generally indicate whether it is light or dark at the time. "Day" روز extends from the very beginning of daylight, and "night" شب، شو starts from the very beginning of darkness (evening).

For example:

۱۲ بجه روز is 12 p.m. and ۱۲ بجه شب is 12 a.m.

5. In colloquial Dari, since days are counted as extending from 4 a.m. until 3:59 a.m., you account for nights in a completely different manner: the upcoming night belongs to the current day and the night that has just passed belongs to the day before. So, in colloquial Dari, if it is during the day on Saturday, then the upcoming night (Sunday night in the western standard) is considered Saturday night.

6. In standard Dari, if it is Saturday during the day, then Saturday night is the night that has just passed.

### 5.3 Telling Time in Afghanistan (cont'd.)

7. In colloquial Dari, people have some specific terms for telling parts of the hour.

For example:

| | | | |
|---|---|---|---|
| 1:15 | یک و پانزده دقیقه | quarter past one | پاو بالا یک |
| 1:45 | یک و چهل وپنج دقیقه | quarter to two | پاو کم دو |
| 1:30 | یک و سی دقیقه | half past one | یک و نیم |

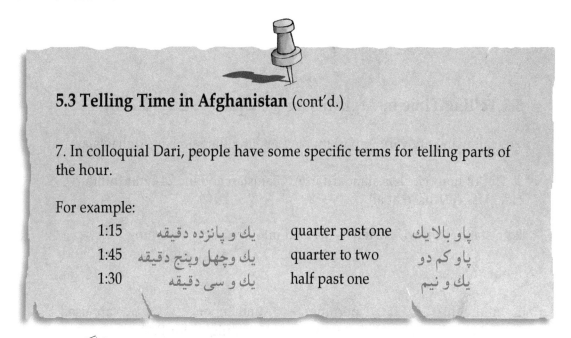

Exercise 7:    تمرین ۷:

Read the following times and guess which one is a.m. and which one is p.m.; then, write a.m. or p.m. beside it.

| یازده صبح | دوازده شب | هشت صبح | دو نیم بعد از ظهر |
|---|---|---|---|
| ۴ | ۳ | ۲ | ۱ |

| ۱۱ | ۱۲ | ۸ | ۲:۳۰ |
|---|---|---|---|
| ۸ | ۷ | ۶ | ۵ |

## 5.4 Calendar جنتری

In Afghanistan, the main calendar used by the people is the Hijri solar calendar هجری خورشیدی or هجری شمسی, and the secondary calendar used is the Gregorian calendar, which is called جنتری میلادی (calendar of the 'birth of Jesus') or جنتری عیسوی / مسیحی (Christian calendar).

Several years ago, during the Taliban regime, the main calendar was the Islamic lunar calendar هجری قمری. Today this calendar is still used for tracking Islamic events and by the media (as the third date given), however, it is rarely used in people's day to day life to track time.

When giving or writing the date in Dari, you give the day, month, and then year. For example:

English

2/17/2012

Dari

۱۷/۲/۲۰۱۲

Exercise 8:    تمرین ۸:

A. The beginning of the solar calendar, meaning the first day of the month of حمل, generally falls on March 20th or 21st. This day coincides with the Spring Equinox, the first day of spring, and is called نوروز meaning "new day."

Look at the following table. Match the month names in the solar column to the month names in the Gregorian calendar.

| Gregorian Calendar | Solar Calendar |
|---|---|
| جنوری | حمل |
| فبروری | ثور |
| مارچ | جوزا |
| اپریل | سرطان |
| می | اسد |
| جون | سنبله |
| جولای | میزان |
| آگست | عقرب |
| سپتمبر | قوس |
| اکتوبر | جدی |
| نوامبر | دلو |
| دسامبر | حوت |

B.  The following dates are written in the order that they're used in the US. Convert the dates to how they are written in Afghanistan.

| | | |
|---|---|---|
| 01/02/2012 | _____ | ١ |
| 04/05/2011 | _____ | ٢ |
| 10/11/2004 | _____ | ٣ |
| 06/07/2009 | _____ | ۴ |

## 5.5 Using Ordinal Numbers

Ordinal numbers (1st, 2nd, 3rd, etc.) are used in Dari to give the days of the month, months in a year, and numbers in order. Just as in English, ordinal numbers vary slightly from the original numbers they represent, taking the suffix ـُم [om] to form the ordinal form. For example:

| | | | | | |
|---|---|---|---|---|---|
| second | [do-wom] | دوم | first | [awal/yakom] | اول/ یکم |
| fourth | [čārom] | چارم | third | [se-wom] | سوم |
| sixth | [se-wom] | ششم | fifth | [panjom] | پنجم |
| eighth | [se-wom] | هشتم | seventh | [haftom] | هفتم |
| tenth | [da-hom] | دهم | ninth | [no-hom] | نهم |

Note that the ordinal numbers always come after titles. For example:

March 2nd  [dowom-e mārč]   مارچ دوم
March 1st  [awal-e mārč]   اول مارچ

Exercise 9:  تمرین ۹:

Write the following phrases in Dari.

1. Today is January 21st, 2010. _____

2. Yesterday was January 20th, 2012. _____

3. Tomorrow is January 19th, 2013. _____

4. Two thousand twelfth. _____

5. Fourth hour _____

6. Fifth hour _____

Exercise 10: تمرین ۱۰:

Solve the following equations. Then check your answers with a partner, taking turns giving your answer in Dari.

34 + 14 = _____ ۳

112 + 312 = _____ ۲

13 + 13 = _____ ۱

15 + 25 = _____ ۶

26 + 36 = _____ ۵

38 + 48 = _____ ۴

27 + 47 = _____ ۹

29 + 29 = _____ ۸

311 + 411 = _____ ۷

Exercise 11: تمرین ۱۱:

You will hear three short conversations on the audio recording in which people ask one another about the date, day, and year. Listen and then practice with a partner.

کدام سال است؟
Which year is it?

سبا تاریخ چند است؟
What is tomorrow's date?

امروز تاریخ چند است؟
What is today's date?

سال ۲۰۱۲
2012

سبا سوم مارچ است.
Tomorrow is March 3rd.

امروز دوم مارچ است.
Today is the 2nd of March.

## 5.6 Time Adverbs قید زمان

Common adverbs of time in Dari are:

| | | | | | |
|---|---|---|---|---|---|
| year | سال | night | شب | day | روز |
| this year | امسال | tonight | امشب | today | امروز |
| last year | پارسال | last night | دیشب | yesterday | دیروز |
| next year | سال آینده | tomorrow night | فردا شب / صباح شب | tomorrow | فردا / صباح |

Adverbs of time usually come at the beginning of the sentence in Dari. However, they can also come after the subject. For example:

Today is the first of Hamal.    امروز تاریخ اول حمل است.
تاریخ امروز اول حمل است.

Note: the word صباح also spells out as followings: سبا /صبا.

Exercise 12:    تمرین ۱۲:

A. Write the following questions in Dari. Then ask your classmates the questions.

| | | |
|---|---|---|
| What time do you go to class today? | _____ | ۱ |
| What time do you leave class today? | _____ | ۲ |
| What is today's date? | _____ | ۳ |
| What is next year? | _____ | ۴ |
| Are you watching a movie tonight? | _____ | ۵ |
| What are you doing tonight? | _____ | ۶ |

B.  Complete the following sentences with the proper adverbs of time. Then translate them into English.

| | |
|---|---|
| ــــــ ــــــ من به صنف میروم. | ۱ |
| ــــــ ــــــ ما به کابل میرویم. | ۲ |
| ــــــ ــــــ من آن فلم را سیل میکنم. | ۳ |
| ــــــ ــــــ شما کتاب را میخوانید. | ۴ |
| ــــــ ــــــ ساعت ۱۰ من نوشته میکنم. | ۵ |
| ــــــ ــــــ ساعت ۳ کجا هستید؟ | ۶ |

## 5.7 Function of the Present–Tense Verbs in the Future

In Dari, when the future time adverbs are used, the present form of the verb functions as the future tense. For example:

| | | |
|---|---|---|
| صباح تاریخ دوم ثور است. | tomorrow | فردا/ صباح |
| صباح شب ما فلم تماشا میکنیم. | tomorrow night | فردا شب/ صباح شب |
| هفتهٔ آینده کار نمیکنم. | next week | هفته آینده |
| ماه آینده به کابل میرویم. | next month | ماه آینده |
| سال آینده ۲۰۱۳ است. | next year | سال آینده |

Exercise 13: تمرین ۱۳:

Write the following questions in Dari.  Then pick 3 classmates and ask them the questions, filling in the chart with their answers.

| Student 3 | Student 2 | Student 1 | | |
|---|---|---|---|---|
| _____ | _____ | _____ | What are you doing tomorrow at 11 a.m.? | ۱ |
| _____ | _____ | _____ | What are you doing tonight at 8 p.m.? | ۲ |
| _____ | _____ | _____ | Where are you next week? | ۳ |
| _____ | _____ | _____ | What is the date for tomorrow? | ۴ |
| _____ | _____ | _____ | What year is next year? | ۵ |
| _____ | _____ | _____ | What time do you go to class tomorrow? | ۶ |

Exercise 14: تمرین ۱۴:

You will hear a conversation between میرویس and شریف on the audio recording. Listen and choose the best answer for the following questions.

| | | | | |
|---|---|---|---|---|
| | | | ۱  ساعت چند بجه است؟ | |
| ۱:۳۰ | ۱:۴۰ | ۱:۵۰ | ۱:۲۰ | |
| | | | ۲  فردا تاریخ چند است؟ | |
| ۲/۳/۲ | ۲۰۱۱/۲/۳ | ۲۰۱۰/۲/۳ | ۲۰۱۰/۳/۲ | |
| | | | ۳  شریف فردا چی میکند؟ | |
| کتاب میخواند. | نوشته میکند. | تلویزیون سیل میکند. | در صنف است. | |
| | | | ۴  کدام سال است؟ | |
| ۲۰۱۰ | ۲۰۱۱ | ۲۰۱۲ | ۲۰۱۳ | |

# درس دوم: شما چند بجه بیدار میشوید؟

## Lesson Two: What time do you wake up?

In this section, you will learn to talk about your daily routine, including your morning, afternoon, and evening activities.

Exercise 1: تمرین ۱:

A. Mirwais میرویس describes his daily morning activities on the audio recording. Listen to him, and number the pictures in order of his typical day. Then translate each into English.

من هرصبح معمولاً ساعت ۷ بجه بیدار میشوم.

ساعت ۷:۱۰ شاور میگیرم.

ساعت ۷:۳۰ کالایم را میپوشم.

من از ساعت ۸ تا ۱۲ در مکتب، درس میخوانم.

ساعت ۷:۵۰ به مکتب میروم.

ساعت ۷:۴۰ چای صبح را میخورم.

| مکتب | از ... تا ... | معمولاً |
|---|---|---|
| school | from ... to ... | usually |

B. Look at Mirwais's morning activities in part A. For each of the steps in his morning routine, choose one of the infinitives below and write it underneath the corresponding picture.

| شاور گرفتن | کالاپوشیدن | درس خواندن |
|---|---|---|
| چای صبح خوردن | مکتب رفتن | بیدار شدن |

Exercise 2: تمرین ۲:

A. Ask a few of your classmates the following questions about Mirwais's daily activities and then complete the chart by filling in their responses.

| شاگرد سوم | شاگرد دوم | شاگرد اول | | |
|---|---|---|---|---|
| _____ | _____ | _____ | میرویس ساعت چند بجه مکتب میرود؟ | ۱ |
| _____ | _____ | _____ | میرویس چند ساعت در مکتب است؟ | ۲ |
| _____ | _____ | _____ | میرویس ساعت ۷:۱۰ چی میکند؟ | ۳ |
| _____ | _____ | _____ | میرویس چند بجه چای صبح را میخورد؟ | ۴ |
| _____ | _____ | _____ | میرویس ساعت ۷:۳۰ چی میکند؟ | ۵ |

B. Which one of the following activities do you do every morning, and at what time? First, mark the activities you do. Then, write a sentence saying the time that you do the activity. Finally, report your results to the class.

| | | |
|---|---|---|
| _____ | بیدار شدن (بیدار شو) | ۱ |
| _____ | شاور گرفتن (شاور گیر) | ۲ |
| _____ | کالاپوشیدن (کالاپوش) | ۳ |
| _____ | چای صبح خوردن (چای صبح خور) | ۴ |
| _____ | به مکتب رفتن (به مکتب رو) | ۵ |
| _____ | در مکتب بودن (در مکتب هست) | ۶ |

C. Working with a partner, create a conversation by asking each other about your morning activities. Then come in front of the class and act it out.

Exercise 3: تمرین ۳:

A. Now, میرویس describes his activities on the audio recording for every afternoon as he returns from school. Listen and number the pictures in the order he describes them.

از ساعت ۱۲:۳۰ تا ۴ بجه کار میکنم.

من معمولاً بعد از مکتب، نان چاشت را میخورم.

باز ساعت ۱۲:۳۰ به کار میروم.

باز ساعت ۵ ورزش میکنم.

ساعت ۴:۳۰ به خانه میروم.

در خانه کالای رسمی ام را میکشم.

| کالای رسمی | خانه | باز | بعد از |
|---|---|---|---|
| formal dress | home | then | after the ... |

B. Look at میرویس afternoon activities in part A. For each of the activities, choose one of the verbs below and write it under the corresponding picture.

| | | |
|---|---|---|
| to work | to eat lunch | to go to work |
| to go home | to work out | to undress |

C. Working with a partner, write an appropriate answer to the
following questions.

| | |
|---|---|
| ۱ | میرویس بعد از نان چاشت چی میکند؟ |
| ۲ | میرویس ساعت ۴:۳۰ چی میکند؟ |
| ۳ | میرویس درکجا کالایی رسمی اش را میکشد؟ |
| ۴ | میرویس بعد از مکتب چی میکند؟ |
| ۵ | میرویس ساعت چند ورزش میکند؟ |
| ۶ | میرویس کدام ساعت ها کار میکند؟ |

Exercise 4:  تمرین ۴:

Ask a few of your classmates the following questions about Mirwais's daily
activities and complete the chart by filling in their responses.

| شاگرد سوم | شاگرد دوم | شاگرد اول | | |
|---|---|---|---|---|
| | | | What time do you go to work? | ۱ |
| | | | What do you do after work? | ۲ |
| | | | When do you work out? | ۳ |
| | | | What do you do after working out? | ۴ |

Exercise 5: تمرین ۵:

A. Now, میرویس describes his evening activities on the audio recording. Listen and number the pictures in the order he describes them. Then translate each into English.

بازساعت ۹ کارخانگی ام را انجام میدهم.

گاهی کتاب میخوانم.

من همیشه به موسیقی گوش میکنم.

بعد از ورزش، معمولاً ساعت ۷:۳۰ نان شب را میخورم.

از ساعت ۸ تا ۹ تلویزیون سیل میکنم.

و ساعت ۱۱ شب خواب میشوم.

| گاهی | همیشه | نان شب | کار خانگی |
|---|---|---|---|
| sometimes | always | dinner | homework |

B. Look at میرویس daily activities in part A. For each of the activities, choose one of the verbs below and write it underneath the corresponding picture.

| خواب شدن (خواب شو) |
|---|
| نان شب خوردن (نان شب خور)    کتاب خواندن (کتاب خوان) |
| سیل کردن (سیل کن) |
| به موسیقی گوش کردن (به موسیقی گوش کن)    کارخانگی انجام دادن (کارخانگی انجام ده) |

Exercise 6: تمرین ۶:

You will hear a conversation on the audio recording between لیلا and شریف as they talk about their evening activities. Listen, and then mark each of the following statements as true or false.

| غلط | صحیح | جمله ها | |
|---|---|---|---|
| ـــــ | ـــــ | لیلا همشیه به موسیقی گوش میکند . | ۱ |
| ـــــ | ـــــ | لیلا ساعت ۹ کارخانگی اش را انجام میدهد . | ۲ |
| ـــــ | ـــــ | لیلا بعد از نان شب، تلویزیون سیل میکند . | ۳ |
| ـــــ | ـــــ | لیلا بعد از کتاب خواندن ، خواب میشود . | ۴ |

Exercise 7: تمرین ۷:

Look at the following verbs and their present stems. Conjugate each one. The first example is done for you.

| | | | |
|---|---|---|---|
| من بیدار میشوم، ما بیدارمیشویم، تو بیدار میشوی، شما بیدار میشوید ، او بیدار میشود ، آنها بیدار میشوند | بیدار می+شو | بیدار شدن* | ۱ |
| _____ | شاورمی+گیر | شاورگرفتن | ۲ |
| _____ | می+پوش | پوشیدن | ۳ |
| _____ | می+ خور | خوردن | ۴ |
| _____ | می+ رو | رفتن | ۵ |
| _____ | کارمی+ کن | کارکردن | ۶ |
| _____ | کالامی+ کش | کالاکشیدن | ۷ |
| _____ | ورزش می+ کن | ورزش کردن | ۸ |
| _____ | سیل می+ کن | سیل کردن | ۹ |
| _____ | انجام می+ ده | انجام دادن | ۱۰ |
| _____ | گوش می+ کن | گوش کردن | ۱۱ |
| _____ | می+ خوان | خواندن | ۱۲ |
| _____ | خواب می+ شو | خواب شدن* | ۱۳ |

Exercise 8:  تمرین ۸:

Look at the following pictures showing Ajmal's daily activities. In the spaces provided, write short sentences to describe his habits.

## 5.8 Compound Verbs بیدارشدن، خواب شدن

The simple verb شدن 'to become, to be, to happen' is often combined with adjectives like 'awake' بیدار, 'asleep' خواب, to create new, compound verbs. For example:

| | | |
|---|---|---|
| to wake up (to become awake) | بیدارشو | بیدارشدن |
| to sleep (to become asleep) | خواب شو | خواب شدن |

Exercise 9: تمرین ۹:

A. Conjugate the following infinitives in the present tense.

| زمان حال | مصدر |
|---|---|
| | بیدار شدن |
| | خواب شدن |

B.  Write the following questions in Dari. Then pick 3 classmates and ask them the questions, filling in the chart with their answers.

| شاگرد سوم | شاگرد دوم | شاگرد اول | | |
|---|---|---|---|---|
| | | | What time do you wake up everyday? | ۱ |
| | | | What time do you go to sleep everyday? | ۲ |
| | | | What time did you wake up yesterday? | ۳ |
| | | | What time did you got to sleep yesterday? | ۴ |

## 5.9 The Prepositions "From ... Until"  از .... تا

The prepositions 'from' از and 'until' تا are used together to describe the length of time or a distance. For example:

از ساعت ۱۲ تا ۴ کار میکند.    He works from 12 to 4.

Exercise 10:  تمرین ۱۰:

Write the following questions in Dari. Then pick 3 classmates and ask them the questions, filling in the chart with their answers.

| شاگرد سوم | شاگرد دوم | شاگرد اول | | |
|---|---|---|---|---|
| | | | What do you do from 7:00 p.m. to 9:00 p.m.? | ۱ |
| | | | Where are you tonight from 10 a.m. to 2 p.m.? | ۲ |
| | | | What time do you watch TV every night? | ۳ |
| | | | What time do you exercise everyday? | ۴ |

## 5.10 Adverbs of Time قید های زمان

In order to explain the daily routines in a paragraph, you will need the following adverbs of time.

| I *sometimes* read a book. | من بعضی وقتها کتاب میخوانم. | sometimes | گاهی، بعضی وقتها |
|---|---|---|---|
| I *often* listen to music. | من اکثراً موسیقی گوش میکنم. | most of the time, often | اکثراً |
| We work *every* day. | ما هر روز کارمیکنیم. | every (every day, every time) | هر (هر روز، هر بار) |
| I *usually* don't work on Fridays. | من معمولاً روز های جمعه کار نمیکنم. | usually | معمولاً |
| *After* working out, I usually take a shower. | بعد از ورزش، من معمولاً شاور میگیرم. | after | بعد از |
| *Before* breakfast, I usually wear my formal clothes. | پیش از چای صبح، من معمولاً کالایی رسمی ام را میپوشم. | before | پیش از |
| *How many times* a day do you eat? | شما روز چند بار نان میخورید؟ | how many times, several times | چندبار |
| I eat *twice* a day. | من روز دوبار نان میخورم. | once, twice | یک بار، دو بار |
| She *always* works. | او همیشه کار میکند. | always | همیشه |

Exercise 11: تمرین ۱۱:

A. Listen to لیلا talk about her routine, and then circle the appropriate answer for each question. .

1. How many days a week does Layla usually go to the university?
   a) 3 days    b) 4 days    c) 5 days    d) 6 days

2. How often does she write at the university?
   a) always    b) sometimes    c) mostly    d) once a day

3. Where does she go after work?
   a) home    b) to work out    c) to class    d) to school

4. When does she sleep?
   a) after watching TV
   b) after doing homework
   c) after reading a book
   d) after taking a shower

5. How often does she do her homework?
   a) one hour a night
   b) two hours a night
   c) three hours a night
   d) four hours a night

6. How many times a week does she watch TV in the classroom?
   a) once a week
   b) twice a week
   c) three times a week
   d) everyday for one hour

B. Now read about لیلا's daily routine and check your answers.

نام من لیلا است، من محصل هستم، معمولاً هفتهٔ شش روز به پوهنتون میرووم، در پوهنتون همیشه کتاب میخوانم، گفتگو میکنم و گاهی نوشته میکنم. معمولابعداز پوهنتون به کار میروم و برایِ چارساعت کار میکنم. بعد از کار، گاهی ورزش میکنم، و بعد از ورزش اکثراً به خانه میروم. همچنان معمولاهرشب یک ساعت کارخانگی ام را انجام میدهم، و بعد از آن خواب میشوم.  در صنف معمولاهفتهٔ یک بار تلویزیون سیل میکنیم.

Exercise 12:   تمرین ۱۲:
Using the given adverbs, write a proper answer for each of the following questions.

| | |
|---|---|
| What do you do every Tuesday between 4 p.m. and 6 p.m.? | ۱ معمولاً |
| How many times a week do you read a book? | ۲ معمولاً، چار بار |
| How often do you watch TV? | ۳ اکثراً، هرشب |
| What do you usually do before you sleep? | ۴ معمولاً، پیش از |
| What do you usually do after school? | ۵ معمولاً، بعد از |
| How often do you wear formal clothing? | ۶ بعضی وقتها |
| When do you work? | ۷ هر روز |
| How often do you read a book in the classroom? | ۸ همیشه |

Exercise 13:   تمرین ۱۳:
You will hear a conversation on the audio recording between لیلا and شریف
in which they are talking about their daily activities. Listen and then answer the
questions that follow.

| | |
|---|---|
| What does Sharif do between 6 and 7 a.m.? | ۱ |
| What does Sharif do at 7:30 a.m.? | ۲ |
| What does Sharif do at 1:30 p.m.? | ۳ |
| What does Sharif do between 8 p.m. and 1 p.m.? | ۴ |
| What does Sharif do at 7 p.m.? | ۵ |
| What does Sharif do at 10 p.m.? | ۶ |
| What does Sharif do at 5 p.m.? | ۷ |

Exercise 14: تمرین ۱۴ :

First, jot down in Dari all the activities that you do throughout a typical day. Then exchange your list with a classmate. Each of you will summarize the daily routine of the other.

Exercise 15: تمرین ۱۵ :

A. You will hear a short conversation on the audio recording between لیلا and شریف discussing their daily activities.

لیلا ـ شما معمولاً هر دوشنبه، از ساعت ۱ تا ۷ چی میکنید؟

شریف ـ من معمولاً هر دوشنبه ساعت ۱ به خانه میروم، باز ساعت یک و نیم نان چاشت را میخورم بعد از نان چاشت کارخانگی هایم را انجام میدهیم، باز گاهی ورزش میکنم و یا تلویزیون سیل میکنم.

لیلا ـ شما معمولاً هفتهٔ چند بار ورزش میکنید؟

شریف ـ معمولاً چار بار در هفته ورزش میکنم.

B. Working with a partner, make a similar conversation. Practice it. Then act it out in front of the class.

# درس سوم: در روزهای رخصتی چی میکنید؟

## Lesson Three: What do you do on weekends?

In this section, you will talk about your schedule and what you like to do during your free time. You will learn to express your likes and dislikes and will also learn about Buzkashi, a traditional Afghan sport.

Exercise 1: تمرین ۱:

A. Read لیلا and میرویس schedules.

| | |
|---|---|
| بیدار میشوم. | ساعت ۹ صبح |
| چای صبح را آماده میکنم. | ساعت ۹ و نیم صبح |
| چای صبح را میخورم. | ساعت ۱۰ صبح |
| خانه را پاک میکنم. | ساعت ۱۱ صبح |
| نان چاشت را میپزم. | ساعت ۱۲ ظهر |
| شاور میگیرم و کالایم را میپوشم. | ساعت ۱۲ و نیم بعد از ظهر |
| نان چاشت را میخورم. | ساعت ۱ بعد از ظهر |
| به پارک میروم. و دوش میکنم. | ساعت ۲ بعد از ظهر |
| کتاب میخوانم و استراحت میکنم. | ساعت ۳ بعد از ظهر |
| به کتابخانه میروم و باز به خانه میروم. | ساعت ۴ دیگر |
| کارخانگی ام را انجام میدهم. | ساعت ۵ شام |

| ساعت ۹ صبح | بیدار میشوم. |
| ساعت ۹ و نیم صبح | شاور میگیرم. |
| ساعت ۱۰ صبح | چای صبح را میخورم. |
| ساعت ۱۱ صبح | کالایم را میپوشم. |
| ساعت ۱۲ ظهر | نان چاشت را میخورم. |
| ساعت ۱۲ و نیم بعد از ظهر | به مسجد میروم. |
| ساعت ۱ بعد از ظهر | سودا میخرم. |
| ساعت ۲ بعد از ظهر | به میله میروم. |
| ساعت ۳ بعد از ظهر | والیبال بازی میکنم و آببازی میکنم. |
| ساعت ۴ دیگر | به خانه میروم. |
| ساعت ۵ شام | به سینما میروم و باز به رستورانت میروم. |

B. Which of the following activities are done by لیلا or میرویس? As you read the schedule above, put a checkmark for each person in the box below stating who does what activity.

| میرویس | لیلا | افعال | |
|---|---|---|---|
| | | به مسجد رفتن | ۱ |
| | | به سینما رفتن | ۲ |
| | | به کتابخانه رفتن | ۳ |
| | | به پارک رفتن | ۴ |
| | | به رستورانت رفتن | ۵ |
| | | به میله رفتن | ۶ |
| | | والیبال بازی کردن | ۷ |
| | | آببازی کردن | ۸ |
| | | استراحت کردن | ۹ |
| | | پاک کردن | ۱۰ |
| | | دوش کردن | ۱۱ |
| | | نان پختن | ۱۲ |
| | | سودا خریدن | ۱۳ |

Exercise 2: 🎧 تمرین ۲ :

You will hear زرغونه and شریف describe their free time activities on the audio recording. Listen and mark true or false for the statements that follow.

| غلط | صحیح | جملات | |
|---|---|---|---|
| ـــــ | ـــــ | زرغونه در روز های رخصتی معمولاً به کتابخانه میرود . | ۱ |
| ـــــ | ـــــ | زرغونه در روز های رخصتی بعضی وقتها سینما میرود . | ۲ |
| ـــــ | ـــــ | زرغونه در روز های رخصتی اکثراً به پارک میرود . | ۳ |
| ـــــ | ـــــ | شریف در روز های رخصتی اکثراً دوش میکند . | ۴ |
| ـــــ | ـــــ | شریف در روز های رخصتی بعضی وقتها به پارک میرود . | ۵ |
| ـــــ | ـــــ | شریف در روز های رخصتی همیشه آببازی میکند . | ۶ |

Exercise 3: 📝 تمرین ۳ :

Go around the room and find out what your classmates do on the weekends, filling in the chart below as you go. For example:

[šahr-e šikāgo dar kojā ast?] شهر شیکاگو در کجا است؟

[šahr-e šikāgo dar ělinōy ast.] شهر شیکاگو در ایلینوی است.

| فعالیت های روز های رخصتی | نام شاگرد |
|---|---|
| | |
| | |
| | |
| | |

Exercise 4: تمرین ۴:

A. You will hear شریف and میرویس talking about their weekends on the audio recording. Listen and write down each of their activities as you hear them.

شریف

میرویس

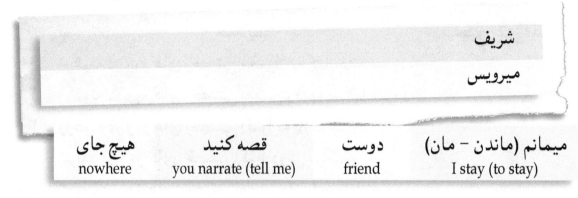

| هیچ جای | قصه کنید | دوست | میمانم (ماندن - مان) |
|---|---|---|---|
| nowhere | you narrate (tell me) | friend | I stay (to stay) |

B. Write a short paragraph in Dari about the activities that you like to do on the weekends. Present it to the class.

### 5.11 Negative Adverbs

In Dari, one can add هیچ to the beginning of some adverbs to create a negative adverb. For example:

| nowhere, anywhere | هیچ جا | please | جای |
|---|---|---|---|
| never | هیچوقت | time | وقت |
| no one, nobody | هیچکس | person | کس |

When using a negative adverb in Dari, you use the negative verb.

من امروز هیچ جای نمیروم.
من هیچوقت سینما نمیروم.
در صنف ما هیچکس کار نمیکند.

Exercise 5: تمرین ۵:

A. Answer the following questions using negative adverbs.

| | |
|---|---|
| ۱ | شما روز جمعه کجا میروید؟ |
| ۲ | شما در یک هفته چند بار به رستورانت میروید؟ |
| ۳ | در صنف شما کی از ایران است؟ |

B. Write the following statements in Dari.

| | | |
|---|---|---|
| You never go to a movie. | | ۱ |
| Every weekend she stays home and doesn't go anywhere. | | ۲ |
| This weekend nobody played soccer. | | ۳ |

Exercise 6: تمرین ۶:

Conjugate the verbs (مان) ماندن 'to stay', (قصه کن) قصه کردن 'to narrate'.

Exercise 7: تمرین ۷:

A. Which sports do you like? Listen to the short conversation on the audio recording between شریف and میرویس discussing sports. Then practice it with a partner.

شریف جان، شما کدام ورزشها را خوش دارید؟
من فوتبال امریکایی و باسکیتبال را خوش دارم.
شما کدام سپورت ها را خوش دارید؟
من آببازی، کاراته و کرکیت را خوش دارم.

B. Go around the classroom and ask your classmates which sports they like
and dislike using the following list. For example, ask:

آیا شما فوتبال خوش دارید؟
نه من فوتبال خوش ندارم، من باسکتبال خوش دارم.

بزکشی    شمشیر بازی    وزنه برداری    مشت‌زنی،بوکسینگ

فوتبال امریکایی    فوتبال    کاراته    آبازی، شنا

دوش    اسب دوانی    بایسکل دوانی    باسکتبال

بیسبال    کرکیت

## Cultural Note تبصرهٔ فرهنگی
## Buzkashi بزکشی

Buzkashi بزکشی 'goat game or pulling a goat' is a very traditional Afghan game. It is one of the most ancient and famous games in Afghanistan, especially in the central and northern regions. Previously, Buzkashi didn't have regular rules, but recently the Afghanistan Olympic committee developed official rules for the game.

For example, the game must be played with two teams of 15 horsemen. The horsemen are called چاپ انداز. The field must be 350 square meters. Each team will try to pull the goat from the circle, called 'Helal circle' دایرهٔ حلال, and to the other side of the field and then bring it back to that circle. The team that succeeds wins.

## 5.12 The Verb 'To Like' خوش داشتن and Adverbs

To express likes and dislikes in Dari, you use the compound verb 'to like' (خوش دار خوش) داشتن. This verb consists of a simple verb داشتن 'to have' and the word خوش 'happy, pleasant, well, like'. For example:

من فوتبال خوش دارم.
من والیبال خوش دارم.

However, if you want to say that you like something very much or a little, then the following adverbs come before the verb. For example:

| | | |
|---|---|---|
| من فوتبال را کم خوش دارم. | little | کم |
| من والیبال را بسیار خوش دارم. | very, a lot | بسیار زیاد |
| من آبازی را بسیار زیاد خوش دارم. | very very much | بسیار زیاد |
| من باسکیتبال را بسیار کم خوش دارم. | very little | بسیار کم |

Exercise 8: تمرین ۸:

Answer the following questions saying you 'like' or 'dislike' something, and how much.

| | |
|---|---|
| ۱ | آیا شما ورزش سکی را خوش دارید؟ |
| ۲ | آیا شما ورزش کاراته را خوش دارید؟ |
| ۳ | آیا شما ورزش بزکشی را خوش دارید؟ |
| ۴ | آیا شما ورزش کشتی گیری را خوش دارید؟ |
| ۵ | آیا شما ورزش فوتبال را خوش دارید؟ |
| ۶ | آیا شما ورزش باسکیتبال را خوش دارید؟ |
| ۷ | آیا شما ورزش جودو را خوش دارید؟ |
| ۸ | آیا شما ورزش دوش را خوش دارید؟ |

Exercise 9: تمرین ۹:

Read the following text about کریم and زرمینه. Then answer the following questions.

نام من زرمینه است، من در کابل زنده گی میکنم و در پوهنتون کابل درس میخوانم، من در بین هفته هرروز از ساعت ۸ تا ساعت ۱۲ بجه در پوهنتون هستم، در پوهنتون معمولاً من کتاب میخوانم، به گپ های استادم گوش میکنم، نوت میگیرم و گفتگو میکنم. در پوهنتون صنف های ما هر پنجاه دقیقه یک تفریح دارد و ما در ساعت ۱۲ بجه از پوهنتون رخصت میشویم. من وزرش والیبال را بسیار خوش دارم اما ورزش فوتبال را خوش ندارم.

آن مرد کریم است، او هم در کابل زنده گی میکند، اما اصلاً از هرات است، او ورزشکار است، او فوتبال بازی میکند و ورزش باسکتبال را بسیار خوش دارد اما ورزش والیبال را کم خوش دارد. معمولاً او در روز های رخصتی فوتبال میکند و گاهی هم به پارک میرود و آببازی میکند. او همصنفی من است.

| تفریح | درس خواندن (درس خوان) | ورزشکار | رخصت شدن (رخصت شو) | اما | گذشته |
|---|---|---|---|---|---|
| break | to study | athlete | to be released | but | last, past |

| | |
|---|---|
| According to the text, what does کریم like? | ١ |
| According to the text, what does کریم not like? | ٢ |
| According to the text, what does زرمینه like? | ٣ |
| According to the text, what does زرمینه not like? | ۴ |
| What does زرمینه do at the university? | ۵ |
| What happens at the university at 12 p.m.? | ۶ |
| What happens every 50 minutes at the university? | ٧ |

Exercise 10: تمرین ۱۰:

A. Using the list of sports given in Exercise 7B, ask a partner which sports they like/dislike.  For example:

کم، بسیار، بسیار زیاد، بسیار کم

B. Write a short paragraph in Dari detailing which sports you like, really like, don't like, and really don't like.  Then present it to the class.

### 5.13 The Conjunction اما 'but'

The conjunction اما 'but' is connected to sentences which express two different feelings about something or somebody. For example:

I like the sport soccer, but I don't like volleyball.

Ajmal likes running, but I don't.

من ورزش فوتبال را خوش دارم اما ورزش والیبال را خوش ندارم.
اجمل ورزش دوش را خوش دارد اما من خوش ندارم.

تمرین ۱۱: Exercise 11:

A. The following table shows ملالی and اجمل likes and dislikes. Using اما, talk about their likes and dislikes with a classmate. For example:

اجمل بزکشی را خوش دارد اما مشت زنی را خوش ندارد.

| کم خوش دارد | بسیار زیاد خوش دارد | بسیار کم خوش دارد | هیچ خوش ندارد |
|---|---|---|---|
| فوتبال | باسکیت بال | سینما رفتن | غذا پختن |
| سودا خریدن | استراحت کردن | کاراته | والیبال |
| نام | خوش دارد | خوش ندارد | بسیار خوش دارد |
| ملالی | والیبال | آببازی | بسیار خوش دارد |
| اجمل | بزکشی | مشت زنی | اسپ دوانی |

B.   With a partner, make three sentences in Dari about اجمل and ملالی
likes and dislikes. Then compare your sentences with a classmate. S/he will tell you
whether your statement is صحیح است. or این غلط است.

## 5.14 More Verbs to Express Likes and Dislikes

In Dari, the compound verb (خوش آمدن(آی is used to express likes and
dislikes. It literally means 'welcome', but for expressing likes and dislikes,
its meaning changes to 'to like, to enjoy'. When this verb is used for
expressing likes and dislikes, the verb doesn't take the personal ending, but
instead the possessive pronouns are used to indicate the person, and the
verb always follows the preposition از . For example:

من از ورزش فوتبال خوشم میآید.

ما از ورزش فوتبال خوش ما میآید.

شما از ورزش فوتبال خوش تان میآید.

تو از ورزش فوتبال خوش ات میآید.

او از ورزش فوتبال خوش اش میآید.

آنها از ورزش فوتبال خوش شان میآید.

Exercise 12: تمرین ۱۲:

The following questions ask about likes and dislikes with the verb خوش داشتن. Use the verb خوش آمدن instead to answer each of the following questions.

| | |
|---|---|
| ۱ | آیا شما ورزش اسکی را خوش دارید؟ |
| ۲ | آیا او ورزش کاراته را خوش دارد؟ |
| ۳ | آیا آنها ورزش بزکشی را خوش دارند؟ |
| ۴ | آیا تو ورزش اسب دوانی را خوش داری؟ |
| ۵ | آیا شما ورزش فوتبال را خوش دارید؟ |

Exercise 13: تمرین ۱۳:

You will hear a conversation on the audio recording between میرویس and شریف.
Listen to their conversation and answer the following questions.

| | |
|---|---|
| ۱ | آیا شریف از فلم پاکستانی خوش اش میآید؟ |
| ۲ | آیا میرویس از فلم امریکایی خوش اش میآید؟ |
| ۳ | آیا شریف از فلم امریکایی خوش اش میآید؟ |
| ۴ | میرویس از کدام فلم خوش اش میآید؟ |

## Cultural Note تبصرهٔ فرهنگی

### Future tense prayers
### دعایه های زمان آینده

In Afghanistan, people use some prayer phrases for things they will do in the future. Some of these words are borrowed from the Arabic language. Using these words simply means that the person is wishing that the action will happen peacefully and safely. Here are some phrases which are commonly used:

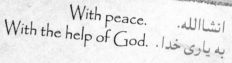

| | |
|---|---|
| God willing. | انشاالله. |
| With peace. | بخیر. |
| If God wants.. | اگر خدا بخواهد. |

| | |
|---|---|
| With peace. | انشاالله. |
| With the help of God. | به یاری خدا. |

These phrases are used at the beginning of the sentences. For example:

| | |
|---|---|
| انشاالله، صباح به میله میرویم. | انشاالله |
| بخیر، آنها صبا میایند. | بخیر |
| اگر خدا بخواهد، فردا به کابل میرویم. | اگر خدا بخواهد |
| کتی خیر، هفتهٔ آینده به پارک میرویم. | کتی خیر |
| به یاری خدا، سال آینده به مزار میرویم. | به یاری خدا |

# مرور فصل پنجم
## Review of Chapter Five

In this section you will review the vocabulary, phrases, grammar, and cultural elements that you learned throughout the chapter.

Exercise 1: تمرین ۱:

A. You will hear لیلا describe her daily activities on the audio recording. Listen and answer the following questions.

| | |
|---|---|
| ۱ | ساعت هفت لیلا چی میکند؟ |
| ۲ | لیلا چی وقت چای صبح را میخورد؟ |
| ۳ | از ساعت ۹ تا ۱۲ لیلا چی کرد؟ |
| ۴ | معمولاً لیلا در روزهای رخصتی چی میکند؟ |
| ۵ | اکثراً لیلا کدام ورزش را انجام میدهم؟ |
| ۶ | لیلا در روزهای رخصتی بعد از پارک چی میکند؟ |
| ۷ | فردا کدام تاریخ است؟ |
| ۸ | فردا لیلا به کجا خواهد رفت؟ |
| ۹ | لیلا چی را خوش دارد؟ |
| ۱۰ | لیلا چی را خوش ندارد؟ |

B. Now read the following text about لیلا activities, and check your answers.

سلام لیلا هستم، من هرروز، ساعت ۷ بیدار میشوم، باز ورزش میکنم، بعد از ورزش، در ساعت ۸ و نیم چای صبح را میخورم، باز کالایی رسمی‌اِم را میپوشم و بعد از آن به پوهنتون میروم. از ساعت ۹ تا ۱۲ در پوهنتون میمانم. من معمولا در روزهای رخصتی به پارک میروم، گاهی آببازی میکنم، اکثرا در پارک والیبال میکنم، بعد از پارک به خانه میروم و غذا میپزم. فردا تاریخ اول حمل است، فردا رخصتی است، من به سینما میروم و یک فلم هندی سیل میکنم، من از فلم هندی بسیار خوشم می‌آید، اما فلم های فرانسوی را خوش ندارم.

Exercise 2: تمرین ۲ :
A. Read the following text and fill in the blanks with the words given.

نام من فرید است، من اصلاً از افغانستان، از شهر مزار هستم و ———— (now) در امریکا
زنده گی میکنم. من در امریکا محصل هستم، من محصل زبان انگلیسی هستم. من صبح
———— (20th) ماه جنوری ۲۰۰۶ به کانادا ———— (to go).
نام پوهنتون من اندیانا است، صنف من در یونین است. شمارۀ صنف من دوصدو چارده است.
ما ———— (every week) پنج روز درس میخوانیم، ———— (most of the time)
در صنف کتاب میخوانیم، گفتگو میکنیم، ویدیو سیل میکنیم، و به گپ های معلم گوش
میکنیم. من گفتگو را ———— (very) خوش دارم و ویدیو را ———— (a little) خوش
دارم.
———— (tonight) تاریخ چارم جولای است، چارم جولای روز استقلال امریکا است،
صباح ———— (holiday) است، من صبح به پارک میروم، در آنجا آببازی میکنم، فوتبال
امریکایی بازی میکنم و کمی ———— (to rest).

B. After you've completed the above text, choose the best answer for each of the following questions.

1. Where will Farid go in 2006?
   a) the USA   b) Canada   c) Kabul   d) Kansas

2. How many days a week does he study at the university?
   a) 2   b) 3   c) 4   d) 5

3. In class, Farid listens to what?
   a) the radio   b) his classmate   c) his teacher   d) the news

4. According to the text, what is tonight's date?
   a) July 1st   b) July 2nd   c) July 3rd   d) July 4th

5. Which sport does he play?
   a) soccer   b) basketball   c) volleyball   d) football

6. What classroom activities does he like?
   a) listening   b) speaking   c) conversation   d) watching videos

7. Where will he go tomorrow?
   a) the movies   b) the park   c) work   d) the university

8. What is the room number of his class?
   a) 142   b) 241   c) 214   d) 412

Exercise 3: تمرین ۳:

Write a few paragraphs about yourself in Dari.  Describe what you do during a typical day, what your likes and dislikes are, and finally write about your future holiday plans (using the future adverbs of the time).

Exercise 4: تمرین ۴:

Role play: Your classmate was absent yesterday. Go to him/her, and start your conversation by greeting your classmate and asking about the time. Then ask what s/he generally does on weekends. Finally, tell him/her that you will go on a picnic tomorrow, and ask him/her if s/he is interested in going with you. Be prepared to answer questions s/he has about where you plan to go and what things you plan to do.

Exercise 5: تمرین ۵:

You will hear a conversation on the audio recording between شریف and میرویس in which they are talking about their future plans. Listen and choose the best answer for the following questions.

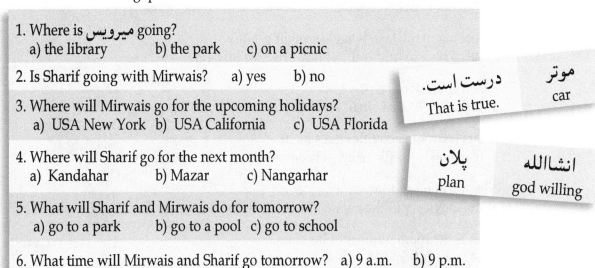

1. Where is میرویس going?
   a) the library        b) the park        c) on a picnic

2. Is Sharif going with Mirwais?        a) yes        b) no

3. Where will Mirwais go for the upcoming holidays?
   a) USA New York    b) USA California        c) USA Florida

4. Where will Sharif go for the next month?
   a) Kandahar        b) Mazar        c) Nangarhar

5. What will Sharif and Mirwais do for tomorrow?
   a) go to a park        b) go to a pool    c) go to school

6. What time will Mirwais and Sharif go tomorrow?    a) 9 a.m.    b) 9 p.m.

موتر
car

درست است.
That is true.

پلان
plan

انشاالله
god willing

# Vocabulary

In this part of the lesson, you will review, listen to, and practice pronunciation of the phrases and vocabulary used in the chapter.

## Phrases اصطلاحات

| | | |
|---|---|---|
| **What time is it?** | sā'at čand baja ast? | ساعت چند بجه است؟ |
| **It is 1:15.** | sā'at yak-o-pānzda daqiqa ast. | ساعت یک و پانزده دقیقه است. |
| **25 past one.** | pāw bālā yak | پاو بالایک |
| **25 past two.** | pāw kam do | پاو کم دو |
| **1:30.** | yak-o-nim | یک و نیم |
| **Excuse me, sorry.** | babaxšed/ babaxšen | ببخشید / ببخشین |
| **If God wants.** | agar xodā baxāhad. | اگر خدا بخواهد. |
| **With peace.** | kate kayr | کتی خیر |
| **With the help of God.** | ba yāri-e xodā | به یاری خدا |

## Vocabulary Words لغات

| | | |
|---|---|---|
| **swimming** | āb-bāzi, šĕnā | آببازی، شنا |
| **to swim** | āb-bāzi kardan (āb-bāzi kon) | آببازی کردن (آببازی کن) |
| **next** | āyenda | آینده |
| **hours riding** | asb dawāni | اسب دوانی |
| **to rest** | estarāhat kardan (estarāhat kon) | استراحت کردن استراحت کن) |
| **most of the time, often** | aksaran | اکثراً |
| **to do a task** | anjām dādan (anjām dah) | انجام دادن (انجام ده) |
| **God willing** | enšālāh | انشاالله |
| **first** | awal | اول |
| **bicycle riding** | bāyskĕl dawāni | بایسکل دوانی |
| **o'clock** | baja | بجه |

| | | |
|---|---|---|
| with peace | baxayr | بخیر |
| buzkashi 'goat game or pulling a goat' | bozkaši | بزکشی |
| to play | bāzi kardan (bazi kon) | بازی کردن (بازی کن) |
| very, a lot | bĕsyār | بسیار |
| very little | bĕsyār kam | بسیار کم |
| very very much | bĕsyār ziyād | بسیار زیاد |
| after | bad az | بعد از |
| afternoon | b'ad az zohr | بعد از ظهر |
| sometimes | ba'ze waqt-ha | بعضی وقتها |
| to | ba | به |
| to wake up | bidār šodan(bidār šaw) | بیدارشدن (بیدارشو) |
| quarter | pāw | پاو |
| to wear | pošidan (poš) | پوشیدن (پوش) |
| before | peš az | پیش از |
| until | tā | تا |
| date | tārix | تاریخ |
| taekwondo | tekwāndō | تکواندو |
| past | tĕr | تیر |
| second | saniya | ثانیه |
| lunch, midday | čāšt | چاشت |
| breakfast | čāy-e sob | چای صبح |
| how many times, several times | čand bār | چندبار |
| home | xāna | خانه |
| to sleep | xāb šodan (xab šaw) | خواب شدن (خواب شو) |
| to read, to sing | xāndan (xān) | خواندن (خوان) |
| to eat | xōrdan (xōr) | خوردن (خور) |
| to like | xōš āmadan (xōš āy) | خوش...آمدن(خوش...آی) |
| to like | xōš dāštan (xōš dār) | خوش داشتن (خوش دار) |

| minute | daqiqa | دقیقه |
|---|---|---|
| running | daweš | دوش |
| to jog | daweš kardan (daweš kon) | دوش کردن (دوش کن) |
| second | dowom | دوم |
| holiday | roxsati | رخصتی |
| to go | raftan (raw) | رفتن (رو) |
| day | rōz | روز |
| watch, clock | sā'at | ساعت |
| to buy groceries | sawdā xaridan (sawdā xar) | سودا خریدن (سودا خر) |
| third | sewom | سوم |
| to watch, to see | sayl kardan (sayl kon) | سیل کردن (سیل کن) |
| to shower | šāwar gěrěftan (šāwar gir) | شاورگرفتن (شاورگیر) |
| night | šab | شب |
| chess | šatranj | شطرنج |
| swordsmanship | šamšer bāzi | شمشیر بازی |
| morning | sob | صبح |
| afternoon | zohr | ظهر |
| to cook food | ğězā poxtan (ğězā paz) | غذا پختن (غذا پز) |
| to work | kār kardan (kār kon) | کار کردن (کار کن) |
| homework | kār-e xānagi | کار خانگی |
| to put on clothes/ to wear | kālā kašidan (kālā kaš) | کالاکشیدن (کالاکش) |
| formal dress | kālāy-e rasmi | کالایی رسمی |
| cricket | kěrket | کرکیت |
| wrestling | košti giri | کشتی گیری |
| little | kam | کم |
| sometimes | gāhe | گاهی |
| to listen | gōš kardan (goš kon) | گوش کردن (گوش کن) |
| left to | mānda | مانده |
| boxing | mošt zani, bokseng | مشت زنی، بوکسینگ |

|  |  |  |
|---|---|---|
| usually | ma'molan | معمولاً |
| school | maktab | مكتب |
| music | mosiqi | موسيقى |
| dinner | nānā-e šab | نان شب |
| lunch | nān-e čāšt | نان چاشت |
| half | nim | نيم |
| midnight, in the middle of the night | nima šab | نيمه شب |
| to sport | warzĕš kār (warzĕš kon) | ورزش كردن (ورزش كن) |
| lifting | wazna bardāri | وزنه بردارى |
| every (everyday, every time) | har (har rōz, har bār) | هر (هر روز، هر بار) |
| always | hameša | هميشه |
| always | hamiša | هميشه |
| once, twice | yak bār | يك بار، دو بار |
| first | yakom | يكم |

## Dari Vocabulary Different from Iranian Persian

| English Translation | Iranian Persian | | Farsi-e Dari | |
|---|---|---|---|---|
| What time is it? | sā'at či ast? | ساعت چى است؟ | sā'at čand baja ast? | ساعت چند بجه است؟ |
| dinner | šām | شام | nān šab | نان شب |
| lunch | nahār | نهار | nān čašt | نان چاشت |
| breakfast | sobhāna | صبحانه | čāy-e sob | چاى صبح |
| to shower | dōš grĕftan (dōš gir) | دوش گرفتن (دوش گير) | šāwar grĕftan (šāwar gir) | شاورگرفتن ( شاورگير) |
| holiday | ta'tilāt | تعطيلات | roxsati | رخصتى |

# فصل ششم
## CHAPTER SIX

# خانواده‌ام
## MY FAMILY

## IN THIS CHAPTER

• **وظایف** Functions

*Talking about family using kinship terms; Addressing others using family titles; Describing others; Comparing people and objects; Using religious titles; Talking about weddings*

• **تبصرهٔ فرهنگی** Cultural Notes

*Prayer against the "evil eye"; Religious titles; Afghan women at work; Afghan wedding traditions*

• **دستور زبان** Language Structure

*The verb 'to be' بودن ; Adjectives; Plural suffix ان; The function verb; Relative pronouns; Forming simple past tense*

• **مرور فصل** Chapter Review

*Describing your family; Reading an email about a honeymoon; Comparing people in a picture*

• **لغات** Vocabulary

*Review phrases and words used in this chapter*

# Chapter Introduction

معرفی فصل

In this chapter, you will learn how to talk about your family, describe people, and give comparisons. You will also learn about prayers to protect against the "the evil eye," the use of religious titles, and wedding ceremony etiquette.

بچهٔ کاکایم از من قد بلندتر است.

My cousin is taller than I.

من کلانترین بچهٔ فامیلم هستم.

I am the oldest child in my family.

من متاهل هستم.

I am married.

# درس اول: من کلانترین بچهٔ فامیلم هستم.

## Lesson One: I am the oldest child in my family.

In this section, you will learn how to talk about your family members, including their ages, occupations, and place in the family. You will also learn to ask others about their family members and how to address elders in Afghan culture.

Exercise 1:  تمرین ۱ :

A. Look at the following picture of a typical Afghan family having dinner. Now think of what a picture of a typical family having dinner in your culture would look like. What are some of the similarities? What are some of the differences?

| یك فامیل افغان | یك فامیل در کشور شما |
|---|---|
|  |  |

B. Working in pairs, read the definitions for some common kinship terms in Dari. Then try to match the term being defined with the person/people in the picture below.

| | |
|---|---|
| mother | مادر |
| daughter (girl) | دختر |
| sister | خواهر |
| child | کودك /طفل |
| children (child) | اولاد |
| grandson/granddaughter | نواسه |

| | |
|---|---|
| family | خانواده/ فامیل |
| grandfather | پدر کلان |
| father | پدر |
| son (boy) | بچه/پسر |
| brother | برادر |
| grandmother | مادر کلان |

C. Read the following text about the شریف family shown in the picture above. Listen to the audio recording as each person is described by their location, name, and kinship. As you are reading, write the name of each person in the boxes above.

خانوادۀ شریف

شریف پدر این خانواده است، او معلم است، او چار اولاد دارد، نام های اولاد هایش زرغونه ، زرمینه ، فرید و نوید است.
در پهلویی چپ شریف پدرش است، نام او حاجی رحیم است. در پهلویی چپ حاجی رحیم نواسه اش زرغونه است او محصل است. در پهلویی چپ زرغونه مادرکلانش است، نام او ماه جان است. در پهلویی چپ ماه جان، مادر زرغونه است، نام او لیلا است، لیلا نرس است، در پیشروی لیلا طفلش نام او نوید است. در پهلویی راست شریف بچه اش است، نام او فرید است و در پهلویی راست فرید زرمینه است، زرمینه شاگرد است.

| چپ | راست |
|---|---|
| left | right |

D. Now, using what you have just read, check "true" or "false" for each statement.

| غلط | صحیح | جملات | |
|---|---|---|---|
| | | حاجی رحیم پدر نوید است. | ۱ |
| | | نوید برادر فرید است. | ۲ |
| | | نوید دو خواهر دارد. | ۳ |
| | | لیلا مادر زرمینه است. | ۴ |
| | | ماه جان مادر لیلا است. | ۵ |
| | | زرمینه خواهر لیلا است. | ۶ |
| | | نوید نواسهٔ حاجی رحیم است. | ۷ |
| | | ماه جان مادر کلان زرغونه است. | ۸ |
| | | حاجی رحیم پدر کلان است. | ۹ |

Note: In colloquial Dari, the following words are pronounced differently.

| بیادر | خووار | شوی | آغا،بابه | بوبو،ننه |
|---|---|---|---|---|
| برادر | خواهر | شوهر | پدر | مادر |
| brother | sister | husband | father | mother |

Exercise 2: تمرین ۲:

A. Using the picture in Exercise 1A, fill in the following family tree with the names and relationships of the people in the picture.

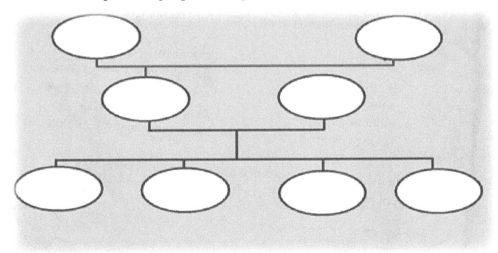

B. Who is in your family? Draw your own family tree, writing the names and relationships of the people in your family.

C.    Write down a few sentences in Dari about your family members.  Then break into small groups and take turns telling your classmates about the people in your family tree.

Cultural Note تبصرهٔ فرهنگی

In Afghan society, when addressing one another in unofficial situations, one typically uses the first name with the honorific [jān] جان or [khān] خان added to the end.

For example:  mirwais jān میرویس جان , laylaa jān لیلا جان ,  yusof khān یوسف خان

When Afghans address someone unfamiliar, depending on that person's age, they typically use one of the following honorific kinship terms:

| | |
|---|---|
| elder man  پدر جان | elder man  کاکا جان |
| younger man  بچه جان | younger man  بچیم (بچه‌ام) |
| same age man  بردار جان | same age woman  خواهر جان |
| elder woman  مادر جان | elder woman  خاله جان |
| younger woman  دختر جان | younger woman  دختریم (دخترم) |

Note: Normally, one does not address an elder person or a person of higher status by his or her first name.

Exercise 3:  تمرین ۳:

How do you address the following people? Their first names are provided in parentheses.

| | |
|---|---|
| 1. Your Dari language classmate. (Navid) | |
| 2. An Afghan female who works in your office. (Laylā) | |
| 3. An elder Afghan man who lives next door to you. (Rahman) | |
| 4. The son of your Afghan landlord. (Omid) | |
| 5. A similar aged Afghan man who lives next door. (Ajmal) | |

Exercise 4: تمرین ۴:

Read the text and answer the questions that follow.

نامم میرویس است، اعضای فامیلم شش نفر میباشند. پدرم، مادرم، دو برادرم و خواهرم. پدرم ۴۵ ساله است ، او معلم است ، مادرم ۳۸ ساله است و او هم معلم است. نام برادرانم نجیب و فرید است، آنها شاگرد مکتب هستند، نجیب هشت ساله و فرید شش ساله است.

نام خواهرم لیلا است، او چار ساله است. و من ۲۴ ساله هستم.

\* The verb (میباشند 'they are') is another version of the verb 'to be'.

| | |
|---|---|
| 1. How many people are in Mirwais's family? | |
| 2. How old are Mirwais's parents? | |
| 3. How many siblings does Mirwais have? | |
| 4. What is Laylā's relationship to Najib? | |
| 5. What is Mirwais's relationship to Farid? | |
| 6. Who is six years old? | |

Exercise 5: تمرین ۵:

A. How old is your brother? Listen to the following short conversation, and then practice it with a partner.

زن – اعضای فامیل تان چند نفر هستند؟

مرد – اعضای فامیلم پنج نفر هستند.

زن – شما چند برادر دارید؟

مرد – من یك برادر دارم.

زن – برادرتان چند ساله است؟

مرد – برادرم بیست ساله است.

B. Role-play: Turn to one of your classmates and talk to him/her about his/her family. Complete the chart below by filling in the information s/he gives. Then ask your classmate to check the chart for accuracy.

| سن | رابطه فامیلی | نام |
|---|---|---|
| | | |
| | | |
| | | |
| | | |
| | | |
| | | |

## 6.1 The Verb 'To Be' بودن

The 'to be' verb in old Dari/Persian has three different infinitives:

1- [hastand/astan] استن/هستن: the present stem of [hast/ast] است/ هست, is called the defective form.

2- [bāšidan] باشیدن: the present stem of [bāš] باش, is also known as the regular 'to be' verb.

3- بودن: the present stem of [bo-wad] بود and past stem [bōd] بود are not used anymore in texts and documents; however, the past stem of this verb is currently used as the past stem of all forms of 'to be', meaning that the infinitives باشیدن, استن/ هستن, and بودن all use the past stem بود.

**The Infinitive** باشیدن [bāšidan]:
The present stem of this verb is باش [bāš] and the prefix می [me] is added to it. This form of 'to be' is interchangeable with هستن /استن [hastand/astan]. For example:

| | | |
|---|---|---|
| I am a teacher. | من معلم میباشم. | من معلم هستم. |
| We are teachers. | ما معلم میباشیم. | ما معلم هستی. |
| You are a teacher. | تو معلم میباشی. | تو معلم هستی. |
| You are a teacher. | شما معلم میباشید. | شما معلم هستید. |
| S/he is a teacher. | او معلم میباشد. | او معلم است. |
| They are teachers. | آنها معلم ها میباشند. | آنها معلم ها هستند. |

However, when in conversation, you will often hear the [hastand/astan] هستن/استن form in the present tense.

Exercise 6:    تمرین ۶:

First, complete the following sentences with the correct form of the verb 'to be.'
Then, translate the meaning of each sentence. The first one has been done for you.

Note: try to use the stem باش.

| | |
|---|---|
| John is Albert's brother. | ۱   جان برادر البرت میباشد. |
| | ۲   من بچه او |
| | ۳   آنها اولاد من |
| | ۴   احمد کاکای من |
| | ۵   ما برادران او |
| | ۶   پدر و مادر احمد داکتر |
| | ۷   تو خواهر آنها |
| | ۸   زرمینه چند ساله |

Exercise 7:    تمرین ۷:

A. You will hear a conversation on the audio recording between احمد and پلوشه.
Listen to their conversation. Then, work with a partner and draw a family tree for
احمد based on what you've heard.

احمد پوپل

B. Now, practice telling who each of the family members is in your family
tree above. Take turns pointing to a family member and asking "Who is this?" Then
your partner should respond, giving the name and relationship to another person in
the family tree.

For example:        او جان است، او برادر دیوید است.        او کیست؟

Exercise 8: 📖 ٨ :تمرین

A population survey is being conducted in your area. Answer the following questions asked by the Census Bureau employee about you and your family.

جمهوری اسلامی افغانستان
ادارهٔ ثبت احوال و نفوس
ولایت کابل

لطفاً فورم زیر را خانه پوری کنید:

نام تان چیست؟
شما مجرد هستید یا متاهل؟
اعضای فامیل تان چند نفر میباشند؟
شما چند برادر دارید؟
شما چند خواهر دارید؟
شما چند بچه دارید؟
شما چند دختر دارید؟
در فامیل شما چند مرد و چند زن هستند؟

تمرین ۹:
Exercise 9:

A. شریف is stating the occupations of his family members on the audio recording. Listen to his monologue and write each of the occupations under the specific family member mentioned.

| | | | |
|---|---|---|---|
| college student | محصل | retired | متقاعد |
| shopkeeper | دوکاندار | teacher | معلم |
| manager | مدیر | nurse | نرس |
| school student | متعلم | unemployed | بیکار |
| kindergarten child | بچهٔ کودکستان | housewife | خانم خانه |

حاجی رحیم　　　　شریف

زرمینه　　　　فرید،

ماه جان　　　　زرغونه

لیلا　　　　نوید

خانواده شریف

B. Listen to the audio recording again. This time check your answers, and also write each person's age beside their name above.

C. Now read the following text and check your answers above.

خانوادهٔ شریف

نامم شریف است من ۴۰ ساله میباشم و من معلم هستم. من بعد از چاشت در یک بانک مدیر هستم.

نام پدرم حاجی رحیم است، او ۷۰ ساله است، او متقاعد است و دوکاندار است. نام مادرم ماه جان است، او بیکار است و خانم خانه است.

من چار اولاد دارم، نام های اولاد هایم زرمینه، زرغونه، فرید و نوید است. کلانترین دخترم زرغونه است او در پوهنتون محصل است و او ۲۳ ساله است. دخترم زرمینه ۱۷ ساله میباشد او متعلم است، نام بچهٔ کلانترم فرید است، او ۱۳ ساله است و متعلم است. نام خوردترین بچه‌ام نوید است، او بچهٔ کودکستان است. مادر اولاد هایم لیلا نام دارد، او ۳۸ ساله است و او نرس است.

| خورد | کلان |
|---|---|
| small | big |

## 6.2 Adjectives صفات

Like most English adjectives, Dari adjectives have three forms:

1- Adjectives (simple form)    big / old کلان
2- Comparative form    bigger / older کلانتر
3- Superlative form    biggest / oldest کلانترین

**Adjectives (simple form):**
This form of adjectives always comes after an object. The *ezāfat* (-e) appears between the object and the adjective to indicate that it's an attribute, "belongs to," or describes the noun. For example:

old brother    برادر کلان
young brother    برادر خورد

**Comparative form:**
The comparative form of adjectives is formed by adding the suffix [-tar] تر; stress moves onto this suffix. Comparative adjectives also come after the noun they modify, which also takes the *ezāfát*. For example:

older brother    برادر کلانتر
younger brother    برادر خوردتر

**Superlative form:**
This form of adjectives is formed by adding the suffix [-tarín] ترین; stress moves onto the last syllable of this suffix. Superlative adjectives appear before the objects, which *does not* take *ezāfát*. For example:

oldest brother    کلانترین برادر
youngest brother    خوردترین برادر

Note: In order to compare two objects, there are two common sentence structures in Dari. For example:

احمد از اجمل کلانتر است اما اجمل کلانتر است    or    احمد از اجمل کلانتر است

In colloquial Dari, there is a different sentence structure for comparing two objects. For example:

Ahmad is older than Ajmal.    احمد از اجمل کرده کلانتراست.

As you can see, the simple verb 'karda' کرده is added to the structure, but this word does not change the meaning of the sentence.

Exercise 10: تمرین ۱۰:

A. For each of the following pairs of pictures, read the adjective pair and write the correct comparative form of each adjective below the associated picture.

 ۴     ۳     ۲     ۱

لاغر/ چاق                                      پیر/ جوان

 ۸     ۷     ۶     ۵

کوتاه/بلند                                      کلان/ خورد

B. Go back to Exercise 9C and re-read Sharif's family description, underlining all of the adjectives.

C. Now, compare the following people using the provided adjective and write your sentences down.

شریف / لیلا (جوان)

زرغونه / زرمینه (کلان)

حاجی رحیم / ماه جان (پیر)

فرید / نوید (خورد)

Exercise 11:

    Write a short introduction of your family.  State their names, ages, and job titles. Then compare them using the above adjectives.

Exercise 12:

    A. You will hear a conversation on the audio recording between an Afghan and an American as they talk about their family members. Before you listen to their conversation, review the discussion you had in Exercise 1A about the differences and similarities between Afghan and American families.  Then jot down some ideas of the things you expect to hear in the conversation.

B. 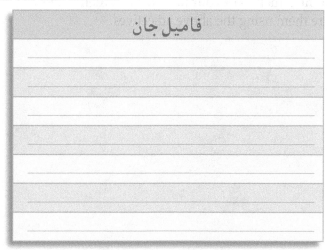 Now, listen again to جان and میرویس's conversation on the audio recording and take notes about their families.

فامیل جان

C. Listen to the audio recording again. Then choose the best answers for the following questions.

| ۱ | مادر فهیم از کجا است؟ | | | |
|---|---|---|---|---|
| | زابل | هرات | کابل | مزار |
| ۲ | آیا فامیل پدر فهیم چی کلان است؟ | | | |
| | بلی | | نه | |
| ۳ | فامیل جان در کجا زنده گی میکنند؟ | | | |
| | افغانستان | اندونیزیا | امریکا | کانادا |
| ۴ | اعضای فامیل جان چند نفر هستند؟ | | | |
| | پنج | چار | سه | دو |
| ۵ | چشم های برادر جان چی رنگ دارد؟ | | | |
| | آبی | سیاه | قهوه یی | سبز |
| ۶ | آیا فامیل پدر و مادر جان همراه آنها زنده گی میکنند؟ | | | |
| | بلی | | نه | |
| ۷ | پدر جان چی وظیفه دارد؟ | | | |
| | مدیر | دوکاندار | انجینر | داکتر |
| ۸ | مادر جان چی وظیفه دارد؟ | | | |
| | متقاعد | بیکار | محصل | معلم |

D.  With a partner, ask and answer similar questions about your own families.

## 6.3 Pluralization with Suffix ان

As you see in the above conversation, the word 'brothers' برادران takes the suffix ان instead of ها. In written Dari, it is very common to use the suffix ان for pluralizing animate objects such as:

| | |
|---|---|
| پدران | پدر |
| مادران | مادر |
| برادران | برادر |
| خواهران | خواهر |

In written Dari, the suffix ها is also used, and it will not be incorrect to use them interchangeably. However, there are some kinship terms that only take the suffix ها. For example:

| | |
|---|---|
| کاکاها | کاکا |
| عمه‌ها | عمه |

## Cultural Note تبصرهٔ فرهنگی

### Prayers for saving someone from the 'evil eye'

Most Afghans believe that people have the power to bestow the evil eye on others simply by looking at a person or object. According to the belief, the evil eye can be given by anyone: a stranger or even your closest friend or family member. The person whom the evil eye is being directed toward is believed to be under some kind of harm.

In order to cure someone or to protect them from the evil eye, there are some prayer words that can be bestowed upon the afflicted (or vulnerable). The closest equivalent to this in American culture is the superstition of knocking on wood to protect you from bad luck.

These prayer words are: 'by the name of God' نام خدا or ("God has willed it.") "Masha'Allah" ما شاء الله. Situations in which you would say these prayers include:

1- When someone is talking about the number of members in your family.

2- If someone compliments you, your family, your properties, and/or any of your belongings.

3- When you want to compliment someone else, his/her family, his/her properties, and/or any of their belongings.

# درس دوم: بچهٔ کاکایم از من قد بلندتر است.

## Lesson Two: My cousin is taller than I am.

In this section, you will learn to explain family relations in more detail and give more details about your family members.

Exercise 1:    تمرین ۱:

A. You will see family terms associated with parents along with their Dari definition. Read the terms, and match them to their definitions.

| | |
|---|---|
| پدر و مادر | ۱  کاکا |
| برادر مادر | ۲  عمه |
| خواهر مادر | ۳  ماما |
| برادر پدر | ۴  خاله |
| خواهر پدر | ۵  والدین |

B. The following terms are about the children in an extended family; match each one to its proper definition.

| | |
|---|---|
| بچهٔ برادر مادر | ۱  بچهٔ کاکا |
| دختر برادر مادر | ۲  دختر کاکا |
| بچهٔ خواهر مادر | ۳  بچهٔ عمه |
| دختر خواهر پدر | ۴  دختر عمه |
| بچهٔ برادر پدر | ۵  بچهٔ ماما |
| دختر برادر پدر | ۶  دختر ماما |
| بچهٔ خواهر پدر | ۷  بچهٔ خاله |
| دختر خواهر پدر | ۸  دختر خاله |

Exercise 2:  تمرین ۲:

A. In the following text زرغونه describes her parents' family members. Working with a partner, read the text and then draw her family tree.

نامم زرغونه است، نام والدینم شریف و لیلا است،  پدرم دو برادر دارد که* نام شان کریم و نسیم است و یك خواهر دارد كه نامش فهیمه است. کریم دو بچه دارد که نام شان  اجمل و ایمل است.

مادرم سه برادر دارد  که نام شان سید صبور، سید ناصر و سید خلیل است،  و او دو خواهر دارد که نام شان گلجان و شاه جان است.  شاه جان یك دختر و یك بچه دارد، نام دخترش شاپری و نام بچه اش جانان است.

فامیل پدر زرغونه            فامیل مادر زرغونه

B.  Answer the following questions about زرغونه family.

| | | |
|---|---|---|
| ۱ | سید صبور چی زرغونه میشود؟* | سید صبور مامایی اجمل است. |
| ۲ | کریم چی زرغونه میشود؟ | _____ |
| ۳ | شاجان چی زرغونه میشود؟ | _____ |
| ۴ | فهیمه چی زرغونه میشود؟ | _____ |
| ۵ | شاپری چی زرغونه میشود؟ | _____ |
| ۶ | زرغونه چی جانان میشود؟ | _____ |
| ۷ | اجمل چی زرغونه میشود؟ | _____ |

## 6.4 The Function of the Verb شدن

In the context of asking about relationships between people, the verb شدن is used and functions semantically like 'to be'. For example:

What is Sayed Sabur's [relation] to Zarghuna?
Sayed Sabur is Zarghuna's uncle.

سید صبور چی زرغونه میشود؟
سید صبور مامایی زرغونه میشود.

The verb شدن in colloquial Dari:

مه بیادر او میشم.
ما خوارهای او میشیم.
تو کاکایم میشی.
شما ماماهایم میشن.
او خاله یم میشه.
آنها کاکاهایم میشن.

Exercise 3:  تمرین ۳:
    A. Write the Dari equivalent of each sentence below using شدن. The first one has been done for you.

| | | |
|---|---|---|
| This woman is my mother. | این زن مادرم میشود. | ۱ |
| That man is our father. | | ۲ |
| This boy is their cousin. (mother's sister's son) | | ۳ |
| That girl is his cousin. (mother's brother's daughter) | | ۴ |
| She is my cousin. (father's sister's son) | | ۵ |
| He is our cousin. (father's sister's son) | | ۶ |
| They are my aunts. (father's sisters) | | ۷ |
| I am your uncle. (mother's brother) | | ۸ |

B.  Read the following descriptions. Then write the relations between the people being described. The first one has been done for you.

| | | |
|---|---|---|
| ۱ | پدر وحید یك برادر دارد که نام او سلطان است، سلطان دو اولاد دارد ، یك بچه و یك دختر. نام بچه اش فواد و نام دخترش شیرین میباشد . | سلطان کاکایی وحید میشود ، شیرین و فواد اولاد های سلطان میشوند |
| ۲ | کریم یك خواهر دارد نام او گل بی بی است، گل بی بی یك بچه دارد ، نامش رحیم است. | |
| ۳ | نام او لیلا است، پدر لیلا دو خواهر دارد ، نام های شان مستوره و مهتاب است. | |
| ۴ | نامم لیلا است و نام مادرم نسرین است، او دو خواهر دارد که نام شان لاله و مریم است. | |

### 6.5 Relative Pronoun که ke

The relative pronoun که is used when describing people (or places and objects). It functions similarly to *that, which, whom, whose,* or *who* in English. For example:

| | |
|---|---|
| My father has two brothers whose names are Karim and Nasim. | پدرم دو برادر دارد که نام های شان کریم و نسیم است. |
| That woman who writes is my sister. | آن زن که نوشته میکند ، خواهرم است. |
| The man who exercises is my brother. | مردی که ورزش میکند برادرم است. |

که can also be used to join two clauses. For example :

| | |
|---|---|
| پدرم دو برادر دارد که نام های شان کریم و نسیم است. | پدرم دو برادر دارد. نام شان کریم و نسیم است. |
| آن زن که نوشته میکند ، خواهرم است. | آن زن خواهرم است. او نوشته میکند . |
| آن مرد که ورزش میکند برادرم است. | آن مرد برادرم است. او ورزش میکند . |

Exercise 4:    تمرین ۴:

A. Working with a partner, write the Dari equivalent of the following sentences in the spaces provided.

| | |
|---|---|
| My mother has one brother whose name is John. | ۱ |
| The boy who is next to Ahmads is my cousin. (father's sister's son) | ۲ |
| The girl who is in front of Laylaa is my cousin. (mother's sister's daughter) | ۳ |
| The man who is behind your brother is my uncle. (mother's brother) | ۴ |
| The woman who is in the class is my aunt. (father's sisters) | ۵ |
| The girl who is working is my cousin. (mother's brother's daughter) | ۶ |

B.    Join the following sentences together using the relative pronoun که.

| | |
|---|---|
| من یک ماما دارم. نام او اسد الله است. | ۱ |
| او دو خاله دارد. نام های آنها فریده و آصفه است. | ۲ |
| ما یک عمه داریم. نام او سیما است. | ۳ |
| آنها یک کاکا دارند. نام او نوراحمد است. | ۴ |
| آن مرد مامایم است. او تلیفون میکند. | ۵ |

Exercise 5: تمرین ۵:

A. Look at the following picture of Sayd-Khalil's family, the uncle of
زرغونه . Working with a partner, discuss his uncle's family. For example:

زرغونه سه ماما دارد که نام مامای خورد او سید خلیل است.

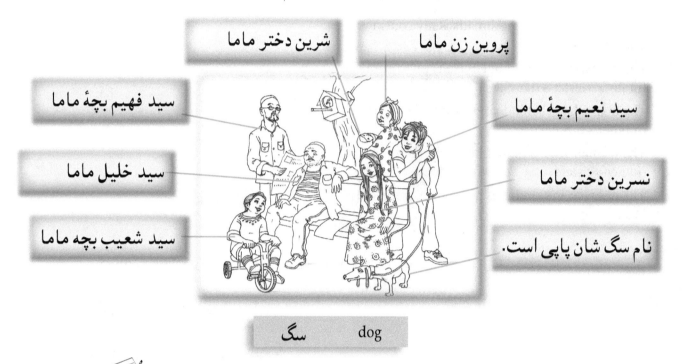

پروین زن ماما

شرین دختر ماما

سید نعیم بچهٔ ماما

سید فهیم بچهٔ ماما

نسرین دختر ماما

سید خلیل ماما

نام سگ شان پاپی است.

سید شعیب بچه ماما

سگ    dog

B. ✎ Now look at the picture of زرغونه uncle's family and write a short
summary about his family. Be sure to include an introduction. Then switch
summaries with a partner and give one another feedback on your work.

## Cultural Note تبصرهٔ فرهنگی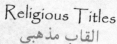

### Religious Titles
القاب مذهبی

In Exercise 5A, Zarghuna's uncle's name is said to be سید
خلیل. The word سید is a religious title. In Dari, there are
many religious titles, and each has its own usage for certain
circumstances. The following are some of the most important
religious titles, their meaning, and usage.

1- [hāji] حاجی is a title used only for those people who have
gone to Mecca in Saudi Arabia for pilgrimage.

2- [sufi] صوف is a title for people who spend most of their time
praying to God.

3- [mulā] ملا , [mulawi] مولوی and [mulānā] مولانا refer to a
religious leader or a person who has mastered Islamic studies.

4- [say-yěd] سید or [āğā-sāyeěb] آغا صاحب refer to people
descended from the prophet of Islam. Say-yéd is used in
writing before a person's name, while [āğā-sāyéb] is used when
speaking to address the individual.

5- [Xāja] خواجه , [hazrát] حضرت and [mir] میر refer to the [Islām]
prophet's close friends. As with other titles, these titles come
before the name of the person.

Exercise 6: تمرین ۶:

A.  You will hear زرغونه introduce her uncle's family by their age and occupations on the audio recording. Match each person to an occupation and fill in the age.

| | |
|---|---|
| بیکار | ۱   مامایم سید خلیل _____ |
| شاگرد مکتب | ۲   زن مامایم پروین _____ |
| محصل | ۳   بچه مامایم سید فهیم _____ |
| منشی | ۴   بچهٔ مامایم سید نعیم _____ |
| خیاط | ۵   دختر مامایم نسرین _____ |
| داکتر | ۶   بچهٔ مامایم سید شعیب _____ |
| آشپز | ۷   دختر مامایم شیرین _____ |
| کودک (child) | ۸   سگ مامایم پاپی _____ |

B.  Now read the following text to check your answers above.  Then answer the following questions.

من زرغونه هستم، من برای شما فامیل مامایم را معرفی میکنم،  نام مامایم سید خلیل است او ۵۴ ساله است و او آشپز است.

زن مامایم پروین نام دارد او ۴۸ ساله است و او خیاط است. مامایم سه بچه و دو دختر دارد.

بچهٔ کلان مامایم سید فهیم نام دارد و او ۳۴ ساله است و او داکتر است،  بعد از سید فهیم، بچهٔ مامایم سید نعیم است، او ۲۴ ساله است او از من یک سال کلانتر است و او محصل است، من و بچهٔ مامایم سید نعیم همصنفی هستیم. او بعد از پوهنتون همراه مامایم کار میکند.

اولاد سوم مامایم نسرین نام دارد، نسرین شاگرد مکتب است، او ۱۶ ساله است. او بعد از مکتب، با برادرش فهیم کار میکند و منشی او است.

اولاد چارم مامایم سید شعیب نام دارد، سید شعیب ۷ ساله است و شاگرد مکتب است، او بیکار است. و خوردترین اولاد مامایم شیرین نام دارد او ۱۰ ماهه است. فامیل مامایم یک سگ هم دارند، نام سگ شان پاپی است و او ۲ ساله است.

| | | |
|---|---|---|
| Who is the oldest child in Zarghuna's uncle's family? | _____ | ١ |
| Who is the youngest child in that family? | _____ | ٢ |
| Who is younger, sayed Na'im or Nasrin? | _____ | ٣ |
| Who is older, sayed Na'im or sayed Sho'ayb? | _____ | ۴ |
| Who works with the head of the family (father)? | _____ | ۵ |
| What is the name of the family dog? | _____ | ۶ |

Exercise 7: تمرین ۷:

A. You will hear some people being described on the audio recording. Using the charts below, mark the characteristics of each of the people you hear being described.

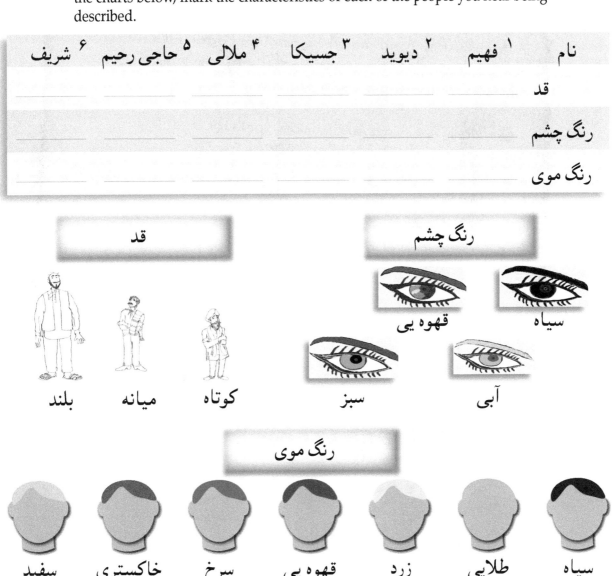

| نام | ۱ فهیم | ۲ دیوید | ۳ جسیکا | ۴ ملالی | ۵ حاجی رحیم | ۶ شریف |
|---|---|---|---|---|---|---|
| قد | | | | | | |
| رنگ چشم | | | | | | |
| رنگ موی | | | | | | |

قد

بلند    میانه    کوتاه

رنگ چشم

سیاه    قهوه یی    سبز    آبی

رنگ موی

سیاه    طلایی    زرد    قهوه یی    سرخ    خاکستری    سفید

## Cultural Note تبصره فرهنگی

### Pets
### حیوانات خانگی

In Afghanistan, keeping pets in the house is very common. Afghans have pets not for companionship, but rather for protective purposes, i.e. having a dog to protect the family from thieves, wild animals, etc. Sometimes, cats are allowed inside an Afghan home, but only for the purpose of catching rodents, and they are never allowed to sleep on the beds. However, some Afghans will allow pet birds in the house.

There are a lot of wild dogs and cats found living in the streets in Afghanistan. Currently the government does not have a good plan for dealing with these animals and, as a result, diseases like rabies are very common among street dogs.

Generally speaking, Afghans have pets for the following reasons:

| | | |
|---|---|---|
| for protection | dogs | سگ |
| for catching rodents | cats | پیشک |
| for singing and sound | song birds (nightingales and canaries) | قناری ، بلبل |
| for the same reason as other cultures, because they can talk | parrots | طوطی |
| for business and hobby; people raise pigeons to sell them for hunting game | pigeons | کبوتر/کفتر |
| for business and hobby, raising them for partridge fighting | partridges | بودنه /کبک |

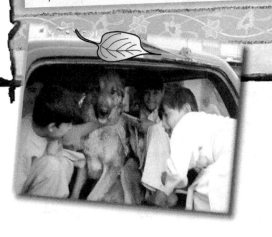

B.  Go around the room marking how many students have the following
characteristics.  Working in pairs, report your findings.  Your partner will check
your answers by saying غلط است. and صحیح است.

| | | | | نام |
|---|---|---|---|---|
| | | | | قد |
| | | | | رنگ چشم |
| | | | | رنگ موی |

C. Look at the following picture and answer the following questions.

صابر          فرید

میوند

اجمل

| | ۱ قد بلندترین بچه کیست؟ |
|---|---|
| | ۲ قد کوتاه ترین بچه کیست؟ |
| | ۳ قد کی میانه است؟ |
| | ۴ کی از کی قدبلند تر است؟ |
| | ۵ کی از کی قد کوتاه تر است؟ |

Exercise 8: تمرین ۸:

A. You will hear on the audio recording a short conversation between جان and فهیم about Afghan and American families. Write down some questions you can expect to hear.

B. Listen to the audio recording and choose the best answer for each question.

1. Who has a bigger family than Fahim's father?
    a) Fahim's uncle.          b) Fahim's friend, John.
    c) Fahim's mother.         d) Fahim's aunt.

2. Fahim has _____ .
    a) one uncle and aunt on his mother's side     b) one uncle and aunt on his
                                                      father's side

3. John's brother has the same eye and hair color as his _____ .
    a) brother        b) father        c) mother        d) grandmother

4. What does John's father do for a living?
    a) He is an engineer.          b) He is a shopkeeper.
    c) He is a manager.            d) He is jobless.

5. Who is the cook in John's family?
    a) His mother.
    b) His aunt on his mother's side.
    c) His aunt on his father's side.
    d) His uncle on his father's side.

6. Which of John's family members is a driver?
    a) His younger aunt.          b) His younger uncle.
    c) His older aunt.            d) His older uncle.

7. Why was Fahim surprised?
    a) Because women are driving in the US.
    b) Because his mother is a shopkeeper in the US.
    c) Because American families are so small.
    d) Because John's family (on his father's side) doesn't live together.

Exercise 9:    تمرین ۹:

A. Who is in your parent's family? Draw your mother's and father's family tree, writing each member's relationship to you.

فامیل پدرتان

فامیل مادرتان

B.    Working in pairs, use your family trees to take turns asking one another about your extended families.  Ask questions about their names, job titles, height, hair color, eye color, etc.

## Cultural Note    تبصرهٔ فرهنگی

### Afghan women at work    زنان افغان در کار

Afghanistan has a conservative and very closed community in which women are not commonly allowed to work outside of the home. However, there are some exceptions:

Women working in urban areas (cities) usually have studied in schools and universities, and as a result they have jobs in the governor's offices or work with NGOs. Most women who didn't go to school and are illiterate remain in the home and mainly work as housewives. However, there are a few who work with private companies, e.g. cleaning, cooking, tailoring, carpet weaving, etc.

In the rural areas (villages and small cities), women are mainly illiterate and rarely work outside the home.  When they do, they are typically working for their male family members in farming and agriculture.

# درس سوم: من متاهل هستم.
## Lesson Three: I am married.

In this section, you will learn more about Afghan marriages and the role in-laws play in an Afghan family. You will also learn how to express yourself in the simple past tense.

Exercise 1: 🎧  تمرین ۱:

A. In the previous lesson, you learned about cousins سید نعیم and زرغونه who are married to one another. Listen to the audio recording to hear Dari terms for سید نعیم and زرغونه in-laws and mark the terms which belong to زرغونه in-laws and the terms which are uses for سیدنعیم's in-laws.

| | سید نعیم | زرغونه | | | سید نعیم | زرغونه |
|---|---|---|---|---|---|---|
| شوهر/ شوی | ___ | ___ | | زن | ___ | ___ |
| داماد | ___ | ___ | | عروس/ سونو | ___ | ___ |
| خسر | ___ | ___ | | خسر | ___ | ___ |
| خشو | ___ | ___ | | خشو | ___ | ___ |
| خسربُره | ___ | ___ | | ایور | ___ | ___ |
| خیاشنه | ___ | ___ | | ننو | ___ | ___ |

B. 📖 Match the following terms with their proper definitions. Note: شوهر 'husband', زن 'wife'.

| | | | |
|---|---|---|---|
| خواهر شوهر | | ۱ خسر |
| برادر شوهر | | ۲ خوشو |
| پدر زن/پدر شوهر | | ۳ ایور |
| مادر زن/ مادر شوهر | | ۴ ننو |
| خواهر زن | | ۵ عروس/ سونو |
| برادر زن | | ۶ داماد |
| زن بچه | | ۷ خسربُره |
| شوهر دختر | | ۸ خیاشنه |

C. ✎ Write down the English equivalent of the following terms.

| | | |
|---|---|---|
| ۱ | خسر | _____ |
| ۲ | خوشو | _____ |
| ۳ | ایور | _____ |
| ۴ | ننو | _____ |
| ۵ | عروس، سونو | _____ |
| ۶ | داماد | _____ |
| ۷ | خسرُبُره | _____ |
| ۸ | خیاشنه | _____ |

Exercise 2: تمرین ۲:
Listen to the audio recording one more time, and this time answer the following questions.

1. Who is Zarghuna's father in-law?
   a) her paternal uncle          b) her maternal uncle

2. Who is Sayed Nahim's father in-law?
   a) his paternal uncle          b) his maternal uncle

3. How many sisters-in-law does Zarghuna have?
   a) one                         b) two

4. How many sisters-in-law does Sayed Nahim have?
   a) one                         b) two

5. How many brothers-in-law does Zarghuna have?
   a) one                         b) two

6. How many brothers-in-law does Sayed Nahim have?
   a) one                         b) two

7. What is the relationship of Sayed Nahim to Zarghuna?
   a) شوهر                        b) زن

8. What is the relationship of Zarghuna to Sayed Nahim?
   a) زن                          b) شوهر

Exercise 3: تمرین ۳:

You will hear a short conversation on the audio recording. Listen and practice the following questions with a partner.

زن: آیا شما مجرد هستید یا متاهل؟

مرد: من متاهل هستم.

زن: چی وقت توی کردید؟

مرد: یک سال پیش توی کردم.

زن: در فامیل خسرتان کیها زندگی میکنند؟

مرد: در فامیل خسرم، خسربوره ام، خیاشنه ام، خوشویم و خسرم زندگی میکنند.

| چی وقت | پیش | توی کردید | توی کردم |
|---|---|---|---|
| when | ago, before | You did marry. | I did marry. |

### 6.6 Forming the Simple Past Tense ساختار زمان گذشته

All infinitives in Dari end with the letter ن. For example:

to be بودن    to do کردن    to become شدن

In order to make the past tense, follow these steps:

First, remove the ending ن. For example:

| | | | |
|---|---|---|---|
| was/were | بود | to be | بودن |
| did | کرد | to do | کردن |
| became | شد | to become | شدن |

Then, conjugate those verbs by adding the appropriate personal endings to each.

| | |
|---|---|
| They were single..آنها مجرد بودند | They did marry..آنها توی کردند |
| S/he was single..او مجرد بود | S/he did marry..او توی کرد |
| You were single..شما مجرد بودید | You did marry..شما توی کردید |
| You were single..تو مجرد بودی | You did marry..تو توی کردی |
| We were single..ما مجرد بودیم | We did marry..ما توی کردیم |
| I was single..من مجرد بودم | I did marry..من توی کردم |

Exercise 4:    تمرین ۴:

Write the past tense of the following infinitives.   Then write a sentence for each.

| | | |
|---|---|---|
| _____ | _____ | ۱   توی کردن |
| _____ | _____ | ۲   ازدواج کردن |
| _____ | _____ | ۳   عروسی کردن |
| _____ | _____ | ۴   نامزد شدن |
| _____ | _____ | ۵   به ماه عسل رفتن |
| _____ | _____ | ۶   دیدن |
| _____ | _____ | ۷   درس خواندن |

Exercise 5:    تمرین ۵:

Working with a partner, read the following text and underline the past tense verbs.

آن زن زرغونه است، او یک سال نیم پیش مجرد بود اما یک سال پیش او همراه بچهٔ ماما‌یش سید نعیم ازدواج کرد. شوهر زرغونه دو ماه پیش محصل بود اما حالا او انجینر است. آنها بعد از توی به ماه عسل رفتند، آنها برای ماه عسل به هندوستان رفتند، در هندوستان آنها تاج محل را دیدند.

Exercise 6: 🎧 تمرین ۶:

A. You will hear on the audio recording a conversation between نعیم and one of his friends, میوند. Listen and draw میوند in-law's family tree.

فامیل خسر میوند

B. 🎧 Now listen again to the audio recording and choose the best answer for each of the following questions.

١   نعیم دیروز کجا بود؟

| خانهٔ خسرو دوستش | خانهٔ خیاشنه اش | خانهٔ خسربره اش | خانهٔ خسرش |

٢   میوند از چی خبر نداشت؟

| توی خسربره نعیم | نامزدی خسربره نعیم | توی نعیم | نامزدی نعیم |

٣   نعیم برای ماه عسل به کجا رفت؟

| به هندوستان | به پاکستان | به ازبکستان | به ترکمنستان |

٤   نعیم کجا را دید؟

| هیچ کدام | تاج محل | شهر اسلام آباد | شهر دهلی |

٥   میوند چی وقت توی کرد؟

| یازده سال پیش | ده سال پیش | نه سال پیش | هشت سال پیش |

٦   چرا خسر میوند دو زن دارد؟

| هیچ کدام | چون زن اولش بچه ندارد. | چون زن اولش ناجور است. | چون او پیسه دارد. |

٧   میوند چند خسربره دارد؟

| چار | سه | دو | یک |

| congratulations | تبریک باشد |

C. 🤝 Working in pairs, ask your classmate about his/her marital status. If s/he is single, ask about the status of her/his family members. Then ask when they were married. Where did they go for their honeymoon? And what things and places did they see?

D. 📝 Write down the English equivalent of the following terms.

١   زرغونه و نعیم چی وقت عروسی کردند؟   _____

٢   نعیم دو ماه پیش کجا بود؟   _____

٣   آنها برای ماه عسل کجا رفتند؟   _____

٤   آنها در هند چی را دیدند؟   _____

### Cultural Note    تبصره فرهنگی

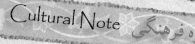

## Marriage among Afghans
### توی در بین افغانها

Because Afghan society is so conservative, most marriages are arranged by the families. First, the family of the man looks for a suitable girl, and after they've found the girl, they will ask about her family and their social situation. Then, they will go to her family and ask for their daughter's hand. The girl's family will not say yes right away, because first they will inquire about the boy and his family. Finally, if they are satisfied, they will respond with a yes or no.

Marriages among Afghans are mostly preferred to be kept among close relatives, i.e. first cousins. But this is not always the case. Also, polygamy is socially acceptable among Afghans, and a man is allowed to marry several times depending on how wealthy he is.

Divorce in Afghan society is not socially acceptable. Despite how the husband and wife feel about each other, they still usually stay together because they (especially the divorced woman) would be looked down upon by their families and society.

Exercise 7: ۷ :تمرین

A. The following text is about زرغونه and her husband سید نعیم on their honeymoon. Number the following places in the order that they visit them.

سفر ماه عسل

من سید نعیم هستم، پارسال به تاریخ پنجم ماه حمل سال ۱۳۹۰ ، من و زنم رزغونه به کشور هندوستان رفتیم، در هندوستان ما به شهر آگره رفتیم. ما در آنجا به یک هوتل رفتیم بعداز آن از تاج محل دیدیم، بعداز آن تحفه خریدیم، و باز به سینما رفتیم. در سینما ما یک فلم هندی تماشا کردیم. ما در هندوستان یک هفته بودیم و بعد از یک هفته به افغانستان آمدیم.

هوتل

بازار

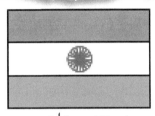

هندوستان

تاج محل

سینما

B. Now write two questions about what the couple did on their honeymoon. Then ask a classmate.

C. What did you do and where did you go for your honeymoon? Or your last date or trip (if you aren't married or didn't go on a honeymoon). Write a few sentences in Dari, and read them to the class.

# مرور فصل ششم
## Review of Chapter Six

In this section you will review the vocabulary, phrases, grammar, and cultural elements that you learned throughout the chapter.

Exercise 1: تمرین ۱:
Read the following text and fill in the blanks with the proper kinship terms.

نامم میوند است. تخلصم پغمانی است ، نام _____ (my father) حاجی عبدالسلام است، _____ (my father) در پوهنتون استاد است. ما سه _____ (brother) و چار _____ (sister) میباشیم. من _____ (married) هستم. نام _____ (my wife) نازنین است، _____ (she) معلمه است. نام _____ (father in-law) احمد است، _____ (he) انجینر است. من دو _____ (son) دارم. نام _____ (My son's) لطیف و صابر است. من همچنان یک _____ (daughter) دارم. نام _____ (my daughter) مرضیه است. _____ (she) متعلمه میباشد. نام _____ (my mother in-law) فریده است. نام _____ (my brothers) متعلم میباشند. نام _____ (my brothers) فواد و فرهاد است و نام _____ (my sisters) مریم، مژده، مژگان و منیژه میباشد.

Exercise 2: تمرین ۲:
Read the text and answer the following questions.

حاجی بریالی پوپل اصلاً از افغانستان، ازولایت کندوز میباشد ، او حالادر امریکا، در ایالت کالیفورنیا ، در شهر لس انجلس زندگی میکند. آقای پوپل متاهل است، نام زنش مستوره پوپل است، حاجی بریالی و مستوره شش اولاد دارند.

اولاد های شان دو بچه و چار دختر است، نام های بچه هایشان توریالی و ننگیالی است و نام های دختر هایشان شکریه، حلیمه، فاطمه و مرضیه میباشد.

توریالی ۲۰ ساله، ننگیالی ۱۸ ساله، شکریه ۱۶ ساله، حلیمه ۱۳ ساله، فاطمه ۱۰ ساله و مرضیه ۷ ساله است.

توریالی در پوهنتون کالیفورنیا ، در پوهنئی انجینری درس میخواند ، ننگیالی متعلم صنف ۱۱ مکتب است، شکریه متعلمهٔ صنف ۹، حلیمه متعلمهٔ صنف ۷، فاطمه متعلمهٔ صنف ۴ و مرضیه متعلمهٔ صنف ۲ میباشد.

حاجی بریالی در پوهنتون استاد پشتو است و زنش مستوره استاد دری است.

١  مستوره چی بریالی میشود؟

٢  بریالی چی فاطمه میشود؟

٣  توریالی چی بریالی میشود؟

٤  ننگیالی چی مرضیه میشود؟

٥  این فامیل در کجا زنده گی میکنند؟

٦  حلیمه چند ساله است؟

٧  بریالی و مستوره چی کار میکنند؟

٨  توریالی و شکریه در کجا درس
میخوانند؟

Exercise 3: تمرین ۳:

A. You will hear two separate monologues on the audio recording in which نازنین
and بابك introduce their family members. Listen and write down the name, kinship
term, and job of each family member.

نازنین

بابك

| وظیفه | رابطۀ فامیلی | نام | | وظیفه | رابطۀ فامیلی | نام |
|---|---|---|---|---|---|---|
| | | | | | | |
| | | | | | | |
| | | | | | | |
| | | | | | | |

B.  نازنین and بابک, got married and are now husband and wife. Based on the information given in their monologues, write a short description about each one's in-laws.

| نازنین | بابک |
|---|---|
| | |

Exercise 4: تمرین ۴:

You will hear a conversation on the audio recording between زرغونه and her brother فرید in which they describe their best friends. Listen and answer the following questions.

| زرغونه | فرید |
|---|---|
| 1. What is Zarghuna's best friend's name? | 1. What is Farid's best friend's name? |
| 2. What is her friend's height? | 2. What is his friend's height? |
| 3. What color are her friend's eyes? | 3. What color are her friend's eyes? |
| 4. What color is her friend's hair? | 4. What color is his friend's hair? |

Exercise 5:  تمرین ۵:

Look at the following pictures:

A. Working in pairs, ask your classmates a few questions about each person.

B. Choose two people from one of the pictures and compare their heights and ages.

زهرا، ۱۴ ساله    مریم، ۱۲ ساله    رحیم، ۵ ساله    کریم، ۱۷ ساله

زلمی، ۱۰ ساله    فرهاد، ۵ ساله    نسیم، ۱۵ ساله    پروین، ۴ ساله

Exercise 6: تمرین ۶:

A. Write a short description of your family members. Then, read it to a classmate.

B. Take turns with your classmate asking one another questions about your family members. Example: Is your mother taller than your father?

Exercise 7: تمرین ۷:

Karim wrote this email message to his best friend, John, about his honeymoon. Read his message carefully and provide an appropriate answer for each question below.

فرستنده: کریم
گیرنده: جان
موضوع: رخصتی های گذشته

دوست عزیزم آقای جان سلام!

هفته گذشته من، پدرم، مادرم و برادر خوردم به خانه خسرم شان، به ولایت مزارشریف رفتیم، در آنجا ما زیارت سخی را دیدیم، میله کردیم و بسیار غذا پختیم. در مزار من اسب دوانی کردم و ورزش بزکشی را هم دیدم.
فامیل خسرم شش نفر هستند، نامزدم، خسرم، خوشویم، خیاشنه ام و خسربره ام و خسر کلانم. من و نامزدم دوسال پیش نامزد شدیم. او محصل است.
برایم نوشته کن که تو در رخصتی های گذشته چی کردی؟

تشکر
دوستت کریم
تاریخ ۱۰ حمل ۱۳۹۱

1. Where did Karim go for his last vacation?
   a) his father-in-law's house
   b) his father's house
   c) his brother-in-law's house
   d) his sister-in-law's house

2. Which sport did Karim take part in?
   a) Buzkashi      b) horse riding      c) football      d) volleyball

3. What did they see there?
   a) زیارت سخی و ورزش بزکشی
   b) مسجد
   c) ورزش بزکشی
   d) زیارت سخی

4. What did Karim do two years ago?
   a) visited his uncle    b) went to Mazar    c) got engaged    d) got married

5. Which of Karim's family members is a university student?
   a) brother-in-law    b) sister-in-law    c) fiancée    d) mother-in-law

Exercise 8: تمرین ۸:

Complete the following sentences with the appropriate form of the verb.

| | | |
|---|---|---|
| to be بودن | ۱ دیروز توی برادرم _____ . | |
| to go رفتن | ۲ دیشب ما به خانهٔ ماهایم _____ . | |
| to be بودن | ۳ پارسال پدرم مدیر مکتب _____ . | |
| to write نامه نوشتن | ۴ من دیشب برای نامزدم _____ . | |
| to come آمدن | ۵ خسرم و فامیلش سال گذشته به کابل _____ . | |
| to retire متقاعد شدن | ۶ پدر کلانم دوسال پیش _____ . | |
| to eat خوردن | ۷ من و زنم دیروز در رستورانت نان _____ . | |
| to have داشتن | ۸ یک سال پیش خواهرم یک بکس کلان _____ . | |

Exercise 9: تمرین ۹:

Rewrite each sentence, changing the adjectives to their comparative (+) or superlative forms (++).

| | | |
|---|---|---|
| _____ | + | ۱ پدر کلانم پیر است. |
| _____ | ++ | ۲ مادرم جوان است. |
| _____ | ++ | ۳ احمد برادر خوردم است. |
| _____ | + | ۴ او خواهر کوچکم است. |
| _____ | + | ۵ فرید برادر کلانم است. |
| _____ | + | ۶ او برادر بزرگم است. |
| _____ | ++ | ۷ نازنین مقبول است. |
| _____ | + | ۸ خاله‌ام لاغر است. |
| _____ | ++ | ۹ شوهرم قد بلند است. |
| _____ | ++ | ۱۰ کاکایم قد کوتاه است. |
| _____ | + | ۱۱ ماهایم قد میانه دارد. |

Exercise 10:  تمرین ۱۰:

Look at the following picture. Choose three people and compare them with one another.

محمد شریف، حاجی کریم، حاجی رحیم،
محمد نعیم

Exercise 11: تمرین ۱۱:

A. The aunt of your Afghan friend is coming to the US. Your friend left a message asking you to pick up her/his aunt from the airport. Before listening, list the information that you expect her/him to tell you about the aunt's description.

B. Now listen to the phone message on the audio recording and write down the description of the aunt.

# Vocabulary

In this part of the lesson, you will review, listen to, and practice pronunciation of the phrases and vocabulary used in the chapter.

## Phrases اصطلاحات

| How old is your brother? | barādar-e tān čand sāla ast? | برادر تان چند ساله است؟ |
| My brother is twenty years old. | barādaram bist sāla ast. | برادرم بیست ساله است. |
| Congratulations. | tabrik bāšad. | تبریك باشد. |
| What is Karim's [relation] to Zarghuna? | karim čiye zarğuna mešawad? | کریم چی زرغونه میشود؟ |

## Vocabulary Words لغات

| blue | ābi | آبی |
| they are ... | ānhā ... mebāšand. | آنها ... میباشند. |
| to marry | ezdĕwāj kardan (ezdĕwāj kon) | ازدواج کردن |
| members | a'zā | اعضا |
| pigeon | kabutar/kaftar | کبوتر/کفتر |
| s/he is ... | ō ... mebāšad. | او ... میباشد. |
| children | awlād | اولاد |
| brother-in-law (for wife) | ewar | ایور |
| son | bača/pasar | بچه/پسر |
| cousin | bačaye a'ma | بچهٔ عمه |
| cousin | bačaye kākā | بچهٔ کاکا |
| kindergarten (age) child | bačaye kodakĕstān | بچهٔ کودکستان |
| cousin | bačaye māmā | بچهٔ ماما |
| cousin | bačaye xāla | بچهٔ خاله |
| brother | barādar | برادر |
| nightingale | bolbol | بلبل |
| tall | bĕland | بلند |

| partridge | bōdana/kabk | بودنه /كبك |
|---|---|---|
| jobless | bikār | بیکار |
| jobless | bikār | بیکار |
| father | padar | پدر |
| grandfather | padar kalān | پدر کلان |
| old | pir | پیر |
| cat | pĕsak | پیشك |
| to marry | tōy kardan (tōy kon) | توی كردن |
| you are ... | tu... mebāše. | تو ... میباشی. |
| young | jawān | جوان |
| fat | čāq | چاق |
| left | čap | چپ |
| gray | xākĕstari | خاكستری |
| uncle (mother's side) | xāl | خاله |
| family | xānawāda | خانواده |
| family | xānawāda/fāmil | خانواده/ فامیل |
| housewife | xānom-e xāna | خانم خانه |
| father-in-law | xosor | خسر |
| brother-in-law (for husband) | xosorbōra | خسربُره |
| mother-in-law | xošō | خشو |
| sister | xāhar | خواهر |
| small/young | xōrd | خورد |
| tailor | xayāt | خیاط |
| sister-in-law (for husband) | xeyāšna | خیاشنه |
| groom | dāmād | داماد |
| daughter | doxtar | دختر |
| cousin | doxtare a'ma | دختر عمه |
| cousin | doxtare kākā | دختر كاكا |
| cousin | doxtare māma | دختر ماما |

| | | |
|---|---|---|
| cousin | doxtare xāla | دختر خاله |
| shopkeeper | dokāndār | دوكاندار |
| right | rāst | راست |
| hair color | rang mōy | رنگ موی |
| eye color | range čěšom | رنگ چشم |
| yellow | zard | زرد |
| woman | zan | زن |
| ... years | sāla ... | ... ساله |
| green | sabz | سبز |
| red | sorx | سرخ |
| white | safed | سفید |
| dog | sag | سگ |
| age | sĕn | سن |
| black | siyā | سياه |
| to get; to grow, to happen, to go, to be | šodan | شدن |
| you are ... | šōmā ... mebāšed. | شما ... میباشید. |
| husband | šawhar/šōy | شوهر/ شوی |
| golden (blonde) | tĕlāye | طلایی |
| parrot | tuti | طوطی |
| bride/daughter in-law | arōs/sōnō | عروس/سونو |
| to marry/to wed | arōsi kardan (arōsi kon) | عروسی کردن |
| aunt (mother's side) | a'ma | عمه |
| family | fāmil | فامیل |
| father-in-law's family | fāmile xosor | فامیل خسر |
| height | qad | قد |
| tall height | qad bĕlan | قد بلند |
| short height | qad kōtā | قد کوتاه |
| canary | qanāri | قناری |

| brown | qahwa ye | قهوه یی |
| parent | kākā | کاکا |
| big | kalān | کلان |
| big | kalān/ bozorg | کلان/بزرگ |
| short | kōtā | کوتاه |
| small/young | kōčak | کوچك |
| child | kōdak/tĕfĕl | کودك/طفل |
| conjunction | kĕ | که |
| skinny | lāğar | لاغر |
| we are ... | mā ... mebāšem. | ما ... میباشیم. |
| mother | mādar | مادر |
| grandmother | mādar kalān | مادر کلان |
| honeymoon | māhe 'asal | ماه عسل |
| uncle (father's side) | māmā | ماما |
| married | motahel | متاهل |
| school student | mota'lem | متعلم |
| retired | motaqā'ad | متقاعد |
| single | mojarad | مجرد |
| college student | mohasĕl | محصل |
| manager | modir | مدیر |
| teacher | mo'lem | معلم |
| i am ... | man ... mebāšam. | من ... میباشم. |
| secretary | monši | منشی |
| to be engaged | nāmzad šodan (nāmzad šaw) | نامزد شدن |
| nurse | nars | نرس |
| sister-in-law (for wife) | nanō | ننو |
| grandchild | nawāsa | نواسه |
| medium/middle/mid | miyāna | میانه |
| aunt (father's side) | wālĕdayn | والدین |

## Dari Vocabulary Different from Iranian Persian

| English Translation | Iranian Persian | | Farsi-e Dari | |
|---|---|---|---|---|
| father-in-law | padar-zan/ padar šawhar | پدر زن/ پدر شوهر | xosor | خسر |
| mother-in-law | mādar-zan/ mādar šawhar | مادر زن/ مادر شوهر | xošō | خشو |
| brother-in-law (husband's side) | barādar šawhar | برادر شوهر | ĕwar | ایور |
| sister-in-law (husband's side) | xāhar šawhar | خواهر شوهر | nanō | ننو |
| brother-in-law (wife's side) | barādar-zan | برادر زن | xosorbōra | خسربُره |
| sister-in-law (wife's side) | xāhar-zan | خواهر زن | xĕyāšna | خیاشنه |
| cat | gorba | گربه | pĕšak | پیشك |
| uncle | 'amō | عمو | kaka | كاكا |
| male cousin (father's side) | pasar 'amō xiyār | پسر عمو | bača-ye kaka | بچهٔ كاكا |
| female cousin (father's side) | doxtar 'amo | دختر عمو | doxtar-e kaka | دختر كاكا |
| child | farzand | فرزند | awlād/farzand | اولاد / فرزند |

# فصل هفتم

## CHAPTER SEVEN

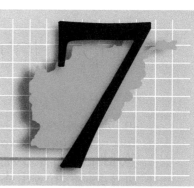

## جای زنده گی من

MY RESIDENCE

# IN THIS CHAPTER

## • وظایف Functions

*Describing your residence; Moving to a new place; Giving locations of rooms within a residence; Asking/giving directions; Describing a university/college campus; Comparing and contrasting one's home/campus to another; Reading and following directions; Talking about daily routine/activities*

## • تبصرهٔ فرهنگی Cultural Notes

*Afghan houses; Giving directions in Afghanistan; Traffic and traffic signs; Significance of directions in Afghan society*

## • دستور زبان Language Structure

*The suffix خانه; The verb نشستن; The verb کوچ کردن; Expressing wishes, wants and abilities; The conjunction بخاطریکه / چونکه; Adjectives describing places; Other prepositions and verbs*

## • مرور فصل Chapter Review

*Describing daily activities; Planning daily schedules; Talking about daily activities/ routines; Giving and receiving directions; Following directions*

## • لغات Vocabulary

*Review phrases and words used in this chapter*

## Chapter Introduction        معرفی فصل

In this chapter, you will learn to describe your residence, ask and give directions, talk about your university/college, and finally talk about your daily routines. Additionally, you will be able to compare and contrast your residence, college, and university with that of other places. By the end of this chapter, you should be able to obtain enough vocabulary in order to hold simple, short conversations about these topics.

ساحهٔ پوهنتون ما کلان است .
Our university campus is big.

من در آپارتمان میشینم .
I live in an apartment.

آدرس خانهٔ تان کجاست؟
Where is your home address?

# درس اول: من در آپارتمان میشینم.

## Lesson One: I live in an apartment.

In this section, you will learn how to tell people about your home and to describe the layout and interior. You will also learn about traditional Afghan homes.

Exercise 1: تمرین ۱:

A. You will hear نعیم describe his home on the audio recording. Listen to his description and find the proper term for each part of the house using the vocabulary table provided below. Then write the term for each part of the house on the blue line.

| garage | گراژ/گراج | kitchen | آشپزخانه | house | خانه |
| --- | --- | --- | --- | --- | --- |
| garden | باغچه | bathroom | تشناب | living room | اتاق نشیمن |
| pathway | راه روی | bath | حمام | bedroom | اتاق خواب |
| stairs | زینه | balcony/porch | برنده | dining room | طعام خانه |
| courtyard | صحن حویلی | tree | درخت | guest room | مهمان خانه |

B. Which of the places in the above table are your favorite? Circle them.

C. Now tell the class which places you have in your house or apartment.

D.     Compare your house or apartment to that of نعیم's house.

| خانهٔ نعیم | خانه شما |
|---|---|
| _____ | _____ |
| _____ | _____ |
| _____ | _____ |
| _____ | _____ |
| _____ | _____ |
| _____ | _____ |
| _____ | _____ |
| _____ | _____ |

E.     What do you generally do in the following places?

| | | |
|---|---|---|
| ۱ | اتاق نشیمن | _____ |
| ۲ | اتاق خواب | _____ |
| ۳ | مهمان خانه | _____ |
| ۴ | طعام خانه | _____ |
| ۵ | آشپزخانه | _____ |
| ۶ | حمام | _____ |

Exercise 2:  تمرین ۲:

A. Read the text and answer the questions that follow.

من سید شریف هستم، من و زنم در یک آپارتمان میشینیم. آپارتمان ما بسیار کلان است، آپارتمان ما دو منزل دارد. منزل اول آن یک اتاق نشیمن، دو اتاق خواب، یک تشناب و یک آشپز خانه دارد. حمام و تشناب آن یکجا است.

منزل دوم نیز مانند منزل اول است. آپارتمان ما گراژ ندارد. من اتاق نشیمن را بسیار خوش دارم، چونکه این اتاق بسیار کلان و آرام است، من در این اتاق کتاب میخوانم، تلویزیون سیل میکنم، چای مینوشم و با فامیلم صحبت میکنم.

| میشینیم | مانند | یکجا بودن | آرام |
|---|---|---|---|
| We live (literally 'to sit'). | like, same as | to be together | calm |

1. How many floors does Sharif's house have?

a) چار منزل   b) سه منزل   c) دو منزل   d) یك منزل

2. Which of the following places are together (in one place) in شریف's apartment?
   a) the kitchen and the living room
   b) the living room and the bedroom
   c) the shower and bathroom
   d) the guest room and living room

3. Which of the following places does NOT exist in شریف's apartment?

a) گراژ   b) آشپزخانه   c) اتاق نشیمن   d) اتاق خواب

4. Which room is very calm and big?

a) طعام خانه   b) اتاق نشیمن   c) اتاق خواب   d) مهمانخانه

B. What does شریف do in his living room? Mark the actions that he does.

کتاب خواندن   خواب شدن   صحبت میکند   تلویزیون سیل کردن   چای نوشیدن

_____   _____   _____   _____   _____

C. Write your own house or apartment's description. Describe how many floors and how many rooms your apartment or house has, and describe your favorite room. Then state the activities that you generally do in each room.

## 7.1 The Suffix خانه

The word خانه means 'room, house, and home'. This word comes at the end of nouns and adjectives and takes the place of a noun. For example:

| kitchen | آشپزخانه | cook | آشپز |
| guest room | مهمانخانه | guest | مهمان |
| storage room | پسخانه | behind | پس |

Exercise 3:    تمرین ۳:

Add the suffix خانه to the following words, and guess a meaning for each.

| | | book | کتاب | ۱ |
|---|---|---|---|---|
| | | medication | دوا | ۲ |
| | | food | طعام | ۳ |
| | | tea | چای | ۴ |
| | | health | شفا | ۵ |

Exercise 4:    تمرین ۴:

A. You will hear a conversation on the audio recording between میرویس and لیلا in which they are talking about their apartment. Listen and draw میرویَس's apartment.

Right side

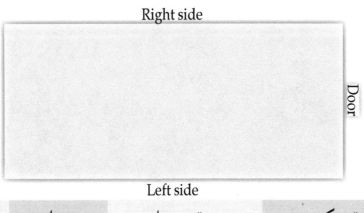

Left side

| سمت چپ | سمت راست | چی قسم جای | وقتیکه |
|---|---|---|---|
| left side | right side | What kind of place? | time adverb (when) |

B.  Listen to the conversation on the audio recording again. This time, using the table below, circle the rooms in میرویس's apartment.

| گراژ/گراج | اتاق خواب | آشپزخانه | اتاق نشیمن |
|---|---|---|---|
| برنده/ بالکین | تشناب صحن حویلی | باغچه | طعام خانه |
| پسخانه | زینه درخت | راه روی حمام | مهمان خانه |

C. Listen to the audio recording and this time mark "true" or "false" for the following statements.

| غلط | صحیح | |
|---|---|---|
| ____ | ____ | ۱  میرویس در یك آپارتمان زندگی میکند . |
| ____ | ____ | ۲  آپارتمان میرویس در پشت مکتب حبیبیه است. |
| ____ | ____ | ۳  آپارتمان میرویس چار منزل دارد . |
| ____ | ____ | ۴  میرویس در منزل سه زندگی میکنند . |
| ____ | ____ | ۵  اتاق خواب میرویس در سمت راست اتاق نشیمن است. |
| ____ | ____ | ۶  آپارتمان میرویس یك برنده دارد . |
| ____ | ____ | ۷  آشپزخانه در سمت راست است. |
| ____ | ____ | ۸  آپارتمان میرویس دو تشناب دارد . |

### 7.2 The Verb نشستن

The verb نشستن/شیشتن has the present stem شین/نشین which literally means 'to sit'. However, it can be used to ask: where do you live? For example:

| Function as (to live) | | Function as (to sit) | |
|---|---|---|---|
| I am living in an apartment. | من در آپارتمان میشینم. | I am sitting on the chair. | من بالای چوکی میشینم. |
| S/he is living in a dorm. | او در لیلیه میشینند . | S/he is sitting on the chair. | او بالاچوکی میشینند. |

Exercise 5: تمرین ۵:

A. Write the Dari equivalent of the following phrases.

| | |
|---|---|
| Where do you live? | ۱ |
| I live in a big house. | ۲ |
| S/he lives on the third floor of an apartment. | ۳ |
| We live in a hotel. | ۴ |
| They live in a bigger house. | ۵ |

B. Ask your classmate to describe his/her house or apartment. Be sure to ask the following questions.

| | |
|---|---|
| Where do you live? | شما در کجا میشینید؟ |
| Which floor do you live on? | شما در منزل چند میشینید؟ |
| How many rooms does your home/apartment have? | آپارتمان/خانهٔ تان چند اتاق دارد؟ |
| Describe your home/apartment. | آپارتمان/خانه تان را برایم توصیف کنید؟ |

C. While your partner is describing his/her house/apartment and the locations of the rooms, draw an image that comes to your mind about his/her place. Then have your partner check your work.

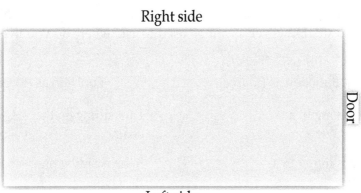

Right side

Left side

Door

## Cultural Note     تبصره فرهنگی

### Afghan houses

In Afghanistan, homes are similar to those in the US. However, the entire house is surrounded by walls and all houses have big entrance gates. Typically, the room that is closest to the entrance is for unknown (strange) guests. Then, there is a courtyard at the end which leads to the main rooms. There is also another guest room in the main living area which is dedicated to guests who are family members or friends. The bathroom and the kitchen are not inside the main living area, but are rather in a corner of the house, outside.

Exercise 6: تمرین ۶:

From what you've read in the cultural note above, and by looking at the picture which demonstrates a typical Afghan house, what differences can you find between an Afghan and an American house? Discuss the similarities and differences with a classmate.

Exercise 7: تمرین ۷:

A. You will hear میرویس describe his classroom on the audio recording. Listen carefully and put the following phrases in the appropriate box that you think best describes it.

۱   رنگ بام صنف ما سیاه است.

۲   رنگ دیوار های صنف ما یاسمنی است.

۳   رنگ سقف صنف ما سفید است.

۴   رنگ کف صنف ما آبی است.

۵   مساحت صنف ما ده متر مربع است.

B. Using the following words, describe your classroom or favorite room in your house.

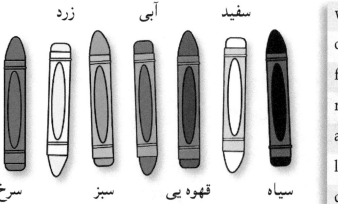

زرد        آبی        سفید

سرخ        سبز        قهوه یی        سیاه

| | |
|---|---|
| wall | دیوار |
| ceiling | سقف |
| floor | کف |
| roof | بام |
| area | مساحت |
| light | روشن |
| dark | تاریک |

Exercise 8: 🎧    تمرین ۸:

A. You will hear a conversation on the audio recording between **زرغونه** and **میرویس** in which they describe their favorite rooms. Listen and draw each room as they describe it.

| Was everything okay? | خیریت بود؟ |
| Yes, everything was okay. | بلی، خیریت بود. |
| to move | کوچ کردن |

B. 🎧 Now listen to the audio recording again, and this time mark "true" or "false" for the statements below.

| غلط | صحیح | | |
|---|---|---|---|
| ــــ | ــــ | ۱ | میرویس دیروز در صنف بود. |
| ــــ | ــــ | ۲ | میرویس به یک آپارتمان بسیار کوچک کوچ کرد. |
| ــــ | ــــ | ۳ | آپارتمان میرویس دو تشناب و دو آشپزخانه دارد. |
| ــــ | ــــ | ۴ | میرویس اتاق نشیمنش را بسیار خوش دارد. |
| ــــ | ــــ | ۵ | دروازه و کلکین هایی اتاق نشیمنش قهوه یی روشن است. |
| ــــ | ــــ | ۶ | کف اتاق نشیمن سفید روشن است. |
| ــــ | ــــ | ۷ | دیوارهای اتاق نشیمن سفید است. |
| ــــ | ــــ | ۸ | مساحت اتاق نشیمن پانزده متر مربع است. |
| ــــ | ــــ | ۹ | آشپزخانه آپارتمان میرویس با اتاق نشیمن یکجا است. |

C. 🤝 Now ask a classmate sitting next to you about the color of his/her favorite room.

## 7.3 The Verb کوچ کردن

The verb 'to move' کوچ کردن is particularly used for moving permanently from a house to another one. For example:

| | |
|---|---|
| Today, I am moving to a new house. | من امروز به خانه نو کوچ میکنم. |
| Today, we are moving to a new house. | ما امروز به خانه نو کوچ میکنیم. |
| Today, you are moving to a new house. | تو امروز به خانه نو کوچ میکنی. |
| Today, you are moving to a new house. | شما امروز به خانه نو کوچ میکنید. |
| Today, s/he is moving to a new house. | او امروز به خانه نو کوچ میکند. |
| Today, they are moving to a new house. | آنها امروز به خانه نو کوچ میکنند. |

If you use this verb for other proposes, e.g. moving from one spot to another, it would be wrong.

Exercise 9: تمرین ۹ :

A. Convert the following phrases to the past form.

| | |
|---|---|
| ۱ | من امروز به خانه نو کوچ میکنم. |
| ۲ | ما امروز به خانه نو کوچ میکنیم. |
| ۳ | تو امروز به خانه نو کوچ میکنی. |
| ۴ | شما امروز به خانه نو کوچ میکنید. |
| ۵ | او امروز به خانه نو کوچ میکند. |
| ۶ | آنها امروز به خانه نو کوچ میکنند. |

B. 🖊 Describe your favorite room. Be sure to describe the location, its color, and the activities that you generally do there, e.g. watch TV, cook, etc.

| | | |
|---|---|---|
| ــــــــــــ | مهمانخانه | ۱ |
| ــــــــــــ | تشناب | ۲ |
| ــــــــــــ | حمام | ۳ |
| ــــــــــــ | آشپز خانه | ۴ |
| ــــــــــــ | گراژ | ۵ |
| ــــــــــــ | اتاق خواب | ۶ |
| ــــــــــــ | باغچه گل | ۷ |
| ــــــــــــ | درخت | ۸ |

تمرین ۱۰: 🎧
Exercise 10:
A. You will hear a conversation on the audio recording between میرویس and زرغونه. Listen to their conversation carefully. Then look at the table that follows the conversation to write the exact number of the following items in Mirwais's house.

| تقریباً | متر مربع | جای شدن | گل |
|---|---|---|---|
| about | square meter | to be placed/to fit | flower |

B. 📖 What does شریف do in his living room? Mark the actions that he does.

| ۱ | خانه میرویس شان چی قسم خانه است؟ |
|---|---|
| الف- حویلی نو | ب- حویلی | ج- آپارتمان |

۲ خانه میرویس شان در کجا موقعیت دارد؟

الف - در بین یك كوچه   ب- در پهلوی سرك فرعی   ج - در پهلوی سرك عمومی

۳ دروازه حویلی میرویس شان چی رنگ است؟

الف - سرخ و آبی   ب- سرخ و سبز   ج- سرخ و گلابی   د- سرخ و سیاه

۴ زمین حویلی میرویس شان چند متر مربع است؟

الف- ۵۲۶   ب- ۵۶۲   ج-۵۳۶   د - ۵۲۷

۵ صحن حویلی میرویس چی دارد؟

الف - سه باغچه گل و دو درخت   ب- دو باغچه گل، سه درخت

۶ مهمانخانه ها در کجا موقعیت دارد؟

الف - در بین خانه و پیشروی حویلی   ب - در بین خانه و در پشت حویلی

# درس دوم: ساحهٔ پوهتنون کابل

## Lesson Two: Kabul University campus

In this section, you will read about and describe a college campus, and you will learn to express wishes, wants, and abilities.

Exercise 1:  تمرین ۱:

A. Look at the map of an Afghan university campus, and mark the places that you have in your university.

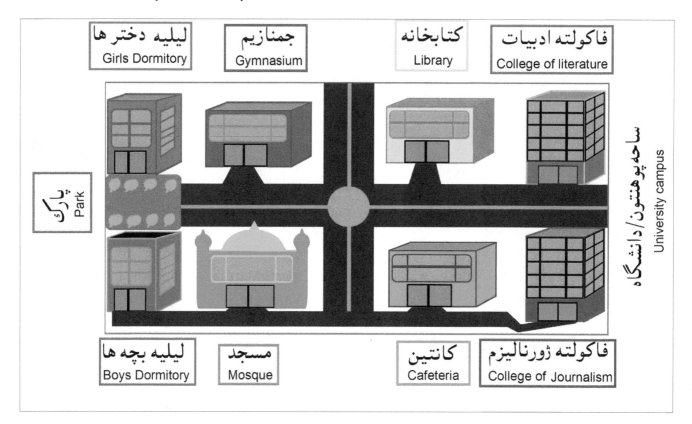

| لیلیه دخترها<br>Girls Dormitory | جمنازیم<br>Gymnasium | کتابخانه<br>Library | فاکولته ادبیات<br>College of literature |

پارک
Park

ساحهٔ پوهتنون / دانشگاه
University campus

| لیلیه بچه ها<br>Boys Dormitory | مسجد<br>Mosque | کانتین<br>Cafeteria | فاکولته ژورنالیزم<br>College of Journalism |

B. Now, with a partner, compare your campus with the Afghan campus and say what places you have in your campus as well as the places you don't have.

Exercise 2: تمرین ۲:

A. You will hear Farid's conversation on the audio recording as he is trying to describe his university campus to his sister زرغونه. Listen and note the questions that are exchanged between them.

| لابراتوار | میدان ورزشی |
|---|---|
| lab | sport field |

B. Listen to the audio recording again. This time choose the best answer for the following.

1. Which of the following best describes the size of the university?
   a) small   b) large   c) among the largest in the country   d) it's the biggest in the country

2. This university has seven ...
   a) labs.          b) colleges.          c) libraries.          d) gymnasiums.

3. Which college library is bigger than the others?
   a) medical          b) engineering          c) literature          d) journalism

4. Does Farid like his university campus?
   a) yes          b) no

Exercise 3: 📖 ٣ تمرین :

A. Read Kabul University's description as presented in the map in Exercise 1. Then complete the sentences that have been started for you.

ساحهٔ پوهنتون کابل

پوهنتون کابل اولین و بزرگترین پوهنتون در افغانستان میباشد. این پوهنتون چارده پوهنځی یا فاکولته دارد . این پوهنتون یک لیلیه برای دخترها و یک لیلیه برای بچه ها دارد . هر لیلیه یک آشپزخانه، یک طعام خانه، یک مسجد ، تشناب ها و حمام های مدرن دارد . این پوهنتون پارک های سر سبز، کتابخانه، لابراتوار، جمنازیم ، کانتین، تالار کانفرانس و میدان های ورزشی دارد .

1. How many colleges does Kabul University have?

2. How many dorms does it have?

3. What amenities do the dorms have?

4. What else did you learn about the university?

B. 📖 Which one of the following places does your campus have? Mark each one and write a sentence about each. The first example is done for you.

| | | | |
|---|---|---|---|
| پوهنتون ما دو جمنازیم دارد . | ☐ | جمنازیم | ۱ |
| | ☐ | فاکولته، پوهنځی، دانشکده | ۲ |
| | ☐ | کتابخانه | ۳ |
| | ☐ | تالار کانفرانس | ۴ |
| | ☐ | لیله | ۵ |
| | ☐ | کانتین | ۶ |

Exercise 4: تمرین ۴:

A. You will hear زرغونه describe the location of her college. Listen and answer the following questions.

| | |
|---|---|
| ۱ | زرغونه محصل کدام فاکولته است؟ |
| ۲ | این فاکولته در کجا موقعیت دارد؟ |
| ۳ | این فاکولته چند منزل دارد؟ |
| ۴ | این فاکولته کدام جای ها را دارد؟ |
| ۵ | دیوار های این فاکولته چی رنگ است؟ |
| ۶ | بام این فاکولته چی رنگ است؟ |
| ۷ | صنف زرغونهٔ چی رنگ است؟ |

B. Now read the description that زرغونه gives about her college and check your answers.

نامم زرغونه است، من محصل فاکولتهٔ انجینری هستم، فاکولته انجینری در غرب ساحه پوهنتون کابل موقعیت دارد، این فاکولته در پیشرویی فاکولته زبانشناسی موقعیت دارد. این فاکولته پنج منزل دارد که در هر منزلش ۵ اتاق است.
فاکولته انجینر دو لابراتوار، یک کتابخانه، یک تالار کانفرانس، یک جمنازیم، و یک کانتین دارد. کانتین در منزل اول موقعیت دارد.
دیوار های این فاکولته رنگ آبی دارد و بام آن رنگ سیاه دارد، صنف ما در منزل دوم این فاکولته است، رنگ دیوارها و سقف صنف ما زرد است اما رنگ کف صنف ما خاکستری است.

C. Describe the college you are studying in. You may use some of your sentences from Exercise 1B.

Exercise 5: تمرین ۵:

A. Listen to the conversation on the audio recording and make three questions about this conversation.

١ _____

٢ _____

٣ _____

B. Listen to the recording one more time. This time, rewrite the questions that are exchanged by speakers.

C. Now check your work with a partner and practice posing questions to each other.

| میخواهم | چرا | بخاطریکه |
|---|---|---|
| I want to | why | because |

D. Now listen to the recording again, and check "true" or "false" for each statement below.

| غلط | صحیح | | |
|---|---|---|---|
| _____ | _____ | آن زن محصل فاکولته ادبیات دری است. | ١ |
| _____ | _____ | چارراهی در آخر سرک است. | ٢ |
| _____ | _____ | پارک در سمت شمال چارراهی است. | ٣ |
| _____ | _____ | برادر زن در مهمانخانه است. | ۴ |
| _____ | _____ | صنف سال دوم در منزل سوم است. | ۵ |
| _____ | _____ | کتابخانه در منزل چهار در پشت راه زینه است. | ۶ |
| _____ | _____ | پوهنځی ادبیات پشتو در همان تعمیر است. | ٧ |
| _____ | _____ | برادر زن محصل سال دوم ادبیات دری است. | ٨ |

## 7.4 Express Wishes, Wants, and Abilities

When you talk about things you want to do or like to do and you want to express your ability, present the main verb in the subjunctive mood. The subjunctive mood of a verb in present tense loses its prefix می and gets replaced with the prefix بـ . For example:

| subjunctive mood | present form | the verb |
|---|---|---|
| برود | میرود | رفتن (رو) |
| بخواند | میخواند | خواندن (خوان) |

When you want to express wants, use the helping verb (خواه) خواستن. For expressing abilities, use the helping verb (توان) توانستن. In both cases, use the relative pronoun که to combine this verb with the main verb. For example:

| Translation | Dari examples | The verbs |
|---|---|---|
| I want to go to the gymnasium. | من میخواهم که به جمنازیم بروم. | خواستن(خواه)/(رفتن) برو |
| We want to visit Indiana University. | ما میخواهیم که پوهنتون اندیانا را ببینم. | خواستن (خواه)/ (دیدن) ببین |
| S/he wants to come to our dormitory. | او میخواهد که به لیلیه ما بیاید. | خواستن (خواه)/ (آمدن) بیآی |
| They could study in the library. | آنها میتوانند که در کتابخانه درس بخوانند. | توانستن (توان)/(خواندن) بخوان |
| You could buy an apartment. | تو میتوانی که یک آپارتمان بخری. | توانستن (توان)/(خریدن) بخر |
| You could write an email message. | شما میتوانید که ایمیل نوشته کنید. | توانستن (توان)/(نوشته کردن) نوشته کن |

Also, the other verbs could be used as helping verbs in the same structure. For example:

| | | | |
|---|---|---|---|
| I would like to study in the library. | من خوش دارم که در کتابخانه درس بخوانم. | to like | خوش داشتن |
| I am going to study in the library. | من میروم که در کتابخانه درس بخوانم. | to go | رفتن |

Remember that, like English, the verb رفتن in this structure functions in the future tense.

Exercise 6: 📖 تمرین ۶ :

A. میرویس wrote the following email message to his best friend in which he describes his university campus and his activities there. Read the text, underline the helping verbs, and circle the main verbs.

---

فرستنده: میرویس
گیرنده: فرید
موضوع: فاکولتهٔ ژورنالیزم

دوست عزیزم فرید جان سلام، میخواهم که برای شما در بارهٔ فاکولتهٔ ژورنالیزم نوشته کنم، فاکولتهٔ ژورنالیزم کابل بسیار کلان است، من در این فاکولتهٔ درس میخوانم. فاکولتهٔ ما در پهلوی فاکولته ادبیات است، این فاکولته دو لابراتوار، دو کتابخانه، یک کانتین، یک میدان ورزشی، یک تالار کانفرانس، بسیت صنف درسی، و یک پارک بسیار کلان دارد.

شاگردان این فاکولته میتوانند که تا ساعت هفت شام در کتابخانه درس بخوانند، و میتوانند که در میدان ورزشی آن والیبال، باسکتبال و فوتبال بازی کنند.

من خوش دارم که در اوقات فراغت به پارک فاکولته بروم، چونکه پارک فاکولته ما بسیار سر سبز است. خلاصه فاکولتهٔ ما بسیار قشنگ و زیبا است. فردا جمعه است، من و شریف میرویم که در میدان ورزشی والیبال کنیم. آیا شما هم پوهنتون تان را خوش دارید؟

لطفاً برایم در بارهٔ پوهنتون تان نوشته کنید.
با احترام دوست تان میرویس

---

| با احترام | خلاصه | زیبا | اوقات فراغت | قشنگ | در بارهٔ |
|---|---|---|---|---|---|
| with respect | in short, summary | beautiful | free times | beautiful | about |

B. 📖 Read the text again, and this time mark "true" or "false" for the following statements.

| غلط | صحیح | |
|:---:|:---:|---|
| ☐ | ☐ | ۱ میرویس میخواهد که در بارهٔ فاکولته ادبیات نوشته کند . |
| ☐ | ☐ | ۲ شاگردان میتوانند که تا ساعت هفت صبح در کتابخانه درس بخوانند . |
| ☐ | ☐ | ۳ آنها همچنان میتوانند که در میدان ورزشی این فاکولته باسکتبال، والیبال و فوتبال کنند . |
| ☐ | ☐ | ۴ میرویس خوش دارد که در اوقات فراغت به کتابخانه برود . |
| ☐ | ☐ | ۵ فردا میرویس و شریف میروند که والیبال بازی کنند . |

C. 📝 Answer the following questions in Dari using helping verbs (توان) توانستن.

| | |
|---|---|
| 1. What could you do in the library? | |
| 2. What could she do in the gymnasium? | |
| 3. What could they do at the university? | |
| 4. What could we do in the dormitory? | |
| 5. What do you want to do this evening? | |
| 6. What do you want to do this afternoon? | |
| 7. What do you want to do tonight? | |
| 8. What do you want to do in an hour? | |
| 9. What do you want to do in class? | |
| 10. Where do you like to exercise? | |
| 11. Where do you like to have lunch? | |
| 12. Where do you like to sleep? | |
| 13. Where do you like to study? | |
| 14. Where are you going to study? | |
| 15. Where is she going to watch a movie? | |
| 16. What are you going to watch at the movies? | |
| 17. When are they going to work out? | |

D.  In the above email message میرویس asks his friend فرید about his university, and he says he likes it there. Now, on behalf of فرید, reply to his email message and provide the information.

فرستنده:
گیرنده:
موضوع:

## 7.5 The Conjunction 'because' بخاطریکه/چونکه

The conjunction (because) بخاطریکه / چونکه connects a subordinate clause to a main clause, and it is used to express the cause or reason of an action expressed in the main clause.

The subordinate clause often begins with the conjunction (because) بخاطریکه / چونکه and follows the main clauses and, in writing, the two clauses are separated by a comma. For example:

من در کتابخانه کتاب میخوانم، بخاطریکه آنجا آرام است.

I'm studying at the library, because it is quiet there.

The question word 'why' چرا is one of the five Ws which requires a detailed answer, and the answer mostly starts with the conjunction 'because' بخاطریکه / چونکه. For example:

Why are you not going to the gym?      چرا جمنازیم نمیروید؟

Because I am studying.      بخاطریکه درس میخوانم.

Exercise 7:    تمرین ۷:

A. Answer the following questions.

| | |
|---|---|
| ۱ | چرا شما زبان دری میخوانید؟ |
| ۲ | چرا در این پوهنتون درس میخوانید؟ |
| ۳ | چرا به کتابخانه رفتید؟ |
| ۴ | چرا دیروز ورزش نکردید؟ |
| ۵ | چرا هر روز قهوه مینوشید؟ |

B. Look at the following sentences and find the subordinate and main clauses. Then combine them using the conjunction چونکه /بخاطریکه.

| | |
|---|---|
| ۱ | من محصل هستم / من هرروز به پوهنتون میروم. |
| ۲ | من به جمنازیم نمیروم/ ورزش را دوست ندارم. |
| ۳ | ما در پوهنتون اندیانا درس میخوانیم/ ساحه پوهنتو کلان دارد . |
| ۴ | یك كتاب ضرورت دارم / من به كتابخانه میروم. |
| ۵ | دیروز ورزش نكردم/ مانده بودم. |
| ۶ | قهوه را خوش ندارم / من قهوه نمینوشم. |

Exercise 8: تمرین ۸:

A. You will hear on the audio recording a conversation between کریم and بصیر. Listen and choose the best answer for each of the following questions.

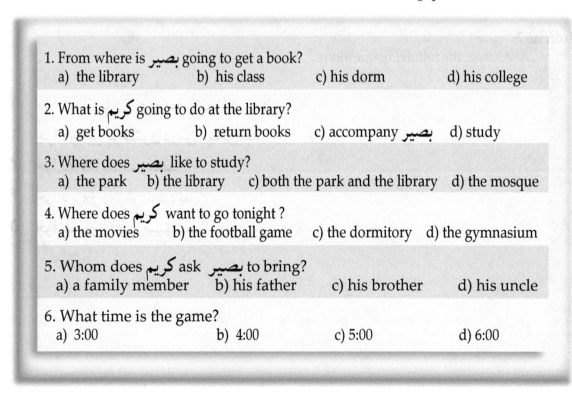

1. From where is بصیر going to get a book?
   a) the library       b) his class       c) his dorm       d) his college

2. What is کریم going to do at the library?
   a) get books       b) return books       c) accompany بصیر       d) study

3. Where does بصیر like to study?
   a) the park    b) the library    c) both the park and the library    d) the mosque

4. Where does کریم want to go tonight ?
   a) the movies       b) the football game       c) the dormitory    d) the gymnasium

5. Whom does کریم ask بصیر to bring?
   a) a family member    b) his father    c) his brother    d) his uncle

6. What time is the game?
   a) 3:00                 b) 4:00                 c) 5:00                 d) 6:00

B. 🎧 Listen to the conversation again and mark the questions that are exchanged between کریم and بصیر.

| | | |
|---|---|---|
| ☐ کجا میروند؟ | ☐ | کجا میروید؟ |
| ☐ آیا من میتوانم که برادرم را نیاورم؟ | ☐ | کجا میرویم؟ |
| ☐ بازی ساعت چند بجه است؟ | ☐ | آیا من میتوانم که برادرم را بیاورم؟ |
| ☐ آیا شما میخواهید که همراه من بروید؟ | ☐ | آیا شما خواهید که همراه من بروید؟ |
| ☐ شما در کجا خوش دارید که درس بخوانید؟ | ☐ | آیا شما میخواهید که همراه من بروید؟ |
| ☐ شما اکثراً در کجا خوش دارید که درس بخوانید؟ | ☐ | شما معمولاً در کجا خوش دارید که درس بخوانید؟ |

C. 🤝 Now practice the same questions with a classmate.

تمرین ۹:

Exercise 9: 🎧

A. زرغونه is studying at Kabul University and she is describing her campus to her brother فرید, who is studying at Herat University. Then فرید describes his university campus. Listen carefully to their conversation on the audio recording and note the differences between the two campuses.

| جداگانه | نو | تعمیر |
|---|---|---|
| separate | new | building |

B. 🎧 Now listen and mark "true" or "false" for each of the following statements.

| غلط | صحیح | | |
|---|---|---|---|
| ☐ | ☐ | ۱ | زرغونه هفتهٔ نو به پوهنتون هرات میرود . |
| ☐ | ☐ | ۲ | برادر زرغونه در کابل است . |
| ☐ | ☐ | ۳ | پوهنتون هرات دوازده فاکولته دارد . |
| ☐ | ☐ | ۴ | زرغونه ساعت ۱۱ صبح روز شنبه به هرات میرسد . |
| ☐ | ☐ | ۵ | زرغونه محصل فاکولتهٔ ادبیات است . |

## 7.6 Adjectives Describing Places

In order to describe places, use the following adjectives:

| wide/extensive | وسیع | new | نو |
|---|---|---|---|
| high, tall | بلند | new | جدید |
| green | سرسبز | old | کهنه |
| modern | مدرن، عصری | ancient | قدیمی |

Exercise 10:  تمرین ۱۰ :

A. **میرویس** wrote the following email message to his best friend in which he describes his university campus and his activities there. Read the text, underline the helping verbs, and circle the main verbs.

فرستنده :زرغونه
گیرنده :لیلا
موضوع: پوهنتون هرات

دوست عزیزم لیلا جان سلام، من دیروز ساعت ۱۰ صبح به هرات رسیدم، در اینجا من با برادرم در یك خانه زندگی میکنم. خانهٔ که ما میشینیم، دو اتاق خواب عصری ، یك اتاق نشیمن عصری ، یك دهلیز کلان دو تشناب، یك حمام و یك آشپز خانه مدرن دارد . این خانه نو است و رنگ سفید دارد من این خانه را بسیار خوش دارم.

من و برادرم دیروز ساعت هشت به پوهنتون رفتیم بخاطریکه صنف هایم را ببینم. پوهنتون هرات یك پوهنتون نو است، تعمیر های بلند  دارد . این پوهنتون را امریکایی ها ساختند ، ساحه این پوهنتون بسیار وسیع نیست و از ساحه پوهنتون کابل خوردتر است. این پوهنتون یك پارك سرسبز  دارد ، یك جمنازیم و یك کانتین کلان و مدرن نیز دارد . من میخواهم که  در جمنازیم این پوهنتون ورزش کنم اما برادرم میخواهد که در پارك ورزش کند. فردا جمعه است  و ما میرویم که به پارك شیدایی برویم. و در آنجا میخواهیم غذا بپزیم و  استراحت کنیم. لطفاً برایم در باره ساحهٔ پوهنتون تان نوشته کنید و آنرا تشریح کنید .

تشکر
خدا حافظ
دوستت زرغونه

B.  Read the above text again. This time, answer the following questions.

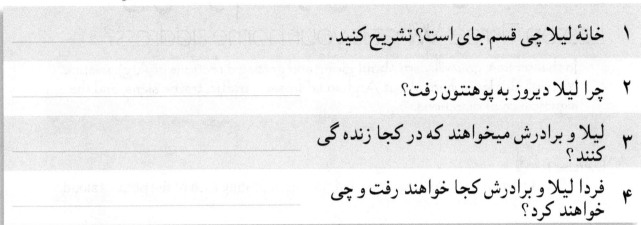

۱   خانهٔ لیلا چی قسم جای است؟ تشریح کنید .

۲   چرا لیلا دیروز به پوهنتون رفت؟

۳   لیلا و برادرش میخواهند که در کجا زنده گی کنند؟

۴   فردا لیلا و برادرش کجا خواهند رفت و چی خواهند کرد؟

C.  Convert the above questions to the second person. Then pose those questions to a classmate. Your partner will answer and give information about him- or herself.

# درس سوم: آدرس خانهٔ تان کجاست؟
## Lesson Three: What is your home address?

In this section, you will learn about giving and getting directions in Afghanistan. You will also learn more about Afghan addresses, traffic, traffic signs, and the significance of directions.

Exercise 1: تمرین ۱:

A.   Listen to the following terms and practice repeating each of the phrases aloud.

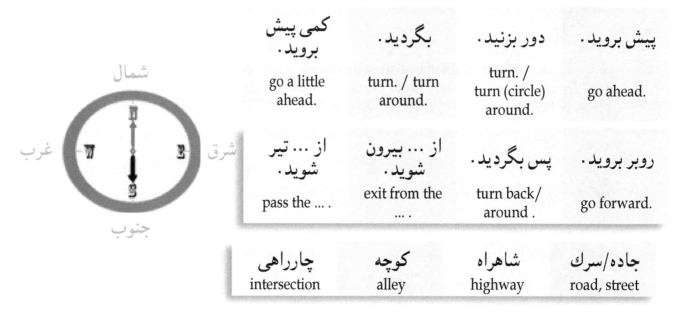

| کمی پیش بروید. | بگردید. | دور بزنید. | پیش بروید. |
|---|---|---|---|
| go a little ahead. | turn. / turn around. | turn. / turn (circle) around. | go ahead. |
| از ... تیر شوید. | از ... بیرون شوید. | پس بگردید. | روبر بروید. |
| pass the ... . | exit from the ... . | turn back/ around . | go forward. |

| چارراهی | کوچه | شاهراه | جاده/سرك |
|---|---|---|---|
| intersection | alley | highway | road, street |

B.   If you want to give someone directions from the university to the hotel, which phrases would you use? Put those phrases together and then ask your classmate to direct you there. Listen to him/her and check your work.

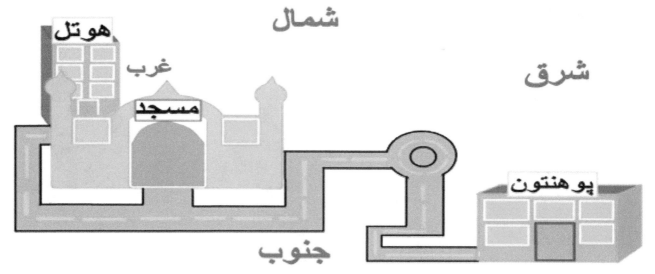

C.  Now you will hear two conversations on the audio recording about the directions in the following pictures. They're marked with green lines. Listen and mark the conversation that the audio is describing.

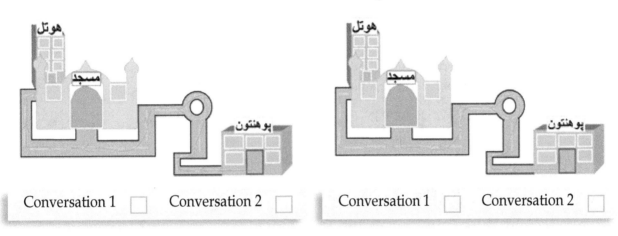

Conversation 1 ☐    Conversation 2 ☐        Conversation 1 ☐    Conversation 2 ☐

D. Now look at the following conversations and check your work.

| الف  ببخشید ، مسجد در کجا است؟ | الف  ببخشید، هوتل در کجا است؟ |
|---|---|
| ب  مسجد ؟ | ب  هوتل؟ |
| الف  بلی! | الف  بلی! |
| ب  از پوهنتون بیرون شوید ، روبرو بروید ، باز سمت راست دور بزنید ، کمی پیش بروید باز به دست راست درو بزن، مستقیم پیش بروید ، در چار راهی به سمت چپ دور بزنید ، کمی پیش بروید باز به سمت چپ بگردید، روبر بروید ، مسجد در دست چپ تان است. | ب  از پوهنتون بیرون شوید، روبرو بروید ، باز سمت راست دور بزنید ، کمی پیش بروید باز به دست راست درو بزن، مستقیم پیش بروید ، در چار راهی به سمت چپ دور بزنید ، کمی پیش بروید باز به سمت چپ بگردید، روبر بروید ، از مسجد تیر شوید ، به دست راست بگردید و کمی پیش بروید ، هوتل در پشت مسجد است. |
| الف  تشکر | الف  تشکر |

## 7.7 The Preposition That Changes the Direction of the Verbs

1- The preposition 'from' از comes before some verbs and shows that the object is moving away from a place, thing, or person that was near to it before. For example:

| | |
|---|---|
| to exit, to come out | بیرون شدن (بیرون شو) |
| Exit the university. | از پوهنتون بیرون شوید . |

| | |
|---|---|
| to get out | برآمدن (بر آی) |
| Get out of the university. | از پوهنتون برآیید . |

2- The preposition به 'to' comes before some verbs and shows that the object is getting closer to a place, thing, or person. For example:

| | |
|---|---|
| to enter, to get in | درون شدن (درون شو) |
| Enter (to) the university. | به پوهنتون داخل شوید . |

| | |
|---|---|
| to get in | درآمدن (در آی) |
| Get into the university. | به پوهنتون میوند درآیید . |

Exercise 2: تمرین ۲:

Look at the following pictures and make a sentence for each one in Dari. Use the verbs above.

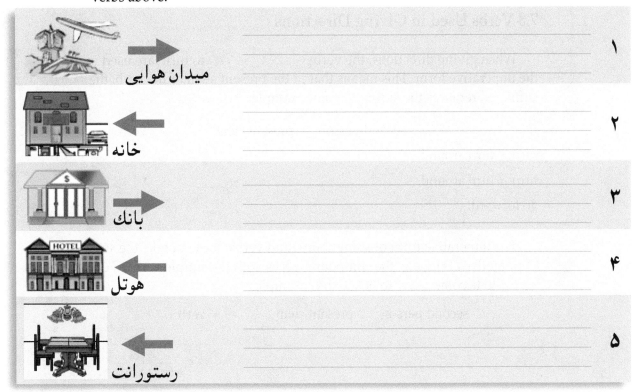

Exercise 3: تمرین ۳:

A. You will hear another conversation on the audio recording between two people. Listen, and follow the directions. Meanwhile, draw an arrow from the starting point to the end point.

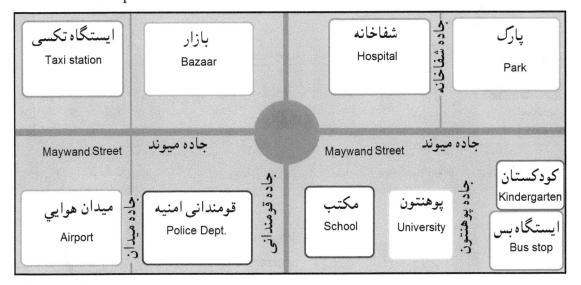

B. Now with a partner, take turns asking each other the address of any place in the map above. Then create a dialogue in which you give directions to at least four places on the map.

## 7.8 Verbs Used in Giving Directions

When giving directions, the verbs گشتن، دور زدن 'to turn' are used in the imperative form. This means that in the present stem of the verb, the suffix 'بـ' replaces the suffix می . For example:

|  | second person | present stem | verb |
|---|---|---|---|
| turn. / turn around. | دور بزنید. | دور میزن | دور زدن(دور زن) |
| turn. / turn around. | بگردید. | میگرد | گشتن (گرد) |
| go forward. | پیش بروید. | پیش میرو | پیش رفتن(پیش رو) |

The imperative form of some compound verbs does not take the suffix 'بـ' in modern Dari, e.g. the compound verbs with the simple verb 'to do' کردن , 'to become شدن' to be'. Other examples:

|  | second person | present stem | verb |
|---|---|---|---|
|  | تیر شوید. | تیر شو | تیر شدن |
|  | بیرون شوید. | بیرون شو | بیرون شدن |
|  | داخل شوید. | داخل شو | داخل شدن |

Exercise 4:   تمرین ۴:

Your classmate is in the cafeteria but wants to go to the gymnasium. Give him/her directions on how to get there. Use the verbs and phrases that you've already learned.

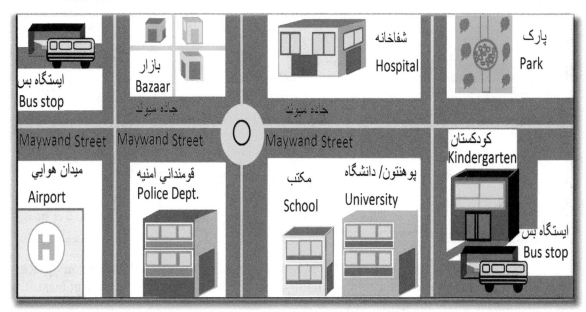

## Cultural Note تبصرهٔ فرهنگی

### Giving directions in Afghanistan

Finding addresses in Afghanistan can at times be tricky and very different from finding them in the US or other countries.

In Afghanistan, there are no zip codes, house numbers, or street names. Therefore, when giving directions, Afghans refer to an address based on its location near major landmarks, e.g. a university, market, or mosque. Also, directions are given using the directional locations (North, South, East, or West) and distance, which is measured in kilometers.

Kabul, Kandahar, Balkh, Jalalabad, and Herat cities are exceptions to this rule. This is because the main streets do have signs and names today. However, many Afghans still do not use these signs, but rather use the traditional ways of giving directions.

Exercise 5: تمرین ۵:

A. You will hear a dialogue on the audio recording between two men. Listen and choose the best answer for each of the questions below.

1. Which address does the first speaker ask for?
   a) college          b) university          c) airport          d) bus stop

2. According to the 2nd speaker, which direction does the first speaker go?
   a) north          b) south          c) east          d) west

3. What will the first speaker see on his left side after going about 5 minutes?
   a) the taxi station    b) an intersection    c) a road          d) a bus station

4. What should the first speaker do in order to get to his final destination?
   a) take the bus      b) take a taxi      c) take the train      d) walk

B. With a partner, create a similar dialogue giving directions in colloquial Dari.

| The word طور means "way, manner" and is widely used in the following compounds. | how | چطور | چی + طور |
| | in this very way, like this | همینطور | همین + طور |
| | in that very way, like that | همانطور | همان + طور |

Exercise 6: تمرین ۶:

Write the Dari equivalent of the following phrases.

| go straight ahead this way for 2 minutes, and then turn left | |
| go straight ahead that way for 2 miles, and then turn right | |
| go a little bit up this way, and then turn left | |

Exercise 7:  تمرین ۷ :
Read the following directions and draw the route on each map.

۱ الف:- ببخشید بازار در کجاست؟

ب:- از استیدیم بیرون شوید ، ۵۰۰ متر پیش بروید ، باز به دست راست دور بزنید تقریباً ۱۰ دقیقه که بروید به یک چاراهی میرسید ، در چار راهی به دست راست بگردید ، در همین سرک در پیشرویی مسجد بازار است.

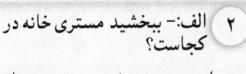

۲ الف:- ببخشید مستری خانه در کجاست؟

ب:- از مسجد تیر شوید ، به دست راست دور بزنید ، رو برو بروید و از چارراهی تیر شوید ، از چار راهی که تیر شدید در دست راست مستری خانه است.

۳ الف:- ببخشید مسجد در کجاست؟

ب:- از بازار بیرون شوید ، در رو بروی تان مسجد است.

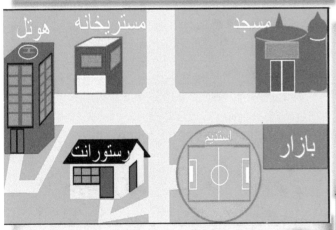

۴ الف:- ببخشید رستورانت در کجاست؟

ب:- از استیدیم بیرون شوید ، رو برو بروید و از چار راهی تیر شوید ، تقریباً پنج دقیقه پیش بروید ، باز به دست راست دور بزنید ، در آخر سرک رستورانت است.

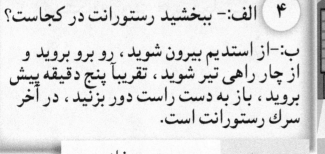

| مستری خانه | مسجد |
|---|---|
| workshop; auto shop | mosque |

الف: ببخشید ، هوتل در کجاست؟

ب:- از رستورانت بیرون شوید ، روبرو بروید ، باز به دست چپ دور بزن.  کمی پیش بروید به یك چار راهی میرسید . در چار راهی باز هم به دست چپ بگردید . تقریبا پنج دقیقه که بروی باز به یك چار راهی دیگر میرسید ، باز هم به دست چپ دور بزنید . در آخر همین سرك در دست چپ هوتل است.

۵

تمرین ۸:    Exercise 8:

A. Listen to the conversation on the audio recording and, write down the names of the places you hear.

B.    Listen to the audio recording again and this time, answer the following questions.

۱    جاوید درکجا میشیند؟

۲    ایستگاهٔ موتر های کارته نو درکجاست؟

۳    ایستگاهٔ سرویس ها درکجاست؟

Exercise 9:  ٩: تمرين

    A. Take turns with a classmate asking for directions to your dorms. Write down the given directions.

B. 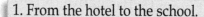 Look at the places given. Then ask a partner to direct you to one of those places. Switch roles and repeat the exercise.

| |
|---|
| 1. From the hotel to the school. |
| 2. From the mosque to the store. |
| 3. From the store to the university. |
| 4. From the mosque to the hotel. |

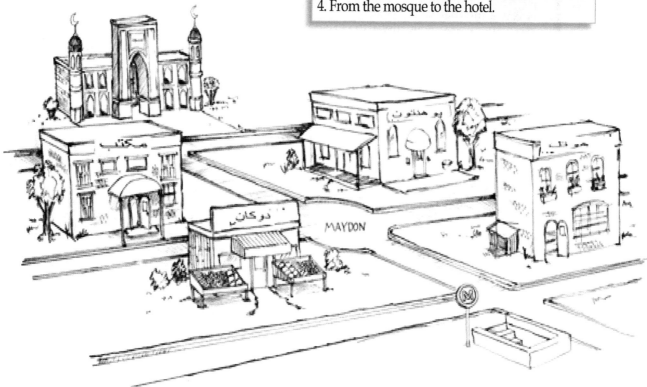

Cultural Note تبصرهٔ فرهنگی

## Traffic and traffic signs

When driving in Afghanistan, you will find that the traffic signs are very much the same as those in the US. There are even a lot of similarities in the actual rules and regulations of traffic in Afghanistan. However, local people don't typically adhere to traffic rules and regulations. In fact, running red lights, entering one-way roads, and making illegal U-turns are very common in most city streets of Afghanistan.

Some other differences:

• Honking at someone several times is not considered rude. You will hear a lot of people honking at each other.
• Most streets don't have traffic lights. On busy streets that don't have traffic lights or roundabouts, you will often see a traffic cop standing in the middle of the road directing cars.
• Due to small roads and big crowds, a distance that generally takes 30 minutes to travel via car in the US will probably take you approximately 1 to 2 hours. Thus, if you have a meeting or need to get to a place across town by a specific time, it is always a good idea to leave well in advance.

Rush hours are typically at 8:00 am, 12:00 pm, and 4:00 pm.

## Cultural Note تبصرهٔ فرهنگی

### Significance of directions in Afghan society

In Afghanistan, the majority of people believe in standard religious regulations and superstitions. Among these are some beliefs about the significance of certain directions. For example, the West is considered to be the direction of prayer, since Mecca (in Saudi Arabia) is located to the West. This is always why, when sleeping, people lie with their heads toward the West and their feet towards the East. If someone sleeps in the opposite position, Afghans say that ghosts will haunt that individual. Although not many people actually believe in that superstition, they do still sleep with their heads toward the West, as a sign of respect to Mecca.

If you are going to work in Afghanistan for a construction company or team, and your task is to build a mosque, you should always remember that it is very important for the prayer direction to be facing the West.

Also, when installing bathrooms in a building, know that the bathrooms must always face the North or South direction.

# مرور فصل هفتم
## Review of Chapter Seven

In this section you will review the vocabulary, phrases, grammar, and cultural elements that you learned throughout the chapter.

Exercise 1:    تمرین ۱:

A. Answer the following questions.

| | |
|---|---|
| ۱ | شما در کجا نان پخته میکنند؟ |
| ۲ | شما با فامیل تان در کجا نان میخورید؟ |
| ۳ | شما با فامیل تان در کجا تلویزیون سیل میکنید؟ |
| ۴ | شما درکجا خواب میشوید؟ |
| ۵ | شما درکجا جان تان را میشویید؟ |
| ۶ | شما از کدام راه به خانه داخل میشوید؟ |
| ۷ | شما موتر تان را در کجا پارک میکنید؟ |

B. The following is taken from زرغونه's journal as are her important activities for the current week. Look at the chart, and write an appropriate Dari answer for each question.

| | | |
|---|---|---|
| شنبه | کتابخانه ساعت ۱۱ | ساعت ۱۲ کانتین، نان چاشت با دوستم لیلا |
| یکشنبه | ساعت ۲ ورزش در جمنازیم | ساعت ۵ کتابخانه کارخانگی |
| دوشنبه | ساعت ۲ بعد از ظهر در لابراتوار کار کنم. | ساعت ۹ شب اخبار |
| سه شنبه | ساعت۱۲ بعد از ظهر در پارک ورزش کنم. | ساعت ۴ دیگر کارخانگی با دوستم لیلا در خانه اش |
| چارشنبه | ساعت ۱۰ شب تلیفون به پدرم | |
| پنجشنبه | ساعت ۸ تا ۱۲ ظهر کار | |
| جمعه | ساعت ۱۰ میله | |

| What will Zarghuna do at 11:00 a.m. on Saturday? | _____ | ۱ |
| What will she do at 2:00 p.m. on Sunday? | _____ | ۲ |
| Where will she go at 12:00 noon on Saturday? | _____ | ۳ |
| Why will she go to her friend's house at 4:00 p.m. on Tuesday? | _____ | ۴ |
| What does she want to do on Monday at 2:00 p.m.? | _____ | ۵ |
| What does she want to do on Wednesday at 10:00 p.m.? | _____ | ۶ |

Exercise 2:     تمرین ۲:
What do you generally do in the following places?

| _____ | classroom | صنف درسی |
| _____ | dormitory | لیله |
| _____ | gymnasium | جمنازیم |
| _____ | park | پارک |
| _____ | library | کتابخانه |
| _____ | laboratory | لابراتوار |

Exercise 3: تمرین ۳:

A. Which one of the following descriptions best describes the directions from point A to point B, as marked with arrows in the picture below?

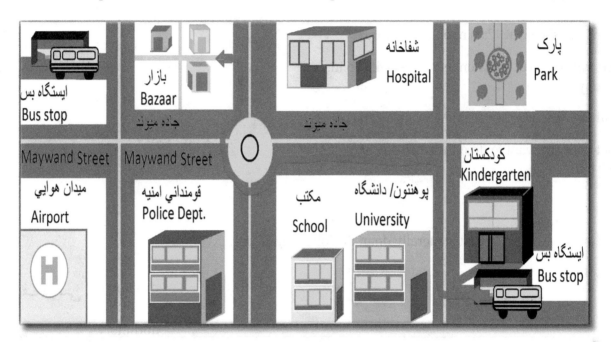

| | |
|---|---|
| از ایستگاه بس تیر شوید ، به سمت چپ دور بزنید ، روبرو بروبید در جادهٔ میوند به سمت باز به سمت چپ دور بزنید ، همانطور پیش بروید درچاراهی بسمت راست بگردید ، ازچار راهی تیر شوید بازار در سمت چپ تان در پشت شفاخانه است. □ | از ایستگاه بس تیر شوید ، به سمت راست دور بزنید ، روبرو بروبید در جادهٔ میوند باز به سمت چپ دور بزنید ، همانطور پیش بروید درچاراهی بسمت راست بگردید ، ازچار راهی تیر شوید بازار در سمت چپ تان در پیشرویی شفاخانه است. □ |

B. ✋ Ask for the following direction from a classmate using the above map.

| |
|---|
| 1. From the police department to the university |
| 2. From the university to the hospital |
| 3. From the hospital to the park |
| 4. From the park to the airport |

Exercise 4: تمرین ۴:

Your friend comes to America; he is at the airport and wants directions to your home. Give him directions to your home but, additionally, give him your address and some specific information about your house so that, if he can't follow your directions, he's able to locate it using the given information. Your classmate will play the role of the friend.

# Vocabulary

In this part of the lesson, you will review, listen to, and practice pronunciation of the phrases and vocabulary used in the chapter.

## Phrases اصطلاحات

| | | |
|---|---|---|
| go straight ahead | peš běrawed. | پیش بروید . |
| make a turn | dawr bězaned. | دور بزنید . |
| make a turn | běgarded. | بگردید . |
| go a little further | kami peš běrawed. | کمی پیش بروید . |
| go forward | rō-barō běrawed. | روبرو بروید . |
| turn back | pas běgarded. | پس بگردید . |
| get off from the ... | az ... birōn šawed. | از ... بیرون شوید . |
| pass the ... | az ... ter šawed. | از ... تیرشوید . |
| sorry, excuse me | běbaxšed./babxšed. | ببخشید . |

## Vocabulary Words لغات

| | | |
|---|---|---|
| blue | ābi | آبی |
| they are ... | ānhā ... mebāšand. | آنها ... میباشند . |
| to marry | ezděwāj kardan (ezděwāj kon) | ازدواج کردن |
| members | a'zā | اعضا |
| pigeon | kabutar/kaftar | کبوتر/کفتر |
| s/he is ... | ō ... mebāšad. | او ... میباشد . |
| children | awlād | اولاد |
| brother-in-law (for wife) | ewar | ایور |
| son | bača/pasar | بچه/پسر |
| cousin | bačaye a'ma | بچهٔ عمه |
| cousin | bačaye kākā | بچهٔ کاکا |
| kindergarten (age) child | bačaye kodakěstān | بچهٔ کودکستان |
| cousin | bačaye māmā | بچهٔ ماما |

| cousin | bačaye xāla | بچۀ خاله |
| brother | barādar | برادر |
| nightingale | bolbol | بلبل |
| tall | bĕland | بلند |
| partridge | bōdana/kabk | بودنه/کبک |
| jobless | bikār | بیکار |
| jobless | bikār | بیکار |
| father | padar | پدر |
| grandfather | padar kalān | پدر کلان |
| old | pir | پیر |
| cat | pĕsak | پیشک |
| to marry | tōy kardan (tōy kon) | توی کردن |
| you are ... | tu ... mebāše. | تو ... میباشی. |
| young | jawān | جوان |
| fat | čāq | چاق |
| left | čap | چپ |
| gray | xākĕstari | خاکستری |
| uncle (mother's side) | xāl | خاله |
| family | xānawāda | خانواده |
| family | xānawāda/fāmil | خانواده/ فامیل |
| housewife | xānom-e xāna | خانم خانه |
| father-in-law | xosor | خسر |
| brother-in-law (for husband) | xosorbōra | خسربُره |
| mother-in-law | xošō | خشو |
| sister | xāhar | خواهر |
| small/young | xōrd | خورد |
| tailor | xayāt | خیاط |
| sister-in-law (for husband) | xeyāšna | خیاشنه |

| | | |
|---|---|---|
| groom | dāmād | داماد |
| daughter | doxtar | دختر |
| cousin | doxtare a'ma | دختر عمه |
| cousin | doxtare kākā | دختر کاکا |
| cousin | doxtare māma | دختر ماما |
| cousin | doxtare xāla | دختر خاله |
| shopkeeper | dokāndār | دوکاندار |
| right | rāst | راست |
| hair color | rang mōy | رنگ موی |
| eye color | range čěšom | رنگ چشم |
| yellow | zard | زرد |
| woman | zan | زن |
| ... years | sāla ... | ... ساله |
| green | sabz | سبز |
| red | sorx | سرخ |
| white | safed | سفید |
| dog | sag | سگ |
| age | sěn | سن |
| black | siyā | سیاه |
| to get; to grow, to happen, to go, to be | šodan | شدن |
| you are ... | šōmā ... mebāšed. | شما ... میباشید. |
| husband | šawhar/šōy | شوهر/شوی |
| golden (blonde) | tělāye | طلایی |
| parrot | tuti | طوطی |
| bride/daughter in-law | arōs/sōnō | عروس/سونو |
| to marry/to wed | arōsi kardan (arōsi kon) | عروسی کردن |
| aunt (mother's side) | a'ma | عمه |
| family | fāmil | فامیل |

| | | |
|---|---|---|
| father-in-law's family | fāmile xosor | فاميل خسر |
| height | qad | قد |
| tall height | qad bělan | قد بلند |
| short height | qad kōtā | قد کوتاه |
| canary | qanāri | قناری |
| brown | qahwa ye | قهوه یی |
| parent | kākā | کاکا |
| big | kalān | کلان |
| big | kalān/ bozorg | کلان/بزرگ |
| short | kōtā | کوتاه |
| small/young | kōčak | کوچک |
| child | kōdak/těfěl | کودک/طفل |
| conjunction | kě | که |
| skinny | lāğar | لاغر |
| we are ... | mā ... mebāšem. | ما ... میباشیم. |
| mother | mādar | مادر |
| grandmother | mādar kalān | مادر کلان |
| honeymoon | māhe 'asal | ماه عسل |
| uncle (father's side) | māmā | ماما |
| married | motahel | متاهل |
| school student | mota'lem | متعلم |
| retired | motaqā'ad | متقاعد |
| single | mojarad | مجرد |
| college student | mohasěl | محصل |
| manager | modir | مدیر |
| teacher | mo'lem | معلم |
| i am ... | man ... mebāšam. | من ... میباشم. |
| secretary | monši | منشی |
| to be engaged | nāmzad šodan (nāmzad šaw) | نامزد شدن |

| nurse | nars | نرس |
|---|---|---|
| sister-in-law (for wife) | nanō | ننو |
| grandchild | nawāsa | نواسه |
| medium/middle/mid | miyāna | میانه |
| aunt (father's side) | wālēdayn | والدین |

## Dari Vocabulary Different from Iranian Persian

| English Translation | Iranian Persian | | Farsi-e Dari | |
|---|---|---|---|---|
| cafe | kāfa | کافه | kāntin | کانتین |
| purple | banafš | بنفش | yāsamani | یاسمنی |
| pink | šōrati | صورتی | golābi | گلابی |
| red | qarmĕz | قرمز | sorx | سرخ |
| hallway | hāl | هال | dahliz | دهلیز |
| floor | tabaqa | طبقه | manzĕl | منزل |
| front yard | hayāt | حیاط | sahn-e haweli | صحن حویلی |
| house/yard | sarā, xuna | سرا، خونه | haweli | حویلی |
| living room | hāl-e pazirāyi | هال پذیرایی | otāq-e našeman | اتاق نشیمن |
| auto repair shop | ta'mir-gāh | تعمیرگاه | mĕstari-xāna | مستری خانه |
| airport | forud-gāh | فرودگاه | maydān-e hawā-ye | میدان هوایی |
| police department | kalāntari | کلانتری | qōmandāni-ye amniya | قومندانی امنیه |
| hospital | bimārestān | بیمارستان | šafāxāna | شفاخانه |
| street, road | xiyābān | خیابان | sarak, jāda | سرک، جاده |
| dorm | xāb-gāh | خوابگاه | layliya | لیله |

# فصل هشتم
## CHAPTER EIGHT

## در بازار
### AT THE BAZAAR

# IN THIS CHAPTER

**• وظایف** Functions

*Buying groceries; Learning names of foods; Expressing likes/dislikes; Talking about daily meals; Asking for food prices; Learning how to use Afghan money; Ordering foods at restaurants; Learning the names of different clothing parts; Shopping/bargaining*

**• تبصرهٔ فرهنگی** Cultural Notes

*Tips for the bazaar; Afghan currency; Weight units; Afghan dishes; Afghan men's clothing; Afghan women's clothing; Clothing sizes*

**• دستور زبان** Language Structure

*The auxiliary verbs* باید ، شاید; *The suffix* فروشی; *The verb 'to like'* خوش آمدن; *Defining relative clause* که; *Using the present perfect of* پوشیدن; *Order of adjectives*

**• مرور فصل** Chapter Review

*Reading clothing ads; Purchasing clothes; Ordering/making food; Buying groceries*

**• لغات** Vocabulary

*Review phrases and words used in this chapter*

## Chapter Introduction

# معرفی فصل

In this chapter, you will learn the names of various foods, learn how to bargain when purchasing groceries, talk about your daily meals, and read menus and order food in Afghan restaurants. Additionally, you will learn the Afghan currency and, finally, learn the names of different clothing parts. By the end of this chapter, you should be able to talk about various foods, talk about your shopping experience, and bargain.

بیا که به رستورانت برویم.

Let's go to the restaurant.

من میخواهم که سودا بخرم.

I want to buy groceries.

او یک پیراهن سیاه خریده است.

She has bought a black shirt.

# درس اول: من میخواهم که سودا بخرم.

## Lesson One: I want to buy groceries.

In this section, you will talk about food, write a grocery list, and bargain at the Bazaar. You will also learn about Afghan money and weight units.

Exercise 1: تمرین ١:

A. لیلا and شریف are discussing what to eat for breakfast on the audio recording. Listen and mark the items that لیلا wants to eat with the [+] mark and the items that شریف wants to eat with a [√] mark.

| لبنیات | نوشیدنی | چای صبح |
|---|---|---|
| dairy | drinks | breakfast |

□ شیر   □ ماست   □ چای   □ قهوه

□ نان خشک   □ تخم مرغ   □ مسکه   □ پنیر

□ بوره   □ مربا   □ کلچه   □ کیک

| یك لحظه صبر کنید . | فقط |
|---|---|
| [Please] wait a moment. | just, only |

B.  Now ask your classmate what s/he likes or doesn't like to eat for breakfast. For example:

| Usually, what do you eat for breakfast? | معمولاً شما برای چای صبح چی میخورید؟ | | Usually, what do you like to eat for breakfast? | برای چای صبح معمولاً شما چی خوش دارید که بخورید؟ |
|---|---|---|---|---|
| I eat (drink) just a cup of coffee with milk and sugar. | من فقط یك پیاله قهوه همراه شیر و بوره میخورم. | | I like to eat..., but I don't like.... | من خوش دارم که ... بخورم. اما ... را خوش ندارم. |

Exercise 2: 🎧   تمرین ۲:

A. لیلا and شریف have overnight guests for breakfast. They are putting together a shopping list. Listen to their conversation on the audio recording and mark the appropriate box based on whether they're available or not available.

| ندارند | دارند | مواد چای صبح | ندارند | دارند | مواد چای صبح |
|---|---|---|---|---|---|
| | | کلچه | | | چای |
| | | تخم مرغ | | | شیر |
| | | بوره | | | ماست |
| | | قهوه | | | مسکه |
| | | نان خشك | | | پنیر |
| | | مربا | | | کیك |

B. 🎧 Listen again to the audio recording. This time circle the items that شریف needs to buy.

C. 🎧 Listen to the audio recording and circle the items that are most needed.

| فکر میکنم | باید | شاید | هیچ چیز |
|---|---|---|---|
| I think | most, should | might, maybe | nothing |

D. Listen to the audio recording again and this time check "true" or "false" for each statement below.

| غلط | صحیح | |
|---|---|---|
| ☐ | ☐ | ۱  مهمانها قهوه خوش دارند . |
| ☐ | ☐ | ۲  زن برای شوهر گفت که زود پس نیایید . |
| ☐ | ☐ | ۳  مهمانها یک ساعت بعد بیدار میشوند . |
| ☐ | ☐ | ۴  زن و شوهر این سودا را برای چای صبح بکار دارند . |

E. Think about what's in your refrigerator, i.e. the things you have or don't have. Then discuss them with a classmate.

## 8.1 The Auxiliary Verb باید

The verb باید 'must, have/has to' is used as an auxiliary verb to help the main verb; the main verb is always in the present tense and comes in the subjunctive mood. This verb is used in the third person singular form of the verb بایستن. The third person singular form of this verb is used for all people in the same form.

See how باید works with different simple verbs in the present tense.

| | Subjunctive mood with باید | Infinitive |
|---|---|---|
| I must eat breakfast. | من باید چای صبح را بخورم. | خوردن (خور) |
| We must drink tea. | ما باید چای بنوشیم. | نوشیدن (نوش) |
| You must buy groceries. | تو باید سودا بخری. | خریدن (خر) |
| You must eat breakfast. | شما باید چای صبح را بخورید . | خوردن (خور) |
| S/he must drink coffee. | او باید قهوه بنوشد. | نوشیدن (نوش) |
| They must eat bread. | آنها باید نان خشک بخرند . | خریدن (خر) |

Exercise 3:    تمرین ۳:

What do you do in the following situations? Use the auxiliary verb باید.

| | |
|---|---|
| You don't have any milk in your fridge. _____ | ۱ |
| She is out of bread. _____ | ۲ |
| I am very tired and sleepy. _____ | ۳ |
| We didn't have breakfast. _____ | ۴ |
| They are very hungry. _____ | ۵ |

Exercise 4:    تمرین ۴:

A. لیلا needs some groceries. She calls her husband and gives him a list of items. She tells him exactly how much of each item is needed. Listen to the audio recording and write down the quantity of each item you hear.

میوه
fruits

ترکاری ، سبزی
vegetables

غذا، نان
foods

_____ گوشت        _____ آب        _____ روغن        _____ نمك

_____ مرچ        _____ سبزی پالك        _____ بادرنگ        _____ بادنجان رومی

_____ پیاز        _____ كچالو        _____ زردك        _____ كاهو

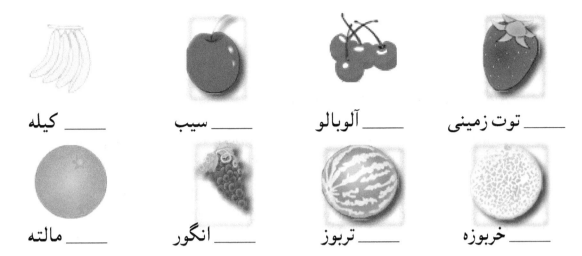

_____ كيله _____ سيب _____ آلوبالو _____ توت زمينی

_____ مالته _____ انگور _____ تربوز _____ خربوزه

B. Sort the foods in Exercises 1A and 4A into the following categories.

نوشيدنی　لبنيات　سبزيجات/ ترکاری باب　ميوه جات

C. Listen to the audio recording from Exercise 4A again and, this time, mark the best answer for each of the following questions.

| | | | |
|---|---|---|---|
| ۱ | چرا ليلا به فريد تليفون کرد؟ | | |
| چونکه او برای چای صبح سودا کار داشت. | چونکه او هم سودا بکار داشت و هم مهمان دارد. | چونکه او امشب مهمان دارد. | چونکه او سودا بکار داشت. |
| ۲ | کی به خانهٔ فريد و ليلا می‌آيد؟ | | |
| خواهر و برادر ليلا | خواهر و برادر فريد | خواهر و داماد ليلا | خواهر و داماد فريد |
| ۳ | چرا ليلا سودا زياد بکار دارد؟ | | |
| چونکه مهمانهايش برای دو روز در خانه اش ميباشند. | چونکه مهمانهايش برای يک ماه در خانه اش ميباشند. | چونکه مهمانهايش برای يک هفته در خانه اش ميباشند. | چونکه بسيار مهمان دارد. |
| ۴ | شريف از کار که بيرون شد بايد چی کند؟ | | |
| بايد به مارکيت برود | بايد به دوکان برود | بايد سودا بخرد | بايد خانه برود |

## 8.2 The Verb خوش آمدن 'To Like'

In order to express likes and dislikes in Dari, use another compound verb: خوش آمدن. For example: "I like apples." من از سیب خوشم میاید.

The verb خوش آمدن doesn't take a personal ending; instead, the possessives are added to the word خوش and the whole phrase, which follows the preposition از. For example:

| من ازسیب خوشم میاید. | من از سیب خوش م میاید. |
|---|---|
| You like apples. | do like    apple   preposition   I |

| I like apples. | من ازسیب خوشم میاید. |
|---|---|
| You like apples. | تو ازسیب خوشت میاید. |
| S/he likes apples. | او ازسیب خوشش میاید. |
| We like apples. | ما ازسیب خوش ما میاید. |
| You like apples. | شما ازسیب خوشتان میاید. |
| They like apples. | آنها ازسیب خوش شان میاید. |

**Exercise 5:** تمرین ۵:

A. Complete the following sentences using the verb خوش آمدن.

| | | |
|---|---|---|
| ۱ | من/ پنیر و نان خشک | _____ |
| ۲ | ما/ شیر | _____ |
| ۳ | تو/ چای و کلچه | _____ |
| ۴ | شما/ قهوه و بوره | _____ |
| ۵ | او/ مسکه و نان خشک | _____ |
| ۶ | آنها / تخم مرغ و نان خشک | _____ |

B. Convert the following sentences from the verb خوش داشتن to the verb از ... خوش آمدن . The first one is done for you.

| | | |
|---|---|---|
| ١ | من چای را همراه شیر خوش دارم. | من از چای همراه شیر خوشم میاید . |
| ٢ | من قهوه را همراه بوره خوش دارم. | |
| ٣ | شما چای را همراه چی خوش دارید؟ | |
| ۴ | شما قهوه را همراه چی خوش دارید؟ | |
| ۵ | او مسکه را همراه نان خشك خوش دارد . | |

C. Working with a partner, go back to Exercises 1 and 4 and take turns naming five items you like and five items you dislike.

D. Turn to a classmate and practice asking likes / dislikes using the following structure.

Which fruits do you like?                شما از کدام میوه ها خوشتان میاید؟
I like ... .                             من از ... خوشم میاید .

Which vegetables do you like?            شما از کدام ترکاری ها خوش تان میاید؟
I like ... .                             من از ... خوشم میاید .

E. You will hear a conversation between two people as they talk about their likes and dislikes. Listen to their conversation on the audio recording and mark the food items in the table below. Then write how much they like each item using: بسیار، کم ، بسیار زیاد ، بسیار کم

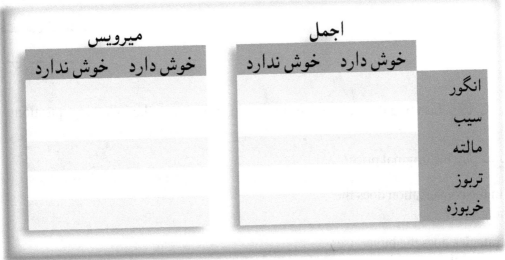

| | میرویس | | اجمل | | |
|---|---|---|---|---|---|
| | خوش دارد | خوش ندارد | خوش دارد | خوش ندارد | |
| | | | | | انگور |
| | | | | | سیب |
| | | | | | مالته |
| | | | | | تربوز |
| | | | | | خربوزه |

Exercise 6:  تمرین ۶:

A. شریف is in the bazaar buying watermelons. Listen to his conversation on the audio recording with the seller, and choose the best answer for the following questions.

---

1. How much was the price at the beginning?
   a) 9 Afghanis        b) 20 Afghanis        c) 10 Afghanis        d) 7 Afghanis

2. When the customer heard the prices, what was his reaction?
   a) He agreed to pay.
   b) He asked for a cheaper price.
   c) He was surprised.

3. How many kilos of the item does the customer need?
   a) 20 kilos        b) 21 kilos        c) 22 kilos        d) 24 kilos

4. How much did the seller buy this item for, originally?
   a) 6 Afghani per kilo
   b) 7 Afghani per kilo
   c) 8 Afghani per kilo
   d) 9 Afghani per kilo

---

B. Listen to the audio recording again. This time, mark the questions that you hear the customer asking by putting a [√] next to them. Then put a [+] mark next to the questions that the seller asks.

| سوال ها | مشتری | فروشنده |
|---|---|---|
| ۱  سودا بکار داشتید؟ | ــــــ | ــــــ |
| ۲  چی بکار دارید؟ | ــــــ | ــــــ |
| ۳  تربوز کیلویی چند است؟ | ــــــ | ــــــ |
| ۴  ارزانتر نمیشود؟ | ــــــ | ــــــ |
| ۵  شما چند میخواهید؟ | ــــــ | ــــــ |
| ۶  پیسه‌اش چند میشود؟ | ــــــ | ــــــ |

C. Listen to the audio recording again and answer the following questions.

---

1. Did شریف pay the original price? _____

2. Where in the conversation does the bargaining start? _____

3. What strategies does the buyer use?
   a) He refused the original price.    b) He stated a higher price.

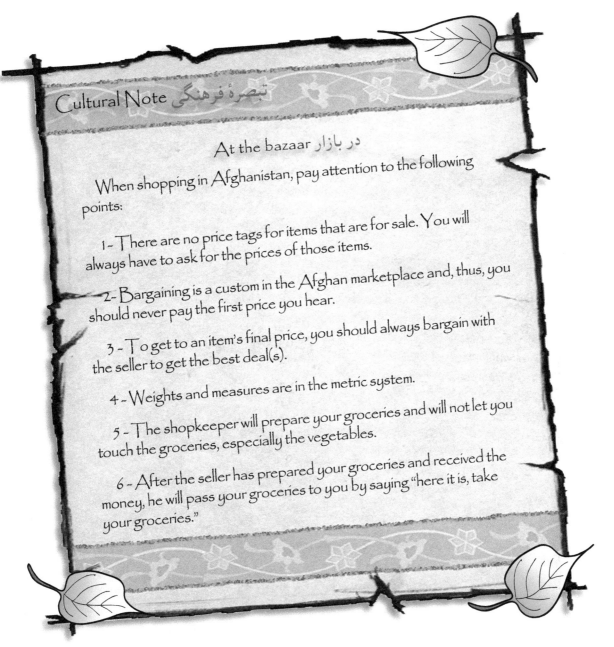

## Cultural Note تبصرهٔ فرهنگی

### در بازار At the bazaar

When shopping in Afghanistan, pay attention to the following points:

1- There are no price tags for items that are for sale. You will always have to ask for the prices of those items.

2- Bargaining is a custom in the Afghan marketplace and, thus, you should never pay the first price you hear.

3 - To get to an item's final price, you should always bargain with the seller to get the best deal(s).

4 - Weights and measures are in the metric system.

5 - The shopkeeper will prepare your groceries and will not let you touch the groceries, especially the vegetables.

6 - After the seller has prepared your groceries and received the money, he will pass your groceries to you by saying "here it is, take your groceries."

D. Play the role of a buyer and seller with a partner. The seller should make a list of foods and drinks taken from Exercise1A and 4A, and the buyer will look at the list and ask for the price of each item. Be sure to use classifiers as well as the following phrases in your conversation.

| دوكاندار | مشتری |
|---|---|
| شما چند میخواهید؟ ...کیلویی... افغانی است. | ارزانتر نمیشود؟ من ... افغانی میخواهم. |
| خیر است. شما ...افغانی بدهید. | نه، قیمت گفتید. |
| من خودم به ... افغانی خریدم. | پیسه اش چند میشود؟ ... کیلو/ دانه بدهید. |
| | ببخشید، ... کیلویی چند است؟ |

## 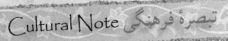 Cultural Note — تبصرهٔ فرهنگی

### Afghan currency

The name of currency in Afghanistan is 'Afghani' افغانی. A long time ago, before 1925, the name of the currency was روپیه or 'Rupees', and some people still use that term when buying or selling things; i.e. they will say روپیه 'rupees' instead of افغانی, 'Afghani'. For example:

How much are apples per kilo?        سیب کیلویی چند روپیه است؟

Apples are 10 rupees per kilo.        سیب کیلویی ده روپیه است.

Both names are used by people on a daily basis. However, official documents must use افغانی 'afghani'. Afghan money (bills and coins) start from 1 AFG and go up to 1000 AFG. For example:

### 8.3 Verbs Used for Shopping

The following verbs are the most commonly used for buying groceries.

| | | | |
|---|---|---|---|
| I am buying groceries. | من سودا میخرم. | to buy | خریدن (خر) |
| The shopkeeper sells groceries. | دوکاندار سودا میفروشد. | to sell | فروختن (فروش) |
| We need fruit. | ما میوه کارداریم. | to need | به کارداشتن (کاردار) |
| Do you want tea? | شما چای میخواهید؟ | to want | خواستن (خواه) |
| Take your groceries. | سودایت را بگیر. | to take | گرفتن (گیر) |
| Give me one kilo of apples. | یک کیلو سیب بدهید. | to give | دادن (ده) |
| Are my groceries ready? | سودایم آماده است؟ | to be ready | آماده بودن (آماده هست) |

Exercise 7:      تمرین ۷:

  A. Complete the following sentences with the present form of the verbs provided in the parentheses, and then write their English equivalent underneath each.

| | | |
|---|---|---|
| ۱ | شما از کجا سودا ———————— خریدن (خر) |
| ۲ | او موترش را ———————— فروختن (فروش) |
| ۳ | ما برای امشب میوه ———————— به کارداشتن (به کاردار) |
| ۴ | آنها برای چای صبح شیر و کلچه ———————— خواستن (خواه) |
| ۵ | من از کانتین برای شما قهوه ———————— گرفتن (گیر) |
| ۶ | من برای او یک دانه سیب ———————— دادن (ده) |
| ۷ | شما ساعت ۷ برای نان شب ———————— آماده بودن (آماده هست) |

B. 📖 Complete the following sentences with the past form of the verbs provided in parentheses, and then write their English equivalent below.

| | |
|---|---|
| ۱ | شما از کجا سودا ——————— خریدن (خر) |
| ۲ | او موترش را ——————— فروختن (فروش) |
| ۳ | ما برای دیشب میوه ——————— به کارداشتن (به کاردار) |
| ۴ | آنها برای چای صبح شیر و کلچه ——————— خواستن( خواه ) |
| ۵ | من از کانتین برای شما قهوه ——————— گرفتن (گیر) |
| ۶ | من برای او یک دانه سیب ——————— دادن (ده) |
| ۷ | شما ساعت ۷برای نان شب ——————— آماده بودن (آماده هست) |

تمرین ۸: 🎧 Exercise 8:

You will hear a dialogue on the audio recording between a shopkeeper and شریف in which شریف wants to buy the rest of his groceries. Listen carefully and mark "true" or "false" for the following statements.

| غلط | صحیح | جمله | |
|---|---|---|---|
| ☐ | ☐ | مشتری ترکاری و نوشیدنی بکار داشت. | ۱ |
| ☐ | ☐ | مشتری ۲ درجن کیله بکار داشت. | ۲ |
| ☐ | ☐ | دوکاندار یک درجن کیله را ۱۲۰ افغانی میفروشد. | ۳ |
| ☐ | ☐ | مشتری سیب را از کیلویی ۸۵ بلندتر نمیخرد. | ۴ |
| ☐ | ☐ | دوکاندار همه سودا را به قیمت دوکان دیگر میفروشد. | ۵ |

Exercise 9: 📖 تمرین ۹ :

A. لیلا wants to go to the bazaar to shop, as her husband شریف didn't buy everything that was on the list. Before going, she sends an email message to her friend ملالی and asks her to come along. Read her email message and answer the following questions.

فرستنده : لیلا
گیرنده : لیلا
موضوع: خریداری

دوست عزیزم لیلا جان سلام! فردا من میخواهم که به بازار بروم و کمی سودا خرید کنم، من به دوکان ترکاری فروشی و کالا فروشی و بوت فروشی میروم. آیا شما هم وقت دارید که همراه من بروید؟

ما فردا به رستورانتِ کابل هم خواهیم رفت، رستورانت کابل غذا های داخلی و خارجی دارد . لطفاً برایم ایمیل و یا تلیفون کنید .

با احترام
دوست تان زرغونه

| با احترام<br>respectfully | کالا فروشی<br>clothing store | خریداری<br>shopping |
|---|---|---|

۱ چرا زرغونه میخواهد که به بازار برود؟

۲ زرغونه به کدام جای ها خواهد رفت؟

۳ چرا زرغونه میخواهد که به رستورانت کابل برود؟

۴ زرغونه برای لیلا گفت که چی کند ؟

B. 🎧 Now you will hear on the audio recording ملالی's voice message for لیلا which is in response to ملالی's email message. Listen and choose the best answer for each of the following questions.

1. Is tomorrow a good day for لیلا to go shopping?    a) yes        b) no

2- What does لیلا ask زرغونه about that wasn't mentioned in her email message?
    a) the place        b) the time        c) the transportation

C.  Now write a short email message to your friend and invite her to go grocery shopping with you. Tell your friend that you also want to look at some clothes at the bazaar. Ask your friend the time and place that she wants to meet. Additionally, see if your friend wants to have lunch as well.

فرستنده:
گیرنده:
موضوع:

## 8.4 The Suffix فروشی

The word فروشی 'sellable,' when combined with a noun, makes a specific name for a store that sells that particular item. For example:

| | | | |
|---|---|---|---|
| ترکاری فروشی | vegetable | ترکاری | |
| آیسکریم فروشی | ice cream | آیسکریم | |
| کالافروشی | clothes | کالا | |
| موتر فروشی | car | موتر | |
| آب میوه فروشی | juice | آب میوه | |

## Cultural Note تبصرهٔ فرهنگی

### Weight units

In Afghanistan, two standard weight measurements are generally used: kilogram and pound. There are, however, some specific weight units which may differ from one place to another.

You will frequently hear these phrases when shopping, but you don't need to memorize them because you can easily avoid using them. Instead, use the standard metric and pound system.

For example:

Approximately 565 kg

خروار

7066 grams in Kabul and in central Afghanistan, but about 100 grams in the western part of the country

سیر

7066 grams in Kabul, about 5000 grams in Kandahar, 4000 grams in western parts of the country

من

this term means "a quarter of"

چاریك/چارك

4.6 grams

مثقال

# درس دوم: بیا که به رستورانت برویم.

## Lesson Two: Let's go to the restaurant.

In this section, you will learn more about Afghan foods, restaurants, and how to read Afghan menus. You will also learn how to say you are thirsty and hungry and ask others about their needs.

Exercise 1: تمرین ۱:

A. With a partner, look at the following pictures and discuss the things you see. Then take a moment to talk about the people in the pictures.

B. Now point out what you find interesting in one of the above pictures. Then talk about it with the class. Be sure you describe everything you see in the picture.

Exercise 2: تمرین ۲ :

Use the following word bank and translate the following phrases for each picture.

| خوردن (خور) | نوشیدن (نوش) | فرمایش دادن (فرمایش ده) | پرداختن (پرداز) | بل/ رسید | مالك |
|---|---|---|---|---|---|
| to eat | to drink | to order | to pay | check | owner |

| گارسون | رستورانت | مینو | سر آشپز | تشنه | گشنه |
|---|---|---|---|---|---|
| waiter/waitress | restaurant | menu | chef | thirsty | hungry |

این مینوی رستورانت افغان است که انواع غذا های افغانی دارد .

اینجا یك رستورانت عصری است و فعلاً مشتری ندارد .

این بچه در یك رستورانت، در نزدیك شاهراه گارسون است.

این مرد کوکاکولامیفروشد ، او تشنه است و چای مینوشد .

این مردها در یك رستورانت نزدیك شاهراه نان خوردند و معطل بل نان شان هستند. آنها چای فرمایش دادند .

این مرد سر آشپز رستورانت است، او همچنان مالك رستورانت است.

Exercise 3: تمرین ۳ :

The following texts are short descriptions of different types of restaurants in Afghanistan. Read each one carefully, and discuss the following questions with a classmate.

# رستورانت های افغانستان

در افغانستان سه قسم رستورانت است، رستورانت مدرن (عصری)، رستورانت معمولی و رستورانت سنتی.

۱- رستورانت های مدرن (عصری): این رستورانت ها مثل رستورانت های امریکا و اروپا است. این رستورانت ها گارسون ، مینویی غذایی، میز، چوکی، قاشق ، پنجه و کارد دارد. این رستورانت ها بسیار کارمندان و آشپزان مسلکی دارد.

۲- رستورانت های معمولی: این رستورانت ها مثل رستورانت های امریکا و اروپا میز، چوکی و گارسون دارد اما مینویی غذایی، قاشق، پنجه و کارد ندارد، و همچنان کارمندان و آشپزان آن مسلکی نیستند.

۳- رستورانت های سنتی: این رستورانت ها مثل دو قسم بالا نیستند. این رستورانت ها معمولا در بین شاهراه ها است، این رستورانت ها مینویی غذایی، میز، چوکی، قاشق، پنجه و کارد ندارند اما گارسون دارند.

| معمولی | سنتی | عصری، مدرن | قسم | قاشق | پنجه | کارد | مسلکی |
|--------|------|------------|-----|------|------|------|-------|
| ordinary | traditional | modern | type, kind | spoon | fork | knife | professional |

1- Which of the above restaurants would you go to and why?

2- Are there any similar restaurants in your city, town, or state? If so, how similar are they?

3- In which of the above restaurants would you find a knife, fork, spoon, and a printed menu?

4- Which of the above restaurants is located alongside highways?

5- Which of the restaurants seats people on the floor?

6- In which of the above restaurants do you eat with your hands?

Exercise 4:  ۴ : تمرین

A. Read the following signs and menu. Then complete the exercise.

رستورانت وقهوه خانه سنتی
کلبه افغان
با داشتن غذاهای داخلی وخارجی درخدمت شما ست

1- What is this sign advertising?
a) a restaurant
b) a restaurant and a coffee shop
c) a restaurant and a tea shop
d) a coffee shop

2- What types of food do they serve?
a) local dishes
b) foreign dishes
c) both foreign and local dishes

مینویی غذایی رستورانت کلبه افغان

| صبحانه (چای صبح) | | نوشیدنی | | نان چاشت و نان شب | | هوسانه | |
|---|---|---|---|---|---|---|---|
| شیر | ۲۵ | چای سبز | ۱۰ | نان خشک | ۵ | بولانی | ۴۵ |
| قیماق | ۴۰ | چای سیاه | ۱۰ | قابلی پلو | ۹۰ | آشک | ۸۰ |
| مسکه | ۳۰ | دوغ | ۵ | پلو | ۹۰ | منتو | ۸۰ |
| پنیر | ۳۰ | آبیخ | ۵ | چلو | ۹۰ | | |
| مربا | ۲۰ | آب لیمو | ۱۰ | کباب گوشت گوسفند | ۱۱۰ | سوپ وسلاته | |
| خاگینه | ۲۰ | آب مالته | ۱۰ | کباب گوشت گاو | ۱۰۰ | یخنی | ۲۰ |
| شیرینی | | آب انار | ۱۰ | شش کباب | ۱۰۰ | آش | ۲۰ |
| فرنی | ۲۰ | کوکاکولا | ۵ | شامی کباب | ۱۴۰ | سوپ مرغ | ۲۰ |
| حلوا | ۲۰ | فانتا | ۵ | چوپان کباب | ۱۴۰ | سلاته | ۱۵ |
| بغلاوه | ۲۰ | پیپسی | ۵ | قورمه گوشت گوسفند | ۴۰ | سلات | ۱۵ |
| روت | ۲۰ | | | قورمه گوشت مرغ | ۳۰ | چتنی | ۱۵ |
| کلچه | ۲۰ | | | قورمه سبزی | ۲۰ | | |
| کیک | ۲۰ | | | قورمه لوبیا | ۲۰ | | |

1 - Which restaurant do you think carries a menu?
  a) modern
  b) casual
  c)  traditional

2 - Read the menu and circle the foods, drinks, appetizers, and desserts you already know or you might have had before. Compare your answers.

3 - Find the Dari version of the following words from the above menu. Then write the Dari equivalent of each on the line provided.

a) drinks                    b) dinner                    c) lunch                    d) breakfast

_____        _____        _____        _____

e) appetizer                 f) dessert                   g) soup and salad

_____        _____        _____

B.   In the above menu you will find the words قورمه (sauce), کباب (kabob), گاو (cow), گوسفند (lamb), and مرغ (chicken). Using these words, list all the sauces and kabobs in the above menu.

_____

_____

_____

C.   Read about some of the traditional Afghan foods on the menu.

52

| | | | |
|---|---|---|---|
| plain white rice dish without meat | چلو | rice dish cooked with meat, e.g. lamb or beef | قابلی پلو |
| dumpling filled with beef or lamb | منتو | dumpling that is filled with vegetables | آشك |
| meat soup | شوربا / یخنی | bread filled with vegetable and meats | بولانی |
| dessert made of corn flour, sugar and milk; usually topped with pistachios | فرنی | soup made of macaroni or spaghetti | آش |
| drink made of yogurt, salt, water and dried mint | دوغ | dessert made of flour, oil, and sugar | حلوا |
| omelet | خاگینه | spicy salsa | چتنی |

## Cultural Note   تبصرۀ فرهنگی

### Afghan dishes   غذا های افغانی

Afghans have several main dishes which are served at different times of the day. For breakfast, Afghans usually drink green tea, black tea, and milk. They also eat cheese, cream cheese, butter, and various types of omelets. What is most common among Afghans, however, is to serve black or green tea for breakfast along with bread and sugar.

For lunch and dinner, Afghans generally serve rice, vegetables, various sauces (meat sauce, bean sauce), bread, and meats, e.g. lamb, beef, chicken, and fish.

Exercise 5:  ۵ : تمرین
Match the following words to their proper definitions.

| | |
|---|---|
| جای که ما در آنجا نان میخوریم. | ۱ گارسون |
| کسی که برای ما نان میدهد. | ۲ رستورانت |
| کسی که برای ما نان پخته میکند. | ۳ آشپز خانه |
| کسی که در رستورانت نان میخورد. | ۴ مینوی غذایی |
| کسی که در رستورانت نان میخورد. | ۵ سرآشپز |
| جای که در آن نان پخته میکنیم. | ۶ مهمان |
| لست غذا های رستورانت است. | ۷ مشتری |

| کسی که | جایی که |
|---|---|
| a person that ... | a place that ... |

## 8.5 Defining Relative Clause که

In Dari, when you want to define an object or a person, you usually use the relative clause که.

کسی که بالایی میز نان میخورد، احمد است.
The person who is eating food at the table is Ahmad.

زنی که نان پخته میکند، زرغونه است.
The woman who is cooking is Zarghuna.

As you can see, suffix ی is added after the word (زن (زنی), کس (کسی).
This suffix works as a definite object marker (the).

Exercise 6: تمرین ۶:
Define the following terms.

| | |
|---|---|
| ۱ | قهوه |
| ۲ | آشپزخانه |
| ۳ | دوکاندار |
| ۴ | حلوا |
| ۵ | قابلی پلو |
| ۶ | منتو |
| ۷ | آشک |
| ۸ | کباب گوسفند |

Exercise 7: تمرین ۷:
You will hear a conversation on the audio recording between لیلا and زرغونه.
Listen and choose the best answer for the following questions.

1. Which meal of the day is being served?
   a) breakfast    b) lunch    c) dinner    d) snack time

2. لیلا is ...
   a) very hungry    b) a little hungry    c) full    d) thirsty

3. Why does لیلا want to go to that restaurant?
   a) because it's very close and زرغونه is very hungry
   b) because it has lots of Afghan dishes
   c) because there is only one restaurant
   d) because this restaurant has cheaper prices

4. What kind of kabob does لیلا mention?
   a) chicken    b) beef    c) lamb    d) shami

## 8.6 The Verb گشنه، تشنه

In Dari, there are two ways to ask someone whether s/he is hungry, thirsty, or full. The first way is the present form of the 'to be' verb. e.g.:

| | |
|---|---|
| بلی من گشنه هستم. | شما گشنه هستید؟ |
| Yes, I am hungry. | Are you hungry? |
| بلی من تشنه هستم. | شما تشنه هستید؟ |
| Yes, I am thirsty. | Are you thirsty? |
| بلی من تشنه هستم. | شما سیر هستید؟ |
| Yes, I am full. | Are you full? |

The second way is to use the past form of the compound verbs گشنه شدن 'to get/become hungry', تشنه شدن 'to become/get thirsty' and سیر شدن 'to become/get full' in the present tense. For example:

| | |
|---|---|
| بلی من گشنه شدم. | شما گشنه شدید؟ |
| Yes, I am hungry. | Are you hungry? |
| بلی من تشنه شدم. | شما تشنه شدید؟ |
| Yes, I am thirsty. | Are you thirsty? |
| بلی من سیر شدم. | شما سیر شدید؟ |
| Yes, I am full. | Are you full? |

The second example is used more in the colloquial rather than in the standard Dari.

Exercise 8: ✎  ۸ تمرین:

   Using the verbs above, with a partner, write the Dari equivalent of the following phrases underneath each.

| | |
|---|---|
| We want to go to a restaurant because we are hungry. | ۱ |
| | |
| She wants to drink a can of Pepsi because she is thirsty. | ۲ |
| | |
| Do you want to go eat lunch because I'm very hungry? | ۳ |
| | |
| They are full and they don't want to eat. | ۴ |
| | |
| Are you hungry? | ۵ |
| | |
| He doesn't want to drink water because he is not thirsty. | ۶ |
| | |
| I want to buy some orange juice because I am thirsty. | ۷ |
| | |
| They want to eat dinner because they are hungry. | ۸ |

Exercise 9: تمرین ۹:

A. Role-play:  With a partner, look at the following menus and choose one. Then state why you've chosen that menu and which foods you would like to have.

| میـــــــــــنوی غذایی | | | | | | | | |
|---|---|---|---|---|---|---|---|---|
| **صبحانه** | | **سوپ و سلاد** | | **غذای چاشت و شب** | | | | |
| ۵۰ افغانی | قیماق | ۵۰ افغانی | یخنی | ۱۲۰ افغانی | قابلی پلو | | | |
| ۲۰ افغانی | شیر | ۳۰ افغانی | آش | ۱۲۰ افغانی | پلو | | | |
| ۳۰ افغانی | مسکه | ۲۰ افغانی | سلاد | ۱۰۰ افغانی | چلو | | | |
| ۳۰ افغانی | پنیر | ۲۰ افغانی | سلاته | ۱۲۵ افغانی | کباب | | | |
| ۴۰ افغانی | خاگینه | ۱۰ افغانی | چتنی | ۱۲۵ افغانی | شش کباب | | | |
| ۱۰ افغانی | مربا | **نوشیدنی** | | ۱۲۵ افغانی | شامی کباب | | | |
| ۵ افغانی | نان خشک | ۳۰ افغانی | چای سبز | ۱۵۰ افغانی | چوپان کباب | | | |
| | | ۳۰ افغانی | چای سیاه | ۷۵ افغانی | قورمهٔ گوشت گوسفند | | | |
| | | ۱۰ افغانی | دوغ | ۵۵ افغانی | قورمهٔ گوشت گاو | | | |
| | | ۱۵ افغانی | کوکاکولا | ۵۵ افغانی | قورمهٔ گوشت مرغ | | | |
| | | ۱۵ افغانی | پیپسی | ۶۵ افغانی | شوربا شوروا | | | |
| | | ۱۵ افغانی | فانتا | | | | | |
| | | مفت | آب یخ | | | | | |

| | | |
|---|---|---|
| خوراک 150 افغانی | قابلی پلو | رستورانت وهوتل کابل |
| خوراک 120 افغانی | چلو | مینوی غذایی |
| خوراک 200 افغانی | کباب دیگی | رستورانت کابل با تهیهٔ بهترین غذا های داخلی وخارجی در خدمت مشتریان عزیز میباشد. |
| خوراک 160 افغانی | کباب سیخی | این رستورانت با بهترین  و با تجربه ترین آشپزان ، گارسونها وپرسونل بیست وچارساعته به روی همه مشتریان باز است. |
| خوراک 150 افغانی | شامی کباب | |
| خوراک 170 افغانی | منتو | |
| خوراک 170 افغانی | آشک | |
| بوتل 20 افغانی | نوشیدنی | |
| کاسه 10 افغانی | سلاته | |
| چاینک 20 افغانی | چای سیاه وسبز | |
| خوراک 60 افغانی | شیربخ | |

B. Using the conversation above as an example, extend the previous conversation by including the following information:

*You and your classmate are outside of your home in Kabul. It's 1:00 p.m., and you are very hungry. Ask your classmate if s/he is also hungry, and introduce him/her to your favorite restaurant. Then tell your classmate about the foods you really like in that restaurant.*

Exercise 10:     تمرین ۱۰:

A. Finally زرغونه and گارسون have arrived at a restaurant. Listen to the first part of their conversation on the audio recording. Then answer the following questions. Be sure to take notes.

1. What type of restaurant are they in?
2. How do you know?

B. Now listen to the whole conversation on the audio recording, and check "true" or "false" for the following questions.

| غلط | صحیح | جملات | |
|---|---|---|---|
| ☐ | ☐ | گارسون برای لیلا و زرغونه گفت: خوش آمدید . | ۱ |
| ☐ | ☐ | زرغونه و لیلا میز سه نفره بکار داشتند . | ۲ |
| ☐ | ☐ | زرغونه و لیلا مینویی غذایی را نخواستند . | ۳ |
| ☐ | ☐ | لیلا برای گارسون گفت که او یك دقیقه وقت برای آنها بدهد . | ۴ |
| ☐ | ☐ | لیلا منتو و سوپ مرغ میخواهد . | ۵ |
| ☐ | ☐ | دوست لیلا قابلی پلو و کباب گوشت گوسفند میخواهد . | ۶ |
| ☐ | ☐ | لیلا نوشیدنی دوغ میخواهد . | ۷ |
| ☐ | ☐ | دوست لیلا نوشیدنی کوکا کولا میخواهد . | ۸ |

C. You will hear a conversation on the audio recording between a waiter and a customer at a restaurant. Briefly summarize what you hear.

D. [icon] Using your notes from Exercise 10A, create a conversation between you and the restaurant waiter or waitress (a partner). Be sure to use the menu in Exercise 9 as a guide.

| Please follow me. | پشت من بیایید . |
|---|---|

Exercise 11: [icon] تمرین ۸:

A. لیلا wrote the following email message to her brother describing her previous bazaar and restaurant experiences. Read her narration carefully and answer the questions that follow.

فرستنده: لیلا
گیرنده : مسعود
موضوع: رستورانت کلبهٔ افغان

برادر عزیزم مسعود جان سلام، من دیروز همراه دوستم زرغونه به بازار رفتیم و در آنجا بسیار چیز ها خریدیم، من برای شما یک تلیفون و کمی سودا خریدم که همراه تان به لیله ببرید .

راستی دیروز ما نان چاشت را در رستورانت کلبهٔ افغان خوردیم، این رستورانت یک ماه پیش باز شد و بسیار غذا هایی خوشمزه دارد . این رستورانت غذایی افغانی و خارجی دارد . من دیروز در نان چاشت منتو و سوپ مرغ خوردم امّا زرغونه قابلی پلو و کباب گوشت گوسفند خورد ، غذایی این رستورانت واقعاً لذیذ و خوشمزه بود . جای تان خالی بود .

بعد از رستورانت ما به دوکان کالافروشی رفتیم و کمی کالاه خریدیم، از دوکان کالافروشی که بیرون شدیم هر دوی ما تشنه شدیم چون کباب و منتو ها کمی شور بود ، بنا ما به آب میوه فروشی رفتیم و آب مالته خوردیم.

لطفاً برایم نوشته کنید که برای تان دیگر چی بخرم.

بااحترام،
خواهرتان لیلا

| واقعاً truly, actually | شور salty | بنا thus, therefore | لذیذ delicious, tasty | خوشمزه tasty, delicious | جای تان خالی بود . This phrase is used when you want to say that a person missed a delicious meal. |
|---|---|---|---|---|---|

1. Who went to the bazaar and restaurant with ليلا؟
   a) her sister     b) her brother     c) her friend     d) her classmate

2. Why did ليلا buy groceries for her brother?
   a) to have him take the groceries to his dorm
   b) to have him take the groceries to his house
   c) to have him take the groceries to his in-laws' house
   d) to have him take the groceries to his school

3. When did the restaurant open?
   a) a week ago     b) a month ago     c) a year ago     d) a decade ago

4. What did ليلا have with the mantu?
   a) lamb soup     b) chicken sauce     c) lamb sauce     d) chicken soup

5. What did زرغونه have with the qabuli?
   a) beef kabob     b) chicken kabob     c) lamb kabob     d) beef sauce

6. Did ليلا like the food?     a) yes     b) no

7. Why did they become thirsty?
   a) the weather was hot
   b) they walked a lot
   c) the food was salty
   d) the food was spicy and salty

B.  Using a similar method as in the exercise above, write a short description of a recent meal you had at a restaurant. In other words, tell about your experience.

Exercise 12: 🎧 تمرین ۱۲:

A. After hearing about the restaurant from his sister لیلا, Masoud wants to celebrate his little brother's birthday in that restaurant along with his family. Thus, he is going to call the restaurant and reserve a table. Listen to his conversation on the audio recording with the restaurant employee and mark the phrases in the box below that مسعود uses with the restaurant employee.

| مالك رستورانت | مسعود | عبارات |
|---|---|---|
| —— | | بلی ، ما میز خالی داریم. شما چی میخواهید که بخورید؟ |
| —— | | برای نوشیدنی، کوکا کولا، چای و آب مالته و برای خوردن کباب گوشت گوسفند همراه نان خشك و سلاته خوب است. |
| —— | | فردا چاشت ساعت چند بجه میآیید؟ |
| —— | | ساعت یك بجه. |
| —— | | بسیار خوب ، تا صباح خدا حافظ! |
| —— | | فردا سالگرهٔ برادر خوردم است، میخواهم که برایش یك كیك كلان آماده کنید. |
| —— | | سلام ، من مسعود هستم، من میخواهم که یك میز چار نفره برای فردا چاشت ریزرف کنم. |
| —— | | به امان خدا! |
| —— | | بسیار خوب برای خوردن و نوشیدن چی میخواهید؟ |
| —— | | هلو به رستورانت كلبهٔ افغان خوش آمدید ، چی خدمت کنم؟ |
| —— | | بسیار خوب ما همه فرمایش های تان را آماده میکنیم. پیسه اش را حالا میپردازید یا فردا. |
| —— | | فردا پیسه تان را میپردازم. |
| —— | | حتما ، میخواهید که بر رویی كیك چیزی نوشته کنیم. |
| —— | | بلی لطفاً نوشته کنید که (سالگره ات مبارك و یا تولدت مبارك). |

B.  Now listen to the audio recording again. This time, complete the following tasks.

1. Masoud asked for what kind of table?
   a) 2-seat table    b) 3-seat table    c) 4-seat table    d) 5-seat table

2. For when is the table reserved?
   a) morning, for breakfast    b) noon, for lunch    c) evening, for dinner

3. What does Masoud want to do while at the restaurant?
   a) reserve an additional table
   b) order a meal
   c) celebrate his brother's birthday

4. What type of restaurant do you think he is calling?
   a) modern    b) casual    c) traditional

5. What phrase will be written on the cake?

6. What kind of food did Masoud order?
   a) lamb kabob with bread and salad
   b) beef kabob with bread and salad
   c) chicken kabob with bread and salad

7. When does Masoud want to pay the check?
   a) right now via phone    b) tomorrow while at the restaurant

C.  Imagine you are in Kabul and you want to celebrate your best friend's birthday at a restaurant. Invite a couple of your friends for dinner. Then, call a restaurant and reserve a table for dinner. Be sure to state the number of people you're inviting, as well as the time and date. Also, be sure to order a cake and ask the restaurant employee to write "happy birthday" on the cake. Lastly, order your meal in advance. Your classmate will play the role of the restaurant employee.

Response:
1. You have a party of 5 people.
2. You want a big cake.
3. Your meal consists of Mantu, lamb kabob, and qabuli palaw.
4. You don't want beef kabob.
5. For drinks, you want orange juice, Pepsi, and dogh.
6. You don't want tea or coffee.
7. Time is tomorrow at 6:00 p.m.

# درس سوم: او یک پیراهن سیاه خریده است.

## Lesson Three: She has bought a black shirt.

In this section, you will learn more about traditional Afghan clothing and shopping in Afghanistan, including clothing sizes, describing colors and materials, and negotiating the price.

Exercise 1: تمرین ۱:

A. The following terms are the names of clothing worn by Afghans in school, offices, and at any official occasion. Listen and write an appropriate definition for each.

| | | | | |
|---|---|---|---|---|
| پیراهن ، یخن قاق | پطلون | کورتی | زیر تنبانی | زیر پیراهنی |
| بالاپوش | نیکر / سنتراج | بلوز | جاکت | جراب |
| کلاه پیکدار | نیکتایی | موزه | بوت | چپلی |

B. You will hear a conversation on the audio recording between زرغونه and her husband نعیم , in which they talk about the clothing they wear during work and school. Listen to the conversation and circle the clothing parts for each person.

زرغونه - نعیم جان، امروز برای کار چی میپوشید؟
نعیم - امروز، کورتی و پطلون سیاه ام همراه یخن قاق آبی و نیکتایی سرخم را میپوشم.
زرغونه - کدام زیر پیراهنی، جراب ها و بوتها را میپوشید؟
نعیم - زیرپیراهنی سفیدم همراه جرابها و بوتهای سیاه ام ، و همان نیکری که دیروز خریدم،
آنرا هم میپوشم. تو امروز چی میخواهی بپوشی؟
زرغونه - من پطلون آسمانی و بلوز زردم را همراۀ چپلی های قهوه یی ام میپوشم.

C. Look at the following pictures and, with a classmate, discuss what each person is wearing. Use the following phrases.

او چی پوشیده است؟
What is s/he wearing?

او پطلون سیاه همراه پیراهن آبی پوشیده است.
S/he is wearing black pants with a blue shirt.

## 8.7 Using the Present Perfect of پوشیدن

The present perfect of the verb پوشیدن "to wear/to put on" is used when telling what someone is wearing, e.g. "she is wearing a blue dress." Thus, in Dari, one says the equivalent of "she has put on a blue dress" instead of "she is wearing a blue dress."

Present perfect is formed using the past participle plus the omitted form of the "to be" verb in the present tense. The past participle is formed by replacing the ending [a] ـه with ending [ـن] of infinitive verbs. The following table shows how the past participle and the omitted form of 'to be' verbs are formed:

| Past Participle | Infinitive verbs |
|---|---|
| پوشیده | پوشیدن |
| omitted form of "to be" in present tense | "to be" |
| ام | هستم |
| ایم | هستیم |
| ای | هستی |
| اید | هستید |
| است | است |
| اند | هستند |

Present perfect

| | |
|---|---|
| I am wearing a white shirt. | من یك پیراهن سفید پوشیده ام. |
| We are wearing white shirts. | ما پیراهن های سفید پوشیده ایم. |
| You are wearing a white shirt. | تو یك پیراهن سفید پوشیده ای. |
| You are wearing white shirts. | شما یك پیراهن سفید پوشیده اید. |
| S/he is wearing a white shirt. | او یك پیراهن سفید پوشیده است. |
| They are wearing white shirts. | آنها پیراهن های سفید پوشیده اند. |

Exercise 2: تمرین ۲:

A. Turn to a classmate sitting next to you and practice asking him/her about what a third classmate is wearing. Be sure to include the color.

B. 🎧 You will hear three conversations on the audio recording between different classmates as they discuss what people are wearing. Listen and practice each one with a partner.

کریم - شریف جان، شما در صنف تان نسیم دارید؟

شریف - بلی، من او را میشناسم.

کریم - او در کجا است؟

شریف - آنجا در پهلوی دروازه است.

کریم - کدامش؟ آنجا دو بچه است.

شریف - همان که بلوز سفید، همراه پطلون سیاه پوشیده و بوتهای قهوه یی هم پوشیده است.

کریم - تشکر.

لیلا - فهیم جان، شما در صنف تان اجمل دارید؟

فهیم - بلی، من او را میشناسم.

لیلا - او در کجا است؟

فهیم - آنجا پیش کمپیوتر نشسته است.

لیلا - کدامش؟ آنجا دو نفر است.

فهیم - همان که یخنقاق آبی، همراه پطلون قهوه یی پوشیده و بوتهای سیاه هم پوشیده است.

لیلا - تشکر.

میرویس - نعیم جان، شما در صنف تان میوند دارید؟

نعیم - بلی، من او را میشناسم.

میرویس - او در کجا است؟

نعیم - آنجا در زیر درخت بالای چوکی نشسته است.

میرویس - کدامش؟ آنجا دو بچه است.

نعیم - همان که کورتی سیاه و پطلون سیاه همراه یخنقاق سبز پوشیده و بوتهای قهوه یی هم پوشیده است.

میرویس - تشکر.

C. 📝 Write the following questions from the previous dialogue in Dari. Then practice asking a partner each question.

| 1. What is your teacher wearing today? | |
|---|---|
| 2. What is your best friend wearing today? | |
| 3. What are you wearing today? | |

Exercise 3: تمرین ۳:

When Afghans are at home and off work, they usually wear the traditional Afghan clothing. زرغونه is describing the clothes her family usually wears. Listen to her monologue on the audio recording and mark the clothing that each of her family members wears.

| ایزار بند | برقعه | شال | چادر | واسکت | چپن | لنگی | پتو | دستمال | کلاه و کلاه پکول | پیراهن و تنبان | |
|---|---|---|---|---|---|---|---|---|---|---|---|
| ☐ | ☐ | ☐ | ☐ | ☐ | ☐ | ☐ | ☐ | ☐ | ☐ | ☐ | زرغونه |
| ☐ | ☐ | ☐ | ☐ | ☐ | ☐ | ☐ | ☐ | ☐ | ☐ | ☐ | شوهر زرغونه |
| ☐ | ☐ | ☐ | ☐ | ☐ | ☐ | ☐ | ☐ | ☐ | ☐ | ☐ | بچهٔ زرغونه |
| ☐ | ☐ | ☐ | ☐ | ☐ | ☐ | ☐ | ☐ | ☐ | ☐ | ☐ | دختر زرغونه |
| ☐ | ☐ | ☐ | ☐ | ☐ | ☐ | ☐ | ☐ | ☐ | ☐ | ☐ | خسر زرغونه |

## Afghan men's clothing 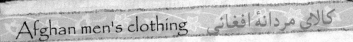 کالای مردانهٔ افغانی

Men's clothes include several parts, depending on the wearer's age and the region in which he resides. Usually, however, all men wear:

پیراهن، تنبان، لنگی، واسکت، کورتی، کلاه، پتو، چپن و پایزار/پایپوش

For example: the following pictures show how men of different ages wear different Afghan clothes.

## Afghan women's clothing کالای زنانهٔ افغانی

The clothes of Afghan women also consist of different parts, e.g. تنبان/ایزار and پایزار and پیراهن، چادر wearer and the region she resides in. For example, the following pictures show how women of different ages wear different Afghan clothes.

Exercise 4: ۴ تمرین :

With a partner, describe the people in the above cultural note and what they're wearing.

آن مرد چی پوشیده است؟

او پیراهن تنبان سیاه همراه کلاه سفید و بوت های سیاه پوشیده است.

Exercise 5: ۵ تمرین :

A. What is he wearing? The following texts are about the two pictures on the right. Read the texts and state which one belongs to حاجی کمال, and which one belongs to محمد یوسف.

حاجی کمال

| | |
|---|---|
| آن مرد پیراهن و تنبان سفید پوشیده است، بالای پیراهن و تنبان کورتی سیاه و چپن قهوه یی پوشیده است، او همچنان لنگی سفید و یک جوره بوت و جراب سیاه پوشیده است. | |
| آن مرد پیراهن سبز خاکی پوشیده، بالای آن جاکت و واسکت سبز خاکی پوشیده است، او همچنان یک پتوی قهوه یی ، کلاه سفید و زیرپیراهنی سفید پوشیده است. | |

محمد یوسف

B. What is she wearing? The following texts are about the two pictures on the right. Read the texts and state which text belongs to مرضیه, and which one belongs to زرمنیه.

| | |
|---|---|
| آن دختر پیراهن و تنبان یاسمنی پوشیده است، او همچنان چادر سرخ ، و چپلی های نارنجی رنگ پوشیده است. | |
| آن دختر پیراهن و تنبان سرخ رنگ پوشیده است، او همچنان جاکت آبی و چادر سیاه پوشیده است. | |

زرمنیه

Note: The words "shirt and pants" پیراهن و تنبان are one name because they're considered a pair.

مرضیه

Exercise 6: تمرین ۶:

Look at the pictures below and write down what the people are wearing.

## Standard Dari vs. Colloquial Dari

The following terms are pronounced differently in colloquial Dari.

For example:

| Colloquial | Standard |
|---|---|
| پیران | پیراهن |
| تمبان | تنبان |
| چادری | رقعه |
| پایزار | بوت |
| چپلك | چپلی |
| دسکش | دستکش |

## 8.8 Order of Adjectives ترتیب صفات

You've already learned that if an object requires an adjective to describe it, the adjectives and comparative adjectives always come after the object and the superlative adjectives come before the objects.

If the object requires more than one adjective, the adjectives come after the object, yet the superlative adjective comes before the object.

In Dari, unlike in English, if the object needs more than one adjective, there is no specific rule to follow when putting those adjectives in order. For example, if you have a jacket which has a large size, made of leather, its color is black, and it is made in China, it could be put in any of the following orders:

من یك جمپر کلان چرمی سیاه چینایی دارم.

من یك جمپر سیاه چرمی کلان چینایی دارم.

من یك جمپر چرمی سیاه دارم که اندازه اش کلان است و ساخت چین میباشد.

The ezafat [-e] is always connected to the adjectives.

Exercise 7:        تمرین ۷:

A. Make your own sentences by putting the following objects and adjectives together. Then compare your work with a partner.

| کتان، پخته | چرمی | تکۀ | پشمی | کلان | میانه | خورد |
|---|---|---|---|---|---|---|
| cotton | leather | fabric | wool | large | medium | small |

| | | |
|---|---|---|
| 1 | She has a large, blue, cotton, Indian sweater. | |
| 2 | I have a medium, white, cotton, Chinese shirt. | |
| 3 | He has a small, brown, wool, American overcoat. | |
| 4 | You had a large, yellow, leather, Italian jacket. | |

B.  With a partner, describe the clothing of two people in your classroom and read your description to the class. The class will then listen and correct you if you miss anything. For example:

او يك كورتى كلان آبى تكهٔ پوشيده است. فكر ميكنم كه ساخت چين است.

S/he is wearing a large, blue, fabric jacket. I think it is made in China.

Exercise 8:  تمرين ۸:

A. You will hear مشترى buy some clothes for her son at a clothing store. Before you listen to the audio recording, write down questions you think will be exchanged between مشترى and the دوكاندار.

B.  Now listen to the audio recording and write down the questions exchanged between them. Check your work.

C. 🎧 Listen to the audio recording again. This time, choose the best answer for the following questions.

| | | | |
|---|---|---|---|
| ۱ | | | مشتری چی نوع کالا بکار داشت؟ |
| زنانه | مردانه | دخترانه | بچه گانه |
| ۲ | | | قیمت یک دانه بلوز چند بود؟ |
| ۴۰۰ افغانی | ۳۰۰ افغانی | ۲۰۰ افغانی | ۱۶۰ افغانی |
| ۳ | | | قیمت پطلون کوبای چند بود؟ |
| ۴۰۰ افغانی | ۳۰۰ افغانی | ۲۰۰ افغانی | ۱۶۰ افغانی |
| ۴ | | | قیمت هر جوره چند بود؟ |
| ۴۰۰ افغانی | ۳۰۰ افغانی | ۲۰۰ افغانی | ۱۶۰ افغانی |
| ۵ | | | مشتری در اخر چند افغانی پرداخت؟ |
| ۶۶۰ افغانی | ۶۳۰ افغانی | ۶۲۰ افغانی | ۶۰۰ افغانی |

| پطلون کوبای | بچه گانه | خیر است |
|---|---|---|
| jeans | boys | That is fine. |

| همشیره | کمی مراعات کنید. | مجموعاً |
|---|---|---|
| sister, title for addressing a strange woman | Give a discount. | in total, in sum, all together |

D. 🤝 You are at a clothing store in Kabul, and you want to buy some clothing for yourself and one of your family members. Greet the seller; tell him/her what is on your list. Then ask for specific colors, size, material, and the country of manufacture. Also, ask for the price and bargain with the seller.

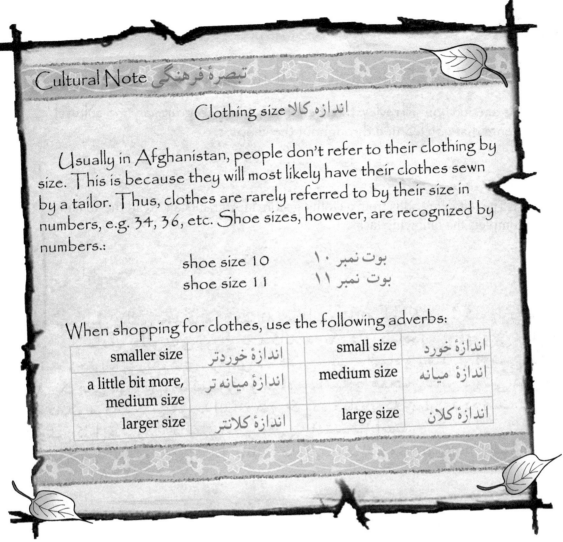

## Cultural Note تبصرهٔ فرهنگی

### اندازه کالا Clothing size

Usually in Afghanistan, people don't refer to their clothing by size. This is because they will most likely have their clothes sewn by a tailor. Thus, clothes are rarely referred to by their size in numbers, e.g. 34, 36, etc. Shoe sizes, however, are recognized by numbers.:

| | |
|---|---|
| shoe size 10 | بوت نمبر ۱۰ |
| shoe size 11 | بوت نمبر ۱۱ |

When shopping for clothes, use the following adverbs:

| smaller size | اندازهٔ خوردتر | small size | اندازهٔ خورد |
|---|---|---|---|
| a little bit more, medium size | اندازهٔ میانه تر | medium size | اندازهٔ میانه |
| larger size | اندازهٔ کلانتر | large size | اندازهٔ کلان |

Exercise 9: تمرین ۹ :

You will hear a conversation on the audio recording between a customer and a salesperson at a clothing store. Listen to their conversation and mark the correct size and color of the following clothing based on the customer's needs.

| زرد | آبی | سیاه | سرخ | اندازه کلان | اندازه میانه | نمبر ۵ | نمبر ۱۰ | | |
|---|---|---|---|---|---|---|---|---|---|
| ☐ | ☐ | ☐ | ☐ | ☐ | ☐ | ☐ | ☐ | men's shoes | ۱ بوت مردانه |
| ☐ | ☐ | ☐ | ☐ | ☐ | ☐ | ☐ | ☐ | women's shirt | ۲ بلوز زنانه |
| ☐ | ☐ | ☐ | ☐ | ☐ | ☐ | ☐ | ☐ | girl's shoes | ۳ بوت دخترانه |
| ☐ | ☐ | ☐ | ☐ | ☐ | ☐ | ☐ | ☐ | boy's pants | ۴ پطلون بچه گانه |

When bargaining, which of the following phrases did the customer use?

a) It's very expensive.   b) Please give me a discount.   c) I am your regular customer.   d) All of the above.

# مرور فصل هشتم
# Review of Chapter Eight

In this section you will review the vocabulary, phrases, grammar, and cultural elements that you learned throughout the chapter.

Exercise 1: تمرین ۱:

A. The following ad is from a clothing store in Afghanistan. Read the ad and complete the following tasks.

لباس فروشی کابل:

لباس فروشی کابل کالای بچه گانه، دخترانه، مردانه و زنانه را از کشور ترکیه وارد کرده است، این کالا شامل پطلونهای کوبای بچه گانه به رنگ های سیاه، آبی و قهوه یی، بلوزهای کتان زنانه و دخترانه به رنگ های سرخ، زرد، گلابی، آبی، سیاه و سفید، و دریشی های مردانه به رنگ های قهوه یی، خاکستری، و سیاه میباشد و همچنان لباس فروشی کابل جمپر های بچه گانه و مردانهٔ چرمی را به اندازه های خورد، میانه و کلان وارد کرده است. لباس فروشی کابل هر روز از ساعت ۸ صبح الی ۱۰ شب باز است.

آدرس: کابل، شهر نو، روبروی کابل بانک، مارکیت میوند، منزل اول دوکان شماره ۱۵

شماره تلیفون: ۰۷۰۰۴۹۲۴۸۲

| اندازه | دریشی | شامل |
|---|---|---|
| size | suit | including |

| | | |
|---|---|---|
| 1 | Which country are the clothes made in? | |
| 2 | What type of boys' clothes does this store have? | |
| 3 | What colors are the men's suits? | |
| 4 | Which clothes come in small, medium, and large sizes? | |
| 5 | Which type of clothing is cotton? | |
| 6 | Which type of clothing is leather? | |
| 7 | What are the operating hours of this store? | |
| 8 | On what floor of this market is Maiwand's store located? | |

B.  You see the above ad and you need the following clothes listed in the table for your younger brother and sister and for yourself. Go to the clothing store and buy those items. Be sure to bargain for the price. A classmate will play the role of the seller.

| me | black suit | large | cotton |
| | white shirt | large | cotton |
| | red tie | | |
| brother | blue jeans | medium | |
| | red shirt | medium | wool |
| | brown jacket | medium | leather |
| sister | yellow shirt | small | cotton |
| | black jeans | small | |
| | white shoes | size 4 | leather |

Exercise 2:   تمرین ۲ :

A. You are living in a dorm with your classmate, and you need some groceries for your room. However, you have an important meeting until 10:00 p.m., and you can't make it to the grocery store. Leave a note to your classmate, and tell him/her to buy those groceries. Be sure to mention the amount of each item.

B. Now go to the grocery store and buy those items. Your classmate will play the role of the shopkeeper.

Exercise 3:    تمرین ۳ :

A. You want to celebrate your brother's graduation (روز فراغت) at a restaurant. Invite your family and friends. Since there are lots of people coming, call a restaurant and make a reservation. Be sure to tell the restaurant employee how many people will attend, the date and time, and what you would like to serve your guests. Finally, order a cake to celebrate the occassion.

Responses:
1- *You have 20 guests.*
2- *You need a private room, and probably for 4 hours, starting from 5:00 and continuing to 9:00 p.m.*
3- *For food, you want lamb kabob, chicken kabob, qaboli palaw, soup, and salad with bread.*
4- *For drinks, you want Coke, Pepsi, yogurt drink, water, and tea.*
5- *For dessert, you want cake and ferni.*

B.    You've invited your friend for dinner in a modern restaurant in Kabul. Have a conversation. Then, ask for the menu, fork, knife, and spoon, and order the meal for yourself and your friend. Then act out the conversation in front of your class.

# Vocabulary

In this part of the lesson, you will review, listen to, and practice pronunciation of the phrases and vocabulary used in the chapter.

## Phrases اصطلاحات

| with regards | bā ĕhtarām | با احترام |
|---|---|---|
| let's go | beyā kĕ bĕrawem. | بیا که برویم. |
| This phrase is used when you want to say that a person was missed during a delicious meal. | jāye tān xāli bōd. | جای تان خالی بود. |
| actually, truly | wāqĕ'an | واقعاً |
| slang for well...umm...hmm... | wallāh | والله |
| That is fine. | xayr ast. | خیر است. |
| Discount the price. | kame ma'āt koned. | کمی مراعات کنید. |

## Vocabulary Words لغات

| water | āb | آب |
|---|---|---|
| juice | āb mewa | آب میوه |
| juice/smoothie shop | ābmewa forōši | آب میوه فروشی |
| flour | ārd | آرد |
| cook | āšpaz | آشپز |
| kitchen | āšpaz xāna | آشپزخانه |
| cherry | ālu bālu | آلوبالو |
| to be ready | āmāda bōdan (āmāda hast) | آماده بودن (آماده هست) |
| ice cream | ayskĕrim | آیسکریم |
| ice cream shop | āyskĕrim forōši | آیسکریم فروشی |
| grape | angur | انگور |
| pomegranate | anār | انار |
| a string that ties the waist of the pants | ezār band | ایزار بند |

| | | |
|---|---|---|
| cucumber | bādrang | بادرنگ |
| for boys | bačagāna | بچه گانه |
| eggplant | bādĕnejān-e siyā (bānejān-e siyā) | بادنجان سیاه |
| tomato | bādĕnjān-e rōmi | بادنجان رومی |
| burqa | borqa, čādari | برقعه، چادری |
| rice | bĕrĕnj | برنج |
| pack | basta | بسته |
| to close | basta kardan (basta kon) | بسته کردن (بسته کن) |
| to need | bakārdāštan (bakārdār) | بکارداشتن (بکار دار) |
| shirt | bōloz | بلوز |
| bottle | bōtal | بوتل |
| boots | but, pāyzār | بوت، پایزار |
| large bags | bōji | بوجی |
| sugar | bōra | بوره |
| oil | rōğan | روغن |
| tasteless | be maza | بی مزه |
| man's shawl | patu | پتو |
| to cook | poxta kardan (poxta kon) | پخته کردن (پخته کن) |
| pants (jeans) | patlun | پطلون |
| jeans/cowboy pants | patlun-e kawbāy | پطلون کوبای |
| cheese | paner | پنیر |
| to wear | pōšidan (pōš) | پوشیدن (پوش) |
| onion | peyāz | پیاز |
| dress/shirt | perāhan | پیراهن |
| change (money) | paysa-e mayda | پیسه میده |
| egg | toxm-e morg | تخم مرغ |
| watermelon | tarbuz | تربوز |
| sour | torš | ترش |

| | | |
|---|---|---|
| vegetable | tarkāri | ترکاری |
| vegetable store | tarkāri forōši | ترکاری فروشی |
| bitter | talx | تلخ |
| pants | tonbān, ezār | تنبان، ایزار |
| spicy, chili | tond | تند |
| strawberry | tōt-e zamini | توت زمینی |
| to prepare, to fix, to make | tayār kardan (tayār kon) | تیار کردن (تیار کن) |
| jacket | jākat | جاکت |
| a place that... | jāy-e kě | جای که |
| socks | jorāb | جراب |
| scarf | čādar | چادر |
| a quarter or a fourth of a unit | čāryak/čārak | چاریك/چارك |
| tea | čāy | چای |
| sandal | čapli | چپلی |
| chapan | čapan | چپن |
| how many kinds, several types | čand naw' | چند نوع |
| omelet | xāgina | خاگینه |
| melon | xarbuza | خربوزه |
| to buy | xarid (xar) | خریدن (خر) |
| to buy | xaridan (xar) | خریدن (خر) |
| shopping | xaridār | خریداری |
| 565 kg | xarwār | خروار |
| to want | xāstan (xāh) | خواستن ( خواه ) |
| edible | xōrāka bāb/xōrdani | خوراکه باب/خوردنی |
| to eat | xōrdan (xōr) | خوردن (خور) |
| to welcome | xōš āmadan (xōš āy) | خوش آمدن (خوش آی) |
| delicious | xōš maza | خوشمزه |
| to give | dādan (dah) | دادن (ده) |

| | | |
|---|---|---|
| piece | dāna | دانه |
| for girls | doxtarāna | دختران |
| dozen | darjan | درجن |
| bunch | dĕsta | دسته |
| gloves | dĕstkaš | دستكش |
| towel/handkerchief | dĕstmāl | دستمال |
| tomato sauce | rob/rob-e badĕnjān-e rōmi | رب/ رب بادنجان رومى |
| restaurant | rastōrant | رستورانت |
| carrot | zarday | زردك |
| rough | zomoxt | زمخت |
| for women, women's (clothing) | zanāna | زنانه |
| undergarments | zer perāni | زیرپیراهنی |
| underpants | zer tonbāni (zer tombāni) | زیرتنبانی |
| spinach | sabzi pālak | سبزی پالك |
| vegetables | sabzijāt/tarkāri | سبزیجات/ ترکاری باب |
| salad | salāta | سلاته |
| groceries | sawdā | سودا |
| apple | seb | سیب |
| 7066 grams in Kabul, but 100 grams in western part of the country. | ser | سیر |
| garlic | sir | سیر |
| shawl | šāl | شال |
| peach | šaftālu | شفتالو |
| turnip | šalğam | شلغم |
| salty | šōr | شور |
| milk | šir | شیر |
| sweet | širin | شیرین |
| glasses | 'aynak | عینك |

| | | |
|---|---|---|
| to sell | forōxtan (forōš) | فروختن (فروش) |
| can | qotti | قطی |
| sauce | qōrma | قورمه |
| coffee | qahwa | قهوه |
| box | kārtan | کارتن |
| clothes | kālā | کالا |
| clothing store | kāla forōši | کالافروشی |
| clothes | kālā, lĕbās | کالا، لباس |
| lettuce | kāho | کاهو |
| kabob | kabāb | کباب |
| potato | kačālu | کچالو |
| cabbage | karam barg | کرم برگ |
| a person who... | kas-e kĕ | کسی که |
| to take off | kašidan (kaš) | کشیدن (کش) |
| hat | kolāh | کلاه |
| hat | kolah-e pik | کلاه پیک |
| cookies | kolča | کلچه |
| to help | komak kardan (komak kon) | کمک کردن (کمک کن) |
| coat | kōrti | کورتی |
| meatball | kofta | کوفته |
| banana | kela | کیله |
| kilo | kelō | کیلو |
| waiter/waitress | ğārsun | گارسون |
| to take | gĕrĕftan (gir) | گرفتن (گیر) |
| meat | gōšt | گوشت |
| beef | gōšt-e gaw | گوشت گاو |
| lamb | gōšt-e gosfand | گوشت گوسفند |
| chicken | gōšt-e morğ | گوشت مرغ |
| dairy | labaniyāt | لبنیات |

| | | |
|---|---|---|
| turban | longi | لنگی |
| yogurt | māst | ماست |
| orange | mālta | مالته |
| 4.6 grams | mĕsqāl | مثقال |
| in total, in sum, all together | majmo'an | مجموعاً |
| pepper | morč | مرچ |
| men's (clothing), for men | mardāna | مردانه |
| butter | maska | مسکه |
| customer | moštari | مشتری |
| radish | moli | ملی |
| 7066 grams in Kabul, about 5000 grams in Kandahar, and 4000 grams in western parts of the country. | man | من |
| menu | menōy-e ğĕzā | منیوی غذا |
| car | mōtar | موتر |
| car sales | mōtar forōši | موتر فروشی |
| boots | mōza | موزه |
| guest | mĕhmān | مهمان |
| fruit | mewa | میوه |
| fruit | mewajāt | میوه جات |
| bread | nān-e xošk | نان خشك |
| salt | namak | نمك |
| to write | nĕwĕšta kardan (nĕwĕšta kon) | نوشته کردن (نوشته کن) |
| to drink | nōšidan (nōš) | نوشیدن(نوش) |
| drinks | nōšidani | نوشیدنی |
| underwear | nekar, sentarāj | نیکر، سنتراج |
| tie | nektāye | نیکتایی |
| vest | wāskat | واسکت |
| sister, title for addressing a strange woman | hamšira | همشیره |

| all | hama | همه |
|---|---|---|
| refrigerator | yaxčāl | يخچال |
| dress shirt | yaxan qāq | يخن قاق |

## Dari Vocabulary Different from Iranian Persian

| English Translation | Iranian Persian | | Farsi-e Dari | |
|---|---|---|---|---|
| cowboy pants | šalvār-e jinz | شلوار جينز | patlun-e kawbāy | پطلون كوباى |
| pants | šalvār | شلوار | patlun | پطلون |
| pajama tie | band-e šalvār | بند شلوار | ezār band | ازار بند |
| tie | karavāt | كروات | niktāye | نيكتايى |
| underwear | šort | شورت | nikar, sĕntarāj | نيكر، سنتراج |
| overcoat | pāltō | پالتو | bālā-poš | بالاپوش |
| turban | 'amāma, dastār | عمامه، دستار | longi | لنگى |
| boots | čakma | چكمه | mōza | موزه |
| dress shirt | pirā-han | پيراهن | yaxan-qāq | يخن قاق |
| underpants | zir-puš | زير پوش | zĕr tonbāni | زيرتنبانى |
| restaurant | rasturan | رستوران | rastōrānt | رستورانت |
| cherry | ālu-gilās | آلوگيلاس | ālu bālu | آلوبالو |
| orange | portaqāl | پرتقال | mālta | مالته |
| watermelon | hĕnduna | هندوانه | tarbuz | تربوز |
| banana | muz | موز | kela | كيله |
| pepper | fĕlfĕl | فلفل | morč | مرچ |
| carrot | havič | هويج | zardak | زردك |
| cucumber | xiyār | خيار | badrang | بادرنگ |
| sugar | šakar | شكر | bura | بوره |

# فصل نهم
## CHAPTER NINE

رخصتی های تابستانی
## SUMMER VACATIONS

# IN THIS CHAPTER

• وظایف Functions

*Talking about the weather; Booking tickets and traveling; Going through the airport and customs; Reserving a hotel room; Talking about travel experiences; Renting a taxi*

• تبصرهٔ فرهنگی Cultural Notes

*Weather in Afghanistan; Hotels in Afghanistan*

• دستور زبان Language Structure

*The verb* باریدن *'; Nominal adjectives with suffix* ی *'i'; Conditional sentences; Past progressive/imperfect tense of verb* وزیدن & باریدن; *Expressing future tense with verb* خواستن; *The generic possessive* خود; *Forming the past perfect*

• مرور فصل Chapter Review

*Talking about the weather; Listening to weather reports; Booking a ticket; Reserving a hotel room; Renting a taxi; Talking about travel plans/experiences*

• لغات Vocabulary

*Review phrases and words used in this chapter*

## Chapter Introduction

# معرفی فصل

In this chapter, you will learn to talk about the weather in various seasons. Additionally, as seasons change, so do plans. Thus, this chapter will also focus on traveling, booking tickets, going to the airport, dealing with customs, reaching a destination, renting a taxi, and, finally, reserving a hotel room.

By the end of this chapter, you should be able to talk about your present, past, or future travels and be able to reserve a hotel room, rent a taxi, and deal with simple situations at airports & with customs.

خریدن تکت برای رخصتی های تابستانی.

Booking a ticket for summer vacation.

هوا چطور است؟

How is the weather?

ریزرف کردن اتاق در هوتل.

Reserving a room at a hotel.

# درس اول: هوا چطور است؟

## Lesson One: How is the weather?

In this section, you will learn how to talk about the seasons, to describe the weather, and to read a weather report in Dari. You will also learn more about the climate of Afghanistan.

Exercise 1: تمرین ۱:

A. Listen to the following terms on the audio recording and repeat the phrases.

| ماه | فصل | سال | آب و هوا |
|-----|-----|-----|----------|
| month | season | year | weather |

| زمستان | خزان | تابستان | بهار |
|--------|------|---------|------|
| winter | fall | summer | spring |

B. In Afghanistan, the solar calendar is the one most frequently used. The solar year starts on the first day of spring. Can you find out which months belong to each season?

| فصل ها | نام ماه ها | فصل ها | نام ماه ها |
|--------|------------|--------|------------|
| | ماه هفتم    میزان | | ماه اول    حمل |
| | ماه هشتم    عقرب | | ماه دوم    ثور |
| | ماه نهم    قوس | | ماه سوم    جوزا |
| | ماه دهم    جدی | | ماه چارم    سرطان |
| | ماه یازدهم    دلو | | ماه پنجم    اسد |
| | ماه دوازدهم    حوت | | ماه ششم    سنبله |

C. What is your favorite season? Why do you like this season? Which months belong to this season? Discuss your responses with a classmate.

Exercise 2: تمرین ۲:

A. Read the following terms and circle the season you think each belongs to. For example, snow belongs to the winter season; thus, circle winter.

B. Now listen to شریف describe Kabul's weather during the four seasons on the audio recording. Then write a description of the weather for each season. For example,  زمستان = برفی

C. Listen again to شریف's monologue on the audio recording, and check "true" or "false" for each of the following statements based on what you hear.

| غلط | صحیح | جملات |
|---|---|---|
| ☐ | ☐ | ۱  در فصلِ بهار هوای کابل معتدل است، آسمان معمولاً ابر و گاهی صاف است. |
| ☐ | ☐ | ۲  در تابستان هوا گرم و مرطوب است. |
| ☐ | ☐ | ۳  در تابستان اکثراً هوا صاف است. |
| ☐ | ☐ | ۴  در بهار گاهی طوفان میشود. |
| ☐ | ☐ | ۵  در خزان هوا سرد است. |
| ☐ | ☐ | ۶  در خزان باران میبارد. |
| ☐ | ☐ | ۷  در زمستان همیشه خنک و سرد است. |

### 9.1 The Verb باریدن 'To Rain, To Pour Down'

In Dari, to describe anything that falls/pours down from the sky, combine the verb باریدن with the falling object to make a new compound verb. For example:

| | | |
|---|---|---|
| to rain | باران باریدن | (to rain, fall down) باریدن + (rain) باران |
| to snow | برف باریدن | (to rain, fall down) باریدن + (snow) برف |
| to hail | ژاله باریدن | (to rain, fall down) باریدن + (hail) ژاله |

Exercise 3:   تمرین ۳:

A. Write the Dari equivalent of the following sentences.

| It is raining today. | _____ | ۱ |
| It is snowing today. | _____ | ۲ |
| It is hailing today. | _____ | ۳ |

B. Describe the weather during your favorite season. Use the following structures.

In the spring, it rains a lot.

در بهار بسیار باران میبارد.

In the summer, it is very hot, but it doesn't rain.

در تابستان هوا بسیار گرم است، اما باران نمیبارد.

In the winter, it snows a lot.

در زمستان بسیار برف میبارد.

C. Using the following verbs, write five sentences about the weather you like or dislike for each season.

| سیل آمدن (سیل آی) | باریدن (بار) | باران میبارد | ژاله میبارد | برف میبارد | باد میوزد |
|---|---|---|---|---|---|
| to flood | to rain, shower | it is raining | it is hailing | it is snowing | the wind is blowing |

D. 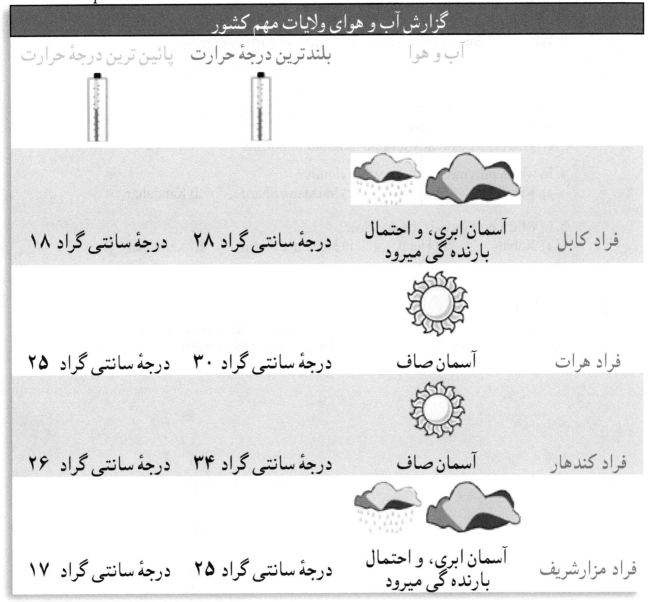 You will hear a short conversation on the audio recording between two people as they talk about the weather. Listen and then practice asking your classmates about the weather.

How is the weather today?

امروز هوا چطور است؟

Today, the weather is cold; the sky is cloudy, and it is raining.

امروز هوا سرد است، آسمان ابری است و باران میبارد.

How was the weather yesterday?

دیروز هوا چطور بود؟

Yesterday, the weather was warm; the sky was cloudy, but it didn't rain.

دیروز هوا گرم بود، آسمان ابر بود اما باران نبارید.

Exercise 4: تمرین: ۴

A. Read the following weather report and discuss the weather in each city with a partner.

| | پائین ترین درجهٔ حرارت | بلندترین درجهٔ حرارت | | آب و هوا | |
|---|---|---|---|---|---|
| | درجهٔ سانتی گراد ۱۸ | درجهٔ سانتی گراد ۲۸ | آسمان ابری، و احتمال بارنده گی میرود | | فراد کابل |
| | درجهٔ سانتی گراد ۲۵ | درجهٔ سانتی گراد ۳۰ | آسمان صاف | | فراد هرات |
| | درجهٔ سانتی گراد ۲۶ | درجهٔ سانتی گراد ۳۴ | آسمان صاف | | فراد کندهار |
| | درجهٔ سانتی گراد ۱۷ | درجهٔ سانتی گراد ۲۵ | آسمان ابری، و احتمال بارنده گی میرود | | فراد مزارشریف |

گزارش آب و هوای ولایات مهم کشور

B. ✎    Based on what you just read in Exercise 4A, what do the following words mean?

_____ ۴ بارنده گی         _____ ۱ درجه سانتی گراد

_____ ۵ گزارش            _____ ۲ ابری

_____ ۶ درجهٔ حرارت       _____ ۳ احتمال رفتن

C. 📖    Now, read the text in exercise 4A again and, this time, circle the best option for each question below.

1. What is the highest temperature in Kabul tomorrow?
   a) 25         b) 28         c) 30         d) 34

2. What is the lowest temperature in Mazaar-e Sharif tomorrow?
   a) 17         b) 18         c) 25         d) 26

3. Which of the following is stated in the text?
   a)  It will rain in Kabul.
   b)  It could rain in Kabul tomorrow.
   c)  There is a possibility for rain in Kabul tomorrow.

4. In which provinces is the weather cloudy?
   a) Kabul         b) Herat         c) Mazaar-e Sharif         d) Kandahar

5. In which provinces is the sky clear?
   a) Kabul         b) Herat         c) Mazaar-e Sharif         d) Kandahar

Exercise 5: 🎧    تمرین ۵:
   A. You will hear a conversation on the audio recording between شریف and his friend میرویس about the weather. Listen and write the name of the city being mentioned and how the weather is in that city.

B.  Go to google.com and find today's weather report for the following provinces of Afghanistan. Then, write down each of the weather reports in the following table.

| | | |
|---|---|---|
| کابل | ۱ | _____ |
| ننگرهار | ۲ | _____ |
| غزنی | ۳ | _____ |
| کندهار | ۴ | _____ |
| غور | ۵ | _____ |
| بدخشان | ۶ | _____ |
| بلخ | ۷ | _____ |
| فاریاب | ۸ | _____ |

C. Working with a partner, make a similar conversation to that of Exercise 2B and ask about the weather in the different provinces of Afghanistan.

## 9.2 Nominal Adjectives with Suffix ى 'i'

As metioned in the text about the weather report, the word ابر 'cloud' takes the suffix ى 'i' and means ابرى 'cloudy'. Thus, in Dari some nouns take the suffix ى 'i' to make an adjective. For example:

| cloudy | ابرى | cloud | ابر |
| rainy | بارانى | rain | باران |

However, remember never to mix the above suffix with the indefinite suffix ى. For example:

| a person, some person | کسى | person | کس |
| sometime, when | وقتى | time | وقت |
| place, somewhere | جایى | place | جاى |

Exercise 6: تمرین ۶:

A. Write the Dari equivalent of the following phrases.

| The weather is cloudy today. | | ۱ |
|---|---|---|
| The weather was rainy yesterday. | | ۲ |
| The weather is snowy today. | | ۳ |
| The weather is sunny tomorrow. | | ۴ |
| There is a full moon in the sky tonight. | | ۵ |

B. 🎧 You will hear a phone conversation on the audio recording between شریف, who lives in Kabul, and his friend کریم, who lives in Herat. Listen to their conversation and write the exact adjectives that you hear for each province in the table below for the different days.

| ۱) کابل امروز | ۲) کابل دیروز | ۳) هرات امروز | ۴) هرات صباح |
|---|---|---|---|
| | | | |

C.  Listen to the conversation again. This time, practice asking the following questions with a partner.

۱   امروز هوایی هرات چطور است؟ _____

۲   صباح هوایی هرات چطور است؟ _____

۳   امروز هوایی کابل چطور است؟ _____

۴   دیروز هوایی کابل چطور بود؟ _____

### 9.3 Conditional Sentences جملات شرطی

In Dari, all conditional sentences are introduced by اگر 'if'. The conditional clause has its verb in the present subjunctive. In Exercise 6C, you just heard the following phrases:

اگر هوا خوب باشد، ساعت ۱۰   If the weather is good, I will
بجه میایم.   come at 10:00 a.m.

Also, sometimes both clauses take a subjunctive verb. The dependent clause (the "if" clause) will always take the subjunctive. When the main clause uses an auxiliary verb (such as "want", "might", "have to", etc.), then it also takes the subjunctive.

اگر هوا خوب باشد میخواهم که   If the weather is good, I
به هرات بیایم.   want to come to Herat.

Note: As you can see in the second sentence, if the second clause starts with an auxiliary, then its verb will also take the subjunctive form. In previous chapters, we learned about the effect of the auxiliary verbs on main verbs.

In colloquial Dari, اگر is pronounced as [aga] اگه .

In Dari, dependent clauses may be marked not only by the word اگر but by words such as the following, which also mean "if":

درصورتیکه        هروقتیکه        چنانچه

Exercise 7:  تمرین ۷:

A. *If the weather is ...* Using the following words, create your own sentences. Use the conditional marker اگر.

| | |
|---|---|
| ۱ | هوا ابری/ سینما رفتن |
| ۲ | هوا سرد / قهوه نوشیدن |
| ۳ | هوا گرم/ آببازی کردن |
| ۴ | هوا برفی/ کالای گرم پوشیدن |
| ۵ | هوا بارانی/ بالاپوش پوشیدن |

B. Listen to the conversation on the audio recording and answer the following questions in Dari.

1. According to the audio recording, what will happen if the weather is good in Herat tomorrow?

2. According to the audio recording, what time will شریف go to Herat if the weather is good tomorrow?

C. The first clause of each sentence below begins with the word اگر. In each case, the second clause starts with an auxiliary verb (such as "want", "might", "have to", etc.). Complete the second clause of the following sentences by using a correct form of the verb.

| | |
|---|---|
| ۱ | اگر صبح باران ببارد ،من میخواهم که در خانه ———— (ماندن). |
| ۲ | اگر صبح آسمان صاف باشد ، ما شاید به میله ———— (رفتن). |
| ۳ | اگر صبح هوا خنک باشد و برف ببارد ، من میخواهم که به مکتب ———— (نه رفتن). |
| ۴ | اگر صبح هوا آفتابی باشد ، ما باید آببازی ———— (کردن). |
| ۵ | اگر صبح برف ببارد ، ما باید کالای گرم ———— (پوشیدن). |

## 9.4  Past Progressive/Imperfect Tense of Verb باریدن & وزیدن

The following verbs are the most commonly used when buying groceries.

| | |
|---|---|
| Yesterday, when I was going to the bazaar, it rained a lot. | دیروز وقتیکه بازار میرفتم، بسیار باران بارید. |

In the following examples, both clauses are in the past progressive. Thus, they explain that the two events happened parallel to each other. In other words, while he was on his way to the bazaar, it was raining at the same time. The time clause وقتیکه 'when, while' is always used in such cases.

| | |
|---|---|
| Yesterday, while I was going to the bazaar, it rained a lot. | دیروز وقتیکه بازار میرفتم، بسیار باران میبارید. |

The past progressive is formed by adding the prefix می to the beginning of the simple past tense of the verb.

Exercise 8: تمرین ۸:

    A. Complete the following sentences with the past progressive form of the verb provided. Then write the English equivalent of each sentence.

| | |
|---|---|
| ۱ | دیشب وقتیکه نان ———— (خوردن) ، ———— (باد وزیدن) |
| ۲ | دیروز وقتیکه مکتب ———— (رفتن) ———— (باران باریدن) |
| ۳ | زمستان گذشته وقتیکه ———— (برف باریدن)، ما در بیرون از خانه ———— (بازی کردن) |
| ۴ | بهار قبل وقتیکه ———— (باران باریدن)، در خانه ما ———— (سیل آمدن) |
| ۵ | بهار گذشته وقتیکه هوا ———— (ژاله باریدن) ما به میله ———— (نرفتن) |
| ۶ | وقتیکه هوا ———— (گرم بودن)، آنها به آببازی ———— (رفتن) |

B. Make a complete sentence using the given elements.

۱ دیروز وقتیکه (باران باریدن) / احمد به مکتب (رفتن)

_____

_____

۲ دیشب وقتیکه ژاله (باریدن) / من (خواب بودن).

_____

_____

۳ هفته گذشته وقتیکه (برف باریدن) زرغونه به خانهٔ ما (آمدن).

_____

_____

۴ زمستان گذشته وقتیکه شما کابل (رفتن) / من در میدان هوایی (بودن)

_____

_____

C. Compare your answers with a classmate. Explain what your sentences suggest about the order of the two events in each sentence. Do they follow each other or are they simultaneous?

D. شریف leaves a voicemail message to his friend کریم. Listen to his message on the audio recording and note the imperfect or progressive form of the verbs below.

Exercise 9:  تمرین ۹:

A. Listen to شریف voicemail message on the audio recording again. This time, answer the following questions.

1. What happened when شریف was talking to کریم on the phone yesterday?
   a) It started raining outside.
   b) It started snowing outside.
   c) It started hailing outside.

2. What tasks was شریف unable to do?
   a) go and buy a ticket
   b) go to Herat
   c) go to the bazaar and shop

3. When does شریف plan to travel?
   a) when there is no rain
   b) when the sky is clear
   c) when the weather is good

4. When does شریف ask his friend to call him?

_____

_____

B. Role-play: Your classmate has invited you to dinner, but suddenly the weather gets really bad. It's stormy, there's lots of snow, and the temperature has dropped down to 30°F. Call your friend, tell him/her that you can't make it, and explain the reasons. Finally, tell your classmate that if the weather gets better, then you can attend the dinner. Then imagine that s/he doesn't answer the phone. Leave a voicemail by recording your message.

Exercise 10: تمرین ۱۰:

A. کریم got شریف voicemail message and is calling him back. Listen to the audio recording and mark the adjectives that you hear.

| برفی | شدید | خنك | سنگین | خراب | خوب | سرد |
|------|------|-----|-------|------|-----|-----|
| snowy | hard | cold | heavy | worse | good | cold |
| | | | | | | |

B. According to the audio recording, which one of the following adjectives goes with the following objects?

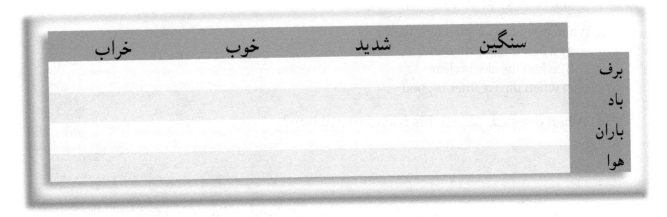

| خراب | خوب | شدید | سنگین | |
|------|-----|------|-------|---|
| | | | | برف |
| | | | | باد |
| | | | | باران |
| | | | | هوا |

C. According to the audio recording, who said the following phrases? Write the name under each phrase.

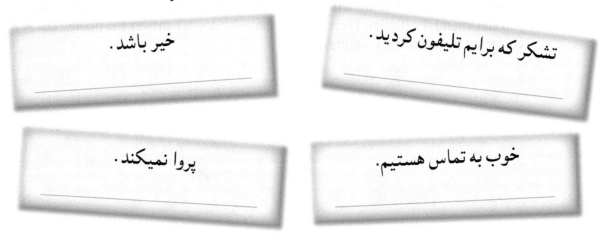

تشکر که برایم تلیفون کردید.

خیر باشد.

خوب به تماس هستیم.

پروا نمیکند.

D.  Listen to the audio recording again and answer the following questions.

1. Where was کریم when شریف called? Answer in Dari.

_____

_____

2. When کریم said "excuse me", what does شریف say in response?

a) پروا نمیکند      b) خیر باشد

3. When شریف wants to end the conversation, which of the following phrases does he use? Put a check mark next to the sentence(s).

_____ خیر باشد     _____ تشکر که برایم تلیفون کردید.

_____ پروا نمیکند     _____ خوب به تماس هستیم.

4. How was the weather in Herat yesterday?

_____

_____

E. In Exercise 9B, your classmate left you a voicemail message stating that s/he can't make it to your dinner party. Call your classmate back and create a conversation. Be sure to include the following:

1. Thank your classmate for the call.
2. Tell your classmate that when s/he was calling you, you were in the shower.
3. If you hear "Excuse me," provide the appropriate response.
4. Tell your classmate that you also noticed the bad weather.
5. Invite your classmate to dinner in an Afghan restaurant at a later date.
6. Tell your classmate that you have checked the weather for that date and that the weather is sunny. Then describe the weather on that date.
7. Wrap up the conversation by stating that you will be in touch.

## Cultural Note    تبصرهٔ فرهنگی

### Traditional Afghan Heater

During the winter season, the weather is extremely cold, especially in the mountainous regions. Because people don't generally have heating and cooling systems in their homes, many Afghans heat their homes using charcoal and a round/square table called a [sandali] صندلی. These tables have hot plates filled with HOT charcoal in the bottom center of the table. A blanket or comforter then covers the table, and when people come home from outside, they sit on the floor near the [sandali] صندلی and crawl under the blanket for warmth. Afghans with better economic status usually buy gas or wood heaters.

When the winter weather conditions become severe, roads will close. As a result, people generally buy several weeks or months of food supplies ahead of time to prepare. People in rural areas are unable to

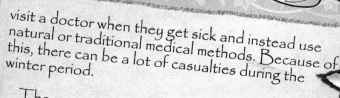

visit a doctor when they get sick and instead use natural or traditional medical methods. Because of this, there can be a lot of casualties during the winter period.

The summer season is very hot and dry. Again, since most Afghans don't have air conditioning or cooling systems, people use electric fans, hand fans, or simply they make a hole in their roof (toward the north section where the wind is most common) to let the wind into the room. Those who have windows leave them open. During summer nights, people generally sleep outside in their yards, on their roofs, or on balconies, using a canopy to protect against mosquitoes.

During the fall and spring season, the weather is mild and enjoyable. People often enjoy it by going on outings with their families—going on picnics, and visiting their relatives' gardens to pick delicious fruit.

# درس دوم : خریدن تکت برای رخصتی های تابستانی

## Lesson Two: Booking a ticket for summer vacation.

In this section, you will learn to discuss travel plans, including talking about destination, transportation, and travel costs.

Exercise 1: تمرین ۱ :

A. Listen to the following short conversations on the audio recording and read the parts aloud with a partner.

شما برای رخصتی های تابستانی به کجا میروید ؟
Where are you going for summer vacation?

شما در مزار چی میکنید ؟
What are you doing in Mazaar?

من برای رخصتی های تابستانی به مزار میروم.
I am going to Mazaar for summer break.

من به موزیم مزار میروم، میله میکنم و استراحت میکنم.
I am going to the Mazaar museum for a picnic and relaxation.

B. Read the following Dari terms and find their English equivalent using the definitions provided in the box below.

میدان هوایی

تکت فروشی

تکت طیاره

ترمینال میدان هوایی

نشست کردن

طیاره

پرواز کردن

پاسپورت

بکس

مسافر

گمرک

پیلوت

استیوردیس

تذکره/ کارت هویت

سفر

plane ticket, travel agency, airport, terminal, airplane, to land, to fly, bag, passenger, passport, customs, flight attendant, ID card, pilot, travel

C. ✋ Imagine you have a local trip planned. Using the list of words above, determine what objects you will need for your trip. Use the following structure and explain it to a classmate.

اگر شما یك سفر داخلی داشته باشید، به کدام چیز ها ضرورت دارید؟

If you take a local trip, what things do you need?

اگر من یك سفر داخلی داشته باشم، من به ... ...... .... ضرورت دارم.

If I take a local trip, I will need ... ... ...

D. ✋ Imagine that you have an overseas trip planned. Using the list of words above, determine what objects you will need for your trip. Use the following structure and explain it to a classmate.

اگر شما یك سفر خارجی داشته باشید، به کدام چیز ها ضرورت دارید؟

If you take a trip overseas, what things do you need?

اگر من یك سفر خارجی داشته باشم، من به ... ...... .... ضرورت دارم.

If I take a trip overseas, I will need ... ... ...

E. ✋ What do you do before a trip? Explain your activities to a classmate. For example: *I go to a travel agency and buy a ticket, then...*

## 9.5  Expressing the Future Tense with the Verb خواستن (خواه)

To describe your future plans, use the verb خواستن (خواه) is used as a future marker.

When the verb خواستن (خواه) is used as a future marker, personal endings are conjugated in the future; unlike the other verbs, this verb doesn't take the prefix می. For example:

| | | | |
|---|---|---|---|
| I will go. | من خواهم رفت. | We will go. | ما خواهیم رفت. |
| You will go. | تو خواهی رفت. | You will go. | شما خواهید رفت. |
| S/he will go. | او خواهد رفت. | They will go. | آنها خواهند رفت. |

As you can see, the main verbs for all cases use the same form, which is also the past form of the third person singular. This means that the personal endings used in the future marker and the main verb do not take any personal endings. For example:

| | | | |
|---|---|---|---|
| I will go. | من خواهم رفت. | We will go. | ما خواهیم رفت. |
| You will go. | تو خواهی رفت. | You will go. | شما خواهید رفت. |
| S/he will go. | او خواهد رفت. | They will go. | آنها خواهند رفت. |

In colloquial Dari, this concept is used as the opposite of the above structure. This means that the personal ending gets conjugated with the main verb, and the future marker stays in the same form as that shown below:

| | | | |
|---|---|---|---|
| I will go. | مه خاد رفتم. | We will go. | ما خاد رفتیم. |
| You will go. | تو خاد رفتی. | You will go. | شما خاد رفتید. |
| S/he will go. | او خاد رفت. | They will go. | اوها خاد رفتن. |

*The colloquial form is never written and is avoided in formal situations.

Exercise 2: 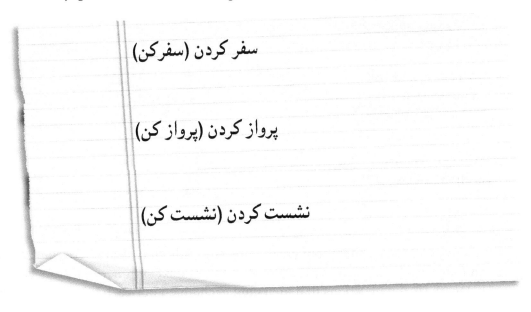 تمرین ۲:

A. Conjugate each of the following verbs in the future tense for all cases.

سفر کردن (سفرکن)

پرواز کردن (پرواز کن)

نشست کردن (نشست کن)

B. Practice asking your classmate what s/he will do on one of the following dates. For example:

شما در دوم جنوری چی خواهید کرد؟

What will you do on January 2nd?

| جنتری | چی خواهم کرد؟ | |
|---|---|---|
| جنوری | بیستم جنوری – شهر کابل  – به سفر رفتن | |
| فبروری | اول فبروری ساعت نه صبح – در میدان هوایی بودن | |
| مارچ | دوم مارچ – پوهنتون – رخصت بودن | |
| اپریل | نهم اپریل – شهر بامیان – بودا را دیدن | |
| می | سی ام می – شهر مزار شریف – موزیم را دیدن | |
| جون | دوازدهم جون – شهر هرات– کالاخریدن | |
| جولای | بیست و یک جولای –  جشن سالگره بودن | |
| اگست | پانزدهم اگست – ساعت شش شام ۔ از میدان هوایی کابل ۔پرواز کردن | |
| سپتمبر | چارم سپتمبر – ساعت پنج صبح– طیاره نشست کردن | |
| اکتوبر | بیست و دوم اکتوبر– از تکت فروشی  – تکت خریدن | |
| نومبر | هفدهم نومبر– از سفارت کابل – ویزه گرفتن | |
| دسمبر | یازدهم دسمبر– بکس بسته کردن | |

52

C.    Provide a Dari response to the following questions.

| | | |
|---|---|---|
| Where will you go on your next holiday? | _____ | ۱ |
| Will you travel by car or by plane? | _____ | ۲ |
| Will you buy your tickets from the internet or a travel agency? | _____ | ۳ |
| If you go on a one week trip to Mazaar, what clothing will you take along? | _____ | ۴ |
| What else will you do during your summer vacation? | _____ | ۵ |

Exercise 3:    تمرین ۳ :

A.  You will hear a short conversation on the audio recording between شریف and his friend میرویس as they talk about their next summer plans. As you listen, mark the questions that are being exchanged between them. Then check your work with a partner.

| | | | |
|---|---|---|---|
| آیا شما زمینی سفرخواهید رفت، یا هوایی؟ | ☐ | شما به کجا خواهید رفت؟ | ☐ |
| هوای مزار شریف در تابستان چطور است؟ | ☐ | شما برای رخصتی های تابستانی تان به کجا سفر خواهید کرد؟ | ☐ |
| شما هوایی سفر خواهید کرد یا زمینی؟ | ☐ | شما در تابستان هندوستان میروید؟ | ☐ |

B.    Listen to the conversation on the audio recording again, and this time check "true" or "false" for each statement below.

| غلط | صحیح | جملات | |
|---|---|---|---|
| ☐ | ☐ | رخصتی های تابستانی یك هفته بعد شروع خواهد شد . | ۱ |
| ☐ | ☐ | میرویس به هندوستان خواهد رفت. | ۲ |
| ☐ | ☐ | میرویس زمینی سفر خواهد کرد. | ۳ |
| ☐ | ☐ | شریف هوایی سفر خواهد کرد. | ۴ |
| ☐ | ☐ | شریف به مزار شریف خواهد رفت. | ۵ |
| ☐ | ☐ | طیاره ها هر هفته به هندوستان پرواز میکند . | ۶ |
| ☐ | ☐ | تکت سفر زمینی بسیار ارزان است. | ۷ |
| ☐ | ☐ | هندوستان جاهای جالب و دیدنی دارد. | ۸ |

C. Now look at the script for the conversation in Exercise 3A provided below. With a partner, practice the dialogue using your names and the places you want to go.

| | |
|---|---|
| میرویس | شریف جان، رخصتی های تابستانی یك هفته بعد شروع خواهد شد. شما به کجا خواهید رفت؟ |
| شریف | والله، میرویس جان، ما به هندوستان خواهیم رفت، چونکه هندوستان بسیار جاهای جالب و دیدنی دارد. |
| میرویس | بلی، آیا شما زمینی سفرخواهید رفت، یا هوایی؟ |
| شریف | هوایی سفرخواهیم کرد، چونکه حالا طیاره های افغانستان هر روز به هندوستان پرواز میکنند. |
| میرویس | شما برای رخصتی های تابستانی تان کجا سفر خواهید کرد؟ |
| شریف | من به مزار شریف خواهم رفت چونکه هوای مزار در تابستان بسیار سرد است. |
| میرویس | شما هوایی سفر خواهید کرد یا زمینی؟ |
| شریف | من زمینی سفر خواهم کرد چونکه زمینی تکت بسیار ارزان است. |

| سفر زمینی | سفر هوایی |
|---|---|
| road trip (traveling via ground transportation) | air travel |

D. Role-play: You and a partner are talking about the future seasonal holidays that you have planned. One of you will ask the other the following questions in Dari about that trip.

1. Where will you go?
2. What will you do during that trip?
3. Will you fly or drive?
4. Why do you want to travel via plane/car?

Exercise 4: 📖 تمرین: ۴

A. شریف and میرویس are looking for travel agencies in the daily paper, and they've found the following ads. Read the ads and complete the following tasks.

شرکت هوایی آریانا!

طیاره های شرکت هوایی آریانا هر روز در ساعت های مختلف به ولایات بزرگ کشور پرواز میکند. تکت همهٔ پرواز های داخلی یک طرفه ۵۰۰۰ افغانی و دو طرفه ۹۵۰۰ افغانی میباشد تقسیم اوقات پرواز های این شرکت هوایی از این قرار است:

کابل – هرات      پرواز ۹ صبح، نشست ۱۱صبح.

کابل – کندهار      پرواز ۱۰ صبح،

شرکت هوایی افغان!

طیاره های شرکت هوایی افغان به کشور های هندوستان، دوبی و ایران هر روز از ساعت.

بعداز ظهر ۲ پرواز دارد.

تکت یک طرفه کابل – دهلی نو ۱۵۰۰۰ افغانی.

تکت یک طرفه کابل – تهران.

| مختلف | شرکت هوایی | دو طرفه | یك طرفه |
|---|---|---|---|
| various | airline | round trip | one way |

1. Which one of the above airlines has overseas flights?

_____

2. Which one of the above airlines has local flights?

_____

3. What is the price of a round-trip ticket from Kabul to Mazaar?
   a) 5000 AF              b) 9500 AF              c) 10000 AF

4. The fare from Kabul to New Delhi (15000 AF) is for a _____ .
   a) round trip       b) one-way trip

5. What is the departure time of the flight from Kabul to Kandahar?
   a) 9 a.m.              b) 10 a.m.              c) 11 a.m.              d) 12 p.m.

6. What is the arrival time of the flight from Kabul to Herat?
   a) 9 a.m.              b) 10 a.m.              c) 11 a.m.              d) 12 p.m.

B. 🎧 شریف wants to go to India and wants to buy a ticket from an Afghan travel agency. Listen to his conversation on the audio recording and complete the following tasks.

1. Who used the following phrases? With a partner, first translate each; then write the name of the speaker next to each phrase.

| | | | |
|---|---|---|---|
| ــــــــــ | چی کمک کرده میتوانم؟ | ــــــــــ | اینه، بفرمایید. |
| ــــــــــ | سفر خوشی را برای تان آرزو میکنیم. | ــــــــــ | به چشم. |
| ــــــــــ | لطفاً چند لحظه صبر کنید. | ــــــــــ | طبعاً. |

| A |
|---|
| چی خدمت کرده میتوانم؟ ☐ |
| شما در کدام تاریخ ها پرواز دارید؟ ☐ |
| شما چند تکت بکار دارید؟ ☐ |
| شما تکت یکطرفه میخواهید یا تکت دوطرفه؟ ☐ |
| قیمت های هرکدامش چند است؟ ☐ |
| برای کدام تاریخ ها میخواهید؟ ☐ |
| ما چند بکس را میتوانیم که همراه خود ببریم؟ ☐ |

2. The following questions in columns A & B have the same meaning. One of the phrases from each person has been stated in the conversation. Place a check mark next to each phrase you hear.

| B |
|---|
| چی کمک کرده میتوانم؟ ☐ |
| شما در کدام روز ها پرواز دارید؟ ☐ |
| شما چند تکت میخواهید؟ ☐ |
| شما چی قسم تکت میخواهید، یکطرفه یا تکت دوطرفه؟ ☐ |
| قیمت های تکت یکطرفه و دوطرفه چند است؟ ☐ |
| برای چی وقت میخواهید؟ ☐ |
| ما چند بکس را همراه خود برده میتوانیم؟ ☐ |

C. Using the following word bank, write the English equivalent of the questions you marked in the above task with a partner.

| حاضربودن | كمك كردن | خارجی | تماس گرفتن | صبر كردن |
|---|---|---|---|---|
| to be present | to help | foreign, foreigner | to contact | to wait |

| طبعاً | خود | آرزو كردن | اينه |
|---|---|---|---|
| obviously | oneself | to wish | Here it is. |

D. Listen to the audio recording again, and mark "true" or "false" for the following statements.

| غلط | صحيح | | |
|---|---|---|---|
| ☐ | ☐ | مسافر تكت براى سفر هند بكاردارد . | ١ |
| ☐ | ☐ | مسافر يك تكت بكار دارد . | ٢ |
| ☐ | ☐ | مسافر تكت دوطرفه بكار دارد . | ٣ |
| ☐ | ☐ | فاميل مسافر سه نفر هستند . | ۴ |
| ☐ | ☐ | مسافر به تاريخ ٢٠ ماه سرطان خواهد رفت. | ۵ |
| ☐ | ☐ | مسافر به تاريخ بيست اسد پس خواهد آمد . | ۶ |
| ☐ | ☐ | شركت هوايى افغان به روزهاى دوشنبه، چارشنبه و جمعه پرواز دارد . | ٧ |
| ☐ | ☐ | تكت فروش پاسپورت هاى مسافر را خواست. | ٨ |
| ☐ | ☐ | مسافر بايد  سه ساعت وقتر به ميدان هوايى بيايد . | ٩ |
| ☐ | ☐ | هر مسافر ٣٢ كيلو وزن همراه خود برده ميتواند . | ١٠ |
| ☐ | ☐ | اگر مسافر پرسان يا سوال داشته باشد ، بايد  به آدرس ايميلى كه تكت فروش داد ، تماس بگيرد . | ١١ |

E. Role-play: You want to go to your favorite place for summer break. Go to a travel agency and book a ticket for yourself and for one other person. Your classmate will play the role of the travel agent. Be sure to include the following:

| مسافر | تکت فروش |
|---|---|
| 1. Tell the travel agent that you need a ticket to your destination. | 1. Greet and welcome the customer. |
| 2. Tell the travel agent the number of people going with you. | 2. Ask about the number of people that the customer wants tickets for. |
| 3. Ask for the price of a one-way and a round-trip flight. | 3. Ask the customer if s/he wants a one-way or a round-trip ticket. |
| 4. Give the travel agent the dates of your travel (departure and arrival). | 4. Ask about the dates that the customer wants to travel. |
| 5. Ask the travel agent about the number of bags allowed. | 5. Tell the customer that s/he is allowed to carry up to 50 pounds per bag for a total of 3 bags per person. |
| 6. Finally, ask for the contact information in case you encounter questions/problems during your flight. | 6. Provide an answer for any additional questions. |

F. 🤝 Now, look at the transcript for the conversation that you have just completed and check your work with a partner.

| | |
|---|---|
| تکت فروش | سلام به شرکت هوایی افغان خوش آمدید! چی کمک کرده میتوانم؟ |
| مسافر | وعلیکم، من یك تکت برای هند بکار دارم، شما در کدام روز ها پرواز دارید؟ |
| تکت فروش | ما در روز های دوشنبه، چارشنبه و جمعه از کابل به هند پرواز داریم. شما چند تکت بکار دارید؟ |
| مسافر | ما سه نفر هستیم. |
| تکت فروش | شما تکت یك طرفه میخواهید یا تکت دوطرفه؟ |
| مسافر | قیمت های تکت یك طرفه و دوطرفه چند است؟ |
| تکت فروش | تکت یك طرفه برای هر نفر ۱۵۰۰۰ افغانی است و تکت دوطرفه ۲۹۵۰۰ افغانی است. |
| مسافر | طبعاً که تکت دوطرفه میخواهم چونکه ارزانتر است. |
| تکت فروش | خوب برای کدام تاریخ ها میخواهید؟ |
| مسافر | ما به تاریخ ۲۰ ماه سرطان خواهیم رفت و به تاریخ ۱۰ ماه اسد پس خواهیم آمد. |
| تکت فروش | بسیار خوب، لطفاً پاسپورتهای تان را بدهید؟ |
| مسافر | اینه بفرمایید. |
| تکت فروش | تشکر، لطفاً چند لحظه صبر کنید. |
| مسافر | به چشم ...... |
| تکت فروش | اینه، تکت های تا آماده شد، لطفاً سه ساعت قبل از پرواز تان در میدان هوایی حاضر باشید. چونکه پرواز تان خارجی است، باید وقتر بیایید. |
| مسافر | ما چند بکس را میتوانیم که همراه خود ما ببریم؟ |
| تکت فروش | هر نفر دو بکس را میتواند که همراه خودش ببرد، وزن هر بکس باید ۳۲ کیلو باشد. |
| مسافر | تشکر. |
| تکت فروش | خواهش میکنم، اگر کدام سوال یا پرسان داشته باشید، به این شماره تلیفون تماس بگیرید. سفر خوشی را برای تان آرزو میکنیم. |
| مسافر | تشکر. |

## 9.6 The Generic Possessive خود

The generic possessive pronoun خود is very frequently used in daily communication (both in colloquial and in standard Dari). It is used with possessive pronouns.  For example:

| | | | |
|---|---|---|---|
| our/ourselves | خود ما | my/myself | خودم |
| them/themselves | خود شان | his/her/herself/himself | خودش |
| your/yourselves | خود تان | your/ yourself | خودت |

As you can see, the above examples can be replaced with the possessives. For example:

من سفرم را کنسل کردم.<br>
من سفر خودم را کنسل کردم.

I cancelled my trip.

Also, these possessives function as reflexive pronouns (myself, ourselves, herself, himself, themselves, yourself, yourselves). For example, consider the conversation in Exercise 4E:

ما چند بکس را میتوانیم که همراه خود ما ببریم؟

How many bags can we take [along with ourselves]?

هر نفر دو بکس را میتواند که همراه خودش ببرد.

Each person can take two bags [with her/himself].

Exercise 5: تمرین ۵:

A. Change the possessive pronoun in each of the following sentences to the generic possessive. Then write its English equivalent.

| | | |
|---|---|---|
| _____ | _____ | ۱  پرواز تان ساعت چند است؟ |
| _____ | _____ | ۲  او تکتش را خریده بود . |
| _____ | _____ | ۳  آنها معطل طیارهٔ شان هستند . |
| _____ | _____ | ۴  من پاسپورتم را گرفتم . |
| _____ | _____ | ۵  تو برادرت را دیدی؟ |

B. Write the Dari equivalent of the following phrases.

| | | |
|---|---|---|
| Please show me your passport. | _____ | ۱ |
| I opened my bag myself. | _____ | ۲ |
| The flight attendant told me herself. | _____ | ۳ |
| I will take my brother with me on that trip. | _____ | ۴ |
| Did you plan your upcoming holiday? | _____ | ۵ |

Exercise 6: تمرین ۶ :

A. A traveler wants to go to Mazaar-e Sharif by bus. You will hear a conversation on the audio recording between him and a travel agent. Listen to their conversation and state which of the following times matches each question.

| | | | |
|---|---|---|---|
| ۱ | | | مسافر چی وقت میرود؟ |
| | پس فردا | فردا | فردا شب |
| ۲ | | | موتر بس چند بجه حرکت میکند؟ |
| | چار شب | چار دیگر | چار صبح |
| ۳ | | | مسافر باید چند بجه حاضر باشد؟ |
| | سه بجهٔ صبح | سه بجهٔ شب | سه بجهٔ دیگر |
| ۴ | | | موتر بس چند بجه به مزار شریف میرسد؟ |
| | ساعت دوازده بجه شب | ساعت دوازده بجه چاشت | ساعت یازده بجه چاشت |
| ۵ | | | تکت فروش برای چی وقت چوکی دارد؟ |
| | صباح شب | دیگرصباح | صباح |

| بس | خالی | مفت | حرکت کردن (حرکت کن) | رسیدن (رس) | چاره نیست. |
|---|---|---|---|---|---|
| bus | empty | free | to move | to reach, to arrive | There is no other choice. |

B. Listen to the audio recording again and mark the questions that are asked by the traveler.

☐ برای شش نفر تکت دارید؟

☐ برای دیگر صباح داریم، آیا میخواهید؟

☐ آیا از بکس هایم پیسه میگیرید؟

☐ چی خدمت کرده میتوانم؟

☐ بس های تان چی وقت حرکت میکند؟

☐ قیمت تکت برای هر نفر چند است؟

C. 🎧 Listen to the audio recording a third time, but this time, answer the following questions.

1. Does the traveller need to pay for his bags?
   a) Yes                    b) No

2. How many seats are available on the bus for today?
   a) 4 seats          b) 6 seats          c) 14 seats

3. How much is the price for each ticket?
   a) 600 AF          b) 1600 AF          c) 6000 AF

D. 🎧 Listen to the audio recording a fourth time and mark "true" or "false" for the following statements.

| غلط | صحیح | | |
|---|---|---|---|
| ☐ | ☐ | مسافر از کابل به مزار شریف میرود . | ۱ |
| ☐ | ☐ | مسافر برای پس فردا تکت خرید چونکه تکت فروشی تکت ندارد . | ۲ |
| ☐ | ☐ | بس ها بکس های مسافر را مفت نمیبرند . | ۳ |
| ☐ | ☐ | تکت فروش تکت های مسافر را نداد . | ۴ |
| ☐ | ☐ | مسافر کارت هویت خودش را به تکت فروش داد . | ۵ |

E. Read the transcript for the conversation you have been listening to and check your work in the previous parts of the exercise.

| | |
|---|---|
| تکت فروش | به شرکت مسافربری کابل خوش آمدید ، چی خدمت کرده میتوانم؟ |
| مسافر | تشکر، من یک تکت به مزار شریف بکار دارم، بس های تان چی وقت حرکت میکند؟ |
| تکت فروش | والله، بس های ما هرروز ساعت ۴ صبح از کابل حرکت میکند و ساعت دوازده بجه چاشت به مزار شریف میرسد. |
| مسافر | خوب برای صباح، برای شش نفر تکت دارید؟ |
| تکت فروش | نه والله، ما فقط برای ۴ نفر دیگر هم چوکی خالی داریم. |
| مسافر | نه ما شش نفر هستیم. |
| تکت فروش | برای دیگر صباح داریم، آیا میخواهید؟ |
| مسافر | بلی چاره نیست. قیمت تکت برای هر نفر چند است؟ |
| تکت فروش | تکت کابل به مزار شریف برای هر نفر ۶۰۰ افغانی است. |
| مسافر | خوب صحیح است، لطفاً شش تکت بدهید. |
| تکت فروش | لطفاً تذکره تا کارت هویت خود را بدهید. |
| مسافر | اینه، بفرمایید. |
| تکت فروش | تشکر. |
| تکت فروش | اینه، تکت های تان را بگیرید، لطفاً دیگرصباح ساعت ۳ بجه اینجا حاضر باشید. |
| مسافر | حتماً آیا از بکس هایم پیسه میگیرید؟ |
| تکت فروش | نه بکس هایتان را مفت خواهیم برد. |
| مسافر | تشکر، دیگر صباح میبینیم. فعلاً به امان خدا. |
| تکت فروش | به امان خدا. |

F.  You are in Kabul and you want to buy bus tickets for yourself and two other friends. Go to the travel agency and book tickets for tomorrow. Your classmate will play the role of a travel agent. Be sure to include the following information:

| تکت فروش | مسافر |
|---|---|
| 1. Welcome the customer and say, "How may I help you?" | 1. Ask the seller if there are tickets available to travel tomorrow from Kabul to Jalalabad. |
| 2. Ask the customer for the number of people traveling. | 2. Tell the seller that there are a total of four people traveling. |
| 3. Tell the customer that you don't have seats for four people; you just have three seats available. In two days, however, you have lots of available seats. | 3. Tell the seller that you want the tickets for the day after tomorrow, and ask for the price of the tickets. |
| 4. Give a price for the tickets, and ask for an ID. | 4. Provide your ID and ask the seller if there is a charge for your luggage. |
| 5. Tell the customer that there is no charge for his bags. | 5. Pay the money and ask when you should arrive at the bus stop. |
| 6. Give the customer the tickets and tell the customer to be at the bus stop the day after tomorrow, at 4:00 a.m. | |

# درس سوم: ریزرف کردن اتاق در هوتل.

## Lesson Three: Reserving a room at a hotel

In this section, you will learn more about Afghan lodging options and practice calling to reserve a hotel room and asking about the hotel amenities.

Exercise 1: ۱ تمرین

A. Read the following words and write a possible definition for each.

 هوتل

 اتاق

 خانه سامان

 مدیر هوتل/ هوتلی

چپرکت

بالشت

کمپل

روجایی

 صابون

جانخشکان/ جانپاك

 اوتو

B.    Read the following ad and answer the following questions.

# هوتل کابل زیبا

هوتل کابل زیبا در مرکز شهر کابل موقعیت دارد ، این هوتل ۲۰ دقیقه از میدان هوایی کابل دور است.

پارک زیبای زرنگار و سفارتخانه ها  در پهلویی این هوتل است.

این هوتل ۱۷۷ اتاق دارد ، هر اتاق یک تشناب، آب گرم، چپرکت های مدرن، روجایی کمپل، بالشت و جانخشکان های پاک دارد .

در پایین این هوتل رستورانت های افغانی و خارجی است. مارکت و بازار کالافروشی در شمال هوتل است.

شما میتوانید از طریق ویب سایت ما اتاق تان را ریزرف کنید .

1. Where is the hotel located?
 a) north of Kabul city            b) in the center of Kabul city

2. How far is this place from the airport?

_____

3. What is next to the hotel?

_____

4. Which of the following items is not mentioned in the above ad?
 a) towel              e) sheet
 b) soap               f) mattress
 c) blanket            g) shampoo
 d) pillow             h) toothpaste

5. Which businesses are located near the hotel?
 a) Afghan restaurants
 b) foreign restaurants
 c) both a & b
 d) a clothing market

6. What style is the hotel?
 a) modern                b) traditional

7. How can you reserve a room in this hotel?

_____

C. You will hear on the audio recording an advertisement from the Mazaar Hotel. Listen and complete the following information in the table below.

| جواب | سوال | نام | |
|---|---|---|---|
| | شما خود را در این چطور احساسس خواهید کرد؟ | هوتل مزار | ۱ |
| | نام او چیست و کدام ساعت ها او کار میکند؟ | مدیر هوتل | ۲ |
| | چند سال تجربهٔ کاری دارند؟ | خانه سامان | ۳ |
| | در هر اتاق چی چیز ها است؟ | اتاق | ۴ |
| | در تشناب چی چیز ها است؟ | تشناب | ۵ |

D. Now read the following advertisement and mark "true" or "false" for each statement below.

قابل توجه مسافرین عزیز!

هوتل مزار که جدیداً تاسیس شده است، در خدمت مسافرین و سیاحان عزیز میباشد.

این هوتل اتاق های یك نفره و دو نفرهٔ مجهز ، پاك و مدرن دارد.

هراتاق با تلویزیون، انترنت، تلیفون، کمپیوتر، چپرکت ، کمپل، بالشت، روجایی و جانخشکان های پاك مجهز میباشد. همچنان هر اتاق یك تشناب و حمام هم دارد که در حمام های آن شامپو، صابون و آب گرم و سرد نیز موجود است.

این هوتل خانه سامان های باتجربه دارد که هر خانه سامان کم از کم ۵ سال در هوتل کار کرده اند.

شما در هوتل مزار خودرا کاملاً راحت احساس خواهید کرد.

آدرس: ولایت بلخ، شهر مزارشریف، روبرویی پارك مولانا صاحب

شماره تلیفون: ۰۷۹۹۱۷۸۲۳ - ۰۷۸۷۶۲۱۶۴۸.

مدیر هوتل: آغای شریف پوپل، اوقات کار- ۹صبح الی ۹ شب.

| کم از کم | کاملاً | راحت | باتجربه | موجود بودن | قابل توجه |
|---|---|---|---|---|---|
| at least | absolutely | comfortable | experienced | to be available | to the attention of |

| اتاق دو نفره | اتاق یك نفره | مجهز بودن | احساس کردن | در خدمت بودن | تاسیس شدن |
|---|---|---|---|---|---|
| double bedroom | single bedroom | to be equipped | to feel | to be in service of | to be established |

| غلط | صحیح | | |
|---|---|---|---|
| ___ | ___ | این یك هوتل مدرن است. | ۱ |
| ___ | ___ | این هوتل با انترنت مجهز نیست. | ۲ |
| ___ | ___ | این هوتل آب گرم و سرد دارد. | ۳ |
| ___ | ___ | خانه سامان های این هوتل با تجربه هستند. | ۴ |
| ___ | ___ | این هوتل بسیار راحت است. | ۵ |
| ___ | ___ | مدیر هوتل هرروز ۸ ساعت کار میکند. | ۶ |
| ___ | ___ | این هوتل در شهر کابل است. | ۷ |

E. Turn to a classmate and talk about the last hotel you stayed in. Then each person should provide a response for the following.

1. The hotel's address

2. The condition of the hotel room

3. The items/furniture in your room

4. The shops and restaurants around the hotel

5. How long you stayed there

6. What kind of room did you stay in? Single bed or double bedroom?

7. Other services that the hotel provided (internet, breakfast, etc.)

## Cultural Note تبصرهٔ فرهنگی

### Hotels in Afghanistan

In Afghanistan, there are three categories of hotels:

1- The Modern Hotel: These hotels are very similar to hotels in other countries, e.g. the US, Europe, etc. Usually, foreign guests stay in hotels such as these. This is because these hotels have higher standards and increased security. The price of these rooms is very high compared to the other types of hotels in Afghanistan. The guests can easily book a room via the internet or phone, and the hotel accepts all types of currencies and bank cards.

2- The Casual Hotel: These hotels are designed to be similar to modern hotels, but have lower standards. For example, the rooms have air conditioning, phone service, internet service, but no private bath (you must go outside the room to a public restroom of the hotel). Booking is usually done on a walk-in basis, and the hotel only accepts certain currencies e.g., the US dollar, the Iranian riyal, and Pakistani and Indian rupees.

3- Hotels located along highways: These businesses are not designed as hotels but as eating establishments. However, when traveling late at night, people stay here informally due to curfews and the dangers of travel. These "hotels" (in Dari, they are called hotels) have large sleeping rooms for 20-40 people. There is no charge to sleep in these rooms; however, the guests have to buy a meal in order to be accommodated. This is the only type of hotel that does NOT require an ID. All others do.

Exercise 2: تمرین ۲:

A. You will hear a conversation on the audio recording between شریف and his friend میرویس, as they talk about their hotel arrangements for their upcoming trips. Listen and circle the correct dates for the following events.

| | | | |
|---|---|---|---|
| ۱ | چی وقت میرویس به هوتل مزار رفته بود؟ | | |
| | سه سال پیش | دو سال پیش | یک سال پیش |
| ۲ | هوتلِ مزار چی وقت جور شده است؟ | | |
| | تقریباً سه سال پیش | تقریباً دو سال پیش | تقریباً یک سال پیش |

B. Listen to the audio recording again and, this time, check each of the accommodations that you hear.

| | | | |
|---|---|---|---|
| clean rooms | ☐ | phone | ☐ |
| fitness center | ☐ | pool | ☐ |
| hot tub | ☐ | restaurant | ☐ |
| internet | ☐ | tv | ☐ |

C. Listen to the audio recording again and complete the following tasks.

1. In which hotel did میرویس reserve a room?

_____

2. Why did میرویس like the hotel?

_____

3. How did میرویس reserve the room for his next vacation?
   a) via phone                 b) via internet

4. How will شریف reserve a room?
   a) via phone                 b) via internet

5. What is the phone number that میرویس suggested to شریف؟

_____

D.  Choose the best hotel in which you ever stayed. Then suggest it to your classmate, who will be traveling there. Talk about the advantages and disadvantages of this hotel and why you like it.

E. Write a description of the hotel that your classmate suggested to you. Then read it to your class.

| جور شدن | رفته بودن | ریزرف کرد | یادداشت کردن | از طریق | پس |
|---|---|---|---|---|---|
| to be built, to be fixed | had gone | to reserve | to take note | via | so, therefore |

## 9.7 Forming of the Past Perfect Tense زمان گذشتهٔ بعید

In Dari, the past perfect is used to describe an action that happened in the far past and was completed at that time. For example, in the above conversation, you heard the phrase شما به مزار شریف رفته بودید. "You had gone to Mazaar-e Sharif." The verb رفته بودید is the past perfect form of the verb رفتن 'to go'. To form the past perfect tense, change the main verb to the past participle and add the past form of the verb 'to be' to it. For example:

| ۴ | ۳ | ۲ | ۱ |
|---|---|---|---|
| رفته بودن (had gone) | رفته | رفتن (رفت) | رفتن |
| 4 | 3 | 2 | 1 |
| The perfective is expressed with the verb 'to be' in Dari, whereas English uses 'to have'; e.g., 'have gone', 'had gone.' Past perfect in Dari uses the past tense of 'to be.' | add the ـه suffix to form the past participle | lose the ـن suffix | the verb 'to go' |

Let's conjugate that same verb and use it in a sentence:

من دو سال پیش به واشنگتن رفته بودم.
ما دو سال پیش به واشنگتن رفته بودیم.
تو دو سال پیش به واشنگتن رفته بودی.
شما دو سال پیش به واشنگتن رفته بودید.
او دو سال پیش به واشنگتن رفته بود.
آنها دو سال پیش به واشنگتن رفته بودند.

Exercise 3:    تمرین ۳:

A. First, change the following verbs to the past participle, and then make a sentence for each in the past perfect form.

| | | |
|---|---|---|
| ۱ | هوتل ریزرف کردن | _____ _____ |
| ۲ | تلیفون کردن | _____ _____ |
| ۳ | ایمیل کردن | _____ _____ |
| ۴ | دیدن | _____ _____ |
| ۵ | شنیدن | _____ _____ |
| ۶ | خریدن | _____ _____ |

B.    Provide a Dari response to the following sentences using the past perfect tense (even if the English equivalent uses an alternate tense, such as past or present perfect).

| | | |
|---|---|---|
| ۱ | _____ | Have you been to Afghanistan before? |
| ۲ | _____ | Have you ever seen the world's biggest hotel? |
| ۳ | _____ | Which hotel have you booked a room in? |
| ۴ | _____ | When did you book a hotel via phone? |
| ۵ | _____ | When was the last time you have traveled on a ship? |

Exercise 4:  تمرین ۴:

A. میرویس wants to reserve a room in the Mazaar Hotel. He calls the hotel and wants to reserve a room over the phone. Listen to his conversation on the audio recording with the hotel manager. Then think about your experience reserving a room and answer the following questions.

1. How do you reserve a room in a hotel?
2. What differences and similarities did you find between reserving a hotel in Afghanistan and in your own country?
3. What are some questions commonly asked by customers? Write down the questions.

B. Listen to the audio recording again. This time, choose the best answer for the following questions.

| | | | | |
|---|---|---|---|---|
| ۱ | میرویس از کجا تلیفون کرد؟ | | | |
| | بلخ | کابل | زابل | مزار شریف |
| ۲ | میرویس اتاق چند نفره بکار دارد؟ | | | |
| | چار نفره | سه نفره | دو نفره | یك نفره |
| ۳ | میرویس در کدام تاریخ باید در هوتل باشد؟ | | | |
| | ۳۰ سرطان | ۱۹ سرطان | ۱۸ سرطان | ۱۷ سرطان |
| ۴ | هوتل در کدام تاریخ اتاق دونفره نداشت؟ | | | |
| | ۳۰ سرطان | ۱۹ سرطان | ۱۸ سرطان | ۱۷ سرطان |
| ۵ | میرویس روز اول را در اتاق چند نفره میماند؟ | | | |
| | چار نفره | سه نفره | دو نفره | یك نفره |
| ۶ | ۲۰۰۰ افغانی کرایۀ اتاق چند نفره است؟ | | | |
| | چار نفره | سه نفره | دو نفره | یك نفره |
| ۷ | آیا اتاق های هوتل انترنت دارد؟ | | | |
| | | نه ندارد | بلی دارد | |
| ۸ | هوتلی از میرویس شمارۀ چی را پرسان کرد؟ | | | |
| | شمارۀ پاسپورت | شمارۀ کارت بانکی | شمارۀ کارت هویت | شمارۀ تلیفون |

C. 🤝 You want to reserve a hotel room. Your classmate will play the role of the hotel employee.  Be sure to include the following:

1. Introduce yourself and tell the hotel employee where you are calling from.
2. Tell the hotel employee the type of bedroom you need and for how long.
3. Ask if there are restaurants and shops close to the hotel.
4. Ask what they charge for a single room and for a double room.
5. Ask which amenities are included with the room (such as TV, hot water, internet, etc.).
6. Give the hotel employee all other needed information.

Exercise 5: 🎧 تمرین ۵:

A. میرویس is at the bus stop in Mazaar-e Sharif, and he wants to take a taxi to go to his hotel. Listen to his conversation with the تکسیوان and discuss the similarities and differences between Afghans and people in your country.

B. 🎧 Listen to the conversation again. This time find the meaning of the following phrase.

How much will you charge to take me to the Mazaar Hotel?

C. 🎧 Listen to the conversation again, and answer the following questions.

1. Does the taxi driver know the address of the hotel?      a) yes      b) no

2. At the beginning, how much does the taxi driver request as a payment?
   a) 100      b) 200      c) 300

3. After they've agreed on the price, what does میرویس say?
   a) Let me take my luggage from the bus.
   b) Let me put my luggage in the trunk.
   c) Please help me put my luggage in the trunk.

4. Did میرویس bargain several times?      a) yes      b) no

| بردن (بر) | بالاشوید. | تکسیوان | کرایه | تولبکس | باشد که |
|-----------|-----------|---------|-------|--------|---------|
| to take | get in | taxi driver | rent | trunk | Let me ... |

D. You are in Afghanistan and want to get a taxi to your hotel. Go to a taxi driver and be sure to include the following in your conversation. Your classmate will play the role of a taxi driver.

| مشتری | تکسیوان |
|---|---|
| 1. Ask the driver how much he charges to go to your hotel. | 1. Tell the passenger that you don't know the address, ask him to give you the address for the hotel. |
| 2. Tell the driver that the hotel is near downtown, on the north side of Maiwand Street, next to the university. | 2. Tell the passenger that you know where it is and offer him 500AFG. |
| 3. Bargain with the taxi driver. | 3. Tell the passenger that your last price is 550 AFG.  Agree somewhere close to that price range. |
| 4. Agree on a price and ask the driver to open the trunk for you to put your luggage in. | |

# مرور فصل نهم
## Review of Chapter Nine

In this section you will review the vocabulary, phrases, grammar, and cultural elements that you learned throughout the chapter.

Exercise 1: تمرین ۱:

A. You will hear weather reports for each of the following provinces. Listen and fill in the following chart.

| ابر | باران | برف | طوفان | باد | بلندترین درجه حرارت | پایین ترین درجه حرارت | |
|-----|-------|-----|-------|-----|------|------|---|
| | | | | | | | ۱.  کابل |
| | | | | | | | ۲.  هرات |
| | | | | | | | ۳.  کندهار |
| | | | | | | | ۴.  مزارشریف |
| | | | | | | | ۵.  جلال آباد |

B. Go to google.com or your preferred site and check the weather reports of the following cities. Then, in Dari, write a short description of the weather.

نیویورک

لندن

پاریس

مسکو

Exercise 2:  تمرین ۲:

A. You will hear a conversation on the audio recording between a passenger and a travel agent. Listen carefully to their conversation and then answer the following questions.

1. Where is the passenger going?  a) Kabul  b) Hamburg

2. On which days of the week are the flights?
   a) Thursday, Wednesday, Friday
   b) Monday, Wednesday, Friday
   c) Tuesday, Wednesday, Friday

3. How much does a one-way ticket cost?
   a) $800   b) $1600   c) $700

4. Did the passenger book his ticket for Tuesday?  a) yes  b) no

5. What did the travel agent want to see?
   a) ID card   b) passport

6. Which type of ticket did the passenger request?
   a) one-way ticket   b) round-trip ticket

B. You want to travel from Kabul to New Delhi. Go to a travel agency and book tickets for you and a family member. Your classmate will play the role of a travel agent. Be sure to include the following:

| تکت فروش | مشتری |
|---|---|
| 1. Greet the customer and ask how you can be of assistance. | 1. Greet and introduce yourself, say that you need two tickets to New Delhi; ask for flight days and times. |
| 2. Say that there are flights every Monday, Wednesday, and Friday at 10 a.m. | 2. Ask for the prices of the tickets. |
| 3. Say that, per-person, a one-way ticket is $200 and a round-trip is $350. | 3. Ask the travel agent to book two round-trip tickets for you for next Wednesday. |
| 4. Ask for documentation. | 4. Give the seller all other needed information. |

Exercise 3:    تمرین ۳:

You and a family member are going on a vacation. Call a hotel and reserve a room for yourself and your family member. Make sure to include the following:

| مدیر هوتل | مشتری |
|---|---|
| 1. Pick up the phone and start with: 'Hello, this is the Mazaar Hotel. How may I help you?' | 1. Say hello, introduce yourself, and say you are calling from Kabul City and you need a room in Mazaar-e Sharif Hotel. |
| 2. Ask the customer for the number of rooms and how many people are going to be staying. | 2. Tell the hotel manager that there are two people and you need one room. |
| 3. Ask the customer whether s/he needs a single-bed room or a double-bed room. | 3. Ask about the price for each room. |
| 4. Tell the customer that single-bed rooms are 2500 AF per night, and double-bed rooms are 3500 AF per night. | 4. Tell the hotel manager that you want a double-bed room. |
| 5. Ask for the customer's arrival and departure dates. | 5. You want a room from the 1st of the month to the 12th of the month. |
| 6. Say that you have a room, book the room, and ask for his/her complete information. | 6. Provide all the other needed information. |

Exercise 4:    تمرین ۴:

In order to travel outside the country, you must provide the travel agent with some more information to book the tickets for you. Provide an appropriate answer for the following.

آیا شما سال گذشته به هندوستان رفته بودید؟

آیا قبلاً ویزهٔ هندوستان را گرفته بودید؟

آیا شما در هندوستان هوتل ریزرف کرده بودید؟

شما کدام شهر ها سفر کرده بودید؟

# Vocabulary

In this part of the lesson, you will review, listen to, and practice pronunciation of the phrases and vocabulary used in the chapter.

## Phrases اصطلاحات

| It's okay. | xayr bāšad. | خیر باشد. |
|---|---|---|
| Don't worry. | parwā namĕkonad. | پروا نمیکند. |
| Here it is, take it please. | ena, bafarmāyed. | اینه، بفرمایید. |
| sure | ba čĕšom | به چشم |
| obviously | tab'an | طبعاً |
| How can I help you? | či komak karda metānom? | چی کمك کرده میتوانم؟ |
| Please wait a few moments. | lotfan čand lahza sabar koned. | لطفاً چند لحظه صبر کنید. |
| There is not another choice. | čāra nest. | چاره نیست. |
| get in | bālā šawed | بالاشوید |
| It is possible. | ehtamāl merawad. | احتمال میرود. |

## Vocabulary Words لغات

| weather | āb ō hawā | آب و هوا |
|---|---|---|
| to wish | ārĕzō kardan (ārĕzō kon) | آرزو کردن |
| sky | āsmān | آسمان |
| sun | āftab, xōr | آفتاب، خورشید |
| cloud | abr | ابر |
| cloudy | abri | ابری |
| room | otāq | اتاق |
| double-bed room | otāq-e do nafara | اتاق دو نفره |
| single-bed room | otāq-e yak nafara | اتاق یك نفره |
| to feel | ehsās kardan (ehsās kon) | احساس کردن (احساس کن) |
| via | az tariq-e | از طریق |
| stewardess | estiwardes | استیوردیس |

| iron | ōtō | اوتو |
|------|-----|------|
| Here it is. | ena. | اینه. |
| experienced | bā tajroba | باتجربه |
| wind | bād, šamāl | باد، شمال |
| rain | bārān | باران |
| to rain | bārān bāridan (bāran bār) | باران باریدن (باران بار) |
| rainy | bārāni | بارانی |
| rainfall | bārĕndagi | بارنده گی |
| to rain, shower | bāridan(bār) | باریدن (بار) |
| let me | bāšad kĕ | باشد که |
| pillow | bālĕšt | بالشت |
| snow | barf | برف |
| to snow | barf bāridan (barf bār) | برف باریدن (برف بار) |
| snowy | barfi | برفی |
| bus | bas | بس |
| spring | bahār | بهار |
| passport | pāsport | پاسپورت |
| flight, take off | parwāz | پرواز |
| to fly | parwāz kardan (parwāz kon) | پرواز کردن (پرواز کن) |
| so | pas | پس |
| pilot | pelōt | پیلوت |
| to be established | tasis šodan (tasis šaw) | تاسیس شدن (تاسیس شو) |
| summer | tābĕstān | تابستان |
| work experience | tajrobaye kāri | تجربهٔ کاری |
| ID card | tĕzkĕra, kārt-e hoyat | تذکره، کارت هویت |
| airport terminal | tarmināl-e maydān-e hawāye | ترمینال میدان هوایی |
| bathroom | tašnāb | تشناب |
| about | taqriban | تقریباً |

| | | |
|---|---|---|
| ticket sales (office/agency) | tĕkĕt forōši | تکت فروشی |
| plane ticket | tĕlĕk-e tayyāra | تکت طیاره |
| taxi driver | tasiwān | تکسیوان |
| to contact | tamās grĕftan (tamās gir) | تماس گرفتن (تماس گیر) |
| trunk | tōlbaks | تولبکس |
| towel | jānxoškān, jānpāk | جانخشکان، جانپاک |
| somewhere, a place | jāye | جایی |
| to build | jōr šodan (jōr šaw) | جور شد |
| to check | čĕk kardan (čĕk kon) | چک کردن (چک کن) |
| bed | čaparkat | چپرکت |
| to be present | hāzĕr bōdan (hāzĕr bāš/ hast) | حاضربودن(حاضرباش/هست) |
| to move | harakat kardan (harakat kon) | حرکت کردن (حرکت کن) |
| overseas, foreign | xārĕji | خارجی |
| empty | xāli | خالی |
| housekeeper, maid | xāna sāmān | خانه سامان |
| bad | sangen | خراب |
| fall | xazān | خزان |
| oneself | xōd | خود |
| myself | xōdam/xōdem | خودم |
| himself/herself | xōdaš/xōdĕš | خودش |
| yourself | xōdat/xōdĕt | خودت |
| ourselves | xōdĕmā | خودما |
| themselves | xōdĕšān | خودشان |
| yourselves | xōdĕtān | خودتان |
| cold, chilly | xonok, sard | خنک، سرد |
| temperature | daraja-e harārat | درجهٔ حرارت |
| centigrade | daraja-e sāntigĕrād | درجه سانتی گراد |
| to be in service of | dar xĕdmat bōdan (dar xĕdmat hast) | در خدمت بودن (در خدمت هست) |

| round-trip | do tarafa | دو طرفه |
|---|---|---|
| comfortable | rāhat | راحت |
| to reach, arrive | rasidan (ras) | رسیدن (رس) |
| lightning | r'ad ō barq | رعد و برق |
| sheet | rōjāye | روجایی |
| to reserve | rezarf /rezarw kardan(rezarf kon) | ریزرف/ریزرو کردن(ریزرو کن) |
| winter | zamēstān | زمستان |
| hail | žāla | ژاله |
| to hail | žāla bāridan (žāla bār) | ژاله باریدن (ژاله بار) |
| year | sāl | سال |
| trip | safar | سفر |
| to travel | safar kardan(safar kon) | سفر کردن (سفرکن) |
| air travel | safar-e hawāye | سفر هوایی |
| road trip | safar-e zamini | سفر زمینی |
| heavy | xarāb | سنگین |
| flood | sel | سیل |
| to flood | sel āmadan (sel āy) | سیل آمدن (سیل آی) |
| hard | šadid | شدید |
| airline | šěrkat-e hawāye | شرکت هوایی |
| soap | sābun | صابون |
| clear | sāf | صاف |
| to wait | sabr kardan(sabr kon) | صبر کردن (صبر کن) |
| to be necessary | zarorat bōdan (zarorat bāš, hast) | ضرورت بودن (ضرورت باش/است) |
| obviously | tab'an | طبعاً |
| storm | tōfān | طوفان |
| plane | tayyāra | طیاره |
| season | fasĕl | فصل |
| to the attention of | qābĕl-e tawajoh | قابل توجه |

| | | |
|---|---|---|
| absolutely | kāmĕlan | کاملاً |
| rent | kĕrāya | کرایه |
| a person, some person | kasi | کسی |
| comforter | kampal | کمپل |
| to help | komak kardan (komak kon) | کمک کردن (کمک کن) |
| warm | garm | گرم |
| report | gozārĕš | گزارش |
| custom | gomrok | گمرک |
| month | māh | ماه |
| to be equipped | mojahaz bōdan (mojahaz hast) | مجهز بودن (مجهز هست) |
| various | motalĕf | مختلف |
| hotel manager | modir-e hotal, hotali | مدیر هوتل، هوتلی |
| foggy | martōb | مرطوب |
| traveler | mosāfĕr | مسافر |
| neutral, mild | mo'tadĕl | معتدل |
| free | moft | مفت |
| to wait | montazĕr bōdan (montazĕr bāš, hast) | منتظر بودن ( منتظر باش، هست) |
| to be available | mawjud bōdan(mawjud hast) | موجود بودن (موجود هست) |
| moon | mahtāb, māh | مهتاب، ماه |
| airport | maydān-e hawāye | میدان هوایی |
| to land | nĕšast kardan (nĕšast kon) | نشست کردن (نشست کن) |
| sometime | waqti | وقتی |
| sky, weather | hawā | هوا |
| hotel | hotal | هوتل |
| to note | yāddāšt kardan (yāddāšt kon) | یادداشت کردن (یادداشت کن) |
| one-way | yak tarafa | یک طرفه |

## Dari Vocabulary Different from Iranian Persian

| English Translation | Iranian Persian | | Farsi-e Dari | |
|---|---|---|---|---|
| taxi driver | šufar | شوفر | tĕxiwān | تکسیوان |
| towel | hawla | حوله | jān-xoškān, jān-pāk | جانخشکان، جانپاك |
| bathroom | dastšoyi | دستشویی | tašnāb | تشناب |
| bed | taxt-e xāb | تخت خواب | čapārkat | چپرکت |
| pilot | xalabān | خلبان | pelōt | پیلوت |
| housekeeper, maid | xedmat-kār | خدمتکار | xāna sāmān | خانه سامان |
| ID card | šanās-nāma | شناسنامه | tazkĕra, kart-e howiyat | تذکره، کارت هویت |
| plane | havāpaymā | هواپیما | tayāra | طیاره |
| plane ticket | balit-e havāpaymā | بلیط هواپیما | tĕkĕt-e tayāra | تکت طیاره |
| airport | forud-gāh | فرودگاه | maydān-e hawā-ye | میدان هوایی |

# فصل دهم
## CHAPTER TEN 10

# در جریان رخصتی هایم
## DURING MY BREAK

# IN THIS CHAPTER

- **وظایف** Functions

  *Checking into a hotel; reading travel brochures/country guidelines; Hiring a tourist company; Going sightseeing; Learning body parts; Handling difficult situations while on vacation; Visiting a doctor, pharmacy, or traditional doctor; Reading health advisories; Writing your own letters and descriptions; Calling a travel agency for tickets, information, delays, flight cancelations, lost luggage, etc.*

- **تبصرهٔ فرهنگی** Cultural Notes

  *Modern vs. traditional doctors; Modern vs. traditional medicines; Traditional health care facilities*

- **دستور زبان** Language Structure

  *Gerunds; Expressions of opinions and decisions; The verb 'to hurt' درد کردن; Derivation of place names using the suffix خانه ; Exclamations and wishing*

- **مرور فصل** Chapter Review

  *Checking into a hotel, reading travel brochures/country guidelines; Visiting a doctor, pharmacy, or traditional doctor about an illness; Calling travel agencies for tickets, information, delays, flight cancelations, lost luggage, etc; Writing about your travel problems to others, e.g. manager, colleagues; Writing about your travel experiences*

- **لغات** Vocabulary

  *Review phrases and words used in this chapter*

## Chapter Introduction

In this chapter, you will read and learn to do the following tasks:

1 - Check into a hotel and read travel brochures/country guidelines
2 - Hire a tourist company, go sightseeing
3 - Talk about your vacations/holidays
4 - Learn various body parts
5 - Handle a difficult situation while on vacation in another country, e.g. getting sick
6 - Visit a doctor, pharmacy, or traditional doctor about an illness
7 - Ask for help from others, buying medicine, talking about an illness
8 - Read health advisories
9 - Write your own letters and descriptions
10 - Call a travel agency for tickets, information, delays, flight cancelations, lost luggage, etc.

By the end of this chapter, you should be able to handle familiar as well as unfamiliar situations.

در روز سوم رخصتی ام مریض شدم.
I got sick on the third day of my vacation.

من دیروز به هوتلم رسیدم.
Yesterday, I arrived at my hotel.

فردا ما پس به کابل خواهیم رفت.
Tomorrow, we will go back to Kabul.

# درس اول: من دیروز به هوتلم رسیدم.

## Lesson One: Yesterday, I arrived at my hotel.

In this section, you will learn more about Afghan hotels, including choosing a hotel based on amenities and accommodations, checking in, and telling others about your vacation.

Exercise 1: تمرین ۱:

A. شریف and his family have reached Mazaar-e Sharif Hotel and want to check in. Listen to the first part of the conversation with the hotel employee on the audio recording and answer the following questions.

1. When did شریف book his hotel room?
   a) one day ago      b) two days ago      c) few days ago

2. What document does the hotel manager ask for?
   a) passport      b) ID card

3. What does the hotel manager want to do with the document he asks for?
   a) He wants to check the information.      b) He wants to make a copy of it.

4. What did the hotel manager ask شریف to do?
   a) read the information on the form
   b) fill out the form
   c) both a and b are correct

B. Now listen to the second part of the conversation on the audio recording and choose the best answer for the following questions.

1. Did the hotel manager give the documents back to شریف?
   a) yes      b) no

2. What is the room number of شریف?
   a) 126      b) 162

3. Which floor is شریف room located on?
   a) 1st floor      b) 2nd floor

4. Who will direct شریف to his room?
   a) the manager himself      b) the maid

C. Listen to both audio recordings again and, this time, repeat each with a partner.

Exercise 2: تمرین ۲:

A. The audio recording will only play the hotel manager's questions. Listen and provide an appropriate answer to each question. Then, write down or record your responses and submit them to your instructor.

| | |
|---|---|
| ۱ | سلام به هوتل مزار خوش آمدید ، چی خدمت کرده میتوانم؟ |
| ۲ | گفتید ، نام تان چیست؟ |
| ۳ | ببخشید ، تخلص تان چیست؟ |
| ۴ | میتوانم که تذکره یا کارت هویت تان را ببینم؟ |
| ۵ | تشکر ، من از تذکره تان یك كاپی میگیرم، لطفاً این فورمه را هم خانه پوری کنید . |
| ۶ | ببخشید ، فورمه را خانه پوری کردید؟ |
| ۷ | تشکر ، اینه تذکرهٔ تان را هم بگیرید و این هم کلید اتاق تان. شماره اتاق تان ۱۲۶ است. |
| ۸ | آیا میخواهید که خانه سامان شما را رهنمایی کند؟ |

B. With a partner, discuss the similarities and differences of the check-in process of the hotels in Afghanistan in comparison with those of your own country.

C. You are in Kabul and you want to check in to your hotel. Go to the front desk and check in. Your classmate will play the role of the hotel manager. Make sure to include the following information:

| مسافر | مدیر هوتل |
|---|---|
| 1. Introduce yourself. | 1. Ask the guest his/her full name. |
| 2. Tell the hotel manager you have reserved a room. | 2. Ask for an ID/passport. |
| 3. Ask for the room number. | 3. Give the guest his/her room key and documentation. |
| 4. Ask for directions to your room. | 4. Say that the guest will be staying in room 213 on the third floor. |

Exercise 3: تمرین ۳ :

A. میرویس saw the following brochure in his room. Read it with a partner and discuss it.

<sup>52</sup>

قابل توجهٔ <u>مسافرین</u> و <u>مهمانان</u> محترم، لطفاً به نکات زیر توجه نمایید :

۱- دروازهٔ اتاق تان را برای <u>اشخاص ناشناس</u> باز نکنید .

۲- <u>درجریان</u> شب بعد از ساعت ۱۰ از هوتل بیرون نشوید .

۳- <u>اسناد</u> ، پیسه ها و <u>چیزهای قیمتی</u> تان را در داخل سیف اتاق تان بمانید .

۴- اگر شما <u>مسافر خارجی</u> هستید و به <u>ترجمان</u> ضرورت دارید ، پس لطفاً به دفتر هوتل تماس بگیرید .

۵- برای <u>پیدا نمودن</u> رستورانت <u>دلخواه</u> تان؛ لست رستورانت ها را از دفتر هوتل بگیرید .

۶- برای دیدن <u>موزیم</u>، زیارت سخی و <u>جاهای دیدنی</u>، در روز های پنجشنبه و جمعه ساعت ۸ صبح بس های هوتل شما را میبرد .

۷- شماره تلیفون های ۰۷۰۴۰۸۰۷۰ و ۰۷۹۹۳۰۲۰۲۰ بیست و چار ساعت در خدمت تان است، شما میتوانید که هر وقت به این شماره <u>تماس بگیرید</u> .

B. Read the brochure above again. Then find the exact Dari equivalent of the following words from those underlined in the brochures.

| | |
|---|---|
| *documents* | *museum* |
| *sights* | *contact* |
| *translators* | *passengers* |
| *finding/to find* | *guests* |
| *favorite* | *unknown people* |
| *valuable things* | *during* |

C. Read the above advisory note again, and check "true" or "false" for the following statements.

| غلط | صحیح | جملات | |
|---|---|---|---|
| ☐ | ☐ | مسافرین و مهمانان باید دروازه اتاق شان را برای اشخاص ناشناس باز کنند . | ۱ |
| ☐ | ☐ | مسافرین و مهمانان باید پیش از ساعت ده شب از هوتل بیرون نشوند . | ۲ |
| ☐ | ☐ | مسافرین و مهمانان لست رستورانت های دلخواه شان را از دفتر باید بگیرند . | ۳ |
| ☐ | ☐ | مسافرین باید چیز های قیمتی شان را در سیف دفتر هوتل بمانند . | ۴ |
| ☐ | ☐ | بس های هوتل هفته دو روز مسافرین و مهمانان را به دیدن جاهای دیدنی میبرد . | ۵ |
| ☐ | ☐ | هوتل دو شماره تلیفون ۲۴ ساعته برای مسافرین دارد . | ۶ |
| ☐ | ☐ | مسافرین خارجی اگر ترجمان بکار دارند ، باید ترجمان را خودشان پیدا کنند . | ۷ |

## 10.1 Gerunds اسم مصدر

In the above text, the words دیدن 'to see' and پیدا نمودن 'to find' are used. In Dari, the infinitive forms (of the verbs in a sentence) function as gerunds. For example:

| Gerunds | | Dari verb | |
|---|---|---|---|
| seeing, visiting | دیدن | to see | دیدن |
| watching | پیدا نمودن | to find | پیدا نمودن |

These types of nouns are the same as the verbs with "-ing" in English; e.g., watching, swimming.

Exercise 4:  تمرین ۴:

A. Write the Dari equivalent of the following sentences.

| | |
|---|---|
| Most people like reserving rooms via the internet. | ۱ |
| He always likes going to an Afghan restaurant to eat lamb kabobs. | ۲ |
| I like working in a hotel. | ۳ |
| To see the زیارت سخی you have to take the hotel's shuttle on Thursday. | ۴ |

B.  You will hear a conversation between a guest and a hotel employee on the audio recording. Listen and find the gerunds. Then, identify which verb they are derived from.

C. Listen to the audio recording of a guest and the hotel employee again. This time, answer the following questions.

| | |
|---|---|
| برای دیدن زیارت سخی و موزیم مزار شریف ، مسافرین باید چی کنند؟ | ۱ |
| بس ها چی وقت برای بردن مسافرین آماده است؟ | ۲ |
| برای راجستر کردن نام و مشخصات، مسافرین باید کجا بروند؟ | ۳ |

Exercise 5:  تمرین ۵:

A. The following texts are taken from tourism company brochures. Read the information inside and complete the following tasks.

شرکت توریزم آریانا:

شرکت توریزم آریانا هر هفته برای سه روز مهمانان و مسافران عزیز را از تمام ولایات کشور به دیدن جاهای دیدنی ولایت بامیان میبرد. خدمات این شرکت قرار ذیل است.

۱ - بوک کردن تکت طیاره برای مسافرین

۲ - برداشتن مسافرین از میدان هوایی کابل و یا مزار شریف

۳ - بردن مسافرین به ولایت بامیان همراه بس ها

۴ - تهیه کردن، چای صبح، نان چاشت و نان شب

۵ - تهیه کردن هوتل در بامیان

۶ - نشان دادن، جاهای دیدنی ولایت بامیان

شرکت توریزم بلخ:

شرکت توریزم بلخ هرروز از ساعت ۸ صبح تا ۴ بجه دیگر مهمانان و مسافرین عزیز را به دیدن جاهای زیر میبرد.

۱ - ساعت ۸ تا ۱۰ زیارت سخی

۲ - ساعت ۱۰ ونیم تا یازده نیم؛ نان چاشت در رستورانت سنتی بلخ

۳ - ساعت ۱۲ تا ۲ بندر حیرتان و دیدن دریایی آمو

۴ - ساعت ۲ ونیم تا چار موزیم ملی بلخ

| شرکت | دریا | موزیم ملی | نشان دادن |
|---|---|---|---|
| company | sea | national museum | to show |

| بندر | خدمات | قرار ذیل | تهیه کردن | برداشتن | زیارت |
|---|---|---|---|---|---|
| seaport | services | as follow | to provide | to pick up | shrine |

1. Which of the above companies in the brochures is inside Mazaar-e Sharif?
   a)  Balkh tourism company            b)  Arianna tourism company

2. Look at the sentences under the services column below. Then place a checkmark next to the appropriate tourism company that provides that service.

| شرکت توریزم بلخ | شرکت توریزم آریانا | خدمات |
|---|---|---|

Takes the passengers to دریایی آمو.

Takes the passengers to the museum between 2 and 4 in the afternoon.

Provides tickets for passengers.

Provides meals three times.

Takes the passenger to a traditional restaurant.

Works every week three times.

Works every day.

3. With a classmate, discuss in Dari which one of the above tourism companies would you most likely use? Why?

4. With a classmate, talk about the most interesting places you've seen or visited. What have you seen? Why is that place so interesting to you?

B. You are in Kabul and you want to go sightseeing. Call the front desk and ask for the schedule of the shuttle that can take you sightseeing. If there is no shuttle, then ask what you should do. Your classmate will play the role of the hotel employee.

Exercise 6:     ۶: تمرین

A. You will hear a conversation on the audio recording between شریف and his wife شیرین as they discuss where they should go for sightseeing. Listen and find out who wants to go sightseeing with which tourism company. Then check the appropriate box.

| شرکت | زن | شوهر |
|---|---|---|
| ۱  بس های هوتل | ___ | ___ |
| ۲  شرکت توریزم بلخ | ___ | ___ |
| ۳  شرکت توریزم آریانا | ___ | ___ |

B.  Now listen to the audio recording again, and check "true" or "false" for each of the following statements.

فکر کردن
to think

تصمیم گرفتن
to decide

| غلط | صحیح | جملات |
|---|---|---|
| ☐ | ☐ | ۱  زن شرکت بلخ را خوش دارد چونکه این شرکت مسافرین را به بندر حیرتان میبرد . |
| ☐ | ☐ | ۲  شریف دریا را خوش دارد . |
| ☐ | ☐ | ۳  شریف با شرکت توریزم آریانا نمیرود چونکه پیسه شان کم است . |
| ☐ | ☐ | ۴  شریف و زنش سه انتخاب دارند . |
| ☐ | ☐ | ۵  شریف و زنش تصمیم گرفتند که با شرکت بلخ به دیدن جاهای دیدنی بروند . |

## 10.2 Expressing Opinions and Decisions

In order to express opinions in Dari, use the verb 'to think' فکر کردن as an auxiliary verb. For example, in the above conversation, you heard:

من فکر میکنم که اگر همراه بس های هوتل برویم بهتر است .
I think that it's better if we go by a hotel bus.

By using this auxiliary verb in the present form, you can put the second clause in the subjunctive mood or in a regular form. For example:

| I think that s/he is going. | من فکر میکنم که او میرود . |
|---|---|
| I think that s/he left. | من فکر میکنم که او رفت . |
| I think that s/he will go. | من فکر میکنم که او خواهد رفت . |
| I think that s/he should go. | من فکر میکنم که او باید برود . |
| I think that s/he might go. | من فکر میکنم که او شاید برود . |
| I think that if s/he goes ... | من فکر میکنم که اگر او برود... |

Exercise 7: تمرین ۷:

A. Listen to **میرویس** and his wife's conversation on the audio recording again. This time, write an appropriate answer to the following questions. Use the auxiliary:

فکر کردن ...

۱ چرا شریف شرکت توریزم آریانا را خوش دارد؟

۲ چرا زن شریف شرکت توریزم بلخ را خوش دارد؟

B. Read the brochures from Exercise 5A again and ask for your classmate's opinions about each.

Exercise 8: تمرین ۸:

A. **شریف** wants to send an email message to his friend **میرویس** who is in India and on vacation. **شریف** describes his vacation in Mazaar-e Sharif. Read his email message and complete the following tasks.

فرستنده: شریف
گیرنده: میرویس
موضوع: رخصتی هایم

دوست عزیز میرویس جان سلام، امیدوارم که رخصتی های تان را با فامیل به خوشی تیر کنید. من هم همراه فامیل، دو روز پیش به مزار آمدم. اینجا هوا بسیار معتدل است، در جریان شب گاهی هم هوا سرد میشود. ما دیروز همراه یك شرکت توریزم به دیدن جاهای دیدنی شهر مزار شریف رفته بودیم. ما از زیارت سخی صاحب، از دریای آمو، موزیم ملی و دیگر جاهای تاریخی این شهر دیدن کردیم.

صباح ما به دیدن آتشکدهٔ نو بهار بلخ خواهیم رفت، من فکر میکنم که این آتشکده چندین قرن تاریخ دارد.

هوتل ما بسیار مدرن است، این هوتل چار منزل دارد و در هر منزل این هوتل تقریباً یك صدو پنجاه اتاق است. ما بخیر سه روز بعد به کابل خواهیم رفت. لطفاً دربارهٔ سفر خود هم برایم نوشته کنید.

با احترام،
دوستتان شریف.

| تاریخی | تاریخ | قرن | آتشکده | تیر کردن | ...امیدوارم که |
|---|---|---|---|---|---|
| historical | history | century | altar | to spend | I hope that... |

1. What is the best translation for the following phrase?

امیدوارم که رخصتی های تان را با فامیل به خوشی تیر کنید .

   a) I hope you may spend your vacation in happiness with your family.
   b) I hope you have spent your vacation in happiness with your family.

2. Where will میرویس go tomorrow for sightseeing?
   a) national museum
   b) Hairatan Seaport
   c) Naw-Bahar Altar
   d) Sakhi Shrine

3. What kind of hotel is میرویس staying in?
   a) modern                b) traditional

4. How is the weather in Mazaar-e Sharif?
   a) mild, but cold in the mornings
   b) mild, but cold during nighttime

5. When will میرویس and his wife be leaving?
   a) in two days
   b) in three days
   c) in four days

B.  Write an email message to a classmate about your most recent trip. Be sure to include the following:

۱ – هوتل و اتاق تان را تشریح کنید .
۲ – آب و هوای آن شهر را تشریح کنید .
۳ – جاهای دیدنی که رفته بودید .
۴ – چند روز آنجا بودید .
۵ – از چی طریق سفر کردید .

فرستنده:
گیرنده:
موضوع:

# درس دوم: در روز سوم رخصتی ام مریض شدم.

## Lesson Two: I got sick on the third day of my vacation.

In this section, you will learn how to talk about body parts, describe an illness, ask others about their symptoms, and discuss medications. You will also learn more about the Afghan health care system and traditions.

Exercise 1:    تمرین ۱:

A. The audio recording will present the following body parts in the order in which they are numbered. Listen and number the appropriate term in the box below.

| | دهان/دهن | | سر |
|---|---|---|---|
| | دست | | گوش |
| | پنجه، انگشت، کلک | | چشم |
| | پا/ پای | | بینی |

B. Listen to the audio recording again and write the exact English translation of each word in the box above.

C. Fill in the following blanks with the appropriate name of a body part.

۴) در _____ ۳) در _____ ۲) آن بچه در ۱) این مرد در _____
های او یک بوتل آب او یک سگرت است. اش _____ هایش عینک است.
است. کلاه پیک است.

۸) در _____ ۷) در _____ ۶) در _____ و ۵) در _____ و
هایش گوشکی است. هایش بوتهای گلابی آن _____ هایشان انگشتر و
است. مرد یک ماسک است. چله است.
است.

Exercise 2: تمرین ۲: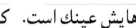

A. شیرین is not feeling well. Listen to her conversation with شریف on the audio recording and put a checkmark next to the each body parts she mentions.

| | | | | | |
|---|---|---|---|---|---|
| _____ | دهان | ۵ | _____ | سر | ۱ |
| _____ | دست | ۶ | _____ | گوش | ۲ |
| _____ | پنجه، انگشت، کلک | ۷ | _____ | چشم | ۳ |
| _____ | پا/ پای | ۸ | _____ | بینی | ۴ |

| طاقت داشتن | مریض | تاثیر | نزدیک | زنگ زدن (زنگ زن) | رد کردن (درد کن) |
|---|---|---|---|---|---|
| to have tolerance, to be tolerant | sick | effect | close, near | to call, to ring | to hurt, to ache |

B.  Now listen to شیرین and شریف's conversation on the audio recording again, and choose the best answer for the following questions.

| | |
|---|---|
| ١ | زن به شوهرش گفت: بخیز که _____ . |
| | مریض نیستم      خوب نیستم      خوب هستم      مریض هستم |
| ٢ | زن فکر میکند که او از تاثیر چی مریض شده است؟ |
| | هوای برفی      هوای آفتابی      گرمی      سردی |
| ٣ | شوهر میخواهد که به کجا زنگ بزند؟ |
| | به کلینیك      به دفتر هوتل      به داکتر      به شفاخانه |
| ٤ | کدام اعضای بدن زن درد میکند؟ |
| | سر، پنجه ها، دستها، پاها |
| | سر، گوش ها، دستها، پاها |
| | سر، دستها، پاها |
| | سر، چشم ها، دستها، پاها |

### 10.3 The Verb درد کردن 'To Hurt'

The compound verb درد کردن 'to hurt/to ache' consists of the word درد 'pain' and the simple verb کردن 'to do'. Thus, any body parts may be added at the beginning of this verb in order to express that the mentioned body part hurts or is in pain. For example:

ترکاری فروشی      to hurt   درد کردن      head   سر

The body part is always followed by a possessive pronoun, and the verb is conjugated only in the third-person singular. This is because each body part is considered in the third person (it). For example:

| | | |
|---|---|---|
| My head hurts. | سرم درد میکند. | سردرد کردن |
| His/her hand hurts. | دستش درد میکند. | دست درد کردن |
| Does your foot hurt? | پایتان درد میکند؟ | پای درد کردن |

Exercise 3: تمرین ۳:

A. Look at Exercise 2A and write down the aching body parts of the wife of شریف.
Then conjugate each part with the verb 'to hurt.'

B. Complete the following sentences using various body parts. For example:

من به پوهنتون نمیتوانم که بروم، چونکه پایم درد میکنم.

I can't go to the university because my foot hurts.

|  |  |  |
|---|---|---|
| My ear hurts. | من نمیتوانم که موسیقی بشنوم چونکه _____ | ۱ |
| His teeth hurt (دندانها). | او نمیتواند که نان بخورد چونکه _____ | ۲ |
| My hand hurts. | من نمیتوانم که نوشته کنم چونکه _____ | ۳ |
| His eyes hurt. | او نمیتواند که فلم ببیند چونکه _____ | ۴ |
| Her ankle hurts. | او نمیتواند که به صنف برود چونکه _____ | ۵ |
| My finger hurts. | من نمیتوانم که تایپ کنم چونکه _____ | ۶ |

Exercise 4: تمرین ۴:

A. شریف is calling the front desk to seek help. Listen to the conversation and answer the following questions.

1. Is there a hospital close to the hotel?
   a) yes                     b) no

2. Which one of the following places is located near the hotel?
   a) Raazi Hospital          b) Raazi Pharmacy

3. Is a doctor available nearby the hotel?
   a) yes                     b) no

4. According to the conversation, which one of these terms means medication?
   a) دواخانه          b) شفاخانه          c) دوا

B. Listen to the conversation again. This time, find the exact Dari term for the following pictures.

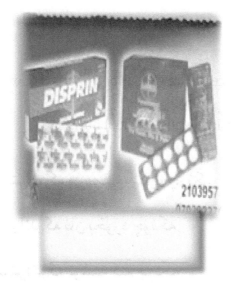

C. 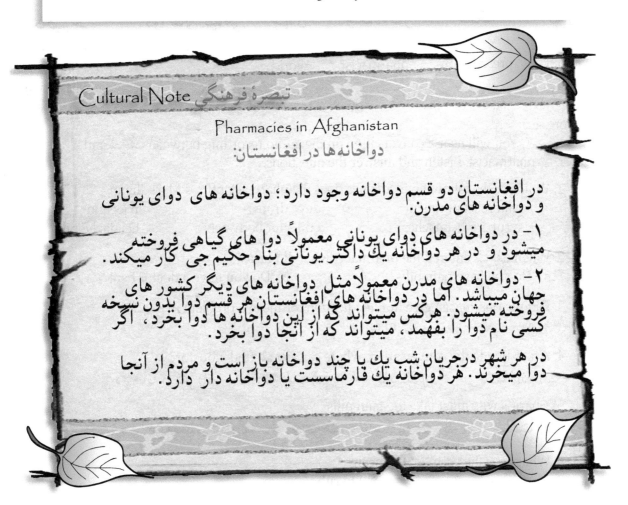 Imagine your ear hurts and you need to buy some medication. You are unfamiliar with the city. Go to the front desk and ask for help. Your classmate will play the role of the hotel manager. Be sure to include the following information:

| مدیر هوتل | مسافر |
|---|---|
| 1. Ask the guest how may you help him/her. | 1. Say that you're a guest from Room 213. |
| 2. Tell the guest that right now, no doctors are available, but tell him/her that a pharmacy is close by the hotel; give the following directions: *When exiting the hotel, turn left, and go straight ahead. After you've reached the intersection, turn left again; you will see Kabul Bank. The pharmacy is on the right side of the bank.* | 2. Tell the hotel manager that your ear hurts and you need to buy some medication. |
| | 3. Ask the hotel manager whether there is a doctor or a pharmacy close by the hotel. |
| | 4. Confirm the directions by repeating them back to the hotel manager. |
| 3. Tell the guest that the pharmacist can help you from there. | 5. Thank the hotel manager and say goodbye. |

Cultural Note  تبصرهٔ فرهنگی

Pharmacies in Afghanistan
دواخانه‌ها در افغانستان:

در افغانستان دو قسم دواخانه وجود دارد؛ دواخانه های دوای یونانی و دواخانه های مدرن.

۱- در دواخانه های دوای یونانی معمولاً دوا های گیاهی فروخته میشود و در هر دواخانه یک داکتر یونانی بنام حکیم جی کار میکند.

۲- دواخانه های مدرن معمولاً مثل دواخانه های دیگر کشور های جهان میباشد. اما در دواخانه های افغانستان هر قسم دوا بدون نسخه فروخته میشود. هرکس میتواند که از این دواخانه ها دوا بخرد، اگر کسی نام دوا را بفهمد، میتواند که از آنجا دوا بخرد.

در هر شهر در جریان شب یک یا چند دواخانه باز است و مردم از آنجا دوا میخرند. هر دواخانه یک فارماسست یا دواخانه دار دارد.

Exercise 5: تمرین ۵:

Answer the folowing true or false statements about the cultural note about pharmacies.

| غلط صحیح | جملات | شماره |
|:---:|:---|:---:|
| ☐ ☐ | There are two types of pharmacies in Afghanistan. | ۱ |
| ☐ ☐ | The traditional pharmacies sell all types of medications. | ۲ |
| ☐ ☐ | The modern pharmacies sell also the herbal medications. | ۳ |
| ☐ ☐ | In Afghanistan, you have to be 18 years old to buy medication. | ۴ |
| ☐ ☐ | You can buy any medication without a prescription. | ۵ |
| ☐ ☐ | All pharmacies are open during the night. | ۶ |
| ☐ ☐ | There is a traditional doctor in each pharmacy. | ۷ |

| بدون | نسخه | دواخانه دار | جهان | دوا های گیاهی | حکیم جی |
|:---:|:---:|:---:|:---:|:---:|:---:|
| without | prescription | pharmacist | world | herbal medicine | traditional doctor (prescribes herbal medications) |

Exercise 6: تمرین ۶:

A. You will hear a conversation on the audio recording between شریف and a pharmacist. Listen and answer the questions.

1. Which of the following medicines does the pharmacy offer ? Mark them.
   ___ pain relief ointment    ___ eye drops    ___ in jection
   ___ syrup for headaches    ___ pills for body aches    ___ headache pills

2. When شریف entered the pharmacy, what did he ask?
   a) Do you have pain pills?    b) Do you have a doctor here?

3. Did the pharmacist give him medication for the eye problem of شیرین؟
   a) yes    b) no

4. According to the conversation, where can شریف find a doctor?
   a) شفاخانه    b) کلینیک    c) دواخانه    d) در خانهٔ داکتر

5. Sharif's wife must take the pain pills _____ .
   a) شش ساعت    b) هر هشت ساعت    c) هر هفت ساعت

6. What does the verb مالیدن mean?
   a) to put    b) to rub

B. 🎧 Place a (+) mark next to the questions that are stated in the audio recording by شریف, and a (√) next to the ones by the pharmacist. Then write a possible English translation of each.

| ترجمه | دواخانه دار | شریف | سوالات |
|---|---|---|---|
| _____ | _____ | | شما در دواخانهٔ تان داکتر دارید؟ |
| _____ | _____ | _____ | چرا خیریت است؟ |
| _____ | _____ | _____ | چی تکلیف دارند؟ |
| _____ | _____ | _____ | حالا به کجا بروم که داکتر را ببینم؟ |
| _____ | _____ | _____ | تشکر چند میشود؟ |

C. 🤝 Imagine you are in Kabul and you need some medication. Go to the pharmacy and purchase the medications you need. Your classmate will play the role of the pharmacist. Use the following information in your conversation:

| دواخانه | مریض |
|---|---|
| 1. Ask the patient what s/he wants. | 1. Tell the pharmacist that your entire body aches and you need some pain-killers. |
| 2. Give the patient the pain killers, and tell him/her to take the pill every 8 hours | 2. Ask the pharmacist what else is good for pain. |
| 3. Give the patient a painkiller ointment and tell him/her to rub it on his arms and feet every night. | 3. Ask for the price of the medicine. |
| 4. Tell the patient that the total price is 300 Afghani. | 4. Pay the money and thank the pharmacist. |

## Cultural Note فرهنگی تبصره

### Traditional Health Care

In addition to the free modern health care that is provided in the cities and countrysides of Afghanistan, there is also an extensive system of private medical care (clinics, hospitals, etc.) that provides service for a fee. Many Afghan people also use traditional medicine techniques. For example, one popular traditional medicine service is a طب یونانی, meaning Greek medicine. The practitioners called (حکیم جی) often prescribe herbs or special diets داکتر یونانی for their patients.

Another traditional medicine practice is visiting a ملا or inviting a mullah to one's home. In these cases, the ملا recites verses of the holy Qur'an قرآن شریف and blows air on the patient. This

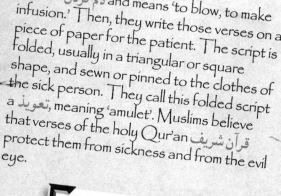

is called دم کردن and means 'to blow, to make infusion.' Then, they write those verses on a piece of paper for the patient. The script is folded, usually in a triangular or square shape, and sewn or pinned to the clothes of the sick person. They call this folded script a تعویذ, meaning 'amulet'. Muslims believe that verses of the holy Qur'an قرآن شریف protect them from sickness and from the evil eye.

Exercise 7: تمرین ۷:

A. The wife of شریف isn't feeling any better, so they are visiting a doctor. Listen to the conversation on the audio recording, and then mark the complaints in the following table that شیرین gives the doctor.

| | | |
|---|---|---|
| سر چرخ هستم. ____ | جانم درد میکند. ____ |
| دلبد هستم. ____ | دست هایم درد میکند. ____ |
| چشم های خارش میکند. ____ | پاهایم درد میکند. ____ |
| بینی ام بند است. ____ | چشمهایم درد میکند. ____ |
| گنس هستم. ____ | سرفه میکنم. ____ |
| کم زور هستم. ____ | استفراغ کردم. ____ |
| شکمم درد میکند. ____ | تب دارم. ____ |

B. Think about the last time you were sick. Which one of the above complaints did you have? Tell them to a classmate.

C. Match the following terms to their proper English equivalents.

| | |
|---|---|
| itch | سرفه |
| dizzy | استفراغ |
| nausea | گنس |
| vomit | دلبد |
| weak | سرچرخ |
| out of it | خارش |
| cough | کم زور |

D. Listen to the audio recording again. Then check the questions the doctor asked.

| | | | |
|---|---|---|---|
| کی مریض است؟ ____ | چی تکلیف دارید؟ ____ |
| آیا استفراغ هم میکنید؟ ____ | آیا گنس هستید؟ ____ |
| آیا سرفه هم میکنید؟ ____ | آیا سرچرخ هستید؟ ____ |

E.  Now look at the following pictures and, in a couple of sentences, explain what has happened to each person.

_____   _____   _____

_____   _____   _____

_____   _____   _____

_____   _____   _____

F.  Listen to the audio recording again and check "true" or "false" for the following.

| غلط | صحیح | جملات | |
|---|---|---|---|
| ☐ | ☐ | داکتر پرسید ( کی مریض است؟) | ۱ |
| ☐ | ☐ | شریف گفت: (زنم مریض است.) | ۲ |
| ☐ | ☐ | زن شریف از دیروز مریض است. | ۳ |
| ☐ | ☐ | او فکر میکند که تب دارد . | ۴ |
| ☐ | ☐ | او سرفه نمیکند . | ۵ |
| ☐ | ☐ | او دلبد است . | ۶ |
| ☐ | ☐ | او چشمایش خارش نمیکند . | ۷ |
| ☐ | ☐ | او بینی اش باز است . | ۸ |
| ☐ | ☐ | داکتر برای معاینه کردن زن میرویس، از او اجازه گرفت. | ۹ |
| ☐ | ☐ | شریف زنش را کمک کرد . | ۱۰ |

G.  Imagine that you're in Kabul and have some health problems. Go to the doctor and explain your problems. Your classmate will play the role of the doctor. Make sure to cover the following:

| داکتر | مریض |
|---|---|
| 1. Ask the patient to sit down and ask him/her what the problem is. | 1. Greet the doctor. |
| 2. Ask the patient if s/he has a stomach ache, nausea, or vomiting. | 2. Tell the doctor that since yesterday your body hurts and that you have a headache. |
| 3. Ask the patient for permission to check him/her, and tell him/her to lie down. | 3. Tell the doctor you that you don't have a stomach ache and you're not vomiting, but you are a little nauseated. |

## 10.4 Deriving Place Names Using the Suffix خانه

The suffix خانه 'home/house' is added to nouns, adjectives, and verbs and forms the name of a place. For example, in the conversations above, you've heard the words شفاخانه and دواخانه. These words consist of one word, along with the suffix خانه, such as the following:

| hospital | شفاخانه | healing, curing, health | شفا |
|---|---|---|---|
| pharmacy | دواخانه | medication | دوا |
| doctor's office, clinic | معاینه‌خانه | check up | معاینه |

Exercise 8: تمرین ۸:
The following words are a list of possible terms that take the suffix خانه. Add the suffix خانه to each, and find their English equivalent.

| | | working | کار | ۱ |
|---|---|---|---|---|
| | | printing | چاپ | ۲ |
| | | tea | چای | ۳ |
| | | guest | مهمان | ۴ |
| | | cook | آشپز | ۵ |
| | | up | بالا | ۶ |
| | | gambling | قمار | ۷ |

Exercise 9: تمرین ۹:

A. You will hear another conversation on the audio recording between a doctor, شریف, and his wife شیرین . Listen and answer the following questions.

---

1. What were the illnesses?

_____ heat stroke          _____ cold          _____ food allergies

---

2. What did they say the weather was like yesterday?
   a) sunny and warm          b) cloudy and rainy

---

3. What was the doctor's advice to شیرین?

---

4. Match the following terms to their English equivalents.
   a) nasal spray
   b) painkiller pills (for the body)
   c) allergy pills
   d) strengthening syrup (multivitamins, etc.)

گولی جان دردی
گولی حساسیت
شربت تقویه
قطرچکان بینی

---

B. Listen to the audio recording again. This time, mark the correct answer for the following medications.

| | | |
|---|---|---|
| روز چار دفعه بعد از نان | روزسه دفعه پیش از نان | ۱ گولی جان دردی<br>روز سه دفعه بعد از نان |
| هرشب دو دانه | هر شب یکدانه | ۲ گولی حساسیت<br>هر شب سه دانه |
| هر شش ساعت سه قاشق | هر شش ساعت دو قاشق | ۳ شربت تقویه<br>هر شش ساعت یک قاشق |
| هر ۲۴ ساعت دو قطره | هر دوازده ساعت دو قطره | ۴ قطرچکان بینی<br>هر هشت ساعت دو قطره |

| شفا عاجل میخواهم<br>I wish for you a quick recovery (get well soon). | فیس<br>doctor's fees | حساسیت کردن<br>to have an allergy | چکاندن<br>to seep / drop (liquid) |
|---|---|---|---|

| نسخه<br>prescription | قطره<br>drop | گرمی زده گی<br>heat stroke | حساسیت<br>allergy | جدی<br>serious | مریضی<br>illness |
|---|---|---|---|---|---|

C.  Ask a classmate about the last time s/he went to a doctor. What did the doctor say? What was the illness? What medication was prescribed?

Exercise 10:  تمرین ۱۰:

A. Read the following health advisory and provide its English equivalent below.

مشوره های صحی برای مهمانان خارجی:

۱- لطفاً وقتیکه هوا بسیار گرم است، کوشش کنید که در اتاق های تان بمانید.

۲- لطفاً غذا های که در روی سرك فروخته میشود ، نخورید.

۳- اگر به غذا حساسیت کردید ، به داکتر بروید.

۴- لطفاً آب های بوتلی را بنوشید چونکه آب های غیر بوتلی پاك نیست.

۵- ما در هوتل دوای سردردی و جان دردی داریم.

۶- اگر در بیرون قدم میزنید ، با ماسك بینی و دهان تان را بپوشانید.

| قدم زدن (قدم زن) | کوشش کردن | پوشاندن (پوشان) | صحی | غیر بوتلی | مشوره |
|---|---|---|---|---|---|
| to walk | to try | to cover | health | without bottle | advice |

B.  Discuss with a partner which of these tips you think are particularly important when you go to Afghanistan. Explain why.

Exercise 11:  تمرین ۱۱:

A. شریف had a chance to check his email messages. He has received a response from his friend میرویس. Read the email message and complete the following tasks.

فرستنده: میرویس
گیرنده: شریف
موضوع: رخصتی ها

دوست عزیز شریف جان سلام،
امیدوار هستم که رخصتی های تان را در پهلوی فامیل محترم تان با خوشی سپری کنید، من ایمیل تان را گرفتم، تشکر.
رخصتی های من هم بخیر میگذرد، ما در اینجا: از جاهای دیدنی شهر آگره دیدن کردیم، مثل تاج محل، معبد ها قدیمی و تاریخی، بحر هند، و بازار های شهر آگره.
من همچنان خودم را به داکتر های هندی نشان دادم، آنها پایم را که درد میکرد معاینه کردند و برایم دوا دادند، حالا درد پایم بسیار خوب است.
ما سه روز بعد از میدان هوایی دهلی نو پرواز خواهیم کرد، پرواز ما ساعت شش صبح است و انشاالله ساعت نه و نیم صبح طیارهٔ ما در میدان هوایی کابل نشست خواهد کرد.

لطفاً در بارهٔ خود و فامیل محترم تان برایم نوشته کنید که چطور هستید؟
با احترام
دوستتان میرویس

1. Which one of the following places did میرویس visit? Place a checkmark next to the appropriate place.

_____ Agra's Bazaar     _____ ancient temples     _____ Indian ocean
_____ zoo              _____ New Dehli's bazaar   _____ Taj Mahal
_____ doctor's office  _____ Indian museum        _____ temple of Agra

2. How is میرویس's foot?
   a) It still hurts.      b) It's a little bit better now.      c) It's completely better now.

3. Write the departure and arrival time of میرویس's flight from New Delhi to Kabul.
Departure from New Dehli _____
Arrival in Kabul _____

B.  In the above email message, میرویس asks شریف to write back about his family vacation. Now شریف has written a response. Read his email message, and check "true" or "false" for each of the following statements.

فرستنده: میرویس
گیرنده: شریف
موضوع: رخصتی ها

دوست عزیز میرویس جان سلام،

تشکر از ایمیلی که برایم نوشته کرده بودید ، من ایمیل تان را گرفتم،  خوشحال شدم که درد پای تان بهتر شده است و شما توانستید که از جاهای دیدنی شهر آگره دیدن کنید .

رخصتی های ما در روز های اول خوب بود اما متاسفانه خانمم در روزهای آخر مریض شد و ما نتواستیم بیرون برویم، ما حالا در هوتل هستیم چونکه خانم باید استراحت کند .

من کوشش کردم که تکت های زمینی خود را پس بفروشم اما کسی آنها را نخرید ، من تکت های زمینی را میفروشم چونکه ما باید هوایی سفر کنیم. من تکت طیاره را برای پس فردا بوک کردم. پرواز ما ساعت هشت بجه خواهد بود و ما ساعت نه و نیم بجه به کابل خواهیم رسید .

حالا من در هوتل هستم، بسیار دق آوردم، من و فامیلم میخواهیم که فلم سیل کنیم، اخبار را ببینیم و برای چای صبح، نان چاشت و نان شب از رستورانت نان فرمایش بدهیم. چونکه خانمم نمیتواند بیرون برود .

راستی اگر میتوانید لطفاً یك جوره کالای هندی زنانه همرایتان برای خانمم بیاورید ، اندازهٔ او را خانم شما میفهمد .

خوب به امید دیدار
با احترام دوستتان شریف

| جملات | صحیح | غلط | |
|---|---|---|---|
| شریف was happy to hear about his friend. | ☐ | ☐ | ١ |
| The vacation of شریف was good at the beginning. | ☐ | ☐ | ٢ |
| شریف sold his bus tickets to someone else. | ☐ | ☐ | ٣ |
| He booked plane tickets for two days later. | ☐ | ☐ | ۴ |
| The flight time of شریف is at 8:00 a.m. | ☐ | ☐ | ۵ |
| The family of شریف will reach Kabul at 9:00 a.m. | ☐ | ☐ | ۶ |
| The family of شریف has been watching movies. | ☐ | ☐ | ٧ |
| شریف asked میرویس to bring a pair of clothes for شریف. | ☐ | ☐ | ٨ |
| میرویس already knows about the (clothing) size of شریف. | ☐ | ☐ | ٩ |

C. Using the above email messages as an example, write an email message to your classmate about your last vacation.

فرستنده:
گیرنده:
موضوع:

D.  Now, have your classmate read the email message you wrote and then write you a response.

فرستنده:
گیرنده:
موضوع:

# درس سوم: فردا ما پس به کابل خواهیم رفت.

## Lesson Three: Tomorrow, we will go back to Kabul.

> In this section, you will learn more about dining out at Afghan restaurants, planning a vacation, arranging travel plans, and expressing wishes.

Exercise 1:    تمرین ۱:

A. شریف and his family are on their last vacation day. Tomorrow, they will be going back to their hometown, Kabul. Listen to the conversation on the audio recording between شریف and his wife شیرین. Then, answer the following questions.

1. شریف said they will leave tomorrow if what happens?
   a)  If his wife gets better.          b) If they find plane tickets.

2. How will the weather be tomorrow?

   _____

3. When will شریف call the travel agency?
   a)  after lunch                    b) after dinner

4. What was the suggestion of شریف about the meal?
   a) He suggested to go to a restaurant.
   b) He suggested to order a meal.
   c) He suggested to cook in the room.

5. The wife of شریف wants to do what?
   a) cook dinner
   b) put on her clothes
   c) take her medication

6. شریف is to get who/what ready?
   a) his wife                    b) his kids                    c) his room

B. 🤝 It's lunch time. You and a classmate are hungry. Discuss where you should go for lunch and what you should eat. For example, you may include the following information in your conversation.

| شاگرد الف | شاگرد ب |
|---|---|
| 1. Tell your classmate that you are very hungry; suggest that he/she join you for lunch. | 1. Tell your classmate that you are also hungry and suggest that he/she order lunch. |
| 2. Tell your classmate that you don't want to order, but want to go to an Afghan restaurant. | 2. Tell your classmate that you agree with him/her, and tell him/her to wait so that you can change your clothes. |
| 3. Tell your classmate that you will go and get the car ready. | |

Exercise 2: 🤝 تمرین ۲:

A. The following ads are about two restaurants. Read each carefully. Then, with a classmate, discuss which one you would like to visit.

رستورانت مزار:

رستورانت مزار خوشمزه ترین غذاهای افغانی، هندی و چینایی را برای شما مهمان عزیز تهیه میکند. این رستورانت همچنان فرمایش های تان را در ۳۰ دقیقه به خانه های تان میآورد، شما فقط با تلیفون کردن به شماره های زیر میتوانید که غذای دلخواه تان را در خانه تان بخورید.

این رستورانت هر روز از ساعت ۱۱ صبح الی ۱۲ شب باز است.

آدرس: شهر کابل، جاده میوند، مقابل فروشگاه افغان

شماره تلیفون: ۰۷۰۰۳۰۳۸۳۸ ـ ۰۷۹۹۳۰۳۸۳۸

رستورانت کابل:

رستورانت کابل با پختن غذا های افغانی از ساعت ۸ صبح الی ۱۲ شب در خدمت مهمانان عزیز میباشد. این رستورانت مینوهای جداگانه برای چای صبح، نان چاشت و نان شب دارد.

این رستورانت برای دوصد مهمان در یک وقت جای دارد، این رستورانت برای مهمانان در نان چاشت و نان شب سوپ مرغ رایگان میدهد.

آدرس: شهر کابل، وزیر اکبر خان، سرک سه، در پهلوی مارکت دوا فروشی

B. 📖 Read the above ads again, and check "true" or "false" for the following statements.

| جملات | صحیح | غلط | |
|---|:---:|:---:|:---:|
| The Mazaar Restaurant cooks food from three different countries. | ☐ | ☐ | ١ |
| You can order food from the Kabul Restaurant. | ☐ | ☐ | ٢ |
| Both restaurants deliver food within 30 minutes of placing an order. | ☐ | ☐ | ٣ |
| The Mazaar Restaurant is open from 11:00 a.m. to 12:00 a.m. | ☐ | ☐ | ۴ |
| Kabul Restaurant has three different menus. | ☐ | ☐ | ۵ |
| For each meal, Kabul Restaurant provides a free cup of chicken soup. | ☐ | ☐ | ۶ |
| The Mazaar Restaurant may seat 200 people at one time. | ☐ | ☐ | ٧ |
| The Mazaar Restaurant is located in the city of Kabul. | ☐ | ☐ | ٨ |

Exercise 3: 🎧 تمرین ٣:
شریف and his wife شیرین are planning their vacation. Listen to their conversation on the audio recording, and choose the best answer for the following questions.

1. What did شیرین wish for?

2. What will شریف do next year?
   a) they will go on another vacation
   b) they will come back to Mazaar

3. What are شیرین's plans for after vacation?
   a) She will go to work and visit her children.
   b) She will go to school and visit her parents.
   c) She will go home and visit her husband's parents.

4. What will شریف do after his vacation?

5. When will they buy gifts?
   a) later          b) after lunch          c) after they buy tickets

| بخیر | پلان داشتن (پلان دار) | تحفه | کاشکی |
|:---:|:---:|:---:|:---:|
| with peace | to have a plan | gift | wishing marker |

## 10.5 Wishes and Exclamations

Wishes are mostly marked by the word کاش که. Sentences expressing wishes are in either of two categories:

1. Realizable: These wishes are for something in the future, and it is possible that the wish may come true. For example:

کاشکه وقت داشته باشم که همه جای ها را ببینم.

I wish that I could see everything in Kabul.

*Note that the verb 'to see' is in the subjunctive.

2. Unrealizable: These wishes are for something that has occurred in the past, and it will therefore never come true. For example, compare the following with the examples above.

کاشکه وقت زیادتر میداشتم که همه جای ها را میدیدیم.

I wish that I could have seen everything in Kabul.

*Note that the verb for this type of sentence is in the past subjunctive (which is the same as the past progressive form).

Exercise 4:  تمرین ۴:

A. Read the following sentences and mark whether each sentence is realizable or unrealizable.

| غیرممکن | ممکن | جملات |
|---|---|---|
| | | ۱ کاشکی مریض نمیبودم که به سینما میرفتم. |
| | | ۲ کاشکی هوا صاف باشد که به سفر برویم. |
| | | ۳ کاشکی به رستورانت افغانی میرفتم که نان میخوردم. |
| | | ۴ کاشکی بازار برویم که کمی تحفه بخرم. |

B. Make a statement of wishing for each of the following sentences.

| | |
|---|---|
| I don't have a car to go to work. | ١ |
| We don't have money to travel to Europe. | ٢ |
| They can't go to the movies because they're sick. | ٣ |
| She couldn't write an email message, because she didn't have internet service. | ٤ |

Exercise 5: تمرین ۵:

A. شریف is calling the travel agency to book a ticket for tomorrow morning. Listen to the audio recording and circle the flight times and landing times from Mazaar-e Sharif to Kabul.

| وقت نشست در کابل | | وقت پرواز از مزار | | روزهای هفته | |
|---|---|---|---|---|---|
| ۱۲:۳۰ بعد از ظهر | ۱۱ صبح | ۹:۳۰ صبح | ۸ صبح | شنبه | ١ |
| ۱۲:۳۰ بعد از ظهر | ۱۱ صبح | ۹:۳۰ صبح | ۸ صبح | یکشنبه | ٢ |
| ۱۲:۳۰ بعد از ظهر | ۱۱ صبح | ۹:۳۰ صبح | ۸ صبح | دوشنبه | ٣ |
| ۱۲:۳۰ بعد از ظهر | ۱۱ صبح | ۹:۳۰ صبح | ۸ صبح | سه شنبه | ٤ |
| ۱۲:۳۰ بعد از ظهر | ۱۱ صبح | ۹:۳۰ صبح | ۸ صبح | چارشنبه | ٥ |
| ۱۲:۳۰ بعد از ظهر | ۱۱ صبح | ۹:۳۰ صبح | ۸ صبح | پنجشنبه | ٦ |
| ۱۲:۳۰ بعد از ظهر | ۱۱ صبح | ۹:۳۰ صبح | ۸ صبح | جمعه | ٧ |

B. Listen to the audio recording again. This time, check "true" or "false" for each statement.

| غلط | صحیح | جملات | |
|---|---|---|---|
| ☐ | ☐ | برای فردا تکت فروشی، تکت دارد. | ١ |
| ☐ | ☐ | برای دیگر صباح تکت فروشی، تکت ندارد. | ٢ |
| ☐ | ☐ | همه تکت ها برای صباح فروخته شده است. | ٣ |
| ☐ | ☐ | شریف برای شش نفر تکت میخواهد. | ٤ |
| ☐ | ☐ | تکت فروشی تا هشت بجه باز است. | ٥ |
| ☐ | ☐ | شریف تا یك ساعت بعد به تکت فروشی میرود. | ٦ |
| ☐ | ☐ | تکت فروشی از طریق تلیفون تکت نمیفروشد. | ٧ |

C.  You are in Mazaar City, and you want to go back to Kabul. Call the travel agency and book tickets. Be sure to include the following:

| مشتری | تکت فروش |
|---|---|
| 1. Ask for the take-off and landing time. | 1. Give the flight and landing times. |
| 2. Ask if they have available seats for tomorrow. | 2. Say that you don't have any available tickets for tomorrow, but you have them for the next day. |
| 3. Say that you want a ticket for the next day. | 3. Provide your hours of operation. |
| 4. Ask for the hours of operation so that you can buy the tickets later. | |
| 5. Say that you will be back in an hour to book the ticket. | |

Exercise 6:  تمرین ۶:

A. شریف has purchased a plane ticket. A day before his flight, he got the following message from the airline. Read the message and answer the following questions.

> به اطلاع مسافران شرکت آریانا پرواز ۲۳، از مزار به کابل رسانیده میشود که شاید پرواز مذکور کنسل شود.
> مسافران عزیز با خبر باشند. برای معلومات بیشتر به شماره تلیفون ۰۷۰۰۳۰۳۰۴۰ تماس بگیرید.

به اطلاع مسافران شرکت آریانا پرواز ۲۳، از مزار به کابل رسانیده میشود که شاید پرواز مذکور کنسل شود.
مسافران عزیز با خبر باشند. برای معلومات بیشتر به شماره تلیفون ۰۷۰۰۳۰۳۰۴۰ تماس بگیرید.

1. What is this message about?
   a) a flight reminder                    b) flight cancellation information

2. How is the weather in Kabul?

_____

3. How can the passenger contact the airline for more information?
   a) calling
   b) emailing
   c) visiting the branch in person

| به اطلاع رساندن(به اطلاع رسان) | معلومات |
|---|---|
| to inform | information |

B. After شریف has received this message, he's contacting the airline to receive further information. Listen to the conversation on the audio recording and mark "true" or "false" for each of the following statements.

| غلط | صحیح | جملات | |
|---|---|---|---|
| ☐ | ☐ | شریف خودش را معرفی کرد. | ۱ |
| ☐ | ☐ | شمارهٔ پرواز ۳۳ است. | ۲ |
| ☐ | ☐ | پرواز کنسل شده چونکه پیلوت مریض است. | ۳ |
| ☐ | ☐ | پرواز شریف شاید دیگر صبح باشد. | ۴ |
| ☐ | ☐ | وقتیکه شریف تلیفون کرد، شب بود. | ۵ |

C.  Imagine that you've received a message from an airline agency in regards to your flight getting canceled. Call the airline agency and find out the reason. Be sure to include the following information.

| مسافر | نماینده |
|---|---|
| 1. Introduce yourself and say you are a passenger on Flight 234, going from Kandahar to Kabul, and you want to know why your flight is canceled. | 1. Welcome the person and ask how you help can the traveler. |
| 2. Ask when your flight will take off again. | 2. Tell the passenger that the weather in Kabul is very stormy; that's why the flight is canceled. |
| 3. Ask how you will be informed. | 3. Tell the passenger to check back tomorrow, but if the flight is to take off before that, the traveler will be informed via phone or email. |

پیام گرفتن(پیام گیر)   پیام
to receive a message   message

D. شریف is going to send a message to his manager to inform him about his flight delay. Read his message and translate his message into English.

مدیر صاحب سلام، امیدوارم که همه در دفتر خوب باشند .
مدیر صاحب من شاید که سبا نتوانم به دفتر بیایم چونکه
پروازم کنسل شده، من پس فردا بخیر خواهم آمد .
با احترام،
شریف

مدیر صاحب سلام، امیدوارم
که همه در دفتر خوب باشند .
مدیر صاحب من شاید که سبا
نتوانم به دفتر بیایم چونکه
پروازم کنسل شده، من پس فردا
اهم آمد .

E. Imagine your flight is being canceled and you can't make it back to your work on time. Write a message to your manager and explain the situation.

Exercise 7:  تمرین ۷:

شریف and his family are ready to leave. Listen to their conversation on the audio recording as they check out. Then complete the following questions.

1. Did شریف like the hotel?
   a) yes              b) no

2. How much does شریف have to pay?
   a) 200 AF          b) 900 AF

3. What is شریف′s money for?
   a) ordering a meal
   b) using the internet
   c) watching movies

4. What did شریف give to the hotel manager?

5. When is the flight for شریف and his family?

6. What did the hotel manager say to شریف at the end?
   a) Have a nice day. Goodbye.
   b) Have a nice trip. Goodbye.
   c) I wish you a nice trip. Goodbye.
   d) I wish you a safe trip. Goodbye.

7. What is the meaning of this phrase?   من میخواهم که حسابم را تصفیه کنم.

# مرور فصل دهم
# Review of Chapter Ten

In this section you will review the vocabulary, phrases, grammar, and cultural elements that you learned throughout the chapter.

Exercise 1:  تمرین ۱:

You have a hotel room reservation. Go to the front desk and check in. Be sure to include the following information. Your classmate will play the role of the hotel manager.

| مدیر هوتل | مسافر |
|---|---|
| 1. Welcome the passenger and say "how can I help you?" | 1. State your name and say that you have a reservation. |
| 2. Ask for his/her complete introduction and identification. | 2. Provide identification. |
| 3. Take the passport, and tell the guest that you are going to make a copy of it. | 3. Tell the hotel manager that it is okay to make a copy of the passport. |
| 4. Give the guest the passport and the room key. The room number is 302 on the third floor. | 4. Tell the hotel manager to have someone direct you to your room. |
| 5. Say that the housekeeper will direct you. | |

Exercise 2:  تمرین ۲:

You're in Kabul and are ill. Go to a doctor and explain your condition. Be sure to include the following information.

| مریض | داکتر |
|---|---|
| 1. Greet the doctor, and say that your head, arms, legs, and ears hurt. | 1. Ask the patient, "what is bothering you?" |
| 2. Say that you're nauseated, but you're not vomiting. | 2. Ask if the patient has nausea or vomiting. |
| 3. Ask the doctor how and when to use the prescribed medication. | 3. Write a prescription for flu, which includes tablets which are also good for body aches and headache. The prescription also includes ear drops. |
| | 4. Tell the patient to take the tablets every six hours, and the ear drops every eight hours by dropping two drops into each ear. |

Exercise 3: تمرین ۳ :

You're in The Kabul Museum and want to go back to your hotel. Go to a taxi driver and ask the following:

1. How much does the driver charge to your hotel?
2. The taxi driver is unfamiliar with your hotel; provide an address.
3. Bargain the initial price.

Exercise 4: تمرین ۴ :

You've just reached Kabul and are waiting at the airport for your next flight to Mazaar. Suddenly, you hear that your flight has been canceled. Go to the airline agent and state that your flight is being canceled. Also, be sure to ask when the next flight will leave, since you have a meeting the next morning.

Exercise 5: تمرین ۵ :

Since your flight has been canceled, you will not make it to your meeting on time. Write an email message to your company's manager, and let him/her know that you will not be able to attend the meeting. Explain your reasoning, and tell the manager that you will arrive a day later.

فرستنده:
گیرنده:
موضوع:

Exercise 6: 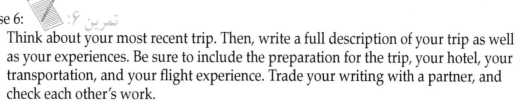 تمرین ۶:

Think about your most recent trip. Then, write a full description of your trip as well as your experiences. Be sure to include the preparation for the trip, your hotel, your transportation, and your flight experience. Trade your writing with a partner, and check each other's work.

# Vocabulary

In this part of the lesson, you will review, listen to, and practice pronunciation of the phrases and vocabulary used in the chapter.

## Phrases اصطلاحات

| How can I be of service? | či xĕdmat karda metānom? | چی خدمت کرده میتوانم؟ |
| I hope that... | omedwāram ke... | امیدوارم که... |
| What is troubling you? | či takllif dāred? | چی تکلیف دارید؟ |
| I wish you a quick recovery (get well soon). | šfāye 'ājĕl mexāham. | شفا عاجل میخواهم |
| If God's willing. | enšālāh | انشاالله |
| I am bored. | man dĕq āwardam! (ma dĕq āwordem!) | من دق آوردم! |
| God willing, with peace. | baxayr | بخیر |

## Vocabulary Words لغتونه

| altar | ātĕškada | آتشکده |
| vomit | estafrāğ | استفراغ |
| unknown people, strangers | ašxās-e nāšanās | اشخاص ناشناس |
| ring, band | angoštar, čĕla | انگشتر، چله |
| finger | angošt | انگشت |
| sea | bahr | بحر |
| without | bĕdōn | بدون |
| to pickup | bardāštan (bardār) | برداشتن (بردار) |
| to contact, to touch base | tamās gĕrĕftan (tamās gir) | تماس گرفتن (تماس گیر) |
| seaport | bandar | بندر |
| herbal medicine | dawā hāy-e giyāye | دوا های گیاهی |
| pharmacist | dawākāna | دواخانه دار |
| pharmacy | dawāxāna | دواخانه |
| to book | bōk kardan (bōk kon) | بوك کردن (بوك کن) |

| to inform | ba etĕlā' rasāndan(ba etĕlā' rasān) | به اطلاع رساندن (به اطلاع رسان) |
| nose | bini | بینی |
| to provide | taheya kardan (taheya kon) | تهیه کردن (تهیه کن) |
| foot | pā/pāy | پا/ پای |
| to have a plane | pĕlān dāštan (pĕlān dār) | پلان داشتن (پلان دار) |
| ointment | pamād | پماد |
| finger | panja | پنجه |
| to cover | pōšāndan (pōšān) | پوشاندن (پوشان) |
| message | payām | پیام |
| to receive a message | payām gĕrĕftan (payām gir) | پیام گرفتن (پیام گیر) |
| injection | pečkāri | پیچکاری |
| finding / to find | paydā namōdan (paydā namāy) | پیدا نمودن (پیدا نمای) |
| effect | tasir | تاثیر |
| history | tārix | تاریخ |
| historical | tārixi | تاریخی |
| fever | tab | تب |
| translator | tarjomān | ترجمان |
| gift | tōhfa | تحفه |
| ID card | tazkĕra | تذکره |
| to decide | tasmim gĕrĕftan (tasmim gir) | تصمیم گرفتن (تصمیم گیر) |
| to spend, to pass | ter kardan (ter kon) | تیر کردن (تیرکن) |
| body | jān | جان |
| sightseeing, places worth seeing | jāhāye didani | جا های دیدنی |
| series | jĕdi | جدی |
| world | jahān | جهان |
| eye | čĕšom/čašom | چشم |
| to seep | čakāndan (čakān) | چکاندن (چکان) |

| expensive, pricey | čiz-e qimati | چیز قیمتی |
| allergy | hasāsiyat | حساسیت |
| to be allergic | hasāsiyat kardan (hasāsiyat kon) | حساسیت کردن (حساسیت کن) |
| traditional doctor (prescribes herbal medications) | hakim ji | حکیم جی |
| itch, itchy | xārĕš | خارش |
| to fill out | xāna pōri kardan (xāna pōri kon) | خانه پوری کردن (خانه پوری کن) |
| housekeeper, maid | xāna sāmān | خانه سامان |
| services | xĕdamāt | خدمات |
| happiness | xōši | خوشی |
| during, among, to be informed | dar jĕryān-e | درجریان |
| to hurt, to have pain, to ache | dard kardan (dard kon) | درد کردن (درد کن) |
| sea | daryā | دریا |
| hand | dĕst | دست |
| nausea | dĕlbad | دلبد |
| favorite | dĕlxā | دلخواه |
| mouth | dahān/dahan | دهان/دهن |
| traditional restaurant | rastōrant-e sonati | رستورانت سنتی |
| to call, to ring | zang zadan (zang zan) | زنگ زدن (زنگ زن) |
| shrine | ziyārat | زیارت |
| to spend | sĕpari kardan (sĕpari kon) | سپری کردن (سپری کن) |
| head | sar | سر |
| dizzy | sarčarx | سرچرخ |
| cough | sorfa | سرفه |
| cough | sorfa kardan (sorfa kon) | سرفه کردن (سرفه کن) |
| cigarette | sĕgrĕt | سگرت |
| document/documents | sanad/asnād | سند/اسناد |

| | | |
|---|---|---|
| syrup | šarbat | شربت |
| company | šĕrkat | شرکت |
| tourism company | šĕrkat-e tōrezom | شرکت توریزم |
| hospital | šafāxāna | شفاخانه |
| stomach | šĕkam | شکم |
| health | sēhi | صحی |
| to have tolerance, to be tolerant | tāqat dāštan (tāqat dār) | طاقت داشتن (طاقت دار) |
| without bottle | ğayr-e botali | غیر بوتلی |
| to order, to demand | farmāyeš dādan (farmāyeš dĕh) | فرمایش دادن (فرمایش ده) |
| to think | fĕkĕr kardan (fĕkĕr kon) | فکر کردن (فکرکن) |
| form | fōrma | فورمه |
| doctor's bill | fis | فیس |
| to walk | qadam zadan (qadam zan) | قدم زدن (قدم زن) |
| as follows | qarār-e zayl | قرار ذیل |
| century | qarn | قرن |
| drop | qatra | قطره |
| drop | qatra čakān | قطره چکان |
| to make a copy of | kāpi gĕrftan (kāpi gir) | کاپی گرفتن (کاپی گیر) |
| ID card | kārt-e hoyat | کارت هویت |
| wishing marker | kāške | کاشکی |
| finger | kĕlk | کلك |
| weak | kamzōr | کمزور |
| to try | kōšĕš kardan (kōšĕš kon) | کوشش کردن (کوشش کن) |
| to pass, to spend, to undergo | gozaštan (gozar) | گذشتن (گذر) |
| sunstroke | garmi zadagi | گرمی زده گی |
| out of it | gans | گنس |
| ear | gōš | گوش |
| pill | guli | گولی |

| | | |
|---|---|---|
| unfortunately | mot'sĕfāna | متاسفانه |
| sick | mariz | مريض |
| illness | marizi | مريضی |
| passenger, traveler | mosāfĕr | مسافر |
| advice | mašwara | مشوره |
| to check up | māyna kardan (māyna kon) | معاينه كردن (معاينه كن) |
| doctor's office | māyna xāna(ma'āyana xāna) | معاينه خانه |
| temple | ma'bad | معبد |
| information | ma'lomāt | معلومات |
| museum | mōziyam | موزيم |
| national museum | mōziyam-e mĕlli | موزيم ملی |
| guest | mehmān | مهمان |
| close, near | nazdik | نزديك |
| prescription | nosxa | نسخه |
| prescription | nosxa | نسخه |
| to show | nĕšān dādan (nĕšān dĕh) | نشان دادن (نشان ده) |
| agent/representative | nomāyenda/namāyenda | نماينده |
| agent/representative | nomāyenda/namāyenda | نماينده |

## Dari Vocabulary Different from Iranian Persian

| English Translation | Iranian Persian | | Farsi-e Dari | |
|---|---|---|---|---|
| I am bored. | dĕlam gĕrĕftĕ | دلم گرفته. | man dĕq āwōrdom. | من دق آوردم. |
| gift | Kādō | کادو | tohfa | تحفه |
| doctor's fees | dastmōza | دستمزد | fis | فیس |
| hospital | bimārĕstān | بیمارستان | šafāxāna | شفاخانه |
| pharmacy | dāruxānĕ | دارو خانه | dawāxāna | دواخانه |
| clinic, doctor's office | matab-e pazĕšk | مطب پزشك | Ma'āyna xāna | معاینه خانه |
| confused, out of it | gič | گیج | gans | گنس |
| nauseated | tahavo | تهوع | dĕlbad | دلبد |
| pill | qōrs | قرص | gōli | گولی |
| band | halğa | حلقه | čĕla | چله |
| museum | muza | موزه | mōziyam | موزیم |
| ID card | kart-e šĕnāsā-yi | کارت شناسایی | kart-e howiyat | کارت هویت |

# APPENDIX A: ANSWER KEY

## CHAPTER ONE

### LESSON 1
Exercise 1:
Conversation 1: Man greets man
Conversation 2: Man greets woman
Conversation 3: Woman greets woman

Exercise 2B:
Conversation 1: shorter     Conversation 2: informal     Conversation 3: formal

Exercise 3A:
Formal: 1, 2, 4, 5, 6      Informal: 3

Exercise 3B:
Conversation 1: formal     Conversation 3: formal
Conversation 2: informal     Conversation 4: informal

Exercise 5A:
Conversation 1: Man greets man
Conversation 2: Man greets woman
Conversation 3: Woman greets woman

Exercise 6A:
1, 7, 3, 6, 5, 2, 4, 8

Exercise 7B:
1. d     4. There is one dot above the letter [ğayn].
2. c     5. There is a line above the letter [alĕf mad].
3. a     6. There are two dots above the letter [qāf] and one dot above the letter [fe].
        7. There are two lines above the letter [gāf] and one line above the letter [kāf].

Exercise 7C:

| | | | | |
|---|---|---|---|---|
| 1. الف (ا) | 2. پ، ت | 3. ج، ح | 4. د | 5. ز |
| 6. س، ص | 7. ط | 8. ع،غ | 9. ق، ك | 10. ن، ی |

Exercise 7D:

| | | | | |
|---|---|---|---|---|
| 1. الف، ب | 2. پ، ت، ث | 3. ج، چ، خ | 4. خ،ذ، ذ | 5. ز، ز، ژ |
| 6. ش،ش،ض | 7. ض، ظ، ظ | 8. ع،غ، ف | 9. گ، ق، ن | 10. ه، ی |

Exercise 8A:
a) Carla    b) John    c) Mike    d) Lily    e) Jessica

Exercise 8B:
a) Parwez    b) Arash    c) Farid    d) Najib    e) Nasrat

## Exercise 12B:

پ  چ  ج  ث<br>
ر  د  د  خ<br>
ش  س  ژ  ذ<br>
ظ  ط  ض  ص<br>
ع  غ

## Exercise 13A:

1. internet    2. nurse    3. email    4. bicycle    5. computer

## Exercise 13B:

| | | | |
|---|---|---|---|
| هستید | س ه د ی ت | [hasted] | answer |
| هستم | ت ه س م | [hastam] | volleyball |
| سلام | ل م م س | [salām] | name |
| چطور | ط رچ و | [četor] | friend |
| نام | ا م ن | [name] | young man |
| چیست | س ی ت چ | [čist] | picture |
| تخلص | ص ل ت خ | [taxalos] | Pashto |
| شام | ش ا م | [šomā] | apartment |

# LESSON 2

## Exercise 2:

1. There are 7 two-form letters and 25 four-form letters.
2. c

## Exercise 5:

| final<br>آخر | medial<br>وسط | initial<br>شروع | isolated<br>مفرد | |
|---|---|---|---|---|
| ـا | ـک | مـ - یـ | ا - ر | امریکا |
| ا - ـا | ـغـ - ـسـ - ـتـ | فـ - ن | ا - ن | افغانستان |
| ا - ـا | | کـ - ن | د - ا | کانادا |
| ـو | ـکـ - ـسـ - ـیـ - ـکـ | مـ | | مکسیکو |

## Exercise 6:

1. مـکـسـیـکـو     2. بـرازیـل     3. روسـیـه

4. تـرکـیـه     5. پـولـنـد     6. کـانـادا

7. فـرانـسـه     8. انـدونـیـزیـا     9. پـاکـسـتـان

Exercise 10:

|  |  |  |  |  |  |  |  |  |
|---|---|---|---|---|---|---|---|---|
| سلام |  |  |  | م | ا | ل | س | 1 |
| وعلیکم |  |  | م | ك | ی | ل | ع | و | 2 |
| خدا حافظ | ظ | ف | ا | ح | ا | د | خ | 3 |
| نام |  |  |  |  | م | ا | ن | 4 |
| شما |  |  |  |  | ا | م | ش | 5 |
| چیست |  |  |  | ت | س | ی | چ | 6 |
| است |  |  |  |  | ت | س | ا | 7 |
| تان |  |  |  |  | ن | ا | ت | 8 |

# LESSON 3
## Exercise 5:

| | | |
|---|---|---|
| 3. ایران | 2. کانادا | 1. اروپا |
| 6. پاکستان | 5. عربستان | 4. افغانستان |
| 9. استرالیا | 8. فرانسه | 7. انگلستان |
| 12. روسیه | 11. جاپان | 10. مصرو |
| | | 13. ازبکستان |

# REVIEW OF CHAPTER 1
## Exercise 1A:
1. Formal          2. Formal

## Exercise 1B:

2. نازنین سلیمی کابل          1. امید فیضی کاپیسا

## Exercise 2:
1. Taksi          2. sĕnfĕ nohom          3. xaybar 'asri hotal
4. rōz rastorānt          5. tool supar āyskĕrim

## Exercise 3:

| | | | |
|---|---|---|---|
| 3. واشنگتن دی سی   4. نیویورك | 2. برلین | 1. انگلستان |
| 7. تگزاسو          8. کابل | 6. کانادا | 5. مکسیکو |

Exercise 4:

| ۱ | وعلیکم سلام | سلام علیکم | 1 |
|---|---|---|---|
| ۲ | وعلیکم | سلام | 2 |
| ۳ | نام من صادق است. | نام تان چیست؟ | 3 |
| ۴ | نام من زلمی است. | نام شما چیست؟ | 4 |
| ۵ | خدا حافظ! | خدا حافظ! | 5 |

Exercise 5:

| Country Name | امریکا | کانادا | اندونیزیا | پاکستان | برازیل | روسیه | ترکیه | چین | پولند | فرانسه |
|---|---|---|---|---|---|---|---|---|---|---|
| City Name | کابل | نیویورک | برلین | واشنگتن | کندهار | | | | | |
| First Name | لیلی | کارلا | جان | مایک | پرویز | آرش | جسیکا | فرید | نجیب | نصرت |

# CHAPTER TWO

## LESSON 1

Exercise 1:

۹-۸-۷-۶-۵-۴-۳-۲-۱-۰

Exercise 3:

۱۰-۹-۸-۷-۶-۵-۴-۳-۲-۱-۰

Exercise 4:

1-[sě]  2-[hašt]  3-[noh]  4-[čār]  5- [šaš]  6-[haft]  7-[dah]  8-[dō]  9-[panj]  10-[sěfěr]  11-[yak]

Exercise 6:

| a (۵ | ā (۴ | ě (۳ | a (۲ | ě (۱ |
|---|---|---|---|---|
| a (۱۰ | o (۹ | a (۸ | a (۷ | a (۶ |

Exercise 7:

| nār (۵ | xar (۴ | tār (۳ | kār (۲ | Bam (۱ |
|---|---|---|---|---|
| tir (۱۰ | pas (۹ | jāl (۸ | zěr (۷ | muš (۶ |
| šir (۱۵ | por (۱۴ | sir (۱۳ | pār (۱۲ | dur (۱۱ |

Exercise 8:

| [ ābaw ] | آبرو | ۴ | | [ sayr ] | سیر | ۱ |
|---|---|---|---|---|---|---|
| [ aftaw ] | افتو | ۵ | | [ xaw ] | خو | ۲ |
| [ may ] | نی | ۶ | | [ kay ] | کی | ۳ |

## Exercise 9:

| ğolām (۱) | xĕlāf (۲) | ğayr (۳) | ğam (۴) | xār (۵) |
|---|---|---|---|---|
| qāri (۶) | qand (۷) | kamar (۸) | qalam (۹) | qār (۱۰) |

## Exercise 10A:

11-yāz-dah,  12-dōwāz-dah,  13-sĕz-dah,  14-čār-dah,  15-pānz-dah,  16-šānz-dah,
17-haf-dah,  18-haž-dah,  19-nōz-dah,  20-bist

## Exercise 10B:

| (۱۶) | شانزده | | | (۱۱) | یازده |
|---|---|---|---|---|---|
| (۱۷) | هفده | | | (۱۲) | دوازده |
| (۱۸) | هژده | | | (۱۳) | سیزده |
| (۱۹) | نوزده | | | (۱۴) | چارده |
| (۲۰) | بیست | | | (۱۵) | پانزده |

# LESSON 2

## Exercise 1:

Farid: ۰۷۹۹۲۰۲۰۴۴          Laylā: ۰۷۰۰۴۰۰۲۸۴

## Exercise 4:

۱) ماری ۰۷۸۶۷۸۹۹۰۳          ۲) کریم ۰۷۹۹۱۱۲۲۰۰

۳) لیلا ۰۷۰۰۲۳۱۴۸۹          ۴) رحیم ۰۷۷۷۹۱۰۲۴۸

۵) فرید ۰۷۰۰۲۱۳۹۹۰          ۶) میوند ۰۷۹۹۷۷۱۲۰۳

## Exercise 5:

Business card #1:
1. 799012282
2. a
3. burgers and ice cream

Business card #2:
1. restaurant
2. Rōz
3. 070010030, 0799308000

Business card #3:
1. Zalmai Aziz
2. doctor
3. 070034671, 0799112345
4. Afghanistan
5. Kabul

Business card #4:
1. افغانستان
2. Kabul
3. ۰۷۹۹۲۳۱۵۴۴

## Exercise 6A:

۱) رادیو   ۲) تلیفون   ۳) کمپیوتر   ۴) تلویزیونو   ۵) پنسل
۶) والیبال   ۷) کاراته /تکواندو   ۸) مبایل/ سلفون   ۹) تکسی   ۱۰) بایسکل
۱۱) بس

## Exercise 6B:

1. engineer    2. pilot    3. doctor    4. hotel    5. printer    6. glass    7. bicycle    8. video

## Exercise 7:

1. پروین    2. اسلم    3. ۰۷۹۹۰۷۷۲۳۸    4. ۰۷۸۶۲۳۰۹۸۴

## Exercise 9:

| | | |
|---|---|---|
| 1. Abdul Matin Faizi | 3. 0799303729 | 5. Kabul |
| 2. Abdul Salām | 4. 2022346281 | 6. engineer |

## Exercise 10:

1, 4, 3, 7, 5, 2, 6

## Exercise 11:

[joma] جمعه    [čā-ršanbe] چارشنبه    [dō-šanbe] دوشنبه

## Exercise 12B:

| جمعه | پنجشنبه | چار شنبه | سه‌شنبه | دوشنبه | یکشنبه | شنبه |
|---|---|---|---|---|---|---|
| Friday | Thursday | Wednesday | Tuesday | Monday | Sunday | Saturday |

## Exercise 13:

افغانستان یك كشور محاط به خشكه است كه در اطراف آن كشور های ایران، پاكستان، چین، تاجكستان، ازبكستان و تركمنستان واقع میباشد . افغانستان یك كشور زراعتی است و دارای باغ های مثمر میباشد .

مردم این كشور پركار و زحمتكش اند ، آنها از نظر اقتصادی بسیار غریب و ضعیف میباشند . كشور مذكور سرشار از منابع طبیعی میباشد . سیستم تحصیلی این كشور، سیستم دولتی و خصوصی است . مشهورترین پوهنتون های آن پوهنتون كابل، هرات، مزار، جلال آباد و قندهار است كه هر یك شامل چندین پوهنځی میباشد .

| Arabic loanwords | محاط، اطراف، واقع، زراعتی، مثمر، زحمتكش، نظر، اقتصادی، دولتی، خصوصی، مشهورترین، شامل |
|---|---|
| English loanwords | سیستم، سیستم |
| Pashto loanwords | پوهنتون، پوهنتون، پوهنځی |

# LESSON 3

## Exercise 4:

| | | |
|---|---|---|
| ۳) شاگرد ها school students | ۲) همصنفی ها classmates | ۱) معلم ها teachers |
| ۶) محصل ها college students | ۵) زنها women | ۴) بچه ها boys |
| | | ۷) دختر ها girls |

## Exercise 5:

۱) پنج بچه   ۲) چارمعلم   ۳) هشت زن   ۴) نه بچه   ۵) یازده دختر   ۶) هژده همصنفی

## Exercise 6A:

۱) این زن است.   ۲) این مرد است.   ۳) این دختر معلم است.
۴) آن بچه محصل است.   ۵) این زن استاد است.

## Exercise 6B:

۱) آن مرد جان است.   ۲) این دختر مارتا است.   ۳) این زن لیلا است.
۴) این بچه کریم است.   ۵) آن مرد میوند است.

## Exercise 8A:

۱   آن دخترها کیستند؟   آن دخترها لیلا و نسرین هستند.
   [ān doxtar-hā kistand]   [ān doxtar-hā laylā wa nasrin hastand]

۲   اینها کیستند؟   اینها اجمل و پروین هستند.
   [ĕn-hā kistand]   [ĕn-hā ajmal wa parwin hastand]

## Exercise 9:

۱) اینها شریف، فرزانه، خلیل و کریم هستند.
۲) اینها زرمینه و زرغونه هستند.
۳) اینها میوند، نازنین، میرویس و شیرین هستند.
۴) اینها مرضیه و شگوفه هستند.

## Exercise 11A:

۱) او احمد است؟   ۲) نام تان میرویس است؟   ۳) شما از کابل هستید؟
۴) امروز دوشنبه است؟   ۵) نمبر تلیفون تان ۰۷۷۷۲۰۵۴۵۸ است؟
۶) تخلص تان کریمی است؟

# REVIEW OF CHAPTER 2

## Exercise 1:

1. Parwin Rahimi
2. Mohammad Karim, Mohammad Rahim
3. Afghanistan
4. Kabul
5. Paghman
6. 10 Afghanis
7. 234
8. 1263541

## Exercise 2:

1. radio and TV workshop
2. Saturday, Sunday, Monday, Tuesday, Wednesday, and Thursday
3. Maywand Radio and TV Workshop
4. 2207576235     5. 123
6. 0700403267     7. Ghazni

## Exercise 5:

| | | |
|---|---|---|
| وعلیکم السلام! | السلام و علیکم ! | ۱ |
| نامم ... است. | نام تان چیست؟ | ۲ |
| تخلصم ... است. | تخلص تان چیست؟ | ۳ |
| من از ... هستم. | شما از کجا هستید؟ | ۴ |
| شمارۀ تلیفونم ... است. | شمارۀ تلیفون تان چند است؟ | ۵ |
| امروز ... شنبه است. | امروز چند شنبه است؟ | ۶ |
| تشکر | تشکر | ۷ |
| خدا حافظ | خدا حافظ | ۸ |

# CHAPTER THREE

# LESSON 1

## Exercise 1:
Conversation One: 1, 3, 6, 4, 2, 5
Conversation Two: 6, 5, 1, 3, 4, 2
Conversation Three: 5, 6, 2, 3, 4, 1

## Exercise 3A:
1. They embrace and shake hands.
2. He puts his right hand on his chest and greets someone.
3. He kisses his grandfather's hands, hugs him, and shakes hands with both hands.
4. They shake hands.
5. They shake hands.
6. He puts his right hand on his chest and greets them.
7. Not a proper greeting.

## Exercise 4A:

| شما | ۴ | ما | ۱ |
|---|---|---|---|
| او | ۵ | تو | ۲ |
| آنها | ۶ | من | ۳ |

## Exercise 4B:

| Formal form: | Singular form: | |
|---|---|---|
| ما | من | ۱ |
| شما | تو | ۲ |
| آنها | او | ۳ |

## Exercise 5:
A: Standard          B: Colloquial

Exercise 6A:

۱) م- هستم     ۲) یم- هستیم     ۳) ی- هستی

۴) ید- هستید     ۵) ...است     ۶) ند- هستند

Exercise 6B:

۱) هستم     ۲) هستیم     ۳) هستی     ۴) هستید     ۵) است     ۶) هستند

Exercise 7A:

۱) او چطور است؟ او خوب است.     ۲) او خوب است.

۳) تو چطور هستی؟ من خوب هستم.     ۴) آنها چطور هستند؟ آنها خوب هستند.

Exercise 8:

1. Colloquial

Exercise 10:

۱) وعلیکم سلام     ۲) هستید     ۳) شما     ۴) هستم     ۵) جور باشید

Exercise 11A:

۱) وعلیکم سلام

۲) وعلیکم

۳) زنده باشید.، سلامت باشید.، جور باشید.

۴) الحمدالله، خوب هستم.، شُکر فضل خداست.، خوب هستم.

Exercise 12:

1. You meet your friend's father at the bus stop; greet him.

۱    السلام و علیکم پدرجان، مانده نباشید!

2. You meet your Dari instructor on the street; greet him/her.

۲    السلام و علیکم معلم صاحب، مانده نباشید!

3. You see an older relative after one year; greet him/her.

۳    السلام و علیکم ... جان، مانده نباشید!

4. In class, you see your classmate Tom; greet him.

۴    سلام تام چطور هستی، مانده نباشی!

Exercise 14A:

۱) روز بخیر – روز بخیر     ۲) به امید دیدار – به امید دیدار

۳) شب بخیر! – شب بخیر!     ۴) تشکر  – خواهش میکنم.

۵) خوش آمدید! – تشکر

Exercise 15:

۱) لیلا: روز شما هم بخیر، خوش آمدید! ۲) میرویس: تشکر

## Exercise 17:

1. You're leaving for school; say goodbye to your roommate.

۱    خداحافظ ... جان!

2. Your Dari class has ended; say goodbye to your classmates.

۲    خدا حافظ، بچه ها!

3. Your Dari class has ended; say goodbye to your instructor.

۳    خدا حافظ، معلم صاحب!

# LESSON 2

## Exercise 2A:

| | | | | | |
|---|---|---|---|---|---|
| ۳ | نام تو | | ۱ | نامم | |
| ۶ | نام آنها | | ۲ | نام ما | |
| ۴ | نام شما | | ۳ | نامت | |
| ۱ | نام من | | ۴ | نام تان | |
| ۲ | نام ما | | ۵ | نامش | |
| ۵ | نام او | | ۶ | نام شان | |

## Exercise 2B:

| 1 | Her name is Layla. | نامش لیلا است. | ۱ |
| 2 | Your name is Layla. (inf) | تنامت لیلا است. | ۲ |
| 3 | My name is Layla. | تنامم لیلا است. | ۳ |
| 4 | Your name is Layla. (f) | نام تان لیلا است. | ۴ |

## Exercise 2C:

سلام، نامم کریم است، من شاگرد هستم. او مادرم است، نامش رابعه است. او داکتر است. ما افغان هستیم. من جور هستم. مادرم ناجور است.

## Exercise 3:

۱) نامم اجمل است.

۲) نامش سیمین است.

۳) نامت فرهاد است.

۴) نام ما کریم، نجیب و میرویس است.

۵) نام شان پروین، سیمین و نسرین  است.

۶) نام تان عبدالرحیم است.

Exercise 4A:

| | |
|---|---|
| Hello, laylā jan. How are you? | ١ |
| Hello, farid jan. I am fine thanks. Who is he? | ٢ |
| He is Mr. Sharif, my friend. | ٣ |
| Hello, sharif jan, nice to meet you. | ۴ |
| Thanks. Me, too. | ۵ |

Exercise 5:
1. Formal          2. Informal

Exercise 6:

| | |
|---|---|
| 1. | آقای کریم |
| 2. | آقای جان! ایشان خانم لیلا هستند . |
| 3. | پدر جان، نام تان چیست؟ |

Exercise 8:
1. Laylā          2. Parwin          3. Rahim          4. Friend

# LESSON 3
### Exercise 1:
4, 5, 6, 1, 2, 3, 7, 8

### Exercise 3:

۱) قاره: امریکا، اروپا، آسیا

۲) کشور: امریکا، عراق، پاکستان، افغانستان، هندوستان، مکسیکو، فرانسه، ایران

۳) ایالت: فلوریدا، نیویورک

۴) ولایت: کندهار

۵) شهر: پاریس، نیویورک، تهران، منهتن، اسلام آباد، لندن، رم

### Exercise 5:

| | | | |
|---|---|---|---|
| ۲ | رانی از کشور هندوستان است. | ۱ | پروین از ولایت کابل است. |
| ۴ | مارته از ایالت کینتاکی است. | ۳ | کریم از شهر مزار است. |
| ۶ | شریف از ولسوالی پغمان است. | ۵ | فرزانه از کشور تاجکستان است. |

### Exercise 7A:

۱) سلیمی    ۲) فیضی    ۳) کاپیسا    ۴) کابل    ۵) نجراب    ۶) قریهٔ بالا

## Exercise 10:

١) مارته، امریکا، امریکایی      ٢) صادق خان، کابل، افغان

٣) حلیموف، تاجکستان، تاجک      ٤) کریم، بدخشان، افغان

٥) عالیه، ازبکستان، ازبک      ٦) دیوید، لندن، انگلیس

٧) ژاك، فرانسه، فرانسوی      ٨) ثریا، ترکمنستان، ترکمن

## Exercise 11:

| | | | |
|---|---|---|---|
| 1. Paghman district | 3. Afghan | 5. Indiana | 7. Tajik |
| 2. Surab and Rostam | 4. Canada | 6. David | 8. Canadian |

## Exercise 12:

| | | | |
|---|---|---|---|
| 1. false | 2. true | 3. false | 4. true |

## Exercise 13A:

١) ید You live in America.      ٤) م I live in Canada.

٢) یم We live in Kabul.      ٥) د S/he lives in Uzbekistan.

٣) ند They live in France.      ٦) ی You (informal) live in Italy.

## Exercise 13B:

١) اجمل در هندوستان زنده گی میکند .

٢) لیلا در ولسوالی کلمبیا زنده گی میکند .

٣) شما در شیکاگو زنده گی میکنید .

٤) آنها در جرمنی زنده گی میکنند .

٥) ما در کابل زنده گی میکنیم .

٦) شما در ولایت بامیان زنده گی میکنید .

٧) او در امریکا زنده گی میکند .

٨) او قاره افریقا زنده گی میکند .

## Exercise 15:

| | |
|---|---|
| Katrina USA, American, Minneapolis City | ٢ |
| David USA, State of IL, Chicago City | ١ |

# REVIEW OF CHAPTER 3

## Exercise 1:

First column from the right: 6, 7, 1, 2, 3, 4, 5
Second column from the right: 9, 10, 8, 11, 12, 14, 13

Exercise 3:

۶) هم        ۵) هستید        ۴) جور    ۳) مانده    ۲) وعلیکم    ۱)

۱۲) امید      ۱۱) خواهش میکنم.   ۱۰) است    ۹) خوب    ۸) است    ۷)

Exercise 5:

۲) تخلصم وطنوال است.                ۱) نامم اجمل است.

۴) من خوب هستم، تشکر.              ۳) او فرید است.

۶) من از ایالت اوآیو هستم.           ۵) من از امریکا هستم.

۸) من در واشنگتن زنده گی میکنم.      ۷) من از شهر شیکاکو هستم.

Exercise 9B:

1. ید You are from France.        4. م I am from Canada.
2. یم We are from New York.       5. د S/he is from Italy.
3. ند They live in Paris.          6. ی You are from Brazil.

Exercise 10B:

۳) چطور هستید؟      ۲) وعلیکم السلام      ۱) السلام علیکم

۵) تشکر          ۴) خوب هستید؟

Exercise 10C:

۲) فامیل همه خوب هستند؟      ۱) سلامت باشید.

۴) خانه خیریت است؟          ۳) به خیر آمدید؟،

Exercise 11B:

۲) به امان خدا        ۱) خدا حافظ

# CHAPTER FOUR

## LESSON 1

Exercise 5:

| loudspeaker | لودسپیکر | | table | میز |
|---|---|---|---|---|
| monitor | مانیتور | | computer | کمپیوتر |
| mouse | موس | | headphone | گوشکی |
| telephone | تلیفون | | chair | چوکی |
| stapler | ستپلر | | keyboard | کیبورد |
| CD | سی دی | | printer | پرینتر |
| copy machine | ماشین کاپی | | scanner | سکینر |

## Exercise 7:

6, 4, 1, 2, 3, 5

## Exercise 9A:

| | |
|---|---|
| دانه/ تا | خطکش، میز، قلم، گوشکی، پنسل، کتاب، پرینتر، سکینر، دروازه، کلکین، کتابچه، کتاب |
| نفر/ تا | استاد، مرد، معلم، زن، شاگرد |
| پایه | چوکی، کمپیوتر، میز، پرینتر، سکینر |
| جلد | کتابچه، کتاب |
| درجن | کتابچه |

## Exercise 11:

۶) شما ۵) من ۴) تو ۳) ایشان ۲) او ۱) ما

## Exercise 12:

۲) شما یك كتاب دارید.

۴) شما همه یك صنف دارید.

۶) آنها سه معلم دارند.

۷) او یك كتابچه دارد.

۱) من یك میز دارم.

۳) او دو بکس دارد.

۵) ما دو تلیفون داریم.

## Exercise 13:

۱) شش همصنفی

۲) چار بچه

۳) سه میز، هشت دانه چوکی، یك دانه کمپیوتر، یك دانه پرجکتور، دو دانه تخته، سه دانه تخته پاك، و تباشیر

## Exercise 15A:

| | | | | | |
|---|---|---|---|---|---|
| 1. pen | (قلم) | 4. teacher | (معلم) | 7. chair | ( چوکی) |
| 2. classroom | (صنف) | 5. bag | (بکس) | 8. phone | (تلیفون) |
| 3. student | (شاگرد، محصل) | 6. notebook | (کتابچه) | 9. computer | (کمپیوتر) |

# LESSON 2

## Exercise 2A:

| | | |
|---|---|---|
| ۱ | الف | ساعت در روی کتاب است. |
| ۲ | ب | کتاب در روی چوکی است. |
| ۳ | ج | چراغ.در زیر چوکی است. |
| ۴ | د | بکس.در پیشروی چوکی است. |
| ۵ | ه | دستکش در بین بکس است. |

## Exercise 3B:

۲) تخته در بالای کمپیوتر است.      ۱) کمپیوتر در بالای میز است.

۴) یخچال در سمت راست میز است.      ۳) کتاب ها در داخل الماری کتاب است.

۶) چوکی در پیشروی میز است.      ۵) تلیفون در سر یخچال است.

۸) لودسپیکر در سمت راست کمپیوتر است.      ۷) چراغ در بالای یخچال است.

۱۰) الماری کتاب در طرف راست تخته است.      ۹) گیلاس در پیشروی کمپیوتر است.

## Exercise 4:

| English | Combined | | |
|---------|----------|---|---|
| She is the English teacher. | او معلم انگلیسی ام است. | [mo'alem/englisi] معلم/انگلیسی | ۱ |
| The Dari class is over there. | اینجا صنف دری است. | [senf/dari] صنف/دری | ۲ |
| Is he your classmate? | او همصنفی تان است؟ | [hamsĕnfi/tān] همصنفی/تان | ۳ |
| Your pen is on the table. | قلم های تان در روی میز است. | [qalam-hā/tān] قلم ها/تان | ۴ |
| Your book is next to the table. | کتاب تان پهلوی میز است. | [pahlu/mez] پهلو/میز | ۵ |

## Exercise 5:

این صنف دری است، در اینجا سه محصل مرد و دو محصل دختر هستند. در پیشروی صنف، یک تخته، یک میز و یک کمپیوتر است. در بالای میز یک کتاب دری و یک کتاب انگلیسی است. صنف دری ده دانه میز و ده دانه چوکی دارد

## Exercise 6:
1. b      2. a      3. c

## Exercise 7:

| | | |
|---|---|---|
| Students are not in the class. | شاگرد ها در صنف نیستند. | ۱ |
| The book and pen are not on the table. | کتاب و قلم در روی میز نیست. | ۲ |
| S/he is not here. | او اینجا نیست. | ۳ |
| Ajmal doesn't have a notebook. | اجمل سه دانه کتابچه ندارد. | ۴ |
| Karim doesn't live in America. | کریم در امریکا زنده گی نمیکند. | ۵ |

## Exercise 8:

۱) کتاب در پهلوی میز نیست، کتاب در زیر میز است.

۲) آن بچه در پیشروی کلکین نیست، آن بچه در پشت کلکین است.

۳) ساعت در بالای کلکین نیست، ساعت در پهلوی کلکین است.

۴) میز در پهلوی کلکین نیست، میز در زیر کلکین است.

۵) چوکی در پشت میز نیست، چوکی در پیشروی میز است.

۶) ساعت در زیر میز نیست، ساعت در بالای میز است.

Exercise 10A:

1. b          2. a          3. a          4. a          5. c

Exercise 11:

۲) آیا قلم در بالای میز است؟          ۱) آیا معلم در صنف است؟

۴) آیا صنف ما در روبروی دفتر است؟          ۳) آیا کتاب در پشت کمپیوتر است؟

۶) آیا چوکی در پشت میز است؟          ۵) آیا پنسل در بین کتابچه است؟،

Exercise 12A:

| | | |
|:---:|:---:|:---:|
| ۴ | ۲ | ۳ |
| ۱ | ۶ | ۵ |

# LESSON 3

Exercise 1A:

| My name is Omeed. | نامم امید است. |
|---|---|
| I am a Dari language student. | من محصل زبان دری هستم. |
| In Dari class, I read a book. | من در صنف کتاب میخوانم. |
| I converse. | گفتگو میکنم. |
| I write. | نوشته میکنم. |
| I watch a video. | ویدیو سیل میکنم. |
| I listen to conversations. | به گفتگو ها گوش میکنم. |
| I speak. | گپ میزنم. |
| I take notes. | و نوت میگیرم. |

## Exercise 2:

| ۳) تو مینویسی. | ۲) ما نوت میگیریم. | ۱) من کتاب میخوانم. |
|---|---|---|
| ۶) آنها کتاب میخوانند. | ۵) او نوت میگیرد. | ۴) شما گپ میزنید. |

## Exercise 3:

۱) شما در صنف گفتگو میکنید.    ۲) او در کتابچه مینویسد.

۳) ما در صنف تلویزیون تماشا میکنیم.    ۴) آنها در صنف رادیو گوش میکنند.

۵) تو ایمیل را نوشته میکنی.    ۶) من و اجمل گپ میزنیم.

## Exercise 5A:

۱) لیلا :    کتاب میخواند، گفتگو میکند، به گپ های معلم گوش میکند.

۲) فرید :    نوشته میکند، گپ میزند، و ویدیو سیل میکند.

## Exercise 6:

۱) ما کتاب را نوشته میکنیم.    ۲) تو کتاب را میخوانی.

۳) شما کتاب دری را میخوانید.    ۴) آنها فلم ستارترک را سیل میکنند.

۵) من رادیو را گوش میکنم

## Exercise 7:

1. America
2. Indiana University
3. He is a student
4. He writes on the board

## Exercise 8B:

| | | | |
|---|---|---|---|
| 1 | ببخشید. | 5 | اجازه است، داخل شوم؟ |
| 2 | پرسان دارم. | 6 | ببخشید، نفهمیدم. |
| 3 | ببخشید، نفهمیدم. | 7 | ببهخشید. |
| 4 | این واضح است. | | |

## Exercise 10:

| Meaning | Negative | Formal | Informal | |
|---|---|---|---|---|
| Sit down | نشینید | بشینید | بشین | ۱ |
| Get up | نخیزید | بخیزید | بخیز | ۲ |
| Get up | نخوانید | بخوانید | بخوان | ۳ |
| Tell | نگوید | بگوید | بگو | ۴ |
| Come | نیاید | بیاید | بیا | ۵ |
| Go | نروید | بروید | برو | ۶ |
| Listen | گوش نکنید | گوش کنید | گوش کن | ۷ |

| Take | نگیرید | بگیرید | بگیر | ۸ |
|---|---|---|---|---|
| Give | ندهید | بدهید | بده | ۹ |
| Repeat | تکرار نکنید | تکرار کنید | تکرار کن | ۱۰ |
| Open the door | دروازه را باز نکنید | دروازه را باز کنید | دروازه را باز کن | ۱۱ |
| Close the door | دروازه را بسته نکنید | دروازه را بسته کنید | دروازه را بسته کن | ۱۲ |
| Write | نوشته نکنید | نوشته کنید | نوشته کن | ۱۳ |

Exercise 11A:

۴) خاموش کن    ۳) روشن کن    ۲) بردار    ۱) بمان

Exercise 11B:

۳) قلم را بمانید .    ۲) دروازه را بسته کنید .    ۱) کتاب را باز کنید .
۵) پنسل را بدهید .    ۴) تلیفون را بردارید.،

Exercise 12A:

| | بازکن | | بدهید | √ | بفرمایید | √ | بردارید | √ |
|---|---|---|---|---|---|---|---|---|
| | بازکنید | | بده | √ | ببخشید | √ | بردار | |
| √ | پرسان دارم | | بگیرید | √ | بشینید | √ | بمانید | |
| | بروید | | بگیر | | بشین | | بمانید | |
| | برو | | بسته کنید | √ | بخیزید | | بردارید | |
| √ | اجازه است، داخل شوم | | بسته کن | | بخیز | | بردار | |

# REVIEW OF CHAPTER 4

Exercise 3A:

۱) لپتاپ در بین الماری کتاب است.
۲) کتاب انگلیسی در الماری کتاب ها و در زیر کتاب دری است.
۳) مبایل در بین بکس است.

Exercise 3B:

| | بدهید | | بفرمایید | √ | ببین | √ |
|---|---|---|---|---|---|---|
| | بده | | ببخشید | | ببینید | |
| √ | بگیرید | | لطفاً | | بمانید | |
| | بگیر | | بیاور | √ | بمانید | |
| | بسته کنید | | بیاورید | √ | بردارید | |
| | بسته کن | | بخیز | | بردار | |

## Exercise 4A:

| Formal | Informal | | Formal | Informal | |
|---|---|---|---|---|---|
| بروید | برو | ۱۱ | باز کنید | باز کن | ۱ |
| بیایید | بیا | ۱۲ | بسته کنید | بسته کن | ۲ |
| ببرید | ببر | ۱۳ | ببینید | ببین | ۳ |
| بیاورید | بیاور | ۱۴ | بشنوید | بشنو | ۴ |
| بدهید | بده | ۱۵ | گوش کنید | گوش کن | ۵ |
| بگیرید | بگیر | ۱۶ | بگویید | بگوی | ۶ |
| بمانید | بمان | ۱۷ | نوشته کنید | نوشته کن | ۷ |
| بردارید | بردار | ۱۸ | بخوانید | بخوان | ۸ |
| بخورید | بخور | ۱۹ | بشینید | بشین | ۹ |
| بنوشید | بنوش | ۲۰ | بخیزید | بخیز | ۱۰ |
| آرام باشید | آرام باش | ۲۱ | | | |

## Exercise 4B:

| من | ما | تو | شما | او | آنها | Present Stem | |
|---|---|---|---|---|---|---|---|
| بسته میکنم | بسته میکنیم | بسته میکنی | بسته میکنید | بسته میکند | بسته میکنند | بسته کن | ۱ |
| میبینم | میبینیم | میبینی | میبینید | میبیند | میبینند | بین | ۲ |
| میشنوم | میشنویم | میشنوی | میشنوید | میشنود | میشنوند | شنو | ۳ |
| گوش میکنم | گوش میکنیم | گوش میکنی | گوش میکنید | گوش میکند | گوش میکنند | گوش کن | ۴ |
| میگویم | میگوییم | میگویی | میگویید | میگوید | میگویند | گو/گوی | ۵ |
| نوشته میکنم | نوشته میکنیم | نوشته میکنی | نوشته میکنید | نوشته میکند | نوشته میکنند | نوشته کن | ۶ |
| میخوانم | میخوانیم | میخوانی | میخوانید | میخواند | میخوانند | خوان | ۷ |
| میشینم | میشینیم | میشینی | میشینید | میشیند | میشینند | شین | ۸ |
| میخیزم | میخیزیم | میخیزی | میخیزید | میخیزد | میخیزند | خیز | ۹ |
| میروم | میرویم | میروی | میروید | میرود | میروند | رو | ۱۰ |
| میایم | میاییم | میایی | میایید | میاید | میایند | آ/ آی | ۱۱ |
| میبرم | میبریم | میبری | میبرید | میبرد | میبرند | بَر | ۱۲ |
| میاورم | میاوریم | میاوری | میاورید | میاورد | میاورند | آور | ۱۳ |
| میدهم | میدهیم | میدهی | میدهید | میدهد | میدهند | ده | ۱۴ |
| میگیرم | میگیریم | میگیری | میگیرید | میگیرد | میگیرند | گیر | ۱۵ |
| میمانم | میمانیم | میمانی | میمانید | میماند | میمانند | مان | ۱۶ |
| میبردارم | میبرداریم | میبرداری | میبردارید | میبردارد | میبردارند | بردار | ۱۷ |
| میخورم | میخوریم | میخوری | میخورید | میخورد | میخورند | خور | ۱۸ |
| مینوشم | مینوشیم | مینوشی | مینوشید | مینوشد | مینوشند | نوش | ۱۹ |

## Exercise 5:
1. He greets the speaker.
2. He opens the door. He closes the door.
3. He sits on the chair.
4. He look at the map.
5. He picks up the book; he reads it, and he puts it back.
6. He picks up the iPhone, watches a video, and he puts the iPhone back.
7. He picks up the pen. He writes, and he puts the pen back.
8. He picks up the cup, and gives it to the speaker.
9. He takes the CD from the speaker, and he gives it back.
10. He goes back and sits on the chair.
11. He says farewell.

## Exercise 6:

۳) یك دانه ساعت    ۲) پنج دانه کتاب و دو دانه کتابچه    ۱) هشت دانه

۶) بلی    ۵) نه    ۴) نه

۷) دوازده دانه چوکی، شش دانه میز    ۸) یک تخته و دو دانه تخته پاک    ۹) بلی

۱۰) نه

# CHAPTER FIVE

# LESSON 1
## Exercise 1:

| بجه | ساعت | دقیقه | ثانیه |
|------|------|-----------|-------|
| second | minute | hour, watch | clock |

## Exercise 2A:

| 1. Date | تاریخ | 3. Expiration Date | تاریخ ختم | 5. School | تاریخ ختم |
|---------|-------|--------------------|-----------|-----------|-----------|
| 2. Date of issue | تاریخ صدور | 4. Fourth | چارم | | |

## Exercise 2B:
1. Zarghuna
2. Mohammad Sharif
3. Gaw-harshaad
4. fourth
5. March 1st 2012, March 1st 2014

## Exercise 3:

| year of 2012 | two days | five nights | one week | month of January |
|--------------|----------|-------------|----------|------------------|
| ۳ | ۴ | ۵ | ۱ | ۲ |

## Exercise 4A:

۵) ۳۴۰    ۴) ۲۳۴    ۳) ۷۷۳    ۲) ۵۰۰    ۱) ۳۸۳

۱۰) ۵۵۰    ۹) ۷۰۰    ۸) ۱۲۳    ۷) ۴۵۸    ۶) ۴۳۵

Exercise 5A:

| ۱) 1:15 | ۲) 1:10 | ۳) 1:00 | ۴) 1:30 | ۵) 1:40 |

Exercise 5B:

| ۱) 1:20 | ۲) 9:40 | ۳) 5:10 | ۴) 12:05 | ۵) 11:20 |
| ۶) 2:40 | ۷) 10:25 | ۸) 1:15 | ۹) 3:05 | ۱۰) 7:20 |

Exercise 5C:

| ۱ 4:50 | ۲ 3:15 | ۳ 3:15 | ۴ 1:30 |

Exercise 7:

| ۱ p.m. | ۲ a.m. | ۳ a.m. | ۴ a.m. | ۵ p.m. | ۶ a.m. | ۷ a.m. | ۸ a.m. |

Exercise 8A:

| میزان | سپتمبر، اکتوبر | حمل | مارچ، اپریل |
| عقرب | اکتوبر، نوامبر | ثور | اپریل، می |
| قوس | نوامبر، دسامبر | جوزا | می، جون |
| جدی | دسامبر، جنوری | سرطان | جون، جولای |
| دلو | جنوری، فبروری | اسد | جولای، آگست |
| حوت | فبروری، مارچ | سنبله | آگست، سپتمبر |

Exercise 8B:

| ۱ 02/01/2012 | ۲ 05/04/2011 | ۳ 11/10/2004 | ۴ 07/06/2009 |

Exercise 9:

۱) امروز بیست یکم جنوری، ۲۰۱۰ است.  ۲) دیروز بیستم جنوری ۲۰۱۲ بود.
۳) صباح نوزدهم جنوری ۲۰۱۳ است.  ۴) دو هزار و دوازدهم
۵) ساعت چارم  ۶) ساعت پنجم

Exercise 10:

| Solution | ۱ | ۲ | ۳ | ۴ | ۵ | ۶ | ۷ | ۸ | ۹ |
|---|---|---|---|---|---|---|---|---|---|
| | ۲۶ | ۴۲۴ | ۴۸ | ۸۶ | ۶۲ | ۴۰ | ۷۲۲ | ۵۸ | ۷۴ |

Exercise 12A:

۱) شما هرروز چند بچه صنف میروید؟  ۲) امروز شما چند بچه از صنف میروید؟
۳) امروز تاریخ چند است؟  ۴) سال آینده کدام سال است؟
۵) امروز شما فلم سیل میکنید؟  ۶) امشب چی میکنید؟

## Exercise 12B:

|  |  | |
|---|---|---|
| Today, I am going to class. | امروز من به صنف میروم. | ۱ |
| Tomorrow, I am going to Kabul. | سبا ما به کابل میرویم. | ۲ |
| Tonight, I am watching that movie. | امشب من آن فلم را سیل میکنم. | ۳ |
| Today, you are reading the book. | امروز شما کتاب را میخوانید . | ۴ |
| Tonight at 10.p.m, I am writing. | امشب ساعت ۱۰ من نوشته میکنم . | ۵ |
| Where are you tomorrow at 3 o'clock? | سبا ساعت ۳ کجا هستید؟ | ۶ |

## Exercise 13:

۱) شما صبح ساعت ۱۱ صبح چی میکنید؟    ۲) امشب ساعت ۸ شام چی میکنید؟

۳) هفتۀ آینده کجا میروید؟    ۴) صباح/ فردا تاریخ چند است؟

۵) سال آینده کدام سال است؟    ۶) صباح/ فردا شما چند بجه به صنف میروید؟

## Exercise 14:

۱) ۱:۲۰    ۲) ۳/۲/۲۰۱۱    ۳) کتاب میخوانم    ۴) ۲۰۱۱

# LESSON 2

## Exercise 1A:

|  |  | |
|---|---|---|
| I usually wake up every morning at 7:00. | من هر صبح معمولاً ساعت ۷ بیدار میشوم. | ۱ |
| At 7:10, I take a shower. | ساعت ۷:۱۰ شاور میگیرم. | ۲ |
| At 7:30, I put on my clothes. | ساعت ۷:۳۰ کالایم را میپوشم. | ۳ |
| At 7:40, I have tea (breakfast). | ساعت ۷:۴۰ چای میخورم. | ۴ |
| At 7:50, I go to school. | ساعت ۷:۵۰ مکتب میروم. | ۵ |
| I study at school from 8:00 to 12:00. | من از ساعت ۸ تا ۱۲ در مکتب درس میخوانم. | ۶ |

## Exercise 1B:

کالا پوشیدن

شاور گرفتن

بیدار شدن

| درس خواندن | مکتب رفتن | چای صبح خوردن |
|:---:|:---:|:---:|

## Exercise 3A:

|  |  | |
|---|---|:---:|
| After school, I usually eat lunch. | من معمولاً بعد از مکتب، نان چاشت را میخورم. | ۱ |
| Then at 12:30, I go to work. | باز ساعت ۱۲:۳۰ به کار میروم. | ۲ |
| From 12:30 to 4:00 o'clock, I work. | از ساعت ۱۲:۳۰ تا ۴ بجه کار میکنم. | ۳ |
| At 4:30, I go home. | ساعت ۴:۳۰ به خانه میروم. | ۴ |
| At home, I change my (formal) clothes. | در خانه کالای رسمی ام را میکشم. | ۵ |
| Then at 5:00, I exercise. | باز ساعت ۵ ورزش میکنم. | ۶ |

## Exercise 3B:

| to work | to eat lunch | to go to work |
|:---:|:---:|:---:|
| to work out | to go home | to undress |

## Exercise 5A:

|  |  | |
|---|---|:---:|
| After exercise, I usually eat dinner at 7:30. | بعد از ورزش، معمولاً ساعت ۷ و ۳۰ نان شب را میخورم. | ۱ |
| From 8 to 9, I watch television. | از ساعت ۸ تا ۹ تلویزیون سیل میکنم. | ۲ |
| Then at 9, I do my homework. | باز ساعت ۹ کارخانگی ام را انجام میدهم. | ۳ |
| I always listen to the music. | من همیشه به موسیقی گوش میکنم. | ۴ |

| Sometimes I read a book. | ۵ گاهی کتاب میخوانم. |
|---|---|
| And at 11, I go to sleep. | ۶ و ساعت ۱۱ شب خواب میشوم. |

## Exercise 5B:

| | | |
|---|---|---|
| کارخانگی انجام دادن (کارخانگی انجام ده) | کتاب خواندن (کتاب خوان) | به موسیقی گوش کردن (به موسیقی گوش کن) |

| | | |
|---|---|---|
| نان شب خوردن (نان شب خور) | سیل کردن (سیل کن) | خواب شدن (خواب شو) |

## Exercise 6:

۴) صحیح        ۳) غلط        ۲) صحیح        ۱) غلط

## Exercise 7:

| | |
|---|---|
| ۱ | من بیدار میشوم، ما بیدار میشویم، تو بیدار میشوی، شما بیدار میشوید، او بیدار میشود، آنها بیدار میشوند |
| ۲ | من شاور میگیرم، ما شاور میگیریم، تو شاور میگیری، شما شاور میگیرید، او شاور میگیرد، آنها شاور میگیرند |
| ۳ | من میپوشم، ما میپوشیم، تو میپوشی، شما میپوشید، او میپوشد، آنها میپوشند |
| ۴ | من میخورم، ما میخوریم، تو میخوری، شما میخورید، او میخورد، آنها میخورند |
| ۵ | من می روم، ما می رویم، تو می روی، شما می روید، او می رود. آنها می روند |
| ۶ | من کارمیکنم، ما کارمیکنیم، تو کارمیکنی، شما بکارمیکنید، او کارمیکند، آنها کارمیکنند |
| ۷ | من کالا میکشم، ما کالا میکشیم، تو کالا میکشی، شما کالا میکشید، او کالا میکشد، آنها کالا میکشند |

| | |
|---|---|
| ۸ | من ورزش میکنم، ما ورزش میکنیم، تو ورزش میکنی، شما ورزش میکنید، او ورزش میکند، آنها ورزش میکنند |
| ۹ | من سیل میکنم، ما سیل میکنیم، تو سیل میکنی، شما سیل میکنید، او سیل میکند، آنها سیل میکنند |
| ۱۰ | من انجام میدهم، ما انجام میدهیم، تو انجام میدهی، شما انجام میدهید، او انجام میدهد، آنها انجام میدهند |
| ۱۱ | من گوش میکنم، ما گوش میکنیم، تو گوش میکنی، شما گوش میکنید، او گوش میکند، آنها گوش میکنند |
| ۱۲ | من میخوانم، ما میخوانیم، تو میخوانی، شما میخوانید، او میخواند، آنها میخوانند |
| ۱۳ | من خواب میشوم، ما خواب میشویم، تو خواب میشوی، شما خواب میشوید، او خواب میشود، آنها خواب میشوند |

**Exercise 9A:**

| | |
|---|---|
| بیدار شدن | من بیدار میشوم، ما بیدارمیشویم، تو بیدار میشوی، شما بیدار میشوید، او بیدار میشود، آنها بیدار میشوند |
| خواب شدن | من خواب میشوم، ما خواب میشویم، تو خواب میشوی، شما خواب میشوید، او خواب میشود، آنها خواب میشوند |

**Exercise 9B:**

| شاگرد سوم | شاگرد دوم | شاگرد اول | | |
|---|---|---|---|---|
| _____ | _____ | _____ | شما هر روز چند بجه بیدار میشوید؟ | ۱ |
| _____ | _____ | _____ | شما هر روز چند بجه خواب میشوید؟ | ۲ |
| _____ | _____ | _____ | شما دیروز چند ساعت بیدار شدید؟ | ۳ |
| _____ | _____ | _____ | شما دیروز چند ساعت خواب شدید؟ | ۴ |

**Exercise 10:**

| شاگرد سوم | شاگرد دوم | شاگرد اول | | |
|---|---|---|---|---|
| _____ | _____ | _____ | شما از ساعت هفت شام تا نه شب چی میکنید؟ | ۱ |
| _____ | _____ | _____ | امروز از ساعت ۱۰ شب تا ۲ شب کجا هستید؟ | ۲ |
| _____ | _____ | _____ | شما هر شب چند ساعت تلویزیون سیل میکنید؟ | ۳ |
| _____ | _____ | _____ | هر روز شما چند ساعت ورزش میکنید؟ | ۴ |

**Exercise 11A:**

1. d     2. b     3. b     4. b     5. a     6. a

Exercise 13:

| | | | |
|---|---|---|---|
| at university ۴ | lunch ۳ | breakfast ۲ | workout ۱ |
| goes home ۷ | sleeps ۶ | dinner ۵ | |

# LESSON 3

Exercise 1B:

لیلا    به کتابخانه رفتن، به پارک رفتن، استراحت کردن، پاك کردن، دوش کردن،
نان پختن

میرویس به مسجد رفتن،  به مسجد رفتن، به رستورانت رفتن، به میله رفتن،
والیبال بازی کرد، آببازی کردن، سودا

Exercise 2:

۱) صحیح    ۲) غلط    ۳) غلط    ۴) صحیح    ۵) غلط    ۶) صحیح

Exercise 4A:

شریف    هیچ جای نمیرود، در خانه میماند ، کتاب میخواند ، دوش میکند ،
کارخانگی انجام میدهد و استراحت میکند .

میرویس    میله میروند ،به پارک میروند ،غذا میپزند ، والیبال بازی میکنند ، آببازی
میکنند ،استراحت میکنند ،

Exercise 5A:

۱) من روز جمعه هیجای نمیروم.
۲) من هیچوقت به رستورانت نمیروم.
۳) در صنف ما هیچکس ایرانی است.

Exercise 5B:

۱) من هیچوقت سینما نمیروم.
۲) هر آخر هفته او در خانه میماند و هیچ جای نمیرود .
۳) این آخر هفته هیچکس فوتبال بازی نکرد .

Exercise 6:

قصه کردن (قصه کن):  من قصه میکنم، ماقصه میکنیم، توقصه میکنی، شماقصه
میکنید ، او قصه میکند ، آنهاقصه میکنند .

ماندن (مان):    من میمانم، ما میمانیم، تو میمانی، شما میمانید ، او
میماند ، آنها میمانند .

## Exercise 9:

۱. basketball

۲. volleyball

۳. volleyball

۴. football (soccer)

۵. Reads books, listens to her professor's speeches, takes notes, and has conversations.

۶. The university semester ends.

۷. a break

## Exercise 12:

۱) من از ورزش اسکی خوشم میاید .    ۲) او از ورزش کاراته خوشش میاید .

۳) آنها از ورزش بزکشی خوششان میاید .   ۴) من از ورزش اسب دوانی خوشم میاید .

۵) ما از ورزش فوتبال خوش ما(مان) میاید .

## Exercise 13:

۱) شریف از فلم پاکستانی خوشش نمیآید .    ۲) نه، کم خوشش میاید .

۳) بلی، خوشش میاید .    ۴) بلی، خوشش میاید .

# REVIEW OF CHAPTER 5

## Exercise 1A:

۱) بیدار میشود    ۲) هفت و نیم

۳) در پوهنتون میماند .    ۴) به پارک میرود ، گاهی آببازی میکند ، اکثراً والیبال میکند .

۵) اکثراً والیبال میکند .    ۶) به خانه میرود و غذا میپزد .

۷) اول حمل    ۸) به سینما میرود .

۹) او فلم هندی را خوش دارد .    ۱۰) او از فلم فرانسوی خوشش نمیاید .

## Exercise 2A:

| (now) حالا | (20th) بیستم | (to go) میروم |
| --- | --- | --- |
| (every week) هرهفته | (most of the time) اکثر اوقات | (very) بسیار |
| (a little) کمی | (tonight) امشب | (holiday) رخصتی |
| (to rest) استراحت میکنم | | |

## Exercise 2B:

1. b    2. d    3. c    4. d    5. d    6. c    7. b    8. c

## Exercise 5:

1. a    2. a    3. c    4. b    5. a    6. a

# CHAPTER SIX

## LESSON 1
### Exercise 1B:

پدر

پدر کلان

بچه/پسر، برادر، نواسه

دختر، خواهر، نواسه

دختر، خواهر، نواسه

مادر کلان

بچه/پسر، کودك /طفل

مادر

خانواده/ فامیل

### Exercise 1C:

شریف

حاجی رحیم

فرید

زرغونه

زرمینه

ماه جان

نوید

لیلا

خانوادهٔ شریف

### Exercise 1D:

| غلط | صحیح | جملات | |
|---|---|---|---|
| √ | | حاجی رحیم پدر نوید است. | ۱ |
| | √ | نوید برادر فرید است. | ۲ |
| | √ | نوید دو خواهر دارد . | ۳ |

| | | | |
|---|---|---|---|
| | √ | ليلا مادر زرمينه است. | ۴ |
| √ | | ماه جان مادر ليلا است. | ۵ |
| √ | | زرمينه خواهر ليلا است. | ۶ |
| | √ | نويد نواسهٔ حاجی رحيم است. | ۷ |
| | √ | ماه جان مادر کلان زرغونه است. | ۸ |
| | √ | حاجی رحيم پدر کلان است. | ۹ |

## Exercise 2A:

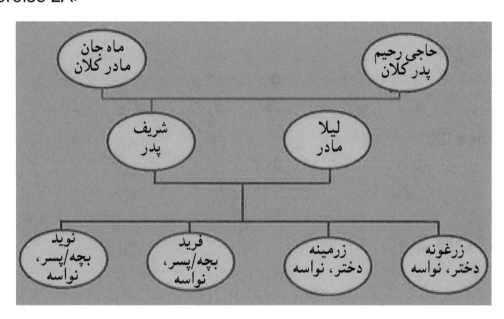

## Exercise 3:

| | |
|---|---|
| 1. Your Dari language classmate. (Navid) | نويد جان |
| 2. An Afghan female who works in your office. (Laylā) | ليلا جان |
| 3. An elder Afghan man who lives next door to you. (Rahman) | رحمان خان |
| 4. The son of your Afghan landlord. (Omid) | اميد جان |
| 5. A similar aged Afghan man who lives next door. (Ajmal) | اجمل خان |

## Exercise 4:

1. six people    2. father 45, mother 38    3. two brothers and one sister
4. brother       5. brother                 6. Farid

## Exercise 6:

| ۴) ميباشد | ۳) ميباشند | ۲) ميباشم | ۱) ميباشد |
|---|---|---|---|
| ۸) ميباشد | ۷) ميباشی | ۶) ميباشند | ۵) ميباشيم |

Exercise 7A:

| | | | |
|---|---|---|---|
| | حاجی عبدالرحیم پدر کلان احمد | | |
| | عبدالکریم پدر احمد | | |
| | احمد پوپل پسر عبدالکریم | | |
| گلالی دختر احمد | ملالی دختر احمد | ایمل بچهٔ احمد | اجمل بچهٔ احمد |
| مرضیه خواهر احمد | هارون برادر احمد | همایون برادر | میرویس برادر احمد |

Exercise 9A:

شریف معلم و مدیر بانک، حاجی رحیم متقاعد و دوکاندار، ماه جان بیکار و خانم خانه، زغونه محصل، زرمینه متعلم، فرید متعلم، نوید بچهٔ کودکستان، لیلا نرس

Exercise 10:

| ۸ | ۷ | ۶ | ۵ | ۴ | ۳ | ۲ | ۱ |
|---|---|---|---|---|---|---|---|
| پیرتر | جوانتر | چاقتر | کلانتر | لاغرتر | خوردتر | بلنتر | کوتاهتر |

Exercise 12C:

| | | | |
|---|---|---|---|
| ۴) چار نفر | ۳) امریکا | ۲) نه | ۱) کابل |
| ۸) بیکار | ۷) انجینر | ۶) نه | ۵) آبی |

# LESSON 2

Exercise 1A:

۱) برادر پدر    ۲) خواهر پدر    ۳) برادر مادر    ۴) خواهر مادر    ۵) پدر و مادر

Exercise 1B:

۱) بچهٔ برادر پدر    ۲) دختر برادر پدر    ۳) بچهٔ خواهر پدر    ۴) دختر خواهر پدر
۵) بچهٔ برادر مادر    ۶) دختر برادر مادر    ۷) بچهٔ خواهر مادر    ۸) دختر خواهر مادر

Exercise 2A:

مادر زرغونه سه برادر دارد که نام شان سید صبور، سید ناصر و سید خلیل است، و او دو خواهر دارد که نام شان گلجان و شاه جان است.

پدر زرغونه دو برادر دارد که* نام شان کریم و نسیم است و یک خواهر دارد که نامش فهیمه است.

Exercise 2B:

۱) ماما    ۲) کاکا    ۳) خاله    ۴) عمه    ۵) دختر خاله    ۶) دختر خاله    ۷) بچهٔ کاکا

Exercise 3A:

۲) آن مرد پدرم میشود .   ۱) این زن ماردم میشود .

۴) آن دختر ، دختر مامایش میشود .   ۳) این بچه، بچهٔ مامای شان میشود .

۶) او بچهٔ عمهٔ ما میشود .   ۵) او دختر عمهٔ ام میشود .

۸) من کاکایتان میشوم.   ۷) آنها عمه هایم میشوند .

Exercise 3B:

۱) سلطان کاکایی وحید میشود ، شیرین و فواد اولاد های سلطان میشوند .

۲) کریم مامای رحیم میشود .

۳) مستوره و مهتاب عمه های لیلا میشوند .

۴) لاله و مریم خاله های لیلا میشوند

Exercise 4A:

۱) مادرم یك برادر دارد که نامش جان است.

۲) بچهٔ که در پهلوی احمد میباشد ، بچهٔ عمهٔ ام است.

۳) دختری که در پیشروی لیلا است، دختر خاله میشود .

۴) مردی که در پشت برادرتان است، مامایم است.

۵) زنی که در صنف است، عمه ام میشود .

۶) دختری که کار میکند ، دختر مامایم است.

Exercise 4B:

۱) من یك ماما دارم که نامش اسدالله است.

۲) او دو خاله دارد که نامهایشان فریده و آصفه است.

۳) ما یك عمه داریم که نامش سیما است.

۴) آنها یك کاکا دارند که نامش نور احمد است.

۵) آن مرد مامایم است که تلیفون میکند .

Exercise 6A:

۲) خیاط چهل و هشت ساله   ۱) آشپز پنجاه وچار ساله

۴) محصل بیست و چار ساله   ۳) داکتر سی و چار ساله

۶) شاگرد مکتب ده ساله   ۵) شاگرد مکتب شانزده ساله

۸) سگ دو ساله   ۷) کودك ده ماهه

Exercise 6B:

۱) سید فهیم   ۲) شیرین   ۳) نسرین   ۴) سید نعیم   ۵) سید نعیم   ۶) پاپی

Exercise 7A:

۱) فهیم قد بلند ، چشم ها و مو ها سیاه

۲) دیوید قد میانه ، چشم ها  و مو ها قهوه یی

۳) جسیکا قد بلند ، چشم هاآبی و مو ها طلایی

۴) ملالی قد کوتاه، چشم ها سیاه و مو ها قهوه یی

۵) حاجی رحیم قد میانه ، چشم هاسیاه  و مو ها سفید

۶) شریف قد بلند ، چشم ها قهوه یی و مو ها خاکستری

Exercise 7C:

۵) اجمل از صابر        ۴) میوند از فرید        ۳) فرید و صابر        ۲) اجمل        ۱) میوند

Exercise 8B:

1. c    2. b    3. c    4. a    5. c    6. c    7. a

# LESSON 3

Exercise 1A:

| | سید نعیم | زرغونه |
|---|---|---|
| شوهر/ شوی | √ | |
| داماد | √ | |
| خسر | √ | |
| خشو | √ | |
| خسربُره | √ | |
| خیاشنه | √ | |

| | سید نعیم | زرغونه |
|---|---|---|
| زن | | √ |
| عروس/ سونو | | √ |
| خسر | | √ |
| خشو | | √ |
| ایور | | √ |
| ننو | | √ |

Exercise 1B:

۴) خواهر شوهر    ۳) برادر شوهر    ۲) مادر زن/مادر شوهر    ۱) پدر زن/پدر شوهر

۸) خواهر زن    ۷) برادر زن    ۶) شوهر دختر    ۵) زن بچه

Exercise 1C:

۱. father-in-law
۲. mother-in-law
۳. brother-in-law (husband's brother)
۴. sister-in-law (husband's sister)

۵. daughter-in-law
۶. son-in-law
۷. brother-in-law (wife's brother)
۸. sister-in-law (wife's sister)

Exercise 2:

1. b    2. a    3. b    4. a    5. a    6. b    7. a    8. a

Exercise 4:

| | | | |
|---|---|---|---|
| ۱ | توی کردن | توی کرد | ما ده سال پیش توی کردیم. |
| ۲ | ازدواج کردن | ازدواج کرد | آنها پارسال توی کردند. |
| ۳ | عروسی کردن | عروسی کرد | هفته گذشته اجمل عروسی کرد. |
| ۴ | نامزد شدن | نامزد شد | آنها دو روز پیش نامزد شدند. |
| ۵ | به ماه عسل رفتن | به ماه عسل رفت | ماه قبل او و شوهرش به ماه عسل رفتند. |
| ۶ | دیدن | دید | آنها در هندوستان تاج محل را دیدند. |
| ۷ | درس خواندن | درس خواند | من در پوهنتون کابل درس خواندم. |

Exercise 5:

آن زن زرغونه است، او یک نیم سال پیش مجرد بود اما یک سال پیش او همراهٔ بچهٔ ماما یش سید نعیم ازدواج کرد. شوهر زرغونه دو ماه پیش محصل بود اما حالا او انجینر است. آنها بعد از توی به ماه عسل رفتند، آنها برای ماه عسل به هندوستان رفتند، در هندوستان آنها تاج محل را دیدند.

Exercise 6A:

میوند:   دو خسربره، سه خیاشنه، یک خسر و دو خوشو

Exercise 6B:

| | | | |
|---|---|---|---|
| ۱) خانهٔ خسرش | ۲) توی نعیم | ۳) به هندوستان | ۴) تاج محل |
| ۵) ده سال پیش | ۶) چون زن اولش بچه ندارد | ۷) دو | |

Exercise 6D:
1. When did Zarghuna and Na'im get married?   3. Where did they go for their honeymoon?
2. Where was Na'im two months ago?   4. What did they see in India?

Exercise 7A:

| ۱) هندوستان | ۲) هوتل | ۳) تاج محل | ۴) بازار | ۵) سینما |
|---|---|---|---|---|

# REVIEW OF CHAPTER 6
Exercise 1:

| | | | |
|---|---|---|---|
| ۱) پدرم | ۲) پدرم | ۳) برادر | ۴) خواهر | ۵) متاهل |
| ۶) زنم | ۷) او | ۸) خسرم | ۹) او | ۱۰) بچه |
| ۱۱) بچه هایم | ۱۲) دختر | ۱۳) دخترم | ۱۴) او | ۱۵) خوشویم |
| ۱۶) برادرانم | ۱۷) برادرانم | ۱۸) خواهرانم | | |

Exercise 2:

۱) زنش میشود.    ۲) پدرش میشود.    ۳) بچه اش میشود.

۴) برادرش میشود.    ۵) در امریکا در ایالت کالیفرنیا    ۶) ۱۳ ساله است.

۷) در پوهنتون استاد هستند.    ۸) توریالی در پوهنتون و شکریه در مکتب

Exercise 3A:

| | نازنین | | | | بابك | |
|---|---|---|---|---|---|---|
| وظیفه | رابطهٔ فامیلی | نام | وظیفه | رابطهٔ فامیلی | نام | |
| نرس | دختر | نازنین | انجینر | بچه | بابك | |
| متقاعد و دكاندار | پدر | اسد الله | مدیر مكتب | پدر | اشرف | |
| خانم خانه | مادر | ماه جبین | خیاط | مادر | توریپیكی | |
| معلم | خواهر | سیمین | آشپز | خواهر | گل مكی | |
| داكتر | برادر | سمیع الله | محصل، منشی | خواهر | ستوری | |
| | | | شاگرد مكتب | خواهر | ملالی | |
| | | | دوكاندار | برادر | برمك | |

Exercise 4:

| زرغونه | فرید |
|---|---|
| 1. Layla | 1. Ahmad |
| 2. tall | 2. average |
| 3. blue | 3. brown |
| 4. brown | 4. black |

Exercise 7:

1. a        2. b        3. a        4. c        5. c

Exercise 8:

۱) بود    ۲) رفتیم    ۳) بود    ۴) نامه نوشتم

۵) آمدند    ۶) متقاعد شد    ۷) خوردیم    ۸) داشت

Exercise 9:

۱) پیرتر    ۲) جوانترین    ۳) خوردترین    ۴) كوچكتر    ۵) كلانتر

۶) بزرگتر    ۷) مقبولترین    ۸) لاغرتر    ۹) قدبلندترین    ۱۰) قد كوتاه ترین،

۱۱) قد میانه تر

Exercise 11B:

قد بلند، چشم ها قهویی، موی های سیاه دارد، در دستش یك بكس زرد میباشد.
نامش سیما است.

# CHAPTER SEVEN

## LESSON 1
Exercise 1A:

خانه

خواندن

تشناب

حمام

اتاق نشیمن،
مهمان خانه

برنده

گراژ/گراج

درخت

آشپز خانه

راه روی

اتاق خواب

زینه

طعام خانه

صحن حویلی

باغچه

Exercise 1E:

| | | |
|---|---|---|
| ۱ | اتاق نشیمن | من تلویزیون میبینم، چای مینوشم، با فامیل صحبت میکنم، کتاب میخوانم. |
| ۲ | اتاق خواب | من خواب میشوم، کتاب میخوانم، موسیقی میشنوم. |
| ۳ | مهمان خانه | با دوست هایم میبینم، با مهمان هایم صحبت میکنم، نان میخورم، چای مینوشم. |
| ۴ | طعام خانه | نان میخورم، چای مینوشم. |
| ۵ | آشپزخانه | نان میپزم، چای دم میکنم، ظرف میشویم. |
| ۶ | حمام | جانم را میشویم، وضو میگیرم، دست ها و رویم را میشویم. |

Exercise 2A:
1. c        2. c        3. a        4. b

Exercise 2B:

| چای نوشیدن | تلویزیون سیل کردن | صحبت میکند | خواب شدن | کتاب خواندن |
|---|---|---|---|---|
| √ | √ | √ | | √ |

Exercise 3:

۱) کتابخانه library          ۲) دواخانه pharmacy          ۳) طعام خانه dining room

۴) چایخانه coffee shop          ۵) شفاخانه hospital

Exercise 4A:

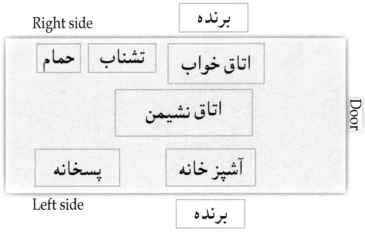

Exercise 4B:

قد اتاق نشیمن، اتاق خواب ، آشپز خانه، تشناب، حمام، برنده، پسخانه

Exercise 4C:

۱) صحیح   ۲) غلط   ۳) غلط   ۴) صحیح   ۵) صحیح   ۶) غلط   ۷) غلط   ۸) غلط

Exercise 5:

| | | |
|---|---|---|
| ۱ | شما کجا میشینید؟ | Where do you live? |
| ۲ | من در یک خانه کلان میشینم. | I live in a big house. |
| ۳ | او در منزل سوم یک آپارتمان میشینند. | S/he lives on the third floor of an apartment. |
| ۴ | ما در یک هوتل میشینیم. | We live in a hotel. |
| ۵ | آنها در یک خانهٔ کلانتر میشینند. | They live in a bigger house. |

Exercise 7A:

۱ بام roof          ۲ سقف ceiling

۳ دیوار wall          ۴ کف اتاق floor

Exercise 8B:

۱) غلط   ۲) غلط   ۳) غلط   ۴) صحیح   ۵) صحیح

۶) غلط   ۷) صحیح   ۸) صحیح   ۹) صحیح

Exercise 9A:

| | | |
|---|---|---|
| من دیروز به خانه نو کوچ کردم. | من امروز به خانه نو کوچ میکنم. | ١ |
| ما دیروز به خانه نو کوچ کردم. | ما امروز به خانه نو کوچ میکنیم. | ٢ |
| تو دیروز به خانه نو کوچ کردم. | تو امروز به خانه نو کوچ میکنی. | ٣ |
| شما دیروز به خانه نو کوچ کردم. | شما امروز به خانه نو کوچ میکنید. | ۴ |
| او دیروز به خانه نو کوچ کردم. | او امروز به خانه نو کوچ میکند. | ۵ |
| آنها دیروز به خانه نو کوچ ر. | آنها امروز به خانه نو کوچ میکنند. | ۶ |

Exercise 10A:

۱) دو مهمانخانه    ۲) سه تشناب    ۳) دو حمام    ۴) دو آشپزخانه

۵) یك گراژ    ۶) چار اتاق خواب    ۷) سه باغچهٔ گل    ۸) دو درخت

Exercise 10B:

| | |
|---|---|
| ب- حویلی، الف- حویلی نو | ١ |
| ج - در پهلوی سرك عمومی | ٢ |
| الف - سرخ و آبی | ٣ |
| الف- ۵۲۶ | ۴ |
| الف - سه باغچه گل و دو درخت | ۵ |
| الف - در بین خانه و پیشروی حویلی | ۶ |

# LESSON 2

Exercise 2B:
1. c        2. b        3. c        4. a

Exercise 3A:
1. fourteen
2. two
3. kitchen, dining room, mosque, bathroom and shower
4. green parks, labs, gymnasiums, cafeteria, conference rooms, and playgrounds

Exercise 4A:

۱) فاکولتهٔ انجینری
۲) در غرب ساحهٔ پوهنتون کابل، در پیشروی فاکولتهٔ زبانشناسی
۳) پنج منزل
۴) دولابراتوار، یك کتابخانه، یك تالار کانفرانس، یك جمنازیم و یك کانتین

۵) آبی
۶) سیاه
۷) دیوار ها و سقف صنف زرد و کف صنف خاکستری است.

## Exercise 5D:

| ۴) غلط | ۳) صحیح | ۲) صحیح | ۱) غلط |
|---|---|---|---|
| ۸) صحیح | ۷) صحیح | ۶) غلط | ۵) صحیح |

## Exercise 6A:

Helping verbs    میخواهم، میتوانند، میتوانند، خوش دارم، میرویم

Main verbs    نوشته کنم، است، میخوانم، است، دارد، بخوانند، بازی کنند، بروم، است، است، است، والیبال کنیم، خوش دارید، نوشته کنید

## Exercise 6B:

| ۵) صحیح | ۴) غلط | ۳) صحیح | ۲) غلط | ۱) غلط |
|---|---|---|---|---|

## Exercise 7A:

| ۱ | چرا شما زبان دری میخوانید؟ | چونکه من به افغانستان میروم. |
|---|---|---|
| ۲ | چرا در این پوهنتون درس میخوانید؟ | بخاطریکه نزدیک خانه ام است. |
| ۳ | چرا به کتابخانه رفتید؟ | چونکه یک کتاب کار داشتم. |
| ۴ | چرا دیروز ورزش نکردید؟ | بخاطریکه مانده بودم. |
| ۵ | چرا هر روز قهوه مینوشید؟ | چونکه قهوه را خوش دارم. |

## Exercise 7B:

۱) من هرروز به پوهنتون میروم چونکه من محصل هستم.
۲) من به جمنازیم نمیروم چونکه ورزش را دوست ندارم.
۳) ما در پوهنتون اندیانا درس میخوانیم چونکه ساحه پوهنتو کلان دارد.
۴) من به کتابخانه میروم چونکه یک کتاب ضرورت دارم.
۵) دیروز ورزش نکردم چونکه مانده بودم.
۶) من قهوه نمینوشم چونکه قهوه را خوش ندارم.

## Exercise 8A:
1. a        2. a        3. c        4. d        5. c        6. c

## Exercise 8B:

کجا میروید؟، آیا من میتوانم که برادرم را بیاورم؟، آیا شما میخوانید که همراه من بروید؟، بازی ساعت چند بجه است؟، شما معمولاً در کجا خوش دارید که درس بخوانید؟

Exercise 9B:

۱) صحیح    ۲) غلط    ۳) غلط    ۴) صحیح    ۵) غلط

Exercise 10A:

Helping verbs    به پوهنتون رفتیم، میخواهم، میخواهد ، میرویم، میخواهیم

Exercise 10B:

| | |
|---|---|
| ۱ | خانهٔ لیلا دو اتاق خواب عصری ، یک اتاق نشیمن عصری ، یک دهلیز کلان دو تشناب، یک حمام و یک آشپز خانه مدرن دارد . |
| ۲ | بخاطریکه صنف هایش را ببیند . |
| ۳ | در یک خانه |
| ۴ | آنها فردا به پارک شیدایی میروند . و در آنجا میخواهند غذا بپزند و استراحت کنند . |

# LESSON 3

Exercise 1C:

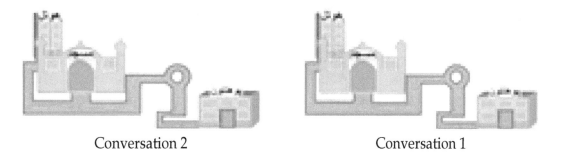

Conversation 2                    Conversation 1

Exercise 3A:

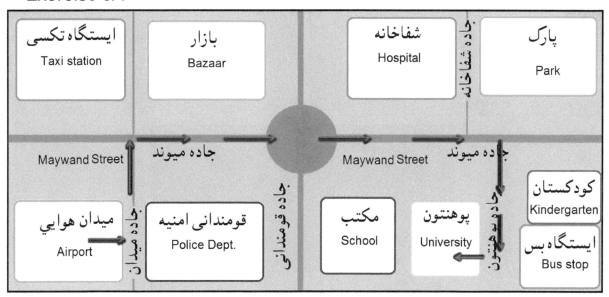

## Exercise 5A:

1. b          2. a          3. d          4. a

## Exercise 6:

| | |
|---|---|
| go straight ahead this way for 2 minutes, and then turn left | برای دو دقیقه به این طرف مستقیم بروید و باز به دست چپ بگردید . |
| go straight ahead that way for 2 miles, and then turn right | برای دو میل به این طرف مستقیم بروید و باز به دست راست بگردید |
| go a little bit up this way, and then turn left | کمی پیش بروید و باز به دست چپ بگردید |

## Exercise 7:

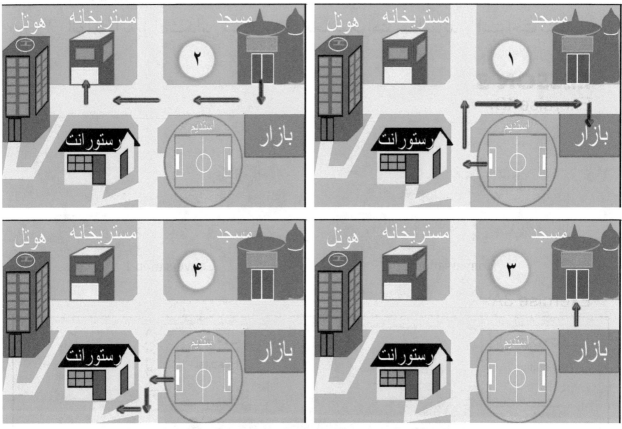

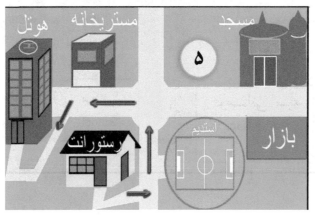

Exercise 8B:

۱) کارته نو

۲) مسجد پل خشتی

۳) از پوهنتون بیرون شو، در دست بگرد، ایستادگاه سرویس ها آنجاست.

# REVIEW OF CHAPTER 7
Exercise 1A:

| | | |
|---|---|---|
| ۱ | شما در کجا نان پخته میکند؟ | من در آشپزخانه نان پخته میکنم. |
| ۲ | شما با فامیل تان در کجا نان میخورید؟ | من با فامیلم در طعام خانه نان میخورم. |
| ۳ | شما با فامیل تان در کجا تلویزیون سیل میکنید؟ | من با فامیلم در اتاق نشیمن تلویزیون سیل میکنم. |
| ۴ | شما در کجا خواب میشوید؟ | من در اتاق خواب، خواب میشوم. |
| ۵ | شما در کجا جان تان را میشویید؟ | من در حمام جانم را میشویم. |
| ۶ | شما از کدام راه به خانه داخل میشوید؟ | من از دهلیز و دروازه راه به خانه داخل میشوم. |
| ۷ | شما موتر تان را در کجا پارک میکنید؟ | من موترم را در گراژ پارک میکنم. |

Exercise 1B:

۱. She goes to the library.
۲. She goes to the gymnasium.
۳. She goes to the cafeteria and will have lunch with her friend Layla.
۴. She goes there to do her homework.
۵. She works in the lab.
۶. She calls her father.

Exercise 3A:

از ایستگاه بس تیر شوید، به سمت راست دور بزنید، روبرو بروید در جادهٔ میوند باز به سمت چپ دور بزنید، همانطور پیش بروید درچاراهی بسمت راست بگردید، ازچار راهی تیر شوید بازار در سمت چپ تان در پیشرویی شفاخانه است.

# CHAPTER EIGHT

# LESSON 1
Exercise 1A:

لیلا:    نان خشک، مربا، پنیر، چای

شریف: قهوه، شیر، بوره، کیک، کلچه، نان خشک، تخم مرغ، مسکه، ماست

Exercise 2A:

دارند:  بوره، چای، تخم مرغ، کیک، کلچه

ندارند: نان خشک، شیر، مسکه، پنیر، مربا، قهوه، ماست

## Exercise 2B:

| | مواد چای صبح | | مواد چای صبح |
|---|---|---|---|
| | کلچه | | چای |
| | تخم مرغ | √ | شیر |
| | بوره | √ | ماست |
| | قهوه | √ | مسکه |
| √ | نان خشك | √ | پنیر |
| √ | مربا | | کیك |

## Exercise 2C:

| | مواد چای صبح | | مواد چای صبح |
|---|---|---|---|
| | کلچه | | چای |
| | تخم مرغ | √ | شیر |
| | بوره | | ماست |
| | قهوه | √ | مسکه |
| √ | نان خشك | √ | پنیر |
| √ | مربا | | کیك |

## Exercise 2D:

۴) صحیح       ۳) صحیح       ۲) غلط       ۱) غلط

## Exercise 3:

۲) او باید نان خشك بخرم.       ۱) من باید شیر بخرم.

۴) ما باید چای صبح بخوریم.       ۳) من باید استراحت کنم.

۵) آنها باید نان بخورند .

## Exercise 4A:

| ۲ کیلو گوشت | ۱۲ بوتل آب | ۱ بوتل روغن | ۲ بسته نمك |
|---|---|---|---|
| ۳۰۰ گرام مرچ | ۴ کیلو سبزی پالك | ۴ دانه بادرنگ | ۳ کیلو بادنجان رومی |
| ۳ کیلو پیاز | ۲ کیلو کچالو | ۱ کیلو زردك | ۲ دسته کاهو |
| ۲ درجن کیله | ۲ کیلو سیب | ۱ کیلو آلوبالو | ۱ کیلو توت زمینی |
| ۴ کیلو مالته | ۳ کیلو انگور | ۱۰ کیلو تربوز | ۱۰ کیلو خربوزه |

## Exercise 4B:

| | |
|---|---|
| ۱ | من از چای همراه شیر خوشم میاید . |
| ۲ | من از قهوه همراه بوره خوشم میاید . |
| ۳ | شما از چای همراه چی خوش تان میاید ؟ |

| | |
|---|---|
| ۴ | شما از قهوه همراه چی خوش تان میاید ؟ |
| ۵ | او از مسکه همراه نان خشك خوشش میاید . |

## Exercise 4C:

۱) چونکه اوهم سودا بکار داشت و هم مهمان دارد .

۲) خواهر و داماد لیلا

۳) چونکه مهمانهایش برای یك هفته در خانه اش میباشند .

۴) باید سودا بخرد

## Exercise 5A:

۱) من از پنیر و نان خشك خوشم میاید . ۲) ما از شیر خوش ما میاید .

۳) تو از چای و کلچه خوشت میاید . ۴) شما از قهوه و بوره خوشتان میاید .

۵) او از مسکه و نان خشك خوشش میاید . ۶)آنها از تخم مرغ و نان خشك خوششان میاید .

## Exercise 5B:

۱) من از چای همراه شیر خوشم میاید . ۲) من از قهوه همراه بوره خوشم میاید .

۳) شما از چای همراه چی خوشتان میاید؟ ۴) شما از قهوه همراه چی خوشتان میاید؟

۵) او از مسکه همراه نان خشك خوشش میاید .

## Exercise 5E:

اجمل: سیب و تربوز را بسیار خوش دارد ، اما خربوزه را خوش ندارد . انگور بسیار زیاد خوش دارد .

میرویس: انگور بسیار خوشش میاید ، از مالته کم خوشش میاید . تربوز و بسیار زیاد خربوزه را خوش دارد . سیب را بسیار کم خوش دارد .

## Exercise 6A:
1. c      2. b      3. a      4. d

## Exercise 6B:

۱) فروشنده ۲) فروشنده ۳) مشتری ۴) مشتری ۵) فروشنده ۶) مشتری

## Exercise 6C:
1. no      2. at the beginning      3. a

## Exercise 7A:

۱) میخرید (you buy)    ۲) میفروشد (he sells)    ۳) به کار داریم (we need)

۴) میخواهند (they want)    ۵) میگیرم (I take)    ۶) میدهم (I give)

۷) آماده هستید (you are ready)

Exercise 7B:

۱) خریدید (you bought) ۲) فروخت (he sold) ۳) به کار داشتیم (we needed)

۴) خواستند (they wanted) ۵) گرفتم (I took) ۶) دادم (I gave)

۷) آماده بودید (you were ready)

Exercise 8:

۱) غلط ۲) صحیح ۳) صحیح ۴) صحیح ۵) صحیح

Exercise 9A:

۱) میخواهد سودا بخرد .

۲) دوکان ترکاری فروشی و کالافروشی و بوت فروشی

۳) چونکه رستورانت کابل غذا های داخلی و خارجی دارد .

۴) گفت که برایش ایمیل روان کند .

Exercise 9B:

1. a      2. b

# LESSON 2

Exercise 2:

|  |  |
|---|---|
| This is the Afghan restaurant menu which has various types of Afghan foods. | این مینوی رستورانت افغان است که انواع غذا های افغانی دارد . |
| This is a modern restaurant and doesn't have any costumer. | اینجا یک رستورانت عصری است و فعلاً مشتری ندارد . |
| This boy is a waiter in a restaurant close to the highway. | این بچه در یک رستورانت، در نزدیک شاهراه گارسون است . |
| This man sells Coca-Cola. He is thirsty, and he drinks tea. | این مرد کوکاکولا میفروشد ، او تشنه است و چای مینوشد . |
| Those men ate in a restaurant close to the highway. They are waiting for their bill. They ordered tea. | این مردها در یک رستورانت نزدیک شاهراه نان خوردند و معطل بل نان شان هستند .آنها چای فرمایش دادند . |
| This man is a chef of the restaurant, and he is the restaurant owner, too. | این مرد سر آشپز رستورانت است، او همچنان مالک رستورانت است . |

Exercise 4A:

Sign#1:    1. b      2. c

Sign#2    1. a      2. student's task

3. a) نوشیدنی    b) نان شب    c) نان چاشت    d) صبحانه/ چای صبح

e) هوسانه    f) شیرینی    g) سوپ و سلاته

## Exercise 4B:

كباب گوشت گوسفند، كباب گوشت گاو، شش كباب، شامی كباب، چوپان كباب

قورمهٔ گوشت گوسفند، قورمهٔ گوش مرغ، قورمهٔ سبزی، قورمهٔ لوبیا

## Exercise 5:
2, 1, 5, 6, 7, 3, 4

## Exercise 6:

| | | |
|---|---|---|
| ۱ | قهوه | نوشیدنی که برای خستگی خوب است. |
| ۲ | آشپز خانه | جای که در آن نان پخته میکنیم. |
| ۳ | دوكاندار | كسی که سودا میفروشد. |
| ۴ | حلوا | شیرینی که از آرد و بوره ساخته میشود. |
| ۵ | قابلی پلو | غذایی که از برنج و گوشت ساخته میشود. |
| ۶ | منتو | غذایی که از خمیر و گوشت ساخته میشود. |
| ۷ | آشك | غذایی که از خمیر و سبزی ساخته میشود. |
| ۸ | كباب گوسفند | غذایی که از گوشت گوسفند ساخته میشود. |

## Exercise 7:
1. b          2. a          3. b          4. c

## Exercise 8:

۱) ما میخواهیم به رستورانت برویم بخاطریکه ما گشنه شدیم.

۲) او میخواهد که یك قطی پیپسی بنوشد چونکه او تشنه شد.

۳) آیا میخواهی که ما نان چاشت را بخوریم بخاطریکه من بسیار گشنه شدم.

۴) آنها سیر شدند و آنها نمیخواهند بخورند.

۵) آیا شما گشنه شدید؟

۶) او نمیخواهد که بنوشد چونکه او تشنه نیست.

۷) من میخواهم که کمی آب نارنج بخرم، چونکه تشنه شدم.

۸) انها میخواهند نان شب را بخورند بخاطریکه آنها گشنه شدند.

## Exercise 10A:
1. modern restaurant          2. because the waiter offers a menu

## Exercise 10B:

| | | | |
|---|---|---|---|
| ۴) غلط | ۳) غلط | ۲) غلط | ۱) صحیح |
| ۸) صحیح | ۷) صحیح | ۶) صحیح | ۵) صحیح |

## Exercise 11A:
1. c          2. a          3. b          4. d          5. c          6. a          7. c

## Exercise 12A:

| مالکرستورانت | مسعود | عبارات |
|---|---|---|
| √ | | بلی ، ما میز خالی داریم. شما چی میخواهید که بخورید؟ |
| | √ | برای نوشیدنی، کوکا کولا، چای و آب مالته و برای خوردن کباب گوشت گوسفند همراه نان خشك و سلاته خوب است. |
| | √ | فردا چاشت ساعت چند بجه میآیید؟ |
| | √ | ساعت یك بجه. |
| | √ | بسیار خوب ، تا صباح خدا حافظ! |
| | √ | فردا سالگرهٔ برادر خوردم است، میخواهم که برایش یك کیك کلان آماده کنید. |
| | √ | سلام ، من مسعود هستم، من میخواهم که یك میز چار نفره برای فردا چاشت ریزرو کنم. |
| √ | | به امان خدا! |
| √ | | بسیار خوب برای خوردن و نوشیدن چی میخواهید؟ |
| √ | | هلو به رستورانت کلبهٔ افغان خوش آمدید ، چی خدمت کنم؟ |
| √ | | بسیار خوب ما همه فرمایش های تان را آماده میکنیم. پیسه اش را.حالا میپردازید یا فردا |
| | √ | فردا پیسه تان را میپردازم. |
| √ | | حتما، میخواهید که بر رویی کیك چیزی نوشته کنیم. |
| | √ | بلی لطفاً نوشته کنید که (سالگره‌ات مبارك و یا تولدت مبارك). |

## Exercise 12B:

سالگره ات مبارک، تولدت مبارک .5

1. c       2. b       3. c       4. a

6. a       7. b

# LESSON 3

## Exercise 1B:

زرغونه - نعیم جان، امروز برای کار چی میپوشید؟

نعیم - امروز، کورتی و پطلون سیاه ام همراه یخن قاق آبی و نیکتایی سرخم را میپوشم.

زرغونه - کدام زیر پیراهنی، جراب ها و بوتها را میپوشید؟

نعیم - زیرپیراهنی سفیدم همراه جرابها و بوتهای سیاه ام ، و همان نیکری که دیروز خریدم، آنرا هم میپوشم. تو امروز چی میخواهی بپوشی؟

زرغونه - من پطلون آسمانی و بلوز زردم را همراه چپلی های قهوه یی ام میپوشم.

Exercise 3:

| | |
|---|---|
| ززغونه | چادر،پیراهن، تنبان ، چپلی ، چادری و یا برقعه |
| شوهر زرغونه | پیراهن، تنبان، واسکت ، کلاه پکول، پتو ، دستمال، ایزار بند |
| بچۀ زرغونه | پیراهن، تنبان،و کلاه، ایزار بند |
| دختر زرغونه | پیراهن، تنبان و شال |
| خسر زرغونه | پیراهن، تنبان، چپن ، لنگی ، ایزار بند |

Exercise 5A:

First Description: حاجی کمال        Second Description: محمد یوسف

Exercise 5B:

First Description: مرضیه        Second Description: زرمینه

Exercise 8C:

۱) بچه گانه     ۲) ۱۶۰ افغانی ۳) ۲۰۰ افغانی ۴) ۳۰۰ افغانی ۵) ۶۰۰ افغانی

Exercise 9:

۱) بوت مردانه نمبر ۱۰ سیاه       ۲) بلوز زنانه کلان زرد

۳) بوت دخترانه نمبر ۵ رنگ سرخ ،      ۴) پطلون بچه گانه میانه آبی

When bargaining, which of the following phrases did the customer use?    a

# REVIEW OF CHAPTER 8

### Exercise 1A:

1. Turkey
2. jeans
3. brown, khaki, black
4. men's and boys' jackets
5. women's and girls' shirts
6. men's and boys' jackets
7. 8:00 a.m. to 10 p.m.
8. first floor

# CHAPTER NINE

## LESSON 1

### Exercise 1B:

| فصل ها | نام ماه ها | فصل ها | نام ماه ها |
|---|---|---|---|
| خزان | میزان — ماه هفتم | بهار | حمل — ماه اول |
| خزان | عقرب — ماه هشتم | بهار | ثور — ماه دوم |
| خزان | قوس — ماه نهم | بهار | جوزا — ماه سوم |
| زمستان | جدی — ماه دهم | تابستان | سرطان — ماه چارم |
| زمستان | دلو — ماه یازدهم | تابستان | اسد — ماه پنجم |
| زمستان | حوت — ماه دوازدهم | تابستان | سنبله — ماه ششم |

### Exercise 2A:

| آسمان | باران | برف | ژاله |
|---|---|---|---|
| sky | rain | snow | hail |
| خزان زمستان / بهار تابستان | خزان زمستان / بهار تابستان | زمستان | زمستان / بهار |

| باد، شمال | طوفان | رعد و برق | سیل |
|---|---|---|---|
| wind | storm | lightning | flood |
| خزان زمستان / بهار تابستان | خزان زمستان / بهار تابستان | تابستان / بهار | زمستان / بهار |

| ابر | صاف | آفتاب، خورشید | مهتاب، ماه |
|---|---|---|---|
| cloud | clear | sun | moon |
| خزان زمستان / بهار | تابستان | تابستان / بهار | خزان زمستان / بهار تابستان |

| خنک، سرد | گرم | معتدل | مرطوب |
|---|---|---|---|
| cold | warm | mild, neutral | humidity |
| خزان زمستان | تابستان / بهار | خزان / بهار | بهار تابستان |

### Exercise 2C:

۱) صحیح ۲) غلط ۳) صحیح ۴) صحیح ۵) غلط ۶) غلط ۷) صحیح

### Exercise 3A:

۱) امروز باران میبارد. / امروز باران است. ۲) امروز برف میبارد. / امروز برف است.

۳) امروز ژاله میبارد. / امروز ژاله است.

### Exercise 4B:

1. degrees celsius   2. cloudy   3. possibility   4. raning   5. report   6. temperature

Exercise 4C:

1. b      2. a      3. c      4. a & c      5. b & d

Exercise 6A:

۱) امروز هوا ابری است.      ۲) دیروز هوا بارانی بود.      ۳) امروز هوا برفی است.

۴) فردا هوا آفتابی است.      ۵) امشب آسمان مهتابی است.

Exercise 6B:

۱) کابل امروز برفی      ۲) کابل دیروز بارانی

۳) هرات امروز ابری، احتمال میرود باران ببارد      ۴) هرات صبح آفتابی

Exercise 6C:

۱) امروز ابری است و احتمال میرود باران ببارد. ۲) صباح هوای هرات آفتابی است.

۳) امروز برفی است.      ۴) دیروز هوای کابل بارانی بود و بسیار باران میبارید.

Exercise 7A:

۱) اگر هوا ابری باشد، سینما نمیروم.      ۲) اگر هوا سرد باشد، قهوهٔ گرم مینوشم.

۳) اگر هوا گرم باشد، آببازی میکنم.      ۴) اگر هوا برفی باشد، کالای گرم میپوشم.

۵) اگر هوا بارانی باشد، بالاپوشم را میپوشم.

Exercise 7B:

۱) اگر هوا خوب باشد، شریف میخواهد به هرات بیاید.

۲) اگر فردا هوا خوب باشد، شریف ساعت ۱۰ بجه میاید.

Exercise 7C:

۱) بمانم      ۲) برویم      ۳) نروم      ۴) آببازی کنیم      ۵) بپوشیم

Exercise 8A:

۱) دیشب وقتیکه نان میخوردیم، باد میوزید.

۲) دیروز وقتیکه مکتب میرفتم، باران میبارید.

۳) زمستان گذشته وقتیکه میبارید، ما در بیرون خانه بازی میکردیم.

۴) بهار قبل وقتیکه باران میبارید، در خانهٔ ما سیل آمد.

۵) بهار گذشته وقتیکه هوا ژاله میبارید، ما به میله نرفتیم،

۶) وقتیکه هوا گرم بود

Exercise 8B:

۱) دیروز وقتیکه باران میبارید، احمد به مکتب رفت.

۲) دیشب وقتیکه ژاله میبارید، من خواب بودم.

۳) هفته گذشته وقتیکه برف میبارید، زرغونه به خانهٔ ما آمد.

۴) زمستان گذشته وقتیکه شما کابل میرفتید، من در میدان هوایی بودم.

## Exercise 9A:
1. b        2. a        3. c        4. after receiving his message

## Exercise 10A:

خنك، شدید، سنگین، خراب

## Exercise 10B:

برف سنگین، باران شدید، باد شدید، هوا خنك، هوا خراب، هوا خوب

## Exercise 10C:

شریف:    تشکر که برایم تلیفون کردید. پروا نمیکند. به تماس هستیم.

کریم:    خیرباشد.

## Exercise 10D:

|  | a) ۳ | ۱ او در صنف بود. |
|---|---|---|
| ۴ دیروز ژالهٔ شدید بارید. |  | ۲ خوب به تماس هستیم. |

# LESSON 2

## Exercise 1B:

| طیاره | پرواز کردن | میدان هوایی | تکت فروشی | تکت طیاره |
|---|---|---|---|---|
| airplane | to fly | airport | travel agency | plane ticket |
| بکس | مسافر | گمرك | ترمینال میدان هوایی | نشست کردن |
| bag | passenger | customs | terminal | to land |
| پیلوت | استیورد/یس | تذکره/کارت هویت | سفر | پاسپورت |
| pilot | flight attendant | ID card | travel | passport |

## Exercise 2A:

| من سفر خواهم کرد.، ما سفر خواهیم کرد. <br> تو سفر خواهی کرد.، شما سفر خواهید کرد. <br> او سفر خواهی کرد.، آنها سفر خواهند کرد. | سفرکردن (سفرکن) |
|---|---|
| طیاره من پرواز خواهد کرد.، طیاره ما پرواز خواهد کرد. <br> تو پرواز خواهد کرد.، طیاره شما پرواز خواهد کرد. طیاره <br> او پرواز خواهد کرد.، طیاره آنها پرواز خواهد کرد. طیاره | پرواز کردن (پرواز کن) |
| طیاره من نشست خواهد کرد.، طیاره ما نشست خواهد کرد. <br> طیاره تو نشست خواهد کرد.، طیاره شما نشست خواهد کرد. <br> طیاره او نشست خواهد کرد.، طیاره آنها نشست خواهد کرد. | نشست کردن (نشست کن) |

Exercise 3A:

۱) شما به کجا خواهید رفت؟   ۲) آیا شما زمینی سفرخواهید رفت، یا هوایی؟

۳) شما برای رخصتی های تابستانی   ۴) شما هوایی سفر خواهید کرد یا زمینی؟
تان به کجا سفر خواهید کرد؟

Exercise 3B:

| ۴) صحیح | ۳) صحیح | ۲) غلط | ۱) صحیح |
|---|---|---|---|
| ۸) صحیح | ۷) صحیح | ۶) غلط | ۵) غلط |

Exercise 4A:

1. Afghan Airline    2. Ariana Airline    3. b    4. b    5. b    6. a

Exercise 4B:

1

| تکت فروش | چی کمک کرده میتوانم؟ | شریف | اینه،بفرمایید. |
|---|---|---|---|
| تکت فروش | سفرِ خوشی را برای تان آرزو میکنیم. | شریف | به چِشم. |
| تکت فروش | لطفاً چند لحظه صبر کنید. | شریف | طبعاً. |

2

| B | | A | |
|---|---|---|---|
| چی کمک کرده میتوانم؟ | √ | چی خدمت کرده میتوانم؟ | |
| شما در کدام روز ها پرواز دارید؟ | √ | شما در کدام تاریخ ها پرواز دارید؟ | |
| شما چند تکت میخواهید؟ | | شما چند تکت بکار دارید؟ | √ |
| شما چی قسم تکت میخواهید، یکطرفه یا تکت دوطرفه؟ | | شما تکت یکطرفه میخواهید یا تکت دوطرفه؟ | √ |
| قیمت های تکت یکطرفه و دوطرفه چند است؟ | √ | قیمت های هرکدامش چند است؟ | |
| برای چی وقت میخواهید؟ | | برای کدام تاریخ ها میخواهید؟ | √ |
| ما چند بکس را همراه خود برده میتوانیم؟ | | ما چند بکس را میتوانیم که همراه خود ببریم؟ | √ |

Exercise 4D:

| ۴) صحیح | ۳) صحیح | ۲) غلط | ۱) صحیح |
|---|---|---|---|
| ۸) صحیح | ۷) صحیح | ۶) غلط | ۵) صحیح |
| | ۱۱) غلط | ۱۰) صحیح | ۹) صحیح |

## Exercise 5A:

| | |
|---|---|
| What time is your flight? | ۱) پرواز خودتان ساعت چند است؟ |
| S/he bought her ticket. | ۲) او تکت خودش را خریده بود. |
| They are waiting for their flight. | ۳) آنها معطل طیارهٔ خودشان هستند. |
| I got my passport. | ۴) من پاسپورت خودم را گرفتم. |
| Did you see your brother? | ۵) تو برادر خودت را دیدی؟ |

## Exercise 5B:

۱) لطفاً پاسپورت خودتان را نشان بدهید.     ۲) من خودم بکسم را باز میکنم.

۳) استیوردیس خودش به من گفت.         ۴) من برادرم را با خودم در این سفر میبرم.

۵) آیا شما رخصتی های آیندهٔ خودتان را پلان کردید؟

## Exercise 6A:

| | | |
|---|---|---|
| ۳) سه بجهٔ صبح | ۲) چار صبح | ۱) پس فردا |
| ۵) دیگرصباح | ۴) ساعت دوازده بجه چاشت | |

## Exercise 6B:

| | |
|---|---|
| | چی خدمت کرده میتوانم؟ |
| √ | بس های تان چی وقت حرکت میکند؟ |
| √ | قیمت تکت برای هر نفر چند است؟ |
| √ | برای شش نفر تکت دارید؟ |
| | برای دیگر صباح داریم، آیا میخواهید؟ |
| √ | آیا از بکس هایم پیسه میگیرید؟ |

## Exercise 6C:
1. b          2. a          3. a

## Exercise 6D:

۵) صحیح     ۴) غلط     ۳) غلط     ۲) صحیح     ۱) صحیح

# LESSON 3
## Exercise 1B:
1. b          2. 20 minutes          3. restaurants, shopping malls, and clothing stores
4. b, f, g, h     5. c & d          6. a                    7. via the hotel's website

## Exercise 1C:

۱) راحت

۲) آغای شریف پویل، از ساعت ۹ صبح تا ۹ شب

۳) پنج سال

۴) ا تلویزیون، انترنت، تلیفون، کمپیوتر، چپرکت ، کمپل، بالشت، روجایی، جانخشکان، تشناب و حمام

۵) شامپو ، صابون و آب گرم و سرد

Exercise 1D:

| ۴) صحیح | ۳) صحیح | ۲) غلط | ۱) صحیح |
|---|---|---|---|
| | ۷) صحیح | ۶) غلط | ۵) صحیح |

Exercise 2A:

| ۲) تقریباً دو سال پیش | ۱) یك سال پیش |
|---|---|

Exercise 2B:
clean rooms, phone, internet

Exercise 2C:
1. Mazaar Hotel
2. It is a modern hotel and has clean rooms, phone, and internet.
3. b
4. a
5. the hotel phone number

Exercise 3A:

۱) هوتل ریزرف کرده او دیروز قبل از ما ، برای خودش یك تكت ریزرف کرده بود .

۲) تلیفون کرده      او هفته گذشته پیش از اینکه بیاید ، برایم تلیفون کرده بود .

۳) ایمیل کرده      دیشب پیش از اینکه خواب شوم، برایش ایمیل کرده بودم.

۴) دیده      من این فلم را تماشا نکردم ، چونکه آنرا قبلاً دیده بودم .

۵) شنیده      من قبلاً شنیده بودم که آنها میایند .

۶) خریده      او برای خودش کالانخرید چون پدرش هفته قبل برایش کالاخریده بود .

Exercise 3B:

۱) آیا شما قبلاً به افغانستان رفته بودید؟

۲) آیا تا به حال کلانترین هوتل جهان را دیده بودید؟

۳) شما در کدام هوتل اتاق ریزرف کرده بودید؟

۴) شما چی وقت از طریق تلیفون اتاق کرایه کرده بودید؟

۵) آخرین باری که با کشتی سفر کرده بودید ، چی وقت بود

Exercise 4B:

١) کابل          ٢) دونفره          ٣) هژدهٔ سرطان          ٤) هژدهٔ سرطان

٥) یک نفره          ٦) دونفره          ٧) بلی          ٨) شمارهٔ کارت بانکی

Exercise 5B:

تا هوتل مزار چند میبری؟

Exercise 5C:

1. a          2. b          3. b          4. a

## REVIEW OF CHAPTER 9

Exercise 1A:

١) کابل : ابری، بلندترین درجهٔ حرارت۲۵ ، پایینترین درجهٔ حرارت ۲۰ ، برف میبارد .

٢) هرات: ابری،باران شدید خواهد بارید، بلندترین درجهٔ حرارت ۲۰ ، پایینترین درجهٔ حرارت۱۷

٣) کندهار:آفتابی و گاهی ابری، بلندترین درجهٔ حرارت ۳۰ ، پایینترین درجهٔ حرارت۲۵، برف میبارد .

٤) مزار شریف: ابری، باد شدید ، برف سنگین خواهد بارید، بلندترین درجهٔ حرارت ۲۰ ، پایینترین درجهٔ حرارت۱۵

٥) جلال آباد: ابری، باران شدید می بارید، احتمال طوفان شدید ، بلندترین درجهٔ حرارت ۳۰ ، پایینترین درجهٔ حرارت ۲۰، برف میبارد .

Exercise 2A:

1. b          2. c          3. a          4. b          5. b          6. a

## CHAPTER TEN

## LESSON 1

Exercise 1A:

1. c          2. b          3. b          4. b

Exercise 1B:

1. a          2. a          3. b          4. b

Exercise 3B:

| | | | | | |
|---|---|---|---|---|---|
| museum | موزیم | ٧ | documents | اسناد٦٦ | ١ |
| contact | تماس بگیرید | ٨ | sights | جاهای دیدنی | ٢ |
| passengers | مسافرین | ٩ | translators | ترجمان | ٣ |
| guests | مهمانان | ١٠ | finding/ to fine | پیدا نمودن | ٤ |

| unknown people | اشخاص ناشناس | ۱۱ | favorite | دلخواه | ۵ |
|---|---|---|---|---|---|
| during | درجریان | ۱۲ | valuable things | چیزهای قیمتی | ۶ |

## Exercise 3C:

۱) غلط     ۲) غلط     ۳) صحیح   ۴) صحیح   ۵) صحیح   ۶) صحیح   ۷) غلط

## Exercise 4A:

۱) اکثر مردم بوک کردن اتاق را از طریق انترنت خوش دارند .

۲) او همیشه رفتن به رستورانت افغان را خوش دارد ، تا کباب گوسفند بخورد .

۳) من از کارکردن در هوتل خوشم میاید .

۴) برای دیدن زیارت سخی شما باید در روز پنجشنبه با بس های هوتل بروید

## Exercise 4B:

دیدن ، بردن، راجستر کردن، نوشیدن

## Exercise 4C:

۱) باید بس های هوتل را بگیرند .     ۲) روز های پنجشنبه و جمعه ساعت هشت صبح.

۳) باید به دفتر هوتل مزار بروند .

## Exercise 5A:

1. a

| شرکت توریزم بلخ | شرکت توریزم آریانا | خدمات |
|---|---|---|
| √ | | Takes the passengers to دریایی آمو |
| √ | | Takes the passengers to the museum between 2 and 4 in the afternoon. |
| √ | √ | Provides tickets for passengers. |
| | √ | Provides meals three times. |
| √ | | Takes the passenger to a traditional restaurant. |
| | √ | Works every week three. |
| √ | | Works every day. |

## Exercise 6A:

شوهر:    بس های هوتل،  شرکت آریانا،  شرکت بلخ.

زن:       بس های هوتل،شرکت بلخ .

## Exercise 6B:

۱) صحیح      ۲) غلط      ۳) غلط      ۴) صحیح      ۵) صحیح

## Exercise 8A:

1. a       2. c       3. a       4. b       5. b

# LESSON 2

## Exercise 1A:

۴) دهان/دهن      ۳) بینی      ۲) چشم      ۱) سر

۸) پا/پای      ۷) پنجه، انگشت ، کلک      ۶) دست      ۵) گوش

## Exercise 1B:

۱. head   ۲. eye   ۳. nose   ۴. mouth   ۵. ear   ۶.hand   ۷.finger   ۸. foot

## Exercise 1C:

۱) چشم   ۲) دست   ۳) دهان   ۴) دست   ۵) کلک   ۶ ) بینی   ۷) پا   ۸ ) گوش

## Exercise 2A:

سر            چشم            دست            پا/پای

## Exercise 2B:

۱) مریض هستم      ۲) گرمی      ۳) به دفتر هوتل      ۴) سر، چشم ها، دستها، پاها

## Exercise 3A:

| | | | |
|---|---|---|---|
| ۳ | دست هایش درد میکند . | ۱ | سرش درد میکند . |
| ۴ | پا هایش درد میکند . | ۲ | چشم هایش درد میکند . |

## Exercise 3B:

۱   من نمیتوانم که موسیقی بشنوم چونکه  گوشم درد میکند . My ear hurts.

۲   او نمیتواند که نان بخورد چونکه  دندانهایش درد میکند . دندانها His teeth hurt

۳   من نمیتوانم که نوشته کنم چونکه   دستم درد میکند . My hand hurts.

۴   او نمیتواند که فلم ببیند چونکه  چشم هایش درد میکند . His eyes hurt.

۵   او نمیتواند که به صنف برود چونکه  پایش درد میکند . Her ankle hurts.

۶   من نمیتوانم که تایپ کنم چونکه   کلک هایم  (انگشتانیم) My finger hurts.
درد میکند .

## Exercise 4A:

1. b        2. b        3. b        4. c

## Exercise 4B:

دواخانه            داکتر            دوا            فارماسست

## Exercise 5:

۱) صحیح ۲) غلط ۳) غلط ۴) غلط ۵) صحیح ۶) غلط ۷) غلط

## Exercise 6A:

1. pills for body aches, headache pills, pain relief ointment     4. a
2. b     5. a
3. b     6. b

## Exercise 6B:

| ترجمه | شریف | دواخانه دار | سوالات |
|---|---|---|---|
| Is there a doctor here in your pharmacy? | √ | | شما در دواخانهٔ تان داکتر دارید؟ |
| Why? Is everything okay? | | √ | چرا خیریت است؟ |
| What illness does she have? | | √ | چی تکلیف دارند؟ |
| Where should I go now to visit a doctor? | √ | | حالا به کجا بروم که داکتر را ببینم؟ |
| Thanks. How much is it? | √ | | تشکر چند میشود؟ |

## Exercise 7A:

| | | |
|---|---|---|
| پاهایم درد میکنند | دست هایم درد میکند | جانم درد میکند |
| سر چرخ هستم. | تب دارم. | چشم هایم درد میکند. |
| بینی ام بند است. | چشم هایم خارش میکند. | دلبد هستم. |
| | کم زور هستم. | استفراغ کردم. |

## Exercise 7C:

| ۱ | cough | سرفه |
|---|---|---|
| ۲ | vomit | استفراغ |
| ۳ | out of it | گنس |
| ۴ | nausea | دلبد |
| ۵ | dizzy | سرچرخ |
| ۶ | itch | خارش |
| ۷ | weak | کم زور |

## Exercise 7D:

| | | | |
|---|---|---|---|
| کی مریض است؟ | √ | چی تکلیف دارید؟ | √ |
| آیا استفراغ هم میکنید؟ | | آیا گنس هستید؟ | |
| آیا سرفه هم میکنید؟ | √ | آیا سرچرخ هستید؟ | √ |

Exercise 7E:

او ریزش کرده.    او تب دارد.    او چشمش درد میکند.

او سرش درد میکند.    او دلش درد میکند.    او سرفه میکند.

Exercise 7F:

| غلط | صحیح | جملات | |
|---|---|---|---|
| | √ | داکتر پرسید (کی مریض است؟) | ۱ |
| √ | | شریف گفت: (زنم مریض است.) | ۲ |
| √ | | زن شریف از دیروز مریض است. | ۳ |
| | √ | او فکر میکند که تب دارد. | ۴ |
| √ | | او سرفه نمیکند. | ۵ |
| | √ | او دلبد است. | ۶ |
| √ | | او چشمایش خارش نمیکند. | ۷ |
| √ | | او بینی اش باز است. | ۸ |
| | √ | داکتر برای معاینه کردن زن میرویس، از او اجازه گرفت. | ۹ |
| | √ | شریف زنش را کمک کرد. | ۱۰ |

Exercise 8:

| coffee shop چایخانه (۳ | publishing house چاپخانه (۲ | factory کارخانه (۱ |
|---|---|---|
| upstairs (room) بالاخانه (۶ | kitchen آشپزخانه (۵ | guest house مهمانخانه (۴ |

casino قمارخانه (۷

## Exercise 9A:
1. heat stroke, food allergies
2. a
3. drink lots of fluids, rest, and have lots of fruits and vegetables
4. a) قطره چکان بینی    b) گولی جان دردی    c) گولی حساسیت    d) شربت تقویه

## Exercise 9B:
۱) روز سه دفعه بعد از نان    ۲) هر شب یکدانه
۳) هر شش ساعت یک قاشق    ۴) هر دوازده ساعت دو قطره

## Exercise 11A:
1. Agra's Bazaar, ancient temples, Indian ocean, Taj Mahal
2. b
3. depart 6:00 a.m.
   arrives 9:30 a.m.

## Exercise 11B:
۱) صحیح    ۲) صحیح    ۳) غلط    ۴) غلط    ۵) صحیح
۶) غلط    ۷) صحیح    ۸) غلط    ۹) غلط

# LESSON 3

## Exercise 1A:
| | | |
|---|---|---|
| 1. b | 3. a | 5. b |
| 2. very hot | 4. b | 6. b |

## Exercise 2B:
۱) صحیح ۲) غلط ۳) غلط ۴) صحیح ۵) صحیح ۶) صحیح ۷) غلط ۸) صحیح

## Exercise 3:
1. to have more time
2. b
3. b
4. He will go to work and visit شیرین parents.
5. b

## Exercise 4A:
۱) غیر ممکن    ۲) ممکن    ۳) غیر ممکن    ۴) ممکن

## Exercise 4B:
۱) کاشکه یک موتر میداشتم.
۲) کاشکه پول میداشتیم که به سفر میرفتیم.
۳) کاشکه جور میبودند که به سینما میرفتند.
۴) کاشکه انترنت میداشت که ایمیل نوشته میکرد.

Exercise 5A:

۱) شنبه، دوشنبه و جمعه پرواز از مزار ۱۱، نشست در کابل ۱۲:۳۰

۲) یکشنبه، سه شنبه و پنجشنبه پرواز از مزار ۸، نشست در کابل نه ونیم صبح

Exercise 5B:

۱) غلط      ۲) غلط      ۳) صحیح      ۴) صحیح      ۵) غلط      ۶) صحیح      ۷) صحیح

Exercise 6A:

1. b                    2. stormy                    3. a

Exercise 6B:

۱) صحیح      ۲) غلط      ۳) غلط      ۴) صحیح      ۵) صحیح

Exercise 7:

1. a                              5. three hours later
2. a                              6. c
3. b                              7. I want to checkout.
4. the keys and money

# APPENDIX B: TRANSCRIPTS

## CHAPTER ONE

## LESSON 1
### Exercise 3B:

| Hello! (Peace be with you) | [asalām ō alaykom!] | السلام عليكم! |
| Hello! (Peace be with you) | [walaykom salām!] | وعليكم السلام! |
| Hello! (Peace be with you) | [asalām ō alaykom!] | السلام عليكم! |
| Hello! (Peace be with you) | [walaykom salām!] | وعليكم السلام! |
| Hello! (Peace be with you) | [salām alaykom!] | سلام عليكم! |
| Hello! (Peace be with you) | [walaykom salām!] | وعليكم السلام! |
| Hello! (Peace be with you) | [salām!] | سلام! |
| Hello! (Peace be with you) | [walaykom!] | وعليكم! |

## REVIEW
### Exercise 1A:

| [asalām ō alaykom! jāwed jān] | السلام عليكم! جاوید جان. |
| [walaykom salām! parwez jān] | وعليكم السلام! پرویز جان. |
| [salām! laylā jān] | سلام! فرید جان. |
| [walaykom! farid jān] | وعليكم! لیلا جان. |

### Exercise 1B:

| ا | السلام عليكم! |
| ب | وعليكم السلام، نام تان چيست؟ |
| ا | نامم اميد است، نام شما چيست؟ |
| ب | نامم نازنين است، تخلص تان چيست؟ |
| ا | تخلصم فيضى است، تخلص شما چيست؟ |
| ب | تخلصم سليمى است، شما از كجا هستيد؟ |
| ا | من از ولايت كاپيسا هستم، شما از كابل هستيد؟ |
| ب | بلى من از كابل هستم. |

# CHAPTER TWO

## LESSON 2
Exercise 1:

| | | |
|---|---|---|
| Farid | سلام، لیلا جان | |
| Laylā | وعلیکم، فرید جان | |
| Farid | نمبر تلیفون تان چند است؟ | |
| Laylā | 07004002848 | |
| Farid | نمبر تلیفون شما چند است؟ | |
| Laylā | 0799202044 | |
| Farid | خدا حافظ | |
| Laylā | خدا حافظ | |

# CHAPTER THREE

## LESSON 1
Exercise 8:

| | | |
|---|---|---|
| لیلا | السلام و علیکم، فرید جان. | |
| فرید | وعلیکم السلام، لیلا جان. | |
| لیلا | چطور هستید؟ | |
| فرید | خوب هستم. تشکر، شما چطور هستید؟ | |
| لیلا | من هم خوب هستم، تشکر.s. | |
| لیلا | مانده نباشید . | |
| فرید | جور باشید . | |
| لیلا | خدا حافظ . | |
| فرید | خدا حافظ . | |

## LESSON 3:
Exercise 7A:

| | | |
|---|---|---|
| نازنین | السلام و علیکم! مانده نباشید . | |
| امید | وعلیکم السلام! زنده باشید . | |

| | |
|---|---|
| نازنین | ببخشین، نام تان چیست؟ |
| امید | نامم امید است. نام شما چیست؟ |
| نازنین | نامم نازنین است. تخلص تان چیست؟ |
| امید | تخلصم فیضی است. تخلص شما چیست؟ |
| نازنین | تخلصم سلیمی است. شما از کجا هستید؟ |
| امید | من از ولایت کاپیسا هستم. شما از ولایت کابل هستید؟ |
| نازنین | بلی، من از ولایت کابل هستم. شما از کدام ولسوالی هستید؟ |
| امید | من از ولسوالی نجراب هستم. |
| نازنین | از کدام قریه هستید؟ |
| امید | از قریه بالا هستم. |
| نازنین | ازدیدن تان خوشحال شدم. |
| امید | من همچنان |
| نازنین | به امان خدا. |
| امید | خدا حافظ. |

## Exercise 12:

| | |
|---|---|
| میوند | سلام احمد جان مانده نباشید، چطور هستید؟ |
| احمد | وعلیکم میوند جان زنده باشید، من خوب هستم، شما چطور هستید؟ |
| میوند | من هم خوب هستم، احمد جان شما از کجا هستید؟ |
| احمد | من از تاجکستان هستم. |
| میوند | شما در کجا زنده گی میکنید؟ |
| احمد | من در شهر بدخشان زنده گی میکنم. شما اصلاً از کجا هستید؟ |
| میوند | من اصلاً از افغانستان هستم. |
| احمد | شما از ولایت کابل هستید؟ |
| میوند | نه، من از ولایت کابل نیستم، من از ولایت کندهار هستم. |
| امید | من از ولسوالی نجراب هستم. |
| نازنین | از کدام قریه هستید؟ |
| امید | از قریه بالا هستم. |

# REVIEW

Exercise 10ABC:

| | |
|---|---|
| زن | السلام علیکم! |
| مرد | وعلیکم السلام، چطور هستید؟ خوب هستید؟ |
| زن | شکر، زنده باشید، شما خوب هستید؟ |
| مرد | تشکر زنده باشید. فامیل خوب هستند؟ |
| زن | شکر، زنده باشید، سلامت باشید، بخیر آمدید؟ |
| مرد | تشکر، بلی، فقط یک ساعت پیش رسیدم. خانه خیریت است؟ فامیل خوب هستند؟ |
| زن | خیر و خیریت است. |
| مرد | من باز همرای شما میبینم، فعلا خدا حافظ! |
| زن | به امان خدا! سلام بگویید. |

Exercise 11AB:

| | |
|---|---|
| زن | السلام علیکم! |
| مرد | وعلیکم السلام، چطور هستید؟ خوب هستید؟ |
| زن | شکر، زنده باشید، شما خوب هستید؟ |
| مرد | تشکر زنده باشید. فامیل خوب هستند؟ |
| زن | شکر، زنده باشید، سلامت باشید، بخیر آمدید؟ |
| مرد | تشکر، بلی، فقط یک ساعت پیش رسیدم. خانه خیریت است؟ فامیل خوب هستند؟ |
| زن | خیر و خیریت است. |
| مرد | من باز همرای شما میبینم، فعلا خدا حافظ! |
| زن | به امان خدا! سلام بگویید. |

# CHAPTER FOUR

# LESSON 1:

Exercise 6A:

نامم زلمی است، من از کابل هستم، حالا من در امریکا زنده گی میکنم. اینجا دفترم است، من در دفترم یک کمپیوتر، یک کیبورد، دو لود سپیکر، یک موس، یک میز، یک چوکی، سه کتاب، دو ستپلر، دو سکاشتیپ، سه تلیفون، یک الماری کتاب، یک پرینتر، یک ماشین کاپی و یک سکینر دارم.

## Exercise 13:

| | | |
|---|---|---|
| لیلا جان، اینجا کجا است؟ | میرویس | |
| اینجا صنفم است. | لیلا | |
| شما چند تا همصنفی دارید؟ | میرویس | |
| من شش تا همصنفی دارم. | لیلا | |
| در صنف، شما چی دارید؟ | میرویس | |
| در صنف ما  سه دانه میز، هشت دانه چوکی،  یک دانه کمپیوتر، یک دانه پروجکتور، دو دانه تخته، سه دانه تخته پاک و تباشیر داریم. | لیلا | |
| در صنف تان چند نفر بچه و چند نفر دختر است؟ | میرویس | |
| در صنف ما،  دو تا دختر و  چار تا بچه است. | لیلا | |

# LESSON 2
## Exercise 6:

| | | |
|---|---|---|
| شریف، شریف،  کتاب انگلیسی تان درکجا ست؟ | نازنین | |
| کتاب انگلیسی ام در بین الماری کتاب ها است. | شریف | |
| الماری کتاب ها؟ | نازنین | |
| بلی. | شریف | |
| اینجا نیست. | نازنین | |
| ها، در روی میز است. | شریف | |
| بلی، اینجا است.  تشکر | نازنین | |
| خواهش میکنم. | شریف | |

## Exercise 10A:

| | | |
|---|---|---|
| سلام، نامم شریف است، نام شما چیست؟ | الف | |
| سلام شریف جان، نام من جاوید است. | ب | |
| جاوید جان، شما از کابل هستید؟ | الف | |
| نی، من از مزار هستم. | ب | |
| من و شما چند نفر همصنفی داریم؟ | الف | |
| ما ۱۲ نفر همصنفی داریم. | ب | |
| همصنفی های ما در کجا هستند؟ | الف | |

| | |
|---|---|
| ب | آنها در بیرون صنف هستند . |
| الف | اینجا ، در صنف چند چوکی داریم؟ |
| ب | ما ۱۳ چوکی داریم. آیا شما کتاب دارید؟ |
| الف | بلی ، من کتاب دارم. |
| ب | کتاب تان در کجا است؟ |
| الف | کتاب در بین بکسم است. کتاب شما درکجا است. |
| ب | من کتاب ندارم. |

# LESSON 3

Exercise 5A:

| | |
|---|---|
| فرید | لیلا جان، شما هر روز در صنف چی میکنید؟ |
| لیلا | ما در صنف کتاب میخوانیم، گفتگو میکنیم، به گپ های معلم گوش میکنیم. |
| فرید | بسیار خوب. |
| لیلا | شما هر روز در صنف چی میکنید؟ |
| فرید | ما نوشته میکنیم، گپ میزنیم، و ویدیو سیل میکنیم. |

Exercise 12A:

| | |
|---|---|
| الف | تك تك تك ... |
| ب | بفرمایید! |
| الف | اجازه است، داخل شوم. |
| ب | بلی، لطفاً بفرمایید . اینجا بالای چوکی بشنید . |
| الف | تشکر! فرید جان، کتاب دری تان در کجاست؟ |
| ب | کتاب دری؟ |
| الف | بلی |
| ب | اینجا است. |
| الف | لطفاً، آن را بدهید. |
| ب | بگیرید . |
| الف | فرید جان، یك پرسان دارم. |
| ب | بفرمایید . |

| | |
|---|---|
| الف | آیا شما کتاب انگلیسی هم دارید . |
| ب | بلی، آنجا بالای میز است . |
| الف | تشکر، |
| ب | رینگ رینگ... میرویس جان لطفاً همان تلیفون را بردارید . و برایم بدهید . |
| الف | بفرمایید . |
| ب | ببخشید . |
| الف | خدا حافظ! |
| ب | به امان خدا! لطفاً همان دروازه را بسته کنید . |

## REVIEW

Exercise 3AB:

| | |
|---|---|
| لیلا | فرید جان، لپتاپ در کجاست؟ |
| فرید | لپتاپ، در بالای میز است . |
| لیلا | در بالای میز نیست . |
| فرید | در بین الماری کتاب ببین . |
| لیلا | ها، اینجا است . تشکر . |
| فرید | لیلا لطفاً همان کتاب انگلیسی را بیاور . |
| لیلا | در کجا است؟ |
| فرید | در الماری کتاب ها و در زیر کتاب دری است . |
| لیلا | ها، اینجا است . دیگر چی کار دارید؟ |
| فرید | لطفاً، تلیفون مبایلم را هم بیاورید . |
| لیلا | تلیفون مبایل؟ |
| فرید | بلی، مبایلم در بین بکسم است . |
| لیلا | اینه، بفرمایید، بگیرید . |
| فرید | تشکر . |
| لیلا | تشکر، |

Exercise 5:

السلام علیکم، دروازه را باز کنید، دروازه را بسته کنید، در روی چوکی بشینید، طرف نقشه ببینید، کتاب را بردارید، کتاب را بخوانید، کتاب را بمانید، آیفون را بردارید و ویدیو را سیل کنید، آیفون را بمانید، قلم را بردارید و نوشته کنید، قلم را بمانید، گیلاس را بدهید، سی دی را بگیرید، سی دی را بدهید، پس بروید و در روی چوکی بنشینید، خدا حافظ.

# CHAPTER FIVE

## LESSON 1

Exercise 4A:

۳۸۳، ۵۰۰، ۷۸۳، ۲۳۴، ۳۴۰، ۴۳۵،۴۵۸، ۱۲۳، ۷۰۰، ۵۵۰

Exercise 5B:

۷:۲۰، ۳:۰۵، ۱:۱۵، ۱۰:۲۵، ۲:۴۰، ۱۱:۲۰، ۱۲:۰۵، ۵:۱۰، ۹:۴۰، ۱:۲۰

Exercise 5C:

| | |
|---|---|
| سلام، | الف |
| وعلیکم، | ب |
| ببخشید، ساعت چند بجه است؟ | الف |
| چار و پنجاه دقیقه | ب |
| تشکر | الف |
| | |
| سلام، | الف |
| وعلیکم، | ب |
| ببخشید، ساعت چند بجه است؟ | الف |
| سه و پانزده دقیقه | ب |
| تشکر | الف |
| | |
| سلام، | الف |
| وعلیکم، | ب |
| ببخشید، ساعت چند بجه است؟ | الف |
| سه و پانزده دقیقه | ب |
| تشکر | الف |
| | |
| سلام، | الف |
| وعلیکم، | ب |
| ببخشید، ساعت چند بجه است؟ | الف |
| ساعت ده و نیم است. | ب |
| تشکر | الف |

Exercise 14:

| | | |
|---|---|---|
| میرویس | شریف، ساعت چند بجه است؟ | |
| شریف | ساعت یک و بیست دقیقه است. | |
| میرویس | شما امروز چی میکنید؟ | |
| شریف | امروز، من کتاب میخوانم، نوشته میکنم و تلویزیون سیل میکنم. | |
| میرویس | شما صبح ساعت دو بجه چی میکنید؟ | |
| شریف | صبح ساعت ۱۲ بجه کتاب میخوانم. | |
| میرویس | صبح تاریخ چند است؟ | |
| شریف | صبح تاریخ سوم فبروری ، سال ۲۰۱۱ است. | |
| میرویس | تشکر. | |

# LESSON 2

Exercise 6:

| | |
|---|---|
| شریف | لیلا جان، شما معمولاً هر شب چی میکنید؟ |
| لیلا | من معمولاً ساعت ۷ بجه نان میخورم، باز کار خانگی ام را انجام میدهم، تا ساعت ۹ بجه کار خانگی ام را انجام میدهم، بعد از کارخانگی یک ساعت تلویزیون سیل میکنم، گاهی به موسیقی گوش میکنم، ساعت ۱۰ و ۳۰ دقیقه کتاب میخوانم و بعد از آن خواب میشوم. |

Exercise 11:

نام من لیلا است، من محصل هستم، معمولاً هفتهٔ شش روز به پوهنتون میروم، در پوهنتون همیشه کتاب میخوانم، گفتگو میکنم و گاهی نوشته میکنم. معمولاً بعد از پوهنتون به کار میروم و چهارساعت کار میکنم. بعد از کار، گاهی ورزش میکنم، و بعد از ورزش اکثراً به خانه میروم. همچنان معمولاً هرشب یک ساعت کارخانگی ام را انجام میدهم ، و بعد از آن خواب میشوم. در صنف معمولاً هفتهٔ یک بار تلویزیون سیل میکنیم.

Exercise 13:

| | |
|---|---|
| لیلا | شریف جان، صبح، تاریخ چند است؟ |
| شریف | صبح سه شنبه ، دوم حمل است. |
| لیلا | شما صبح چی میکنید؟ |

| | |
|---|---|
| شریف | من معمولاً در روز های سه شنبه ساعت ۶ بیدار میشوم، از ساعت ۶ تا ۷ ورزش میکنم، ساعت ۷ شاور میگیرم، ساعت ۷ و ۱۰ دقیقه کالایم را میپوشم، ساعت ۷ و ۳۰ دقیقه چای صبح را میخورم، ساعت ۸ به پوهنتون میروم، از ساعت ۸ تا ۱ بجه در پوهنتون هستم، ساعت ۱ و ۲۰ دقیقه به کار میروم، ساعت ۱ و ۳۰ نان چاشت میخورم، ساعت ۵ بجه خانه میروم، ساعت ۷ نان شب را میخورم، از ساعت ۸ تا ۱۰ کارخانگی ام را انجام میدهم و ساعت ۱۰ خواب میشوم. |
| لیلا | شما تلویزیون سیل نمیکنید؟ |
| شریف | نه چون وقت ندارم. |
| لیلا | آیا شما به موسیقی گوش میکنید؟ |
| شریف | بلی من همیشه به موسیقی گوش میکنم. |
| میرویس | |

# LESSON 3
### Exercise 2:

| | |
|---|---|
| شریف | زرغونه جانه شما در روز ها رخصتی چی میکنید؟ |
| زرغونه | من معمولاً به کتابخانه میروم، گاهی به پارک میروم، به میله میروم، اکثراً به سینما میروم، دوش میکنم، غذا میپزم، و استراحت میکنم. شما در روز ها رخصتی چی میکنید؟ |
| شریف | من اکثراً به مسجد میروم، دوش میکنم، فوتبال بازی میکنم و گاهی به پارک میروم، آببازی میکنم، به رستورانت میروم و سودا میخرم. |

### Exercise 4A:

| | |
|---|---|
| شریف | لسلام علیکم، میرویس جان، چطور هستید؟ |
| میرویس | وعلیکم، شریف جان، من خوب هستم، تشکر شما چطور هستید؟ |
| شریف | من هم خوب هستم، میرویس جان در روزهای رخصتی معمولاً شما کجا میروید؟ |
| میرویس | والله، شریف جان من و دوستهایم معمولاً به میله میرویم. |
| شریف | کجا به میله میروید؟ |
| میرویس | ما اکثراً به پارک زرنگار. |
| شریف | خوب قصه کنید، که در آنجا چی میکنید؟ |
| میرویس | در آنجا غذا میپزیم، والیبال بازی میکنیم، آببازی میکنیم و کمی هم استراحت میکنیم. شما در روزهای رخصتی به کجا میروید؟ |
| شریف | من اکثراً هیچ جای نمیروم و در خانه میمانم. |

| | |
|---|---|
| میرویس | در خانه چی میکنید؟ |
| شریف | در خانه گاهی کتاب میخوانم، معمولاً دوش میکنم، اکثراً کارخانگی ام را انجام میدهم و استراحت میکنم. |

## Exercise 13

| | |
|---|---|
| شریف | میرویس جان، ما امروز ساعت ۱۰ بجه به سینما میرویم، آیا شما همراه ما میروید. |
| میرویس | بلی شریف جان میروم، در سینما کدام فلم است؟ |
| شریف | یک فلم امریکایی است، آیا از فلم امریکایی خوش ات میآید؟ |
| میرویس | بلی از فلم امریکایی خوشم میآید اما از فلم پاکستانی خوشم نمیآید. شما چطور؟ |
| شریف | والله من از فلم امریکایی کم خوشم میاید اما از فلم هندی بسیار خوشم میاید. |

## REVIEW
### Exercise 5A:

| | |
|---|---|
| شریف | میرویس جان، به کجا میروید؟ |
| میرویس | به کتابخانه میروم. |
| شریف | صبر کنید، من هم میروم. خوب، برویم. |
| میرویس | میرویس جان خبر داری، یک ماه بعد پوهنتون رخصت میشود؟ |
| شریف | راستی؟ |
| میرویس | بلی، تو برای رخصتی ها چی پلان داری؟ |
| شریف | انشالله، من ماه آینده به امریکا میروم و در آنجا در ایالت فلوریدا تفریح میکنم. شما در ماه آینده چی پلان دارید؟ |
| میرویس | من ماه آینده به مزار میروم و با فامیلم به میله میروم. |
| شریف | آیا صباح جمعه است؟ |
| میرویس | بلی! |
| شریف | صباح ما به پارک میرویم، آیا شما هم میروید؟ |
| میرویس | بلی، شما ساعت چند بجه میروید؟ |
| شریف | ساعت ۹ بجهٔ صبح |
| میرویس | آیا شما موتر دارید؟ |
| شریف | بلی ما موتر داریم. |
| میرویس | خوب، درست است، صباح میبینم تان. |

# CHAPTER SIX

## LESSON 1
Exercise 7A:

| | |
|---|---|
| احمد | السلام و علیکم، ببخشید! اینجا دفتر ثبت نام است؟ |
| پلوشه | بلی بفرمائید! |
| احمد | مانده نباشید، خواهر جان. |
| پلوشه | تشکر زنده باشید، نام شما چیست؟ |
| احمد | نامم احمد پوپل است. |
| پلوشه | نام پدر تان چیست؟ |
| احمد | نام پدرم عبدالکریم است. |
| پلوشه | نام پدرکلان تان چیست؟ |
| احمد | نام پدرکلانم حاجی عبدالرحیم است. |
| پلوشه | شما مجرد هستید یا متاهل؟ |
| احمد | من مجرد هستم. |
| پلوشه | شما چند اولاد دارید؟ |
| احمد | من چار اولاد دارم. |
| پلوشه | چند بچه و چند دختر دارید؟ |
| احمد | نام خدا! دو بچه و دو دختر دارم. |
| پلوشه | نام های شان چیست؟ |
| احمد | نام بچه هایم اجمل و ایمل است و نام دختر هایم ملالی و گلالی میباشد. |
| پلوشه | شما چند برادر دارید؟ |
| احمد | من سه برادر دارم. نام های شان میرویس، همایون و هارون است. |
| پلوشه | و چند خواهر دارید؟ |
| احمد | من یک خواهر دارم. نامش مرضیه است. |
| پلوشه | تشکر |
| احمد | خواهش میکنم. |

# LESSON 2

Exercise 7A:

| | |
|---|---|
| فهیم قد بلند دارد ، رنگ موی هایش سیاه است و رنگ چشم هایش هم سیاه است. | فهیم |
| دیوید قد بلند دارد ، رنگ موی هایش زرد است، و رنگ چشم هایش سبز است. | دیوید |
| جسیکا قد میانه دارد ، رنگ موی هایش طلایی است، و رنگ چشم هایش آبی است. | جسیکا |
| ملالی قد میانه دارد ، رنگ موی هایش قهوه یی است، و رنگ چشم هایش هم قهوه یی است. | ملالی |
| حاجی رحیم قد کوتاه دارد ، رنگ موی هایش سفید است، و رنگ چشم هایش سیاه است. | حاجی رحیم |
| شریف قد میانه دارد ، رنگ موی هایش خاکستری است، و رنگ چشم هایش قهوه یی است. | شریف |

Exercise 8AB:

| | |
|---|---|
| فهیم، جان والدین تان از کجا هستند؟ | جان |
| پدرم از مزار و مادرم از کابل است. | فهیم |
| فامیل های افغان بسیار کلان هستند. آیا فامیل پدر و مادر تان هم کلان است؟ | جان |
| فامیل پدر بسیار کلان نیستند اما فامیل مادرم کلان است. | فهیم |
| اعضای فامیل پدر تان چند نفر هستند؟ | جان |
| اعضای فامیل پدرم ۴ نفر هستند ، کاکایم، عمهٔ ام، پدر کلان و مادر کلانم. | فهیم |
| فامیل های امریکا چطور ، آیا کلان هستند؟ | فهیم |
| نه، فامیل های امریکایی بسیار کلان نیستند ، مثل فامیل من، فامیل من ۴ نفر هستیم، من ، برادرم، پدرم و مادرم. | جان |
| آیا برادر تان مثل شما، موی های زرد و چشمهای سبز دارد؟ | فهیم |
| نه برادرم چشماهای آبی دارد و موی هایش قهوه یی است. او مثل مادرم است. | جان |
| آیا فامیل پدر و مادرتان همراه شما زنده گی میکنند؟ | فهیم |
| نه، آنها در ایالت های دیگر زنده گی میکنند. من یک کاکا ، دو خاله و یک ماما دارم. من عمه ندارم. | جان |
| آنها چی وظیفه دارند؟ | فهیم |

| | |
|---|---|
| جان | پدرم انجینر است، مادرم بیکار است، کاکایم مدیر بانک است، خالهٔ کلانم دریور است ، خاله خوردم آشپز است. |
| فهیم | خاله ات دریور است؟ |
| جان | بلی، در امریکا همهٔ زنها دریوری میکنند . |

## LESSON 3

### Exercises 1A and 2

زرغونه دختر عمهٔ سید نعیم است، آنها یک سال پیش توی کردند ، زرغونه عروس مامایش است، او یک خسر، یک خشو، یک ایور و دو ننو دارد . و سید نعیم داماد عمهٔ اش است، او یک خسر، یک خشو، دو خسربره و یک خیاشنه دارد .

### Exercise 3

| | |
|---|---|
| زن | آیا شما مجرد هستید ، یا متاهل؟ |
| مرد | من متاهل هستم. |
| زن | چی وقت توی کردید؟ |
| مرد | یک سال پیش توی کردم. |
| زن | در فامیل خسرتان کی ها زندگی میکنند؟ |
| مرد | در فامیل خسرم: خسربره ام، خیشانه ام، خشویم، خشویم و خسرم زندگی میکنند . |

### Exercise 6AB

| | |
|---|---|
| میوند | نعیم جان ، دیروز کجا بودید؟ |
| نعیم | دیروز من و زنم، خانهٔ خسرم رفته بودیم. |
| میوند | شما متاهل هستید؟ |
| نعیم | بلی، من یک سال پیش عروسی کردم. |
| میوند | هو، تبریک باشد . من خبر نداشتم . شما چی وقت عروسی کردید؟ |
| نعیم | تشکر، ما پارسال در تاریخ سوم حمل عروسی کردیم. |
| میوند | راستی ماه عسل کجا رفتید؟ |
| نعیم | ماه عسل ما به هندوستان رفتیم. |
| میوند | در هندوستان در کجا بودید؟ |
| نعیم | در هندوستان ما در شهر آگره بودیم. |
| میوند | خوب آیا تاج محل را هم دیدید؟ |

| | |
|---|---|
| نعیم | بلی تاج محل را هم دیدیم. میوند جان آیا شما مجرد هستید یا متاهل؟ |
| میوند | من متاهل هستم. |
| نعیم | شما چی وقت توی کردید؟ |
| میوند | من تقریباً ده سال پیش توی کردم. |
| نعیم | در فامیل خسرتان کیها زنده گی میکنند؟ |
| میوند | در فامیل خسرم، دو خسربره ام، سه خیاشنه ام، خسر و خوشو هایم. |
| نعیم | خوشو هایتان؟ شما چند خوشو دارید؟ |
| میوند | من دو خوشو دارم، خسرم دو بار ازدواج کرد. |
| نعیم | چرا؟ |
| میوند | چون زن اولش، بچه ندارد. |

## REVIEW
### Exercise 4:

| | |
|---|---|
| فرید | زرغونه در صنف تان کی دوست صمیمی تان است؟ |
| زرغونه | دوست صمیمی ام، لیلا نام دارد، او اصلاً از کابل است؟ |
| فرید | او چی قسم دختر است؟ |
| زرغونه | او قد بلند است، چشم های آبی دارد و موی هایش قهوه یی است. دوست صمیمی تو کیست؟ |
| فرید | دوست صمیمی من احمد نام دارد، او قد میانه دارد، موی هایش سیاه است و چشم هایش قهوه یی است. |

## CHAPTER SEVEN

## LESSON 1
### Exercise 1A:

نامم سید نعیم است، این خانه از من است، خانه من یک مهمانخانه یا اتاق نشیمن، یک آشپز خانه، یک طعام خانه، یک تشناب، یک حمام، دو اتاق خواب، یک گراژ، یک بالکن یا برنده دارد و در زیر برنده یک درخت است. درصحن حویلی من یک باغچه هم است. همچنان در داخل طعام خانه یک راه زینه قرار دارد.

### Exercise 4ABC:

| | |
|---|---|
| لیلا | میرویس جان شما در کجا میشینید؟ |
| میرویس | من در یک آپارتمان میشینم. |
| لیلا | آپارتمان تان در کجاست؟ |

| | |
|---|---|
| میرویس | آپارتمانم در پیشرویی مکتب حبیبیه است. |
| لیلا | خوب، آپارتمان تان چند منزل و چند اتاق دارد؟ |
| میرویس | آپارتمانم سه منزل دارد ما در منزل سوم میشینیم، آپارتمان ما یك اتاق نشیمن، یك اتاق خواب، یك تشناب، یك حمام، یك آشپزخانه ، دو برنده و یك پسخانه دارد . |
| لیلا | لطفاً، کمی آپارتمان تان را تشریح کنید که چی قسم جای است؟ |
| میرویس | آپارتمانم بسیار کلان است، وقتیکه به آپارتمان داخل شوید ، اول اتاق نشیمن است، در سمت راست اتاق نشیمن اتاق خواب، تشناب و حمام است، در سمت چپ آشپز خانه و پسخانه است. یك برنده در پشت اتاق خواب و برنده دوم در پشت آشپزخانه است. |

Exercise 8AB:

| | |
|---|---|
| زرغونه | میرویس جان، خیریت بود؟ دیروز در صنف نبودید؟ |
| میرویس | بلی، خیریت بود ، دیروز به یك آپارتمان جدید کوچ کردم. |
| زرغونه | به آپارتمان کوچ کردید؟ |
| میرویس | بلی، این آپارتمان بسیار کلان است، یك اتاق نشیمن بسیار کلان ، دو اتاق خواب، یك تشناب، یك آشپز خانه، یك حمام و دو برنده دارد . |
| زرغونه | کدام اتاق را شما بسیار خوش دارید؟ |
| میرویس | من در آپارتمانم اتاق نشیمن را بسیار خوش دارم، رنگ کف اتاق نشیمن ام قهوه یی تاریك است، دیوار های سفید است، سقفش هم سفید است، دروازه و کلکین هایش اتاق نشیمن ام قهوه یی روشن است. من از رنگ قهوه یی بسیار خوشم میاید . این اتاق بیسار کلان هم است، تقریباً ۱۵ متر مربع مساحت دارد . در سمت راست این اتاق یك کلکین است، در سمت چپ اتاقهای خواب و تشنابها است. آشپز خانه با اتاق نشیمن یكجا است. |

Exercise 10A:

| | |
|---|---|
| زرغونه | میرویس جان خانه شما در کجا موقیعت دارد؟ |
| میرویس | خانهٔ ما در کارتهٔ پروان موقیعت دارد . |
| زرغونه | آیا خانهٔ تان حویلی است یا آپارتمان؟ |
| میرویس | خانهٔ ما یك حویلی است. |
| زرغونه | آیا میتوانید که خانهٔ تان را تشریح کنید؟ |

| | |
|---|---|
| میرویس | بلی چرا نه، خانهٔ ما یك حویلی نو است، که در پهلوی سرك عمومی موقعیت دارد، دِروازهٔ حویلی ما به رنگ های سرخ و آبی است، زمین حویلی ما تقریباً ۵۳۶ متر مربع است. در داخل صحن حویلی ما ۳ باغچهٔ گل و دو درخت داریم، خانهٔ ما چار اتاق خواب دارد، که هر کدام شش متر مربع میباشد، همچنان خانه ما دو مهمان خانه دارد که یك مهمانخانه در پیشرویی حویلی و دیگرش در بین خانه میباشد. خانه ما دو آشپزخانه، سه تشناب، دو حمام و یك گراژ کلان دارد که در گراژ آن سه موتر جای میشود. |

# LESSON 2

## Exercise 2AB:

| | |
|---|---|
| زرغونه | فرید جان، پوهنتون رفتید؟ |
| فرید | بلی، رفتم. |
| زرغونه | چطور بود؟ خوش تان آمد؟ |
| فرید | بلی، پوهنتون ما بسیار ساحهٔ کلان دارد. |
| زرغونه | خوب، بگویید که پوهنتون تان چی قسم جای است؟ |
| فرید | ساحه پوهنتون ما بسیار کلان است، این پوهنتون ۷ فاکولته، دو کانتین، دو جمنازیم، دو لیلیه، یك مسجد، پارک، چند کتابخانه، لابراتوار و یك میدان ورزشی دارد. |
| زرغونه | آیا کتابخانه های پوهنتون تان کلان است؟ |
| فرید | بلی، کتابخانه های پوهنتون ما بسیار کلان است اما کتاب خانهٔ فاکولتهٔ ادبیات کلانترین کتابخانه است. |

## Exercise 5ABCD:

| | |
|---|---|
| زن | ببخشید، پوهنځی ادبیات دری در کجا است؟ |
| مرد | پوهنځی ادبیات دری، همینطور روبرو پیش بروید، در آخر همین سرك یك چارراهی است، در سمت شمال این چارراهی یك پارك کلان است، از پارك تیر شوید، اولین تعمیر در سمت چپ پارك پوهنځی ادبیات دری است. آیا شما آنجا محصل هستید؟ |
| زن | نه، برادرم در آنجا درس میخواند. آیا شما محصل هستید؟ |
| مرد | بلی، من محصل هستم. |
| زن | شما محصل کدام پوهنځی هستید؟ |
| مرد | من محصل پوهنځی ادبیات پشتو هستم. پوهنځی ما هم در همان تعمیر موقعیت دارد. برادر تان محصل سال چندم است؟ |
| زن | او محصل سال دوم است. چرا؟ |

| | |
|---|---|
| مرد | پرسان کردم، بخاطریکه پوهنئی ما بسیار کلان است.    وقتیکه به تعمیر داخل شدید، از زینه بالا شوید، در منزل سوم به سمت راست دور بزنید، صنف سال دوم در اتاق شماره ۳۱۲ است. |
| زن | آیا پوهنئی تان کتابخانه هم دارد؟ |
| مرد | بلی، چرا؟ |
| زن | بخاطریکه برادرم در آنجاست، من میخواهم که او را ببینم. |
| مرد | کتابخانه در منزل ۴ در روبرویی زینه است. |
| زن | تشکر. |
| مرد | خواهش میکنم. |

**Exercise 8AB:**

| | |
|---|---|
| کریم | بصیر جان کجا میروید؟ |
| بصیر | کریم جان من میروم که از کتابخانه کتاب بگیرم. شما کجا میروید؟ |
| کریم | من هم کتابخانه میروم که این کتاب ها را پس بدهم. |
| بصیر | خو، بیایید که یکجا برویم. |
| کریم | بصیر جان، شما معمولاً خوش دارید که در کجا درس بخوانید؟ |
| بصیر | من معمولاً، خوش دارم که در پارک درس بخوانم و همچنان خوش دارم که در لیله درس بخوانم. |
| کریم | من هم خوش دارم که در پارک درس بخوانم اما کتاب خانه را بیشتر خوش دارم. |
| بصیر | شما میتوانید که در مسجد هم درس بخوانید. |
| کریم | بلی مسجد بسیار آرام است. |
| بصیر | امشب من میخواهم که به جمنازیم بروم و بازی والیبال را سیل کنم، آیا شما میخواهید که همراه من بروید؟ |
| کریم | بلی چرا نه من والیبال را بسیار خوش دارم. بازی چند ساعت بجه است؟ |
| بصیر | بازی ساعت پنج بجه است. |
| کریم | آیا من میتوانم که برادرم را بیاورم؟ |
| بصیر | بلی چرا نه. |
| کریم | خو ساعت پنج در جمنازیم میبینم تان. |

**Exercise 9AB:**

| | |
|---|---|
| زرغونه | هلو، هلو، فرید جان! |
| فرید | بلی، سلام زرغونه خواهر چطور هستید؟ |
| زرغونه | تشکر، من خوب هستم، شما چطور هستید؟ |
| فرید | تشکر، خیریت بود؟ خواهر |
| زرغونه | بلی، من هفته نو به پوهنتون هرات میایم چونکه من در آنجا میخواهم که در فاکولتهٔ ژورنالیزم درس بخوانم. آیا شما هفته نو در هرات هستید؟ |
| فرید | بلی، هفتهٔ نو من در هرات هستم، من شما را به پوهنتون میبرم. |
| زرغونه | تشکر، خوب برایم توصیف کنید که پوهنتون هرات چی قسم جای است. |
| | ساحه پوهنتون هرات بسیار کلان است، پوهنتون هرات در داخل شهر هرات است. پوهنتون هرات ۱۰ فاکولته دارد. هر فاکولته یك تعمیر جداگانه دارد. همچنان این پوهنتون دارای سه کتابخانه، دو جمنازیم، ، دو لابراتوار و پارك های کلان دارد. |
| فرید | لیله پوهنتون هرات از پوهنتون دور است. پوهنتون هرات یك کانتین کلان هم دارد که محصلین در وقت تفریح آنجا چای مینوشند. خوب، هفتهٔ نو چی وقت میایید؟ |
| زرغونه | من هفتهٔ نو، در روز شنبه، ساعت ۱۱ صبح میایم. |
| فرید | خوب، من هم یك آپارتمان کلانتر با دو اتاق خواب میگیرم که شما هم با من زنده گی کنید. |
| زرغونه | تشکر، تا هفتهٔ نو به امان خدا! |
| فرید | خدا حافظ! |

# LESSON 3

**Exercise 3A:**

| | |
|---|---|
| زن | ببخشید، پوهنتون در کجا است؟ |
| مرد | پوهنتون؟ از میدان هوایی که برایید، به سمت چپ دور بزنید، کمی پیش بروید، در آخر میدان هوایی، در جاده میوند به سمت راست دور بزنید. در جاده میوند از قومندانی امنیه تیر شوید، آنجاچاراهی است. از چار راهی تیر شوید، کمی پیش بروید، باز به سمت راست دور بزنید، پوهنتون در سمت راست تان است. |
| زن | تشکر |
| مرد | خواهش میکنم. |

Exercise 5A:

| | |
|---|---|
| سلام | الف |
| وعلیکم | ب |
| ببخشید ، شما میفهمید که پوهنتون کابل در کجاست؟ | الف |
| پوهنتون کابل ؟ | ب |
| بلی | الف |
| ها میفهمم. شما همینطور به سمت شمال پیش بروید. تقریباً پنج دقیقه بعد در سمت چپ تان یك ایستادگاه بس را میبینید ، در آنجا به بس های پوهنتون بالاشوید. آن سرویس شما را به پوهنتون میبرد . | ب |
| تشکر به امان خدا. | الف |
| خواهش میکنم. خدا حافظ. | ب |

# CHAPTER EIGHT

## LESSON 1
Exercise 1A:

| | |
|---|---|
| صبح بخیر شریف جان. | لیلا |
| صبح بخیر لیلا جان، نمیفهمم که برای چای صبح چی داریم؟ | شریف |
| یك لحظه صبر کنید که یخچال را ببینم. امممم؟؟ در یخچال بسیار چیز ها داریم شما چی خوش دارید که بخورید؟ | لیلا |
| من، قهوه و شیر همراه بوره ، کیك و کلچه خوش دارم، همچنان نان خشك همراه تخم مرغ. شما چی میخورید؟ | شریف |
| من نان خشك همراه مربا وپنیر میخورم. | لیلا |
| آیا در یخچال مسکه هم داریم. | شریف |
| بلی ، میخواهید . | لیلا |
| بلی، یك کمی همراه نان خشك میخواهم. شما فقط نان خشك، همراه مربا و پنیر میخورید. | شریف |
| نه، من چای هم میخورم. راستی ماست هم داریم، میخورید؟ | لیلا |
| کمی برای نان چاشت میخورم. تشکر. | شریف |

## Exercise 2ABCD:

| | |
|---|---|
| لیلا | شریف جان، برای چای صبح مهمانها هیچ چیز در یخچال نداریم. بروید و از بازار کمی سودا بخرید. |
| شریف | چی چیزها بکار است که بخرم؟ |
| لیلا | باید نان خشك، شیر، مسکه، پنیر و مربا بخریم. |
| شریف | آیا بوره، تخم مرغ، چای و قهوه داریم. |
| لیلا | بوره، چای و تخم مرغ داریم اما قهوه بکار نیست، چونکه مهمانهای ما قهوه خوش ندارند. فکر میکنم که ماست هم نداریم. لطفاً کمی ماست هم بیاورید. |
| شریف | خو کیك و کلچه هم بخرم یا نه؟ |
| لیلا | نه، کیك و کلچه داریم. دیگر همین ها بس است اما باید زود تر پس بیایید، چونکه یك ساعت بعد مهمانها بیدار میشوند. |
| شریف | بسیار خوب، من میروم. |

## Exercise 4AC:

| | |
|---|---|
| شریف | رینگ، رینگ... هلو بلی، بفرمایید. |
| لیلا | شریف جان من هستم، لیلی. |
| شریف | سلام خیریت است؟ |
| لیلا | ها، امشب خواهرم و شوهرش از مزارشریف خانهٔ ما میایند. کمی سودا بکار داشتم. از دفترت که بیرون شدی باید کمی سودا بخری و بیاوری. |
| شریف | خو چی چیز ها بکار است؟ |
| لیلا | قلم و کاغذ داری؟ |
| شریف | بلی. |
| لیلا | نوشته کن. دو بسته نمك، ۱ بوتل روغن، ۱۲ بوتل آب، دو کیلو گوشت، ۳ کیلو بادنجان رومی، سه دانه بادرنگ، چار کیلو پالك، ۳۰۰ گرام مرچ، ۲ دسته کاهو، ۱ کیلو زردك، ۲ کیلو کچالو، ۳ کیلو پیاز، ۱ کیلو توت زمینی، ۱ کیلو آلوبالو، ۲ کیلو سیب، ۱۰ کیلو خربوزه، ۲ درجن کیله، ۱۰ کیلو تربوز، ۳ کیلو انگور، ۴کیلو مالته |
| شریف | اممم من از تربوز بسیار خوشم میاید، اما این سودا زیاد نیست؟ |
| لیلا | نه، انها برای یك هفته اینجا میباشند. سودا زیاد بکار است. |
| شریف | خو صحیح است، شام میبینم، بخیر، فعلاً خدا حافظ! |
| لیلا | به امان خدا. |

## Exercise 5E:

| | |
|---|---|
| اجمل | میرویس چی میخورید؟ |
| میرویس | والله اجمل جان، کمی انگور میخورم، من از انگور بسیار خوشم میاید . |
| اجمل | من مالته دارم، آیا از مالته خوش تان میاید؟ |
| میرویس | بلی از مالته خوشم میاید اما کم. شما از کدام میوه ها خوشتان میاید؟ |
| اجمل | من سیب و تربوز را بسیار خوش دارم اما از خربوزه خوشم نمیاید. انگور را بسیار زیاد خوش دارم. |
| میرویس | من تربوز و خربوزه را بسیار زیاد خوش دارم، اما سیب را بسیار کم خوش دارم. |

## Exercise 6ABC:

| | |
|---|---|
| مشتری | کاکا جان سلام! |
| دوکاندار | وعلیکم بچیم، سودا بکار داشتید؟ چی بکار دارید؟ |
| مشتری | کاکا جان تربوز کیلوی چند است؟ |
| دوکاندار | تربوز کیلوی ۱۰ روپیه است. |
| مشتری | نه کاکا جان بسیار قیمت گفتی ارزان تر نمیشود؟ |
| دوکاندار | شما چند میخواهید؟ |
| مشتری | من کیلوی هفت روپیه میخواهم، میدهی؟ |
| دوکاندار | من خودم کیلوی ۸ روپیه خریدم چطور ۷ روپیه بدهم؟ |
| مشتری | خیر است کیلوی ۹ روپیه بده. |
| دوکاندار | خو چند کیلو بدهم. |
| مشتری | بیست کیلو بده، پیسه اش چند میشود؟ |
| دوکاندار | بیست ضرب نه مساوی میشود به ۱۸۰ |
| مشتری | این هم پیسه ای تان |
| دوکاندار | خو سودای ایم آماده است. |
| مشتری | بلی اینه سودای تان را بگیرید. |

## Exercise 8:

| | |
|---|---|
| مشتری | سلام! من کمی ترکاری و میوه بکار داشتم؟ |
| دوکاندار | وعلیکم، چی چیز ها بکار دارید؟ |

| | |
|---|---|
| مشتری | ۳ کیلو بادنجان رومی، ۴ دانه بادرنگ، چار کیلو پالك،، ۲ دسته کاهو ، ۲ کیلو سیب، ۲ درجن کیله قیمت هایش چند است؟ |
| دوکاندار | بادنجان رومی کیلوی ۱۰ روپیه ، بادرن۴ دانه ۵ روپیه ، پالك کیلویی ۷ روپیه ،کاهو دسته۳ روپیه ، سیب ۱۰۰ روپیه، کیله درجن ۱۲۰ روپیه |
| مشتری | همه قیمت هایش خوب است، اما سیب و کیله را بسیار قیمت گفتید . |
| دوکاندار | شما چند میخواهید؟ |
| مشتری | من از دوکان دیگر پرسان کردم، سیب را کیلوی ۸۵ و کیله را درجن ۱۰۰ افغانی میدهد . شماهم به آن قیمت میدهید؟ |
| دوکاندار | خیر است شما سیب را کیلوی ۹۰ و کیله را درجن ۱۱۰ بخرید . |
| مشتری | نه من سیب را از ۸۵ و کیله را از ۱۰۰ بلندتر نمیخرم. |
| دوکاندار | خیر است، چند کیلو سیب و چند درجن کیله میخواهید؟ |
| مشتری | ۲ کیلو سیب، ۲ درجن کیله میخواهم. |

Exercise 9B:

سلام زرغونه جان، لیلا هستم،  من ایمیل تان را گرفتم، فردا برایم بسیار خوب است،من همراه تان خواهم رفت،  شما نگفتید که چند بجه میرویم. لطفا برایم زنگ بزنید و وقت را بگویید ، تشکر  به امان خدا .

# LESSON 2
Exercise 7:

| | |
|---|---|
| زرغونه | لیلا جان، دوازده بجه است، چاشت شده، شما گشنه نشدید ؟ |
| لیلا | والله زرغونه جان،  بسیار گشنه شدیم، بیا که برویم و در رستورانت نان بخوریم. |
| زرغونه | به کدام رستورانت برویم؟ |
| لیلا | بیا که به رستورانت، کلبهٔ افغان برویم. |
| زرغونه | رستورانت کلبهٔ افغان؟ |
| لیلا | بلی، این رستورانت غذاهای افغانی بسیار زیاد دارد. |
| زرغونه | چی چیزها دارد؟ |
| لیلا | هر قسم غذای افغانی دارد ، مثل کباب گوشت گوسفند ، منتو، قابلی پلو و دیگر چیز ها. |
| زرغونه | امممم، من بسیار گشنه هستم، بیا که بریم. |

**Exercise 10ABC:**

| | |
|---|---|
| گارسون | سلام به رستورانت کلبهٔ افغان خوش آمدید ، بفرمائید . |
| زرغونه | وعلیکم، تشکر. |
| گارسون | چند نفر هستید؟ |
| زرغونه | ما دو نفر هستیم، یک میز دو نفره بکار داریم. |
| گارسون | بفرمائید از این طرف، پشت من بیایید. |
| زرغونه | تشکر. |
| گارسون | بفرمائید اینجا بشنید . |
| زرغونه | تشکر، لطفاً مینوی تان را بیاورید . |
| گارسون | بفرمائید. |
| زرغونه | لطفاً، به ما یک چند دقیقه وقت بدهید . |
| گارسون | بلی، حتماً..... آیا شما آماده هستید؟ |
| زرغونه | بلی، به من یک خوراک منتو همراه سوپ مرغ بیاورید . به دوستم یک خوراک کباب گوشت گوسفند همراه قابلی پلو بیاورید . |
| گارسون | نوشیدنی چی میخواهید؟ |
| زرغونه | من دوغ میخواهم و برای دوستم یک بوتل کوکاکولا بیاورید . |

# LESSON 3

**Exercise 3:**

سلام؛ من رزغونه هستم، امروز میخواهم که درباره کالایی افغانی معلومات بدهم. افغانها معمولاً بعد از کار، در خانه کالایی افغانی میپوشند ، مثلاً من در خانه معمولاً چادر، پیراهن، تنبان و چپلی میپوشم و گاهی که بیرون میروم، چادری ویا برقعه میپوشم.

شوهرم نعیم در خانه بعد از کار پیراهن وتنبان، واسکت و کلاه پکول میپوشد . بچه ام در خانه معمولاً پیراهن و تنبان همراه کلاه میپوشد . دخترم در خانه پیراهن و تنبان همراه یک شال میپوشد . و خسرم در خانه معمولاً پیراهن و تنبان، چپن و لنگی میپوشد . شوهرم همچنان گاهی پتو و دستمال هم میپوشد . تمام تنبان های کالایی افغانی ایزار بند دارد .

**Exercise 8ABC:**

| | |
|---|---|
| دوکاندار | بفرمایید ، همشیره چی بکار دارید؟ |
| مشتری | من کمی کالایی بچه گانه بکار دارم. |
| دوکاندار | چی قسم کالا بکار دارید؟ |

| | |
|---|---|
| مشتری | یك پطلون كوبای سیاه، دو دانه بلوز آبی و یك جوره بوت كار دارم. |
| دوكاندار | برای بچه چند ساله میخواهید؟ |
| مشتری | برای بچهٔ ۱۰ ساله. |
| دوكاندار | بلی داریم. اینه پطلون كوبای سیاه، دو دانه بلوز و یك جوره بوت. |
| مشتری | قیمت هایش چند است؟ |
| دوكاندار | پطلون ۲۰۰ افغانی، بلوز ها دانهٔ ۱۶۰ افغانی و بوتها جورهٔ ۳۰۰ افغانی |
| مشتری | مجموعاً چند میشود؟ |
| دوكاندار | مجموعاً ۶۶۰ افغانی |
| مشتری | نه، بسیار قیمت است، كمی مراعات كنید. |
| دوكاندار | خیر است شما ۶۳۰ افغانی بدهید. |
| مشتری | نه، پوره ۶۰۰ افغانی میدهم. |
| دوكاندار | خیر است، ۶۲۰. |
| مشتری | نه ، ۶۰۰ بیشتر نمیخرم. |
| دوكاندار | خیر است، بگیرید. |

Exercise 9:

| | |
|---|---|
| دوكاندار | بفرمایید، چی بكار داشتید؟ |
| مشتری | ببخشید، من یك جوره بوت مردانه و یك جوره بوت دخترانه همراه یك پطلون بچه گانه و بلوز زنانه بكار داشتم. |
| دوكاندار | بوت ها كدام رنگ و نمبرش چند باشد؟ |
| مشتری | بوت دخترانه به رنگ سرخ و نمبر ۵ باشد و بوت مردانه نمبر ۱۰ به رنگ سیاه دارید؟ |
| دوكاندار | بلی، این هم بوت دخترانهٔ سرخ و نمبر ۵ و این هم بوت مردانهٔ نمبر ۱۰. خوب پطلون بچه گانه به كدام اندازه میخواهید؟ |
| مشتری | والله بچهٔ ام ۱۲ ساله است، كدام اندازه خوبست؟ |
| دوكاندار | برای بچه ۱۲ ساله اندازه میانه خوبست. كدام رنگش را میخواهید؟ |
| مشتری | كدام رنگ ها را دارید؟ |
| دوكاندار | آبی، سیاه، قهوه یی و سفید. |
| مشتری | یك دانه آبی بدهید لطفاً. |
| دوكاندار | خوب و بولیز زنانه به كدام سایز میخواهید؟ |

| | |
|---|---|
| مشتری | برای زن ۳۰ ساله کدام اندازه خوبست؟ |
| دوکاندار | اندازهٔ کلان خوب است. شما کدام رنگ را خوش دارید؟ |
| مشتری | یك دانه به رنگ زرد بدهید. خوب قیمت هایش چند است؟ |
| دوکاندار | بوت مردانه جورهٔ ۱۰۰۰ روپیه، بوت دخترانه جورهٔ ۴۰۰ روپیه، پطلون بچه گانه ۳۰۰ و بلوز زنانه ۶۰۰ افغانی. |
| مشتری | بسیار قیمت است، کمی مراعات کنید. من مشتری شما هستم. |
| دوکاندار | مجموعاً ۲۳۰۰ روپیه میشود، شما خیراست ۲۲۰۰ روپیه بدهید. |
| مشتری | نه، ۲۰۰۰ پوره میدهم. |
| دوکاندار | ۲۱۵۰ |
| مشتری | نه ۲۰۰۰ بس است. |
| دوکاندار | خوب خیراست، بگیرید. |

# CHAPTER NINE

## LESSON 1

Exercise 2BC:

آب و هوایی کابل در چار فصل سال:

کابل مرکز افغانستان است که در شمال شرق افغانستان موقعیت دارد. این ولایت در بهار یك هوای معتدل دارد، در بهار معمولاً آسمان ابر است ولی گاهی هم آسمان صاف میباشد، اکثراً باران میبارد، رعد و برق میشود و باد میوزد، گاهی طوفان میشود و سیل میآید. وقتیکه آسمان صاف است، آفتاب و مهتاب دیده میشود.

در تابستان هوا گرم است، آسمان اکثراً صاف است، در روز آفتاب و در شب مهتاب دیده میشود. همچنان در تابستان هوا مرطوب نیست.

در خزان هوا گاهی گرم و گاهی سرد است، باد میوزد، آسمان گاهی ابر و گاهی صاف است. اگر آسمان صاف باشد آفتاب و مهتاب هم دیده میشوند.

در زمستان هوا همیشه خنك و سرد است، برف، باران و ژاله میبارد. همچنان آسمان اکثراً ابر است و باد سرد میوزد.

Exercise 5A:

| | |
|---|---|
| شریف | میرویس، بخیر کجا میروید؟ |
| میرویس | شریف جان، بخیر میخواهم که صباح به مزار شریف بروم. میتوانید که آب و هوای صباح را در انترنیت چك کنید؟ |
| شریف | بلی، چرا نه یك لحظه... |

| | |
|---|---|
| میرویس | تشکر |
| شریف | صبح هوای مزار سرد است. آسمان ابری است، بلندترین درجه حرارت ۲۵ و پائین ترین آن ۱۷ درجهٔ سانتی گراد است. |
| میرویس | هوا، بسیار خنک است، من باید کالایی گرم بپوشم. |

## Exercise 6BC:

| | |
|---|---|
| شریف | هلو، هلو کریم جان، من شریف هستم، مانده نباشید، چطور هستید؟ |
| کریم | السلام علیکم، شریف جان. شکر من خوب هستم، شما چطور هستید؟ |
| شریف | فضل خدا من هم خوب هستم. کریم جان هوای هرات چطور است؟ |
| کریم | چرا؟ |
| شریف | اگر هوا خوب باشد میخواهم که به هرات بیایم. |
| کریم | والله، امروز هوا ابری است، احتمال میرود که باران ببارد. |
| شریف | آیا صباح هم باران میبارد؟ |
| کریم | نه صباح آسمان آفتابی است. هوای کابل چطور است؟ |
| شریف | کابل امروز برفی است اما دیروز بارانی بود. دیروز وقتیکه بازار میرفتم، بسیار باران میبارید. |
| کریم | خوب صباح ساعت چند میاید؟ |
| شریف | والله، اگر هوا خوب باشد، ساعت ۱۰ بجه میایم. |
| کریم | خوب فعلاً خدا حافظ، صباح باز میبینیم. |
| شریف | حتماً، خدا حافظ! |

## Exercise 7B:

| | |
|---|---|
| ا | هلو، هلو کریم جان، من شریف هستم، مانده نباشید، چطور هستید؟ |
| ب | السلام علیکم، شریف جان. شکر من خوب هستم، شما چطور هستید؟ |
| ا | فضل خدا من هم خوب هستم. کریم جان هوای هرات چطور است؟ |
| ب | چرا؟ |
| ا | اگر هوا خوب باشد میخواهم که به هرات بیایم. |
| ب | والله، امروز هوا ابری است، احتمال میرود که باران ببارد. |
| ا | آیا صباح هم باران میبارد؟ |
| ب | نه صباح آسمان آفتابی است. هوای کابل چطور است؟ |

| | |
|---|---|
| کابل امروز برفی است اما دیروز بارانی بود. دیروز وقتیکه بازار میرفتم، بسیار باران میبارید. | ا |
| خوب صباح ساعت چند میاید؟ | ب |
| والله، اگر هوا خوب باشد، ساعت ۱۰ بجه میایم. | ا |
| خوب فعلاً خدا حافظ، صباح باز میبینیم. | ب |
| حتماً، خدا حافظ! | ا |

## Exercise 8D:

هلو، کریم جان سلام من شریف هستم، کریم جان دیروز وقتیکه ما در تلیفون صحبت
میکردیم، در بیرون بسیار برف میبارید و من نتوانستم که بروم و تکت بخرم. هوا
اینجا بسیار سرد است و سرک ها را یخ زده، من نمیتوانم که برای صباح به هرات بیایم.
اگر هوا پس صباح خوب شد من بخیر پس صباح میایم. لطفاً اگر پیام من را گرفتید،
برایم تلیفون کنید. خدا حافظ

## Exercise 9A:

هلو، کریم جان سلام من شریف هستم، کریم جان دیروز وقتیکه ما در تلیفون صحبت
میکردیم، در بیرون بسیار برف میبارید و من نتوانستم که بروم و تکت بخرم. هوا
اینجا بسیار سرد است و سرک ها را یخ زده، من نمیتوانم که برای صباح به هرات بیایم.
اگر هوا پس صباح خوب شد من بخیر پس صباح میایم. لطفاً اگر پیام من را گرفتید،
برایم تلیفون کنید. خدا حافظ

## Exercise 10:

| | |
|---|---|
| هلو، شریف جان؟ سلام کریم هستم. | کریم |
| وعلیکم سلام، کریم جان تشکر که برایم تلیفون کردید. | شریف |
| خواهش میکنم، پیام تان را گرفتم، وقتیکه شما تلیفون میکردید من در صنف بودم. ببخشید. | کریم |
| نه، پروا نمیکند کریم جان. | شریف |
| گفتید که هوای کابل خراب است، شما نمیتوانید که بیاید؟ | کریم |
| بلی، در کابل بسیار یک برف سنگین میبارد، و بسیار طوفان است و باد شدید میوزد. | شریف |
| خو، پس چی وقت میاید؟ | کریم |
| اگر آسمان صاف باشد و برف نبارد، بخیر میایم. | شریف |
| خوب خیر باشد، در هرات هم هوا خنک شده، بسیار باران شدید میبارد و سرک ها را یخ زده. دیروز هم بسیار یک ژاله شدید بارید. | کریم |

| | |
|---|---|
| شریف | میفهمم امسال زمستان هوا بسیار سرد شده، خوب به تماس هستیم. فعلاً خدا حافظ. |
| کریم | خدا حافظ! |

# LESSON 2
## Exercise 4BD:

| | |
|---|---|
| تکت فروش | سلام به شرکت هوایی افغان خوش آمدید! چی کمک کرده میتوانم؟ |
| مسافر | وعلیکم، من یک تکت برای هند بکار دارم، شما در کدام روز ها پرواز دارید؟ |
| تکت فروش | ما در روز های دوشنبه، چارشنبه و جمعه از کابل به هند پرواز داریم. شما چند تکت بکار دارید؟ |
| مسافر | ما سه نفر هستیم. |
| تکت فروش | شما تکت یک طرفه میخواهید یا تکت دوطرفه؟ |
| مسافر | قیمت های تکت یک طرفه و دوطرفه چند است؟ |
| تکت فروش | تکت یک طرفه برای هر نفر ۱۵۰۰۰ افغانی است و تکت دوطرفه ۲۹۵۰۰ افغانی است. |
| مسافر | طبعاً که تکت دوطرفه میخواهم چونکه ارزانتر است. |
| تکت فروش | خوب برای کدام تاریخ ها میخواهید؟ |
| مسافر | ما به تاریخ ۲۰ ماه سرطان خواهیم رفت و به تاریخ ۱۰ ماه اسد پس خواهیم آمد. |
| تکت فروش | بسیار خوب، لطفاً پاسپورتهای تان را بدهید؟ |
| مسافر | اینه بفرمایید. |
| تکت فروش | تشکر، لطفاً چند لحظه صبر کنید. |
| مسافر | به چشم ..... |
| تکت فروش | اینه، تکت های تا آماده شد ، لطفاً سه ساعت قبل از پرواز تان در میدان هوایی حاضر باشید . چونکه پرواز تان خارجی است، باید وقتر بیایید. |

| | |
|---|---|
| مسافر | ما چند بکس را میتوانیم که همراه خود ما ببریم؟ |
| تکت فروش | هر نفر دو بکس را میتواند که همراه خودش ببرد،  وزن هر بکس باید ۳۲ کیلو باشد. |
| مسافر | تشکر. |
| تکت فروش | خواهش میکنم، اگر کدام سوال یا پرسان داشته باشید، به این شماره تلیفون تماس بگیرید. سفر خوشی را برای تان آرزو میکنیم. |
| مسافر | تشکر. |

## Exercise 6ABCD:

| | |
|---|---|
| تکت فروش | به شرکت مسافربری  کابل خوش آمدید،  چی خدمت کرده میتوانم؟ |
| مسافر | تشکر،  من یک تکت به مزار شریف بکار دارم،  بس های تان چی وقت حرکت میکند؟ |
| تکت فروش | والله، بس های ما هرروز ساعت ۴ صبح از کابل حرکت میکند و  ساعت دوازده بجه چاشت به مزار شریف میرسد. |
| مسافر | خوب برای صباح، برای شش نفر تکت دارید؟ |
| تکت فروش | نه والله،  ما فقط برای ۴ نفر دیگر هم چوکی خالی داریم. |
| مسافر | نه ما شش نفر هستیم. |
| تکت فروش | برای دیگر صباح داریم، آیا میخواهید؟ |
| مسافر | بلی  چاره نیست.  قیمت تکت برای هر نفر چند است؟ |
| تکت فروش | تکت کابل به مزار شریف برای هر نفر  ۶۰۰ افغانی است. |
| مسافر | خوب صحیح است، لطفاً شش تکت بدهید. |
| تکت فروش | لطفاً تذکره تا کارت هویت  خود را بدهید. |
| مسافر | اینه، بفرمایید. |

| | |
|---|---|
| تکت فروش | تشکر. |
| | اینه، تکت های تان را بگیرید ، لطفاً دیگرصباح ساعت ۳ بجه اینجا حاضر |
| تکت فروش | باشید. |
| مسافر | حتماً آیا از بکس هایم پیسه میگیرید؟ |
| تکت فروش | نه بکس هایتان را مفت خواهیم برد. |
| مسافر | تشکر، دیگر صباح میبینیم.  فعلاً به امان خدا |
| تکت فروش | به امان خدا. |

# LESSON 3

Exercise 2ABC:

| | |
|---|---|
| میرویس | شریف جان، رخصتی های تابستانی یک هفته بعد شروع خواهد شد .  شما به کجا خواهید رفت؟ |
| شریف | والله، میرویس جان،  ما به هندوستان خواهیم رفت، چونکه هندوستان بسیار جاهای جالب و دیدنی دارد . |
| میرویس | بلی، آیا شما زمینی  سفرخواهید رفت، یا هوایی؟ |
| شریف | هوایی سفرخواهیم کرد ، چونکه حالا طیاره های افغانستان هر روز به هندوستان پرواز میکنند . |
| میرویس | شما برای رخصتی های تابستانی تان کجا سفر خواهید کرد؟ |
| شریف | من به مزار شریف خواهم رفت  چونکه هوایی مزار در  تابستان بسیار سرد است. |
| میرویس | شما هوایی سفر خواهید کرد یا زمینی؟ |
| شریف | من زمینی سفر خواهم کرد چونکه زمینی تکت بسیار ارزان است. |

Exercise 4AB:

| | |
|---|---|
| هوتلی | هلو، بفرمایید ، هوتل مزار است، چی خدمت کرده میتوانم؟ |
| میرویس | سلام، نام من میرویس است، از کابل تلیفون میکنم، من یک اتاق دو نفره بکار دارم. |
| هوتلی | شما به کدام تاریخ ها بکار دارید؟ |
| میرویس | من از تاریخ ۱۸ سرطان تا  ۳۰ سرطان بکار دارم. تقریباً ۱۲ شب. |

| | |
|---|---|
| هوتلی | یک لحظه صبر کنید، که من چک کنم. |
| میرویس | بفرمایید. |
| هوتلی | ببخشید، اتاق دو نفره در تاریخ ۱۸ سرطان نداریم، اما در ۱۹ سرطان داریم. آیا میخواهید؟ |
| میرویس | نه در تاریخ ۱۸ سرطان من باید آنجا باشم، آیا دیگر راه است؟ |
| هوتلی | بلی، اگر شما بخواهید. برای یک شب ما برایتان یک اتاق یک نفره میدهیم، باز سر از روز دیگر شما میتوانید که در اتاق دونفر بروید. |
| میرویس | بسیار خوب، پس لطفاً یک اتاق برایم ریزرف کنید، راستی کرایه یک اتاق شب چند است؟ |
| هوتلی | یک اتاق دو نفره شب ۲۰۰۰ افغانی است. |
| میرویس | آیا اتاق های تان انترنت، تلویزیون، تشناب، حمام، آب گرم و سرد دارد. |
| هوتلی | بلی اتاق های ما بسیار مجهز است. |
| میرویس | خوب مجموعاً چند شد؟ |
| هوتلی | مجموعاً ۲۴۰۰۰ افغانی میشود،  شما کارت بانکی دارید؟ |
| میرویس | بلی، |
| هوتلی | لطفاً شمارهٔ اش را بدهید. |
| میرویس | خوب نوشته کنید. |

### Exercise 5ABC:

| | |
|---|---|
| مسافر | کاکا تکسیوان، تا هوتل مزار چند میبری؟ |
| تکسیوان | هوتل مزار؟ هوتل مزار در کجا است؟ |
| مسافر | در ربروریی پارک مولانا. |
| تکسیوان | ها، میفهمم که در کجا است،  بلی میبرم تان. |
| مسافر | چند کرایه میگیری؟ |
| تکسیوان | تا هوتل مزار ۲۰۰ روپیه میشود. |
| مسافر | نه کاکا جان چی میگویی؟ بسیار قیمت است. |
| تکسیوان | خوب، شما چند میدهید؟ |
| مسافر | ۱۰۰ روپیه میدهم. |
| تکسیوان | نه، ۱۵۰ روپیه میبرمتان،  اگر میروید بیایید و بالاشوید. |
| مسافر | خیر است، بیایید که برویم. |
| تکسیوان | باشد که همی بکس هایم را در تولبکس بمانم. |

# REVIEW

Exercise 1A:

لطفاً به گزارش آب و هوای چند ولایت مهم کشور توجه کنید:

فردا کابل،  آسمان ابری،  بلندترین درجهٔ حرارت ۲۵ و پائین ترین درجهٔ حرارت ۲۰ درجهٔ سانتی گراد میباشد وهمچنان فردا در کابل برف خواهد بارید .

هرات، آسمان ابری و باران شدید خواهد بارید ، بلندترین درجهٔ حرارت ۲۰ و پائین ترین درجهٔ حرارت ۱۷ درجهٔ سانتی گراد میباشد .

کندهار، آسمان آفتابی و گاهی ابری، بلندترین درجهٔ حرارت ۳۰ و پائین ترین درجهٔ حرارت ۲۵ درجهٔ سانتی گراد میباشد .

مزار شریف، آسمان ابری، باد شدید خواهد وزید و برف سنگین خواهد بارید . بلندترین درجهٔ حرارت ۲۰ و پائین ترین درجهٔ حرارت ۱۵ درجهٔ سانتی گراد میباشد .

جلال آباد آسمان ابری، باران شدید  میبارد و احتمال طوفان شدید است . بلندترین درجهٔ حرارت ۳۰ و پائین ترین درجهٔ حرارت ۲۰ درجهٔ سانتی گراد میباشد .

Exercise 2A:

| | |
|---|---|
| مسافر | سلام، ببخشین شما از کابل به هامبورک پروازدارید؟ |
| نماینده | وعلیکم، بلی ما برای هامبورک پرواز داریم. |
| مسافر | کدام روزها پرواز دارید ؟ |
| نماینده | روز های سه شنبه ، چار شنبه و جمعه |
| مسافر | بسیار خوب قیمت تکت کابل به هامبورک چند است؟ |
| نماینده | یك طرفه یا دو طرفه؟ |
| مسافر | یك طرفه. |
| نماینده | قیمت یك تکت یك طرفه ۸۰۰ دالر امریکایی است. |
| مسافر | بسیار خوب، یك تکت به روز چارشنبه آینده بوك کنید . |
| نماینده | لطفاً پاسپورت تان را بدهید؟ |
| مسافر | اینه بفرمائین. |
| نماینده | تشکر، چند دقیقه صبر کنید ... اینه بفرمائین تکت تان آماده شد . |
| مسافر | تشکر به امان خدا! |
| نماینده | به امان خدا! |

# CHAPTER TEN

## LESSON 1

Exercise 1ABC:

| | |
|---|---|
| هوتلی | سلام به هوتل مزار خوش امدید ، چی خدمت کرده میتوانم؟ |
| شریف | سلام نامم شریف است، چند روز پیش من یك اتاق سه نفری بوك کرده بودم. |
| هوتلی | گفتید ، نام تان شریف است؟ |
| شریف | بلی |
| هوتلی | ببخشید ، تخلص تان چیست؟ |
| شریف | شریف حبیبی |
| هوتلی | بلی، میتوانم که تذکره یا کارت هویت تان را ببینم؟ |
| شریف | بلی بفرمایید . |
| هوتلی | تشکر، من از تذکره تان یك کاپی میگیرم، لطفاً این فورمه را هم خانه پوری کنید . |
| شریف | بسیار خوب. |

Exercise 4BC:

| | |
|---|---|
| مامور هوتل | هلو، دفتر هوتل مزارشریف است، بفرمایید . |
| مسافر | سلام، من از اتاق شماره ۱۲۶ تماس میگیرم. |
| مامور هوتل | سلام بفرمایید ، چی خدمت کرده میتوانم؟ |
| مسافر | من و فامیل میخواهیم که به دیدن زیارت سخی و موزیم مزار شریف برویم. بس ها چی وقت برای بردن مسافرین آماده است؟ |
| مامور هوتل | بس ها معمولاً در روز های پنجشنبه و جمعه ساعت هشت صبح مسافرین را میبرند . شما باید اول نام تان را راجستر کنید. |
| مسافر | برای راجستر کردن، من باید چی بکنم؟ |
| مامور هوتل | شما باید به دفتر هوتل بیایید و نام و مشخصات خود را نوشته کنید. |
| مسافر | تشکر، ببخشید، ما در اتاق خود برای نوشیدن آب نداریم، میتوانید کمی آب برای ما روان کنید. |
| مامور هوتل | چرا نه، خانه سامان تا چند دقیقه بعد آب خواهد آورد . |
| مسافر | تشکر. |

| | |
|---|---|
| مامور هوتل | خواهش میکنم، دیگر سوال ندارید؟ |
| مسافر | نه، تشکر، فعلاً به امان خدا! |
| مامور هوتل | خداحافظ! |

**Exercise 6AB:**

| | |
|---|---|
| زن | تصمیم گرفتی که باید به کجا برویم؟ |
| شوهر | والله، ما سه انتخاب داریم، ما میتوانیم که همراه بس های هوتل برویم، یا همراه شرکت توریزم بلخ و هم آریانا برویم. |
| زن | کدامش بهتر است؟ و تو کدامش را خوش کردی؟ |
| شوهر | من شرکت توریزم آریانا را خوش کردم، چونکه ما را به جای های دیدنی ولایت بامیان میبرد اما ما وقت کم داریم. پس من فکر میکنم که اگر همراه بس های هوتل برویم بهتر است. |
| زن | من هم دربارهٔ شرکت های آریانا و بلخ خواندم، من فکر میکنم که اگر همراه شرکت توریزم بلخ برویم بهتر است، چونکه این شرکت ما را به بندر حیرتان هم میبرد، من دریا را بسیار خوش دارم. |
| شوهر | بسیار خوب، پس بیا که یک تکسی بگیریم و به شرکت توریزم بلخ برویم. |

# LESSON 2

**Exercise 2AB:**

| | |
|---|---|
| شیرین | پدر ایمل جان، او پدر ایمل جان بیدار هستی، یا نه؟ الله... بخیز که خوب نیستم...اههه، الله وی. |
| شریف | چرا؟ چی شده؟ مادر ایمل. |
| شیرین | نمیفهمم بسیار مریض هستم، سرم، چشم هایم، دست ها و پاهایم همهٔ اش درد میکند. من فکر میکنم که تاثیر گرمی است. |
| شریف | باشد که من به دفتر هوتل زنگ بزنم و پرسان کنم که در این نزدیکها دواخانه و یا کلینیک است، یا نه؟ |
| شیرین | خوب زود کن که طاقت ندارم. |

## Exercise 4AB:

| | |
|---|---|
| هوتلی | هلو بفرمایید ، دفتر هوتل مزار است. چی خدمت کرده میتوانم؟ |
| شریف | سلام من مهمان اتاق شماره ۱۲۶ هستم. خانمم کمی مریض است. آیا در این نزدیك ها دواخانه یا شفاخانه است؟ |
| هوتلی | در این نزدیك ها شفاخانه نیست اما یك دواخانه در زیر هوتل ماست. شما میتوانید از آنجا دوا بخرید . |
| شریف | نام این دواخانه چیست؟ |
| هوتلی | دواخانهٔ رازیو که از هوتل بیرون شدید ، در دست راست تان بعد از دوکان دوم است. |
| شریف | آیا این دواخانه داکتر دارد؟ |
| هوتلی | فکر میکنم که داکتر ندارد ، اما فارمسست دارد. او شما را كمك کرده میتواند . |
| شریف | تشکر از همکاری تان. |

## Exercise 6AB:

| | |
|---|---|
| شریف | سلام، ببخشید ، شما در دواخانهٔ تان داکتر دارید؟ |
| دواخانه دار | سلام، نه ما داکتر نداریم، چرا خیریت است؟ |
| شریف | والله، خانمم کمی مریض است. |
| دواخانه دار | چی تکلیف دارند؟ |
| شریف | سرش، چشم هایش، دستها و پاهایش درد میکند. |
| دواخانه دار | والله برای سردردی، جان دردی، من میتوانم که برای شما دوا بدهم، اما برای چشم های شان شما باید داکتر را ببینید . |
| شریف | حالا به کجا بروم که داکتر ببینم؟ |
| دواخانه دار | حالا فقط در شفاخانه داکتر است، اگر خانم تان بیشتر مریض شدند ، میتوانید ایشان را به شفاخانه ببرید . |
| شریف | بسیار خوب، پس لطفاً کمی دوای سردردی و جان دردی برایم بدهید . |
| دواخانه دار | اینه، یك پاکت گولی سردردی وجان دردی و یك پماد درد برایتان میدهم،  برای خانم تان هر شش ساعت یك تابلیت بدهید که بخورند و پماد را بالای دستها و پاهایشان بمالید. |
| شریف | تشکر چند میشود؟ |
| دواخانه دار | ۱۰۰ افغانی |
| شریف | بفرمایید . |

## Exercise 7ADF:

| | | |
|---|---|---|
| شریف | داکتر صاحب سلام! | |
| داکتر | وعلیکم، بفرمایید، داخل بیایید. کی مریض است؟ | |
| شریف | داکتر صاحب مادر اولادهایم مریض است. | |
| داکتر | بفرمایید، خواهر جان اینجا بشینید. چی تکلیف دارید؟ | |
| شیرین | داکتر صاحب، از دیشب تمام جانم، دست هایم، پاهایم و چشم هایم درد میکند. فکر میکنم که کمی تب هم دارم. | |
| داکتر | آیا سرچرخ هستید؟ | |
| شیرین | بلی، سرچرخ هستم و کمی دلبدهستم و چشم هایم خارش میکند و همچنان بینی ام بند است. | |
| داکتر | آیا سرفه هم میکنید؟ | |
| شیرین | نه سرفه نمیکنم، اما یك دفعه استفراغ کردم. و بسیار کمزور هستم. | |
| داکتر | خوب اگر اجازه باشد، من میخواهم شما را معاینه کنم. لطفاً اینجا سر میز دراز بکشید. | |
| شریف | مادر ایمل صبر کن که کمکت کنم. | |
| شیرین | خیر بینی. | |

## Exercise 9AB:

| | | |
|---|---|---|
| داکتر | بسیار خوب مریضی تان بسیار جدی نیست، این گرمی زدگی است و شما به غذا ها حساسیت کردید. | |
| شیرین | ها، داکتر صاحب راست میگویید، ما دیروز بسیار در بیرون پیاده روی کردیم، هوا بسیار گرم و آفتابی بود. | |
| داکتر | بلی کوشش کنید که بسیار آب بنوشید و برای دو روز استراحت کنید، میوه جات و سبزیجات بسیار بخورید. | |
| شیرین | داکتر صاحب دوا برایم نوشته میکنید؟ | |
| داکتر | بلی، من در نسخه برای شما یك قسم گولی جان دردی، یك قسم گولی حساسیت و شربت تقویه نوشته کردم، و همچنان یك قطره چکان بینی. | |
| شیرین | داکتر صاحب این دوا هارا چی قسم استفاده کنم؟ | |
| داکتر | گولی های جاندردی را روز سه دفعه بعد از نان، گولی حساسیت را هر شب یکدانه، شربت تقویه را هر شش ساعت یك قاشق بخورید، و قطره چکان را اگر بینی تان بند بود هر ۱۲ ساعت در بینی تان دو قطره بچکانید. | |
| شیرین | تشکر داکتر صاحب، بفرمایید، فیس تان را بگیرید. | |
| داکتر | تشکر، شفای عاجل میخواهم برایتان. | |

# LESSON 3

Exercise 1A:

| | |
|---|---|
| شیرین | خوب یك روز دیگر مانده، صباح باید پس برویم بخیر. |
| شریف | ها اگر تكت طیاره پیدا شود. انشا الله صباح میرویم. |
| شیرین | چرا ما زمینی نمیرویم. |
| شریف | نه شما مریض هستید و سفر زمینی برای شما خوب نیست. |
| شیرین | پروا ندارد. من میتوانم كه زمینی سفر كنم. |
| شریف | نه، داكتر گفت كه هوای گرم برای شما خوب نیست. و صباح هوا بسیار گرم خواهد بود. |
| شیرین | خو، به تكت فروشی چی وقت زنگ خواهد زدی؟ |
| شریف | بعد از نان چاشت زنگ میزنم. حالا باید نان بخوریم، شما چی خوش دارید كه من فرمایش بدهم. |
| شیرین | بیا كه بیرون برویم و در یك رستورانت افغانی نان بخوریم. |
| شریف | آیا شما میتوانید كه راه بروید. |
| شیرین | ها حالا بهتر هستم. باش كه كالایم را بپوشم باز میبرایم. |
| شریف | بسیار خوب من هم بچه ها را آماده میكنم. |

Exercise 3:

| | |
|---|---|
| شریف | خوب چطور بود، از مزار شریف خوشتان آمد؟ |
| شیرین | بلی، بسیار خوب بود، اما كاشكی وقت زیادتر میداشتم كه همه جای ها را میدیدیم. |
| شریف | پروا نمیكند، انشاالله سال نو باز خواهیم آمد. خوب بعد از رخصتی ها چی پلان دارید؟ |
| شیرین | من اگر جور باشم باید مكتب بروم و دیدن پدرم و مادرم بروم. |
| شریف | ها، من هم به كار خواهم رفت، و همراه تو به دیدن پدر و مادرتان خواهم رفت. آیا برای شان تحفه خریدید؟ |
| شیرین | نه، نخریدم، خوب شد كه گفتید. بعد از نان بخیر خواهیم رفت. |

Exercise 5AB:

| | |
|---|---|
| تكت فروش | هلو بفرمایید، شركت هوایی آریانا ست، چی خدمت كرده میتوانم؟ |
| شریف | سلام، من شریف هستم، ببخشید، شما در كدام روز ها به كابل پرواز دارید؟ |

| | |
|---|---|
| تکت فروش | طیاره های ما روزهای شنبه، دوشنبه، چارشنبه و جمعه ساعت ۱۱ بجه از مزار شریف پرواز میکند و ساعت ۱۲ ونیم بجه در میدان هوایی کابل نشست میکند و در روز های یکشنبه، سه شنبه و پنجشنبه ساعت ۸ پرواز میکند و ساعت ۹ و نیم در میدان هوایی مزار شریف نشست میکند . |
| شریف | آیا برای صباحِ، برای شش نفر تکت دارید؟ |
| تکت فروش | یك دقیقه لطفاً.…. نه، برای صباح همه تکت ها فروخته شده است، اما برای دیگر صباحِ داریم، میخواهید؟ |
| شریف | بلی، لطفاً شش تکت بوك کنید . |
| تکت فروش | شما باید به تکت فروشی بیاید ، چونکه ما از طریق تلیفون تکت نمیفروشیم . |
| شریف | شما تا چند بجه باز هستید؟ |
| تکت فروش | تا پنج بجه . |
| شریف | خوب، من تا یك ساعت بعد میایم. فعلاً خدا حافظ! |
| تکت فروش | به امان خدا! |

## Exercise 6B:

| | |
|---|---|
| نماینده | هلو سلام، شرکت هوایی آریانا است، بفرمایید . |
| شریف | سلام، نامم شریف است، من یکی از مسافرین پرواز شماره ۲۳ هستم، من یك پیام گرفتم که پرواز مزار به کابل کنسل خواهد شد ، این درست است؟ |
| نماینده | بلی، این پرواز کنسل شده است ، چونکه هوای کابل خوب نیست. |
| شریف | پس چی وقت پرواز میکنیم؟ |
| نماینده | ما برای شما باز هم پیام روان میکنم، شاید دیگر صباح پرواز کنیم. |
| شریف | خوب تشکر |
| نماینده | خواهش میکنم، شب خوشی داشته باشید . خدا حافظ! |
| شریف | به امان خدا! |

Exercise 7:

| | |
|---|---|
| نماینده | هلو سلام، شرکت هوایی آریانا است، بفرمایید . |
| شریف | سلام، نامم شریف است، من یکی از مسافرین پرواز شماره ۲۳ هستم، من یك پیام گرفتم که پرواز مزار به کابل کنسل خواهد شد ، این درست است؟ |
| نماینده | بلی، این پرواز کنسل شده است، چونکه هوای کابل خوب نیست. |
| شریف | پس چی وقت پرواز میکنیم؟ |
| نماینده | ما برای شما باز هم پیام روان میکنم، شاید دیگر صباح پرواز کنیم. |
| شریف | خوب تشکر |
| نماینده | خواهش میکنم، شب خوشی داشته باشید . خدا حافظ! |
| شریف | به امان خدا! |

## Dari to English دری به انگلیسی

| | | |
|---|---|---|
| If God wants. | agar xodā baxāhad. | اگر خدا بخواهد . |
| Thanks be to God, I am fine. | al-hamdolelā, xub hastam. | الحمدالله، خوب هستم. |
| Hello! (Peace be with you.) | asalām ō alaykom! | السلام وعلیکم! |
| from Afghanistan | az afğānĕstān | از افغانستان |
| Nice meeting you. | az didan-e tān xōšāl šodom. | از دیدن تان خوشحال شدم. |
| get off from the ... | az... birōn šawed. | از ... بیرون شوید . |
| pass the ... | az... ter šawed. | از ... تیرشوید . |
| It is possible. | ehtamāl merawad. | احتمال میرود . |
| May I come in? | ĕjāza ast dāxĕl šawam? | اجازه است داخل شوم؟ |
| May I? | ĕjāza ast? | اجازه است؟ |
| What day is today? | ĕmroz Čand šanbe ast? | امروز، چند شنبه است؟ |
| Today is Monday. | ĕmroz do šanbe ast. | امروز دوشنبه است. |
| This is clear. | ĕn wāzĕh ast. | این واضح است. |
| Here it is, take it please. | ena, bafarmāyed. | اینه، بفرمایید . |
| If God's willing | Enšālāh | انشاالله |
| I hope that... | omedwāram ke... | امیدوارم که... |
| Sure. | ba čĕšom. | به چشم |
| with regards | bā ĕhtarām | با احترام |
| Hope to see you soon. | ba omeede dídār. | به امید دیدار . |
| With the help of God | ba yāri-e xodā | به یاری خدا |
| Excuse me! (Forgive me.) | babaxšed! | ببخشید! |
| Excuse me, sorry. | babaxšed/ babaxšen | ببخشید / ببخشین |
| Please (when offering something) | bafarmāyed | بفرمایید! |
| get in | bālā šawed. | بالاشوید . |
| My brother is twenty years old. | barādaram bist sāla ast. | برادرم بیست ساله است. |
| How old is your brother? | barādar-e tān čand sāla ast? | برادر تان چند ساله است؟ |
| God willing, with peace | Baxayr | بخیر |

| sorry, excuse me | bĕbaxšed./babxšed. | ببخشید . |
| make a turn | bĕgarded. | بگردید . |
| let's go | beyā kĕ bĕrawem. | بیا که برویم . |
| Don't worry. | parwā namĕkonad. | پروا نمیکند . |
| Turn back. | pas bĕgarded. | پس بگردید . |
| 25 past one. | pāw bālā yak | پاو بالایک |
| 25 past two. | pāw kam do | پاو کم دو |
| go straight ahead | peš bĕrawed. | پیش بروید . |
| I have a question. | porsān dāram. | پرسان دارم. |
| Congratulations! | tabrik bāšad! | تبریک باشد! |
| Thanks. | tašakor | تشکر |
| This phrase is used when you want to say that a person was missed during a delicious meal. | jāye tān xāli bōd. | جای تان خالی بود . |
| Be well. Live healthy! | jōr bāšed. | جور باشید . |
| There is not another choice. | čāra nest. | چاره نیست. |
| How are you? | četor hasted? | چطور هستید؟ |
| How can I help you? | či komak karda metānom? | چی کمک کرده میتوانم؟ |
| What is troubling you? | či takllif dāred? | چی تکلیف دارید؟ |
| How can I be of service? | či xĕdmat karda metānom? | چی خدمت کرده میتوانم؟ |
| My pleasure! | xāheš mekonam! | خواهش میکنم! |
| That is fine. | xayr ast. | خیر است. |
| It's okay. | xayr bāšad. | خیر باشد . |
| Goodbye. | xodā hāfĕz. | خدا حافظ! |
| Goodbye! | xodā hāfĕz! | خدا حافظ! |
| Welcome! | xoš āmaded! | خوش آمدید! |
| I am fine. | xub hastam. | خوب هستم. |
| Make a turn. | dawr bĕzaned. | دور بزنید . |
| Go forward. | rō-barō bĕrawed. | روبرو بروید . |
| Good day! | roz baxayr! | روز بخیر! |
| Be alive. | zĕnda bāšed. | زنده باشید . |

| | | |
|---|---|---|
| What time is it? | sā'at Čand baja ast? | ساعت چند بجه است؟ |
| It is 1:15. | sā'at yak-o-pānzda daqiqa ast. | ساعت یک و پانزده دقیقه است. |
| Hello! (Peace be with you.) | salām! | سلام! |
| Live healthy. | salāmat bāšed. | سلامت باشید. |
| Goodnight! | šab baxayr! | شب بخیر! |
| I wish you a quick recovery (get well soon). | šfāye 'ājĕl mexāham. | شفا عاجل میخواهم |
| Thanks, it's God's will. | shokor fazle xodāst. | شُکر فضلِ خداست. |
| Where are you originally from? | šomā as-lan an az kojā hasted? | شما اصلاً از کجا هستید؟ |
| Which city are you from? | šomā az kodām šahr hasted? | شما از کدام شهرهستید؟ |
| Where are you from? | šomā az kojā hasted? | شما از کجا هستید؟ |
| How many phones do you have? | šomā Čand dāna tĕlefun dāred? | شما چند دانه تلیفون دارید؟ |
| Which state do you live in? | šomā dar kodām ayālat zendagi me-koned? | شما در کدام ایالت زنده گی میکنید؟ |
| obviously | tab'an | طبعاً |
| I understood. | fahmidan. | فهمیدم. |
| Discount the price. | kame ma'āt koned. | کمی مراعات کنید . |
| Go a little further. | kami peš bĕrawed. | کمی پیش بروید . |
| What is Karim's relation to Zarghuna? | karim čiye zarğuna mešawad? | کریم چی زرغونه میشود؟ |
| with peace | kate kayr | کتی خیر |
| Please. | lotfan | لطفاً . |
| Please wait a few moments. | lotfan čand lahza sabar koned. | لطفاً چند لحظه صبر کنید . |
| I am from Kabul City. | man az šahr kabol hastam. | من ازشهر کابل هستم. |
| I am bored! | man dĕq āwardam! (ma dĕq āwordem!) | من دق آوردم! |
| Me too. | man hamčenān. | من همچنان . |
| I have one phone. | man yak dāna tĕlefun dārom. | من یک دانه تلیفون دارم. |
| Don't be tired. | mānda nabāšed?(mānda nabāšen?) | مانده نباشید . |
| I didn't understand. | nafamidam. | نفهمیدم. |

| My name is Farid. | nām-am farid ast. | نامم فرید است. |
| What is your phone number? | nambar-e telefun-e tān čand ast? | نمبر تلیفون تان چند است؟ |
| What is the name of your city? | nām-e šahr tān čist? | نام شهرتان چیست؟ |
| The name of my city is Kabul. | nām-e šahr-am kābol ast. | نام شهرم کابل است. |
| What is your name? | nām-e tān čist? | نام تان چیست؟ |
| Hello! (Peace be with you.) | walaykom | وعلیکم! |
| Hello! (Peace be with you.) | walaykom salām! | وعلیکم السلام! |
| slang for well...umm...hmm... | wallāh | والله |
| actually, truly | wāqě'an | واقعاً |
| one thirty (one and half) | yak-o-nim | یك و نیم |

## English to Dari انگلیسی به دری

| | | |
|---|---|---|
| actually, truly | wāqĕ'an | واقعاً |
| Congratulations. | tabrik bāšad. | تبریك باشد . |
| Discount the price. | kame ma'āt koned. | کمی مراعات کنید . |
| Excuse me! | babaxšed/ babaxšen | ببخشید / ببخشین |
| from Afghanistan | az afğānĕstān | از افغانستان |
| get in | bālā šawed. | بالاشوید . |
| get off from the ... | az... birōn šawed. | از... بیرون شوید . |
| Go a little further. | kami peš bĕrawed. | کمی پیش بروید . |
| Go forward. | rō-barō bĕrawed. | روبرو بروید . |
| Go straight ahead. | peš bĕrawed. | پیش بروید . |
| God willing, with peace | baxayr | بخیر |
| Good day. | roz baxayr! | روز بخیر! |
| Goodbye. | xodā hāfĕz! | خدا حافظ! |
| Goodbye. | xodā hāfĕz! | خدا حافظ! |
| Goodnight! | šab baxayr! | شب بخیر! |
| Hello! (Peace be with you.) | asalām ō alaykom! | السلام وعلیکم! |
| Hello! (Peace be with you.) | walaykom salām! | وعلیکم السلام! |
| Hello! (Peace be with you.) | salām! | سلام! |
| Hello! (Peace be with you.) | walaykom! | وعلیکم! |
| Here it is, take it please. | ena, bafarmāyed. | اینه، بفرمایید . |
| Hope to see you soon. | ba omeede dídār. | به امید دیدار . |
| How are you? | četor hasted? | چطور هستید؟ |
| How can I be of service? | či xĕdmat karda metānom? | چی خدمت کرده میتوانم؟ |
| How can I help you? | či komak karda metānom? | چی کمک کرده میتوانم؟ |
| How many phones do you have? | šomā čand dāna tĕlefun dāred? | شما چند دانه تلیفون دارید؟ |
| How old is your brother? | barādar-e tān čand sāla ast? | برادر تان چند ساله است؟ |
| I am bored. | man dĕq āwardam! (ma dĕq āwordem!) | من دق آوردم! |
| I am fine. | xub hastam. | خوب هستم . |

| | | |
|---|---|---|
| I am from Kabul City. | man az šahr kabol hastam. | من از شهر کابل هستم. |
| I didn't understand. | nafamidam. | نفهمیدم. |
| I have a question. | porsān dāram. | پرسان دارم. |
| I have one phone. | man yak dāna tělefun dārom. | من یك دانه تلیفون دارم. |
| I hope that... | omedwāram ke... | امیدوارم که... |
| I understood. | fahmidan. | فهمیدم. |
| I wish you a quick recovery (get well soon). | šfāye 'ājěl mexāham. | شفا عاجل میخواهم |
| If God wants. | agar xodā baxāhad. | اگر خدا بخواهد . |
| If God's willing | enšālāh | انشاالله |
| It is 1:15. | sā'at yak-o-pānzda daqiqa ast. | ساعت یك و پانزده دقیقه است. |
| It is possible. | ehtamāl merawad. | احتمال میرود . |
| It's okay. | xayr bāšad. | خیر باشد . |
| Let's go | beyā kě běrawem. | بیا که برویم. |
| Live healthy. | salāmat bāšed | سلامت باشید . |
| Make a turn. | dawr bězaned. | دور بزنید . |
| Make a turn. | běgarded. | بگردید . |
| May I come in? | ějāza ast dāxěl šawam? | اجازه است داخل شوم؟ |
| May I? | ějāza ast? | اجازه است؟ |
| May you not be tired. | mānda nabāšed? (mānda nabāšen?) | مانده نباشید . |
| Me too. | man hamčenān. | من همچنان . |
| My brother is twenty years old. | barādaram bist sāla ast. | برادرم بیست ساله است. |
| My name is Farid. | nām-am farid ast. | نامم فرید است. |
| My pleasure! | xāheš mekonam! | خواهش میکنم! |
| Nice meeting you. | az didan-e tān xōšāl šodom. | از دیدن تان خوشحال شدم. |
| No problem. (It doesn't matter.) | parwā naměkonad. | پروا نمیکند . |
| obviously | tab'an | طبعاً |
| one thirty (one and half) | yak-o-nim | یك و نی |
| pass the... | az... ter šawed. | از ... تیرشوید . |
| Please (when offering something). | bafarmāyed. | بفرمایید . |

| | | |
|---|---|---|
| Please wait a few moments. | lotfan čand lahza sabar koned. | لطفاً چند لحظه صبر کنید. |
| Please. | lotfan. | لطفاً. |
| slang for well...umm...hmm... | wallāh | والله |
| Sorry, excuse me. | běbaxšed./babxšed. | ببخشید. |
| Sure. | ba čěšom. | به چشم. |
| Thank you. (Be alive.) | zěnda bāšed. | زنده باشید. |
| Thank you. (Be prosperous.) | jōr bāšed. | جور باشید. |
| Thanks be to God, I am fine. | al-hamdolelā, xub hastam. | الحمدالله، خوب هستم. |
| Thanks, it's God's will. | shokor fazle xodāst. | شُكر فضل خداست. |
| Thanks. | tašakor. | تشکر. |
| That is fine. | xayr ast. | خیر است. |
| The name of my city is Kabul. | nām-e šahr-am kābol ast. | نام شهرم کابل است. |
| There is not another choice. | čāra nest. | چاره نیست. |
| This is clear. | ěn wāzěh ast. | این واضح است. |
| This phrase is used when you want to say that a person was missed during a delicious meal. | jāye tān xāli bōd. | جای تان خالی بود. |
| Today is Monday. | ěmroz do šanbe ast. | امروز دوشنبه است. |
| Turn back. | pas běgarded. | پس بگردید. |
| Twenty-five past one. | pāw bālā yak | پاو بالایک |
| Twenty-five past two. | pāw kam do | پاو کم دو |
| Welcome! | xoš āmaded! | خوش آمدید! |
| What day is today? | ěmroz čand šanbe ast? | امروز، چند شنبه است؟ |
| What is Karim's relation to Zarghuna? | karim čiye zarğuna mešawad? | کریم چی زرغونه میشود؟ |
| What is the name of your city? | nām-e šahr tān čist? | نام شهرتان چیست؟ |
| What is troubling you? | či takllif dāred? | چی تکلیف دارید؟ |
| What is your name? | nām-e tān čist? | نام تان چیست؟ |
| What is your phone number? | nambar-e telefun-e tān čand ast? | نمبر تلیفون تان چند است؟ |
| What time is it? | sā'at čand baja ast? | ساعت چند بجه است؟ |
| Where are you from? | šomā az kojā hasted? | شما از کجا هستید؟ |

| Where are you originally from? | šomā as-lan an az kojā hasted? | شما اصلاً از کجا هستید؟ |
|---|---|---|
| Which city are you from? | šomā az kodām šahr hasted? | شما از کدام شهر هستید؟ |
| Which state do you live in? | šomā dar kodām ayālat zendagi me-koned? | شما در کدام ایالت زنده گی میکنید؟ |
| with peace | kate kayr | کتی خیر |
| with regards | bā ĕhtarām | با احترام |
| with the help of God | ba yāri-e xodā | به یاری خدا |

# APPENDIX D: PERSIAN PHRASES

## Dari to English

| English | Iranian Persian | | Farsi Dari | |
|---------|-----------------|--|------------|--|
| | | الف ، الف مد | | |
| cherry | ālu-gilās | آلوگیلاس | ālu bālu | آلوبالو |
| Indonesia | andonizi | اندونیزی | andoniziyā | اندونیزیا |
| child | farzand | فرزند | awlād/farzand | اولاد / فرزند |
| brother-in-law (husband's side) | barādar šawhar | برادر شوهر | ĕwar | ایور |
| pajama tie | band-e šalvār | بند شلوار | ezār band | ایزار بند |
| living room | hāl-e pazirāyi | هال پذیرایی | otāq-e našeman | اتاق نشیمن |
| | | ب | | |
| male cousin (father's side) | pasar 'amō | پسر عمو | bača-ye kaka | بچۀ کاکا |
| cucumber | xiyār | خیار | badrang | بادرنگ |
| overcoat | pāltō | پالتو | bālā-poš | بالاپوش |
| sugar | šakar | شکر | bura | بوره |
| | | پ | | |
| pants | šalvār | شلوار | patlun | پطلون |
| cowboy pants | šalvār-e jinz | شلوار جینز | patlun-e kawbāy | پطلون کوبای |
| pilot | xalabān | خلبان | pelōt | پیلوت |
| pencil | medād | مداد | pĕnsĕl | پنسل |
| eraser | medādpāk-kon | مداد پاک کن | pĕnsĕl-pāk | پنسل پاك |
| cat | gorba | گربه | pĕšak | پیشك |
| | | ت | | |
| watermelon | hĕnduna | هندوانه | tarbuz | تربوز |
| toilet | dastshoyi | دستشویی | tašnāb | تشناب |
| last name | esme fāmili | اسم فامیلی | taxalos | تخلص |
| airplane | havāpaymā | هواپیما | tayāra | طیاره |
| ID card | šanās-nāma | شناسنامه | tazkĕra, kart-e howiyat | تذکره، کارت هویت |

| airplane ticket | balit-e havāpaymā | بلیط هواپیما | tĕkĕt-e tayāra | تکت طیاره |
| taxi driver, chauffer | šufar | شوفر | tĕxiwān | تکسیوان |
| gift | kādō | کادو | tohfa | تحفه |
| | | ج | | |
| towel | havla | حوله | jān-xoškān, jān-pāk | جانخشکان، جانپاك |
| | | ح | | |
| house/yard | sarā, xuna | سرا، خونه | haweli | حویلی |
| | | خ | | |
| housekeeper, maid | xedmat-kār | خدمتکار | xāna sāmān | خانه سامان |
| sister-in-law (wife's side) | xāhar-zan | خواهر زن | xĕyāšna | خیاشنه |
| mother-in-law | mādar-zan/ mādar šawhar | مادر زن/ مادر شوهر | xošō | خشو |
| father-in-law | padar-zan/ padar šawhar | پدر زن/ پدر شوهر | xosor | خسر |
| brother-in-law (wife's side) | barādar-zan | برادر زن | xosorbōra | خسربُره |
| | | د | | |
| hallway | hāl | هال | dahliz | دهلیز |
| door | dar | در | darwāza | دروازه |
| pharmacy | dāru xāna | دارو خانه | dawā-xāna | دواخانه |
| nauseated | tahavo' | تهوع | dĕl-bad | دلبد |
| female cousin (father's side) | doxtar 'amo | دختر عمو | doxtar-e kaka | دختر کاکا |
| | | ر | | |
| restaurant | rasturan | رستوران | rastōrānt | رستورانت |
| holiday | ta'tilāt | تعطیلات | roxsati | رخصتی |
| | | ز | | |
| carrot | hawĕč | هویج | zardak | زردك |
| underpants | zir-puš | زیر پوش | zĕr tonbāni | زیرتنبانی |

|  |  | س |  | س |
|---|---|---|---|---|
| What time is it? | sā'at či ast? | ساعت چی است؟ | sā'at čand baja ast? | ساعت چند بجه است؟ |
| street, road | xiyābān | خیابان | sarak, jāda | سرک، جاده |
| red | qarmĕz | قرمز | sorx | سرخ |

|  |  | س |  | س |
|---|---|---|---|---|
| hospital | bimārestān | بیمارستان | šafāxāna | شفاخانه |
| hospital | bimārestān | بیمارستان | šafāxāna | شفاخانه |
| Saturday | šanba | شنبه | šanbe | شنبه |
| to shower | dōš grĕftan (dōš gir) | دوش گرفتن (دوش گیر) | šāwar grĕftan (šāwar gir) | شاورگیر ( شاورگرفتن) |

|  |  | ص |  |  |
|---|---|---|---|---|
| class | kalās | کلاس | sĕnf | صنف |
| front yard | hayāt | حیاط | sahn-e haweli | صحن حویلی |

|  |  | ط |  |  |
|---|---|---|---|---|
| airplane | havāpaymā | هواپیما | tayāra | طیاره |

|  |  | ف |  |  |
|---|---|---|---|---|
| doctor's fees | dastmozd | دستمزد | fis | فیس |

|  |  | ق |  |  |
|---|---|---|---|---|
| pen | xudkār | خودکار | qalam | قلم |
| village | ahrestānš | شهرستان | qari-ya | قریه |
| pencil sharpener | medād-tarāš | مداد تراش | qlam-tarāš | قلمتراش |
| police department | kalāntari | کلانتری | qōmandāni-ye amniya | قوماندانی امنیه |

|  |  | ک |  |  |
|---|---|---|---|---|
| uncle | 'amō | عمو | kaka | کاکا |
| cafe | kāfa | کافه | kāntin | کانتین |
| banana | muz | موز | kela | کیله |
| window | panjarah | پنجره | kĕlkin | کلکین |
| notebook | daftar | دفتر | kĕtāb-ča | کتابچه |

|  |  | گ |  |  |
|---|---|---|---|---|

| confused, out of it | geč | گیج | gans | گنس |
|---|---|---|---|---|
| pink | šōrati | صورتی | golābi | گلابی |
| pill | qors | قرص | gōli | گولی |

ل

| dorm | xāb-gāh | خوابگاه | layliya | لیله |
|---|---|---|---|---|
| turban | 'amāma, dastār | عمامه، دستار | longi | لنگی |

م

| Mexico | mak-zik | مکزیك | maksikō | مکسیکو |
|---|---|---|---|---|
| orange | portaqāl | پرتقال | mālta | مالته |
| I am bored. | dělam gěrěfta. | دلم گرفته | man děq āwardam. | من دق آوردم. |
| floor | tabaqa | طبقه | manzěl | منزل |
| airport | forud-gāh | فرودگاه | maydān-e hawā-ye | میدان هوایی |
| clinic, doctor's office | matab-e pazěšk | مطب پزشك | māyna-xāna | معاینه خانه |
| auto repair shop | ta'mir-gāh | تعمیرگاه | městari-xāna | مستری خانه |
| pepper | fělfěl | فلفل | morč | مرچ |
| boots | čakma | چکمه | mōza | موزه |
| museum | muza | موزه | mōziyam | موزیم |

ن

| lunch | nahār | نهار | nān čašt | نان چاشت |
|---|---|---|---|---|
| dinner | šām | شام | nān šab | نان شب |
| sister-in-law (husband's side) | xāhar šawhar | خواهر شوهر | nanō | ننو |
| grandchild | nava | نوه | nawāsa | نواسه |
| underwear | šort | شورت | nikar, sěntarāj | نیکر، سنتراج |
| tie | karavāt | کروات | niktāye | نیکتایی |

و

| province | ostān | استان | walāyat | ولایت |
|---|---|---|---|---|
| district | farmāndāri | فرمانداری | waloswāli | ولسوالی |
| Washington | vāšeng-tōn | واشنگتون | wāšěngtan | واشنگتن |

| | | ه | | |
|---|---|---|---|---|
| classmate | ham-kelāsi | همکلاسی | ham-senfi | همصنفی |
| eighteen | haj-dah | هجده | haž-dah | هژده |
| | | ی | | |
| purple | banafš | بنفش | yāsamani | یاسمنی |
| dress shirt | pirā-han | پیراهن | yaxan-qāq | یخن قاق |

## English to Dari

| English | Iranian Persian | | Farsi Dari | |
|---|---|---|---|---|
| | | A | | |
| airplane | havāpaymā | هواپیما | tayāra | طیاره |
| airplane ticket | balit-e havāpaymā | بلیط هواپیما | tĕkĕt-e tayāra | تکت طیاره |
| airport | forud-gāh | فرودگاه | maydān-e hawā-ye | میدان هوایی |
| | | B | | |
| banana | muz | موز | kela | کیله |
| band | halqa | حلقه | čĕla | چله |
| bed | taxt-e xāb | تخت خواب | čapārkat | چپرکت |
| boots | čakma | چکمه | mōza | موزه |
| breakfast | sobhāna | صبحانه | čāy-e sob | چای صبح |
| brother-in-law (husband's side) | barādar šawhar | برادر شوهر | ĕwar | ایور |
| brother-in-law (wife's side) | barādar-zan | برادر زن | xosorbōra | خسربُره |
| | | C | | |
| cafe | kāfa | کافه | kāntin | کانتین |
| auto repair shop | ta'mir-gāh | تعمیرگاه | mĕstari-xāna | مستری خانه |
| carrot | havĕč | هویج | zardak | زردك |
| cat | gorba | گربه | pĕšak | پیشك |
| chair | sandali | صندلی | čawki | چوکی |
| cherry | ālu-gilās | آلوگیلاس | ālu bālu | آلوبالو |
| child | farzand | فرزند | awlād/farzand | اولاد / فرزند |

| class | kalās | كلاس | sĕnf | صنف |
|---|---|---|---|---|
| classmate | ham-kelāsi | همكلاسى | ham-senfi | همصنفى |
| clinic, doctor's office | matab-e pazĕšk | مطب پزشك | māyna-xāna | معاينه خانه |
| confused, out of it | geč | گيج | gans | گنس |
| cowboy pants | šalvār-e jinz | شلوار جينز | patlun-e kawbāy | پطلون كوباى |
| cucumber | xiyār | خيار | badrang | بادرنگ |
| | | D | | |
| dinner | šām | شام | nān šab | نان شب |
| district | farmāndāri | فرماندارى | waloswāli | ولسوالى |
| doctor's fees | dastmozd | دستمزد | fis | فيس |
| door | dar | در | darwāza | دروازه |
| dorm | xāb-gāh | خوابگاه | layliya | ليله |
| dress shirt | pirā-han | پيراهن | yaxan-qāq | يخن قاق |
| | | E | | |
| eighteen | haj-dah | هجده | haž-dah | هژده |
| eraser | medādpāk-kon | مداد پاك كن | pĕnsĕl-pāk | پنسل پاك |
| | | F | | |
| father-in-law | padar-zan/ padar šawhar | پدر زن/ پدر شوهر | xosor | خسر |
| female cousin (father's side) | doxtar 'amo | دختر عمو | doxtar-e kaka | دختر كاكا |
| floor | tabaqa | طبقه | manzĕl | منزل |
| four | čahār | چهار | čār | چار |
| fourteen | čahār-dah | چهارده | čār-dah | چارده |
| front yard | hayāt | حياط | sahn-e haweli | صحن حويلى |
| | | G | | |
| gift | kādō | كادو | tohfa | تحفه |
| grandchild | nava | نوه | nawāsa | نواسه |
| | | H | | |
| hallway | hāl | هال | dahliz | دهليز |
| holiday | ta'tilāt | تعطيلات | roxsati | رخصتى |

| hospital | bimārestān | بیمارستان | šafāxāna | شفاخانه |
| hospital | bimārestān | بیمارستان | šafāxāna | شفاخانه |
| house/yard | sarā, xuna | سرا، خونه | haweli | حویلی |
| housekeeper, maid | xedmat-kār | خدمتکار | xāna sāmān | خانه سامان |

| I | | | | |
| --- | --- | --- | --- | --- |
| I am bored. | dělam gěrěfta. | دلم گرفته | man děq āwardam. | من دق آوردم. |
| ID card | šanās-nāma | شناسنامه | tazkěra, kart-e howiyat | تذکره، کارت هویت |
| Indonesia | andonizi | اندونیزی | andoniziyā | اندونیزیا |
| last name | esme fāmili | اسم فامیلی | taxalos | تخلص |

| L | | | | |
| --- | --- | --- | --- | --- |
| living room | hāl-e pazirāyi | هال پذیرایی | otāq-e našeman | اتاق نشیمن |
| lunch | nahār | نهار | nān cast | نان چاشت |

| M | | | | |
| --- | --- | --- | --- | --- |
| male cousin (father's side) | pasar 'amō | پسر عمو | bača-ye kaka | بچۀ کاکا |
| Mexico | mak-zik | مکزیك | maksikō | مکسیکو |
| mother-in-law | mādar-zan/ mādar šawhar | مادر زن/ مادر شوهر | xošō | خشو |
| museum | muza | موزه | mōziyam | موزیم |

| N | | | | |
| --- | --- | --- | --- | --- |
| nauseated | tahavo' | تهوع | děl-bad | دلبد |
| notebook | daftar | دفتر | kětāb-ča | کتابچه |

| O | | | | |
| --- | --- | --- | --- | --- |
| orange | portaqāl | پرتقال | mālta | مالته |
| overcoat | pāltō | پالتو | bālā-poš | بالاپوش |

| P | | | | |
| --- | --- | --- | --- | --- |
| pajama tie | band-e šalvār | بند شلوار | ezār band | ایزار بند |
| pants | šalvār | شلوار | patlun | پطلون |
| pen | xudkār | خودکار | qalam | قلم |
| pencil | medād | مداد | pěnsěl | پنسل |

| pencil sharpener | medād-tarāš | مداد تراش | qlam-tarāš | قلمتراش |
|---|---|---|---|---|
| pepper | fĕlfĕl | فلفل | morč | مرچ |
| pharmacy | dāru xāna | دارو خانه | dawā-xāna | دواخانه |
| pill | qors | قرص | gōli | گولی |
| pilot | xalabān | خلبان | pelōt | پیلوت |
| pink | šōrati | صورتی | golābi | گلابی |
| police department | kalāntari | کلانتری | qōmandāni-ye amniya | قومندانی امنیه |
| province | ostān | استان | walāyat | ولایت |
| purple | banafš | بنفش | yāsamani | یاسمنی |

| R | | | | |
|---|---|---|---|---|
| red | qarmĕz | قرمز | sorx | سرخ |
| restaurant | rasturan | رستوران | rastōrānt | رستورانت |

| S | | | | |
|---|---|---|---|---|
| Saturday | šanba | شنبه | šanbe | شنبه |
| sister-in-law (husband's side) | xāhar šawhar | خواهر شوهر | nanō | ننو |
| sister-in-law (wife's side) | xāhar-zan | خواهر زن | xĕyāšna | خیاشنه |
| street, road | xiyābān | خیابان | sarak, jāda | سرك، جاده |
| sugar | šakar | شکر | bura | بوره |

| T | | | | |
|---|---|---|---|---|
| taxi driver, chauffeur | šufar | شوفر | tĕxiwān | تكسیوان |
| tie | karavāt | کروات | niktāye | نیكتایی |
| to shower | dōš grĕftan (dōš gir) | دوش گرفتن (دوش گیر) | šāwar grĕftan (šāwar gir) | شاور گرفتن (شاور گیر) |
| toilet | dastshoyi | دستشویی | tašnāb | تشناب |
| towel | hawla | حوله | jān-xoškān, jān-pāk | جانخشكان، جانپاك |
| turban | 'amāma, dastār | عمامه، دستار | longi | لنگی |

| U | | | | |
|---|---|---|---|---|
| uncle | 'amō | عمو | kaka | كاكا |

| underpants | zir-puš | زیر پوش | zĕr tonbāni | زیرتنبانی |
| underwear | sort | شورت | nikar, sĕntarāj | نیکر، سنتراج |
| | | V | | |
| village | ahrestānš | شهرستان | qari-ya | قریه |
| | | W | | |
| Washington | vāšeng-tōn | واشنگتون | wāšĕngtan | واشنگتن |
| watermelon | hĕnduna | هندوانه | tarbuz | تربوز |
| Wednesday | čahār- šanba | چهارشنبه | čār- šanbe | چار شنبه |
| What time is it? | sā'at či ast? | ساعت چی است؟ | sā'at čand baja ast? | ساعت چند بجه است؟ |
| window | panjarah | پنجره | kĕlkin | کلکین |

# APPENDIX E: DARI-ENGLISH GLOSSARY

Dari to English دری به انگلیسی

| | الف مد | |
|---|---|---|
| water | āb | آب |
| swimming | āb-bāzi, šěnā | آببازی، شنا |
| to swim | āb-bāzi kardan (āb-bāzi kon) | آبیازی کردن (آبیازی کن) |
| juice | āb mewa | آب میوه |
| juice/smoothie shop | ābmewa forōši | آب میوه فروشی |
| weather | āb ō hawā | آب و هوا |
| blue | ābi | آبی |
| blue | ābi | آبی |
| altar | ātěškada | آتشکده |
| to calm/silent | ārām bōdan (ārām bāš/ ārām hast) | آرام بودن (آرام باش /هست) |
| flour | ārd | آرد |
| to wish | ārězō kardan (ārězō kon) | آرزو کردن |
| sky | āsmān | آسمان |
| kitchen | āšpaz xāna | آشپز خانه |
| cook | āšpaz | آشپز |
| kitchen | āšpaz xāna | آشپز خانه |
| sun | āftab, xōr | آفتاب، خورشید |
| Mr./Gentleman, Sir | āqā | آقا |
| cherry | ālu bālu | آلوبالو |
| to be ready | āmāda bōdan (āmāda hast) | آماده بودن (آماده هست) |
| to come | āmadan (āy) | آمدن (آی) |
| there | ānjā | آنجا |
| they are ... | ān-hā ... hastand. | آنها ... هستند. |
| they | ān-hā | آنها |
| they are ... | ānhā ... mebāšand. | آنها ... میباشند. |

| | | |
|---|---|---|
| to bring | āwordan (āwar) | آوردن (آور) |
| ice cream | ayskĕrim | آیسکریم |
| ice cream shop | āyskĕrim forōši | آیسکریم فروشی |
| next | āyenda | آینده |
| | الف | |
| cloud | abr | ابر |
| cloudy | abri | ابری |
| your (singular) | at | ات |
| living room | otāq-e našiman | اتاق نشیمن |
| bedroom | otāq-e xāb | اتاق خواب |
| room | otāq | اتاق |
| double-bed room | otāq-e do nafara | اتاق دو نفره |
| single-bed room | otāq-e yak nafara | اتاق یك نفره |
| to feel | ehsās kardan (ehsās kon) | احساس کردن (احساس کن) |
| to marry | ezdĕwāj kardan (ezdĕwāj kon) | ازدواج کردن |
| via | az tariq-e | از طریق |
| hours riding | asb dawāni | اسب دوانی |
| college instructor | ostād | استاد |
| stewardess | estiwardes | استیوردیس |
| vomit | estafrāğ | استفراغ |
| to rest | estarāhat kardan (estarāhat kon) | استراحت کردن (استراحت کن) |
| her/his | aš | اش |
| unknown people, strangers | ašxās-e nāšanās | اشخاص ناشناس |
| members | a'zā | اعضا |
| most of the time, often | aksaran | اکثراً |
| ring, band | angoštar, čĕla | انگشتر، چله |
| grape | angur | انگور |
| bookshelf | almāri kĕtāb | الماری کتاب |
| my | am | ام/مَ |
| entrance exam | emtĕhān kānkōr | امتحان کانکور |

| America | mrikā | امریکا |
|---|---|---|
| today | ĕmroz | امروز |
| female, feminine | onās, zanāna | اناث، زنانه |
| pomegranate | anār | انار |
| to do a task | anjām dādan (anjām dah) | انجام دادن (انجام ده) |
| Indonesia | andoniziyā | اندونیزیا |
| God willing | enšālāh | انشاالله |
| finger | angošt | انگشت |
| s/he is... | o ... ast. | او ... است. |
| s/he, it | o | او |
| s/he is ... | ō ... mebāšad. | او ... میباشد . |
| iron | ōtō | اوتو |
| first | awal | اول |
| children | awlād | اولاد |
| state | ayālat | ایالت |
| a string that ties the waist of the pants | ezār band | ایزار بند |
| here | ĕnjā | اینجا |
| taxi station | estgāh-e taxi | ایستگاه تکسی |
| bus station/bus | estgāh-sarwes/estgāh-e bas | ایستگاه سرویس/ بس |
| they | ĕšān | ایشان |
| Here it is. | ena. | اینه. |
| brother-in-law (for wife) | ewar | ایور |
| | ب | |
| experienced | bā tajroba | باتجربه |
| cucumber | bādrang | بادرنگ |
| wind | bād, šamāl | باد ، شمال |
| rain | bārān | باران |
| to rain | bārān bāridan (bāran bār) | باران باریدن (باران بار) |
| rainy | bārāni | بارانی |
| rainfall | bārĕndagi | بارنده گی |

| to rain, shower | bāridan(bār) | باریدن (بار) |
|---|---|---|
| to open | bāz kardan (bāz kon) | باز کردن (باز کن) |
| bazaar | bāzār | بازار |
| let me | bāšad kĕ | باشد که |
| roof | bām | بام |
| garden | bāğča | باغچه |
| upward, up | bālā | بالا |
| pillow | bālĕšt | بالشت |
| eggplant | bādĕnejān-e siyā (bānejān-e siyā) | بادنجان سیاه |
| tomato | bādĕnjān-e rōmi | بادنجان رومی |
| bicycle riding | bāyskĕl dawāni | بایسکل دوانی |
| to play | bāzi kardan (bazi kon) | بازی کردن (بازی کن) |
| o'clock | baja | بجه |
| boy | bača | بچه |
| son | bača/pasar | بچه/پسر |
| cousin | bačaye a'ma | بچهٔ عمه |
| cousin | bačaye kākā | بچهٔ کاکا |
| kindergarten (age) child | bačaye kodakĕstān | بچهٔ کودکستان |
| cousin | bačaye māmā | بچهٔ ماما |
| cousin | bačaye xāla | بچهٔ خاله |
| for boys | bačagāna | بچه گانه |
| sea | bahr | بحر |
| because | baxātĕr-e kĕ/čōn kĕ | بخاطریکه/چونکه |
| with peace | baxayr | بخیر |
| without | bĕdōn | بدون |
| to exit, to come out of (infinitive) | bar āmadan (bar āy) | برآمدن (بر آی) |
| Brazil | barāzíl | برازیل |
| brother | barādar | برادر |
| to pickup | bardāštan (bardār) | برادشتن (بردار) |
| to pick up/to leave | bardāštan (bardār) | برداشتن (بردار) |

| to carry | bordan (bar) | بردن (بر) |
|---|---|---|
| snow | barf | برف |
| to snow | barf bāridan (barf bār) | برف باریدن (برف بار) |
| snowy | barfi | برفی |
| burqa | borqa, čādari | برقعه، چادری |
| balcony/porch | baranda/bālkĕn | برنده/بالکن |
| rice | bĕrĕnj | برنج |
| buzkashi 'goat game or pulling a goat' | bozkaši | بزکشی |
| bus | bas | بس |
| to close | basta kardan (basta kon) | بسته کردن (بسته کن) |
| package | basta | بسته |
| pack | basta | بسته |
| to close | basta kardan (basta kon) | بسته کردن (بسته کن) |
| very, a lot | bĕsyār | بسیار |
| very little | bĕsyār kam | بسیار کم |
| very very much | bĕsyār ziyād | بسیار زیاد |
| after | bad az | بعد از |
| afternoon | b'ad az zohr | بعد از ظهر |
| sometimes | ba'ze waqt-ha | بعضی وقتها |
| to need | bakārdāštan (bakārdār) | بکارداشتن (بکار دار) |
| book bag/backpack/case | baks | بکس |
| nightingale | bolbol | بلبل |
| tall | bĕland | بلند |
| shirt | bōloz | بلوز |
| seaport | bandar | بندر |
| bottle | bōtal | بوتل |
| boots | but, pāyzār | بوت، پایزار |
| large bags | bōji | بوجی |
| sugar | bōra | بوره |
| partridge | bōdana/kabk | بودنه/کبک |

| oil | rōğan | روغن |
| to book | bōk kardan (bōk kon) | بوك كردن (بوك كن) |
| to | ba | به |
| spring | bahār | بهار |
| to inform | ba etĕlā' rasāndan(ba etĕlā' rasān) | به اطلاع رساندن (به اطلاع رسان) |
| to wake up | bidār šodan(bidār šaw) | بیدارشدن (بیدارشو) |
| to exit (infinitive) | birōn šodan (birōn šaw) | بیرون شدن (بیرون شو) |
| twenty | bist | بیست |
| unemployed | bi-kār | بیکار |
| jobless | bikār | بیکار |
| jobless | bikār | بیکار |
| tasteless | be maza | بی مزه |
| in between, middle | bayn | بین |
| nose | bini | بینی |

پ

| park | pārk | پارك |
| park | pārk | پارك |
| fifteen | pānz-dah | پانزده |
| passport | pāsport | پاسپورت |
| Pakistan | pākĕstān | پاكستان |
| quarter | pāw | پاو |
| capital | pāye-taxt | پایتخت |
| classifier for objects that 'stand' (e.g. table, chair, bed) | pā-ya | پایه |
| downward, down | pāyen | پایین |
| foot | pā/pāy | پا/پای |
| man's shawl | patu | پتو |
| to cook | poxta kardan (poxta kon) | پخته كردن (پخته كن) |
| father | padar | پدر |
| grandfather | padar kalān | پدر كلان |

| flight, take off | parwāz | پرواز |
| to fly | parwāz kardan (parwāz kon) | پرواز کردن (پرواز کن) |
| printer | parentar | پرینتر |
| so | pas | پس |
| storage room | pas xāna | پسخانه |
| boy | pasar | پسر |
| behind | pĕšt/pošt | پشت |
| pants (jeans) | patlun | پطلون |
| jeans/cowboy pants | patlun-e kawbāy | پطلون کوبای |
| to have a plane | pĕlān dāštan (pĕlān dār) | پلان داشتن (پلان دار) |
| ointment | pamād | پماد |
| five | panj | پنج |
| Thursday | panj-šanbe | پنجشنبه |
| finger | panja | پنجه |
| pencil | pĕnsĕl | پنسل |
| eraser (pencil) | pĕnsĕl-pāk | پنسل پاک |
| cheese | paner | پنیر |
| to wear | pošidan (poš) | پوشیدن (پوش) |
| to wear | pōšidan (pōš) | پوشیدن (پوش) |
| to cover | pōšāndan (pōšān) | پوشاندن (پوشان) |
| Poland | poland | پولند |
| college | pōhanzay | پوهنځی |
| onion | peyāz | پیاز |
| message | payām | پیام |
| to receive a message | payām gĕrĕftan (payām gir) | پیام گرفتن (پیام گیر) |
| injection | pečkāri | پیچکاری |
| finding /to find | paydā namōdan (paydā namāy) | پیدا نمودن (پیدا نمای) |
| old | pir | پیر |
| dress/shirt | perāhan | پیراهن |
| change (money) | paysa-e mayda | پیسه میده |

| before | peš az | پیش از |
|---|---|---|
| cat | pĕsak | پیشك |
| in front of (infinitive) | peš raftan (peš borō) | پیش رفتن (پیش رو) |
| in front of | pešrōye | پیشرویی |
| pilot | pelōt | پیلوت |
| | ت | |
| until | tā | تا |
| effect | tasir | تاثیر |
| date | tārix | تاریخ |
| history | tārix | تاریخ |
| historical | tārixi | تاریخی |
| to be established | tasis šodan (tasis šaw) | تاسیس شدن (تاسیس شو) |
| summer | tābĕstān | تابستان |
| conference hall | tālār-e kānfarāns | تالارکانفرانس |
| your | tān | تان |
| your (plural) | tān | تان |
| fever | tab | تب |
| chalk | tabāšir | تباشیر |
| translator | tarjomān | ترجمان |
| work experience | tajrobaye kāri | تجربهٔ کاری |
| gift | tōhfa | تحفه |
| board | taxta | تخته |
| eraser (board) | taxta-pāk | تخته پاك |
| last name | taxalos | تخلص |
| egg | toxm-e morg | تخم مرغ |
| ID card | tĕzkĕra, kārt-e hoyat | تذکره، کارت هویت |
| ID card | tazkĕra | تذکره |
| watermelon | tarbuz | تربوز |
| sour | torš | ترش |
| Turkey | torki-ya | ترکیه |

| | | |
|---|---|---|
| vegetable | tarkāri | ترکاری |
| vegetable store | tarkāri forōši | ترکاری فروشی |
| airport terminal | tarmināl-e maydān-e hawāye | ترمینال میدان هوایی |
| bathroom | tašnāb | تشناب |
| to decide | tasmim gĕrĕftan (tasmim gir) | تصمیم گرفتن (تصمیم گیر) |
| building | ta'mir | تعمیر |
| about | taqriban | تقریباً |
| about | taqriban | تقریباً |
| ticket sales (office/agency) | tĕkĕt forōši | تکت فروشی |
| plane ticket | tĕlĕk-e tayyāra | تکت طیاره |
| taxi driver | tasiwān | تکسیوان |
| taekwondo | tekwāndō | تکواندو |
| bitter | talx | تلخ |
| to contact, to touch base | tamās gĕrĕftan (tamās gir) | تماس گرفتن (تماس گیر) |
| to contact | tamās grĕftan (tamās gir) | تماس گرفتن (تماس گیر) |
| pants | tonbān, ezār | تنبان، ایزار |
| spicy, chili | tond | تند |
| you are... | tu ... hasti. | تو ... هستی. |
| you | tu | تو |
| you are ... | tu ... mebāše. | تو ... میباشی. |
| strawberry | tōt-e zamini | توت زمینی |
| trunk | tōlbaks | تولبکس |
| to marry | tōy kardan (tōy kon) | توی کردن |
| to provide | taheya kardan (taheya kon) | تهیه کردن (تهیه کن) |
| to prepare, to fix, to make | tayār kardan (tayār kon) | تیار کردن (تیار کن) |
| past | tĕr | تیر |
| to pass (infinitive) | ter šodan (ter šaw) | تیر شدن (تیر شو) |
| to spend, to pass | ter kardan (ter kon) | تیر کردن (تیرکن) |
| | ث | |
| second | saniya | ثانیه |

| | | |
|---|---|---|
| register | sabt | ثبت |
| | ج | |
| road | jādda | جاده |
| jacket | jākat | جاكت |
| towel | jānxoškān, jānpāk | جانخشكان، جانپاك |
| body | jān | جان |
| sightseeing, places worth seeing | jāhāye didani | جا های دیدنی |
| to be placed | jāy šodan (jāy šaw) | جای شدن (جای شو) |
| a place that... | jāy-e kĕ | جای كه |
| somewhere, a place | jāye | جایی |
| separate | jodāgāna | جداگانه |
| series | jĕdi | جدی |
| socks | jorāb | جراب |
| island | jazira | جزیره |
| book cover | jeld | جلد |
| Friday | joma | جمعه |
| gymnasium | jĕmnāziyam | جمنازیم |
| south | jonub | جنوب |
| young | jawān | جوان |
| healthy | jōr | جور |
| to build | jōr šodan (jōr šaw) | جور شد |
| world | jahān | جهان |
| | چ | |
| scarf | čādar | چادر |
| four | čār | چار |
| Wednesday | čār- šanbe | چار شنبه |
| fourteen | čār-dah | چارده |
| a quarter or a fourth of a unit | čāryak/čārak | چاریك/چارك |
| lunch, midday | čāšt | چاشت |
| fat | čāq | چاق |

| well | čah-e āb | چاه آب |
| breakfast | čāy-e sob | چای صبح |
| tea | čāy | چای |
| left | čap | چپ |
| bed | čaparkat | چپرکت |
| sandal | čapli | چپلی |
| chapan | čapan | چپن |
| why | čarā | چرا |
| eye | čěšom/čašom | چشم |
| how | četór | چطور |
| how | čětōr | چطور |
| to seep | čakāndan (čakān) | چکاندن (چکان) |
| to check | čěk kardan (čěk kon) | چك كردن (چك كن) |
| how many times, several times | čand bār | چندبار |
| how many kinds, several types | čand naw' | چند نوع |
| chair | čawki | چوکی |
| what | či | چی |
| expensive, pricey | čiz-e qimati | چیز قیمتی |
| China | čin | چین |

ح

| to be present | hāzěr bōdan (hāzěr bāš/hast) | حاضربودن (حاضر باش/هست) |
| to move | harakat kardan (harakat kon) | حرکت کردن (حرکت کن) |
| allergy | hasāsiyat | حساسیت |
| to be allergic | hasāsiyat kardan (hasāsiyat kon) | حساسیت کردن (حساسیت کن) |
| traditional doctor (prescribes herbal medications) | hakim ji | حکیم جی |
| bathhouse/ shower | hamām | حمام |
| house | haweli | حویلی |

خ

| overseas, foreign | xārěji | خارجی |
| itch, itchy | xārěš | خارش |

| gray | xākĕstari | خاکستری |
| gray | xākĕstari | خاکستری |
| omlet | xāgina | خاگینه |
| uncle (mother's side) | xāl | خاله |
| empty | xāli | خالی |
| Mrs./Lady | xānom | خانم |
| home | xāna | خانه |
| family | xānawāda | خانواده |
| family | xānawāda/fāmil | خانواده/فامیل |
| housewife | xānom-e xāna | خانم خانه |
| housekeeper, maid | xāna sāmān | خانه سامان |
| to fill out | xāna pōri kardan (xāna pōri kon) | خانه پوری کردن (خانه پوری کن) |
| housekeeper, maid | xāna sāmān | خانه سامان |
| God | xodā | خدا |
| services | xĕdamāt | خدمات |
| bad | sangen | خراب |
| melon | xarbuza | خربوزه |
| 565 kg | xarwār | خروار |
| to buy | xarid (xar) | خریدن (خر) |
| to buy | xaridan (xar) | خریدن (خر) |
| shopping | xaridār | خریداری |
| fall | xazān | خزان |
| father-in-law | xosor | خسر |
| brother-in-law (for husband) | xosorbōra | خسربُره |
| mother-in-law | xošō | خشو |
| ruler | xatkaš | خطکش |
| cold, chilly | xonok, sard | خنك، سرد |
| to read | xāndan (xān) | خواندن (خوان) |
| to sleep | xāb šodan (xab šaw) | خواب شدن (خواب شو) |
| to read, to sing | xāndan (xān) | خواندن (خوان) |

| | | |
|---|---|---|
| sister | xāhar | خواهر |
| to want (infinitive) | xāstan (xāh) | خواستن(خواه) |
| to want | xāstan (xāh) | خواستن (خواه) |
| edible | xōrāka bāb/xōrdani | خوراکه باب/خوردنی |
| well/fine | xub | خوب |
| oneself | xōd | خود |
| myself | xōdam/xōdem | خودم |
| himself/herself | xōdaš/xōděš | خودش |
| yourself | xōdat/xōdět | خودت |
| ourselves | xōděmā | خودما |
| themselves | xōděšān | خودشان |
| yourselves | xōdětān | خودتان |
| to eat | xōrdan (xōr) | خوردن (خور) |
| small/young | xōrd | خورد |
| to eat | xōrdan (xōr) | خوردن (خور) |
| to be happy | xōšāl šodan | خوشحال شدن |
| to like | xōš āmadan (xōš āy) | خوش... آمدن (خوش ... آی) |
| happiness | xōši | خوشی |
| to welcome | xōš āmadan (xōš āy) | خوش آمدن (خوش آی) |
| to like | xōš dāštan (xōš dār) | خوش داشتن (خوش دار) |
| delicious | xōš maza | خوشمزه |
| tailor | xayāt | خیاط |
| sister-in-law (for husband) | xeyāšna | خیاشنه |
| to eat | xordan (xor) | خوردن (خور) |
| to stand up | xestan (xez) | خیستن (خیز) |
| | د | |
| to enter (infinitive) | dāxěl šodan (dāxěl šaw) | داخل شدن (داخل شو) |
| to give | dādan (děh) | دادن (ده) |
| to give | dādan (dah) | دادن (ده) |
| college | dāněškada | دانشکده |

| groom | dāmād | داماد |
|---|---|---|
| piece | dāna | دانه |
| daughter | doxtar | دختر |
| cousin | doxtare a'ma | دختر عمه |
| cousin | doxtare kākā | دختر کاکا |
| cousin | doxtare māma | دختر ماما |
| cousin | doxtare xāla | دختر خاله |
| for girls | doxtarāna | دخترانه |
| in, in the, at | dar | در |
| to enter (infinitive) | dar āmadan (dar āy) | درآمدن (در آی) |
| around the | dar atrāf-e | در اطراف |
| next to the | dar baǧal-e | در بغل |
| on the, at the top of the | dar bālāy-e | در بالای |
| between the | dar bayn-e | در بین |
| outside of the | dar birōn-e | در بیرون |
| next to the | dar pahlōy-e | در پهلوی |
| in front of the | dar pĕšrōy-e | در پیشروی |
| behind the | dar pĕšt-e | در پشت |
| behind the | dar pōšt-e sar-e | در پشت سر |
| dozen | darjan | درجن |
| dozen | darjan | درجن |
| temperature | daraja-e harārat | درجهٔ حرارت |
| centigrade | daraja-e sāntigĕrād | درجه سانتی گراد |
| during, among, to be informed | dar jĕryān-e | درجریان |
| around the | dar čār taraf-e | در چار طرف |
| tree | daraxt | درخت |
| outside of the | dar xārĕj-e | در خارج |
| to be in service of | dar xĕdmat bōdan (dar xĕdmat hast) | در خدمت بودن (در خدمت هست) |
| inside the | dar dāxĕle | در داخل |

| | | |
|---|---|---|
| to hurt, to have pain, to ache | dard kardan (dard kon) | درد کردن (درد کن) |
| across the | dar rōbarōy-e | در روبروی |
| on top of the/on the | dar rōy-e | در رویی |
| under the | dar zĕr-e | در زیر |
| on the left side of the | dar samt-e čap-e | در سمت چپ |
| on the right side of the | dar samt-e rāst-e | در سمت راست |
| on the, on top of the | dar sar-e | در سر |
| on the left side of the | dar taraf-e čap-e | در طرف چپ |
| on the right side of the | dar taraf-e rāst-e | در طرف راست |
| behind the | dar aqĕb-e | در عقب |
| around the | dar gerd-e, dar dawr-e | در گرد، در دور |
| inside of the | dar mābayn-e | در مابین |
| in front of the | dar moqābĕl-e | در مقابل |
| door | darwāza | دروازه |
| to enter (infinitive) | darōn šodan (darōn šaw) | درون شدن (درون شو) |
| sea | daryā | دریا |
| bunch | desta | دسته |
| left hand side | dĕst-e čap | دست چپ |
| right hand side | dĕst-e rāst | دست راست |
| bunch | dĕsta | دسته |
| gloves | dĕstkaš | دستکش |
| hand | dĕst | دست |
| towel/handkerchief | dĕstmāl | دستمال |
| minute | daqiqa | دقیقه |
| nausea | dĕlbad | دلبد |
| favorite | dĕlxā | دلخواه |
| two | do | دو |
| herbal medicine | dawā hāy-e giyāye | دوا های گیاهی |
| pharmacist | dawākāna | دواخانه دار |
| pharmacy | dawāxāna | دواخانه |

| twelve | dōwāz-dah | دوازده |
|---|---|---|
| turn | dawr | دور |
| far | dur | دور |
| to turn (infinitive form) | dawr zadan (dawr zan) | دور زدن (دور زن) |
| running | dawĕš | دوش |
| to jog | dawĕš kardan (dawĕš kon) | دوش کردن (دوش کن) |
| Monday | do-šanbe | دو شنبه |
| round-trip | do tarafa | دو طرفه |
| shopkeeper | dokāndār | دوکاندار |
| second | dowom | دوم |
| ten | dah | ده |
| mouth | dahān/dahan | دهان/دهن |
| hall | dahlez | دهلیز |
| meeting, seeing (to see) | didan | دیدن |
| to see | didan (bin) | دیدن (بین) |
| wall | diwār | دیوار |
| ذ | | |
| male, masculine | zokōr, mardāna | ذکور، مردانه |
| ر | | |
| comfortable | rāhat | راحت |
| classifier for cattle (head) | ra's | رأس |
| right | rāst | راست |
| pathway | rāh rawi | راه روی |
| tomato sauce | rob/rob-e badĕnjān-e rōmi | رب/رب بادنجان رومی |
| holiday | roxsati | رخصتی |
| restaurant | rastōrant | رستورانت |
| traditional restaurant | rastōrant-e sonati | رستورانت سنتی |
| to reach, arrive | rasidan (ras) | رسیدن (رس) |
| lightning | r'ad ō barq | رعد و برق |
| to go | raftan (raw) | رفتن (رو) |

| | | |
|---|---|---|
| hair color | rang mōy | رنگ موی |
| eye color | range čĕšom | رنگ چشم |
| sheet | rōjāye | روجایی |
| day | rōz | روز |
| Russia | rōsiya | روسیه |
| to reserve | rezarf/rezarw kardan(rezarf kon) | ریزرف/ریزرو کردن (ریزرو کن) |
| | ز | |
| language, tongue | zabān | زبان |
| yellow | zard | زرد |
| carrot | zarday | زردک |
| rough | zomoxt | زمخت |
| winter | zamĕstān | زمستان |
| woman | zan | زن |
| for women, women's (clothing) | zanāna | زنانه |
| to live | zendagi kardan | زندگی کردن |
| to call, to ring | zang zadan (zang zan) | زنگ زدن (زنگ زن) |
| shrine | ziyārat | زیارت |
| undergarments | zer perāni | زیرپیراهنی |
| underpants | zer tonbāni (zer tombāni) | زیرتنبانی |
| stairs | zina | زینه |
| | ژ | |
| hail | žāla | ژاله |
| to hail | žāla bāridan (žāla bār) | ژاله باریدن (ژاله بار) |
| | س | |
| watch, clock | sā'at | ساعت |
| ... years | sāla ... | ساله ... |
| year | sāl | سال |
| green | sabz | سبز |
| spinach | sabzi pālak | سبزی پالک |

| vegetables | sabzijāt/tarkāri | سبزیجات/ترکاری باب |
| to spend | sĕpari kardan (sĕpari kon) | سپری کردن (سپری کن) |
| staple | ĕstĕblar | ستپلر |
| head | sar | سر |
| dizzy | sarčarx | سرچرخ |
| red | sorx | سرخ |
| cough | sorfa | سرفه |
| cough | sorfa kardan (sorfa kon) | سرفه کردن (سرفه کن) |
| street | sarak | سرک |
| trip | safar | سفر |
| to travel | safar kardan(safar kon) | سفر کردن (سفرکن) |
| air travel | safar-e hawāye | سفر هوایی |
| road trip | safar-e zamini | سفر زمینی |
| white | safed | سفید |
| ceiling | saqf | سقف |
| scanner | ĕskenar | سکینر |
| dog | sag | سگ |
| cigarette | sĕgrĕt | سگرت |
| salad | salāta | سلاته |
| left side | samt-e čap | سمت چپ |
| right side | samt-e rāst | سمت راست |
| age | sĕn | سن |
| document/documents | sanad/asnād | سند/اسناد |
| heavy | xarāb | سنگین |
| to buy groceries | sawdā xaridan (sawdā xar) | سودا خریدن (سودا خر) |
| groceries | sawdā | سودا |
| third | sewom | سوم |
| three | se | سه |
| Tuesday | se-šanbe | سه شنبه |
| black | siyā | سیاه |

| | | |
|---|---|---|
| black | siyāh | سیاه |
| apple | seb | سیب |
| CD | si di | سی دی |
| 7066 grams in Kabul, but 100 grams in western part of the country. | ser | سیر |
| garlic | sir | سیر |
| thirteen | sĕz-dah | سیزده |
| to watch, to see | sayl kardan (sayl kon) | سیل کردن (سیل کن) |
| flood | sel | سیل |
| to flood | sel āmadan (sel āy) | سیل آمدن (سیل آی) |
| | ش | |
| student | šāgerd | شاگرد |
| shawl | šāl | شال |
| sixteen | šānz-dah | شانزده |
| their | šān | شان |
| to shower | šāwar gĕrĕftan (šāwar gir) | شاورگرفتن (شاورگیر) |
| night | šab | شب |
| to get; to grow, to happen, to go, to be | šodan | شدن |
| hard | šadid | شدید |
| syrup | šarbat | شربت |
| east | šarq | شرق |
| airline | šĕrkat-e hawāye | شرکت هوایی |
| company | šĕrkat | شرکت |
| tourism company | šĕrkat-e tōrezom | شرکت توریزم |
| six | šaš | شش |
| chess | šatranj | شطرنج |
| hospital | šafāxāna | شفاخانه |
| peach | šaftālu | شفتالو |
| stomach | šĕkam | شکم |
| turnip | šalğam | شلغم |

| you (your) | šomā | شما |
|---|---|---|
| you are ... | šomā ... hasted. | شما ... هستید . |
| you are ... | šōmā ... mebāšed. | شما ... میباشید . |
| north | šamāl | شمال |
| swordsmanship | šamšer bāzi | شمشیر بازی |
| Saturday | šanbe | شنبه |
| to listen | šanidan (šanaw) | شنیدن (شنو) |
| salty | šōr | شور |
| husband | šawhar/šōy | شوهر/شوی |
| city | šahr, šār | شهر |
| milk | šir | شیر |
| sweet | širin | شیرین |
| | ص | |
| soap | sābun | صابون |
| madam | sā-heb, sā-heba | صاحب/صاحبه |
| sir | sā-heb | صاحب |
| clear | sāf | صاف |
| morning | sob | صبح |
| to wait | sabr kardan(sabr kon) | صبر کردن (صبر کن) |
| courtyard | sahn-e haweli | صحن حویلی |
| health | sĕhi | صحی |
| zero | sefer | صفر |
| classroom/class | sĕnf | صنف |
| synagogue | somĕ'a | صومعه |
| | ض | |
| to be necessary | zarorat bōdan (zarorat bāš, hast) | ضرورت بودن (ضرورت باش/ است) |
| | ط | |
| to have tolerance, to be tolerant | tāqat dāštan (tāqat dār) | طاقت داشتن (طاقت دار) |
| obviously | tab'an | طبعاً |

| | | |
|---|---|---|
| dining room | ta'ām xāna | طعام خانه |
| golden (blonde) | tĕlāye | طلایی |
| parrot | tuti | طوطی |
| storm | tōfān | طوفان |
| plane | tayyāra | طیاره |

ظ

| | | |
|---|---|---|
| afternoon | zohr | ظهر |

ع

| | | |
|---|---|---|
| classifier for vehicles (vehicle) | 'arāda | عراده |
| bride/daughter in-law | arōs/sōnō | عروس/سونو |
| to marry/to wed | arōsi kardan (arōsi kon) | عروسی کردن |
| aunt (mother's side) | a'ma | عمه |
| glasses | 'aynak | عینك |

غ

| | | |
|---|---|---|
| to cook food | ğĕzā poxtan (ğĕzā paz) | غذا پختن (غذا پز) |
| west | ğarb | غرب |
| without bottle | ğayr-e botali | غیر بوتلی |

غ

| | | |
|---|---|---|
| college | fākolta | فاكولته |
| family | fāmil | فامیل |
| father-in-law's family | fāmile xosor | فامیل خسر |
| France | faransa | فرانسه |
| to order, to demand | farmāyeš dādan (farmāyeš dĕh) | فرمایش دادن (فرمایش ده) |
| to sell | forōxtan (forōš) | فروختن (فروش) |
| season | fasĕl | فصل |
| to think | fĕkĕr kardan (fĕkĕr kon) | فکر کردن (فکرکن) |
| form | fōrma | فورمه |
| doctor's bill | fis | فیس |

ق

| | | |
|---|---|---|
| to the attention of | qābĕl-e tawajoh | قابل توجه |

| | | |
|---|---|---|
| continent | qārra | قاره |
| height | qad | قد |
| tall height | qad bĕlan | قد بلند |
| short height | qad kōtā | قد کوتاه |
| to walk | qadam zadan (qadam zan) | قدم زدن (قدم زن) |
| as follows | qarār-e zayl | قرار ذیل |
| century | qarn | قرن |
| village | qari-ya | قریه |
| part, section | qĕsmat | قسمت |
| drop | qatra | قطره |
| drop | qatra čakān | قطره چکان |
| classifier for picture (piece of ) | qeťa | قطعه |
| can | qotti | قطی |
| pen | qalam | قلم |
| canary | qanāri | قناری |
| sauce | qōrma | قورمه |
| security headquarters | qōmandāniye amniya | قوماندانی امنیه |
| brown | qahwa ye | قهوه یی |
| coffee | qahwa | قهوه |
| | ک | |
| Kabul | kābol | کابل |
| to make a copy of | kāpi gĕrftan (kāpi gir) | کاپی گرفتن (کاپی گیر) |
| to work | kār kardan (kār kon) | کار کردن (کار کن) |
| homework | kār-e xānagi | کار خانگی |
| box | kārtan | کارتن |
| ID card | kārt-e hoyat | کارت هویت |
| wishing marker | kāške | کاشکی |
| paper | kāğaz | کاغذ |
| parent | kākā | کاکا |
| to put on clothes/ to wear | kālā kašidan (kālā kaš) | کالا کشیدن (کالا کش) |

| | | |
|---|---|---|
| clothes | kālā | کالا |
| clothes | kālā, lĕbās | کالا، لباس |
| clothing store | kāla forōši | کالافروشی |
| formal dress | kālāy-e rasmi | کالایِ رسمی |
| absolutely | kāmĕlan | کاملاً |
| Canada | kānādā | کانادا |
| cafeteria | kāntin | کانتین |
| lettuce | kāho | کاهو |
| kabob | kabāb | کباب |
| pigeon | kabutar/kaftar | کبوتر/کفتر |
| book | kĕtāb | کتاب |
| notebook | kĕtāb-ča | کتابچه |
| library | kĕtāb xāna | کتابخانه |
| where | kojā | کجا |
| potato | kačālu | کچالو |
| rent | kĕrāya | کرایه |
| cricket | kĕrket | کرکیت |
| cabbage | karam barg | کرم برگ |
| creamy, cream color | kĕrimi | کریمی |
| a person who... | kas-e kĕ | کسی که |
| a person, some person | kasi | کسی |
| wrestling | košti giri | کشتی گیری |
| country | kešwar | کشور |
| to take off | kašidan (kaš) | کشیدن (کش) |
| floor | kaf | کف |
| big | kalān/bozorg | کلان/بزرگ |
| hat | kolāh | کلاه |
| hat | kolah-e pik | کلاه پیک |
| cookies | kolča | کلچه |
| window | kalkin | کلکین |

| finger | kĕlk | كلك |
|---|---|---|
| church | kalisā | كليسا |
| little | kam | كم |
| comforter | kampal | كمپل |
| computer | kampi-yutar | كمپيوتر |
| weak | kamzōr | كمزور |
| to help | komak kardan (komak kon) | كمك كردن (كمك كن) |
| short | kōtā | كوتاه |
| small/young | kōčak | كوچك |
| to move (infinitive) | kōč-kardan (kōč kon) | كوچ كردن (كوچ كن) |
| child | kōdak/tĕfĕl | كودك/طفل |
| coat | kōrti | كورتى |
| to try | kōšĕš kardan (kōšĕš kon) | كوشش كردن (كوشش كن) |
| meatball | kofta | كوفته |
| conjunction | kĕ | كه |
| who | ki | كى |
| when | kay | كى |
| keyboard | kibōrd | كيبورد |
| banana | kela | كيله |
| kilo | kelō | كيلو |

گ

| waiter/waitress | ğārsun | گارسون |
|---|---|---|
| sometimes | gāhe | گاهى |
| to speak | gap zadan (gap zan) | گپ زدن (گپ زن) |
| to pass, to spend, to undergo | gozaštan (gozar) | گذشتن (گذر) |
| garage | garāž/garāj/garāč | گراژ/گراج/گراچ |
| to take | gĕrĕftan (gir) | گرفتن (گير) |
| to take | gĕrĕftan (gir) | گرفتن (گير) |
| warm | garm | گرم |
| sunstroke | garmi zadagi | گرمى زده گى |

| report | gozāreš | گزارش |
|---|---|---|
| to turn, to search for (infinitive) | gaštan (gard) | گشتن (گرد) |
| to converse | goftago kardan (goftago kon) | گفتگو کردن (گفتگو کن) |
| to tell | goftan (goy) | گفتن (گوی) |
| flower | gol | گل |
| pink | golābi | گلابی |
| custom | gomrok | گمرك |
| out of it | gans | گنس |
| ear | gōš | گوش |
| to listen | goš kardan (goš kon) | گوش کردن (گوش کن) |
| headphone | gošaki | گوشکی |
| to listen | gōš kardan (goš kon) | گوش کردن (گوش کن) |
| meat | gōšt | گوشت |
| beef | gōšt-e gaw | گوشت گاو |
| lamb | gōšt-e gosfand | گوشت گوسفند |
| chicken | gōšt-e morğ | گوشت مرغ |
| pill | guli | گولی |

ل

| laboratory | lābrātowār | لابراتوار |
|---|---|---|
| skinny | lāğar | لاغر |
| dairy | labaniyāt | لبنیات |
| turban | longi | لنگی |
| loudspeaker | lōd-espikar | لودسپیکر |
| dorm | layliya | لیله |

م

| we | mā | ما |
|---|---|---|
| our | mā, mān | ما/مان |
| we are... | mā ... hastem. | ما ... هستیم. |
| we are ... | mā ... mebāšem. | ما ... میباشیم. |
| mother | mādar | مادر |

| grandmother | mādar kalān | مادر کلان |
|---|---|---|
| yogurt | māst | ماست |
| copy machine | māšin ěsāb | ماشین کاپی |
| orange | mālta | مالته |
| to put down | māndan (mān) | ماندن (مان) |
| monitor (computer screen) | mānitor (safha-e kampi-yutar) | مانیتور (صفحهٔ کمپیوتر) |
| left to | mānda | مانده |
| honeymoon | māhe 'asal | ماه عسل |
| uncle (father's side) | māmā | ماما |
| month | māh | ماه |
| cell phone | mobā-yel | مبایل |
| married | motahel | متاهل |
| unfortunately | mot'sěfāna | متاسفانه |
| square meter | mětěr morab' | متر مربع |
| school student | mota'lem | متعلم |
| retired | motaqā'ad | متقاعد |
| 4.6 grams | měsqāl | مثقال |
| single | mojarad | مجرد |
| in total, in sum, all together | majmo'an | مجموعاً |
| to be equipped | mojahaz bōdan (mojahaz hast) | مجهز بودن (مجهز هست) |
| Mr. | moh-taram | محترم |
| Ms./Mrs. | moh-tarama | محترمه |
| college student | mohasěl | محصل |
| various | motalěf | مختلف |
| manager | modir | مدیر |
| hotel manager | modir-e hotal, hotali | مدیر هوتل، هوتلی |
| pepper | morč | مرچ |
| man | mard | مرد |
| men's (clothing), for men | mardāna | مردانه |
| foggy | martōb | مرطوب |

| | | |
|---|---|---|
| sick | mariz | مریض |
| illness | marizi | مریضی |
| traveler | mosāfĕr | مسافر |
| passenger, traveler | mosāfĕr | مسافر |
| car repair shop | mĕstari xāna | مستری خانه |
| mosque | masjĕd | مسجد |
| butter | maska | مسکه |
| boxing | mošt zani, bokseng | مشت زنی، بوکسینگ |
| customer | moštari | مشتری |
| advice | mašwara | مشوره |
| to check up | māyna kardan (māyna kon) | معاینه کردن (معاینه کن) |
| doctor's office | māyna xāna(ma'āyana xāna) | معاینه خانه |
| temple | ma'bad | معبد |
| neutral, mild | mo'tadĕl | معتدل |
| school teacher | mo'lem | معلم |
| information | ma'lomāt | معلومات |
| usually | ma'molan | معمولاً |
| free | moft | مفت |
| school | maktab | مکتب |
| Mexico | maksikō | مکسیکو |
| radish | moli | ملی |
| I, my | man | من |
| I am ... | man ... hastam. | من ... هستم. |
| I am ... | man ... mebāšam. | من ... میباشم. |
| 7066 grams in Kabul, about 5000 grams in Kandahar, and 4000 grams in western parts of the country. | man | من |
| to wait | montazĕr bōdan (montazĕr bāš, hast) | منتظر بودن (منتظر باش، هست) |
| second floor | manzĕl-e dowom | منزل دوم |
| lower floor | manzĕl-e pāyen | منزل پائین |

| secretary | monši | منشى |
|---|---|---|
| menu | menōy-e ğĕzā | منيوی غذا |
| car | mōtar | موتر |
| car sales | mōtar forōši | موتر فروشی |
| to be available | mawjud bōdan(mawjud hast) | موجود بودن (موجود هست) |
| boots | mōza | موزه |
| museum | mōziyam | موزیم |
| national museum | mōziyam-e mĕlli | موزیم ملی |
| (computer) mouse | maws | موس |
| music | mosiqi | موسیقی |
| to have location, to be located | moqĕ'yat dāštan (moqĕ'yat dār) | موقعیت داشتن (موقعیت دار) |
| moon | mahtāb, māh | مهتاب، ماه |
| guest | mĕhmān | مهمان |
| guest room | mehmānxāna | مهمان خانه |
| medium/middle/mid | miyāna | میانه |
| airport | maydān-e hawāye | میدان هوایی |
| airport | maydān-e hawāye | میدان هوایی |
| table/desk | mez | میز |
| fruit | mewa | میوه |
| fruit | mewajāt | میوه جات |

| | ن | |
|---|---|---|
| name | nām | نام |
| to be engaged | nāmzad šodan (nāmzad šaw) | نامزد شدن |
| dinner | nānā-e šab | نان شب |
| lunch | nān-e čāšt | نان چاشت |
| bread | nān-e xošk | نان خشك |
| nurse | nars | نرس |
| close, near | nazdik | نزدیک |
| prescription | nosxa | نسخه |
| to show | nĕšān dādan (nĕšān dĕh) | نشان دادن (نشان ده) |

| | | |
|---|---|---|
| to sit down | nešastan (šin) | نشستن (شین) |
| to sit, to live | nešastan/šeštan (šen, našen) | نشستن/شیشتن (شین/نشین) |
| to land | nĕšast kardan (nĕšast kon) | نشست کردن (نشست کن) |
| brown | naswāri | نصواری |
| people classifier (individual, person) | nafar, tan | نفر، تن |
| golden | noqraye | نقره یی |
| agent/representative | nomāyenda/namāyenda | نماینده |
| salt | namak | نمك |
| sister-in-law (for wife) | nanō | ننو |
| grandchild | nawāsa | نواسه |
| to take note | nōt gĕrĕftan (nōt gir) | نوت گرفتن (نوت گیر) |
| nineteen | nōz-dah | نوزده |
| to write | nawĕšta kardan (nawĕšta kon) | نوشته کردن (نوشته کن) |
| to write | naweštan (dĕh) | نوشتن (نویس) |
| to write | nĕwĕšta kardan (nĕwĕšta kon) | نوشته کردن (نوشته کن) |
| to drink | nōšidan (nōš) | نوشیدن(نوش) |
| drinks | nōšidani | نوشیدنی |
| to drink | nošidan (noš) | نوشیدن (نوش) |
| nine | noh | نه |
| underwear | nekar, sentarāj | نیکر، سنتراج |
| tie | nektāye | نیکتایی |
| half | nim | نیم |
| midnight, in the middle of the night | nima šab | نیمه شب |
| New York | neyō-yōrk | نیویورك |
| | و | |
| and | wa | و |
| vest | wāskat | واسکت |
| Washington | wāšĕngtan | واشنگتن |
| aunt (father's side) | wālĕdayn | والدین |

| to sport | warzĕš kār (warzĕš kon) | ورزش کردن (ورزش کن) |
|---|---|---|
| lifting | wazna bardāri | وزنه برداری |
| etc. | wa ğqyra | وغیره |
| sometime | waqti | وقتی |
| province | walāyat | ولایت |
| district | waloswāli | ولسوالی |

ه

| every (everyday, every time) | har (har rōz, har bār) | هر (هر روز، هر بار) |
|---|---|---|
| eighteen | haž-dah | هژده |
| eight | hašt | هشت |
| seven | haft | هفت |
| seventeen | haf-dah | هفده |
| in that very way, like that | hamāntōr | همانطور |
| also, too | hamčanān | همچنان |
| also | hamčenān | همچنان |
| sister, title for addressing a strange woman | hamšira | همشیره |
| classmate | ham-senfi | همصنفی |
| all | hama | همه |
| in this very way, like this | hamintōr | همینطور |
| always | hameša | همیشه |
| sky, weather | hawā | هوا |
| hotel | hotal | هوتل |

ی

| to note | yāddāšt kardan (yāddāšt kon) | یادداشت کردن (یادداشت کن) |
|---|---|---|
| eleven | yāz-dah | یازده |
| purple | yāsamani | یاسمنی |
| refrigerator | yaxčāl | یخچال |
| dress shirt | yaxan qāq | یخن قاق |
| one | yak | یك |
| once, twice | yak bār | یك بار، دو بار |

| Sunday | yak-šanbe | يك شنبه |
|--------|-----------|---------|
| one-way | yak tarafa | يك طرفه |
| first | yakom | يكم |

# APPENDIX F: ENGLISH-DARI GLOSSARY

English to Dari   انگلیسی به دری

| | A | |
|---|---|---|
| a person who ... | kas-e kě | کسی که |
| a person, some person | kasi | کسی |
| a place that ... | jāy-e kě | جای که |
| a quarter or a fourth of a unit | čāryak/čārak | چاریك/چارك |
| a string that ties the waist of the pants | ezār band | ایزار بند |
| about | taqriban | تقریباً |
| about | taqriban | تقریباً |
| absolutely | kāmělan | کاملاً |
| across the | dar rōbarōy-e | در روبروی |
| advice | mašwara | مشوره |
| after | bad az | بعد از |
| afternoon | zohr | ظهر |
| afternoon | b'ad az zohr | بعد از ظهر |
| age | sěn | سن |
| agent/ representative | nomāyenda/namāyenda | نماینده |
| air travel | safar-e hawāye | سفر هوایی |
| airline | šěrkat-e hawāye | شرکت هوایی |
| airport | maydān-e hawāye | میدان هوایی |
| airport | maydān-e hawāye | میدان هوایی |
| airport terminal | tarmināl-e maydān-e hawāye | ترمینال میدان هوایی |
| all | hama | همه |
| allergy | hasāsiyat | حساسیت |
| also | hamčenān | همچنان |
| also, too | hamčanān | همچنان |
| altar | ātěškada | آتشکده |
| always | hamiša | همیشه |

| always | hameša | همیشه |
|---|---|---|
| America | amrikā | امریکا |
| and | wa | و |
| apple | seb | سیب |
| around the | dar atrāf-e | در اطراف |
| around the | dar čār taraf-e | در چار طرف |
| around the | dar gerd-e, dar dawr-e | در گرد، در دور |
| as following | qarār-e zayl | قرار ذیل |
| aunt (father's side) | wālĕdayn | والدین |
| aunt (mother's side) | a'ma | عمه |
| | B | |
| bad | sangen | خراب |
| balcony/porch | baranda/bālkĕn | برنده/ بالکن |
| banana | kela | کیله |
| bathhouse/ shower | hamām | حمام |
| bathroom | tašnāb | تشناب |
| bathroom | tašnāb | تشناب |
| bazaar | bāzār | بازار |
| because | baxātĕr-e kĕ/čōn kĕ | بخاطریکه/ چونکه |
| bed | čaparkat | چپرکت |
| bedroom | otāq-e xāb | اتاق خواب |
| beef | gōšt-e gaw | گوشت گاو |
| before | peš az | پیش از |
| behind | pĕšt/ pošt | پشت |
| behind the | dar aqĕb-e | در عقب |
| behind the | dar pĕšt-e | در پشت |
| behind the | dar pōšt-e sar-e | در پشت سر |
| between the | dar bayn-e | در بین |
| bicycle riding | bāyskĕl dawāni | بایسکل دوانی |
| big | kalān | کلان |

| big | kalān/ bozorg | کلان/بزرگ |
| big | kalān | کلان |
| bitter | talx | تلخ |
| black | siyā | سیاه |
| black | siyāh | سیاه |
| blue | ābi | آبی |
| blue | ābi | آبی |
| board | taxta | تخته |
| body | jān | جان |
| book | kĕtāb | کتاب |
| bookbag/backpack/ case | baks | بکس |
| book cover | jeld | جلد |
| bookshelf | almāri kĕtāb | الماری کتاب |
| boots | mōza | موزه |
| boots | but, pāyzār | بوت، پایزار |
| bottle | bōtal | بوتل |
| box | kārtan | کارتن |
| boxing | mošt zani, bokseng | مشت زنی، بوکسینگ |
| boy | bača | بچه |
| boy | pasar | پسر |
| Brazil | barāzíl | برازیل |
| bread | nān-e xošk | نان خشک |
| breakfast | čāy-e sob | چای صبح |
| bride/daughter-in-law | arōs/sōnō | عروس/سونو |
| brother | barādar | برادر |
| brother-in-law (for wife) | ewar | ایور |
| brother-in-law (for husband) | xosorbōra | خسربُره |
| brown | qahwa ye | قهوه یی |
| brown | naswāri | نصواری |
| building | ta'mir | تعمیر |

| | | |
|---|---|---|
| bunch | desta | دسته |
| bunch | děsta | دسته |
| burqa | borqa, čādari | برقعه، چادری |
| bus | bas | بس |
| bus station/bus | estgāh-sarwes/ estgāh-e bas | ایستگاه سرویس/ بس |
| butter | maska | مسکه |
| buzkashi 'goat game or pulling a goat' | bozkaši | بزکشی |

C

| | | |
|---|---|---|
| cabbage | karam barg | کرم برگ |
| cafeteria | kāntin | کانتین |
| can | qotti | قطی |
| Canada | kānādā | کانادا |
| canary | qanāri | قناری |
| capital | pāye-taxt | پایتخت |
| car | mōtar | موتر |
| car repair shop | městari xāna | مستری خانه |
| car sales | mōtar forōši | موتر فروشی |
| carrot | zarday | زردك |
| cat | pěsak | پیشك |
| CD | si di | سی دی |
| ceiling | saqf | سقف |
| cell phone | mobā-yel | مبایل |
| centigrade | daraja-e sāntigěrād | درجه سانتی گراد |
| century | qarn | قرن |
| chair | čawki | چوکی |
| chalk | tabāšir | تباشیر |
| change (money) | paysa-e mayda | پیسه میده |
| chapan | čapan | چپن |
| cheese | paner | پنیر |
| cherry | ālu bālu | آلوبالو |

| chess | šatranj | شطرنج |
| chicken | gōšt-e morğ | گوشت مرغ |
| child | kōdak/tĕfĕl | کودک /طفل |
| children | awlād | اولاد |
| China | čin | چین |
| church | kalisā | کلیسا |
| cigarette | sĕgrĕt | سگرت |
| city | šahr šār | شهر |
| classifier for cattle (head) | ra's | رأس |
| classifier for objects that stand (like chair, table, computer) | pā-ya | پایه |
| classifier for picture (piece of ), frame | qet'a | قطعه |
| classifier for vehicles (vehicle) | 'arāda | عراده |
| classmate | ham-senfi | همصنفی |
| classroom/ class | sĕnf | صنف |
| clear | sāf | صاف |
| close, near | nazdik | نزدیک |
| clothes | kālā | کالا |
| clothes | kālā, lĕbās | کالا، لباس |
| clothing store | kāla forōši | کالافروشی |
| cloud | abr | ابر |
| cloudy | abri | ابری |
| coat | kōrti | کورتی |
| coffee | qahwa | قهوه |
| cold, chilly | xonok, sard | خنک، سرد |
| college | fākolta, pōhanzay, dānĕškada | فاکولته، پوهنځی، دانشکده |
| college instructor | ostād | استاد |
| college student | mohasĕl | محصل |
| comfortable | rāhat | راحت |
| comforter | kampal | کمپل |

| company | šĕrkat | شرکت |
| computer | kampi-yutar | کمپیوتر |
| conference hall | tālār-e kānfarāns | تالارکانفرانس |
| conjunction | kĕ | که |
| continent | qārra | قاره |
| cook | āšpaz | آشپز |
| cookies | kolča | کلچه |
| copy machine | māšin ĕsāb | ماشین کاپی |
| cough | sorfa | سرفه |
| cough | sorfa kardan (sorfa kon) | سرفه کردن (سرفه کن) |
| country | kešwar | کشور |
| courtyard | sahn-e haweli | صحن حویلی |
| cousin | bačaye kākā | بچۀ کاکا |
| cousin | doxtare kākā | دختر کاکا |
| cousin | bačaye a'ma | بچۀ عمه |
| cousin | doxtare a'ma | دختر عمه |
| cousin | bačaye māmā | بچۀ ماما |
| cousin | doxtare māma | دختر ماما |
| cousin | bačaye xāla | بچۀ خاله |
| cousin | doxtare xāla | دختر خاله |
| creamer | xāgina | خاگینه |
| creamy, cream color | kĕrimi | کریمی |
| cricket | kĕrket | کرکیت |
| cucumber | bādrang | بادرنگ |
| custom | gomrok | گمرک |
| customer | moštari | مشتری |
| | D | |
| dairy | labaniyāt | لبنیات |
| date | tārix | تاریخ |
| daughter | doxtar | دختر |

| | | |
|---|---|---|
| day | rōz | روز |
| delicious | xōš maza | خوشمزه |
| dining room | ta'ām xāna | طعام خانه |
| dinner | nānā-e šab | نان شب |
| district | waloswāli | ولسوالی |
| district | wolaswāli | ولسوالی |
| dizzy | sarčarx | سرچرخ |
| doctor's bill | fis | فیس |
| doctor's office | māyna xāna(ma'āyana xāna) | معاینه خانه |
| document/documents | sanad/asnād | سند/اسناد |
| dog | sag | سگ |
| door | darwāza | دروازه |
| dorm | layliya | لیله |
| double bedroom | otāq-e do nafara | اتاق دو نفره |
| downward, down | pāyen | پائین |
| dozen | darjan | درجن |
| dozen | darjan | درجن |
| dress shirt | yaxan qāq | یخن قاق |
| dress/shirt | perāhan | پیراهن |
| drinks | nōšidani | نوشیدنی |
| drop | qatra čakān | قطره چکان |
| drop | qatra | قطره |
| during, among, to be informed | dar jĕryān-e | درجریان |
| | **E** | |
| ear | gōš | گوش |
| east | šarq | شرق |
| edible | xōrāka bāb/xōrdani | خوراکه باب/خوردنی |
| effect | tasir | تاثیر |
| egg | toxm-e morg | تخم مرغ |
| eggplant | bādĕnejān-e siyā (bānejān-e siyā) | بادنجان سیاه |

| eight | hašt | هشت |
|---|---|---|
| eighteen | haž-dah | هژده |
| eleven | yāz-dah | یازده |
| empty | xāli | خالی |
| entrance exam | emtěhān kānkōr | امتحان کانکور |
| eraser (board) | taxta-pāk | تخته پاك |
| eraser (pencil) | pěnsěl-pāk | پنسل پاك |
| etc. | wa ğqyra | وغیره |
| every (everyday, everytime) | har (har rōz, har bār) | هر (هر روز، هر بار) |
| expensive, pricey | čiz-e qimati | چیز قیمتی |
| experienced | bā tajroba | باتجربه |
| eye | čěšom/čašom | چشم |
| eye color | range čěšom | رنگ چشم |

| | F | |
|---|---|---|

| fall | xazān | خزان |
|---|---|---|
| family | xānawāda/fāmil | خانواده/ فامیل |
| family | fāmil | فامیل |
| family | xānawāda | خانواده |
| far | dur | دور |
| fat | čāq | چاق |
| father | padar | پدر |
| father-in-law | xosor | خسر |
| father-in-law's family | fāmile xosor | فامیل خسر |
| favorite | dělxā | دلخواه |
| female, feminine | onās, zanāna | اناث، زنانه |
| fever | tab | تب |
| fifteen | pānz-dah | پانزده |
| finding/to find | paydā namōdan (paydā namāy) | پیدا نمودن (پیدا نمای) |
| finger | panja, angošt, kělk | پنجه، انگشت، کلك |
| first | awal | اول |

| first | yakom | یکم |
| five | panj | پنج |
| five hundred and sixty five kilograms (565 kg) | xarwār | خروار |
| flight, take off | parwāz | پرواز |
| flood | sel | سیل |
| floor | kaf | کف |
| flour | ārd | آرد |
| flower | gol | گل |
| foggy | martōb | مرطوب |
| foot | pā/pāy | پا / پای |
| for boys | bačagāna | بچه گانه |
| for girls | doxtarāna | دخترانه |
| for women, women's (clothing) | zanāna | زنانه |
| form | fōrma | فورمه |
| formal dress | kālāy-e rasmi | کالایی رسمی |
| four | čār | چار |
| four point six grams (4.6 gr) | měsqāl | مثقال |
| fourteen | čār-dah | چارده |
| France | faransa | فرانسه |
| free | moft | مفت |
| Friday | joma | جمعه |
| fruit | mewa | میوه |
| fruit | mewajāt | میوه جات |
| | G | |
| garage | garāž/garāj/garāč | گراژ/گراج/ گراچ |
| garden | bāğča | باغچه |
| garlic | sir | سیر |
| gift | tōhfa | تحفه |
| glasses | 'aynak | عینک |
| gloves | děstkaš | دستکش |

| God | xodā | خدا |
|---|---|---|
| God willing | enšālāh | انشاالله |
| golden | noqraye | نقره یی |
| golden (blonde) | tĕlāye | طلایی |
| grandchild | nawāsa | نواسه |
| grandfather | padar kalān | پدر کلان |
| grandmother | mādar kalān | مادر کلان |
| grape | angur | انگور |
| gray | xākĕstari | خاکستری |
| gray | xākĕstari | خاکستری |
| green | sabz | سبز |
| green | sabz | سبز |
| groceries | sawdā | سودا |
| groom | dāmād | داماد |
| guest | mĕhmān | مهمان |
| guest | mehmān | مهمان |
| guest room | mehmānxāna | مهمان خانه |
| gymnasium | jĕmnāziyam | جمنازیم |

## H

| hail | žāla | ژاله |
|---|---|---|
| hair color | rang mōy | رنگ موی |
| half | nim | نیم |
| hall | dahlez | دهلیز |
| hand | dĕst | دست |
| happiness | xōši | خوشی |
| hard | šadid | شدید |
| hat | kolah-e pik | کلاه پیک |
| hat | kolāh | کلاه |
| head | sar | سر |
| headphone | gošaki | گوشکی |

| health | sĕhi | صحی |
| healthy | jōr | جور |
| heavy | xarāb | سنگین |
| height | qad | قد |
| her/his | aš | اش |
| herbal medicine | dawā hāy-e giyāye | دوا های گیاهی |
| here | ĕnjā | اینجا |
| Here it is. | ena | اینه |
| himself/herself | xōdaš/xōdĕš | خودش |
| historical | tārixi | تاریخی |
| history | tārix | تاریخ |
| holiday | roxsati | رخصتی |
| home | xāna | خانه |
| homework | kār-e xānagi | کار خانگی |
| honeymoon | māhe 'asal | ماه عسل |
| hospital | šafāxāna | شفاخانه |
| hospital | šafāxāna | شفاخانه |
| hotel | hotal | هوتل |
| hotel manager | modir-e hotal, hotali | مدیر هوتل، هوتلی |
| hours riding | asb dawāni | اسب دوانی |
| house | haweli | حویلی |
| housekeeper, maid | xāna sāmān | خانه سامان |
| housekeeper, maid | xāna sāmān | خانه سامان |
| housewife | xānom-e xāna | خانم خانه |
| how | četór | چطور |
| how | čĕtōr | چطور |
| how many kinds, several types | čand naw' | چند نوع |
| how many times, several times | čand bār | چندبار |
| husband | šawhar/šōy | شوهر/ شوی |

| | | |
|---|---|---|
| I | man | من |
| I am ... | man ... mebāšam. | من ... میباشم. |
| I am... | man ... hastam. | من ... هستم. |
| I, my | man | من |
| ice cream shop | āyskĕrim forōši | آیسکریم فروشی |
| ice cream | ayskĕrim | آیسکریم |
| ID card | tĕzkĕra, kārt-e hoyat | تذکره، کارت هویت |
| ID card | tazkĕra | تذکره |
| ID card | kārt-e hoyat | کارت هویت |
| illness | marizi | مریضی |
| in between, middle | bayn | بین |
| in front of | pešrōye | پیشرویی |
| in front of the | dar moqābĕl-e | در مقابل |
| in front of the | dar pĕšrōy-e | در پیشروی |
| in front of (infinitive) | peš raftan(peš borō) | پیش رفتن(پیش رو) |
| in that very way, like that | hamāntōr | همانطور |
| in this very way, like this | hamintōr | همینطور |
| in total, in sum, all together | majmo'an | مجموعاً |
| in, in the, at | dar | در |
| Indonesia | andoniziyā | اندونیزیا |
| information | ma'lomāt | معلومات |
| injection | pečkāri | پیچکاری |
| inside of the | dar mābayn-e | در مابین |
| inside the | dar dāxĕle | در داخل |
| iron | ōtō | اوتو |
| island | jazira | جزیره |
| itch, itchy | xārĕš | خارش |

| | J | |
|---|---|---|
| jacket | jākat | جاکت |
| jeans/cowboy pants | patlun-e kawbāy | پطلون کوبای |
| jobless | bikār | بیکار |
| jobless | bikār | بیکار |
| juice | āb mewa | آب میوه |
| juice/smoothie sales shop | ābmewa forōši | آب میوه فروشی |

| | K | |
|---|---|---|
| kabob | kabāb | کباب |
| Kabul | kābol | کابل |
| keyboard | kibōrd | کیبورد |
| kilo | kelō | کیلو |
| kindergarten (age) child | bačaye kodakěstān | بچهٔ کودکستان |
| kitchen | āšpaz xāna | آشپز خانه |
| kitchen | āšpaz xāna | آشپز خانه |

| | L | |
|---|---|---|
| laboratory | lābrātowār | لابراتوار |
| lamb | gōšt-e gosfand | گوشت گوسفند |
| language, tongue | zabān | زبان |
| large bags | bōji | بوجی |
| last name | taxalos | تخلص |
| left | čap | چپ |
| left-hand side | děst-e čap | دست چپ |
| left side | samt-e čap | سمت چپ |
| left to | mānda | مانده |
| let me | bāšad kě | باشد که |
| lettuce | kāho | کاهو |
| library | kětāb xāna | کتابخانه |
| lifting | wazna bardāri | وزنه برداری |
| lightning | r'ad ō barq | رعد و برق |

| little | kam | کم |
|---|---|---|
| living room | otāq-e našiman | اتاق نشیمن |
| loudspeaker | lōd-espikar | لودسپیکر |
| lower floor | manzěl-e pāyen | منزل پائین |
| lunch | nān-e čāšt | نان چاشت |
| lunch, midday | čāšt | چاشت |
| | M | |
| male, masculine | zokōr, mardāna | ذکور، مردانه |
| man | mard | مرد |
| man's shawl | patu | پتو |
| manager | modir | مدیر |
| married | motahel | متاهل |
| meat | gōšt | گوشت |
| meatball | kofta | کوفته |
| medium/middle/mid | miyāna | میانه |
| meeting, seeing (to see) | didan | دیدن |
| melon, cantaloupe | xarbuza | خربوزه |
| members | a'zā | اعضا |
| men's (clothing), for men | mardāna | مردانه |
| menu | menōy-e ğēzā | منیوی غذا |
| message | payām | پیام |
| Mexico | maksikō | مکسیکو |
| midnight, in the middle of the night | nima šab | نیمه شب |
| milk | šir | شیر |
| minute | daqiqa | دقیقه |
| Monday | do-šanbe | دو شنبه |
| monitor (computer screen) | mānitor (safha-e kampi-yutar) | مانیتور (صفحهٔ کمپیوتر) |
| month | māh | ماه |
| moon | mahtāb, māh | مهتاب، ماه |
| morning | sob | صبح |

| | | |
|---|---|---|
| mosque | masjĕd | مسجد |
| most of the time, often | aksaran | اكثراً |
| mother | mādar | مادر |
| mother-in-law | xošō | خشو |
| mouse (computer) | maws | موس |
| mouth | dahān/dahan | دهان/دهن |
| Mr. | moh-taram | محترم |
| Mrs., lady | xānom | خانم |
| Ms., Mrs. | moh-tarama | محترمه |
| museum | mōziyam | موزیم |
| music | mosiqi | موسیقی |
| my | am | ام / مَ |
| myself | xōdam/xōdem | خودم |

N

| | | |
|---|---|---|
| name | nām | نام |
| national museum | mōziyam-e mĕlli | موزیم ملی |
| nausea | dĕlbad | دلبد |
| near | nazdik | نزدیك |
| neutral, mild | mo'tadĕl | معتدل |
| New York | neyō-yōrk | نیویورك |
| next | āyenda | آینده |
| next to the | dar bağal-e | در بغل |
| next to the | dar pahlōy-e | در پهلوی |
| night | šab | شب |
| nightingale | bolbol | بلبل |
| nine | noh | نه |
| nineteen | nōz-dah | نوزده |
| north | šamāl | شمال |
| nose | bini | بینی |
| notebook | kĕtāb-ča | کتابچه |

| | | |
|---|---|---|
| nurse | nars | نرس |

O

| | | |
|---|---|---|
| o'clock | baja | بجه |
| obviously | tab'an | طبعاً |
| oil | rōğan | روغن |
| ointment | pamād | پماد |
| old | pir | پیر |
| on the, at the top of the | dar bālāy-e | در بالای |
| on the, on top of the | dar sar-e | در سر |
| on the left side of the | dar samt-e čap-e | در سمت چپ |
| on the left side of the | dar taraf-e čap-e | در طرف چپ |
| on the right side of the | dar samt-e rāst-e | در سمت راست |
| on the right side of the | dar taraf-e rāst-e | در طرف راست |
| on top of the, on the | dar rōy-e | در رویی |
| once, twice | yak bār | یك بار، دو بار |
| one | yak | یك |
| one-way | yak tarafa | یك طرفه |
| oneself | xōd | خود |
| onion | peyāz | پیاز |
| orange | mālta | مالته |
| our | mā , mān | ما/ مان |
| ourselves | xōdĕmā | خودما |
| out of it | gans | گنس |
| outside of the | dar birōn-e | در بیرون |
| outside of the | dar xārĕj-e | در خارج |
| overseas, foreign | xārĕji | خارجی |

P

| | | |
|---|---|---|
| pack | basta | بسته |
| package | basta | بسته |
| Pakistan | pākĕstān | پاكستان |

| | | |
|---|---|---|
| pants | tonbān, ezār | تنبان، ایزار |
| pants (jeans) | patlun | پطلون |
| paper | kāğaz | کاغذ |
| parent | kaka | کاکا |
| park | pārk | پارك |
| park | pārk | پارك |
| parrot | tuti | طوطی |
| part, section | qĕsmat | قسمت |
| partridge | bōdana/kabk | بودنه /کبك |
| passenger, traveler | mosāfĕr | مسافر |
| passport | passport | پاسپورت |
| past | tĕr | تیر |
| pathway | rāh rawi | راه روی |
| peach | šaftālu | شفتالو |
| pen | qalam | قلم |
| pencil | pĕnsĕl | پنسل |
| people classifier (individual, person) | nafar, tan | نفر، تن |
| pepper | morč | مرچ |
| pharmacist | dawākāna | دواخانه دار |
| pharmacy | dawāxāna | دواخانه |
| piece | dāna | دانه |
| pigeon | kabutar/kaftar | کبوتر/کفتر |
| pill | guli | گولی |
| pillow | bālĕšt | بالشت |
| pilot | pelōt | پیلوت |
| pink | golābi | گلابی |
| plane | tayyāra | طیاره |
| plane ticket | tĕlĕk-e tayyāra | تکت طیاره |
| Poland | poland | پولند |
| pomegranate | anār | انار |

| | | |
|---|---|---|
| potato | kačālu | کچالو |
| prescription | nosxa | نسخه |
| prescription | nosxa | نسخه |
| printer | parentar | پرینتر |
| province | walāyat | ولایت |
| province | walāyat | ولایت |
| purple | yāsamani | یاسمنی |
| | Q | |
| Quarter | pāw | پاو |
| | R | |
| radish | moli | ملی |
| rain | bārān | باران |
| rainfall | bārĕndagi | بارنده گی |
| rainy | bārāni | بارانی |
| red | sorx | سرخ |
| red | sorx | سرخ |
| refrigerator | yaxčāl | یخچال |
| register | sabt | ثبت |
| rent | kĕrāya | کرایه |
| report | gozārĕš | گزارش |
| restaurant | rastōrant | رستورانت |
| retired | motaqā'ad | متقاعد |
| rice | bĕrĕnj | برنج |
| right | rāst | راست |
| right-hand side | dĕst-e rāst | دست راست |
| right side | samt-e rāst | سمت راست |
| ring, band | angoštar, čĕla | انگشتر، چله |
| road | jādda | جاده |
| road trip | safar-e zamini | سفر زمینی |
| roof | bām | بام |
| room | otāq | اتاق |

| rough | zomoxt | زمخت |
|---|---|---|
| round-trip | do tarafa | دو طرفه |
| ruler | xatkaš | خطکش |
| running | dawĕš | دوش |
| Russia | rōsiya | روسیه |

## S

| s/he is … | ō … mebāšad. | او ... میباشد. |
|---|---|---|
| s/he is… | o … ast. | او ... است. |
| s/he/it | o | او |
| salad | salāta | سلاته |
| salt | namak | نمك |
| salty | šōr | شور |
| sandal | čapli | چپلی |
| Saturday | šanbe | شنبه |
| sauce | qōrma | قورمه |
| scanner | ĕskenar | سكینر |
| scarf | čādar | چادر |
| school | maktab | مكتب |
| school student | mota'lem | متعلم |
| school teacher | mo'lem | معلم |
| sea | daryā | دریا |
| sea | bahr | بحر |
| seaport | bandar | بندر |
| season | fasĕl | فصل |
| second | saniya | ثانیه |
| second | dowom | دوم |
| second floor | manzĕl-e dowom | منزل دوم |
| secretary | monši | منشی |
| security headquarters | qōmandāniye amniya | قومندانی امنیه |
| separate | jodāgāna | جداگانه |
| series | jĕdi | جدی |

| services | xĕdamāt | خدمات |
|---|---|---|
| seven thousand sixty-six grams (7066 gr) in Kabul, about five thousand grams (5000 gr) in Kandahar, and four thousand grams (4000 gr) in western parts of the country | man | من |
| seven thousand sixty-six grams (7066 gr) in Kabul, but one hundred grams (100 gr) in western parts of the country | ser | سیر |
| seven | haft | هفت |
| seventeen | haf-dah | هفده |
| shawl | šāl | شال |
| sheet | rōjāye | روجایی |
| shirt | bōloz | بلوز |
| shopkeeper | dokāndār | دوکاندار |
| shopping | xaridār | خریداری |
| short | kōtā | کوتاه |
| short height | qad kōtā | قد کوتاه |
| shrine | ziyārat | زیارت |
| sick | mariz | مریض |
| sightseeing, places worth seeing | jāhāye didani | جا های دیدنی |
| single | mojarad | مجرد |
| single-bed room | otāq-e yak nafara | اتاق یک نفره |
| Sir | sā-heb | صاحب |
| Sir, Mr., gentleman | āqā | آقا |
| Sir/Madam | sā-heb, sā-heba | صاحب / صاحبه |
| sister | xāhar | خواهر |
| sister-in-law (for wife) | nanō | ننو |
| sister, title for addressing a strange woman | hamšira | همشیره |
| sister-in-law (for husband) | xeyāšna | خیاشنه |
| six | šaš | شش |

| sixteen | šānz-dah | شانزده |
|---|---|---|
| skinny | lāğar | لاغر |
| sky | āsmān | آسمان |
| sky, weather | hawā | هوا |
| small/young | xōrd | خورد |
| small/young | kōčak | کوچك |
| snow | barf | برف |
| snowy | barfi | برفی |
| so | pas | پس |
| soap | sābun | صابون |
| socks | jorāb | جراب |
| sometime | waqti | وقتی |
| sometimes | gāhe | گاهی |
| sometimes | ba'ze waqt-ha | بعضی وقتها |
| somewhere, a place | jāye | جایی |
| son | bača/pasar | بچه/پسر |
| sour | torš | ترش |
| south | jonub | جنوب |
| spicy, chili | tond | تند |
| spinach | sabzi pālak | سبزی پالك |
| spring | bahār | بهار |
| square meter | mĕtĕr morab' | متر مربع |
| stairs | zina | زینه |
| stapler | ĕstĕblar | ستپلر |
| state | ayālat | ایالت |
| stewardess | estiwardes | استیوردیس |
| stomach | šĕkam | شكم |
| storage room | pas xāna | پسخانه |
| storm | tōfān | طوفان |
| strawberry | tōt-e zamini | توت زمینی |

| | | |
|---|---|---|
| street | sarak | سرك |
| student | šāgerd | شاگرد |
| sugar | bōra | بوره |
| summer | tābĕstān | تابستان |
| sun | āftab, xōr | آفتاب، خورشید |
| Sunday | yak-šanbe | يك شنبه |
| sunstroke | garmi zadagi | گرمی زده گی |
| sweet | širin | شيرين |
| swimming | āb-bāzi, šĕnā | آببازی، شنا |
| swordsmanship | šamšer bāzi | شمشير بازی |
| synagogue | somĕ'a | صومعه |
| syrup | šarbat | شربت |

T

| | | |
|---|---|---|
| table/desk | mez | ميز |
| taekwondo | tekwāndō | تكواندو |
| tailor | xayāt | خياط |
| tall | bĕland | بلند |
| tall (height) | qad bĕlan | قد بلند |
| tasteless | be maza | بی مزه |
| taxi driver | tasiwān | تكسيوان |
| taxi station | estgāh-e taxi | ايستگاه تكسی |
| tea | čāy | چای |
| teacher | mo'lem | معلم |
| temperature | daraja-e harārat | درجۀ حرارت |
| temple | ma'bad | معبد |
| temple | ma'bad | معبد |
| ten | dah | ده |
| their | šān | شان |
| themselves | xōdĕšān | خودشان |
| there | ānjā | آنجا |

| they | ān-hā | آنها |
| they | ĕšān | ايشان |
| they are ... | ānhā ... mebāšand. | آنها ... ميباشند . |
| they are... | ān-hā ... hastand. | آنها ... هستند . |
| third | sewom | سوم |
| thirteen | sĕz-dah | سيزده |
| three | se | سه |
| Thursday | panj-šanbe | پنجشنبه |
| ticket sales (office/agency) | tĕkĕt forōši | تکت فروشی |
| tie | nektāye | نيکتايی |
| to | ba | به |
| to be allergic | hasāsiyat kardan(hasāsiyat kon) | حساسيت کردن (حساسيت کن) |
| to the attention of | qābĕl-e tawajoh | قابل توجه |
| to be available | mawjud bōdan(mawjud hast) | موجود بودن (موجود هست) |
| to be engaged | nāmzad šodan (nāmzad šaw) | نامزد شدن |
| to be equipped | mojahaz bōdan (mojahaz hast) | مجهز بودن(مجهز هست) |
| to be established | tasis šodan (tasis šaw) | تاسيس شدن(تاسيس شو) |
| to be happy | xōšāl šodan. | خوشحال شدن |
| to be in service of | dar xĕdmat bōdan (dar xĕdmat hast) | در خدمت بودن(در خدمت هست) |
| to be necessary | zarorat bōdan(zarorat bāš, hast) | ضرورت بودن (ضرورت باش/ است) |
| to be placed | jāy šodan(jāy šaw) | جای شدن(جای شو) |
| to be present | hāzĕr bōdan (hāzĕr bāš/hast) | حاضربودن (حاضر باش/هست) |
| to be ready | āmāda bōdan (āmāda hast) | آماده بودن (آماده هست) |
| to book | bōk kardan (bōk kon) | بوک کردن (بوک کن) |
| to bring | āwordan (āwar) | آوردن(آور) |
| to build | jōr šodan (jōr šaw) | جور شد |
| to buy | xarid (xar) | خريدن (خر) |
| to buy | xaridan (xar) | خريدن (خر) |

| to buy groceries | sawdā xaridan (sawdā xar) | سودا خریدن (سودا خر) |
|---|---|---|
| to call, to ring | zang zadan (zang zan) | زنگ زدن (زنگ زن) |
| to calm/silence | ārām bōdan (ārām bāš/ ārām hast) | آرام بودن(آرام باش /هست) |
| to carry | bordan (bar) | بردن(بر) |
| to check | čĕk kardan (čĕk kon) | چك كردن (چك كن) |
| to check up | māyna kardan (māyna kon) | معاینه کردن (معاینه کن) |
| to close | basta kardan (basta kon) | بسته کردن(بسته کن) |
| to close | basta kardan (basta kon) | بسته کردن(بسته کن) |
| to come | āmadan (āy) | آمدن(آی) |
| to contact | tamās grĕftan (tamās gir) | تماس گرفتن (تماس گیر) |
| to contact, to touch base | tamās gĕrĕftan (tamās gir) | تماس گرفتن (تماس گیر) |
| to converse | goftago kardan (goftago kon) | گفتگو کردن (گفتگو کن) |
| to cook | poxta kardan (poxta kon) | پخته کردن(پخته کن) |
| to cook food | ğĕzā poxtan (ğĕzā paz) | غذا پختن (غذا پز) |
| to cover | pōšāndan (pōšān) | پوشاندن (پوشان) |
| to decide | tasmim gĕrĕftan (tasmim gir) | تصمیم گرفتن (تصمیم گیر) |
| to do a task | anjām dādan (anjām dah) | انجام دادن (انجام ده) |
| to drink | nošidan (noš) | نوشیدن(نوش) |
| to drink | nōšidan (nōš) | نوشیدن(نوش) |
| to eat | xordan (xor) | خوردن(خور) |
| to eat | xōrdan(xōr) | خوردن (خور) |
| to eat | xōrdan(xōr) | خوردن(خور) |
| to enter (infinitive) | dāxĕl šodan (dāxĕl šaw) | داخل شدن (داخل شو) |
| to enter (infinitive) | darōn šodan (darōn šaw) | درون شدن (درون شو ) |
| to enter (infinitive) | dar āmadan (dar āy) | درآمدن (در آی) |
| to exit (infinitive) | birōn šodan (birōn šaw) | بیرون شدن(بیرون شو) |
| to exit, to come out of (infinitive) | bar āmadan (bar āy) | برآمدن (بر آی) |
| to feel | ehsās kardan (ehsās kon) | احساس کردن(احساس کن) |
| to fill out | xāna pōri kardan (xāna pōri kon) | خانه پوری کردن (خانه پوری کن) |

| to flood | sel āmadan (sel āy) | سیل آمدن (سیل آی) |
|---|---|---|
| to fly | parwāz kardan (parwāz kon) | پرواز کردن (پرواز کن) |
| to get; to grow, to happen, to go, to be | šodan | شدن |
| to give | dādan (děh) | دادن(ده) |
| to give | dādan (dah) | دادن (ده) |
| to go | raftan (raw) | رفتن(رو) |
| to go | raftan(raw) | رفتن (رو) |
| to hail | žāla bāridan (žāla bār) | ژاله باریدن(ژاله بار) |
| to have a plane | pělān dāštan (pělān dār) | پلان داشتن (پلان دار) |
| to have a location, to be located | moqě'yat dāštan (moqě'yat dār) | موقعیت داشتن (موقعیت دار) |
| to have tolerance, to be tolerant | tāqat dāštan (tāqat dār) | طاقت داشتن (طاقت دار) |
| to help | komak kardan (komak kon) | کمک کردن (کمک کن) |
| to help | komak kardan (komak kon) | کمک کردن (کمک کن) |
| to hurt, to have pain, to ache | dard kardan(dard kon) | درد کردن (درد کن) |
| to inform | ba etělā' rasāndan(ba etělā' rasān) | به اطلاع رساندن(به اطلاع رسان) |
| to jog | dawěš kardan (dawěš kon) | دوش کردن(دوش کن) |
| to land | něšast kardan (něšast kon) | نشست کردن (نشست کن) |
| to like | xōš dāštan (xōš dār) | خوش داشتن (خوش دار) |
| to like | xōš āmadan (xōš āy) | خوش... آمدن (خوش ... آی) |
| to listen | goš kardan (goš kon) | گوش کردن(گوش کن) |
| to listen | šanidan (šanaw) | شنیدن(شنو) |
| to listen | gōš kardan (goš kon) | گوش کردن (گوش کن) |
| to live | zendagi kardan | زنده گی کردن |
| to make a copy of | kāpi gěrftan (kāpi gir) | کاپی گرفتن(کاپی گیر) |
| to marry | tōy kardan (tōy kon) | توی کردن |
| to marry | ezděwāj kardan (ezděwāj kon) | ازدواج کردن |
| to marry/to wed | arōsi kardan (arōsi kon) | عروسی کردن |
| to move | harakat kardan (harakat kon) | حرکت کردن (حرکت کن) |
| to move (infinitive) | kōč-kardan (kōč kon) | کوچ کردن (کوچ کن) |

| | | |
|---|---|---|
| to need | bakārdāštan (bakārdār) | بکارداشتن (بکار دار) |
| to note | yāddāšt kardan (yāddāšt kon) | یادداشت کردن (یادداشت کن) |
| to open | bāz kardan (bāz kon) | باز کردن (باز کن) |
| to order, to demand | farmāyeš dādan (farmāyeš děh) | فرمایش دادن (فرمایش ده) |
| to pass (infinitive) | ter šodan(ter šaw) | تیر شدن (تیر شو) |
| to pass, to spend, to undergo | gozaštan (gozar) | گذشتن (گذر) |
| to pick up/to leave | bardāštan (bardār) | برداشتن(بردار) |
| to pick up | bardāštan (bardār) | برادشتن (بردار) |
| to play | bāzi kardan (bazi kon) | بازی کردن (بازی کن) |
| to prepare, to fix , to make | tayār kardan (tayār kon) | تیار کردن(تیار کن) |
| to provide | taheya kardan (taheya kon) | تهیه کردن (تهیه کن) |
| to put down | māndan (mān) | ماندن(مان) |
| to put on clothes/to wear | kālā kašidan (kālā kaš) | کالاکشیدن (کالاکش) |
| to rain | bārān bāridan (bāran bār) | باران باریدن(باران بار) |
| to rain, to shower | bāridan(bār) | باریدن (بار) |
| to read | xāndan(xān) | خواندن(خوان) |
| to read, to sing | xāndan (xān) | خواندن (خوان) |
| to receive a message | payām gěrěftan (payām gir) | پیام گرفتن(پیام گیر) |
| to reserve | rezarf /rezarw kardan(rezarf kon) | ریزرف/ریزرو کردن(ریزرو کن) |
| to rest | estarāhat kardan (estarāhat kon) | استراحت کردن(استراحت کن) |
| to reach, to arrive | rasidan (ras) | رسیدن (رس) |
| to see | didan (bin) | دیدن(بین) |
| to seep | čakāndan (čakān) | چکاندن(چکان) |
| to sell | forōxtan (forōš) | فروختن (فروش) |
| to show | něšān dādan (něšān děh) | نشان دادن (نشان ده) |
| to shower | šāwar gěrěftan (šāwar gir) | شاورگرفتن (شاورگیر) |
| to sit down | nešastan (šin) | نشستن(شین) |
| to sit, to live | nešastan/šeštan (šen, našen) | نشستن/شیشتن (شین، نشین) |
| to sleep | xāb šodan(xab šaw) | خواب شدن (خواب شو) |
| to snow | barf bāridan (barf bār) | برف باریدن(برف بار) |

| to speak | gap zadan (gap zan) | گپ زدن (گپ زن) |
| to spend | sĕpari kardan (sĕpari kon) | سپری کردن (سپری کن) |
| to spend, to pass | ter kardan (ter kon) | تیر کردن(تیرکن) |
| to sport, to exercise | warzĕš kār (warzĕš kon) | ورزش کردن (ورزش کن) |
| to stand up | xestan (xez) | خیستن(خیز) |
| to swim | āb-bāzi kardan (āb-bāzi kon) | آببازی کردن(آببازی کن) |
| to take | gĕrĕftan (gir) | گرفتن(گیر) |
| to take | gĕrĕftan (gir) | گرفتن (گیر) |
| to take note | nōt gĕrĕftan (nōt gir) | نوت گرفتن (نوت گیر) |
| to take off | kašidan (kaš) | کشیدن (کش) |
| to tell | goftan (goy) | گفتن(گوی) |
| to think | fĕkĕr kardan (fĕkĕr kon) | فکر کردن (فکرکن) |
| to travel | safar kardan(safar kon) | سفر کردن (سفرکن) |
| to try | kōšĕš kardan (kōšĕš kon) | کوشش کردن (کوشش کن) |
| to turn (infinitive) | dawr zadan (dawr zan) | دور زدن (دور زن) |
| to turn, to search for (infinitive) | gaštan (gard) | گشتن(گرد) |
| to wait | montazĕr bōdan (montazĕr bāš, hast) | منتظر بودن( منتظر باش، هست) |
| to wait | sabr kardan(sabr kon) | صبر کردن(صبر کن) |
| to wake up | bidār šodan(bidār šaw) | بیدارشدن (بیدارشو) |
| to walk | qadam zadan (qadam zan) | قدم زدن(قدم زن) |
| to want | xāstan (xāh) | خواستن( خواه ) |
| to want (infinitive) | xāstan (xāh) | خواستن(خواه) |
| to watch | sayl kardan (sayl kon) | سیل کردن ( سیل کن) |
| to watch, to see | sayl kardan (sayl kon) | سیل کردن (سیل کن) |
| to wear | pōšidan (pōš) | پوشیدن (پوش) |
| to wear | pōšidan (pōš) | پوشیدن (پوش) |
| to welcome | xōš āmadan (xōš āy) | خوش آمدن (خوش آی) |
| to wish | ārĕzō kardan (ārĕzō kon) | آرزو کردن |
| to work | kār kardan (kār kon) | کار کردن (کار کن) |
| to write | nawĕšta kardan (nawĕšta kon) | نوشته کردن(نوشته کن) |

| to write | naweštan (děh) | نوشتن (نویس ) |
| to write | něwěšta kardan (něwěšta kon) | نوشته کردن(نوشته کن) |
| today | ěroz | امروز |
| tomato | bāděnjān-e rōmi | بادنجان رومی |
| tomato sauce | rob/rob-e baděnjān-e rōmi | رب/ رب بادنجان رومی |
| tourism company | šěrkat-e tōrezom | شرکت توریزم |
| towel | jānxoškān, jānpāk | جانخشکان، جانپاك |
| towel/handkerchief | děstmāl | دستمال |
| traditional doctor (prescribes herbal medications) | hakim ji | حکیم جی |
| traditional restaurant | rastōrant-e sonati | رستورانت سنتی |
| translator | tarjomān | ترجمان |
| traveler | mosāfěr | مسافر |
| tree | daraxt | درخت |
| trip | safar | سفر |
| trunk | tōlbaks | تولبکس |
| Tuesday | se- šanbe | سه شنبه |
| turban | longi | لنگی |
| turkey | torki-ya | ترکیه |
| turn | dawr | دور |
| turnip | šalğam | شلغم |
| twelve | dōwāz-dah | دوازده |
| twenty | bist | بیست |
| two | do | دو |
| | U | |
| uncle (father's side) | mama | ماما |
| uncle (mother's side) | xāl | خاله |
| underpants | zer tonbāni (zer tombāni) | زیرتنبانی |
| under the | dar zěr-e | در زیر |
| undergarments | zer perāni | زیرپیراهنی |
| underwear | nekar, sentarāj | نیکر، سنتراج |

|  |  |  |
|---|---|---|
| unemployed | bi-kār | بیکار |
| unfortunately | mot'sěfāna | متاسفانه |
| university student | mohasel | محصل |
| unknown people, strangers | ašxās-e nāšanās | اشخاص ناشناس |
| until | tā | تا |
| upward, up | bālā | بالا |
| usually | ma'molan | معمولاً |

V

|  |  |  |
|---|---|---|
| various | motalěf | مختلف |
| vegetable | tarkāri | ترکاری |
| vegetable store | tarkāri forōši | ترکاری فروشی |
| vegetables | sabzijāt/tarkāri | سبزیجات/ ترکاری باب |
| very, a lot | běsyār | بسیار |
| very little | běsyār kam | بسیار کم |
| very very much | běsyār ziyād | بسیار زیاد |
| vest | wāskat | واسکت |
| via | az tariq-e | از طریق |
| village | qari-ya | قریه |
| vomit | estafrāğ | استفراغ |

W

|  |  |  |
|---|---|---|
| waiter/waitress | ğārsun | گارسون |
| wall | diwār | دیوار |
| warm | garm | گرم |
| Washington | wāšěng-tan | واشنگتن |
| watch | sěnf | صنف |
| watch, clock | sā'at | ساعت |
| water | āb | آب |
| well | čah-e āb | چاه آب |
| watermelon | tarbuz | تربوز |
| we | mā | ما |

| | | |
|---|---|---|
| we are ... | mā ... mebāšem. | ما ... میباشیم. |
| we are... | mā ... hastem. | ما ... هستیم. |
| weak | kamzōr | کمزور |
| weather | āb ō hawā | آب و هوا |
| Wednesday | čār- šanbe | چار شنبه |
| well/fine | xub | خوب |
| west | ğarb | غرب |
| what | či | چی |
| where | kojā | کجا |
| white | safed | سفید |
| white | safed | سفید |
| who | ki | کی |
| who | ki | کی |
| why | čarā | چرا |
| wind | bād, šamāl | باد، شمال |
| window | kalkin | کلکین |
| winter | zaměstān | زمستان |
| to wish | kāške | کاشکی |
| with peace | baxayr | بخیر |
| without | bĕdōn | بدون |
| without bottle | ğayr-e botali | غیر بوتلی |
| woman | zan | زن |
| woman | zan | زن |
| work experience | tajrobaye kāri | تجربهٔ کاری |
| world | jahān | جهان |
| wrestling | košti giri | کشتی گیری |
| | Y | |
| year | sāl | سال |
| years old... | sāla... | ...ساله |
| yellow | zard | زرد |

| | | |
|---|---|---|
| yellow | zard | زرد |
| yogurt | māst | ماست |
| you | šomā | شما |
| you | tu | تو |
| you (your) | šomā | شما |
| you are ... | tu... mebāše. | تو ... میباشی. |
| you are ... | šōmā ... mebāšed. | شما ... میباشید. |
| you are... | šomā ... hasted. | شما ... هستید. |
| you are... | tu ... hasti. | تو ... هستی. |
| young | jawān | جوان |
| your | tān | تان |
| your (plural) | tān | تان |
| your (singular) | at | ات |
| yourself | xōdat / xōdĕt | خودت |
| yourselves | xōdĕtān | خودتان |
| | Z | |
| zero | sefer | صفر |

# Index of grammar terms, topics, and language functions

## - C -

## - N -

## - P -

## - V -

## - W -